DOCUMENTS
ON POLISH-SOVIET RELATIONS
1939–1945

VOLUME I
1939–1943

GENERAL SIKORSKI HISTORICAL INSTITUTE

DOCUMENTS
ON
POLISH–SOVIET RELATIONS
1939–1945

VOLUME I
1939–1943

HEINEMANN

LONDON MELBOURNE TORONTO

Printed and bound in Great Britain by Butler & Tanner Ltd., Frome and London

Contents

Contents

Preface

THE General Sikorski Historical Institute in London has, since its foundation in the year 1945, worked methodically to collect in its Archives all available material on the political and military history of Poland at the time of the Second World War. These endeavours of the Institute were actively supported by a Research Committee called into being on the Institute's initiative and composed of Polish men of learning, former diplomats and members of the Polish Armed Forces. The Research Committee has taken the view that the publication of the records held by the Sikorski Institute was urgently necessary in order to place in the hands of students of history a full picture of events. The Committee decided to give pride of place to 'Documents on Polish-Soviet Relations 1939–1945'. The choice was dictated by the importance of the problems involved and the full documentary evidence at hand. This collection, originally started as far back as 1943, was gradually enlarged and completed, revised and re-edited in order to embrace all available sources. Also the number of documents appended or quoted in part was substantially increased. The publication was made possible thanks to a generous donation received by the Institute for that purpose.

The present series of documents and records covers a period of just over six years. It also includes the texts of a few basic agreements binding the two countries such as that of the Treaty of Riga of March 18, 1921, the Treaty of Non-Aggression of July 25, 1932, and the Convention on the Definition of Aggression of July 3, 1933. Since 1921 Polish-Soviet relations had at times been strained. They were adversely affected by the German-Soviet Rapallo Agreement signed in May, 1922. The Polish-Soviet Treaty of Non-Aggression of 1932 was the outcome of protracted Polish endeavours to place relations with our eastern neighbour on a stable footing and to increase in both countries a sense of security. The multilateral London Convention on the Definition of Aggression was designed to serve the same purpose. I happened to be its signatory on behalf of Poland. Article 2, point 2, of the Convention stated in particular that the 'aggressor' in an international conflict shall be considered to be that State which is the first to commit 'invasion by its armed forces, with or without a declaration of war, of the territory of another State'. And Article 3 states, 'no political, military, economic or other considerations may serve as an excuse or justification for the aggression referred to in Article 2'. Both Conventions so carefully drawn were violated by the Soviet Union in co-operation with Hitler's Third Reich. Hence the persistence with which on September 17, 1939, the day of the Soviet attack on Poland, the Moscow Government pretended to treat the Polish Government as non-existent. As the Polish Government is non-existent—ran the argument—obligations contracted in regard to this

vii

Government are no more binding on the USSR! A fine example of Communist dialectic!

The history of the following years can be closely followed on the testimony of the documents collected in this book. It shows how, by secret agreement with Hitler, Moscow was able to annex half of Poland's pre-war territory together with the Baltic States and parts of Rumania. How in 1941 after Hitler's attack, Russia, dependent on Allied support, signed an agreement with the Polish Government in London which, on the face of it, undid the effects of Moscow's compact with the Third Reich and restored the pre-war relationship between the Soviet Union and Poland. How thereafter Moscow worked stubbornly and persistently to deprive this document of its meaning. How finally no longer as Hitler's Ally but as a member of the United Nations Russia imposed her will and social system on Poland, another member of the United Nations, which, for its part, remained true to its obligations to its Western Allies and fought on their side from the first to the last day of the war.

The Polish-Soviet Agreement of July 30, 1941, laid the foundation for the establishment in the USSR of welfare delegations entrusted with the protection of the masses of deportees numbering about 1½ million and scattered over large regions of the Union from the Arctic to Central Asia. It also laid the foundation for the creation within the Soviet Union of a new Polish Army out of the 181,000 Polish prisoners of war captured in September, 1939, and out of deportees. Difficulties were encountered from the start. The setting up of Polish delegations entrusted with the welfare of Polish deportee masses did not proceed without friction. The status of the delegates who acted as members of the Polish Embassy in Moscow was confirmed only on December 23, 1941.

As regards the army, differences of opinion cropped up from the start, first of all regarding numbers. On August 14, 1941 a Military Agreement between the Polish and Soviet High Command was signed in Moscow which in its Article 4 made the strength and number of Polish military units dependent on manpower, equipment and supplies available but otherwise set no limit to their expansion. In fact such limits were imposed. The Soviet Ambassador Bogomolov impressed on me in London that no more than two Polish divisions could be formed on Soviet territory. Later this number was nominally increased to 11 divisions before the figure was again drastically reduced. One major difficulty which cropped up from the start and which is reflected in the documents published was the lack of any information about the many thousands of Polish officers of all ranks captured by the Russians in 1939. Out of about 14 thousand officers including generals, colonels, etc., more than eleven thousand could not be traced and enquiries made by Prime Minister Sikorski, General Anders and others were left unanswered.

As the situation in the field of battle was gradually changing in Russia's favour, Moscow grew more intractable in all questions. This evolution can be traced very soon after the signature of the Polish-Soviet Agreement. Already on December 1, 1941, on the eve of General Sikorski's visit to

Moscow, the Soviet Government addressed a note to the Polish Embassy in Moscow in which it refused to recognize the Polish nationality of several categories of our citizens. In a later note of January 17, 1942, it openly laid claim to a number of cities of eastern Poland. Also in December, 1941, during General Sikorski's visit to the Soviet Union the Soviet Government convened the first meeting of Polish Communists in Saratov who organized themselves as the Union of Polish Patriots—the nucleus of the so-called Lublin Committee and later of the present Polish Communist régime. On January 1, 1942, the so-called Kościuszko Radio Station in the Soviet Union was first heard as a medium of propaganda in support of the Union of Polish Patriots. Soon the activities of the Polish welfare delegates were more and more hampered, and in July, 1942, arrests followed. In March, 1942, Stalin informed General Sikorski that contrary to previous agreements the Polish Army would be reduced to a total of 44,000 men. This threat was followed by the evacuation of the entire Polish Army and a number of civilians from the Soviet Union across the Persian border. In January, 1943, with a further improvement in Russia's military situation, Stalin's pressure on the Polish Government increased. The Soviet Government declared all Polish deportees to be Soviet citizens. Three months later news about the massacre of Polish officers in the Katyń Wood startled the world and Moscow broke off relations with the Polish Government in London. It gave for its reason that the Polish request addressed to the International Red Cross in Geneva for an investigation of the circumstances of this massacre was an offence to the Soviet Union.

Parallel with its policy of unrelenting pressure on the Polish Government Moscow followed a similar line with regard to its Western Allies, with the patent aim of legalizing the conquest of half of Poland's territory and obtaining the Western Powers' consent to the subjugation of the whole of our country. The Western Powers proved incapable of countering this pressure with equal energy. They were obsessed by anxiety as to the loyalty of the Soviet Ally and feared to provide him with an excuse for a separate deal with Germany. They also lacked sufficient knowledge of Soviet-Russian psychology, and thought that they could achieve satisfactory results by humouring Moscow. Such was no doubt, *inter alia* the intention of the Anglo-American mission headed by Lord Beaverbrook and Ambassador Averil Harriman which visited Moscow in October, 1941, in order to discuss the problem of Western military supplies to Russia and which left entirely in the hands of Stalin the apportionment of equipment and armaments for the Polish Armed Forces on Soviet territory. This decision must have done much at the time to embolden the Soviet dictator. Demands regarding the recognition of Russian conquests in Eastern Europe were made as early as the Spring of 1942 in the course of negotiations on the British-Soviet Treaty (signed May 26, 1942). Moscow then demanded the recognition of its conquests in the Baltic countries and Rumania. This demand was turned down at the time but was upheld by the Moscow Government and later extended to comprise eastern Poland. Western statesmen limited their reaction to offers of mediation. I remember the British Prime Minister saying in 1944 that he did not find it possible to secure the respect of Poland's territorial integrity but that he would put up a fight to preserve its independence. The different phases of the tragedy are reflected in these records. They deserve close study particularly at a time when the Soviet Union is redoubling its efforts to force the free world to recognize the colonial system it has implanted in the heart of Europe as legal and final.

It is my pleasant duty to acknowledge the scholarly research and editorial work done with competence and devotion by The Editorial Board: Mr. E. Weese, LL.M. and T. Jankowski, Ph.D., responsible for the compiling of the basic set of documents; Col. S. Bieganski, Ph.D. who completed the material through extensive research, outlined the form of the publication and made the final selection, and with Dr. Jankowski, prepared the Editorial Notes; Mrs. R. Oppman, M.A., whose thorough knowledge of the valuable material greatly facilitated research work and who made the final adjustment of documents for print; Professor T. Komarnicki, LL.D., who shouldered the task of organizing and controlling the English translations of the documents; Lt.-Gen. M. Kukiel, Ph.D., who with his great competence and authority co-ordinated the team work and supervised its progress. The devoted co-operation of the Staff of the General Sikorski Historical Institute proved most helpful as well as the Translations Universal Agency.

We feel greatly indebted to Mr. Alexander Frere, Chairman of Heinemann Publishers, for his kind interest in the publication, and to his Personal Assistant Mr. B. Glazebrook for his helpful co-operation throughout.

London, June 1960   Edward Raczyński

Editorial Note

THE aim of the present publication was to make available to the students of contemporary history the documentary evidence relating to the policies of the Polish and Soviet Governments during the Second World War. The influence of the Western Powers on the development of these policies also had to be taken into account. The editors were allowed complete freedom in research and selection. They were free to include in this series all valuable evidence. The Soviet documentary materials could not be utilized to the full extent, due to the fact that only certain sections of sources were available. These above included the entire correspondence of the USSR with Poland. The actual policy of the Kremlin, their plans, aims and decisions were not known, but they can be indirectly studied from relevant Polish and British reports on Soviet actions.

The work on this set of documents started in January, 1958. It was planned by the Research Committee of the General Sikorski Historical Institute as a part of a larger work, which would include publication of sources (documents and materials) referring to the History of Poland in the Second World War. Preliminary publications had been undertaken before by members of the Polish Ministry of Foreign Affairs, who published in Washington, 1944, a selection of 90 documents from diplomatic correspondence entitled *Polish-Soviet Relations, 1918–1943*; this work was made by Mr. Tadeusz Jankowski, Ph.D. and Mr. Eugeniusz Weese, LL.M.

A larger set entitled 'Stosunki polsko-sowieckie', extending up to activities of 1945, was compiled by the latter, containing about 450 documents and materials, bound in two volumes, and prepared in the Polish language for the most part. This work was issued in mimeographed form in London, 1946.

The Board of Editors made a review of the materials available in the General Sikorski Historical Institute and of the possibilities of their completion from records preserved elsewhere. Enquiries and research were undertaken by the Keeper of the Archives of the Institute and the Board of Editors to recover important diplomatic materials, which was largely achieved.

The general plan of the publication was to observe strictly the chronological order of documents, to treat the problems and the selection of documents relating to them with liberalism and objectivity, and not to indulge in deductions and judgements and to restrain from referring to posterior controversies and polemics. Several texts serving for understanding official documents were included also, e.g. speeches and broadcasts of political leaders, many proceedings of and reports on conferences held between Polish and British or Soviet Military authorities, and the Polish-British correspondence relating to the USSR. Those materials might be an important contribution to the understanding of the diplomatic correspondence.

As a result of that preparatory work the Board of Editors could find sufficient evidence to present in full the developments of 1940–45. The situation proved less satisfactory for the earlier period of the activities of the Polish Government in France, 1939–40; there was scant correspondence on the subject and still less was preserved of it. The documentation of the pre-war period proved to be still more fragmentary. There is yet hope for future improvement of that situation. For the time being it was necessary to fill some gaps with documents from foreign publications. This was especially the case of the 'Introductory Documents', i.e. preceding the outbreak of the war.

The editors have utilized the following Polish sources:

Prime Minister's Office,
Central Military Authorities, i.e. the records of Commanders in Chief, of the General Staff and of the War Ministry (later Ministry of National Defence),
Ministry for Foreign Affairs with some parts of documents of the Embassy of Poland in the USSR,
Polish Army Command in the Middle East,
Polish Legation and Agencies in the Middle East,
The Chancery of the President of Poland (for supplementary materials),
Collection of documents of General Anders, Col. Zamoyski and others.

In all these groups original documents were searched or their carbon copies. In a few cases, marked 'M.S.Z. Coll.', typewritten copies of documents of the Ministry of Foreign Affairs, made from originals in 1943–46 for official use, had to replace the wanted originals. Their authenticity was carefully checked in each case.

Documents or passages in documents relating to personal subjects or internal controversies have been omitted if not important for understanding the course of events. Documents on general politics were also omitted if Polish-Soviet problems were only incidentally involved. A selection of them will be included in the projected series of 'Political and Military Correspondence of General Sikorski.'

Besides originals of unpublished documents the Editors have been consulted and utilized the following printed collections:

1. Correspondence between the Chairman of the Council of Ministers of the USSR and the Presidents of the USA and the Prime Ministers of Great Britain. Two vols. in one. London, 1958 [Engl. transl.].
2. Jane Degras: *Soviet Documents on Foreign Policy*. Royal Institute of International Affairs, London, 1951 and 1953, vols. I and III.
3. *Documents on British Foreign Policy, 1919–1939*, ed. E. L. Woodward and Rohan Butler, Third Series, London, 1951–4, vols. IV, V, VI, VII.
4. *Documents on German Foreign Policy, 1918–1945*. [Board of editors changed.] Series 'D', London, H.M.S.O., 1951–6, vols. V, VI, VII, VIII.
5. 'Dziennik Ustaw Rzeczypospolitej Polskiej' [*Journal of Laws of the Polish Republic*], Warsaw, 1923, 1929, 1932, 1933, 1934.
6. *Izvestia* ['News', official daily of the USSR], Moscow, 1939, 1943.

7. Wacław Jędrzejewicz: *Poland in the British Parliament, 1939–1945*, New York, 1946–59, vols. I–II.
8. J. V. Kluchnikov and A. Sabanin: *Mezhdunarodnaya politika noveishovo vremeni v dogovorakh, notakh i deklaratsiakh*. ['International Policy of Contemporary Times in Treaties, Notes and Declarations']. Moscow, 1928, vol. III.
9. League of Nations: *Monthly Summary of the . . .*, Genève, 1923, 1934, 1939, vols. III, XIV, XIX, with Special Supplements.
10. League of Nations: *Treaty Series*, Genève, 1921, 1923, 1928, 1929, vols. VI, XV, XXXIX, LXXXIX, XC.
11. *Mirovoye Khoziaistvo i Mirovaya Politika* ['World Economy and World Politics'], Moscow, 1939.
12. *Monitor Polski* ['Polish Monitor', Official reports], Paris-Angers, 1939, 1940.
13. *Official Documents concerning Polish-German and Polish-Soviet Relations, 1933–1939* ('Polish White Book'), London [1940]. Published by authority of the Polish Government.
14. Parliamentary Debates [Hansard], House of Commons, Official Report, vols. 351, 355, 365, 372, 373. London, 1939–41.
15. *Polish-Soviet Relations, 1918–1943*. Official Documents, issued by the Polish Embassy in Washington by authority of the Government of the Republic of Poland. [1944].
16. *Pravda* ['Truth', official daily of Soviet Communist Party], Moscow, 1934, 1939, 1941, 1943.
17. Report of the International Committee of the Red Cross (September 1, 1939–June 30, 1947), vol. I, Genève, 1948.
18. *The Times*, London, 1934, 1939, 1941, 1943.

In the later phase of the work of the Editorial Board the attention was concentrated upon a proper selection of documents, especially on crucial problems like the restoration of diplomatic relations of Poland and the USSR in 1941 and their severing in 1943; the military collaboration and formation of the Polish Army in the USSR (1941); the difficulties met in this field in 1942; the organization of relief-work for Polish citizens and its later suppression; the controversies over the acquisition of Polish citizenship as applied to the inhabitants of Eastern Poland; and finally a constant enigma of missing war prisoners.

The continuity of documentary evidence for each problem was carefully checked and it was the Editors' concern to throw full light on such crucial cases as the conclusion of the agreement of July 30, 1941, the declaration of December 4, 1941, both the phases of the evacuation of the Polish Army to the Middle East and the problem of further protection and relief for Polish exiles in autumn 1942.

The Editors abstained from historical comments on the subjects of the published documents. Short footnotes only are given at the end of some records with reference to their origin and their relation to other texts. However, in many cases concerning the 'Preliminary Documents' (1918–39) explanatory notes were considered necessary for factual reference. Some notes relating to military problems and to the relief for the Poles in the USSR seemed also helpful for their elucidation or fuller representation. Those notes are given in a group following the Documents with references to their Nos.

The documents on foreign policy are given as a rule in their full text and in English or French. Those not strictly of diplomatic character are given in extracts, confined to what concerned the Polish-Soviet relations. Some documents important for the understanding of that subject, but not belonging to it, are given in Appendices. The addresses, compliments, signatures and office marks in documents are omitted, treaties and conventions excepted.

The English texts of the documents are either original or translated from Polish or Russian. A part of them are given in official contemporary translations. The main part appears in translations made specially for this publication. The documents in French are given in their original version. There is in the heading of each included document an indication to which of the three categories it belongs.

The editorial work was organized as follows:

The Editorial Board, presided over by Count E. Raczyński, LL.D., with Lt.-General M. Kukiel, Ph.D. and Prof. T. Komarnicki, LL.D. as Deputies, and Col. St. Biegański, Ph.D. as Asistant Editor, was responsible for the conception of the publication, its planning and supervision. The Editors, Mr. T. Jankowski, Ph.D., and Mr. E. Weese, LL.M., have collected the basic material; Col. Biegański extended the documentary material by further research, made the final selection of texts and provided explanatory notes together with Dr. Jankowski. The checking of many documents with the original texts, their final arrangement and preparing for print was done by Mrs. R. Oppman, M.A. assisted by Miss D. Jurkiewicz, M.A. Professor Komarnicki took care of the large amount of translation into English.

STANISŁAW BIEGAŃSKI

xiv

Abbreviations

used in headings of documents and editors' notes

(*a*) ARCHIVAL SOURCES

1. Ch. Pres. P.R. Documents from the Chancery of the President of Polish Republic.

2. GSHI General Sikorski Historical Institute in London. Archives with notations and numbers of records, groups and files.

(*b*) PRINTED PRIMARY SOURCES

1. Cor. Churchill-Roosevelt-Stalin *Stalin's Correspondence with Churchill, Attlee, Roosevelt and Truman, 1941–1945.* London, 1958, Lawrence and Wishart.

2. Degras Jane Degras: *Soviet Documents on Foreign Policy, 1917–1941.* 3 vols. Oxford Univ. Press for Royal Institute of International Affairs, 1951–3.

3. D. Brit. F.P. *Documents on British Foreign Policy, 1919–1939*, ed. E. L. Woodward and Rohan Butler. Third Series, vols. IV, V, VI, VII. London, 1951–4, H.M.S.O.

4. D. Germ. F.P. *Documents on German Foreign Policy, 1918–1945*, publ. by The British Foreign Office and the U.S. Department of State. Series D (1937–45), vols. V, VI, VII, VIII. Washington, U.S., G.P.O., and London, H.M.S.O., 1951–6.

5. Dz. U.R.P. *Dziennik Ustaw Rzeczypospolitej Polskiej* [Journal of Laws of the Polish Republic]. Warsaw, 1918–39, and London, 1940–5.

6. H.C. Deb. *Parliamentary Debates* [Hansard]. House of Commons. Official Report. London, H.M.S.O.

7. H.L. Deb. *Parliamentary Debates* [Hansard]. House of Lords. Official Report. London, H.M.S.O.

8. H.M.S.O., Cmd. *His Majesty's Stationery Office.* Command Paper. London.

9. I.M.T., Nur. *The Trial of German Major War Criminals before the International Military Tribunal at Nuremberg, 1945–1946.* London, 1947, H.M.S.O.

10. Jędrzejewicz, Poland Wacław Jędrzejewicz: *Poland in the British Parliament, 1939–1945.* Vol. I, N. York, 1946; vol. II, with the assistance of P. C. Ramsey, N. York, 1959. J. Pilsudski Institute of America.

11. Keesing's, C.A. *Keesing's Contemporary Archives.* Weekly Diary of World Events. Vol. III, 1937–40; vol. IV, 1940–3. London, Keesing's Contemporary Archives.

12. Kluchnikov, M.p.	I. V. Kluchnikov and A. Sabanin ed.: *Mezhdunarodnaya politika noveishovo vremeni v dogovorakh, notakh i deklaratsiakh.* Vol. III, Moscow, 1928, N.K.I.D.
13. Kot, Listy	Stanisław Kot: *Listy z Rosji do Gen. Sikorskiego.* London, 1955. 'Jutro Polski.'
14. Kot, Rozmowy	Stanisław Kot: *Rozmowy z Kremlem.* London, 1959. 'Jutro Polski.'
15. L.N., M.S.	League of Nations, *Monthly Summary of the . . .*, vols. III, XIV, XIX with Special Supplements. Genève, 1923, 1934, 1939.
16. L.N., T.S.	League of Nations, *Treaty Series*, vols. VI, XV, XXXIX, LXXXIX, XC, Genève, 1921, 1923, 1928, 1929.
17. MSZ., Coll.	*Stosunki polsko-sowieckie. Zbiór dokumentów MSZ, 1939–1946* [Collection of Polish Ministry for Foreign Affairs]. London, 1948, 2 vols. [mimeographed].
18. Nazi-Sov. R.	*Nazi-Soviet Relations, 1939–1941.* Documents from the Archives of the German Foreign Office. Ed. R. J. Sontag and J. S. Beddie. Department of State, 1948.
19. Pol.-Sov. R.	*Polish-Soviet Relations, 1918–1943.* Official Documents. Issued by the Polish Embassy in Washington by authority of the Government of the Republic of Poland [1944].
20. Pol. W.B.	*Official Documents concerning Polish-German and Polish-Soviet Relations, 1933–1939* (Polish White Book) issued by the Polish Ministry for Foreign Affairs. London [1940], Hutchinson and Co.
21. S. Zak. R.	*Sobranie zakonov i rasporiazhenii Raboche-Krestianskovo Pravitelstva SSSR.* Moscow, 'Gosizdat'. Annual.
22. U.S.A., Dipl., 1941	*Foreign Relations of U.S.A., Diplomatic Papers, 1941.* Vol. I, General. The Soviet Union. Washington, 1958. Department of State Publication 6642.
23. U.S.A., Sov. Union	*Foreign Relations of U.S.A., Diplomatic Papers. The Soviet Union, 1933–1939.* Washington, 1952. Department of State Publication 4539.

(c) PRINTED SECONDARY SOURCES

1. Anders, Army	Lt.-General W. Anders: *An Army in Exile.* The Story of the Second Polish Corps. London, 1949, Macmillan and Co., Ltd.
2. Beck, D. rap.	Colonel Joseph Beck: *Dernier rapport.* Politique polonaise, 1926–39. Editions de la Baconnière, Neuchatel, 1951.
3. Churchill, S.W.W.	Winston S. Churchill: *The Second World War*, vols. III–IV. London, 1950–1, Cassell and Co., Ltd.
4. Ciechanowski, D.V.	Jan Ciechanowski: *Defeat in Victory.* New York, 1947. Doubleday and Company, Inc.

5. Komarnicki, Rebirth   Titus Komarnicki: *Rebirth of the Polish Republic*. London, 1957, William Heinemann Ltd.

6. Langer-Gleason, U.W.   William L. Langer and S. Everett Gleason: *The Undeclared War, 1940–1941*. New York, 1953, Harper and Brothers.

7. Lenin, Soch.   V. I. Lenin: *Sochinienia* [Works], Ned. Vols. 30, 31, Moscow, 1950, Institute of Marx, Engels and Lenin.

8. Matuszewski, G.B.O.   Ignacy Matuszewski: *Great Britain's Obligations towards Poland and some facts about the Curzon Line*. New York, 1945. National Committee of Americans of Polish Descent.

9. Stalin, Soch.   J. W. Stalin: *Sochinienia* [Works], Moscow, 1946–8. Vols. IV, XI. Institute of Marx, Engels and Lenin.

10. Toynbee, Eve   Arnold Toynbee and Veronica M. Toynbee (edit.): 'The Eve of War 1939'. Publ. *Survey of International Affairs, 1939–1946*. Oxford Univ. Press, 1958.

11. Weinberg, Germany   Gerhard L. Weinberg: *Germany and the Soviet Union, 1939–1941*. Ed., *Studien zur Geschichte Osteuropas*. Leiden, 1954.

List of Principal Persons

ANDERS, Władysław, Lt.-Gen., C.-in-C. Polish Army in the USSR (1941–2) in the Middle East (1942–4) and Italy (1944–5).

ASTAKHOV, Georgyi, Chargé d'Affaires of the USSR in Berlin (1939).

ATTLEE, Clement Richard, Parliamentary Leader of the Labour Party (since 1935), Lord Privy Seal (1941–2), Deputy Prime Minister (1942–45), Prime Minister (since 1945).

BECK, Joseph, Polish Minister of Foreign Affairs (1932–9).

BOGOMOLOV, Alexander Y., Ambassador of the USSR to the Polish Govt. (1941–3).

CADOGAN, Sir Alexander, Permanent Under-Secretary of State at Foreign Office (1938–46).

CHAMBERLAIN, Neville, British Prime Minister (1937–1940).

CHICHAYEV, Ivan, Counsellor of the Soviet Embassy to the Polish Govt. (1941–3).

CHURCHILL, Winston, British Prime Minister (1940–5).

CIECHANOWSKI, Jan, Polish Ambassador to the USA (1941–5).

CRIPPS, Sir Stafford, British Ambassador to the USSR (1940–2).

EDEN, Anthony, British Secretary of State for War (1940), for Foreign Affairs (Dec. 1941–5).

GRZYBOWSKI, Wacław, Ph.D., Polish Ambassador in the USSR (1936–9).

HALIFAX, Viscount, Secretary of State for Foreign Affairs (1938–41).

HITLER, Adolf, Chancellor of the German Reich (1933–45).

HULL, Cordell, Secretary of State of the USA (1933–44).

ISMAY, Sir Hastings, General, British Chief of Staff to Minister of Defence (1940–6).

KOT, Stanisław, Polish Ambassador to the USSR (1941–2), Minister of Information (1943–4).

LITVINOV, Maxim, Soviet Commissar for Foreign Affairs (1930—May 3, 1939).

MACFARLANE, Sir Frank Noel Mason, Lt.-Gen., Head of Military Mission to Moscow (1941–2), Governor of Gibraltar (1942–4).

MAISKY, Ivan M., Ambassador of the USSR to Great Britain (1932–43).

MOLOTOV, Vyacheslav M., Commissar for Foreign Affairs (since May 3, 1939), Chairman, later Deputy Chairman of the Council of People's Commissars of the USSR.

PAPÉE, Kazimierz, Polish Ambassador to the Holy See (from 1939).

POTEMKIN, Vladimir, Soviet Deputy Commissar for Foreign Affairs (1937–40).

RACZKIEWICZ, Władysław, President of Polish Republic (1939–47).

RACZYŃSKI, Count Edward, Polish Ambassador to Great Britain (1934–45) and acting Foreign Minister (Aug. 22, 1941–July 14, 1943).

RETINGER, Joseph H., Ph.D., Private Secretary to Polish Prime Minister (1941–3), Chargé d'Affaires in Moscow (1941), Counsellor Polish Embassy, London (1943–5).

RIBBENTROP, Joachim v., German Minister of Foreign Affairs (1938–45).

ROMER, Tadeusz, Polish Ambassador to Japan (1937–41), to the USSR (1942–3).

ROOSEVELT, Franklin Delano, President of the USA (1933–45).

SCHNURRE, Karl, Dr., Head East-European Section, Dept. of Economic Policy, German Ministry of Foreign Affairs (1939).

SCHULENBURG, Friedrich v., German Ambassador to the USSR (1934–41).

SHARONOV, Nikolay, Soviet Ambassador to the Polish Republic (1939).

SIKORSKI, Władysław, General, Polish Prime Minister (from Sept. 30, 1939) and C.-in-C. Polish Forces (from Nov. 1939). Killed July 4, 1943.

SOKOLNICKI, Henryk, Minister Plenipotentiary, Counsellor Polish Embassy in the USSR (1941–3).

STALIN, Joseph, General Secretary of the Central Committee of the Communist Party (from 1922). Chairman of the Council of People's Commissars (1941–1946), Commissar for Defence and C.-in-C. (1941–6).

SZEMBEK, Jan, Polish Deputy Minister of Foreign Affairs (1932–9).

SZYSZKO-BOHUSZ, Zygmunt, Maj.-Gen., Chief of Polish Military Mission to the USSR (1941–2).

VALKOV, Vassily, Counsellor at Soviet Embassy to the Polish Government (1941–1943).

VASSILEVSKY, Alexander, General, Plenipotentiary of the Soviet High Command for the organization of the Polish Army in the USSR (1941).

VOROSHILOV, Klimentiy E., People's Commissar for Defence of the USSR (1925–1944).

VYSHINSKY, Andrei J., Deputy Commissar for Foreign Affairs of the USSR (1940–9).

WEIZSÄCKER, Ernst v., State Secretary, German Ministry of Foreign Affairs (1938–43).

ZALESKI, August, Polish Minister of Foreign Affairs (1939–Aug. 22, 1941).

Summaries

INTRODUCTORY DOCUMENTS

1918-1939

DOCUMENTS

September 1939–April 1943

xxix

APPENDICES

INTRODUCTORY DOCUMENTS

1918-1939

No. 1

Extract from the Decree of the Council of People's Commissars . . . annulling the agreements of the Government of the former Russian Empire with the Governments of the German and Austro-Hungarian Empires, the Kingdoms of Prussia, etc., concerning the partitions of Poland[1]

Moscow, August 29, 1918　　　　　S.Zak.R., 1917–18, No. 64 of
　　　　　　　　　　　　　　　　　　September 9, 1918
　　　　　　　　　　　　　　　Transl. from Russian: Degras, I/98

[. . .] Art. 3. All agreements and acts concluded by the Government of the former Russian Empire with the Governments of the Kingdom of Prussia and the Austro-Hungarian Empire referring to the partitions of Poland are irrevocably annulled by the present decree, since they are contrary to the principle of the self-determination of peoples and to the revolutionary-legal conceptions of the Russian people, which recognizes the inalienable right of the Polish nation to independence and unity. [. . .]

Signed: Chairman of the Council of People's Commissars:
V. Ulyanov-Lenin
Deputy People's Commissar for Foreign Affairs:
L. Karakhan
Executive Secretary of the Council of People's Commissars:
Vlad. Bontch-Bruyevitch

[1] See Note No. 1.

No. 2

Declaration of the Council of People's Commissars of RSFSR to the Polish Government and the Polish Nation, proposing the actual front-line as the armistice line[1]

Moscow, January 28, 1920　　　　　Kluchnikov, III, No. 2
　　　　　　　　　　　　　　Transl. from Russian: Pol.-Sov.R., No. 2

Poland is now confronted with a decision that for many years to come may have grave repercussions on the lives of both nations. Everything shows that the extreme imperialists of the Entente, the supporters and agents of Churchill and Clemenceau, are directing at present all their efforts to draw Poland into a futile, ill-considered and criminal war with Soviet Russia.

Conscious of its responsibility for the fate of the Russian working masses

[1] See Note No. 2.

and wishing to prevent new and innumerable disasters, sacrifices and devastation threatening the two nations:—

1. The Council of People's Commissars declares that the policy of the USSR towards Poland is based not on any occasional, transient considerations of war or diplomacy but on the inviolable principle of self-determination of nations and it has recognized and recognizes unreservedly the independence and sovereignty of the Polish Republic and declares this recognition to be the basis of all its relations with Poland from the moment of the formation of an independent Polish State.

2. While regarding the last peace proposal of December 22 put forward by the People's Commissariat for Foreign Affairs as still fully valid, the Council of People's Commissars, which has no aggressive intentions whatever, declares that the Red Army will not cross the present line of the White-Ruthenian front that passes near the following points: Dryssa, Dzisna, Polock, Borysow, Parycze, Railroad Stations Ptycz and Bialokozowice. As regards the Ukrainian front, the Council of People's Commissars declares in its own name and in the name of the provisional Ukrainian Government that the army of the Federated Soviet Republic will not engage in military operations to the West of the present line, running near the localities of Bodouwa, Pilawy, Deraznia and Bar.

3. The Council of the People's Commissars declares that the Soviet Government has not entered into any agreements or pacts, with Germany or any other country, aimed directly or indirectly against Poland, and that the character and spirit of international policy of the Soviet authorities excludes the very possibility of similar agreements, as well as attempts to exploit eventual conflict between Poland and Germany or Poland and other countries in order to violate Poland's independence and her territorial integrity.

4. The Council of People's Commissars declares that so far as the essential interests of Poland and Russia are concerned there is not a single question, territorial, economic or other, that could not be solved in a peaceful way, through negotiation, mutual compromise or agreement, as is now the case in the negotiations with Estonia.

While recommending to the People's Commissariat for Foreign Affairs that it obtain at the next session of the All-Russian Central Executive Committee in February, a confirmation by the Supreme Body of the Republic of the above stated basis of Soviet policy towards Poland, the Council of People's Commissars considers on its part that by this categorical declaration it is fulfilling its duty towards the peace interests of the Russian and Polish nations and hopes that all controversial matters will be settled by friendly negotiations between Russia and Poland.

Chairman of the Council of People's Commissars:
V. Ulyanov-Lenin
People's Commissar for Foreign Affairs:
Chicherin
People's Commissar for Army and Navy:
Trotsky

No. 3

Treaty of Peace between Poland, Russia and the Ukraine[1]

Riga, March 18, 1921 Dz.U.R.P., 1921, No. 49/300, 301;
paras: 1, 2, 3, 5 and 10
Kluchnikov, III, No. 58 [excerpts]
Transl. from Polish: L.N., T.S.,
Vol. VI, No. 149, pp. 122–169

Preamble

Poland—on the one hand—and Russia and the Ukraine—on the other—being desirous of putting an end to the war and of concluding a final, lasting and honourable peace based on a mutual understanding and in accordance with the peace preliminaries signed at Riga on October 12, 1920, have decided to enter into negotiations and have appointed for this purpose as plenipotentiaries:

The Government of the Polish Republic: MM. Jean Dąbski, Stanislas Kauzik, Edouard Lechowicz, Henri Strasburger and Leon Wasilewski.

The Government of the Federal Socialist Republic of the Russian Soviets, on its own behalf and with the authorization of the Government of the White-Ruthenian Socialist Republic of Soviets and of the Government of the Ukrainian Socialist Republic of Soviets: MM. Adolphe Joffe, Jacob Ganet-ski, Emmanuel Kviring, Leonide Obolenski and Georges Kotshoubinski.

The above-mentioned plenipotentiaries met at Riga, and having exchanged their full powers, which were recognized as sufficient and found to be in good and due form, agreed to the following provisions:[2]

Article 1

The two Contracting Parties declare that a state of war has ceased to exist between them.

Article 2

The two Contracting Parties, in accordance with the principle of national self-determination, recognize the independence of the Ukraine and of White Ruthenia and agree and decide that the eastern frontier of Poland, that is to say, the frontier between Poland on the one hand, and Russia, White Ruthenia and the Ukraine on the other, shall be as follows:

The frontier shall follow the course of the Zapadnaia Dźwina [Dvina][3] from the frontier between Russia and Latvia, to the point at which the frontier of the former Government of Wilno meets the frontier of the former Government of Witebsk; thence it shall follow the frontier between the former Governments of Wilno and Witebsk as far as the road running from

[1] See Note No. 3.

[2] Ratification of this Treaty took place on April 30, 1921, and the registration with the Secretariat of the League of Nations on August 12, 1921.

[3] The place names other than Polish are given in brackets in a French transliteration from Treaty Series of the League of Nations as above.

the village of Drozdy to the town of Orzechowno [Oriekhovno], leaving the road and the town of Orzechowno to Poland;

it shall then cross the railway line near the town of Orzechowno, and, turning towards the South-West, shall run along the railway line, leaving the station of Zahacie [Zagatié] to Poland, the village of Zahacie to Russia, and the village of Stelmachowo [Stolmakhovo] to Poland;

thence it shall follow the eastern frontier of the former Government of Wilno as far as the meeting point of the districts of Dzisna, Lepel and Borysow;

thence it shall follow the frontier of the former Government of Wilno at an approximate distance of one kilometre, as far as the point at which this frontier turns westward near Sosnowiec;

thence the frontier shall continue in a straight line towards the sources of the river Czernica to the east of Hornów [Gornov], and thereafter it shall follow the Czernica river as far as the village of Wielka-Czernica [Bolshaia Tchernitsa] which it shall leave to White Ruthenia;

thence it shall continue in a south-westerly direction, across the Lake of Miadziol, to the village of Zarzeczyck [Zarietchitsk] which shall be left to White Ruthenia together with the village of Chmielewszczyzna [Khmielevchtchizna]; on the other hand, the villages of Starosiele and of Turowszczyzna [Tourovchtchizna] shall belong to Poland;

thence the frontier shall run in a south-westerly direction to the confluence of the river Wilja [Wilia] with an unnamed stream on the west of the village of Drohomicze [Drogomitchi], leaving to White Ruthenia the following villages: Uhly [Ougli], Wolbarowicze [Volbarovitchi], Borowe [Borovie], Szunówka [Chounovka], Beztrock [Biestrotsk], Daleka [Dalekaia], Klacz-kówek [Klatchkovek], Zazantów [Ziazantov], Maciejowce [Matviéievtsi], and the following to Poland: Komajsk Raszkówka [Raschkovka], Osowa [Osova], Kusk, Wardomicze [Vardomitchi], Sołone [Solonoie], Milcz [Miltcha];

thence the line shall follow the river Wilia to the road on the south of the town of Dołhinowo [Dolginov];

thence it shall pass to the south as far as the village of Baturyn [Botourino], leaving to White Ruthenia all that road and the villages of Rahozin [Ragozin], of Tokary [Tokari], of Połosy and of Hłuboczany [Gloubotchani], and to Poland the following villages: Owsianiki, Czarnorucze [Tchernor-outchie], Żurawa [Jourava], Ruszczyce [Rouchitsé], Zaciemień [Zatiemie], Borki, Czerwiaki and Baturyn [Botourino];

thence it shall run to the town of Radoszkowicze [Radochkovitchi], leaving to White Ruthenia the villages of Papysze [Papichi], Sieliszcze, Podworany [Podvorani], Trusowicze-North [Trusovitchi], Doszki, Cyganowo, Dwor-zyszcze [Dvorischzi], and Czyrewicze [Tchirévitchi], and to Poland the villages of Łukawiec [Loukoviets], Mordasy, Rubce [Roubtsi], Ławcowicze North and Ławcowicze South [Lavtsovitchi], Budzki [Boutski], Klimonty, Wielkie Bakszty [Bolchiie-Bakchté], and the town of Radoszkowicze [Radochkovitchi];

4

thence it shall follow the river Wiązówka [Viazovka] to the village of Lipienie [Lipieni], leaving the latter village to Poland, then running in a south-westerly direction, crossing the railway and leaving the station of Radoszkowicze [Radochkovitchi] to White Ruthenia;

thence it shall run to the east of the town of Raków [Rakov], leaving to White Ruthenia the villages of Wiekszyce [Viekchitchi], Dołżenie [Dolgeni], Mietkowa, Wielka Borozdynka [Bolchaia Borodinka], and Kozielszczyzna [Kozelchchizna], and to Poland the villages of Szypowały [Chipouvali], Macewicze [Matsévitchi], Stary Raków [Starii Rakov], Kuczkuny and the town of Raków;

thence the frontier shall continue as far as the town of Wołma [Volma], leaving to White Ruthenia the villages of: Wielkie Sioło [Vielikoje Siélo], Malawka [Malavka], Łukasze [Loukachi] and Szczepki, and to Poland the villages of Duszkowo [Douchkovo], Chimorydy [Himarydy], Jankowce [Jankovtsi], and the town of Wołma;

thence it shall follow the road from the town of Wolma as far as the town of Rubieżewicze [Roubiegevitchi], leaving that road and the town to Poland;

thence it shall continue south as far as the unnamed inn situated at the point at which the Baranowicze-Mińsk railway crosses the Nowy Swierzeń-Mińsk road [see map, scale one English inch to ten versts, above the letter 'M' at the beginning of the word Mieżinówka, and map, scale one English inch to twenty-five versts, near Kołosowo] leaving the inn to Poland; the villages of Papki, Żywica [Givitsa], Połoniewicze [Polonievitchi], Osinówka [Osinovka] shall go to White Ruthenia and the villages of Lichacze [Likhatchi] and of Rożanka shall go to Poland;

thence the frontier shall pass across the centre of the Nieśwież-Cimkowicze [Niesvige-Timkovitchi] road to the west of Kukowicze [Koukovitchi], leaving the villages of Swerynowo [Swérinovo], Kutiec, Łunina [Lounina], Jaźwina [Jasvina] North, Bieliki, Jaźwin [Jasvine], Rymasze [Rymachi], and Kukowicze [all three] to White Ruthenia; the villages of Kul, Buczne [Boutchnoie], Dwianopol, Żurawy, Posieki, Juszewicze [Jouchévitchi], Lisuny-North and Lisuny-South, Sułtanowszczyzna [Soultanovchtchina], and Pleszewicze [Pléchévitchi] to Poland;

thence it shall pass halfway between Kleck [Kletsk] and Cimkowicze [between the villages of Puzowo and Prochody], leaving to White Ruthenia the villages of Rajówka [Raiouvka], Sawicze [Savitchi], Zarakowce [Zarakovtsi], and Puzowo, and to Poland the villages of Marusin, East Smolicze [Smolitchi], Lecieszyn [Letiéchine] and Prochody;

thence it shall continue as far as the Warsaw-Moscow road, crossing it to the west of the village of West Filipowicze [Filipovitchi], and leaving the village of Ciechowa [Tiekhova] to White Ruthenia and the village of Jodczyce [Jodtchitsi] to Poland;

thence it shall run south as far as the Morocz river [Morotch], near Choropol [Khoropol], leaving the villages of Stare Mokrany [Starye Mokrany], Zadwórze [Zadvorie], Mokrany and Choropol to White

Ruthenia, and the villages of Ciecierowiec, Ostaszki, Łozowicze [Lozovitchi], and Nowe Mokrany [Nowye Mokrany] to Poland;

thence it shall follow the Morocz river as far as its confluence with the river Słucz [Sloutch] of Mińsk;

thence it shall follow the river Słucz as far as its confluence with the river Prypeć [Pripet];

thence it shall continue towards the village Bereźce [Bierestsi], leaving the villages of Lubowicze [Loubovitchi], Chilczyce [Khilchitsi], and Bereźce to White Ruthenia, and the villages of North Lutki and South Lutki to Poland;

thence it shall follow the road from the village of Bukcza [Bouktcha], leaving the road and the village of Bukcza to White Ruthenia and the village of Korma to Poland;

thence it shall continue as far as the Sarny–Olewsk railway which it shall cross between the stations of Ostki and Snowidowicze [Snovidovitchi], leaving to the Ukraine the villages of Wojtkowicze [Voitkovitchi], Sobiczyn [Sobitchine], Michałówka [Mikhailovka], and Budki Snowidowickie [Boudki Snovidovitskié], and to Poland the villages of Radziwiłowicze [Radzivilovitchi], Raczków [Ratchkov], Białowiska [Bialovichskaja], Białowiż [Bielovija], and Snowidowicze [Snovidovitchi];

thence the frontier shall continue towards the village of Myszakówka [Michakovka], leaving to the Ukraine the villages of Majdan Hołyszewski [Maidan Golichevski], Zaderewie [Zadiérevie], Mariampol, Żolny, Klonowa [Klenovaia] and Rudnia Klonowska [Rudnia Klenovska], and to Poland the villages of Derc [Diert], Okopy, Netreba [Niétreva], Woniacze, Perełysianka, Nowa Huta [Novaia Gouta] and Myszakówka [Michakovka];

thence it shall continue as far as the mouth of the river Korczyk [Kortchik], leaving the village of Młynek [Mlinok] to the Ukraine;

thence it shall run up the river Korczyk, leaving the town of Korzec [Koriets—Novoié Miesto] to Poland;

thence it shall continue as far as the village of Milatyn [Milatin], leaving to the Ukraine the villages of Poddubce [Poddoubtsi], Kilikijów, Dołżki, Narajówka [Narajevka], Ulaszanówka [Oulasianovka], and Marianówka [Marianovka], and the villages of Bohdanówka [Bogdanovka], Czernica [Tchernitsa], Kryłów [Krilov], Majków, Dołha, Friederland, Poręba Kuraska [Kurachsku Poroub], and Milatyn to Poland;

thence it shall follow the road leading from the village of Milatyn to the town of Ostróg, leaving the villages of Moszczanówka [Mochtchanovka], Krzywin [Krivine] and Sołowie to the Ukraine and the villages of Moszczanica [Mochtchanitsa], Bodówka [Bodovka], Wilbowno, the town of Ostróg and the road to Poland;

thence it shall run up the river Wilja [Vilia] as far as the village of Chodaki, which remains to Poland;

thence it shall continue as far as the town of Białozórka [Bielozorka], leaving to the Ukraine the villages of Wielka Borowica [Vielikaia Borovitsa], Stepanówka [Stiepanovka], North Bajmaki and South Bajmaki, Liski, Siwki, Wołoski, the town of Jampol, the villages of Didkowce [Diedkovtsi],

6

Wiazowiec [Viazoviets] and Krzywczyki [Krivtchiki] and to Poland the villages of Bołozówka [Bologevka], Sadki, Obory, Szkrobotówka [Chkrobotovka], Pańkowce [Pankovtsi], Grzybowa [Gribova], Łysohorka [Lysogorka], Mołodzków [Molodkov] and the town of Białozórka [Bielozorka];

thence it shall continue as far as the river Zbrucz, leaving the road and the village of Szczęsnówka [Chtchasnovka] to Poland;

thence it shall follow the river Zbrucz, as far as its confluence with the river Dniester.

Article 3

Russia and the Ukraine abandon all rights and claims to the territories situated to the west of the frontier laid down by Article 2 of the present Treaty. Poland, on the other hand, abandons in favour of the Ukraine and of White Ruthenia all rights and claims to the territory situated to the east of this frontier. The two Contracting Parties agree that, in so far as the territory situated to the west of the frontier fixed in Article 2 of the present Treaty includes districts which form the subject of a dispute between Poland and Lithuania, the question of the attribution of these districts to one of those two States is a matter which exclusively concerns Poland and Lithuania. [. . .].

Article 5

Each of the Contracting Parties mutually undertakes to respect in every way the political sovereignty of the other Party, to abstain from interference in its internal affairs, and particularly to refrain from all agitation, propaganda or interference of any kind, and not to encourage any such movement.

Each of the Contracting Parties undertakes not to create or protect organizations which are formed with the object of encouraging armed conflict against the other Contracting Party or of undermining its territorial integrity, or of subverting by force its political or social institutions, nor yet such organizations as claim to be the Government of the other Party or of a part of the territories of the other Party. The Contracting Parties, therefore, undertake to prevent such organizations, their official representatives and other persons connected therewith, from establishing themselves on their territory, and to prohibit military recruiting and the entry into their territory, and transport across it, of armed forces, arms, munitions and war material of any kind destined for such organizations. [. . .].

Article 10

1. Each of the Contracting Parties guaranties to the subjects of the other Party a full amnesty for political crimes and offences. Attacks directed against the system of government and the security of the State, as well as all acts committed in the interest of the other Party, shall be regarded as political crimes and offences within the meaning of this article.
2. The amnesty shall also apply to acts which have been made the subject of administrative proceedings or proceedings other than before a court

7

of law and to contraventions of provisions in force as regards prisoners of war and interned civilians and, generally, as regards subjects of the other Party.

3. The putting into effect of the amnesty under points 1 and 2 of this Article entails the obligation to institute no new judicial investigations, to discontinue proceedings which have already been instituted and to suspend execution of sentences which have already been passed.

4. The suspension of the execution of a sentence does not necessarily imply that the prisoner shall be set at liberty, but in such an event he must be immediately handed over, with all papers referring to his case, to the authorities of the State of which he is a national.

Nevertheless, if such person states that he desires not to be repatriated, or if the authorities of the country of which he is a national refuse to admit him, such person may be again placed in custody.

5. Persons against whom legal proceedings have been taken, or a preliminary judicial investigation has been instituted, or who have been summoned to appear before a court of justice for any breach of the law, or who have been sentenced for such an offence, shall forthwith be handed over, on application being made by the State of which they are nationals, together with all the papers relating to their case.

6. The amnesty referred to in this Article shall also apply to all the above-mentioned offences that have been committed up to the time when this Treaty is ratified.

Sentence of death passed upon persons found guilty of one of the offences referred to above shall be suspended as from the date of the signature of this Treaty. [. . .].

No. 4

Decision of the Conference of Ambassadors on the subject of the frontiers between Poland and Soviet Russia and Lithuania[1]

Paris, March 15, 1923   Dz.U.R.P., 1923, No. 49/333
                          L.N., T.S., Vol. XV, No. 398, pp. 260–265

L'Empire Britannique, la France, l'Italie et le Japon, signataires avec les États Unis d'Amérique, comme Principales Puissances alliées et associées, du Traité de Paix de Versailles,

Considérant qu'aux termes de l'Article 87, alinéa 3, dudit Traité, il leur appartient de fixer les frontières de la Pologne, qui n'ont pas été spécifiées par ce Traité;

Considérant que le Gouvernement polonais a adressé, le 15 février 1923, à la Conférence des Ambassadeurs, une demande tendant à voir les Puissances, qui s'y trouvent représentées, faire usage des droits que leur confère ledit article;

[1] See Note No. 4. The Government of the United States of America have acknowledged this decision on 5 April, 1923/Pol.-Sov.Rel. No. 5/.

Que, de son côté, le Gouvernement lithuanien s'était déjà, par sa note du 18 novembre 1922, montré soucieux de voir lesdites Puissances faire usage desdits droits;

Considérant qu'aux termes de l'Article 91 du Traité de Paix de Saint-Germain-en-Laye, l'Autriche a renoncé, en faveur des principales Puissances alliées et associées, à tous ses droits et titres sur les territoires, qui appartenaient antérieurement à l'ancienne Monarchie austro-hongroise et qui, situés au delà des nouvelles frontières de l'Autriche, telles qu'elles sont décrites à l'Article 27 dudit Traité, ne sont actuellement l'objet d'aucune autre attribution;

Considérant qu'il est reconnu par la Pologne, qu'en ce qui concerne la partie orientale de la Galicie, les conditions ethnographiques nécessitent un régime d'autonomie;

Considérant que le Traité conclu entre les Principales Puissances alliées et associées et la Pologne, le 28 juin 1919, a prévu pour tous les territoires placés sous la souveraineté polonaise, des garanties spéciales en faveur des minorités de race, de langue ou de religion;

Considérant qu'en ce qui concerne sa frontière avec la Russie, la Pologne est entrée directement en rapport avec cet État en vue d'en déterminer le tracé;

Qu'en ce qui concerne la frontière de la Pologne avec la Lithuanie, il y a lieu de tenir compte de la situation de fait résultant notamment de la résolution du Conseil de la Société des Nations du 3 février 1923,

Ont chargé la Conférence des Ambassadeurs du règlement de cette question. En conséquence, la Conférence des Ambassadeurs:

I.—Décide de reconnaître comme frontières de la Pologne:

1º Avec la Russie:

La ligne tracée et abornée d'accord entre les deux États et sous leur responsabilité à la date du 23 Novembre 1922.

2º Avec la Lithuanie:

La ligne ci-dessous décrite (d'après la carte allemande au 1/100,000ᵉ):

Depuis le point où la limite administrative septentrionale du district de Suwalki rencontre la frontière de Prusse orientale (point commun à la Prusse orientale, à la Pologne et à la Lithuanie) et jusqu'au point le plus au sud du rentrant de la limite du district de Suwalki, point situé à environ 7 kilomètres au N.-O. de Punsk la limite administrative septentrionale du district de Suwalki;

de là, vers le S.-E. jusqu'à un point de la route Berzniki-Kopciowo situé à environ 2 kilomètres au S.-E. de Berzniki;

une ligne à déterminer sur le terrain laissant Punsk à la Pologne, traversant le lac Galadusya depuis son extrémité N.-O. jusqu'à un point situé à environ 2 kilomètres au nord de Zegary, se dirigeant ensuite vers l'est, puis parallèlement à la ligne de petits lacs situés entre Berzniki et Zegary à environ 2 kilomètres à l'est de ces lacs;

9

de là, jusqu'à un point à environ 2 km. 500 à l'est de Zelwa sur la Marycha, une ligne à déterminer sur le terrain;

de là, en aval, le cours de la Marycha jusqu'au confluent d'un petit affluent situé sur la rive gauche de cette rivière et immédiatement en amont de Sztudjanka;

de là, une ligne à déterminer sur le terrain jusqu'à la source de la rivière Igorka, puis le cours de cette rivière qui passe à Warwischki jusqu'à son confluent avec le Niémen;

de là, en aval, le cours du Niémen jusqu'au confluent de la rivière Grawe;

de là, la rivière Grawe jusqu'au point où elle se croise avec la chaussée Merecs-Rudnica (Rotnica);

de là, une ligne à déterminer sur le terrain jusqu'au confluent de la rivière Skroblis avec la rivière Mereczanka;

de là, le cours de la Mereczanka jusqu'à un point à environ 800 mètres au sud-est de Podkamien;

de là et jusqu'à la cote 142 à environ 2 kilomètres au N.-E. de Strzelciszki;

une ligne à déterminer sur le terrain laissant en Lithuanie les localités de Podkamien, Karpiszki, Strzelciszki; en Pologne, celles de Bortele, Kukle, et passant par la croisée des routes allant de Bobryszki à Olkieniki et d'Orany à Wojtowo sur la voie ferrée de Grodno à Vilna;

de là et jusqu'à un point à déterminer sur le cours de la Wilia à environ 800 mètres à l'ouest de Surmance;

une ligne à déterminer sur le terrain laissant en Lithuanie les localités de: Kalance, Spengleniki, Gieceniszki, Uzuleje, Prybance, Greczowka, Wismance, Jagielany, Dergiance, Kopciszki, Zailgi, Chwoszczyzna, Niedzwiedowka, Janczuny, Daniliszki, Jerzowka, Nowy Dwor, Promyslowka, Walakiszki, Kurkliszki, Kalejkiemie, Wiluniszki, Kiermanczyszki, Bialolesie et Owsieciszki; et laissant en Pologne les localités de: Wojtowo, Vw-Puskarnia, Czarnokowale, Kol-Lejpuny, Wejksztelance, Ejgielance, Markowszczyzna, Skobska, Wizgirdy, Dombrowo, Dembniaki, Stanislawowka, Kotysz, Staskuniszki, Lebiedzie, Mejluszki, Podworance, Glity, Piektoniszki, Kiermeliszki, Kudrany, Poniewiezka, Majdany, Miciuny, Lojziszki, Megryszki, Borcie, Jateluny, Puzanowo, Kazimirowka et Surmance;

de là, le cours de la Wilia jusqu'à un point situé à environ 1 km. 200 au sud de Sejmieniszki;

de là et jusqu'à un point à déterminer à l'extrémité sud-ouest de lac Oswie au sud de Zoltynie;

une ligne à déterminer sur le terrain, laissant en territoire lithuanien les localités de: Sejmieniszki, Kliszebloto, Podozierce, Pojodzie, Pospierze, Kejmince, Skietery, Olinowo, Pory, Kontromiszki, Kiele, Awizance, Nieczance, Borowy, Olany, Palki, Ollis, Okmiana, Towkiele, Alexandryszki, Gawejki, Zoltynie; et, en territoire polonais les localités de: Podworzance, Podgajem, Drawcze, Mejluny, Papiernia, Bortkuszki, Uzyblindzie, Lipowko, Poblyndzie, Zyndule, Astyki, Szelkowszczyzna, Romaskance, Pogiry, Borowka, Sontoki, Pulstylki, Rudejki, Stolewszczyzna, Zemwiszki, Smilgi, Gawejki, Sidabry;

de là, une ligne traversant le lac Oswie jusqu'à un point à déterminer sur sa rive N.-E., à 1,500 mètres environ au sud-est d'Olka;

de là, et jusqu'à un point à déterminer sur la rive sud du lac Prowa à l'est de Surgance;

une ligne à déterminer sur le terrain, laissant en territoire lithuanien les localités de: Olka, le lac Boloma, Labejszyski, Mlynek, Janiszki, Szerajkiszki, Surgance; et, en territoire polonais les localités de: Jankuniszki, Purwiniszki, Szarkiszki, Maciejewa, Orniany, Skardze, Nowosiolka Grybiance;

de là, et jusqu'à un point à déterminer sur la rive méridionale du lac au bord duquel se trouve Antolkony et à 500 mètres à l'ouest de cette localité;

une ligne à déterminer sur le terrain laissant en territoire lithuanien les localités de: Madejki, Mazule, Szykaliszki, Andrulance, Shukowschtschisna, Shemeityschki, Prudsischki, Polukno, Poshenis, Shwirblischki, Rgt-Sidori-schki, Mineischany; et, en territoire polonais les localités de: Maldziuny, Rutowschtschisna, Baranowo, Antaledse, Bernjuny, Lyngmjany, Antolkony;

de là, et jusqu'à la frontière de Lettonie;

une ligne à déterminer sur le terrain se dirigeant vers le nord-est puis vers le nord, passant entre le lac de Boloscha et le lac Dringis, et laissant en territoire lithuanien les localités de: Rgt-Ashusseniz Achramjanzy, Reipe, Ashany, Sadsjuny, Bol-Derewnja, Suntupe, Kalnischki, Schablowisna, Muglischki, Junkokalne, Gut-Nowo-Smolwy, Werugischki; et, en territoire polonais les localités de: Kosatschisna, Meiluny, Wardsikeme, Aliejuny, Sakischki, Poshemischki, Karatschuny, Smolwy, Paukschte-Lischki, Gut Smolwy (nord), Dulzischki, Matelischki.

Le tracé de cette ligne sur le terrain est laissé aux soins des deux Gouvernements intéressés, qui auront toute latitude pour procéder, d'un commun accord, aux rectifications de détail qu'ils reconnaîtraient, sur place, indispensables.

II.—Décide de reconnaître à la Pologne, qui accepte, tous droits de souveraineté sur les territoires compris entre les frontières ci-dessus définies et les autres frontières du territoire polonais, sous réserve des dispositions du Traité de Paix de Saint-Germain-en-Laye concernant les charges et obligations incombant aux États auxquels un territoire de l'ancienne Monarchie austro-hongroise est transféré.

Fait à Paris, le quinze mars mil neuf cent vingt-trois.

Eric Phipps   R. Poincaré
Romano Avezzana   M. Matsuda

Le soussigné dûment autorisé, déclare, au nom du Gouvernement polonais, accepter les dispositions ci-dessus.

Fait à Paris, le quinze mars mil neuf cent vingt-trois.

Maurice Zamoyski

No. 5

Protocol between Estonia, Latvia, Poland, Rumania and the USSR for the immediate entry into force of the Treaty of Paris, of August 27, 1928, regarding Renunciation of War as an Instrument of National Policy[1]

Moscow, February 9, 1929   Dz.U.R.P., 1929, No. 29/283, 284 and No. 63/489, 490

L.N., T.S., Vol. LXXXIX, No. 2028, pp. 369–375

Protocole

signé à Moscou, le 9 février 1929 entre l'Estonie, la Lettonie, la Pologne, la Roumanie et l'Union des Républiques Soviétiques Socialistes, relatif à la mise en vigueur du Traité de renonciation à la guerre, signé à Paris, 27 août 1928.

Le Gouvernement de la République Estonienne, le Président de la République de Lettonie, le Président de la République de Pologne, sa Majesté le Roi de Roumanie et le Comité Central Exécutif de l'Union des Républiques Soviétiques Socialistes,

animés du désir de contribuer au maintien de la paix existante entre leurs Pays et de mettre à ces fins sans délai en vigueur entre les peuples de ces Pays le Traité de renonciation à la guerre, en tant qu'instrument de politique nationale, signé à Paris, le 27 août 1928,

ont décidé de réaliser ces intentions par l'effet du présent Protocole et ont nommé comme Plénipotentiaires, savoir:

Le Gouvernement de la République Estonienne:

Monsieur Julius Seljamaa, Envoyé Extraordinaire et Ministre Plénipotentiaire d'Estonie à Moscou;

Le Président de la République de Lettonie:

Monsieur Charles Ozols, Envoyé Extraordinaire et Ministre Plénipotentiaire de Lettonie à Moscou;

Le Président de la République de Pologne:

Monsieur Stanisław Patek, Envoyé Extraordinaire et Ministre Plénipotentiaire de Pologne à Moscou;

Sa Majesté le Roi de Roumanie:

Monsieur Charles A. Davila, Son Envoyé Extraordinaire et Ministre Plénipotentiaire à Varsovie et

Le Comité Central Exécutif de l'Union des Républiques Soviétiques Socialistes:

Monsieur Maxime Litvinoff, Membre du Comité Central Exécutif, Commissaire du Peuple ad interim aux Affaires Etrangères,

[1] (*a*) French official text communicated by the Polish Delegate accredited to the League of Nations and the Estonian Minister for Foreign Affairs.

(*b*) Instruments of ratification: Latvia, March 5, 1929; Estonia, March 16, 1929; Poland, March 30, 1929; Rumania, March 30, 1929. The registration of this Protocol took place June 3, 1929.

(*c*) Among the signatories of this Protocol Poland only was the co-partner of the Treaty of Paris of August 27, 1928.

Lesquels, après s'être communiqué leurs pleins pouvoirs, reconnus en bonne et due forme, sont tombés d'accord sur ce qui suit:

Article I

Le Traité de renonciation à la guerre en tant qu'instrument de politique nationale, signé à Paris le 27 août 1928, dont copie est jointe au présent Protocole comme sa partie intégrante, entre en vigueur entre les Parties Contractantes après la ratification dudit Traité de Paris de 1928 par les organismes législatifs compétents des États Contractants respectifs.

Article II

La mise en vigueur par le présent Protocole du Traité de Paris de 1928 dans les relations mutuelles des Parties au présent Protocole sera valable indépendamment de l'entrée en vigueur du Traité de Paris de 1928, comme elle est stipulée par l'article III de ce dernier.

Article III

1. Le présent Protocole sera ratifié par les organismes législatifs compétents des Parties Contractantes, conformément aux exigences de leurs constitutions respectives.

2. Les instruments de ratifications seront déposés par chacune des Parties Contractantes au Gouvernement de l'Union des Républiques Soviétiques Socialistes dans le délai d'une semaine à partir de la date de la ratification du présent Protocole par la Partie respective.

3. Dès le jour du dépôt de l'instrument de ratification par deux des Parties Contractantes le présent Protocole entrera en vigueur entre ces deux Parties. Dans les relations mutuelles des autres Parties Contractantes et des États pour lesquels le Protocole est déjà entré en vigueur, il entrera en vigueur au fur et à mesure du dépôt de leur instrument de ratification.

4. Le Gouvernement de l'Union des Républiques Soviétiques Socialistes notifiera immédiatement chaque dépôt à tous les signataires du présent Protocole.

Article IV

Afin de donner effet à l'Article premier du présent Protocole, chaque Partie Contractante après ratification par ses organismes législatifs du Traité de Paris de 1928, en notifiera immédiatement par voie diplomatique le Gouvernement de l'Union des Républiques Soviétiques Socialistes et toutes les autres Parties au présent Protocole.

Article V

Le présent Protocole est ouvert à l'adhésion des Gouvernements de tous les pays. La notification de l'adhésion définitive devra être faite au nom du Gouvernement de l'Union des Républiques Soviétiques Socialistes qui en notifiera toutes les autres Parties au présent Protocole. Dès la réception de ladite notification concernant l'adhésion, le présent Protocole sera mis en

13

vigueur dans les relations mutuelles de l'État adhérant et de toutes les autres Parties au présent Protocole.

Article VI

La mise en vigueur par l'effet du présent Protocole du Traité de Paris de 1928 dans les relations mutuelles de l'État adhérant et de toutes les autres Parties au présent Protocole devra être réalisée dans la voie prévue à l'article IV du présent Protocole.

Article VII

Le présent Protocole est dressé en un seul exemplaire, dont copie authentique sera communiquée par le Gouvernement de l'Union des Républiques Soviétiques Socialistes à chacun des États signataires ou adhérants.

En foi de quoi les Plénipotentiaires susnommés ont signé le présent Protocole et y ont apposé leurs sceaux.

No. 6
Pact of Non-Aggression between Poland and the USSR[1]

Moscow, July 25, 1932 Dz.U.R.P., 1932, No. 115/951/953
Transl. from Polish: Pol.-Sov.R., No. 7

The President of the Polish Republic, of the one part, and the Central Executive Committee of the Union of Soviet Socialist Republics, of the other part,

Desirous of maintaining the present state of peace between their countries, and convinced that the maintenance of peace between them constitutes an important factor in the work of preserving universal peace;

Considering that the Treaty of Peace of March 18, 1921, constitutes, now as in the past, the basis of their reciprocal relations and undertakings;

Convinced that the peaceful settlement of international disputes and the exclusion of all that might be contrary to the normal condition of relations between States are the surest means of arriving at the goal desired;

Declaring that none of the obligations hitherto assumed by either of the Parties stands in the way of the peaceful development of their mutual relations or is incompatible with the present Pact;

Have decided to conclude the present Pact with the object of amplifying and completing the pact for the renunciation of war signed at Paris on August 27, 1928, and put into force by the Protocol signed at Moscow on February 9, 1929, and for that purpose have designated as their Plenipotentiaries. [. . .][2]

Who, after exchanging their full powers, found in good and due form, have agreed on the following provisions:

[1] See Note No. 6.
[2] The Plenipotentiaries: Min. Stanisław Patek and Deputy Commissar Nikolai Krestinsky.

Article 1

The two Contracting Parties, recording the fact that they have renounced war as an instrument of national policy in their mutual relations, reciprocally undertake to refrain from taking any aggressive action against or invading the territory of the other Party, either alone or in conjunction with other Powers.

Any act of violence attacking the integrity and inviolability of the territory or the political independence of the other Contracting Party shall be regarded as contrary to the undertakings contained in the present Article, even if such acts are committed without declaration of war and avoid all possible warlike manifestations.

Article 2

Should one of the Contracting Parties be attacked by a third State or by a group of other States, the other Contracting Party undertakes not to give aid or assistance, either directly or indirectly, to the aggressor State during the whole period of the conflict.

If one of the Contracting Parties commits an act of aggression against a third State the other Contracting Party shall have the right to be released from the present Treaty without previous denunciation.

Article 3

Each of the Contracting Parties undertakes not to be a party to any agreement openly hostile to the other Party from the point of view of aggression.

Article 4

The undertakings provided for in Articles 1 and 2 of the present Pact shall in no case limit or modify the international rights and obligations of each Contracting Party under agreements concluded by it before the coming into force of the present Pact, so far as the said agreements contain no aggressive elements.

Article 5

The two Contracting Parties, desirous of settling and solving, exclusively by peaceful means, any disputes and differences, of whatever nature or origin, which may arise between them, undertake to submit questions at issue, which it has not been possible to settle within a reasonable period by diplomatic channels, to a procedure of conciliation, in accordance with the provisions of the Convention for the application of the procedure of conciliation, which constitutes an integral part of the present Pact and shall be signed separately and ratified as soon as possible simultaneously with the Pact of Non-Aggression.[3]

[3] The Convention for Conciliation between the Republic of Poland and the Union of Soviet Socialist Republics was signed at Moscow, November 23, 1932.

Article 6

The present Pact shall be ratified as soon as possible, and the instruments of ratification shall be exchanged at Warsaw within thirty days following the ratification by Poland and the Union of Soviet Socialist Republics, after which the Pact shall come into force immediately.

Article 7

The Pact is concluded for three years. If it is not denounced by one of the Contracting Parties, after previous notice of not less than six months before the expiry of that period, it shall be automatically renewed for a further period of two years.

Article 8

The present Pact is drawn up in Polish and Russian, both texts being authentic.

In faith whereof the above-named Plenipotentiaries have signed the present Pact and have thereto affixed their seals.[4]

Done at Moscow, in two copies, July 25, 1932.

Protocol of Signature No. 1

The Contracting Parties declare that Article 7 of the Pact of July 25, 1932, cannot be interpreted as meaning that the expiry of the time-limit or denunciation before the expiry of the time-period under Article 7 could have as a result the limitation or cancellation of the obligations arising out of the Pact of Paris of 1928.

Done at Moscow, in two copies, July 25, 1932.

Protocol of Signature No. 2

On signing the Pact of Non-Aggression this day, the two Parties having exchanged their views on the draft Conciliation Convention submitted by the Soviet Party, declare that they are convinced that there is no essential difference of opinion between them.

Done at Moscow, in two copies, July 25, 1932.

[4] Entry into force of this Pact took place on December 23, 1932.

No. 7
Convention for the Definition of Aggression[1]

London, July 3, 1933   Dz.U.R.P., 1933, No. 93/712, 713

Le Président de la République de Pologne, le Président de la République d'Estonie, le Président de la République de Lettonie, Sa Majesté le Roi de Roumanie, le Président de la République de Turquie, le Comité Central Exécutif de l'Union des Républiques Soviétiques Socialistes, Sa Majesté Impériale le Shah de Perse et Sa Majesté le Roi d'Afghanistan,

[1] See Note No. 7. Ratification of this Convention by the Polish Government took place on November 4, 1933.

Désireux de renforcer la Paix existante entre leurs pays;

Considérant que le Pacte Briand-Kellog, dont ils sont signataires, interdit toute agression;

Estimant nécessaire, dans l'intérêt de la sécurité générale de définir de manière aussi précise que possible l'agression afin de prévenir tout prétexte pour sa justification;

Constatant que tous les États ont également droit à l'indépendance, à la sécurité, à la défense de leurs territoires, et au libre développement de leurs institutions;

Animés du désir, dans l'intérêt de la paix générale d'assurer à tous les peuples l'inviolabilité du territoire de leur pays;

Jugeant utile, dans l'intérêt de la paix générale, de mettre en vigueur entre leurs pays des règles précises définissant l'agression, en attendant que ces dernières deviennent universelles,

Ont décidé, dans ces buts, de conclure la présente Convention et ont dûment autorisé à cet effet:

Le Président de la République de Pologne:

M. Edouard Raczyński, Délégué permanent auprès de la Société des Nations, Envoyé Extraordinaire et Ministre Plénipotentiaire;

Le Président de la République d'Estonie:

M. le Dr. Oskar Kallas, Envoyé Extraordinaire et Ministre Plénipotentiaire à Londres;

Le Président de la République de Lettonie:

M. Waldemaras Salnais, Ministre des Affaires Étrangères;

Sa Majesté le Roi de Roumanie:

M. Nicolas Titulesco, Ministre des Affaires Étrangères;

Le Président de la République de Turquie:

Tevfik Rüstü bey, Ministre des Affaires Étrangères;

Le Comité Central Exécutif de l'Union des Républiques Soviétiques Socialistes:

M. Maxime Litvinoff, Commissaire du Peuple aux Affaires Étrangères;

Sa Majesté Impériale le Shah de Perse:

Fatollah Khan Noury Esfandiary, Chargé d'Affaires à Londres;

Sa Majesté le Roi d'Afghanistan:

Ali Mohammed Khan, Ministre de l'Instruction Publique:

Lesquels ont convenu des dispositions suivantes:

Article I

Chacune des Hautes Parties Contractantes s'engage à accepter dans ses rapports mutuels avec chacune des autres et à partir du jour de la mise en vigueur de la présente Convention la définition de l'agression telle qu'elle a été expliquée dans le rapport du Comité pour les questions de sécurité en date du 24 Mai 1933 (Rapport Politis) à la Conférence pour la réduction et la limitation des armements, rapport fait à la suite de la proposition de la Délégation Soviétique.

Article II

En conséquence, sera reconnu comme agresseur dans un conflit international, sous réserve des accords en vigueur entre les parties en conflit, l'État qui, le premier, aura commis l'une des actions suivantes:

1. Déclaration de guerre à un autre État;
2. Invasion par ses forces armées, même sans déclaration de guerre, du territoire d'un autre État;
3. Attaque par ses forces terrestres, navales ou aériennes, même sans déclaration de guerre, du territoire, des navires, ou des aéronefs d'un autre État;
4. Blocus naval des côtes ou des ports d'un autre État;
5. Appui donné à des bandes armées qui, formées sur son territoire, auront envahi le territoire d'un autre État, ou refus, malgré la demande de l'État envahi, de prendre, sur son propre territoire, toutes les mesures en son pouvoir pour priver lesdites bandes de toute aide ou protection.

Article III

Aucune considération d'ordre politique, militaire, économique ou autre ne pourra servir d'excuse ou de justification à l'agression prévue à l'Article II (A titre d'exemple voir l'Annexe).

Article IV

La présente Convention sera ratifiée par les Hautes Parties Contractantes conformément à la législation de chacune d'entre elles.

Les instruments de ratification seront déposés par chacune des Hautes Parties Contractantes auprès du Gouvernement de l'Union des Républiques Soviétiques Socialistes.

Aussitôt que les instruments de ratification auront été déposés par deux des Hautes Parties Contractantes, la présent Convention entrera en vigueur entre ces deux Parties. Elle entrera en vigueur pour toutes les autres Hautes Parties Contractantes à mesure que ces dernières déposeront à leur tour leurs instruments de ratification.

Chaque dépôt des instruments de ratification sera immédiatement notifié par le Gouvernement de l'Union des Républiques Soviétiques Socialistes à tous les signataires de la présente Convention.

Article V

La présente Convention a été signée en huit exemplaire dont chacune des Hautes Parties Contractantes en a reçu un.

En foi de quoi les Plénipotentiaires énumérés ci-dessus ont signé la présente Convention et y ont apposé leurs sceaux.

Annexe

à l'Article III de la Convention relative à la définition de l'agression.

Les Hautes Parties Contractantes signataires de la Convention relative à la définition de l'agression,

Désirant, sous la réserve expresse de ne restreindre en rien le portée absolue de la règle posée à l'Article III de ladite Convention, fournir certaines indications de nature à déterminer l'agresseur,

Constatent qu'aucun acte d'agression au sens de l'Article II de ladite Convention ne pourra, entre autre, être justifié par l'une des circonstances suivantes:

A. La situation intérieure d'un État.

Par exemple

sa structure politique, économique ou sociale; les défauts allégués de son administration; les troubles provenant de grèves, révolutions, contre-révolutions ou guerre civile.

B. La conduite internationale d'un État.

Par exemple

la violation ou le danger de violation des droits ou intérêts matériels ou moraux d'un État étranger ou de ses ressortissants; la rupture des relations diplomatiques ou économiques; les mesures de boycottage économique ou financier; les différends relatifs à des engagements économiques, financiers ou autres envers des États étrangers; les incidents de frontière ne rentrant pas dans un des cas d'agression indiqués dans l'Article II.

Les Hautes Parties Contractantes sont d'autre part d'accord pour reconnaître que la présente Convention ne devra jamais servir à légitimer les violations du droit des gens qui pourraient être impliquées dans les circonstances comprises dans l'énumération ci-dessus.

Protocole de Signature

Il est convenu entre les Hautes Parties Contractantes que si ultérieurement un ou plusieurs des autres États immédiatement voisins de l'Union des Républiques Soviétiques Socialistes adhère à la présente Convention, cette adhésion lui ou leur conférera les mêmes droits et imposera les mêmes obligations que ceux des signataires originaires.

No. 8

Statement made by Minister Beck to the Representative of the 'Iskra Press Agency' on the Convention of the Eastern Powers for the Definition of Aggression

Warsaw, July 3, 1933   Pol.W.B., No. 153

I consider the Convention for the definition of Aggression, which has been signed today by the Representatives of Poland, Afghanistan, Estonia, Latvia,

Persia, Rumania, Turkey and the USSR, as an important political and outstandingly creative act. In the system of Eastern regional pacts it is a synthesis of individual efforts towards the effective organization of a peaceable co-existence. The geographical scope of this Convention is the best indication of its true political significance.

In Poland's foreign policy the Convention for the definition of Aggression is a logical sequence to a whole series of political agreements which are the basis of the constantly improving Polish-Soviet relations. I have in mind the Protocol signed at Moscow in 1929 accelerating the bringing into force of the Kellogg Pact, the Pact of Non-Aggression and the Conciliation Agreement.

In view of our Alliance with Rumania and relations with the Soviet Union, the signatures of Soviet Russia, Rumania and Poland on the same political Agreement are a source of special satisfaction to us.

No. 9

Official communiqué issued in connection with Minister Beck's visit to Moscow[1]

Moscow, February 15, 1934   'Pravda', February 16, 1934
Transl. from Russian: Pol.W.B., No. 156

The three-day visit to Moscow of the Minister for Foreign Affairs of the Republic of Poland, M. Beck, afforded him and the People's Commissar for Foreign Affairs, M. Litvinov, an opportunity of having several long conversations.

During these conversations both ministers carried out a survey and considered not only the general political international situation, but also the international problems arising from it, and in particular those which interest or may interest the Republic of Poland and the Union of Soviet Socialist Republics.

The exchange of views between M. Beck and M. Litvinov revealed a community of views in regard to many of these problems, as well as the lasting decision of the Governments they represent to continue their endeavours for a further improvement in mutual relations between the Republic of Poland and the Union of Soviet Socialist Republics, as also for a *rapprochement* between the peoples of both States. The foundation of any such *rapprochement* is the Pact of Non-Aggression and the Convention for the Definition of Aggression concluded between both countries, which it is recognized as desirable to give as permanent a character as possible. In the spirit of these acts both Governments are ready to co-operate in the preservation and reinforcement of a general peace, in this co-operation directing special attention to the maintenance of peaceful and normal relations in the eastern part of Europe which more closely interests them.

Taking into consideration the present state of Polish-Soviet relations, together with the increasing possibilities and importance of the international

[1] See Note No. 9.

co-operation of both States, in the name of his Government M. Beck proposed the reciprocal elevation of the diplomatic representations of both States in Warsaw and Moscow to the status of embassies. M. Litvinov completely associated himself with M. Beck's opinion and accepted the proposal in the name of his Government.

No. 10

Protocol renewing the Pact of Non-Aggression of July 25, 1932, between Poland and the USSR until December 31, 1945

Moscow, May 5, 1934 Dz.U.R.P., 1934, No. 53/487, 488
Transl. from Polish: Pol.W.B., No. 157

The President of the Republic of Poland, and The Central Executive Committee of the Union of Soviet Socialist Republics,

Being desirous of providing as firm a basis as possible for the development of the relations between their countries;

Being desirous of giving each other fresh proof of the unchangeable character and solidity of the pacific and friendly relations happily established between them;

Moved by the desire to collaborate in the consolidation of world peace and also for the stability and peaceful development of international relations in Eastern Europe;

Noting that the conclusion on July 25, 1932, at Moscow, of the Treaty between the Republic of Poland and the Union of Soviet Socialist Republics has had a beneficial influence on the development of their relations and on the solution of the above-mentioned problems;

Have decided to sign the present Protocol, and have for this purpose appointed as their Plenipotentiaries [. . .].[1]

Who, having communicated their full powers, found in good and true form, have agreed on the following provisions:

Article 1

In modification of the provisions of Article 7 of the Treaty of Non-Aggression concluded at Moscow on July 25, 1932, between the Republic of Poland and the Union of Soviet Socialist Republics concerning the date and manner in which that Treaty shall cease to have effect, the two Contracting Parties decide that it shall remain in force until December 31, 1945.

Each of the High Contracting Parties shall be entitled to denounce the Treaty by giving notice to that effect six months before the expiry of the above-mentioned period. If the Treaty is not denounced by either of the Contracting Parties, its period of validity shall be automatically prolonged for two years; similarly, the Treaty shall be regarded as prolonged on each occasion for a further period of two years, if it is not denounced by either of the Contracting Parties in the manner provided for in the present Article.

[1] The Plenipotentiaries: Ambassador Juliusz Łukasiewicz and Member of C.C. Maxim M. Litvinov.

Article 2

The present Protocol is drawn up in duplicate, each copy being in the Polish and Russian languages and both texts being equally authentic.

The present Protocol shall be ratified as soon as possible, and the instruments of ratification shall be exchanged between the Contracting Parties at Warsaw.[2]

The present Protocol shall come into force on the date of the exchange of the instruments of ratification.

In faith whereof the above-mentioned Plenipotentiaries have signed the present Protocol and have thereto affixed their seals.

Done at Moscow in duplicate, in the Polish and Russian languages, the 5th day of May, 1934.

Final Protocol

In connection with the signature on this date of the Protocol prolonging the Treaty of Non-Aggression between the Republic of Poland and the Union of Soviet Socialist Republics of July 25, 1932, each of the High Contracting Parties, having again examined all the provisions of the Peace Treaty concluded at Riga on March 18, 1921, which constitutes the basis of their mutual relations, declares that it has no obligations and is not bound by any declarations inconsistent with the provisions of the said Peace Treaty and in particular of Article 3 thereof.

Consequently, the Government of the Union of Soviet Socialist Republics confirms that the note from the People's Commissar, G. V. Chicherin, of September 28, 1926, to the Lithuanian Government cannot be interpreted to mean that the note implied any intention on the part of the Soviet Government to interfere in the settlement of the territorial questions mentioned therein.

Done at Moscow in duplicate, in the Polish and Russian languages, the 5th day of May, 1934.

[2] Ratification of the present Protocol by the Polish Government took place on June 16, 1934.

No. 11

Note from Chargé d'Affaires Sokolnicki to Commissar Krestinsky in connection with the admission of the USSR into the League of Nations[1]

Moscow, September 10, 1934   Pol.W.B., No. 158

In connection with the eventuality of the entry of the Union of Soviet Socialist Republics into the League of Nations, the Government of the Republic of Poland proposes to the Government of the Union of Soviet Socialist Republics a reciprocal recognition that after the Union of Soviet Socialist Republics has entered the League of Nations the relations between the Republic of Poland and the Union of Soviet Socialist Republics will in all

[1] See Note No. 11.

their extent continue on the basis of all existing agreements between them, including the Pact of Non-Aggression and the Convention for Definition of Aggression.

No. 12

Note from Commissar Krestinsky to Chargé d'Affaires Sokolnicki in reply to his Note of the same day

Moscow, September 10, 1934   Pol.W.B., No. 158

In reply to your note of today's date, I have the honour to communicate to you in the name of my Government that the Government of the Union of Soviet Socialist Republics completely agrees with the Polish Government on the question that, after the eventual invitation to and entry of the Union of Soviet Socialist Republics into the League of Nations the relations between the Union of Soviet Socialist Republics and the Republic of Poland will remain on the basis of the treaties existing between them, all of which, including the Pact of Non-Aggression and the Convention for the Definition of Aggression, will continue to preserve all their force.

No. 13

Telegram from Minister Beck to all Polish Diplomatic Missions abroad concerning the Anti-Comintern Pact[1]

Warsaw, November 9, 1937   GSHI, A.12.53/18
                                           Transl. from Polish: Pol.W.B., No. 159

So far no proposals to join the Italo-German-Japanese Protocol have been received by Poland. In any case, Poland could not be a party to that Protocol in view of her special position as neighbour of the USSR, as well as her objection in principle to the formation of any bloc.

If inquiries are made on this subject please reply in the above sense.

[1] See Note No. 13.

No. 14

Joint Communiqué issued by the Polish and Soviet Governments on the subject of Polish-Soviet relations[1]

Warsaw, November 26, 1938   Pol.W.B., No. 160

A series of conversations recently held between the USSR People's Commissar for Foreign Affairs, M. Litvinov, and the Polish Ambassador in Moscow, M. Grzybowski, has led to the following statement:

1. Relations between the Polish Republic and the Union of Soviet Socialist Republics are and will continue to be based to the fullest extent on all the existing Agreements, including the Polish-Soviet Pact of Non-Aggression

[1] See Note No. 14.

23

dated July 25, 1932. This Pact, concluded for five years and extended on May 5, 1934, for a further period ending December 31, 1945, has a basis wide enough to guarantee the inviolability of peaceful relations between the two States.

2. Both Governments are favourable to the extension of their commercial relations.

3. Both Governments agree that it is necessary to settle a number of current and longstanding matters which have arisen in connection with the various agreements in force, and, in particular, to dispose of the various frontier incidents which have lately been occurring.

No. 15

Official Commentary issued by the PAT on the Joint Polish-Soviet Communiqué regarding Polish-Soviet relations

Warsaw, November 26, 1938   Pol.W.B., No. 161

Conversations recently held between M. Litvinov, the People's Commissar for Foreign Affairs, and M. Grzybowski, the Polish Ambassador in Moscow, and the Communiqué recently issued as their result, are the expression of the enduring and unalterable will of both Governments to regulate their mutual relations in accordance with the existing bilateral Agreements, and loyally to observe them. This mutual tendency appears to provide a sufficient guarantee for stabilization of conditions on the Polish-Soviet frontier.

No. 16

Communiqué issued by the PAT on the signing of the Polish-Soviet Commercial Agreement in Moscow[1]

Warsaw, February 19, 1939   Pol.W.B., No. 162

Negotiations which have been taking place for some time past between Poland and the USSR, have led to the signing of the following Agreements embodying economic relations between Poland and the USSR: a Commercial Agreement, an Understanding with regard to trade turnover, and an Understanding with regard to clearing operations.

The Agreements were signed on behalf of Poland by M. Grzybowski, Polish Ambassador in Moscow, and M. Łychowski, the head of the Trade Delegation, and on behalf of the Soviets by M. A. J. Mikoyan, the USSR People's Commissar for Foreign Trade. This Agreement is the first general Polish-Soviet Commercial Agreement to be based on the most favoured nation principle. It includes a number of points of principle concerning trade turnover and also maritime transport.

The Agreement with regard to trade turnover provides for a considerable extension of trading operations between the two countries. The main articles of Polish imports from the USSR will be cotton and cotton by-products, furs,

---

[1] See Note No. 16.

apatites, tobacco, manganese ore, asbestos, graphite, etc. Poland, for her part, will supply the Soviet Union with coal, iron manufactures, zinc and sheet zinc, textiles, textile machinery, tanned leather and viscose.

The clearing Agreement stipulates that financial payments will be effected through a Polish Clearing Institution.

No. 17

Statement by Mr. Chamberlain in the House of Commons regarding the British guarantee to Poland

London, March 31, 1939   H.C.Deb., 345/2415–2417, 2419

The Prime Minister [Mr. Chamberlain]: The Right Hon. Gentleman the Leader of the Opposition asked me this morning whether I could make a statement as to the European situation. As I said this morning, His Majesty's Government have no official confirmation of the rumours of any projected attack and they must not, therefore, be taken as accepting them as true.

I am glad to take this opportunity of stating again the general policy of His Majesty's Government. They have constantly advocated the adjustment, by way of free negotiation between the parties concerned, of any differences that may arise between them. They consider that this is the natural and proper course where differences exist. In their opinion there should be no question incapable of solution by peaceful means, and they would see no justification for the substitution of force or threats of force for the method of negotiation.

As the House is aware, certain consultations are now proceeding with other Governments. In order to make perfectly clear the position of His Majesty's Government in the meantime before those consultations are concluded, I now have to inform the House that during that period, in the event of any action which clearly threatened Polish independence, and which the Polish Government accordingly considered it vital to resist with their national force, His Majesty's Government would feel themselves bound at once to lend the Polish Government all support in their power. They have given the Polish Government an assurance to this effect.

I may add that the French Government have authorized me to make it plain that they stand in the same position in this matter as do His Majesty's Government.

No. 18

Record of a conversation between Minister Beck and Lord Halifax on the Polish undertakings in case of a Four Powers Pact. Present also: Sir Alexander Cadogan, Mr. Strang, Ambassador Raczyński, M. Potocki[1]

London, April 4, 1939   D.Brit.F.P., V, No. 1

[. . .] Lord Halifax said that he would now turn to Soviet Russia.

He was glad to hear M. Beck say that His Majesty's Government had

[1] See Note No. 18.

appreciated the position of Poland vis-à-vis Soviet Russia. Would he be right in thinking that the Polish Government would not be sorry if His Majesty's Government could manage to keep on fair terms with Soviet Russia?

M. Beck said that Poland attached great importance to preserving correct relations with Soviet Russia. The Polish Government had signed a pact of non-aggression with her.[2] After a period of tension last autumn, the necessary steps had been taken to bring about a détente. The two countries had even signed a satisfactory commercial treaty. For that reason, the Polish Government could understand that His Majesty's Government should also attach importance to having good relations with Soviet Russia.

He wished, however, to say that any pact of mutual assistance between Poland and Soviet Russia would bring an immediate hostile reaction from Berlin and would probably accelerate the outbreak of a conflict. Poland had succeeded in 1934 in putting Polish-German relations on a normal and satisfactory basis, and this in spite of the existence of the Polish-French Treaty, of which they had never made any secret. But the Polish Government realized that, if they similarly engaged themselves towards their eastern neighbour, matters would be brought to a breaking-point.

Lord Halifax asked whether M. Beck thought that a mutual assistance arrangement between Poland and Great Britain would have a provocative effect on Germany.

M. Beck said he could not give a definite answer. Such an agreement would be a very important matter for Germany, though not so important as a Polish-Russian agreement. He thought the Polish-French Treaty was a good analogy and he recalled that Hitler himself had said that he had nothing to say against that Treaty, as he had no intention of attacking either Poland or France and had no objection to their making a treaty with each other. The same might apply to a Polish treaty with Great Britain.

Lord Halifax said that, making full allowance for these considerations, which he fully understood, it might well be that Poland, Great Britain and France might all be in trouble together and, if so, it might be important to Poland to be able to use the Russian route for the supply of war material. Was the appropriate course not, therefore, to look upon the problem facing Poland and Great Britain and France as the problem of how to get a maximum degree of collaboration from Soviet Russia without entailing dangerous consequences?

M. Beck appreciated this argument, but insisted that the aim of the efforts which were now being made should be the maintenance of peace, and that every care should be taken not to do anything to make the danger of war more imminent. Poland, for her part, was ready to improve her relations with Soviet Russia, but not to extend them. It was important not to provoke a conflict, though it was, of course, difficult to say whether, indeed, a conflict was unavoidable.

Lord Halifax asked how far it would be an embarrassment to the Polish Government, and open to objection from their point of view, if relations

[2] See doc. No. 10.

26

between France and Soviet Russia, or even between Great Britain and Soviet Russia, were made closer.

M. Beck recalled that during the negotiations between France and the Soviet Union which led up to the Franco-Soviet Pact, the Polish Government made an arrangement with M. Laval by which the latter accepted a Polish declaration to the effect that no undertaking entered into by France towards the Soviet Union could extend Polish liabilities. If France and Great Britain now undertook obligations towards the Soviet Union, Poland would find it necessary to make some similar declaration.

He thought that France had made a bad bargain under the Franco-Soviet Pact, which brought few concrete results and made a détente with Berlin and Rome more difficult.

Lord Halifax asked whether, if France decided to simplify the Franco-Soviet Pact and make its operation more automatic, M. Beck would feel it necessary to do or say something to show that Poland was not affected and was keeping out of it.

M. Beck said that he would.

Lord Halifax asked what value M. Beck placed upon the Soviet military forces and upon the Soviet transport system as a means of transit.

M. Beck replied that the second question was really one for experts, but the Polish Government had not a very high opinion of Soviet Russia from either point of view. In the autumn of 1938 four Soviet army corps had moved towards the Polish frontier, but Poland had not thought it necessary to move a single detachment.

Lord Halifax said that his information was that the Red army might be efficient for purposes of defence, but not for purposes of offensive operations.

M. Beck said that this was also the view of the Polish General Staff.

Lord Halifax explained that one of the difficulties about Soviet Russia in this country was that some members of the Labour party believed that, if Great Britain and the Soviet Union could join hands, the world would be safe for ever more.

M. Beck said he doubted the validity of this theory. There was no common frontier between Germany and Soviet Russia.

Discussion then turned on Roumania.

M. Beck said that he wished to consult the Roumanian Foreign Minister before coming to any final conclusion as regards the Roumanian aspect of our proposal.

Lord Halifax fully appreciated what M. Beck had said about Roumania and Hungary and about the danger of throwing Hungary into Germany's arms. On the other hand, he thought that there was great danger in having no concerted plan as to what to do if Roumania were the object of an attack, either directly, or indirectly through Hungary.

M. Beck thought that it was desirable to give Roumania some backing. Poland had done so from the military point of view. Great Britain could do so from the economic and other points of view. This would be a different thing from a rigid political system like the Little Entente which would automatically throw Hungary into the other camp. Poland was anxious for good relations between Roumania and Hungary, and had even threatened Hungary a short time ago that there would be trouble if Hungary did anything to endanger Roumania. At the same time the Polish Government were loath to waste what little political capital they possessed in Budapest.

Lord Halifax was sure that it was M. Beck's view that Great Britain and Poland had a common interest in preventing Roumania from being swallowed up by Germany like Czecho-Slovakia.

M. Beck entirely agreed.

Lord Halifax explained that what His Majesty's Government had suggested was the establishment of a deterrent by means of a preliminary understanding between Great Britain, France and Poland, against an attack upon Roumania. He understood that M. Beck felt that this would cause trouble by throwing Hungary the wrong way.

A third point was, if the case which Lord Halifax had been putting was sound, would not M. Beck think it important that the Polish Government and His Majesty's Government and, if possible, the French Government, should arrive at a common decision as to what they would be prepared to do in the event of Roumania being threatened?

M. Beck replied that he would like to think this point over. He was awaiting further information from Bucharest as to the Roumanian attitude.

No. 19

Telegram from Minister Beck to the Polish Embassy in Paris on his conversation with Deputy-Commissar Potemkin regarding the Soviet attitude in the event of an armed conflict between Poland and Germany[1]

Warsaw, May 13, 1939   Pol.W.B., No. 163

The conversations with M. Potemkin during his stay in Warsaw on the 10th inst. have made it clear that the Soviet Government takes an understanding attitude to our point of view with regard to Polish-Soviet relations, which are now developing quite normally.

The Soviets realize that the Polish Government is not prepared to enter into any agreement with either one of Poland's great neighbours against the other, and understand the advantages to them of this attitude.

M. Potemkin also stated that in the event of an armed conflict between Poland and Germany the Soviets will adopt '*une attitude bienveillante*' towards us.

As M. Potemkin himself indicated, his statements were made in accordance with special instructions which the Soviet Government sent to Warsaw for him.

[1] See Note No. 19.

28

No. 20

Extracts from Ambassador Schulenburg's letter to State Secretary Weiz-
säcker transmitting a memorandum on his conversation with Commissar
Molotov on the necessity of a political basis for the economic negotiations in
course[1]

Moscow, May 22, 1939   D.Germ.F.P., VI, No. 424

I have the honour to transmit to you as an enclosure a copy of the memorandum[2] which gives the gist and course of my interview with M. Molotov
on May 20. I have also sent the memorandum as a despatch.

The Reich [Foreign] Minister directed me to maintain extreme caution
in my conference with Molotov. As a result I contented myself with saying
as little as possible, the more so as the attitude of M. Molotov seems to me
quite suspicious. It cannot be understood otherwise than that the resumption
of our economic negotiations does not satisfy him as a political gesture and
that he obviously wants to obtain from us more extensive proposals of a
political nature. We must, I think, be extremely cautious in this field as
long as it is not certain that any possible proposals from our side will not be
used by the Kremlin only to exert pressure on Britain and France. On the
other hand, if we want to accomplish something here it may well be unavoidable that we sooner or later take some action.

[1] See Note No. 20.
[2] See D.Germ.F.P., No. 424, the above letter covers the tenor of the Memorandum [not
printed].

No. 21

Extracts from the speech by Commissar Molotov at the Supreme Council of the
USSR on the Anglo-Franco-Soviet negotiations

Moscow, May 31, 1939   The Times, June 1, 1939,
                                                 supplemented by Pol.W.B., No. 164

The Soviet Government entered into negotiations with the British and
French Governments regarding the measures necessary for combating
aggression. This was as far back as the middle of last April. The negotiations
then begun are not yet ended. [. . .].

While guaranteeing themselves from direct attack on the part of aggressors
by pacts of mutual assistance between themselves and with Poland, and while
trying to secure for themselves the assistance of the USSR in the event of an
attack by the aggressors on Poland and Rumania, the British and French
left open the question of whether the USSR in its turn might count on their
assistance in the event of it being directly attacked by the aggressors, as they
likewise left open another question—namely, whether they could take part
in guaranteeing small States bordering on the USSR and covering the north-
western frontier of the USSR, should they prove unable to defend their
neutrality from an attack of aggressors. [. . .].

As regards the question of guaranteeing the countries of Central and Eastern Europe, the proposals mentioned make no progress whatever, if regarded from the standpoint of reciprocity. They provide for assistance being given by the USSR to five countries, which the British and French have already promised to guarantee, but they say nothing about the assistance being given by them to the three countries on the north-western frontier of the USSR which may prove unable to defend their neutrality in the event of attack by aggressors. But the Soviet Union cannot assume obligations in regard to the five countries mentioned unless it receives the guarantee in regard to the three countries situated on its north-western frontier. [. . .].

It is almost a direct invitation to Germany to leave Poland and other countries alone for the time being and to attack instead the other States on the Soviet borders by the time-honoured Nazi methods of the instigation and financing of internal disturbances and revolts and then marching in on the 'invitation' of a puppet Government. [. . .].

As is known, a special communiqué was published in February last confirming the development of good neighbourly relations between the USSR and Poland. A certain general improvement is now noticeable in our relations with Poland. Furthermore, the Trade Agreement concluded in March with Poland may considerably increase the trade turnover between the USSR and Poland. [. . .].

No. 22

Minute made by Under-Secretary Szembek after his conversation with Ambassador Sharonov concerning a further improvement of Polish-Soviet relations[1]

Warsaw, June 14, 1939   Pol.W.B., No. 166

In his talk with me, M. Sharonov laid stress on the satisfactory state of Polish-Soviet relations. He pointed out the necessity for their further improvement. He emphasized that the objective must be complete fulfilment of the Trade Agreement. At the moment there are certain difficulties in this respect, for the Agreement has not long been in force, and both sides are anxious for a mutual exchange of commodities at the most favourable prices. M. Sharonov hopes that in this respect also the situation will develop satisfactorily. Finally he stated that M. Potemkin's visit to Warsaw and his conversation with M. Beck had been very beneficial to Polish-Soviet relations.

Subsequently we discussed the international situation. When I remarked that it was difficult and complicated, the Ambassador said that in his opinion there would be no armed conflict in Europe.

When I asked him about Soviet-Japanese relations M. Sharonov told me that these relations are always and by their very nature very difficult. In any case, Japan is at present greatly occupied with her difficult situation in China.

[1] See Note No. 22.

No. 23

Telegram from Ambassador Schulenburg to the German Ministry for Foreign Affairs concerning a suggested political basis for German-Soviet relations

Moscow, July 3, 1939   D.Germ.F.P., VI, No. 607

[. . .] Molotov received me in the Kremlin three hours after I had asked for an interview. [. . .].

I opened the discussion with the statement that on the basis of the talks in Berlin, particularly with the Foreign Minister, I had the impression that we would welcome a normalization of relations with the Soviet Union. The State Secretary had very clearly acquainted M. Astakhov with our attitude. The following were indicative of this attitude:

The correct tone of the German press towards the Soviet Union, the conclusion of Non-Aggression Pacts with the Baltic States, and our desire for the resumption of economic negotiations.

Molotov listened with interest, and stated that he took note of my communication with satisfaction. I continued that since the conversation of the State Secretary with Astakhov, we had waited for a Soviet statement as to what Molotov had meant in his conversation with me on May 20 by the words 'construction of a political basis for the resumption of economic negotiations'. I must also point out to him that the attitude of the Soviet press in all questions concerning Germany still gave cause for serious objections.

M. Astakhov had been told that M. Molotov wished to answer me personally. Among other things I had come to enquire whether he had anything to tell me.

In his answer, Molotov did not go into the question as to the meaning of the term 'political basis' but he declared that the Soviet Government, in accordance with the public statements of their leaders, desired good relations with all countries and therefore—provided there was reciprocity—would also welcome a normalization of relations with Germany. It was not the fault of the Soviet Government if these relations had become bad. He could not accept the charge against the Soviet press, since he was not aware of any hostile attitude of the press towards Germany.

I replied that much could be said about these questions; that I had not, however, come to talk of the past, but of the future.

Thereupon Molotov asked how we visualized further developments and what changes had occurred recently in the relations between Germany and the Soviet Union. As to the Non-Aggression Pacts, Germany had concluded them in the first place in her own interest, and they concerned only Germany and the countries participating, but not the Soviet Union. Moreover, judging by Poland's experiences, he must doubt the permanence of such treaties.

I replied that our Non-Aggression Pacts provided the Baltic States with additional security, in which the Soviet Union was very much interested. Poland had herself brought about the termination of the treaty with us by

31

behaving irresponsibly and by joining a combination of Powers hostile to us, which was incompatible with friendly relations with us. To this Molotov stated that in his opinion the treaty concluded by Poland with Britain[1] was a purely defensive instrument.

I contradicted this, and pointed out that the word 'defensive' in this connection was of only academic significance. Then I returned to Molotov's question as to how we visualized further developments and said that, in my opinion, the main task in the future would be that both countries should avoid everything that would lead to a further deterioration of relations and do everything that might result in their improvement. Germany harboured no evil intentions against the Soviet Union; one of the proofs of that was the Treaty of Berlin, which we had extended.

Thereupon Molotov asked: 'Are you convinced that the Berlin Treaty really is still in force and has not been superseded by later treaties concluded by Germany?' I replied: 'I know of no such treaties and have no reason to doubt the validity of the Treaty of Berlin.'

[. . .] The conversation closed in a friendly spirit with my repeated request that Molotov influence the attitude of the Soviet press.

[1] Evidently a reference to the Anglo-Polish Conferences of April 4–6, 1939. See doc. No. 18.

No. 24

Extract from Under-Secretary Szembek's minute of his conversation with Ambassador Sharonov on the rumours about the Soviet-German trade negotiations[1]

Warsaw, July 8, 1939   Pol.W.B., No. 167

When I asked him the position in regard to the Soviet-German trade negotiations, concerning which there have been rumours in the press, M. Sharonov told me that no such negotiations were taking place.

[1] See Note No. 24.

No. 25

Telegram from Minister Ribbentrop to Ambassador Schulenburg referring to his conversation with the Soviet Chargé d'Affaires on the normalization of German-Soviet relations and the necessity of an agreement on the future of Poland[1]

Berlin, August 3, 1939   D.Germ.F.P., VI, No. 760

For the Ambassador personally.

Last night I received the Russian Chargé d'Affaires, who had previously called at the Ministry on other matters. [. . .]. I considered that, in so far as

[1] See Note No. 25.

32

the Russians so desired, a remoulding of our relations would be possible on two conditions:

a/ Non-interference in the internal affairs of the other State [M. Astakhov believes that he can promise this forthwith].

b/ Abandonment of a policy directed against our vital interests. To this Astakhov was unable to give an entirely clear-cut answer, but he thought his Government had the desire to pursue a policy of understanding with Germany.

I continued that our policy was an unswerving and long-range one; we were in no hurry. We were favourably disposed towards Moscow; it was, therefore, a question of what direction the rulers there wished to take. If Moscow took . . . attitude, we should know where we stood and how to act. If the reverse were the case, there was no problem from the Baltic to the Black Sea that could not be solved between the two of us. I said that there was room for the two of us on the Baltic and that Russian interests by no means needed to clash with ours there. As far as Poland was concerned, we were watching further developments attentively and ice cold. In case of Polish provocation we would settle accounts with Poland in the space of a week. For this contingency, I dropped a gentle hint at our coming to an understanding with Russia on the fate of Poland, I described German-Japanese relations as good and friendly; these relations were lasting ones. As to Russian-Japanese relations, however, I had my own special ideas (by which I meant a long-term *modus vivendi* between the two countries) [. . .].

Addition for Count Schulenburg:

I conducted the conversation without showing any haste. The Chargé d'Affaires, who seemed interested, tried several times to pin the conversation down to more concrete terms, whereupon I gave him to understand that I would be prepared to make it more concrete as soon as the Soviet Government officially communicated their fundamental desire for remoulding our relations. Should Astakhov be instructed in this sense, we for our part should be interested in coming to more concrete terms at an early date. This exclusively for your personal information.

No. 26

Telegram from Minister Ribbentrop to Ambassador Schulenburg containing the detailed instruction for his negotiations aiming to restore German-Soviet friendship and jointly clear up the territorial questions in Eastern Europe

Berlin, August 14, 1939   D.Germ.F.P., VII, No. 56

For the Ambassador personally.

I request you to call upon M. Molotov and communicate to him the following:

1. The contradiction between the national idea, exemplified by National

Socialist Germany, and the idea of world revolution, exemplified by the USSR, has in past years been the sole cause for the alignment of Germany and Russia in ideologically separate and hostile camps. The developments of the recent period seem to show that differing philosophies do not prohibit a reasonable relationship between the two States, and the restoration of new, friendly co-operation. The period of opposition in foreign policy could therefore be brought to an end once and for all and the way opened to a new future for both countries.

2. There exist no real conflicts of interests between Germany and Russia. The living spaces of Germany and Russia touch each other, but in their natural requirements they do not overlap. Thus there is lacking all cause for an aggressive attitude on the part of one country against the other. Germany has no aggressive intentions against the USSR. The Reich Government are of the opinion that there is no question between the Baltic Sea and the Black Sea which cannot be settled to the complete satisfaction of both countries. Among these are such questions as: the Baltic Sea, the Baltic States, Poland, South-Eastern questions, etc. Over and above such matters political co-operation between the two countries can only have a beneficial effect. The same applies also to the German and Russian economies, which are complementary in every sphere.

3. There is no doubt that German-Russian policy today has come to an historic turning-point. The decisions with respect to policy to be made in the immediate future in Berlin and Moscow will be of decisive importance for the development of relations between the German and the Russian peoples for generations. On these decisions will depend whether the two peoples will some day, again and without any compelling reason, take up arms against each other, or whether they pass again into a new friendly relationship. It has gone well with both countries previously when they were friends and badly when they were enemies.

4. It is true that Germany and Soviet Russia, as a result of years of ideological opposition, today face each other distrustfully. A great deal of accumulated rubble will have to be cleared away. It must be said, however, that even during this period the natural sympathy of the Germans for the Russians never disappeared. The policy of both States can be built anew on that basis.

5. The Reich Government and the Soviet Government must, judging from past experience, take into account that the capitalistic Western democracies are the implacable enemies of both National Socialist Germany and Soviet Russia. They are today trying again, by the conclusion of a military alliance, to drive Russia into war against Germany. In 1914 the Russian régime collapsed as a result of this policy. It is the compelling interest of both countries to avoid for all future time the destruction of Germany and of Russia in the interests of Western democracies.

6. The crisis which has been produced in German-Polish relations by English policy, as well as English agitation for war and the attempts at an alliance which are bound up with that policy, make a speedy clarification of

German-Russian relations necessary. Otherwise matters might, without Germany contributing thereto, take a turn which would deprive both Governments of the possibility of restoring German-Russian friendship and in due course clarifying jointly territorial questions in Eastern Europe. The leadership of both countries, therefore, should not allow the situation to drift, but should take action at the proper time. It would be fatal if, through mutual ignorance of views and intentions, the two peoples should finally drift apart.

As we have been informed, the Soviet Government also feel the desire for a clarification of German-Russian relations. Since, however, according to previous experience the clarification can be achieved only slowly through the usual diplomatic channels, I am prepared to make a short visit to Moscow in order, in the name of the Führer, to set forth the Führer's views to M. Stalin. In my view, only through such a direct discussion can a change be brought about, and it should not be impossible thereby to lay the foundations for a final settlement of German-Russian relations.

Annex: I request that you do not give M. Molotov these instructions in writing, but that you read them to him verbatim. I consider it important that they reach M. Stalin in as exact a form as possible and I authorize you, if occasion arises, to request from M. Molotov on my behalf an audience with M. Stalin, so that you may be able to make this important communication directly to him also. In addition to a conference with Molotov, a detailed discussion with Stalin would be a condition for my making the trip.

No. 27

Telegram from Ambassador Schulenburg to the German Ministry for Foreign Affairs on his conversation with Commissar Molotov held on 15 August in order to explore the possibility of concluding a non-aggression pact and of jointly guaranteeing the Baltic States

Moscow, August 16, 1939   D.Germ.F.P., VII, No. 70

With reference to your telegram No. 175 of August 14.

Molotov received with greatest interest the information I had been instructed to convey, designated it as extremely important, and declared that he would report it to his Government at once and give me an answer shortly. He could already state that the Soviet Government warmly welcomed German intentions of improving relations with the Soviet Union and, in view of my communication of today, now believed in the sincerity of these intentions.

In the matter of the Reich Foreign Minister coming here, he wanted to state tentatively, as his own opinion, that such a trip required adequate preparation in order that the exchange of opinions might lead to results.

In this connection, he was interested in the question of how the German Government were disposed towards the idea of concluding a non-aggression pact with the Soviet Union, and further, whether the German Government were prepared to influence Japan for the purpose of improving Soviet-Japanese relations and eliminating border conflicts, and whether a possible joint guarantee of the Baltic States was contemplated by Germany.

With regard to the sought-for expansion of economic relations, Molotov admitted that negotiations were progressing successfully in Berlin and approaching a favourable conclusion.

Molotov repeated that if my communication of today included the idea of a non-aggression pact, or something similar, this question must be discussed in concrete terms, in order that, should the Reich Foreign Minister come here, it will not be a matter of an exchange of opinions but of making concrete decisions.

Molotov recognized that speed was necessary in order not to be confronted with accomplished facts, but stressed that adequate preparation of the problems mentioned by him was indispensable.

A detailed memorandum on the course of the conversation will follow on Thursday by special air courier.

No. 28

Telegram from Minister Ribbentrop to Ambassador Schulenburg expressing readiness to conclude a non-aggression pact with the USSR to guarantee the Baltic States and to come to Moscow to speed up the completion of Soviet-German talks

Berlin, August 16, 1939   D.Germ.F.P., VII, No. 75

For the Ambassador personally.

I request that you arrange to call again upon M. Molotov, with the statement that you have to communicate to him, in addition to yesterday's message for M. Stalin, supplementary instructions just received from Berlin, which relate to the questions raised by M. Molotov. Please then state to M. Molotov the following:

1. The points brought up by M. Molotov are in accordance with German desires. That is, Germany is prepared to conclude a non-aggression pact with the Soviet Union and, if the Soviet Government so desire, one which would be undenounceable for a term of twenty-five years. Further, Germany is ready to guarantee the Baltic States jointly with the Soviet Union. Finally, it is thoroughly in accord with the German position, and Germany is prepared to exercise influence for an improvement and consolidation of Russian-Japanese relations.

2. The Führer is of the opinion that, in view of the present situation, and of the possibility of the occurrence, any day, of serious events (please at this point explain to M. Molotov that Germany is determined not to endure Polish provocation indefinitely), a basic and rapid clarification of German-Russian relations, and of each country's attitude to the questions of the moment, is desirable. For these reasons I am prepared to come by aeroplane to Moscow at any time after Friday, August 18, to deal, on the basis of

full powers from the Führer, with the entire complex of German-Russian questions, and if the occasion arises, to sign the appropriate treaties.

Annex: I request that you again read these instructions word for word to M[olotov] and ask for the views of the Russian Government and of M. Stalin immediately. Entirely confidentially, it is added for your guidance that it would be of very special interest to us if my Moscow trip could take place at the end of this week or the beginning of next week.

No. 29

Report of Ambassador Schulenburg to the German Ministry for Foreign Affairs containing Soviet reply to German proposals of 15 August for improving German-Russian relations[1]

Moscow, August 17, 1939   D.Germ.F.P., VII, No. 105

[. . .] Molotov read out the answer of the Soviet Government, which, in the text given to me, is as follows: 'The Soviet Government has taken note of the statement of the German Government transmitted by Count Schulenburg on 15 August[2] concerning their desire for a serious improvement in the political relations between Germany and the Soviet Union.

In view of the official statements of several representatives of the German Government, which have not infrequently had an unfriendly and even hostile character with reference to the Soviet Union, the Soviet Government up till very recently has proceeded on the assumption that the German Government is seeking an occasion for a clash with the Soviet Union, is preparing itself for such a clash, and not infrequently justified the need for its increasing armament by the inevitability of such a clash. Not to mention the fact that the German Government by using the so-called Anti-Comintern Pact was endeavouring to and did establish the united front of a number of States against the Soviet Union, into which with especial persistence it enticed Japan.

It is understandable that such a policy on the part of the German Government has compelled the Soviet Union to take serious steps in the preparation of defence against possible aggression by Germany against the Soviet Union and consequently to participate in the organization of a defensive front of a number of States against such aggression.

If, however, the German Government now undertakes a change from the old policy in the direction of a serious improvement in political relations with the Soviet Union the Soviet Government can only welcome such a change and is for its part prepared to revise its policy in the sense of a serious improvement in respect of Germany.

Adding to this the fact that the Soviet Government has never had and will not have any sort of aggressive intentions towards Germany, and that now, as previously, the Soviet Government considers a peaceful solution of the questions at issue in the field of relations between Germany and the Soviet

---

[1] See Note No. 29.   [2] See doc. No. 26.

Union as entirely possible, and that the principle of the peaceful co-existence of various political systems represents a long established principle of the foreign policy of the Soviet Union, the conclusion can be reached that for the re-establishment of new, improved political relations between the two countries there are at hand not only a real basis but also the prerequisites for undertaking serious and practical steps in this direction already now.

The Government of the Soviet Union holds that the first step towards such an improvement in relations between the Soviet Union and Germany could be the conclusion of a trade and credit agreement.

The Government of the Soviet Union holds that the second step, to be taken shortly thereafter, could be the conclusion of a non-aggression pact or the re-affirmation of the neutrality pact of 1926, with the simultaneous conclusion of a special protocol defining the interests of the contracting parties in this or that question of foreign policy, and forming an integral part of the pact.'

No. 30

TASS statement on the negotiations for a non-aggression pact with Germany

Moscow, August 22, 1939   Mirovoye Khoziaistvo, 1939, 9, p. 246
Transl. from Russian: Degras, III/359

After the conclusion of the Soviet-German trade and credit agreement there arose the question of improving political relations between Germany and the USSR. An exchange of views on this subject, which took place between the Governments of Germany and the USSR, established that both parties desire to relieve the tension in their political relations, eliminate the danger of war, and conclude a non-aggression pact. Consequently the German Minister for Foreign Affairs, Herr von Ribbentrop, will shortly arrive in Moscow for the relevant negotiations.

No. 31

Treaty of Non-Aggression between Germany and the USSR stipulating their future collaboration on problems concerning their common interests[1]

Moscow, August 23, 1939   D.Germ.F.P., VII, No. 228

The Government of the German Reich and the Government of the Union of Soviet Socialist Republics, desirous of strengthening the cause of peace between Germany and the USSR, and proceeding from the fundamental provisions of the Treaty of Neutrality, which was concluded between Germany and the USSR in April 1926, have reached the following agreement:

Article I

The two Contracting Parties undertake to refrain from any act of violence, any aggressive action and any attack on each other either severally or jointly with other Powers.

[1] See Note No. 31.

Article II

Should one of the Contracting Parties become the object of belligerent action by a third Power, the other Contracting Party shall in no manner lend its support to this third Power.

Article III

The Governments of the two Contracting Parties will in future maintain continual contact with one another for the purpose of consultation in order to exchange information on problems affecting their common interests.

Article IV

Neither of the two Contracting Parties will join any grouping of Powers whatsoever which is aimed directly or indirectly at the other Party.

Article V

Should disputes or conflicts arise between the Contracting Parties over questions of one kind or another, both Parties will settle these disputes or conflicts exclusively by means of a friendly exchange of views or if necessary by the appointment of arbitration commissions.

Article VI

The present Treaty shall be concluded for a period of ten years with the proviso that, in so far as one of the Contracting Parties does not denounce it one year before the expiry of this period, the validity of this Treaty shall be deemed to be automatically prolonged for another five years.

Article VII

The present treaty shall be ratified within the shortest possible time.[2] The instruments of ratification will be exchanged in Berlin. The treaty shall enter into force immediately upon signature.

Done in duplicate in the German and Russian languages. Moscow, August 23, 1939

For the Government of the German Reich: v. Ribbentrop	With full power of the Government of the USSR: V. Molotov

[2] Instruments of ratification were exchanged on September 24; see Reichsgesetzblatt, 1939, Part II, p. 968.

No. 32

Secret Additional Protocol to the Treaty of Non-Aggression between Germany and the USSR concerning delimitation of German and Soviet spheres of interest in Eastern Europe

Moscow, August 23, 1939   D.Germ.F.P., VII, No. 229

On the occasion of the signature of the Non-Aggression Treaty between the German Reich and the Union of Soviet Socialist Republics, the under-signed plenipotentiaries of the two Parties discussed in strictly confidential conversations the question of the delimitation of their respective spheres of interest in Eastern Europe. These conversations led to the following result:

1. In the event of a territorial and political transformation in the territories belonging to the Baltic States (Finland, Estonia, Latvia, Lithuania), the northern frontier of Lithuania shall represent the frontier of the spheres of interest both of Germany and the USSR. In this connection the interest of Lithuania in the Vilna territory is recognized by both Parties.

2. In the event of a territorial and political transformation of the territories belonging to the Polish State, the spheres of interest of both Germany and the USSR shall be bounded approximately by the line of the rivers Narew, Vistula, and San.

The question whether the interests of both Parties make the maintenance of an independent Polish State appear desirable and how the frontiers of this State should be drawn can be definitely determined only in the course of further political developments.

In any case both Governments will resolve this question by means of a friendly understanding.

3. With regard to South-Eastern Europe, the Soviet side emphasizes its interest in Bessarabia. The German side declares complete political dés-intéressement in these territories.

4. This Protocol will be treated by both parties as strictly secret.

Moscow, August 23, 1939

For the Government of   With full power of the
the German Reich: Government of the USSR:
  v. Ribbentrop   V. Molotov

No. 33

Extracts from Marshal Voroshilov's interview on the Anglo-French-Soviet military negotiations in Moscow

Moscow, August 27, 1939   Izvestia, August 27, 1939
                                              Transl. from Russian: Pol.W.B., No. 170

[. . .] Help in the form of raw materials and war materials is a commercial question, and no Pact of Mutual Assistance whatever, far less a Military Convention, is needed in order to supply Poland with these materials.

The United States of America and several other States have neither a Pact of Mutual Assistance nor a Military Convention with Japan, yet for the past two years they have been selling raw materials and war materials to the Japanese, irrespective of the fact that Japan is in a state of war with China. [. . .].

No. 34

Telegram from Under-Secretary Szembek to Ambassador Raczyński on the German-Soviet Agreement

Warsaw, August 29, 1939   Pol.W.B., No. 169

On the strength of instructions from Berlin, the German representative at Bucharest recently told Rumanian political circles that German-Soviet conversations regarding a Non-Aggression Pact have been in progress for some two and a half months, and that all the details of the Pact have been settled for some time.

Please utilize this information, in view of Marshal Voroshilov's statement that the understanding with Germany was brought about only by Poland's negative attitude towards the Staff conversations between the Soviets and Great Britain and France.

No. 35

Extracts from Commissar Molotov's speech on the ratification of the Soviet-German Non-Aggression Pact delivered at the fourth session of the Supreme Council of the USSR

Moscow, August 31, 1939   D.Brit.F.P., VII/615

Since the third session of the Supreme Soviet the international situation has shown no change for the better. On the contrary it has become even more tense. Steps taken by various governments to put an end to this state of tension have obviously proved inadequate. They have proved fruitless. This is true of Europe. Nor has there been any change for the better in eastern Asia. Japanese troops continue to occupy the principal cities and a considerable part of the territory of China. Nor is Japan refraining from hostile acts against the USSR. Here, too, the situation has shown further deterioration.

In view of this state of affairs the conclusion of a pact of non-aggression between the USSR and Germany is of tremendous positive value, eliminating the danger of war between Germany and the Soviet Union. In order more fully to define the significance of this pact I must first dwell on the negotiations which have taken place in recent months in Moscow with representatives of Great Britain and France.

As you are aware, Anglo-French-Soviet negotiations for the conclusion of a pact of mutual assistance against aggression in Europe began as far back as April. True, the initial proposals of the British Government were, as you know, entirely unacceptable. They ignored the prime requisites for such negotiations—they ignored the principle of reciprocity and of equal obligations.

DOCUMENTS
1·9·39—30·4·43

No. 36

Telegram from Minister Beck to the Polish Embassy in London concerning his conversation with Ambassador Sharonov on prospective Soviet supplies to Poland

Warsaw, September 2, 1939   Pol. W.B., No. 171

The Soviet Ambassador has called on me and asked why we were not negotiating with the Soviets regarding supplies, as the 'Voroshilov interview' has opened up the possibility of getting them.

I have instructed Moscow to investigate the situation.[1]

[1] This instruction was sent by special courier, but owing to difficulties of communication he did not arrive in Moscow until September 6, 1939. M. Grzybowski replied to the instruction with the telegram printed below. See doc. No. 39.

No. 37

Telegram from Minister Ribbentrop to Ambassador Schulenburg urging Soviet invasion of Eastern Poland

Berlin, September 3, 1939   D.Germ.F.P., VII, No. 567

Exclusively for the Ambassador: For the Head of Mission or his representative personally. Special security handling. To be decoded by himself. Most secret.

We definitely expect to have beaten the Polish Army decisively in a few weeks. We should then keep the territory that was fixed at Moscow as a German sphere of interest under military occupation. We should naturally, however, for military reasons, have to continue to take action against such Polish military forces as are at that time located in the Polish territory belonging to the Russian sphere of interest.

Please discuss this at once with Molotov and see if the Soviet Union does not consider it desirable for Russian forces to move at the proper time against Polish forces in the Russian sphere of interest and, for their part, to occupy this territory. In our estimation this would be not only a relief for us, but also be in the sense of the Moscow agreements, and in the Soviet interest as well.

In this connection please determine whether we may discuss this matter with the officers who have just arrived here and what the Soviet Government generally intend their position to be.

No. 38

Telegram from Ambassador Schulenburg to the German Ministry for Foreign Affairs containing Commissar Molotov's reply on Soviet invasion of Eastern Poland

Moscow, September 5, 1939   D.Germ.F.P., VIII, No. 5

With reference to my telegram No. 261 of September 4.

Molotov asked me to call on him today at 12.30 and transmitted to me the following reply of the Soviet Government:

'We agree with you that at a suitable time it will be absolutely necessary for us to start concrete action. We are of the view, however, that this time has not yet come. It is possible that we are mistaken, but it seems to us that through excessive haste we might injure our cause and promote unity among our opponents. We understand that as the operations proceed, one of the parties or both parties might be forced temporarily to cross the line of demarcation between the spheres of interest of the two parties; but such cases must not prevent the strict execution of the plan adopted.'

No. 39

Telegram from Ambassador Grzybowski to Minister Beck on conversation with Commissar Molotov and the Soviet refusal to supply arms to Poland

Moscow, September 8, 1939   Pol.W.B., No. 172

M. Sharonov's suggestions are no longer opportune. M. Molotov has informed me that the intervention of Great Britain and France has created an entirely new situation, which Marshal Voroshilov did not know and could not take into consideration when giving the interview. At present the Soviets are compelled to safeguard first and foremost their own interests, remaining outside the conflict. For us Poland, said M. Molotov, is now synonymous with England. In regard to the practical question which I raised of supply of raw materials and the eventual supply of war materials, he maintains the position of a strict observance of the agreements existing between us. In consequence the Soviets are prepared to supply us only with those raw materials which are provided for in the quotas for the current year. As to war materials, in face of the changed situation, he does not consider that the Soviet Government could supply them at present. On the transit question he informed me that all transit of a military character might be in contradiction with the Pact concluded with Germany, and so he does not consider that the Soviet Government could allow it. In answer to my reference to previous promises, he repeated once more that the situation had changed, and that the Soviet Union must care first and foremost for its own security.

No. 40

TASS Communiqué on partial Soviet mobilization

Moscow, September 10, 1939   Degras, III/372

In connexion with the German-Polish war, which is taking on a broader and more threatening character, the Government has decided for the purpose of further strengthening the defences of the country on the partial call-up into the army of certain age groups.

The mobilization of the reserves into the Red Army has been effected in the Ukraine, White Russia, Leningrad, Moscow, Kalinin, and Orlov military districts.

No. 41

Telegram from Minister Ribbentrop to Ambassador Schulenburg proposing the publication of a joint communiqué on the necessity of protection of the nationalities living in the former Polish State[1]

Berlin, September 15, 1939   D.Germ.F.P., VIII, No. 70

For the Ambassador personally.

I request that you communicate the following to M. Molotov at once:

1) The destruction of the Polish Army is rapidly approaching its conclusion, as appears from the review of the military situation of September 14 which has already been communicated to you. We count on the occupation of Warsaw in the next few days.

2) We have already stated to the Soviet Government that we consider ourselves bound by the definition of spheres of influence agreed upon in Moscow, entirely apart from purely military operations, and the same applies, of course, to the future as well.

3) From the communication made to you by Molotov on September 14, we assume that the Soviet Government will take a hand militarily, and that it intends to begin its operation now. We welcome this. The Soviet Government thus relieves us of the necessity of annihilating the remainder of the Polish Army by pursuing it as far as the Russian boundary. Also the question is disposed of whether, in the absence of a Russian intervention, a political vacuum might not occur in the area lying to the east of the German zone of influence. Since we on our part have no intention of undertaking any political or administrative activities in these areas, apart from what is made necessary by military operations, without such an intervention by the Soviet Government, new states might possibly be formed there.

4) For the political support of the advance of the Soviet Army, we propose the publication of a joint communiqué of the following contents:

'In view of the obvious splitting apart of the nationalities living in the former Polish state, the Reich Government and the Government of the USSR consider it necessary to bring to an end the intolerable political and economic

---

[1] See Note No. 41.

conditions existing in these territories. They regard it as their joint task restore peace and order in these, their natural spheres of influence, and to bring about a new order by the creation of natural frontiers and viable economic organizations.'

5) We assume in proposing such a communiqué that the Soviet Government has already given up the idea, expressed by Molotov in an earlier conversation with you, of taking the threat to the Ukrainian and White Russian populations by Germany as a ground for Soviet action. The assignment of a motive of that sort would indeed be out of the question in practice. It would be directly contrary to the true German intentions, which are confined exclusively to the realization of well-known German vital interests. It would also be in contradiction to the arrangements made in Moscow, and finally, would—in opposition to the desire for friendly relations expressed on both sides—make the two States appear as enemies before the whole world.

6) Since the military operations must be concluded as soon as possible because of the advanced season of the year, we would be gratified if the Soviet Government would now set a day and hour on which their Army would begin their advance, so that we on our part might govern ourselves accordingly. For the necessary co-ordination of military operations on both sides, a representative of each Government, along with German and Russian officers, should fly to some meeting place in the operations zone—we propose Białystok—to agree on what must be done.

I request an immediate reply by telegraph. The change in text discussed by Gaus with Hilger has already been taken care of.

No. 42

Telegram from Ambassador Schulenburg to the German Ministry for Foreign Affairs about his conversation with Stalin on the entry of the Soviet Army into Poland

Moscow, September 17, 1939   D.Germ.F.P., VIII, No. 80

With reference to my telegram No. 371 of September 16.

Stalin received me at 2 o'clock at night in the presence of Molotov and Voroshilov and declared that the Red Army would cross the Soviet border this morning at 6 o'clock along the whole line from Polotsk to Kamenets-Podolsk.

In order to avoid incidents, Stalin urgently requested that we see to it that German planes as of today do not fly east of the Białystok–Brest Litovsk–Lwów line. Soviet planes would begin today to bomb the district east of Lwów.

I promised to do my best with regard to informing the German Air Force but asked in view of the little time left that Soviet planes not approach the above-mentioned line too closely today.

The Soviet commission will arrive in Białystok tomorrow or day after tomorrow at the latest.

Stalin read me a note that is to be handed to the Polish Ambassador tonight, to be sent in copy to all the missions in the course of the day and then published. The note contains a justification for the Soviet action. The draft read to me contained three points unacceptable to us. In answer to my objections, Stalin with the utmost readiness so altered the text that the note now seems satisfactory for us. Stalin stated that the issuance of a German-Soviet communiqué could not be considered before 2 or 3 days.

In future all military matters that come up are to be handled by Lieutenant General Köstring directly with Voroshilov.

No. 43

Note of the Soviet Government to the Polish Embassy in Moscow announcing that the USSR regards the Polish State as having ceased to exist and all their agreements as invalid, therefore claiming rights of occupation of borderlands

Moscow, September 17, 1939   Livre Blanc Polonais, No. 175

La guerre germano-polonaise a montré la faillite intérieure de l'État polonais. Au cours de dix jours d'opérations militaires, la Pologne a perdu tous ses bassins industriels et ses centres culturels. Varsovie, en tant que capitale de la Pologne, n'existe plus. Le Gouvernement polonais s'est effondré et ne manifeste aucun indice de vie. Cela signifie que l'État polonais et son Gouvernement ont, de fait, cessé d'exister. Par cela même, les traités conclus entre l'URSS et la Pologne ont perdu leur valeur. Abandonnée à son propre sort et privée de ses dirigeants, la Pologne est devenue un champ d'action facile pour toutes sortes de menées et de surprises susceptibles de devenir une menace pour l'URSS. C'est pourquoi, ayant observé la neutralité jusqu'a présent, le Gouvernement soviétique ne peut plus rester neutre en présence de ces faits.

Le Gouvernement soviétique ne peut pas non plus rester indifférent alors que ses frères de sang Ukrainiens et Blancs-Russiens, habitant le territoire de la Pologne, abandonnés à leur sort, sont restés sans défence.

Prenant cette situation en considération, le Gouvernement soviétique a donne des instructions au Commandement Suprême de l'Armée Rouge d'ordonner aux troupes de franchir la frontière et de prendre sous leur protection, la vie et les biens de la population de l'Ukraine et de la Russie-Blanche Occidentale.

Dans le même temps, le Gouvernement soviétique a l'intention de faire tous ses efforts pour libérer le peuple polonais de la malheureuse guerre ou l'ont jeté ses dirigeants insensés et pour lui donner la possibilité de vivre d'une vie paisible.

No. 44

Telegram from Ambassador Grzybowski to the Polish Ministry for Foreign Affairs on the Soviet aggression against Poland

Moscow, September 17, 1939   Pol.W.B., No. 174

M. Potemkin sent for me today, September 17, at 3 a.m., and read me a note from his Government, signed by Premier Molotov. The note communicates that the Soviet Government has ordered its troops to cross the Polish frontier. The motives given in the note were of such a nature that I refused to take it into cognizance and categorically protested against its contents. In view of the absence of Soviet diplomatic representatives from Poland I agreed only to transmit the above information. I await instructions.

No. 45

Communiqué by the Polish Government protesting against the Soviet aggression

Kuty, September 17, 1939   Monitor Polski, No. 213, September 25, 1939
                                   Transl. from Polish: Pol.-Sov.R., No. 15

The Polish Ambassador in Moscow has refused to accept the Note presented to him today by the Soviet Government.

The Polish Government has approved this attitude of their Ambassador who has asked the Soviet Government for his passports.

The Polish Government solemnly protest against the unilateral violation of the Non-Aggression Pact by Russia and against the invasion of Polish territory at a moment when the whole Polish Nation is making a supreme effort to repel the German aggressor.

The Polish Government protest against the motives alleged in the Note of the Soviet Government because the Polish Government are carrying on their normal activities and the Polish Army is successfully resisting the enemy.

No. 46

Extracts from Commissar Molotov's broadcast on the Soviet invasion of Poland

Moscow, September 17, 1939   Mirovoye Khoziaistvo, 1939, 9, p. 13
                                     Transl. from Russian: Degras, III/374-376

Events arising out of the Polish-German war have revealed the internal insolvency and obvious impotence of the Polish State. Polish ruling circles have suffered bankruptcy. All this has happened in the briefest space of time.

A mere fortnight has passed and Poland has already lost all its industrial centres, the greater part of its large towns and cultural centres. Warsaw as the capital of the Polish State no longer exists. No one knows the whereabouts of the Polish Government. The population of Poland have been

47

abandoned by their ill-starred leaders to their fate. The Polish State and its Government have virtually ceased to exist. In view of this state of affairs, treaties concluded between the Soviet Union and Poland have ceased to operate.

A situation has arisen in Poland which demands of the Soviet Government especial concern for the security of its State. Poland has become a fertile field for any accidental and unexpected contingency that may create a menace to the Soviet Union. Until the last moment the Soviet Government has remained neutral. But in view of the circumstances mentioned, it can no longer maintain a neutral attitude towards the situation that has arisen.

Nor can it be demanded of the Soviet Government that it remain in-different to the fate of its blood brothers, the Ukrainians and White Russians inhabiting Poland, who even formerly were nations without rights and who now have been utterly abandoned to their fate. The Soviet Government deems it its sacred duty to extend the hand of assistance to its brother Ukrainians and White Russians inhabiting Poland.

In view of all the above, the Government of the Soviet Union this morning handed a note to the Polish Ambassador in Moscow announcing that the Soviet Government has instructed the high command of the Red Army to order the troops to cross the frontier and to take under their protection the lives and property of the population of western Ukraine and western White Russia.

The Soviet Government also stated in its note that it intends at the same time to take every step to deliver the Polish people from the disastrous war into which they have been plunged by their unwise leaders and to give them the opportunity to live a peaceful life.

In the early part of September, when a partial mobilization of Red Army reserves was effected in the Ukraine, White Russia, and four other military districts, the situation in Poland was not clear, and this step was taken as a precautionary measure. Nobody could have imagined that the Polish State would reveal such impotence and collapse as quickly as it has already done throughout Poland. But since this collapse has occurred, and Polish leaders have revealed their complete bankruptcy and are unable to change the situation in Poland, our Red Army, having been strongly reinforced by the recent mobilization of reserves, must perform with credit the honourable duty assigned to it.

The Government expresses the firm conviction that our workers' and peasants' Red Army will on this occasion too display its fighting strength, its sense of responsibility and discipline, and that in carrying out its great task of liberation it will distinguish itself by new feats of heroism and glory.

At the same time the Soviet Government transmitted copies of its note to the Polish Ambassador to all Governments with which it has diplomatic relations, stating that the Soviet Union will pursue a policy of neutrality towards all these countries.

It was these considerations which determined the recent measures we took in the field of foreign policy.

Statement issued by the British Ministry of Information regarding Soviet action in Poland

London, September 18, 1939   The Times, September 19, 1939

The British Government have considered the situation created by the attack upon Poland ordered by the Soviet Government. This attack made upon Great Britain's ally at a moment when she is prostrate in face of overwhelming forces brought against her by Germany cannot in the view of His Majesty's Government be justified by the arguments put forward by the Soviet Government. The full implication of these events is not yet apparent, but His Majesty's Government take the opportunity of stating that nothing that has occurred can make any difference to the determination of His Majesty's Government with the full support of the country, to fulfil their obligations to Poland and to prosecute the war with all energy until their objectives have been achieved.

No. 48

Telegram from Ambassador Schulenburg to the German Ministry for Foreign Affairs on the Soviet proposal to partition Poland along the four rivers line: Pissa–Narew–Vistula–San

Moscow, September 20, 1939   D.Germ.F.P., VIII, No. 104

Molotov stated to me today that the Soviet Government now considered the time has come to establish definitively, jointly with the German Government, the structure of the Polish area. In this regard, Molotov hinted that the original inclination entertained by the Soviet Government and Stalin personally to permit the existence of a residual Poland had given way to the inclination to partition Poland along the Pissa–Narew–Vistula–San line. The Soviet Government wishes to commence negotiations on this matter at once, and to conduct them in Moscow, since such negotiations must be conducted on the Soviet side by persons in the highest positions of authority who cannot leave the Soviet Union. Request telegraphic instructions.

No. 49

Extracts from the speech by Mr. Chamberlain in the House of Commons on the Soviet aggression against Poland

London, September 20, 1939   H.C.Deb., 351/975–1003

The Prime Minister [Mr. Chamberlain]: Events have occured in the last week of such far-reaching importance that there has not yet been time to estimate their effect on the fortunes of war and on the attitudes of other countries.

In my statement on September 13 I referred to the relentless German pressure on the Polish army which had so far been frustrated by the indomitable spirit of the Poles. This pressure and this resistance continued during the week, and is still continuing in many parts of Poland. The tide of German invasion eastwards has reached an approximate north-south line through Brest-Litovsk and Lemberg, though there still remain islands of Polish resistance, such as Warsaw, which refuse to be submerged. On September 17 an event occurred which has inevitably had a decisive effect upon the war on the Eastern Front. On the morning of September 17 Russian troops crossed the Polish frontier at points along its whole length and advanced into Poland.

I cannot say that the action of the Soviet Government was unexpected. For some time past Soviet troops have been mobilized and concentrated on the western frontiers of the Soviet Union, and statements have appeared in the Soviet Press and wireless referring to the position of White Russians and Ukrainians in Poland, which bore the interpretation that the Soviet Government were preparing for intervention.

On September 17 a note was handed to the Polish Ambassador in Moscow to the effect that Warsaw as the capital of Poland no longer existed, that the Polish Government had disintegrated, and that the Polish State and its Government had ceased to exist. In the same way the agreements concluded between the Soviet Union and Poland had come to an end.

Poland had become a suitable field for all manner of hazards and surprises which might constitute a threat to the Soviet Union. The Soviet Union could, therefore, no longer preserve a neutral attitude, and the Soviet Government had ordered their troops to cross the frontier and take under their protection the life and property of the population of the Western Ukraine and Western White Russia. The Polish Ambassador in Moscow refused to accept this note, and has since been instructed to ask for his passports.

A copy of this communication was sent to His Majesty's Ambassador in Moscow with a note stating that the Soviet Government would pursue a policy of neutrality in the relations between the USSR and Great Britain. A similar communication was made to the diplomatic representatives of foreign Powers in Moscow.

In this situation, His Majesty's Government authorized the issue of a statement on September 18 that this attack by the Soviet Government upon Poland (a country with whom she had a non-aggression pact) at a moment when Poland was prostrate in the face of overwhelming forces brought against her by Germany could not be justified by the arguments put forward and, that while the full implication of these events was not yet apparent, nothing which had occurred would make any difference to the determination of His Majesty's Government to fulfil their obligations to Poland and to prosecute the war with all energy until these obligations had been achieved.

The effects of the Russian invasion upon the hard-pressed Poles have naturally been very serious. Caught between two vast armies, and with their communications to the South cut off, the Polish forces are still continuing their courageous resistance. According to a communiqué issued on September 18 the Polish Government have requested the Rumanian Government to accord hospitality to the Head of the Polish State and to his Ministers who have taken refuge on Rumanian territory. [. . .].

It is still too early to pronounce any final verdict on the motives or consequences of the Russian action. For the unhappy victim of this cynical attack the result has been a tragedy of the grimmest character. The world which has watched the vain struggle of the Polish nation against overwhelming odds with profound pity and sympathy admires their valour which even now refuses to admit defeat. If Britain and France have been unable to avert the defeat of the armies of Poland they have assured her that they have not forgotten their obligations to her nor weakened in their determination to carry on the struggle.

No. 50

German-Soviet Communiqué on the demarcation line between the German and the Soviet military zones[1]

Moscow, September 22, 1939   The Times, September 23, 1939

The German Government and the Government of the Union of Soviet Socialist Republics have established a demarcation line between the German and Soviet armies which passes along the course of the river Pissa up to its confluence with the river Narew, then along the Narew up to its confluence with the river Bug, then along the Bug up to its confluence with the river Vistula, then along the Vistula up to the mouth of the river San, and then along the San up to its source.

[1] See Note No. 50.

No. 51

Telegram from Ambassador Schulenburg to the German Ministry for Foreign Affairs concerning M. Stalin's proposal to erase Poland as a state and to fix the new frontier on the river Bug

Moscow, September 25, 1939   D.Germ.F.P., VIII, No. 131

Stalin and Molotov asked me to come to the Kremlin at 8 p.m. today. Stalin stated the following: In the final settlement of the Polish question anything that in the future might create friction between Germany and the Soviet Union must be avoided. From this point of view, he considered it wrong to leave an independent residual Poland. He proposed the following: From the territory to the east of the demarcation line, all the Province of Lublin and that portion of the Province of Warsaw which extends to the Bug should be added to our share. In return, we should waive our claim to Lithuania.

Stalin designated this suggestion as a subject for the forthcoming negotiations with the Reich Foreign Minister and added that, if we consented, the Soviet Union would immediately take up the solution of the problem of the Baltic countries in accordance with the Protocol of August 23,[1] and expected

[1] See doc. No. 32.

in this matter the unstinting support of the German Government. Stalin expressly indicated Estonia, Latvia and Lithuania, but did not mention Finland.

I replied to Stalin that I would report to my Government.

No. 52

German-Soviet Boundary and Friendship Treaty[1]

Moscow, September 28, 1939   D.Germ.F.P., VIII, No. 157

The Government of the German Reich and the Government of the USSR consider it as exclusively their task, after the disintegration of the former Polish state, to re-establish peace and order in these territories and to assure to the peoples living there a peaceful life in keeping with their national character. To this end, they have agreed upon the following:

Article I

The Government of the German Reich and the Government of the USSR determine as the boundary of their respective national interests in the territory of the former Polish state the line marked on the attached map, which shall be described in more detail in a supplementary protocol.[2]

Article II

Both parties recognize the boundary of the respective national interests established in article I as definitive and shall reject any interference of third powers in this settlement.

Article III

The necessary reorganization of public administration will be effected in the areas west of the line specified in article I by the Government of the German Reich, in the areas east of this line by the Government of the USSR.

Article IV

The Government of the German Reich and the Government of the USSR regard this settlement as a firm foundation for a progressive development of the friendly relations between their peoples.

Article V

This treaty shall be ratified and the ratification shall be exchanged in Berlin as soon as possible. The treaty becomes effective upon signature.

Done in duplicate in the German and Russian languages.

For the Government of the German Reich:	By authority of the Government of the USSR:
v. Ribbentrop	W. Molotov

[1] See Note No. 52.   [2] See doc. No. 59.

Confidential Protocol to the German-Soviet Boundary and Friendship Treaty of September 28, 1939, dealing with the transfer of persons of German, Ukrainian and Byelorussian descent

Moscow, September 28, 1939   D.Germ.F.P., VIII, No. 158

The Government of the USSR shall place no obstacles in the way of Reich nationals and other persons of German descent residing in its sphere of influence if they desire to migrate to Germany or to the German sphere of influence. It agrees that such removals shall be carried out by agents of the Government of the Reich in cooperation with the competent local authorities and that the property rights of the emigrants shall be protected.

A corresponding obligation is assumed by the Government of the German Reich in respect to the persons of Ukrainian or White Russian descent residing in its sphere of influence.[1]

For the Government   By authority of the
of the German Reich: Government of the USSR:
  v. Ribbentrop   W. Molotov

[1] An agreement implementing this Protocol was signed in Moscow on November 16, 1939.

No. 54

Secret Additional Protocol to the German-Soviet Boundary and Friendship Treaty of September 28, 1939, containing an alteration to the Secret Additional Protocol of August 23, 1939, relating to Poland and Lithuania[1]

Moscow, September 28, 1939   D.Germ.F.P., VIII, No. 159

The undersigned plenipotentiaries declare the agreement of the Government of the German Reich and the Government of the USSR upon the following:

The Secret Additional Protocol signed on August 23, 1939,[2] shall be amended in item I to the effect that the territory of the Lithuanian state falls to the sphere of influence of the USSR, while, on the other hand, the province of Lublin and parts of the province of Warsaw fall to the sphere of influence of Germany (cf. the map attached to the Boundary and Friendship Treaty signed today). As soon as the Government of the USSR shall take special measures on Lithuanian territory to protect its interests, the present German-Lithuanian border, for the purpose of a natural and simple boundary delineation, shall be rectified in such a way that the Lithuanian territory situated to the southwest of the line marked on the attached map falls to Germany.

Further it is declared that the economic agreements now in force between Germany and Lithuania shall not be affected by the measures of the Soviet Union referred to above.

For the Government   By authority of the
of the German Reich: Government of the USSR:
  v. Ribbentrop   W. Molotov

[1] See Note No. 54.   [2] See doc. No. 32.

Secret Additional Protocol to the German-Soviet Boundary and Friendship Treaty of September 28, 1939, on the solidarity of both parties in the suppression of Polish agitation on their territories

Moscow, September 28, 1939   D.Germ.F.P., VIII, No. 160

The undersigned plenipotentiaries, on concluding the German-Russian Boundary and Friendship Treaty, have declared their agreement upon the following:

Both parties will tolerate in their territories no Polish agitation which affects the territories of the other party. They will suppress in their territories all beginnings of such agitation and inform each other concerning suitable measures for this purpose.

For the Government   By authority of the
of the German Reich: Government of the USSR:
  v. Ribbentrop   W. Molotov

No. 56

Declaration of the Government of the German Reich and the Government of the USSR on the settlement of problems arising from the 'disintegration' of the Polish State

Moscow, September 28, 1939   D.Germ.F.P., VIII, No. 161

After the Government of the German Reich and the Government of the USSR have, by means of the treaty signed today, definitely settled the problems arising from the disintegration of the Polish state and have thereby created a firm foundation for a lasting peace in Eastern Europe, they mutually express their conviction that it would serve the true interest of all peoples to put an end to the state of war existing at present between Germany on the one side and England and France on the other. Both Governments will therefore direct their common efforts, jointly with other friendly powers if occasion arises, toward attaining this goal as soon as possible.

Should, however, the efforts of the two Governments remain fruitless, this would demonstrate the fact that England and France are responsible for the continuation of the war, whereupon, in case of the continuation of the war, the Governments of Germany and of the USSR shall engage in mutual consultations with regard to necessary measures.

For the Government   By authority of the
of the German Reich: Government of the USSR:
  v. Ribbentrop   W. Molotov

No. 57

Protest of the Polish Government against the German-Soviet Agreement of September 28, 1939, presented by Ambassador Raczyński to the Foreign Office

London, September 30, 1939   Pol.W.B., No. 180

In face of the flagrant violation of the sacred rights of the Polish State and the Polish Nation constituted by the Agreement of September 28 between Germany and the USSR, disposing of territories of the Polish Republic to the benefit of the two aggressor States, in the name of the Polish Government I make the most formal and solemn protest against this machination woven between Berlin and Moscow in contempt of all international obligations and all human morality.

Poland will never recognize this act of violence, and, strong in the justice of her cause, she will not cease to struggle for the day when, her territory liberated from the invaders, her legitimate rights will be established in their entirety.

By the heroic resistance of her army, by the patriotic sacrifice of all her population which has been demonstrated in the heroic defence of the capital city of Warsaw, of Lwów, of Wilno, of Gdynia, of Modlin and of so many other towns, the Polish Nation has clearly proved to the world her steadfast will to live in freedom and independence.

Basing herself on the unanimous sympathy of all the countries which respect liberty and good faith in relations between the peoples, and confiding in the steadfast support which is guaranteed her by her treaties of alliance, Poland will continue the struggle by all means in her power, confident in her future and in the ultimate victory.[1]

[1] A similar protest was presented by all the Polish diplomatic representatives abroad to the respective governments to which they are accredited.

No. 58

Extracts from speeches by Mr. Chamberlain, Mr. Attlee and Mr. Lloyd George made in the House of Commons on the subject of the Soviet aggression against Poland

London, October 3, 1939   H.C.Deb., 351/1855–1912

The Prime Minister [Mr. Chamberlain]: [. . .]. The agreement between Germany and Russia and the subsequent partition of Poland between them has, of course, changed the position in Poland, but it by no means follows that the arrangement will endure to the ultimate advantage of Germany, and still less should it affect the aims of His Majesty's Government. There is nothing in that agreement that should cause us to do anything other than what we are doing now—mobilizing all the resources and all the might of the British Empire for the effective prosecution of the war.

The reason for which this country entered the war has been frequently proclaimed. It was to put an end to the successive acts of German aggression which menaced the freedom and the very security of all the nations of Europe.

The immediate cause of the war was the deliberate invasion of Poland by Germany, the latest, but by no means the only, act of aggression planned and carried through by the German Government.

But if Poland was the direct occasion of war, it was not the fundamental cause. That cause was the overwhelming sense in this country and in France of the intolerable nature of a state of affairs in which the nations of Europe were faced with the alternative of jeopardizing their freedom or of mobilizing their forces at regular intervals to defend it.

The passage in the Russo-German declaration about the liquidation of the war is obscure, but it seems to combine a suggestion of some proposal for peace with a scarcely veiled threat as to the consequences if the proposal should be refused.

I cannot anticipate what the nature of any such proposal might be. But I can say at once that no threat would ever induce this country or France to abandon the purpose for which we have entered upon this struggle.

And I would add one thing more. No more assurances from the present German Government could be accepted by us. For that Government have too often proved in the past that their undertakings are worthless when it suits them that they should be broken. If, therefore, proposals are made, we shall certainly examine them and we shall test them in the light of what I have just said. Nobody desires the war to continue for an unnecessary day, but the overwhelming mass of opinion in this country, and I am satisfied also in France, is determined to secure that the rule of violence shall cease, and that the word of Governments, once pledged, must henceforth be kept. [. . .].

Mr. Attlee [Lab.]: I welcome the statement made by the Prime Minister with regard to the situation that has arisen through the forcible division of Poland between two great Powers. That fact does not really alter the situation which caused us to enter upon this war, and the fact that Poland has been overrun is not different from the fact that almost all Belgium was overrun in the last war or that Serbia was overrun. Belgium rose again: Poland will rise again. The spirit of the Polish people is not defeated. The Prime Minister is right, in my view, in saying that we must examine carefully every kind of proposal for peace, but we must deal with realities. It is no good saying that there is peace when there is no peace, and the mere reversion to a situation of the last year or so would not bring the world back to peace, because, in fact, this war began long before there was any formal declaration of war. We shall require deeds, and not merely words, before we can get any substantial basis for peace when we look at what has happened previously. I, therefore, welcome the Prime Minister's statement that this country and France stand where we are, because we are standing essentially for a real peace and not a sham peace, and for the safety of all peoples, and not merely considering only our own people. With that, as the Prime Minister said, every one of us would welcome any real possibility of ending this war, and no one would wish to prolong it any longer than is absolutely necessary [. . .].

Mr. Lloyd George [Ind.L.]: [. . .] it is quite clear from what appears in the Press . . . that there has been a discussion between the parties concerned, I mean Russia and Germany and Italy, of more detailed terms of Peace. There is a good deal that we do not know. We do not know, for instance, what is proposed to be done with Poland, and that is a very vital matter. I was very glad that the First Lord of Admiralty [Mr. Churchill] in his powerful broadcast on Sunday night [October 1] did draw a distinction between the attitude of the Russian Government and that of the German Government. I could give many reasons, but this is not the opportunity for doing so, for treating even the partition of Poland, in so far as the Russian part is concerned, in a totally different spirit from that part which appertains to Herr Hitler and the German Government. Whether the parts of Poland which they have annexed are truly Russian is a matter for discussion. Since the announcement that it was proposed that peace terms should be proffered there has been detailed discussion in Moscow between the German Government and Mr. Stalin. What happened we do not know. There have been discussions at the invitation of Herr Hitler with the Italian Government, and let me say that I do not think the Italian Government have shown any hostility towards this country during the last few days; on the whole they have shown a friendly disposition.

No. 59

Supplementary Protocol to the German-Soviet Boundary and Friendship Treaty of September 28, 1939, on the delineation of the frontiers between Germany and the USSR

Moscow, October 4, 1939   D.Germ.F.P., VIII, No. 193

The undersigned, being duly empowered thereto by the German Government and the Government of the USSR, pursuant to article I of the Boundary and Friendship Treaty concluded in Moscow on September 28, 1939, between Germany and the USSR,[1] have agreed upon the following:

I

The boundary line between the respective national interests in the territory of the former Polish state shall have the following course:

Beginning at the point located on the Igorka River at the mouth of a nameless brook which comes before the village of Pschetok and which flows into the Igorka River at a distance of about 2,300 metres northeast of the intersection of this river with the Shondowy-Kopzewo road, the boundary shall run in a southwesterly direction, on a straight line to be determined, to the point located on the Tschernaja Gantscha River opposite the northwestern edge of the village of Shondowy.

[1] See doc. No. 52.

Thence the boundary ascends along the Tschernaja Gantscha River to the mouth of the Marycha River. From this mouth the boundary shall follow a southwesterly direction, on a straight line to be determined, to the northern shore of Jedryno Lake. Thence the boundary shall follow a straight line to be determined to the point located opposite the mouth of the Wolkushanka River on the Tschernaja Gantscha River, and further, ascending this latter river, to the point lying south of the village of Ostrynske. Thence the boundary shall run at first in a southwesterly and then in a northwesterly direction along the ravine to its northwestern end and then, on a straight line to be determined, running in a northwesterly direction to the point lying at the northeastern edge of the village of Tscharny Brud. From here the boundary shall run in a northwesterly direction, on a straight line to be determined, to the railroad bridge across the Blisna River at the northern edge of the village of Schtschebra so that the village of Schtschebra shall be on the USSR side and the village of Blisna on the German side. Continuing the boundary shall descend the Blisna River to the junction of the roads Suwałki-Schtschebra II and Ratschki Schtschebra II, so that the fork of the road and the village of Schtschebra II, shall remain on the German side and the village of Schtschebra I on the USSR side.

Thence the boundary shall continue in a northwesterly direction, on a straight line to be determined, to a point located north of the village of Topilowka and then shall bend slightly in a southwesterly direction and run, on a straight line to be determined, to a point located on the former Russo-German Reich border, which is located at a distance of about 900 metres southwest of the village of Pruska Mala, which shall remain on the German side.

Thence the boundary shall continue generally in a south-westerly direction along the former Russo-German border up to the point where the latter intersects the Pissa River.

Thence the aforesaid boundary shall descend along the Pissa River to its confluence with the Narew River and then descend this river to the mouth of a nameless brook which flows into the Narew River between the town of Ostrolenka and the village of Ostrowa. Thence the boundary shall ascend the brook to the eastern edge of the village of Lawy (South). From the eastern edge of the village of Lawy (South), the boundary shall continue in a southeasterly direction, on a straight line to be determined, to the southern edge of the village of Sussk, and continue, also on a straight line to be determined, to a point situated on the Troschyn-Rabendy road approximately 400 metres southwest of the edge of the village of Troschyn. Thence the boundary runs in a south-southeasterly direction, on a straight line to be determined, to the crossroads south of the village of Stylengi and then shall turn towards the southeast and continue, on a straight line to be determined, to a point on the Osh River south of the village of Butschin, so that this village shall remain on the USSR side, and the village of Saoshe on the German side.

Thence the boundary shall ascend the Osh River to a tributary on the left which flows into the Osh River between the villages of Sokolowo and Rogowek, then along this tributary to a point located 1,200 metres east of the village of Malinowa-Stare. Thence the boundary shall continue in a southeasterly direction, on a straight line to be determined, to a point on the Ostruw-Masowezka-Schabikowo road, approximately 700 metres south of the brick works, so that the Salesze estate, the village of Lubejewo-Nowe and the aforesaid brick works shall be on the USSR side; the village of Salesze, the village of Pshiimy and the village of Lubejewo on the German side.

Thence the boundary shall continue in a southeasterly direction, on a straight line to be determined, up to a point on the Brotschisko River, approximately 500 metres northwest of the western edge of the village of Nowa Zolotorija, so that the village of Ugnewo shall remain on the German side.

Thence, the boundary shall continue in a southeasterly direction, on a straight line to be determined, to a point on the road, approximately 350 metres south of the village of Petzki.

Thence the boundary shall run in a southeasterly direction to a point on the Sapadnyi Bug River approximately 1,500 metres east of the edge of the village of Nadbushne.

Thence the boundary shall ascend the Sapadnyi Bug River to the mouth of the Solokija River.

From the mouth of the Solokija River, the boundary shall run along this river to a point located opposite the north-western edge of the village of Ugnuw.

Thence the boundary shall continue in a northwesterly direction, on a straight line to be determined, to the southern edge of the village of Chody-wantze, so that the village of Pschedno and the village of Nowossjulki shall remain on the USSR side and the village of Mysljatin and Chodywantze on the German side.

Thence the boundary shall continue in a northwesterly direction, on a straight line to be determined, to a point located approximately 1,300 metres north of the northeast edge of the village of Shurawze.

Thence the boundary shall continue in a southwesterly direction, on a straight line to be determined, to a point located on the Krinitza Brook, opposite the southeastern edge of the village of Shilka.

Thence the boundary shall continue in a southwesterly direction, on a straight line to be determined, to the southeastern edge of the village of Bshesina, then the boundary shall continue in a southwesterly direction, on a straight line to be determined, to a point approximately 800 metres northwest of the village of Pisuny.

Thence the boundary shall continue in a southwesterly direction, on a straight line to be determined, up to Luwtscha Brook and shall reach this brook opposite the southwestern edge of the village of Garby and thence shall ascend along this brook up to the Sigly farm.

Thence the boundary shall continue in a southwestern direction, on a straight line to be determined, to a point on the Gnoinik Brook opposite the southeastern edge of the village of Gorajetz and shall then descend this brook to its intersection with the Gorajetz–Zetschanuw road.

Thence the boundary shall continue in a southwesterly direction, on a straight line to be determined, to the eastern edge of the village of Zetschanuw.

Thence the boundary shall continue in a southwesterly direction, on a straight line to be determined, to the western edge of the village of Dachnuw, so that the Novy farm shall remain on the German side.

Thence the boundary shall continue in a southwesterly direction, on a straight line to be determined, to the southeastern edge of the village of Futory and thence approximately westward, on a straight line to be determined, to a point on the northwestern edge of the village of Sabjala, so that the Ljatoschin farm and the village of Uschkowtze shall remain on the USSR side.

Thence the boundary shall continue in a northwesterly direction, on a straight line to be determined, to a point on the Pschikopa Brook opposite the northwestern edge of the village of Dobtscha, so that the village of Milkuw shall remain on the USSR side and the village of Degelnja on the German side.

Thence the boundary descends the course of the Pschikopa Brook to its confluence with the Pschiluben River and then follows this river downstream to its confluence with the San River.

Thence the boundary shall ascend the course of the San River to its source, so that the Sjanki and Ushok railroad stations shall remain on the USSR side.

Note 1: At nonnavigable rivers and brooks the boundary line shall be the middle of the main branch of such rivers and brooks. At navigable rivers, the boundary line shall be the middle of the main channel of navigation.

Note 2: Those portions of the boundary which have been determined by lines to be agreed upon, shall be defined in detail at the demarcation of the boundary. [...].

II

The boundary line determined in section I of this Protocol shall be marked on the ground by a mixed German-Russian commission.

The commission shall erect boundary monuments, prepare a detailed description of this line and enter it on a map to the scale of 1:25,000.

This commission shall commence its work on October 9 of this year.

The description of the course of the boundary prepared by the foregoing commission and a map of this line shall be confirmed by both Governments.

III

This Protocol, which is subject to ratification, takes effect immediately upon signature. The exchange of ratification shall take place in Berlin within the shortest time possible.

This Protocol has been done in four copies, of which two are in the German and two in the Russian language, both texts being equally authentic. Signed in Moscow, on October 4, 1939.

By authority of the
Government of the USSR:
W. Molotov

For the Government
of the German Reich:
F. Schulenburg

No. 60

Telegram from Minister Ribbentrop to Ambassador Schulenburg on the German claim to the territory of Suwałki

Berlin, October 5, 1939   D.Germ.F.P., VIII, No. 196

With reference to today's telephonic communication from the Ambassador. The Legation in Kaunas is being instructed as follows:

1) Solely for your personal information, I am apprising you of the following: At the time of the signing of the German-Russian Non-Aggression Pact on August 23, a strictly secret delimitation of the respective spheres of influence in Eastern Europe was also undertaken. In accordance therewith, Lithuania was to belong to the German sphere of influence, while in the territory of the former Polish state, the so called four-river line, Pissa-Narew-Vistula-San, was to constitute the border. Even then I demanded that the district of Vilna go to Lithuania, to which the Soviet Government consented. At the negotiations concerning the Boundary and Friendship Treaty on September 28, the settlement was amended to the extent that Lithuania, including the Vilna area, was included in the Russian sphere of influence, for which in turn, in the Polish area, the province of Lublin and large portions of the province of Warsaw, including the pocket of territory of Suwałki, fell within the German sphere of influence. Since, by the inclusion of the Suwałki tract in the German sphere of influence a difficulty in drawing the border line resulted, we agreed that in case the Soviets should take special measures in Lithuania, a small strip of territory in the southwest of Lithuania, accurately marked on the map, should fall to Germany.

2) Today Count von der Schulenburg reports that Molotov, contrary to our own intentions, notified the Lithuanian Foreign Minister last night of the confidential arrangement. Please now, on your part, inform the Lithuanian Government, orally and in strict confidence, of the matter, as follows:

As early as at the signing of the German-Soviet Non-Aggression Pact of August 23, in order to avoid complications in Eastern Europe, conversations were held between ourselves and the Soviet Government concerning the delimitation of German and Soviet spheres of influence. In these conversations I had recommended restoring the Vilna district to Lithuania, to which the Soviet Government gave me its consent. In the negotiations concerning the Boundary and Friendship Treaty of September 28, as is apparent from the German-Soviet boundary demarcation which was published, the pocket of territory of Suwałki jutting out between Germany and Lithuania had fallen to Germany. As this created an intricate and impractical boundary, I had reserved for Germany a border correction in this area, whereby a small strip of Lithuanian territory would fall to Germany. The award of Vilna to Lithuania was maintained in these negotiations also. You are now authorized to make it known to the Lithuanian Government that the Reich Government does not consider the question of this border revision timely at this moment. We make the proviso, however, that the Lithuanian Government treat this matter as strictly confidential. End of instruction for Kaunas.

I request you to inform M. Molotov of our communication to the Lithuanian Government. Further, please request of him, as already indicated in the preceding telegram, that the border strip of Lithuanian territory involved be left free in the event of a possible posting of Soviet troops in Lithuania and also that it be left to Germany to determine the date of the implementing of the agreement concerning the cession to Germany of the territory involved. Both of these points at issue should be set forth in a secret exchange of letters between yourself and Molotov.

No. 61

Note from Commissar Molotov to Ambassador Schulenburg concerning the incorporation of the Suwałki region to Lithuania

Moscow, October 8, 1939   D.Germ.F.P., VIII, No. 218

I have the honour hereby to confirm that in connection with the Secret Additional Protocol,[1] concluded on September 29 [28], 1939, between the USSR and Germany, concerning Lithuania, the following understanding exists between us:

1) The Lithuanian territory mentioned in the Protocol and marked on the map attached to the Protocol shall not be occupied in case forces of the Red Army should be stationed [in Lithuania];

2) It shall be left to Germany to determine the date for the implementing of the agreement concerning the cession to Germany of the above-mentioned Lithuanian territory.

[1] See doc. No. 54.

No. 62

Extract from the Soviet-Lithuanian Agreement

Moscow, October 10, 1939   Mirovoye Khoziaistvo, 1939, 10, p. 5
                        Transl. from Russian: Degras, III/380–381

The Presidium of the Supreme Soviet of the USSR on the one side, and the President of the Lithuanian Republic on the other,

For the purpose of developing the friendly relations established by the peace treaty of 12 July 1920, based on the recognition of independent State existence and of non-intervention in the internal affairs of the other party;

Recognizing that the peace treaty of 12 July 1920, and the pact on non-aggression and the peaceful settlement of conflicts of 28 September 1926, continue to provide a firm basis for their mutual relations and undertakings;

Convinced that it is in the interests of both contracting parties to define the exact conditions of ensuring mutual security and to make a just settlement of the question to which State the City of Vilna and the Vilna region (unlawfully wrested from Lithuania by Poland) belong;

Have found it necessary to conclude the following treaty on the transfer of the city of Vilna and the Vilna region to the Lithuanian Republic and on mutual assistance between the Soviet Union and Lithuania, and have appointed for this purpose as their plenipotentiaries;

The Presidium of the Supreme Soviet of the USSR: V. M. Molotov, Chairman of the Council of People's Commissars for Foreign Affairs;

The President of the Lithuanian Republic: Jouzas Urbsys, Minister for Foreign Affairs; who, having presented their credentials, which were found to be drawn up in due form and proper order, agreed on the following:

October 1939
Article I

For the purpose of consolidating the friendship between the USSR and Lithuania, the city of Vilna and the Vilna region are transferred by the Soviet Union to the Lithuanian Republic and included in the territory of the Lithuanian State, the frontier between the USSR and the Lithuanian Republic being established in accordance with the map appended hereto, which frontier shall be specified in more detail in a supplementary protocol.

Article II

The Soviet Union and the Lithuanian Republic undertake to render each other every assistance, including military assistance, should Lithuania be attacked or in danger of attack, or should the Soviet Union be attacked or in danger of attack through Lithuanian territory by any European Power. [...].

No. 63

Protest of the Polish Government against the Soviet-Lithuanian Agreement sent to Allied and Neutral Governments through Polish diplomatic representatives[1]

Paris, October 18, 1939   GSHI, MSZ Coll.49/Sow., No. 10

J'ai l'honneur de communiquer à Votre Excellence que le Gouvernement Polonais, ayant eu connaissance du pacte d'assistance mutuelle entre la Lithuanie et l'Union des Républiques Soviétiques Socialistes, signé le 10 octobre 1939 a fait parvenir au Gouvernement Lithuanien une protestation formelle contre l'acceptation par ce Gouvernement de tout territoire cédé par l'Union des Républiques Soviétiques Socialistes et n'appartenant pas à cette Union.

[1] See Note No. 63.

No. 64

Protest of the Polish Government against the holding of a plebiscite by the Soviet Government on Polish territory, temporarily occupied by USSR, sent to Allied and Neutral Governments through Polish diplomatic representatives

Paris, October 21, 1939   GSHI, MSZ Coll.49/Sow., No. 11

Le Gouvernement Polonais vient d'apprendre que sur le territoire de la Pologne temporairement occupé par l'Union des Républiques Soviétiques Socialistes doit avoir lieu un plébiscite ayant pour but la constatation de la volonté de la population relativement au rattachement de ce territoire à l'Union des Républiques Soviétiques Socialistes. Le Gouvernement Polonais constate dès à présent que l'organisation d'un tel plébiscite sous l'occupation militaire est contraire au droit international, qu'il le considérera par conséquent comme nul et non avenu et qu'il ne reconnaîtra en aucun cas son résultat comme ayant force légale.

No. 65

Protest of the Polish Government to the League of Nations against the Soviet-German agreements on the partition of Poland[1]

Geneva, October 27, 1939   The Monthly Summary of the League
of Nations, October, 1939, Vol. XIX,
No. 10, p. 375

The Governments of Germany and of the Union of Soviet Socialist Republics recently published an Agreement concerning the delimitation of the 'imperial interest' of their States in the territory of the Republic of Poland.

The Polish Government duly addressed through the diplomatic channel an energetic protest to all States against this Agreement, declaring that it can have no legal effect whatever, being absolutely contrary to the fundamental principles of the international law in force. The Agreement, in fact, contains stipulations disposing of the territory of a State Member of the League of Nations which has been the victim of unprovoked aggression.

I am instructed by my Government to reiterate before the League of Nations a solemn protest against the Agreement in question and to declare that it will always be regarded by the Polish nation and by the Polish Government as null and void.

I have the honour to request you to be good enough to bring the present communication to the knowledge of all the States Members of the League of Nations.[2]

[1] See Note No. 65.

[2] The Polish Government addressed this protest to the League of Nations, through the Consul-General Kazimierz Trębicki in Geneva.

Extracts from Commissar Molotov's speech on the partition of Poland and Soviet Foreign Relations made at the V extraordinary session of the Supreme Council of the USSR[1]

Moscow, October 31, 1939   Degras, III/388–395

There have been important changes in the international situation during the past two months. This applies above all to Europe but also to countries far beyond the confines of Europe. In this connection we have to bear in mind three principal circumstances which are of decisive importance. Firstly, mention should be made of changes that have taken place in the relations between the Soviet Union and Germany. Since the conclusion of the Soviet-German non-aggression pact on 23 August, an end has been put to the abnormal relations that have existed between the Soviet Union and Germany for a number of years. Instead of the enmity which was fostered in every way by certain European powers, we now have a rapprochement and the establishment of friendly relations between the USSR and Germany.

The further improvement of these new and good relations found its reflection in the German-Soviet frontier and friendship treaty signed in Moscow on 28 September. This radical change in the relations between the Soviet Union and Germany, the two biggest States in Europe, was bound to have its effect on the entire international situation. Furthermore, events have entirely confirmed the estimation of the political significance of the Soviet-German rapprochement given at the last session of the Supreme Soviet.

Secondly, mention must be made of such a fact as the military defeat of Poland and the collapse of the Polish State. The ruling circles of Poland boasted quite a lot about the 'stability' of their State and the 'might' of their army. However, one swift blow to Poland, first by the German Army and then by the Red Army, and nothing was left of this ugly offspring of the Versailles treaty which had existed by oppressing non-Polish nationalities. The 'traditional policy' of unprincipled manœuvring between Germany and the USSR, and the playing off of one against the other, has proved unsound and suffered complete bankruptcy.

Thirdly, it must be admitted that the big war that has flared up in Europe has caused radical changes in the entire international situation. This war began as a war between Germany and Poland and turned into a war between Germany on the one hand, and Britain and France on the other. The war between Germany and Poland ended quickly owing to the utter bankruptcy of the Polish leaders. As we know, neither British nor French guarantees were of help to Poland. To this day, in fact, nobody knows what these 'guarantees' were. The war between Germany and the Anglo-French bloc is only in its first stage and has not yet really developed. It is nevertheless clear that a war like this was bound to cause radical changes in the situation in Europe and not in Europe alone. [. . .].

[1] See Note No. 66.

Today, as far as the European great Powers are concerned Germany's position is that of a State which is striving for the earliest termination of war and for peace, while Britain and France, which but yesterday were declaiming against aggression, are in favour of continuing the war and are opposed to the conclusion of peace. The roles as you see are changing.

The efforts of the British and French Governments to justify this new position of theirs on the ground of their undertakings to Poland are, of course, obviously unsound. Everybody realizes that there can be no question of restoring old Poland. It is, therefore, absurd to continue the present war under the flag of restoration of the former Polish State.

Although the Governments of Britain and France understand this they do not want the war to end and peace to be restored, but are seeking new excuses for continuing the war with Germany. The ruling circles of Britain and France have lately been attempting to depict themselves as champions of the democratic rights of nations against Hitlerism, and the British Government has announced that its aim in the war with Germany is nothing more nor less than the 'destruction of Hitlerism'. It amounts to this, that the British and with them the French supporters of the war have declared something in the nature of an 'ideological' war on Germany, reminiscent of the religious wars of olden times. [. . .].

In any case under the 'ideological' flag there has now been started a war of even greater dimensions and fraught with even greater danger for the peoples of Europe and of the whole world. But there is absolutely no justification for a war of this kind. One may accept or reject the ideology of Hitlerism as well as any other ideological system; that is a matter of political opinion. But everybody should understand that an ideology cannot be destroyed by force, that it cannot be eliminated by war. It is therefore not only senseless but criminal to wage such a war as a war for the 'destruction of Hitlerism' camouflaged as a fight for 'democracy'. [. . .].

The real reason for the Anglo-French war with Germany is not that Britain and France have vowed to restore the old Poland, and not, of course, that they decided to undertake a fight for democracy. The ruling circles of Britain and France have of course other and more effective motives for going to war with Germany. These motives do not lie in any ideology but in their profoundly material interests as mighty colonial Powers. . . . The possession of these colonies, which makes possible the exploitation of hundreds of millions of people, is the foundation of the world supremacy of Great Britain and France. It is the fear of Germany's claims to these colonial possessions that is behind the present war of Britain and France with Germany, a fear that has become substantially stronger lately as the result of the collapse of the Versailles Treaty. It is the fear of losing world supremacy that dictates to the ruling circles of Great Britain and France a policy of fomenting war with Germany.

Thus the imperialist character of this war is obvious to anyone who wants to face realities and does not close his eyes to facts. One can see from all this who is interested in this war that is being waged for world supremacy.

Certainly not the working class. This war promises nothing to the working class but bloody sacrifice and hardship. Well, now judge for yourselves whether the meaning of such concepts as 'aggression' and 'aggressor' has changed recently or not. [. . .].

As I have said, our relations with Germany have radically improved. Here development has proceeded along the line of strengthening our friendly relations, extending our practical co-operation, and rendering Germany political support in her efforts for peace. The non-aggression pact concluded between the Soviet Union and Germany bound us to maintain neutrality should Germany participate in a war. We have consistently pursued this course, which was in no wise contradicted by the entry of our troops into the territory of former Poland, which began on 17 September. It will be sufficient to recall the fact that on that same day, 17 September, the Soviet Government sent a special note to all States with which it maintains diplomatic relations, declaring that the USSR would continue its policy of neutrality in its relations with them.

As is well known, our troops entered the territory of Poland only after the Polish State had collapsed and had in fact ceased to exist. Naturally we could not remain neutral towards these facts, since as a result of these events we were confronted with urgent problems concerning the security of our State. Furthermore, the Soviet Government could not but reckon with the exceptional situation created for our brothers in Western Ukraine and Western White Russia, who had been abandoned to their fate as a result of the collapse of Poland.

Subsequent events fully confirmed that the new Soviet-German relations were based on a firm foundation of mutual interest. After the Red Army units entered the territory of the former Polish State serious questions arose relating to the delimitation of the State interests of the USSR and Germany. These questions were promptly settled by mutual agreement. The German-Soviet treaty on amity and delimitation of the frontiers between the two countries which was concluded at the end of September has consolidated our relations with the German State. [. . .].

Permit me now to dwell on events directly connected with the entry of our troops into the territory of the former Polish State. There is no need for me to describe the course of these events. They have been reported in detail in our press, and you, comrade deputies, are well acquainted with the facts. I shall only dwell on what is most essential. There is no need to prove that, at the moment when the Polish State was completely collapsing, our Government was obliged to extend a helping hand to our brother Ukrainians and White Russians inhabiting the territory of Western Ukraine and Western White Russia. That is what it did.

When the Red Army marched into these regions it was greeted with general sympathy by the Ukrainian and White Russian population who welcomed our troops as liberators from the yoke of the gentry, from the yoke of the Polish landlords and capitalists. As the Red Army advanced through these districts there were serious encounters in some places between our troops and the Polish troops, and consequently there were casualties. These casualties were as follows: On the White Russian front, counting both officers and men of the Red Army, there were 246 killed and 503 wounded, or a total of 749. On the Ukrainian front there were 491 officers and men killed and 1,359 wounded, or a total of 1,850. Thus the total casualties of the Red Army on the territory of White Russia and Western Ukraine were 737 killed and 1,862 wounded, or a total of 2,599.

As for our war trophies in Poland, they consisted of over 900 guns, over 10,000 machine-guns, over 300,000 rifles, over 150 million rifle cartridges, over 1 million artillery shells, about 300 aeroplanes, etc.

The territory which has passed to the USSR is equal in area to a large European State. Thus the area of Western White Russia is 108,000 square kilometres, and its population is 4,800,000. The area of Western Ukraine is 88,000 square kilometres, and its population 8 million. Hence together the territories which have passed to us have an area of 196,000 square kilometres, and a population of about 13 million, of whom there are more than 7 million Ukrainians, more than 3 million White Russians, over 1 million Poles, and over 1 million Jews.

The political significance of these events can scarcely be overrated. All reports from Western Ukraine and Western White Russia show that the population greeted their liberation from the yoke of the gentry with indescribable enthusiasm and warmly hailed this great new victory of the Soviet Power. [. . .].

I shall now pass on to our relations with the Baltic countries. As you know, important changes have taken place here as well. Soviet relations with Estonia, Latvia, and Lithuania are based on the peace treaties concluded with the respective countries in 1920. By those treaties Estonia, Latvia, and Lithuania became independent States, and ever since then the Soviet Union has invariably pursued a friendly policy towards these newly created small States. This was a reflection of the radical difference between the policy of the Soviet Government and the policy of Tsarist Russia, which brutally oppressed the small nations, denied them every opportunity of independent national and political development, and left them with most painful memories.

It must be recognized that the experience of the past two decades of the development of Soviet-Estonian, Soviet-Latvian, and Soviet-Lithuanian friendly relations has created favourable conditions for the further consolidation of political and all other relations between the USSR and its Baltic neighbours, and this was shown in the recent diplomatic negotiations with their representatives and in the treaties[1] which were signed in Moscow as a result of those negotiations.

As you know, the Soviet Union has concluded pacts of mutual assistance with Estonia, Latvia, and Lithuania, which are of major political significance. The principles underlying all these pacts are indentical. They are based on mutual assistance between the Soviet Union on the one hand and Estonia, Latvia, and Lithuania on the other, and they include military assistance

[1] League of Nations Treaty Series, CXCVIII, pp. 223, 381.

should any of these countries be attacked. In view of the special geographical position of these countries, which form a kind of approach to the USSR, particularly from the Baltic, these pacts allow the Soviet Union to maintain naval bases and aerodromes at specified points of Estonia and Latvia, and in the case of the pact with Lithuania, provides for the defence of the Lithuanian border jointly with Soviet Union. [. . .].

The special character of these mutual assistance pacts in no way implies any interference by the Soviet Union in the affairs of Estonia, Latvia, or Lithuania, as some foreign newspapers are trying to make out. On the contrary, all these pacts strictly stipulate the inviolability of the sovereignty of the signatory States and the principle of non-interference in each other's affairs. They are based on mutual respect for the political, social and economic structure of the contracting parties and are designed to strengthen the foundations for peaceful neighbourly co-operation between our peoples. [. . .].

The principles of Soviet policy towards small countries have been demonstrated with particular force by the treaty providing for the transfer of the city of Vilna and the Vilna region to the Lithuanian Republic. The Lithuanian State with its population of $2\frac{1}{2}$ million thereby considerably extends its territory, increases its population by 550,000, and receives the city of Vilna, whose population is almost double that of the present Lithuanian capital. The Soviet Union agreed to the transfer of the city of Vilna to the Lithuanian Republic not because it has a predominantly Lithuanian population. No, the majority of the inhabitants of Vilna are not Lithuanians. But the Soviet Government took into consideration the fact that the city of Vilna, which was forcibly wrested from Lithuania by Poland, ought to belong to Lithuania as a city with which are associated both the historical past of the Lithuanian State and the national aspirations of the Lithuanian people. [. . .].

No. 67

Decree of the Supreme Council of the USSR concerning the incorporation of Western Ukraine into the USSR[1]

Moscow, November 1, 1939   GSHI, A.11. 49/Sow./3
                                       Transl. from Russian: Pol.-Sov.R., No. 24

The Supreme Council of the Union of Soviet Socialist Republics having heard the report of the Authorized Committee of the National Assembly of Western Ukraine has decided as follows:[2]

1. To comply with the petition of the National Assembly of Western Ukraine to incorporate it in the Union of Soviet Socialist Republics and to unite it with the Ukrainian Soviet Socialist Republic.

2. To instruct the Presidium of the Supreme Council to fix a date for the election of representatives of Western Ukraine to the Supreme Council of the USSR.

[1] See Note No. 67.
[2] The Supreme Council of the Ukrainian SSR took cognizance of this Decree on November 15, 1939.

3. To propose to the Supreme Council of the Ukrainian Soviet Socialist Republic the admission of Western Ukraine to the Ukrainian SSR.

4. To instruct the Supreme Soviet of the Ukrainian SSR to submit to the Supreme Soviet of the USSR for examination a plan for the demarcation of boundaries between the provinces and districts on the borders of the Ukrainian Soviet Socialist Republic and the White Ruthenian Soviet Socialist Republic.

Chairman of the Presidium of the Supreme
Council of the USSR:
M. Kalinin
Secretary of the Presidium of the Supreme
Council of the USSR:
A. Gorkin

No. 68

Decree of the Supreme Council of the USSR concerning the incorporation of Western White Ruthenia into the USSR

Moscow, November 2, 1939   GSHI, A.11. 49/Sow./3
Transl. from Russian: Pol.-Sov.R., No. 25

The Supreme Council of the Union of Soviet Socialist Republics having heard the report of the Authorized Committee of the National Assembly of Western White Ruthenia has decided as follows:[1]

1. To comply with the petition of the National Assembly of Western White Ruthenia to incorporate Western White Ruthenia into the Union of Soviet Socialist Republics and to unite it with the White Ruthenian Soviet Socialist Republic.

2. To instruct the Presidium of the Supreme Council to fix a date for the election of representatives of Western White Ruthenia to the Supreme Council of the USSR.

3. To propose to the Supreme Council of the White Ruthenian Soviet Socialist Republic the admission of Western White Ruthenia to the White Ruthenian SSR.

4. To instruct the Supreme Council of the White Ruthenian SSR to submit to the Supreme Council of the USSR for examination a plan for the demarcation of boundaries between the provinces and districts on the borders of the Ukrainian Soviet Socialist Republic and the White Ruthenian Soviet Socialist Republic.

Chairman of the Presidium of the Supreme
Council of the USSR:
M. Kalinin
Secretary of the Presidium of the Supreme
Council of the USSR:
A. Gorkin

[1] The Supreme Council of the White Ruthenian SSR took cognizance of this Decree on November 14, 1939.

No. 69

Final Report presented to the Minister for Foreign Affairs by former Ambassador Grzybowski

Paris, November 6, 1939 Pol.W.B., No. 184

The act of aggression which the Soviet Union committed against Poland on September 17, 1939, without declaring war, without breaking off diplomatic relations, and without denouncing the pact of non-aggression, is a simple phenomenon regarded from the moral aspect. Considered as a political decision, however, it is much more complex, for it constitutes a consequential step in M. Stalin's policy.

I

I began my mission in Moscow on July 1, 1936. In the absence of M. Litvinov, who was in Geneva, I was received by M. Krestinsky. Our talk was brief, but not without import. M. Krestinsky informed me in plain terms that my mission had begun at a most unfortunate time.

'The political relations between us could not be worse. We are working,' said M. Krestinsky, 'to increase the prestige of the League of Nations, and for collective security; we are combating all forms of aggression and all forms of fascism. At the present time we are pursuing an anti-German, anti-Italian, and anti-Japanese policy. Poland is pursuing a diametrically contrary policy, tending to weaken the League of Nations, combating attempts to realize collective security, supporting Italy and sympathizing with Japan. Poland is within the orbit of German policy.'

I replied that to define our position as being within the German orbit was an erroneous interpretation, unsupported by any facts whatever. I declared that Poland was pursuing a policy based above all on bilateral agreements, and was working first and foremost for correct and good relations with her neighbours. Not all conceptions of international co-operation carried conviction to our minds. I considered that the differences between our views in this regard should not influence the ordering of our neighbourly relations. The tendency which existed on our side towards good relations with the USSR was the best proof that our policy was independent of Germany.

It was in this talk with M. Krestinsky that I first noted the fact which afterwards I was continually to come up against: irrespective of Polish policy, the Soviets constantly interpreted it so as to contrapose it to their own policy.

II

I presented my credentials to M. Kalinin on July 4, 1936. On this occasion I had a long conversation with him, M. Krestinsky taking part.

M. Kalinin's remarks were in no way aggressive. He talked of the important role which Polish engineers had played in Russian industry in responsible positions. He himself had been a foreman in a factory run by

Polish specialists, and admitted that on their departure the enterprise had suffered considerably. He inquired as to my intentions. I told him that I attached major importance to the development of economic relations. In many spheres our industrial and agricultural production could mutually complement each other. M. Kalinin readily took up this theme. He held the view that the tendency to autarchy was absurd, and that the USSR possessed a sufficiently large production of gold and a sufficient reserve of gold to develop imports satisfying the population's consumption needs. Poland would be a natural source of such imports, for Polish production had long adapted itself to the needs of the Russian market. M. Krestinsky remarked that Polish-Soviet political relations were not propitious to the development of economic relations, but M. Kalinin warmly objected, declaring that it was necessary to *begin* with economic relations. He argued that Germany, which was effecting its political expansion primarily by economic means, set an example to be followed. Yet, apparently making some concession to M. Krestinsky's opinion, he complained that Poland isolated herself from cultural co-operation with the Soviets, and that despite their high level, the Soviet theatre, music and literature were not made sufficiently accessible to the Polish masses.

I answered that the revival of cultural relations was possible only as a final stage, after the achievement of a lasting improvement in the economic and political spheres. I report this conversation at length, since the head of the Soviet State expounded the basic prerequisites of a political programme expressing the Soviets' tendency towards expansion and treating Poland as an object of that expansion.

Events in Europe, however, turned Soviet efforts in another direction. A few months later M. Krestinsky returned to this conversation, and felt obliged to tell me that when M. Kalinin was talking of the intention to abandon autarchy, and to improve supplies in the Soviets by resorting to increased exports, he was revealing the actual plans of the Government. However, European events and Germany's policy forced the USSR to abandon these plans and to apply all resources to the swiftest possible increase in armaments. More or less about this time Marshal Tukhachevski told me of the progress achieved in the sphere of mechanizing the army.

In my report to Count Szembek on November 4, 1936, I made the following remarks:

'. . . Owing to the progress achieved by the Soviets in the development of production and a relative internal stabilization, signs of a growing dynamism are observable. This dynamism will probably take the form not only of expansion but also of aggression. It can be described by the term: doctrinal imperialism, but the choice of the moment at which that aggression will be applied is solely and simply a tactical question.

'. . . It is an error to apply the term "evolution" to the present stage of development of the situation in the Soviets. What is being achieved in the USSR today is nothing but a revolution from above, and a revolution which is continually advancing. The entire economic and industrial activity of the

Soviets is not the result of natural development nor of the needs of the population. It is a realization of doctrinaire plans enforced from above. Soviet industry is wholly directed towards the future war, and is concentrating its efforts on the up-to-date equipment and motorization of the Red Army. The intensive construction of strategic roads is also characteristic. In the direction of the Latvian frontier three parallel roads have been built, of which only one is given over to normal exploitation. In the direction of Poland two motor roads, one from Moscow to Minsk, and a second from Kiev towards Polish Volhynia are being constructed.

'. . . Russian imperialism is still laying down a road for itself by means of the "Emancipation of the proletariat". The method by which it works towards this end is by supporting all and every conflict in Europe.

'. . . So far as we are concerned, despite their ostensible desire to establish good neighbourly relations, the Soviets are doing their best to arouse hatred for Poland with the help of propaganda. By its very nature Soviet expansion is directed against us, for we constitute a natural barrier to the realization of their designs.'

III

The summers of 1936 and 1937, of little importance in the foreign policy of the Soviets and equally of little importance in the establishment of Polish-Russian relations, were undoubtedly the period of final crystallization of Stalinist Russia.

(a) The features of the new Stalinist régime were revealed most of all in the trials, which staggered the whole world. The 'purges' which accompanied them engulfed hundreds of thousands of victims, disorganizing the army and the State apparatus. They were a primitive system which had as object the complete subjection of individuals to the needs of the State, which in turn was dependent on the will of one man—Stalin.

(b) In the new situation, parallel with the system of terror developed a system of bluff. This latter system was born of the necessity to hide the reality from foreigners, but it led to the wholesale necessity to justify that reality at home. Anyone who has not lived for some length of time in Soviet Russia is not in a position to realize the degree and dimensions of the bluff which prevails in that country.

(c) It is not surprising, either, that anyone who has resided in the Soviets outside the charmed circle of 'Intourist' cannot resist a continual feeling of living in an atmosphere of universal suffering. Human speech possesses no words or phrases sufficiently striking to express that which is to be read in the eyes of a large proportion of the people one meets. Beyond a certain small group of people intoxicated with authority and momentary success, almost all eyes reveal anxiety as well as suffering, and often an animal terror. For in the Soviets uncertainty as to the morrow is almost as universal as suffering.

Here it has to be borne in mind that in the period under discussion the process of destruction of all the sanctuaries of religious faith had been completed. Almost all the churches were closed. The few remaining Polish

73

priests had been sentenced to imprisonment or exile. Persecutions and purges had affected the clergy and the faithful of all creeds.

With complete disregard the people of the Soviets had been cut off from all contact with foreigners and foreign countries.

Against this general background definite problems were equally abnormal in their development.

In a personal report to the Minister for Foreign Affairs, M. Beck, dated April 8, 1938, I wrote:

'In every State and in every period of development the governing authorities have to deal with the opposition of elements of the past and elements of the future, which are active and at work in the given political situation. This is particularly so in the periods of creation of new régimes and new systems. The solution depends customarily on an appropriate estimate of the correlation of forces between the elements of the past and the elements of the future, and takes the line of a corresponding compromise.

'. . . It has to be stated that in the USSR the method of compromise was at once rejected and the method of mechanical resolution was applied on the widest scale. The Russian revolution laid down the road to the future by shooting tens of thousands of officers, officials and specialists, priests, and all "bourgeoisie". The collective farm system has been built up on the extermination and enforced emigration of millions of peasants. The problem of national minorities and the problem of the "homeless children" have been resolved in the same way.

'During the Stalin period the technique of government has not changed.

'Stalin has come up against the problem of the influence of elements of the past simply because twenty years of revolution could not but create a certain number of people possessing their own political state of ownership, their own stage of services, and hence the right to regard themselves not only as participators in but masters of the Soviet State. We would be making a mistake if we described them as an opposition in the usual meaning of the word. They were exclusively isolated individuals and small desperate groups. We have no data whatever which would justify the view that they had a common aim and programme. One can only recognize that on very numerous problems they did not agree with the Stalin "line" and opposed a number of current solutions. In very many cases their "wrecking" did not arise from political impulses. They were simply a steadily increasing legion of people who in future could not or did not want to march along the Politbureau line. In so far as it is a question of active people psychologically unadapted to the given stage of development of the State, life deals with them more effectively than do the police. But Stalin regards them as a considerable danger, because the discontent to which they give expression of one kind or another is shared by millions.

'Stalin's mechanical method of dealing with these "opponents" has lasted for almost two years. During the past year changes occurring in the governing positions have been amazing in their number and frequency. There are military regions which in ten months have had five commanders in succession.

In the case of the highest authorities in White Russia the average period of authority during the last year has been two months. . . .

'Two very important consequences arise from this:

'The first is the disintegration of the State apparatus owing to the disastrous handling of the personnel problem. Since 1917 there have been numerous experimental attempts to solve this problem. Certain of them had signs of a tendency to be based on the objective criteria of specialized knowledge and patriotism. These criteria have now been replaced by the criterion of absolute and uncritical fidelity to Stalin. . . .

'This has created a decidedly desperate situation in all parts of the State apparatus, but particularly in the army, which in the past year has lost the majority of its previous higher command. Despite the knowledge that the "cadres decide everything", Stalin has not resolved the problem of cadres.

'The next consequence consists of certain anticipations for the future. In the Leninist period the mass executions eliminated the possibility of a monarchist and capitalist restoration. The present mass executions make impossible any restoration of Leninism. . . .'

In the same report I further wrote:

'One of the basic tasks of every administration is the struggle to adapt the psychology of the individual citizen to the needs of the State, the struggle to strike the necessary effort out of the human masses. There are periods when this task is modest and is limited to changing the attitude or certain tendencies of the community.

'The tremendous Soviet effort to create a new psychological type, to "reforge" the Russian man, is in accordance with the unusual aims they have set themselves. The aims imposed on the State must, however, spring out of reality. In the USSR they grow out of a simplicistic doctrine. Conforming to the law that the less internal discipline man possesses, the greater his need of external discipline, Stalin has developed an autocratic system peculiar to the Russians. Nevertheless, the demands he made on the Soviet citizen in the realm of labour and production were inadequately justified by the reality, and it grows more and more clear that these demands are unreal and will be incapable of achievement.

'A system demanding great organizing ability, a pedantic exactitude, prolonged, systematic effort and sacrifice on the part of those who have to apply it is incompatible with the characteristics of the Russian spirit.

'To combat this an enormous propaganda effort has been put into operation in the USSR. One cannot but recognize both the unusual scale of this effort, and the great success achieved. Propaganda is an effective means only in a strictly defined, and therefore narrow sphere. If Stalin had restricted his propaganda, it would probably have remained effective. But he applied it too extensively. In the Soviets propaganda has become a falsification of reality, and by placing a gulf between the State and reality it is thereby weakening the State. The Soviets live in an incredible condition of propaganda bluff. The new human type which has been thus created has been admitted by the authorities themselves to be a product of the hot-house.

75

And so before our eyes there is occurring a process of insulation of the Soviet citizen from all external influences. Not only foreign consulates, but also the most communistic foreign members of the Comintern are being liquidated. Anyone who has ever had any kind of contact with foreigners or foreign countries is dangerous. . . . The best proof of the deception which has been caused by this almost inhuman propaganda effort is the lasting necessity of continual resort to terror, as the sole stimulus in whose effectiveness the authorities continue to believe. . . .'

I ended this report with the following words:

'From the several features of Soviet administration which I have outlined, one conclusion results: we have to deal with an extremely primitive system of government. A half-educated governor possesses only one, not always useful quality. Nothing is impossible to him. This is simply because, with his very one-sided and narrow view of reality, the complexity of that reality does not enter his consciousness. In the USSR it is considered that to mechanize agriculture it is sufficient to build a certain number of tractors, that to achieve a certain level of professional culture it is sufficient to build the requisite number of schools, that to overcome the supplies difficulties it is sufficient to multiply rabbits to tens of millions, that the political commissars decide the standard of the army, and so on. This is a continual taking the part for the whole. Always fresh factors are revealed which had not been reckoned with in the original account. The struggle to overcome them causes a weakening of effort in regard to factors previously recognized as the most important. Of the themes which have been regarded in the Soviets as the most important during the past two years one could make an encyclopaedia. . . .'

This primitive method of government is to be observed in two other spheres also.

Following in the steps of Russian Tsarism, Stalinist autocracy is based entirely and completely on the bureaucracy.

Nevertheless, so far no solution has been found to the organizational problems of administration. In the above-quoted report I said:

'The administrative apparatus is in a state of flux and is the subject of experimentation. . . . There are continual vacillations from individual authority to administration by collective groups, from non-political to political government, from concentration to deconcentration, from centralization to decentralization. . . . The all-powerful bureaucracy does not yet possess an established structure. During the last year there have been numberless examples of reorganization of the administration. . . . Weighed down with the excess of its tasks, the bureaucratic Soviet apparatus cannot achieve equilibrium.'

Again in complete analogy with Tsarist Russia, the Stalinist régime stands impotent in face of the problems of national minorities. All that is vociferated in this sphere is a monstrous bluff. As to the practical applications, I informed M. Beck in my report dated March 10, 1939:

'The process of Russification is being continued with complete lack of regard and with the utmost consistency. The most important factors of the policy in regard to minorities are: (*a*) The minority areas are ruthlessly being rendered economically dependent on the Russian areas; (*b*) The minority elements are being dispossessed and the Russian element is being settled in the minority areas; (*c*) The minority Press is gradually being replaced by the Russian Press; (*d*) There is steadily decreasing instruction in the local language and steadily increased emphasis on teaching the Russian language; (*e*) Religious cults which might strengthen the feeling of separate nationality are being destroyed; (*f*) All the most eminent representatives of national minorities are being transferred to the interior of Russia; (*g*) A terror unflagging in its cruelties is being applied even to the least tendency towards independence. . . .'

Simultaneously it has to be recognized that all these methods, despite their intensification, have not advanced the solution of the minorities problem, but, on the contrary, are causing an underground ferment, which in favourable conditions would lead to an overthrow of the régime.

IV

Phenomena and facts met with in the sphere of economic affairs confirm the foregoing observations on political problems in the USSR.

In its application of a policy of integral State capitalism the Soviet Government has based itself primarily on two factors.

The first of these is the so-called State Plan, which has become a fundamental element of governmental activity in the Soviets.

This plan was intended to be an adaptation of the State production and economy to the needs of the State. Obviously, it is to a considerable extent dependent on the actual possibilities of the State itself. As the existing possibilities are not adequate to meet the satisfaction of all needs, it becomes necessary to establish a strict grading of needs and a rota for their satisfaction. So constructed, the Plan remained an ideal on paper. It is true that the first two Five Year Plans, at the cost of incredible outlay, achieved certain results, but since 1936 we have observed a slowing up and even retrogression in this process.

Little by little the number of needs satisfied is diminishing. The State Plan broke down both in quantitative and in qualitative aspects. On the former count, for instance, a dangerous shortage of coal and oil fuel arose.

The qualitative failure to achieve the plan is the result of a whole series of factors. It arises from the deficit production of many raw materials, which have to be replaced by substitutes, from the failure of the financial plan, from the lack of co-ordination of production, but above all else from the immense exploitation and the poverty of the toiling masses and the irrationally allocated production charges. The system of bureaucratic government burdens the workshops with disproportionate administrative charges. In the chase after financial equilibrium a tendency develops to produce that which pays the best, despite the demands of the plan. The ills of Soviet economic life are creating such a complexity of reasons for the non-fulfilment of the

77

State plan that already today nobody is able to foresee what will be the final result of the processes of production and exchange. The plans are ceasing to be plans, and are becoming more and more a source of disorientation. What should be the foundation of the Soviets' economic structure is becoming a necessary evil.

Another overestimated factor in the Soviets is the role which machinery was to play in the reconstruction of economic life.

A lack of faith in man has become the starting-point for the cult of the machine. Certainly with the aid of machinery it was possible to start new methods of production, and in particular it would have been impossible to imagine collective agricultural production in the form of the collective farms without the mechanization of agriculture.

Yet machinery can play a decisive role only at the beginning of these processes. Life proved that in order to stabilize and further develop these forms of creative activity machinery was not sufficient. For machinery can fulfil various kinds of functions, sometimes very complex, but, unfortunately for Soviet conditions, it is not able to mind itself, or mend itself. This factor proved to be an unusually heavy burden on the development of production in the Soviets. The Soviet tractor or lorry's normal 'life', it now appears, is three times shorter than the State plan provided for. The same unusually short life is possessed by machinery, locomotives, railway trucks. . . . The most striking example of the mechanization drive is the Army, which depends on an enormous number of aeroplanes and tanks. All other factors appear to be neglected.

The situation in agriculture seems to be analogical. Mechanization has made tremendous progress, but production is in an increasingly worse state.

In the endeavour to break down the resistance which the most numerous section of the population in the USSR, the mass of peasantry, has made and is still making to the Stalinist régime, a mechanical system of ruinous exploitation has been created which is leading to smaller and smaller harvests.

So it is not surprising that, while during the period 1909 to 1913 Tsarist Russia exported an average of 104 million quintals of grain, during the period 1929 to 1933 the USSR exported an average of 26 million, after which date a further severe decline in exports set in.

In a report dated March 8, 1938, I wrote:

'The longer I observe the Soviet Government's methods the more I come to the conclusion that their particular feature is an inability to solve the simplest of fundamental problems. Elementary factors which in other systems of production are the basis, the starting-point, in the Soviet system become peak points. The same symptom is observable in all the spheres of State life. In supplies and in education, in heavy industry and in transport, in agriculture and in politics. Administration proceeds more or less satisfactorily only in the higher regions, remote from reality. In contact with the reality "below" it grows more and more delusive.

'One can assume without fear of error that whether as contracting party, ally or aggressor, the USSR must in *any* case reveal the fundamental inefficiency of its structure, an intrinsic weakness instead of an intrinsic strength.'

V

Anyone who thinks that the system of government in the Soviets arises only from inefficiency and primitivism would be making a fundamental mistake. In addition to these two psychological factors, the unchanging features of the oriental mentality and Stalin's semi-mystical attitude to the doctrine of world revolution have no less influence. The very structure of the pseudo-Socialistic State is noteworthy. No other totalitarian system has achieved such complete absolutism.

In Italy the Duce, Benito Mussolini, has united in his person the functions of head of the Government and leader of the party, but the royal dynasty has remained the symbol and expression of the continuity of State sovereignty. In addition to leadership of the party and headship of the Government, Chancellor Hitler has assumed the position of head of the State. Stalin has placed himself a step higher. The head of the State (a collective body) and the Government are only emanations of the Communist Party, and the head of that party, Stalin, stands above the State and can in principle exert unlimited rule in relation to an unlimited number of States, so long as their Governments are exponents of Communism. So one must take account of the fact that the entire Government in the Union of Soviet Socialist Republics is nothing but a system for the preparation within the Soviets of an instrument for revolution and the conquest of Europe. Only viewed from this angle does the picture become completely intelligible.

Political murders, the enslavement of the soul and the universal bluff, terror and misery, the bureaucratic autocracy, the torture of national minorities, are all crimes arising from a gloomy revolutionary doctrine.

Residing in the USSR, one cannot resist a feeling of compassion not only for the fettered peoples of the Ukraine, the Caucasus, Turkestan and White Russia, but also for the Russian people on whom, by a new turn of history, the role of invader, and destroyer of all the achievements of human culture, is once more being imposed.

In relation to such a reality, in relation to the rule of Stalin and his clique, what policy could Poland have pursued?

It is obvious that with such a state of affairs on the side of the Soviet partner certain definite limits were imposed upon Polish policy and upon the possibility of Polish collaboration with the Soviets. To exceed those limits would have been to destroy all that Poland had stood for for centuries in the east of Europe.

Even so, in its persistent striving for correct neighbourly relations, in its respect for basic agreements and the Riga Peace Treaty which had been concluded, Polish policy remained invariably faithful to three principles:

1. Abstention from any form of intervention in the internal affairs of the USSR.

79

2. The persistent attempt to regulate bilateral relations in a spirit of goodwill to the USSR.

3. Non-participation in any action or in international understandings directed against the USSR. Most important of all, Poland resolutely rejected numerous German proposals directed against the Soviets.

The course of diplomatic negotiations during the last year of my mission in Moscow was as follows:

(a) A turning point rendering possible greater diplomatic activity in our relations with the Soviets, arrived only with the series of international agreements concluded at Munich. Without consulting the USSR and without her participation, the four Western Powers regulated among themselves the question of the Sudeten Germans and Czechoslovakia.

Poland also took no part in these agreements.

Local Polish-Soviet relations were in a state of some exacerbation. M. Potemkin's declaration on September 23, 1938, to our Chargé d'Affaires, and our Government's sharp reply were accompanied by a certain amount of ill-will and hardly friendly demonstrations on the part of the Soviet Government. When the European and local atmosphere had undergone a certain appeasement, I decided during the first ten days of October that the time had come to take the initiative in lessening the political tension, acting on the outline instructions I possessed. I called on M. Potemkin, and by virtue of the custom established between us of from time to time having talks which were not binding (having the character of a personal exchange of views, 'thinking aloud', as M. Potemkin put it), I had a long conversation with him on the general situation.

I for my part expressed the opinion that, in the European situation now created, in the interests of both parties an improvement in the existing Polish-Soviet relations was desirable.

M. Potemkin did not express any opinion, but told me that he would like to return to this talk.

Some days later M. Litvinov invited me to call on him. He told me that he had before him a note of my talk with M. Potemkin. The conversation had greatly interested him, and he desired to ask me a few questions. Most of all he wished to know whether my initiative was of a personal character, or whether it originated from my Government. I told him: 'I think that that depends entirely on your answer. If your answer is positive I have no doubt that the initiative will originate from my Government. But if your answer is negative, then don't you think it would probably be better that we should have to deal with the personal initiative of M. Grzybowski?' M. Litvinov agreed, and wished to know what was the political premiss on which I based my proposal. I answered that it was a very simple premiss. I thought, namely, that good neighbourly Polish-Soviet relations were an adequate factor to ensure peace in this part of Europe.

M. Litvinov's next question was: 'What conditions do you regard as most important to achieve this end?' I answered that the reply to this question would probably be better indicated when I knew his Government's attitude.

Two days later M. Litvinov sent for me again, and informed me that his Government willingly took up the initiative of. . . . I said: 'The Polish Government.' He asked that we should present our views.

I answered that in foreign policy I did not trust to improvizations, and I counted on a permanent lessening of tension and improvement in relations only after the realization of a series of conditions which in my view were fundamental. I regarded the strict observation of existing agreements as a fundamental condition. The Soviet Government had a tendency towards their one-sided modification, as in the case of the cancellation of the train running between the Polish frontier and Kiev, the endless procrastination over our admitted claims to property, and finally the frontier regulations, which were slowly becoming a dead letter, while incidents and violations of the regulations were multiplying endlessly.

The second condition, in my view, was an increase in trade turnover, which had fallen to a few millions, and I proposed as a basis of discussion that it should be raised to the sum of a hundred million zlotys on each side.

M. Litvinov answered with some animation that what I called the foundation was, in his view, the roof. In order to make it possible to realize the desiderata I had postulated, it was necessary, first and foremost, to create a corresponding atmosphere by some political step. He would regard a corresponding joint declaration as the most modest form of such a step.

I told him that I personally did not reject the idea of such a declaration, but I could recommend it to my Government only when I knew the Soviet Government's positive attitude to the conditions I had put forward.

Again after some days (about October 25, 1938) M. Litvinov informed me that his Government did take a positive attitude to the realization of the conditions I had put forward, and handed me a draft declaration he had ready. I read it through, and at once made a certain number of reservations and changes which I regarded as indispensable. But I accepted the matter *ad referendum*.

In the last days of October occurred the unfortunate incident of the Soviet Government's destruction of the Polish military cemetery in Kiev.

This affair, together with the necessity to agree certain details of our conditions with the departments of the Ministry for Foreign Affairs, had a braking effect on the course of negotiations. Only on November 24, 1938, did M. Litvinov finally accept the text of the declaration we had proposed and a memorandum containing the agreed conditions of the understanding. To the list of matters 'pending and not settled' was added also the restitution *ad integrum* of the cemetery at Kiev. We agreed that the declaration was to be published on November 26, 1938.

This declaration possesses undoubted political significance for, made as the result of Polish initiative, it is a precise summary of our fundamental position in regard to the Soviets. To our eastern neighbour we guaranteed the complete loyalty of our policy, its sincere striving for improvement in neighbourly relations, and the development of economic relations. In return we required respect for existing agreements and that the Soviet authorities should adapt their conduct to these agreements. At the same time we fully realized that our partner's intentions were rather more complex, that his ambitions went considerably further, and that his aim was not only to worsen relations between Poland and Germany, but also to win us over to his own political system. But we had the right to expect that we would be able to protect ourselves against that.

(b) The most important of the agreed practical conditions of the declaration concerned trade turnover.

The peculiar economic system of the Soviets had resulted in our never having a full trade treaty with them. Exchange was effected only on the basis of quotas established from year to year.

Only the introduction of foreign exchange regulation in Poland created an equal opportunity for both partners, giving the governmental factors of both States the same possibility of regulating turnover.

In view of the importance of the question we set to work on its realization as early as the middle of December 1938. On the Soviet side the negotiations were conducted by the Vice-Premier M. Mikoyan, and the *pactum de contrahendo* signed by him opened hopeful prospects.

Truly, once more it transpired that, as M. Mikoyan put it, 'the Soviets have everything to buy, but really nothing to sell'; but simultaneously with the commercial Treaty we were to have a settlement of the, for us, very important transit agreement; exchange was to be based on the clearing system, assuring equilibrium in the goods balances; and the quotas on the Soviet side were to consist of raw materials of value to us and amounting to a sum of not less than sixty million zlotys. The atmosphere in which the negotiations were conducted could not have been more friendly. The Soviets desired to extend them to the sphere of war industry also, which, however, proved to be impracticable, owing to the fact that their requirements in this direction exceeded our export possibilities.

It must also be noted that immediately after the publication of the declaration the Soviet Government dealt with a number of the desiderata I had advanced. Steps were taken to restore the cemetery in Kiev, an express train began to run regularly between the Polish frontier and Kiev, a certain number of frontier incidents were adjusted. But all the other minor postulates were in practice subjected to the tactic of endless procrastination.

But the definite improvement in the atmosphere of relations with Poland did not last long on the Soviet side. The traditional New Year reception for the diplomatic corps in Berlin brought an unexpected incident. Chancellor Hitler talked with the Soviet Ambassador longer than with anyone else. In Moscow this fact was given quite considerable publicity. M. Potemkin told me about it in detail and with some delight. He also declared that the conversation touched purely on the Ambassador's personal and family affairs. On the other hand, M. Litvinov, in our conversation on January 8, advised me to hasten the trade negotiations, in order 'to forestall German intrigues'. Soon afterward, information was spread through Moscow of the impending arrival of a German economic delegation with M. Schnurre at its head.

I note as a characteristic fact that this delegation did indeed arrive—at Warsaw about January 25, ostensibly en route to Moscow, but then it chose the road to the west and returned straight to Berlin.

So one must assume that in this first period of contacts there was quite a considerable vacillation in Berlin as well as in Moscow.

Our trade negotiations were opened on January 19, 1939. After only a couple of meetings between our delegations it was possible to deduce that since the time of the conclusion of the *pactum de contrahendo* a change had occurred in the attitude of the Soviet delegation. Not only did they manifest a disposition to chaffer very ardently over every point of the agreement, but such an important issue for us as the transit question was subjected to postponement.

I must state that our economic representatives attached great importance to the achievement of a trade Treaty with the Soviets, and so, naturally, our attitude was compliant. I can state definitely that after a month of tedious negotiations we achieved a trade Treaty primarily owing to the concessions we made to the Soviets as against the *pactum de contrahendo*. Except for the postponement of the transit question (which the Soviet said was indispensable because of other negotiations on the same issue) these concessions were not considerable, but they expressively emphasized that every signature of the Soviet Government would have only a relative value.

We signed the first Polish-Soviet Trade Treaty on February 19, 1939. So-called branch discussions on the fulfilment of quotas were to begin without delay. In fact they began in March, but they came up against such considerable difficulties on the Soviet side that they were never concluded. In a letter to Count Szembek dated May 23, 1939, I wrote: 'At times I have the impression that in our persistent striving for practical things we are overlooking the possibilities of this country. It looks also as if, when making any kind of agreement with this State, we have to consider only the actual fact that it is made, and not the gain which may result from its conclusion.'

(c) At the beginning of May M. Litvinov himself vanished from the political scene. Today we realize that the Soviets' imperialistic plans must have been already sufficiently formulated for them to retain a final and decisive understanding with Chancellor Hitler as a trump card in their policy of instigation of war. It is obvious that such an understanding could not be negotiated by M. Litvinov.

For the time being the Soviets' external activity seemed to be turned in another direction. In face of England's and France's widespread diplomatic activity they regarded it as sound to extend their own activities also. Vice-Commissar Potemkin was delegated to Ankara with the object of assuring that the USSR would have the strict solidarity of Turkish policy. On this journey M. Potemkin halted at Bucharest and Sofia. On his return journey he made his way to Warsaw and, after previous agreement with M. Beck, halted there to carry on conversations. Both M. Beck and M. Arciszewski received favourable impressions from these conversations. M. Potemkin seemed to understand the reservations which restrained us from direct participation in the Anglo-Franco-Soviet negotiations. In the name of his Government he assured M. Beck of the Soviet Government's decision to adopt a benevolent attitude to Poland. Recapitulating these conversations to me in Moscow, he stressed with satisfaction M. Beck's declaration that in the event of such a conflict we would rely inevitably on the Soviets. In my private letter of May 25 to Count Szembek I stressed that in conversations with the diplomatic corps M. Potemkin laid great emphasis on M. Beck's words.

M. Molotov took over the Commissariat for Foreign Affairs on May 5th. On Sunday, the 7th, he invited me to call on him. He began with warm compliments on M. Beck's speech of two days previously, and especially emphasized how much he had been impressed by his words on national honour.

He then talked about the conversations between the Soviet Union and Great Britain and France. I answered that I could not precisely state our views on this subject until I had received instructions. But I could already state, I added, that we adopted a pacific and loyal attitude to all our neighbours and that only clearly aggressive acts committed by any one of them could modify this attitude. As to the proposed collaboration between the USSR and the Western Powers, we regarded it sympathetically. I also observed that we intended to maintain our alliance with Rumania.

Some days later (more or less at the time of M. Potemkin's stay in Warsaw) I gave M. Molotov a résumé of our attitude.

We could not accept a one-sided Soviet guarantee. Nor could we accept a mutual guarantee, because in the event of a conflict with Germany our forces would be completely engaged, and so we would not be in any position to give help to the Soviets. Also we could not accept collective negotiations, and made our adoption of a definite attitude conditional on the result of the Anglo-Franco-Soviet negotiations. We rejected all discussion of matters affecting us other than by the bilateral method. Our alliance with Rumania, being purely defensive, could not in any way be regarded as directed against the USSR.

In addition I indicated our favourable attitude to the Anglo-Franco-Soviet negotiations, and once more emphasized our entire loyalty in relation to the Soviets. In the event of conflict we by no means rejected specified forms of Soviet aid, but considered it premature to determine them definitely. We considered it premature to open bilateral negotiations with the Soviets before the Anglo-Franco-Soviet negotiations had achieved a result. M. Molotov made no objection whatever.

(d) In June there was a series of offers on the part of the Soviets to supply us with armaments materials. It has to be admitted that they were always accompanied by unacceptable conditions. The Soviet propaganda never ceased to urge us to resist the German demands.

It is true that when we raised the question of accelerating the transit negotiations we met with a refusal, but M. Potemkin assured me that obviously everything would change in the event of a conflict, and that in that case we could count on transit. It has to be borne in mind that so long as the Anglo-French-Soviet negotiations lasted it was almost impossible for us to go beyond a waiting attitude. We felt no optimism whatever in regard to the result of those negotiations. It was difficult to expect that the Soviets would do anything in the direction of preventing a conflict or even rendering its outbreak difficult. We observed rather that their tactics aimed at the exact opposite.

The German-Soviet Pact of Non-aggression justly made a deep impression. The fact that two mutually contradictory sets of negotiations had been carried on simultaneously was a true measure of the cynicism of Soviet policy. The conclusion of the pact was beyond all doubt an encouragement to Germany to make war. The scope of the obligations undertaken, the extent of the understanding between the Soviets and Germany remained vague.

The Soviets endeavoured to give it the appearance of a pact assuring them peace, but not effecting any fundamental change in their policy. In this regard M. Molotov even appealed to Poland's example.

The undefined character of the obligations resulting from the pact was emphasized by M. Voroshilov's interview given a few days later. Evidently influenced by news emanating from Berlin and London of the conversations between the British Ambassador and Chancellor Hitler, Marshal Voroshilov gave the Soviet Press an interview, in which he stated that the Anglo-Franco-Soviet negotiations were only suspended, and that their renewal would not be in contradiction with the Soviet-German pact.

Moreover, Marshal Voroshilov simultaneously stated that the supply of raw material and war material to Poland in the event of a conflict was a 'commercial matter', equally not in contradiction with the pact.

The warning was understood in Berlin.

(e) On Saturday, September 2, I received instructions to give official notification of the German aggression and the ensuing state of war between Poland and Germany. On the 3rd I was received by M. Molotov. He did not question our statement that it was a case of unprovoked aggression committed without previous declaration of war, by a surprise attack during negotiations. He agreed in recognizing Germany as the aggressor. He asked whether we counted on the intervention of Great Britain and France, and whether we expected any time-limit. I told him I had no official information, but I anticipated their declaration of war to follow a day later, on the 4th. M. Molotov smiled sceptically. 'Well, we shall see, Monsieur l'Ambassadeur. . . .'

In the meantime the Soviet Ambassador in Warsaw had stressed the importance of Marshal Voroshilov's interview, and had inquired at the Ministry for Foreign Affairs whether steps had already been taken in Moscow with the object of utilizing Marshal Voroshilov's promises in regard to us. As the result of these suggestions, on the 6th I received instructions to investigate the practical possibilities in this direction. Simultaneously I received a list of required materials, which I was to put forward in the event of M. Molotov's adopting a favourable attitude. I was not afforded the opportunity to negotiate on this list. M. Molotov was difficult to get hold of, and received me only on the 8th. Referring to previous official statements and Marshal Voroshilov's interview, I put to him the question of buying the additional raw materials we needed and the eventual supply of war material.

M. Molotov answered that Marshal Voroshilov's interview had been made public in totally different circumstances. Marshal Voroshilov did not and could not know that Britain and France's intervention would follow. The situation had now radically changed. 'Poland', said M. Molotov, 'is now synonymous with England, so far as we are concerned.' The Soviet Union was compelled to safeguard first and foremost its own interests, and to remain outside the conflict.

On the practical question of supplies, which I had raised, the Soviet Government maintained the position of a strict observance of the existing agreements. The fulfilment of our trade agreement had not been satisfactory, but for their part the Soviet Government were prepared to do all that was necessary for that agreement to function normally. Nevertheless, M. Molotov did not think that the Soviet Government could go beyond the quotas established for the current year, either in regard to quantities or in regard to the categories of goods. To this I replied that given good will the difficulties were not so great after all, because, in the first place, the clearing quotas could always be complemented by quotas of purchases for cash, while, secondly, we could even establish supplementary clearing quotas, for the fourth quarter or for the following year, and anticipate with their supply.

M. Molotov said again that he did not anticipate that his Government could introduce any changes whatever in the existing agreements.

I then passed to the transit question and, referring to former Soviet declarations, I asked what facilities could be granted us in this sphere. M. Molotov answered that he was afraid the transit of military materials would be in contradiction with the Pact of Non-aggression concluded with Germany.

So there was nothing else to be done than to inform him that I would communicate his attitude to my Government. At the end of the conversation M. Molotov stated that all he had said had been said in present conditions, but that circumstances might change. The phrase 'in present conditions' was several times repeated in his answers.

Almost simultaneously (September 11) M. Sharonov took a friendly leave of the Ministry for Foreign Affairs, 'in view of his departure for a few days to have contact with his Government'. He communicated to Count Szembek that he had just granted visas to our specialists to travel to Moscow to purchase medical supplies, and he did not doubt that the supplies would be swiftly forthcoming.

Next day *Pravda* published a leading article violently attacking the condition of our minorities in the eastern areas. It stressed that the fate of these minorities could not be a matter of indifference to the Soviet public.

I drew the Ministry for Foreign Affairs' attention to this article, stating that it might be in preparation for eventual decisions.

September 16 was already ended when the telephone rang. I looked at my watch: it was 2.15 a.m. M. Potemkin's secretariat notified me that the Commissar wished to inform me of an important statement by his Government, and asked whether I could come to him at three o'clock. I answered that I would. I ordered a car, and warned Councillor Jankowski that I should need him and Colonel Brzeszczyński as well as the cypher officer for four o'clock. As I drove out of the Embassy the militia-man on duty at the gate saluted with obvious surprise and rushed to the wall-telephone. For the first time in all my term as Ambassador I drove through Moscow without a police escort.

As I went I was prepared for bad news. I thought that under one pretext or another the denunciation of our Pact of Non-aggression was about to follow. That which awaited me was far worse.

M. Potemkin slowly read to me the text of a note signed by M. Molotov. When he had finished I told him at once that I refused to take the contents of the note into cognizance, I refused to communicate it to my Government, and expressed the most categorical protest against its content and form.

I protested against the unilateral abrogation of existing and binding agreements. None of the arguments intended to justify the transformation of those agreements into 'scraps of paper' would withstand criticism. According to my information the head of the Polish State and the Government were within the territory of the Republic. The functioning of the Government was by the nature of things restricted by the state of war. 'You will not demand that at such a time the Minister for Agriculture should carry out agricultural reforms?' For that matter the question of the Government was not so essential at that moment. The sovereignty of the State existed so long as a single regular soldier was still fighting. 'You will not maintain that the Polish soldiers are no longer fighting!'

That which the note said about the position of the minorities within our borders was nonsense. All the minorities, including the Jews, had not only given expression to their loyalty, but were actively proving it by their complete solidarity with Poland in her struggle against Germanism. 'More than once in our conversations,' I told him, 'you have appealed to Slavonic solidarity. At our side at this moment not only Ukrainians and White Russians, but also Czech and Slovak legions are fighting the Germans. Where is your Slavonic solidarity?

'So many times has the USSR indignantly condemned and stigmatized the Germans' perfidy. The note which you have read to me would signify that you had taken the same road.

'During the Great War the territories of Serbia and Belgium were occupied, but it entered no one's head to regard their obligations to these States as non-existent on that account. Napoleon was once in Moscow, but so long as Kutuzov's army existed it was considered that Russia existed.'

M. Potemkin tried to explain that my historic responsibility would be very great if I refused to accept a document of such importance. Besides, the Soviet Government no longer possessed any representative in Poland, and were not in a position to communicate their decision to the Polish Government by any other way.

I said: 'Monsieur le Commissaire, if I agreed to communicate the contents of the note to my Government it would be not only a proof that I had no respect for my Government, but it would also be a proof that I had lost all respect for the Soviet Government. I understand that I am in duty bound to inform my Government of the aggression probably already committed, but I will do no more than that. But I still hope that your Government will restrain the Red Army from invasion, and will not stab us in the back at the moment of our struggle against the Germans.'

M. Potemkin said that evidently I did not take into account the impossibility of our resisting the German onslaught. On the basis of the reports of their military attaché the Soviet Government considered that the German army would inevitably march to the frontiers of the Union.

I told him: 'The most pessimistic reports of military attachés have not the power to release from international agreements. The German troops' advance into the heart of Poland may be the source of great difficulties for them. A similar situation occurred in 1812.'

M. Potemkin replied that in face of the attitude I had taken up he must discuss the matter with his Government. It was four o'clock. I waited for further developments for half an hour.

Finally, M. Potemkin informed me that he had communicated with the utmost precision all that I had said, but his Government could not alter the decisions taken.

I declared that I also could not change my decision, and would inform my Government only of the fact of the aggression.

I sent my telegram *en clair* at a few minutes past five. It did not reach the Ministry for Foreign Affairs until 11 a.m. The Soviet troops invaded Poland at 6 a.m.

(*f*) On September 18 I received approval of the attitude I had adopted and instructions to demand my passports. At my request the Ambassador of one of the Powers had already obtained the agreement of his Government to take over charge of the Embassy building.

On the 19th I called on M. Potemkin and told him that I regarded my mission as ended. I had only to regulate the transference of the charge of the Embassy to a third Power, and to carry out the evacuation of the outlying posts. I asked that it might be made possible for the personnel of the Consulates to arrive at a definite date, and also for the appointment of a special official to carry out the details of the evacuation in agreement with the Embassy. M. Potemkin answered that, as they did not recognize the existence of the Polish State, they would not be able to agree to a third State taking over the protection of our property. He also warned me that they would not be able to recognize the diplomatic privileges of my personnel. The rest he promised to settle without delay.

In fact, after some days the Director of 'Biurobin' (Bureau for Relations with Foreigners), M. Nazarov, was appointed 'plenipotentiary for evacuation', and he opened negotiations with the railway authorities. (For understandable reasons, railway communications at this period were unusually difficult.)

The question of our safety and departure became a subject of lively interest to the entire diplomatic corps. The situation was complicated a little by the fact that the doyen of the corps was the German Ambassador, Count von der Schulenburg, while I was the vice-doyen. Owing to events my functions passed to the Italian Ambassador, M. Rosso, and to him, more than anyone else, we owe the handling of our affairs through diplomatic channels. I must stress that although my position prohibited my communicating with the doyen, Count von der Schulenburg effectively intervened on our behalf several times with the Government. In reply to his intervention M. Molotov stated that *les usages diplomatiques* would be observed at our departure, and he also communicated to him that that departure would not take place so long as the staff of the Soviet Embassy, who had voluntarily remained in Warsaw and who, owing to the bombardment of the building, were spending their time in the cellars, did not return from the besieged city safe and sound. Realizing that I for my part was utterly helpless, Count von der Schulenburg caused communication on the question to be opened between the German Command and the Warsaw Command and on September 25 the staff of the Soviet Embassy, to the unexpected number of sixty-two persons, arrived in Koenigsberg.

On September 26 the Consulate staff in Minsk were allowed to depart, being deprived of half their cases on the pretext of lack of room in the train. Certain officials arrived in Moscow without anything whatever. Despite our protests we did not recover this baggage.

A more dramatic incident occurred in Kiev. At two in the morning of September 30 the Councillor of the Embassy, and acting consul-general, Matusiński, was summoned to the plenipotentiary of the Soviet Foreign Office, ostensibly to agree the final details of his departure. He went at once, with two chauffeurs and accompanied by two police cars. From that moment Councillor Matusiński, the two chauffeurs and the car vanished without trace.

Ambassador Rosso intervened with M. Potemkin in this affair. M. Potemkin stated that he had no information so far from the local authorities, but he must point out that as M. Matusiński had already lost his diplomatic privileges, he could be called to account by the Soviet authorities if it appeared that he had committed some crime against the Soviet Union.

Ambassador Rosso justly replied that he saw no possibility of that, for down to September 18 M. Matusiński had enjoyed full diplomatic privileges, while from that day he had been in fact interned and could commit no crime whatever.

In view of the above-stated position of the affair I asked Ambassador Rosso to communicate to the Soviet Government that I would not leave Moscow so long as M. Matusiński was not set free, and that I demanded formulation of the charge against him.

The intervention with M. Molotov gave a result completely different. M. Molotov informed the doyen of the corps most categorically that the Soviet authorities had no information whatever as to the place of residence and the fate of M. Matusiński. 'I assure you', said M. Molotov, 'that he is not in our hands. I am myself personally making investigations in order to clear up this affair. To hold up the Ambassador's departure on this account is pointless, and I cannot agree to it.'

In view of the Soviet Government's obvious intention to avoid formulating any charge against M. Matusiński there was really nothing to wait for, since one could no longer expect him to be found.

Thanks to the kindness of the Finnish Legation and authorities, the railway difficulties were overcome and our departure took place on the evening of October 10.

The train placed at our disposition by the Soviet authorities had one special feature. It was a sealed train. No one was allowed to alight from it at the stops. The following evening we crossed the Finnish frontier.

I cannot but note that from the Diplomatic Corps and from very numerous colleagues we received a great amount of sympathy and assistance. The cordiality of the leave-taking at the station went far beyond anything known on normal occasions. In addition to Ambassador Rosso special thanks are due to the Ambassador of Great Britain, Sir William Seeds, and the entire personnel of his Embassy.

In conclusion one remark prompts itself. A diplomat accredited to Moscow, cut off from all contacts and all sources of information, can get an orientation on the course of general processes, but knows only facts which come to the surface. Any estimate of the Soviets' foreign policy relies upon very inadequate sources. But there can be no doubt that, equally with their internal policy, it is subversive. Is it at the same time a bad policy? Life would be simpler if the directors of foreign policy could be divided into two definite categories: those who commit only errors and those who render only services. Certain features of Stalin's policy have been marked by great ability. But it must be stated that his policy of invasion of Poland, his entente with Nazi Germany and his tactic of keeping us deceived until the last moment, will bring effects of the most negative kind to Stalin and the USSR. One may repeat with Talleyrand: *'C'est pire qu'un crime, c'est une faute.'*

No. 70

Extract from the record of the conversation between General Sikorski and Lord Halifax concerning Soviet policy

London, November 14, 1939   GSHI, PRM, 3

[. . .] At this point the conversation turned into more general channels, and after General Sikorski had reaffirmed the determination of the Poles to continue the struggle and received from Lord Halifax an assurance that this country was equally determined, Lord Halifax asked whether General Sikorski had any more information than we had as to the development of Soviet policy.

General Sikorski said that it was difficult to give a satisfactory answer, since Soviet policy was many-sided, but he was convinced that the aim of the Soviet Government was the bolshevisation of Europe. The attitude of the Germans to Russia was definitely subservient. Russia was taking advantage of the opportunity to increase her grip on the Baltic in order to assure the maintenance of her position in the territory she had taken from Poland, a territory which included 5 million Poles and many million Ukrainians, and others who rejected Russia's anti-Christian philosophy. For the moment there were rumours that the Bukovina and Bessarabia would be occupied in the spring. If it were possible for the British and French Governments to bring pressure to bear on Rumania to revise her treatment of the Poles interned in that country, it might be possible for the Polish forces in that event to be of assistance to Rumania.

Lord Halifax said that he thought there were also large numbers of Poles interned in Hungary.

General Sikorski said that that was so, and that Hungarians under German pressure had closed their frontiers to prevent the exit of all Poles, whether interned soldiers or civilian refugees.

He went on to say that, a year and a half ago, he had written an article drawing attention to the danger of Russo-German co-operation, and he still thought it a mistake to take the association of the two countries too lightly. It was true that Russian troops in occupied Poland were talking of conquering Red Berlin, and that the Russian army of occupation was not treating the Poles so badly as they were treating the Ukrainians. But, nevertheless, despite any indications to the contrary, he still thought that Russo-German co-operation represented a real danger, since there were too many similarities between the two systems.

Lord Halifax said that if an extension of Soviet influence in Germany took place, it must be either with Hitler's approval or against it. In the first event Hitler would have to say publicly that National Socialism approximated to bolshevism, or, in the second event, there would be real trouble in Germany.

General Sikorski said that he thought the second hypothesis the more likely, but although there was real opposition to Hitler and to Hitler's Russian policy, he did not think that it was likely to be articulate for the moment.

91

Hitler's popularity and prestige seemed possibly to have fallen recently and a new outburst might therefore be expected. [. . .].

No. 71

Decree of the Presidium of the Supreme Council of the USSR concerning the acquisition of citizenship of the USSR by the inhabitants of the Western districts of the Ukraine and Byelorussia

Moscow, November 29, 1939   GSHI, A.11. 49/Sow./5
                                                                                    Pol.-Sov.R., No. 26

1. In conformity with the Citizenship of the USSR Act of August 19th, 1938, it is decreed that the following are henceforth citizens of the USSR.

a) former Polish citizens who were on the territory of the Western districts[1] of the Ukraine and White Ruthenia when these became part of the USSR (November 1 and 2, 1939).

b) persons who arrived in the USSR on the basis of the agreement of November 16, 1939, between the Government of the USSR and the German Government as well as those who arrived as a result of the cession by the USSR to Lithuania of the city of Wilno and the district[1] of Wilno in accordance with the agreement of October 10, 1939.

2. Former Polish citizens resident in the Western districts[1] of the Ukraine and White Ruthenia who were not present in the territory of these districts[1] on November 1 and 2, 1939, and do not possess Soviet citizenship can acquire the citizenship of the USSR by the procedure provided in Article 3 of the Citizenship of the USSR Act.

3. Such persons enumerated in Paragraph 1 of the present Decree as were deprived of Soviet citizenship under the Decree of the All-Russian Central Executive Committee and the Council of People's Commissars of the RSFSR of December 15th 1921 may acquire citizenship of the USSR by the procedure provided in Article 3 of the Citizenship of the USSR Act.

Chairman of the Presidium of the Supreme
Council of the USSR:
M. Kalinin
Secretary of the Presidium of the Supreme
Council of the USSR:
A. Gorkin

[1] *Oblast.*

No. 72

Statement made in the House of Commons by Mr. Chamberlain on the aggression against Poland by Germany and the USSR[1]

London, December 6, 1939   H.C.Deb., 355/657

Mr. Pritt [Lab.] asked the Prime Minister whether the statement by

[1] See Note No. 72.

General Sikorski,[2] the Prime Minister of Poland, that his Government made no difference between the seizure of Polish territories by Russia and their seizure by Germany and that they had no reason to believe that their Allies took a contrary view, is in accord with the policy of His Majesty's Government?

The Prime Minister: The views of His Majesty's Government about the invasion of Poland have already been stated to the House, and there can be no difference of opinion about an unprovoked attack followed by the seizure of the territory of another State.

[1] See *The Times*, November 20, 1939.

No. 73

Protest of the Polish Government to the Allied and Neutral Governments against the conscription of Polish citizens by the Red Army

Paris, February 3, 1940   GSHI, MSZ Coll.49/Sow.I, No. 15

D'ordre de mon Gouvernement j'ai l'honneur de porter à la connaissance de Votre Excellence ce qui suit:

Les autorités soviétiques viennent de procéder sur les territoires de la République de Pologne occupés par les armées de l'URSS au récensement du point de vue militaire de tous les hommes agés de 18 à 50 ans ainsi que de toutes les femmes ayant suivi des cours d'infirmières et ceci comme action préliminaire à leur service militaire.

Comme suite à la protestation élevée contre la décision de l'incorporation à l'URSS des territoires susmentionnés et se référant aux dispositions en vigueur du droit international le Gouvernement Polonais élève une protestation contre cette nouvelle violation des lois et coutumes internationales.

En attirant l'attention sur le fait que l'exercice de la contrainte à l'égard des ressortissants polonais pour les forcer à servir dans l'armée d'un État qui occupé par la violence une partie du territoire de la Pologne entraînera un grand nombre de victimes, le Gouvernement Polonais dès maintenant en rend responsable le Gouvernement de l'URSS.

No. 74

Protest of the Polish Government against the confiscation by the Soviet authorities of objects of artistic and historical value belonging to the Polish State and its citizens

London, March 29, 1940   GSHI, MSZ Coll.49/Sow.I, No. 16

D'ordre de mon Gouvernement j'ai l'honneur de porter à la connaissance de Votre Excellence ce qui suit:

Les autorités soviétiques d'occupation en Pologne procèdent actuellement à la confiscation générale des objets appartenant à l'État Polonais et aux ressortissants polonais et ayant une valeur historique ou artistique (tableaux, livres et manuscrits, argenteries, porcelaines, tapis etc.). Cette mesure constitue une violation flagrante de l'art. 46 al. 2 de l'annexe à la IV Convention de la Hague sur les lois et coutumes de la guerre sur terre dont la teneur est la suivante: 'La propriété privée ne peut pas être confisquée', ainsi que de l'art. 56 de l'annexe à ladite Convention ainsi conçu: 'Les biens des communes, ceux des établissement consacrés aux cultes, à la charité et à l'instruction aux arts et aux sciences, même appartenant à l'État, seront traités comme la propriété privée.'

'Toute saisie, destruction ou dégradation intentionelle de semblables établissements, de monuments historique, d'œuvres d'art et de sciences, est interdite et doit être poursuivie.'

Le Gouvernement Polonais se référant à sa protestation en date du 21 octobre 1939 au sujet de l'incorporation illégale par l'URSS de certains territoires polonais qui continuent conformément au droit international de faire partie de la Pologne, élève une nouvelle protestation contre la violation du droit international dont se rend coupable le Gouvernement de l'URSS, en confisquant des biens appartenant à l'État et aux ressortissants polonais.

Le Gouvernement Polonais se réserve le droit d'exiger au moment opportun la réparation complète des dommages infligés ainsi par l'URSS à l'État et aux ressortissants polonais. Cependant dès à présent il tient à mettre en garde les Gouvernements et les ressortissants des pays tiers contre des tentatives soviétiques de vente à l'étranger des objets confisqués illégalement par l'URSS et vendus ensuite à l'étranger, une vente pareille ne pouvant créer pour les acheteurs aucun droit sur les objets provenant du pillage soviétique.

No. 75

Extracts from a conversation on Soviet problems between General Sikorski and Mr. Churchill

London, June 19, 1940   GSHI, PRM, 20
                                                    Transl. from Polish

[. . .]. After their mutual statements that both governments would carry on the war to its final conclusion, they passed on to the Russian problems. [. . .]. The Soviet attitude was outlined, General Sikorski emphasizing that he was not advocating a policy which might provoke Russia, but he warned against cherishing any illusions regarding the Soviets and their policy towards the Allies. Mr. Churchill stated that Sir Stafford Cripps's conversation in Moscow 'did not turn out badly'. The British Prime Minister emphasized that 'he had no illusions' regarding Moscow's intentions. On the other hand, he seemed to hope that 'once England would defend herself against an invasion', the following spring Hitler might be tempted to strike against Russia, if only to employ his big armies which he neither wished nor was able to send home.

No. 76

Aide-mémoire from General Sikorski to the British Government concerning the situation of the Polish population in Eastern Poland and in Russia and the possibility of creating a Polish army in Soviet-occupied Poland in the event of a Soviet-German war[1]

London, June 19, 1940   Ch.Pres.P.R.

Le Gouvernement Polonais qui considère la défaite de l'Allemagne comme but principal de la guerre n'a pas l'intention de provoquer des difficultés destinées à gêner les discussions entre le Gouvernement Britannique et Soviétique, entamée à l'occasion de l'envoi de Sir Stafford Cripps en qualité d'Ambassadeur à Moscou.

D'autre part le Gouvernement Polonais est décidé à n'épargner aucun effort afin d'améliorer la situation tragique de la population polonaise soumise à l'occupation soviétique. Il est d'avis que cette condition une fois remplie, il serait possible d'utiliser les élements précieux de reserves instruites et d'officiers, existant dans ce territoire et aussi en dehors de lui [prisonniers de guerre détenus en territoire soviétique] afin de créer avec le consentement des autorités soviétiques une armée polonaise de 300,000 hommes environ à utiliser contre l'Allemagne.

Dans le présent état des choses le Gouvernement Polonais se permet de suggérer d'attacher au personel de l'ambassade de Grande Bretagne à Moscou à titre non officiel et confidentiel une personalité polonaise, qui aurait pour devoir d'étudier le point de vue soviétique et les possibilités de réalisation du projet indiqué plus haut. Cette personne, que le Gouvernement Polonais choisirait parmi celles qui possédent une connaissance approfondie des conditions soviétiques et de la mentalité russe, pourrait en même temps être utile à Sir Stafford Cripps dans l'exécution de sa mission. Le Gouvernement Soviétique devrait être évidemment renseigné par l'Ambassade Britannique sur son véritable caractère.

Il va sans dire, que les considérations émises dans le présent aide-mémoire ne sauraient en aucune manière être interpretées comme impliquant une résignation des droits imprescriptibles de l'État Polonais, lésés par l'agression de l'Union Soviétique.

[1] See Note No. 76.

No. 77

Protest of the Polish Government against the annexation of the district of Wilno by the USSR, sent to Allied and Neutral Governments

London, July 25, 1940   GSHI, MSZ Coll.49/Sow.I, No. 17

D'ordre de mon Gouvernement j'ai l'honneur de porter à la connaissance de Votre Excellence ce qui suit:

Le Gouvernement de l'URSS vient de procéder à l'annexion des territoires de trois républiques baltes. Cette annexion comprend également le territoire de Wilno qui avait été déja illégalement occupé par les troupes soviétiques en septembre 1939 et fut rétrocédé au mois d'octobre 1939 au Gouvernement Lithuanien et réoccupé actuellement par les troupes soviétiques en même temps que le territoire lithuanien.

Le Gouvernement Polonais proteste solennellement contre cette nouvelle violation par l'URSS du droit international et réserve formellement tous ses droits par rapport aux territoires de la République de Pologne occupés par les troupes soviétiques, soit en septembre 1939, soit tout récemment. L'acte de violence commis par l'URSS ne saurait lui donner aucun droit sur les territoires ainsi occupés et le Gouvernement Polonais se réserve le droit de réclamer au moment opportun du Gouvernement Soviétique la réparation de tous les dommages que l'occupation soviétique a provoqués ou provoquera au détriment de la Pologne ou des ressortissants.

No. 78

Speech by Commissar Molotov at the seventh session of the Supreme Council of the USSR dealing with the incorporation of Baltic States and Soviet foreign relations[1]

Moscow, August 1, 1940   Degras, III/464-466

[. . .]. I now come to our relations with Lithuania, Latvia, and Estonia. Since the mutual assistance pacts concluded with Lithuania, Latvia, and Estonia had not produced the expected results, our relations with the Baltic countries have lately taken a new turn. [. . .].

Proof that the Governments of these countries were grossly violating the mutual assistance pacts concluded with the USSR kept piling up. It became utterly impossible to tolerate such a state of affairs any longer, particularly in the present international situation. This was the reason why the Soviet Government presented the demands, of which you are aware, concerning changes in the Governments of Lithuania, Latvia, and Estonia, and the dispatch of additional Red Army units to these countries. You know the results of these steps taken by our Government.

The most important measure carried out by the Governments friendly to the Soviet Union that were set up in Estonia, Latvia, and Lithuania, was the holding of free parliamentary elections. Democratic elections were held in July, and the results proved that the ruling bourgeois cliques of Lithuania, Latvia, and Estonia did not express the will of their peoples but represented only a small group of exploiters.

The Diets of Lithuania and Latvia and the State Duma of Estonia were elected by secret ballot on the basis of universal direct and equal suffrage, and have already expressed their unanimous opinion on fundamental political questions. We note with satisfaction that the peoples of Estonia, Latvia, and Lithuania voted solidly for their representatives, who unanimously pronounced in favour of introducing the Soviet system and of the incorporation of Lithuania, Latvia, and Estonia in the Union of Soviet Socialist Republics.

Thus relations between Lithuania, Latvia, and Estonia and the Soviet

[1] See Note No. 78.

Union must be placed on a new basis. The Supreme Soviet will examine the question of Lithuania, Latvia, and Estonia joining the Soviet Union as Union of Soviet Socialist Republics of the USSR. [. . .].

As the figures of the population show, the USSR will now be able to speak in the powerful voice of a population of 193 million, which does not include the natural increase in the population of the USSR in 1939 and 1940. The fact that the frontier of the Soviet Union will now be shifted to the Baltic coast is of first-rate importance for our country. At the same time we shall now have ice-free ports in the Baltic of which we stand so much in need.

The successes of Soviet foreign policy are all the more significant because we achieved them all by peaceful means; the peaceful settlement of questions both with the Baltic countries and Bessarabia was achieved with the active co-operation and support of the broad masses of the peoples of these countries. [. . .].

No. 79

Statement made by Mr. Churchill in the House of Commons on the non-recognition of any territorial changes effected during the war

London, September 5, 1940   H.C.Deb., 365/40

The Prime Minister [Mr. Churchill]: [. . .]. We have not at any time adopted, since the war broke out, the line that nothing could be changed in the territorial structure of various countries. On the other hand, we do not propose to recognize any territorial changes which take place during the war, unless they take place with the free consent and goodwill of the parties concerned.

No. 80

Letter from Lord Halifax to Minister Zaleski concerning Anglo-Soviet relations[1]

London, November 27, 1940   GSHI, PRM, 20

When I saw you on the 18th November I promised to let you have some account of our policy towards the Soviet Union, with particular reference to the proposals for an understanding, which, as I told you, we recently made to the Soviet Government.

These proposals included an offer on the part of His Majesty's Government to recognize, on a temporary basis pending a general settlement of all such outstanding questions at the end of the war, Soviet de facto control of the areas which have been occupied by the Red Army since the beginning of the war. The question of sovereignty would of course remain unaffected by such recognition.

In this connection, I would draw your attention to the Prime Minister's declaration of the 5th September last that: 'We don't propose to recognize any territorial changes which take place during the war unless they take

[1] See Note No. 80.

place with the free consent and goodwill of the parties concerned', and to my own statement to this effect of the same date. Our proposal to the Soviet Government in no way invalidates or weakens this principle to which we are fully resolved to adhere.

In general our proposals to the Soviet Government were only tentative, and you may rest assured that it was our intention to approach the Polish Government before any agreement affecting Polish interests was reached. In the course of the conversations which we have been conducting with the Soviet Government with the object of effecting some improvement in Anglo-Soviet relations, it had, however, become quite clear that, so long as we refused to admit that the Soviet authorities were in fact in control of the areas occupied by the Red Army since the beginning of the war at the expense of other countries, it would, for purely practical reasons, be difficult to find any basis for discussion. In actual fact the existence of British interests in certain of the areas in question had already made it necessary for us to treat with the Soviet Government and local authorities on the assumption that they were in control of these areas, and our proposals therefore only implies the acknowledgement on our part of a state of affairs which already existed in fact.

As I have already pointed out, however, the proposals made by us to the Soviet Government only contemplated a temporary arrangement, based on an existing state of affairs, which we cannot deny or ignore if we are to protect British interests in the territories concerned. But, in our view, the definite settlement of the future of the territories concerned, which have of course in no way been prejudiced by our proposals, can only be effected at the end of the war. As it would clearly be impossible to exclude the Soviet Government from such a settlement, our offer to consult them about it may be regarded as a necessary consequence of our refusal to recognize enforced territorial changes which take place during the war.

No. 81

Reply of Minister Zaleski to the letter from Lord Halifax of November 27 on Anglo-Soviet relations

London, December 14, 1940   GSHI, A.12. 49/WB.Sow./1

In reply to your letter of November 27th 1940 I wish to thank you for having kindly informed me of the attitude taken up by the British Government in their negotiations with the Government of Soviet Russia. In this respect I note with satisfaction the British Government's decision to consult with the Polish Government before reaching any agreement with the Government of Soviet Russia.

It is not quite clear to me from your letter, what was implied by the offer made by His Majesty's Government to recognize 'on a temporary basis pending a general settlement of all such outstanding questions at the end of the war Soviet de facto control of the areas which have been occupied by the

Red Army since the beginning of the war'.—It appears to me that The Hague Convention of 1907 provides a sufficiently clear definition of the rights and duties of an occupying Power on territories temporarily under its control. If the offer made to USSR by the British Government only reaffirms the stipulations of the above Convention, I cannot help thinking that such a reaffirmation might be regarded as superfluous. If, on the other hand, it implies the grant of additional prerogatives to the occupying Power, it would, I feel sure, constitute a dangerous precedent. This precedent may, for instance, be exploited by Germany in relation to Neutral States as regards an analogous 'de facto' recognition of her temporary territorial acquisitions.

I note with pleasure your reference to your own and the Prime Minister's speech of the 5th September last in which you declared: 'that His Majesty's Government do not propose to recognize any territorial changes which take place during the war, unless they take place with the free consent and good-will of the parties concerned'.—I need hardly assure you that I appreciate very highly the spirit expressed in this declaration, nevertheless, I think that the expression of 'free consent and goodwill of the parties concerned' can only take place through official and constitutional channels of the States concerned.

While I admit the necessity of Soviet participation in the discussion of the liquidation of the Russian temporary occupation of the territories concerned, after the war, I think that it would be premature to take any decision in this matter at the present moment. I feel sure that British consultation with Russia at that stage may be of great value to Poland, as I have no doubt that we can count on Great Britain to support Poland's territorial and sovereign rights.

I avail myself of this opportunity to define the views of my Government with regard to the occupation of her territories by Soviet Russia:

1/ In March 1939, the Polish Government rejected the German proposals both for national reasons and because they were aware that their acceptance would force Poland into a permanent system of collaboration with Germany directed against the interests of other European States and particularly against Soviet Russia. In taking this vital decision the Polish Government preferred to accept war with the German Reich, rather than sacrifice territorial integrity and essential rights of Poland.

2/ It has become more evident in the light of recent events on other European fronts, how effective was the armed resistance of Poland against overwhelming German forces in September 1939, especially in view of the fact that Poland's Allies were not prepared to give her the support she was entitled to expect.

3/ At a crucial moment of the war in Poland, in violation of the Soviet-Polish pacts of non-aggression of July 25th 1932 and May 5th 1934, Soviet Russia attacked the Polish Army in the rear. Thereby Russia, a neutral Power, assumed with regard to Poland the same part as was later assumed in June 1940 by Italy with regard to France and Great Britain, with the only difference that Italy frankly declared herself a belligerent Power.

4/ It must be observed that the Polish-Russian frontier was fixed by virtue of the Treaty concluded in Riga on March 18th 1921, freely negotiated by the plenipotentiaries of Poland and Soviet Russia and recognized officially by Great Britain at the Conference of Ambassadors of March 5th 1923.

It should be remembered that on September 9th 1918 the Soviet Government cancelled all Treaties concerning the partitions of Poland of 1772, 1793 and 1795 as well as all subsequent Treaties relating to Poland up to 1833. Article 3 of this Resolution states:

'All agreements and acts concluded by the Government of the late Russian Empire with the Governments of Prussia and of the Austro-Hungarian Empire relating to the partitions of Poland are for ever annulled by the present Resolution, considering that they are contrary to the principle of free determination of peoples as well as to the juridical revolutionary conception of the Russian Nation which has recognized to the Polish Nation the "imprescriptable" right to decide of its own fate and its unification.'

This Resolution signed by Lenin, Karakhan and Bontch-Bruyevitch was communicated to the Government of the German Reich on October 3rd 1918.

In virtue of this Resolution Poland had the right to the restitution of all the territories which belonged to her before 1772, but by the Treaty of Riga, Poland renounced her right to a substantial part of these territories. This is clearly evident from Article III of the Treaty which stipulates:

'Russia and the Ukraine renounce all rights and claims as regards the territories situated westward of the frontier, as defined under Article II of the present Treaty. Poland on her side renounces, in favour of the Ukraine and White Russia, all rights and claims as regards the territories situated eastward of the aforesaid frontier.

'Should the area situated westward of the frontier as fixed by Article II of the present Treaty include territories being under dispute between Poland and Lithuania, the question of the sovereignty of either of the two States over these territories concerns exclusively Poland and Lithuania.' [. . .].

5/ After occupying Eastern Poland militarily in 1939, the Soviet Government concluded with the German Reich in Moscow, on September 28th 1939, a Treaty changing the occupation into definite annexation of Polish territories by the two Parties. Later, on October 10th 1939, contrary to international law, part of this territory was ceded by Soviet Russia to Lithuania, and once again reannexed by the USSR in July 1940 together with the whole of Lithuania.

On each of these occasions the Polish Government addressed official and solemn protests to all allied and neutral Governments against these violations.

6/ In addition to this, any recognition of the Soviet annexation of Lithuanian territory would not only involve the recognition of the annexation of the Wilno area, which is an integrant part of the Polish Republic, but would constitute in itself a matter of great importance for Poland. This results clearly from Article 2 par. b/ of the Secret Protocol attached to the Agreement of Mutual Assistance signed between the United Kingdom and Poland on August 25th 1939 which states that similarly as Belgium and

Holland represent a vital interest of Great Britain, so Lithuania lies within the vital interests of Poland.

I am sure you will agree with me that, under these circumstances, the Polish Nation could never understand any action on the part of His Majesty's Government which could be interpreted as an acceptance or an approval of the seizure of Polish national territory at the end of a victorious war in the course of which Poland unfalteringly fulfilled her obligations as an active and loyal Ally of Great Britain.

In conclusion I would like to call your attention to Article 1 par. b/ and Article 3 of the aforesaid Secret Protocol.

In accordance with these stipulations, shortly after taking office in the Polish Government, I had the pleasure of a conversation with you in October 1939 at the Foreign Office, in the course of which we agreed upon the line to be followed by both our Governments with respect to Soviet Russia.

Later, this was once more confirmed in our correspondence of the same month.

I need hardly add that should you think it desirable, I am always ready to continue our exchange of views on this subject in the same spirit of frank and friendly collaboration in which it was started.

No. 82

Secret German-Soviet Protocol containing German renunciation of claim to the district of Suwałki

January 10, 1941   Nazi-Sov.R., 267–8

The German Ambassador, Count von der Schulenburg, Plenipotentiary of the Government of the German Reich, on the one hand, and the Chairman of the Council of People's Commissars of the USSR, V. M. Molotov, Plenipotentiary of the Government of the USSR, on the other hand, have agreed upon the following:

1. The Government of the German Reich renounces its claim to the strip of Lithuanian territory which is mentioned in the Secret Supplementary Protocol of September 28, 1939,[1] and which has been marked on the map attached to this Protocol;

2. The Government of the Union of Soviet Socialist Republics is prepared to compensate the Government of the German Reich for the territory mentioned in Point 1 of this Protocol by paying 7,500,000 gold dollars or 31,500,000 Reichsmarks to Germany.

The amount of 31,5 million Reichsmarks will be paid by the Government of the USSR in the following manner: one-eighth, that is, 3,937,500 Reichsmarks, in non-ferrous metal deliveries within three months after the signing of this Protocol, the remaining seven-eighths, or 27,562,500 Reichsmarks, in gold by deduction from the German gold payments which Germany is to make by February 11, 1941, in accordance with the correspondence exchanged between the Chairman of the German Economic Delegation, Dr. Schnurre,

[1] See doc. No. 54.

and the People's Commissar for Foreign Trade of the USSR, Herr A. I. Mikoyan, in connection with the 'Agreement of January 10, 1941, concerning reciprocal deliveries in the second treaty period on the basis of the Economic Agreement between the German Reich and the Union of Soviet Socialist Republics of February 11, 1940.'

3. This Protocol has been executed in two originals in the German language and two originals in the Russian language and shall become effective immediately upon signature.

Moscow, January 10, 1941

For the Government   By authority of the
of the German Reich: Government of the USSR:
Schulenburg   V. Molotov

No. 83

Protest of the Polish Government against the imposition of Soviet citizenship upon Polish citizens, sent to Allied and Neutral Governments[1]

London, February 21, 1941   Pol.-Sov.R., No. 29

By order of my Government I have the honour to submit the following for Your Excellency's information:

The Polish Government has recently been informed that the Soviet authorities acting now on the Polish territories occupied by the USSR are proceeding to register the population and are forcing Polish citizens, under threat of reprisals, to renounce formally their Polish nationality, to cease all activity aimed at the restoration of the independence of Poland, and to declare that they will henceforward consider themselves loyal citizens of the USSR.

The Polish Government protests against this new and flagrant breach of the elementary principles of international law and justice.

[1] See Note No. 83.

No. 84

Letter and aide-mémoire from General Sikorski to Mr. Churchill concerning future German aggression against USSR

London, May 23, 1941   GSHI, PRM, 39-a

Referring to our conversation on May 20th on the subject of a possible German attack on Soviet Russia, I have the honour to forward you a memorandum on this question, prepared on the basis of the data of the Polish General Staff and the Polish Ministry of Foreign Affairs.

Memorandum.

A. Military Considerations

[. . .]. 3) Is German aggression against Russia feasible?

(a) The German preparations for a war against Russia appear to be so advanced, that only the time necessary for the arrival of the air force and armoured units separates them from a complete war readiness, viz.:

—There are at present about 60 Great Units in Poland, including two armoured and two motorized units; in East Prussia about a dozen Great Units; in Rumania, Hungary and Slovakia most of the Great Units, which were used in the Balkans, can easily be massed. They amounted to about 50 Great Units, ten of which armoured and ten motorized.

—The construction of new air-fields, and substantial increase of ground staffs, liaison and A.A. artillery on the airfields.

—An intensified construction of defence lines along the rivers Bug and Narew.

—An important development of roads and railways carried out solely for strategical reasons. It is of a strong offensive character.

—Organization of hospitals and stores of supplies, moving up of munitions nearer to the frontier zone and transports of river crossing material dispatched in the direction of the river Bug.

—An increase in the intelligence work in Russia.

—The propagating among German soldiers of rumours to the effect that aggression against Soviet Russia is imminent. Owing to pre-war propaganda, this is a very popular slogan in the German Army.

(b) What time is required by the Germans for completing all their preparation for a war against Russia?

Assuming that:

1) the views as to the complete German readiness in the East with the exception of the arrival of armoured units and air forces are right,
2) the Germans need between one and two weeks for the concentration of armoured units and air forces in Poland.
3) News from Poland has been lacking since about four weeks; it may be concluded that if the Germans continued their war preparations for the last month they may now be completely ready for this war.

The grouping of German forces in the East is not so clear as that of the Russian forces. This is typical for all German concentrations as the German High Command prefers to postpone until the very last hour the actual concentration required for the opening of offensive operations. [. . .].

No. 85

Note made by General Sikorski on his conversation with Sir Stafford Cripps on the imminent outbreak of the war between Germany and the USSR. Present also Dr. Retinger[1]

London, June 18, 1941 GSHI, PRM, 39–b
Transl. from Polish

General Sikorski's conversation with Sir Stafford Cripps was a very frank exchange of information and views. Sir Stafford seemed to be well informed

[1] See Note No. 85.

on General Sikorski's pre-war activity which, as he stated to Dr. Retinger before the conversation, had been watched by him from afar with the greatest admiration.

The account given by Sir Stafford was based on information gathered by himself or by his colleagues from the British Embassy in Moscow, on information provided by the Foreign Office from all over the world, on the reports of the British Intelligence Service, and on the observations made by himself in the course of conversations with prominent Russian personalities, such as Stalin, Molotov, Vyshinsky, Zhdanov, etc., as well as with high-ranking Russian officers, and, in the last instance, with neutral diplomatists in Moscow and Stockholm, on his return voyage. He also saw the Polish envoy in Stockholm.

General Sikorski, after having thanked Sir Stafford for calling on him, said that he was in possession of confidential reports from Poland from which it appeared that German troops were concentrating in the strength of more than a hundred divisions and about 2,000 supporting aircraft, in the proximity of the Russian frontier. The General commanding the German forces in the East, von Brauchitsch, had established his headquarters in a well-known Polish locality. There should be mentioned also information concerning the transfer of three or may be even five divisions to Finland, without supporting air-force, as well as the concentration of considerable forces in Rumania from where the main attack might be launched. All this information showed that the Germans were well prepared to start an offensive against Russia very shortly. Hitler was convinced that he would be able to finish that war very quickly, and then attack Britain also before winter.

In reply Sir Stafford said that he believed that the Russo-German war would start within a few days. 'Today there are even rumours'—he said—'that General Antonescu has already declared war and invaded Russia.'

Sir Stafford heard from an utterly reliable source in Stockholm a few days ago that Goering had telephoned to his friend, reminding him of his forecast of April, that the contest with Russia would begin in mid-June.

About the end of April, according to Cripps, the anti-war party among Hitler's associates was prevailing over the others, and the German Ambassador in Moscow, von Schulenburg, who returned from Berlin on the 1st of May, said to a friend of Cripps that, at last, he had succeeded in convincing Hitler of the necessity of coming to terms with Stalin. The best evidence of that improvement in Russo-German relations was the return of the wives and children of German diplomatic and consular officials to Moscow after that date. This period of lull lasted till mid-May.

It was only a month ago—according to Cripps—that Hitler finally yielded to Goering's war party, and decided to strike against Russia.

'Consequently, it happened'—observed General Sikorski—'just before Hess' flight to England which, as a matter of fact, was caused by the conviction that the anti-Russian party around Hitler had failed in its endeavours.'

'Hitler wants war'—asserted Cripps—'and not an understanding with Stalin made under a menace of war.' This is not a sort of colossal blackmail but the wish to crush Russia's military power, as the latter, by adopting an ambiguous attitude towards the Reich, constituted a constant menace to it. He is no longer interested in economic considerations or concessions, as they cannot replace requests of military nature. Hitler wants to dispose of the Russian military danger once and for all, and thus to remove the possibility of a Russian attack at the time of his final struggle against England.

He thinks also that an anti-Soviet crusade might turn the scale in American public opinion in Germany's favour.

General Sikorski observed that during his last voyage to the USA he had occasion to state that the great chiefs of American industry, who were rabid Republicans, opposed to Roosevelt's liberal policy, might be inclined to give such support.

Emphasizing the fact that Russia had for such a long time co-operated with Germany in military, propaganda and economic fields in Poland, the Baltic States and Rumania, General Sikorski asked the Ambassador for his explanation of this fact.

Cripps' answer was that it was due to the conviction that, for the time being, Russia was unable to defend herself against Germany, and that she would not be in a position to offer resistance before 1942. The occupation of the Baltic States and of Bessarabia was prompted by strategic reasons, that is to say that the shortening of the line of defence mattered above all. In fact, contrary to various rumours, Russia did not believe in the possibility of a Communist upheaval in Germany, and was not preparing a Communist crusade in the West. She was waiting for the time when Germany would be weakened in her struggle against the Western countries, and would start her action at that moment only.

For the time being, continued Sir Stafford, as long as Hitler has not become a master of the seas, he cannot win. Such was also Stalin's opinion, expressed not long ago.

'So far'—said General Sikorski—'Germany has won on the land, lost on the seas, and there is a draw in the air.'

'How long can the Russian resistance last?' asked General Sikorski, adding that his information was rather pessimistic on that point. 'The Russian soldiers are very numerous,' ran Sir Stafford's answer, 'and their morale is good, because for the last 9 months Stalin has been building up a very clever patriotic propaganda. There is plenty of military equipment but the means of communication are awful and, consequently, should the Russians consider it proper to retreat to a more distant line of defence, for strategic reasons, a catastrophe could easily occur, causing the total collapse of the Russian army and régime. The Russians have never held any army manœuvres, and they have not behind them—as Germany has—six successful campaigns. They are bound, therefore, to be weaker than the Germans from the operational point of view.'

'By executing Tukhachevsky and other army commanders,' said General Sikorski, 'Stalin killed the soul of the Red Army. Timoshenko is not a commander on Tukhachevsky's scale. Such misdeeds cannot be made good within one year's time. The Red Army will probably fight, but it will not be able to stand the impact.'

'It will not'—replied Sir Stafford—'and it will surely break down. For some time Timoshenko has been working hard in order to rebuild the Russian military organization, which he had to start from the bottom, from the lowest military units. Timoshenko is a good and diligent soldier.'

'But unripe for military operations'—observed General Sikorski, and Cripps agreed.

In connection with the recent trends in Russo-German relations, Sir Stafford stated that 'it would be best for ourselves and for you if the Germans should advance into Russia and occupy all Polish territories, and then be stopped by the Russians beyond that line. That would remove from the agenda the Polish question which has so far weighed heavily on Anglo-Soviet relations.'

'What was the position adopted by the Russian leaders towards Poland in the course of conversations with British representatives?' asked General Sikorski.

'We spoke with them at length about the Baltic States and Bessarabia, but I have to emphasize that the Russians never mentioned Poland in those conversations,' answered Sir Stafford.

'What may be the reason for this?' asked General Sikorski. 'Did they expect a sharp rebuke on the part of the British Government or was it due to the fact that in their strategic plans Poland plays quite a different part from that of the Baltic States and Bessarabia? The latter protect the Russian flanks and Leningrad, shortening their line of defence. Bessarabia is, moreover, a bulwark of the Ukraine. It is further very advantageous for the Soviet Union to have a common frontier with Hungary. The Polish space is but a vacuum from the strategic point of view, and does not constitute a serious military obstacle.'

'It was, of course, for that reason in the first instance,' stated Cripps, 'but one has to take also into account the Russian mentality, which is very sensitive as regards legalistic and technical issues. The Baltic republics have actually joined the Soviet Union, and Bessarabia has always been a bone of contention between Rumania and Russia, while Poland's position is totally different both from the political and military point of view.'

'What will Great Britain do in the event of the outbreak of the Russo-German war?' asked General Sikorski.

'She will, of course, assist Russia. However, this assistance must be reduced to sending to Russia of a military mission which I shall accompany because, of course, I shall return immediately to my post in Russia after the outbreak of the war,' said Sir Stafford. He added that Poland's assistance could be more effective because of the great number of Polish officers and soldiers in Russia, and the Polish gift for organization. At that moment Cripps began to complain of the disorder reigning in Russia, and the total lack of whatever organization in the Soviet Union.

General Sikorski informed Sir Stafford that there were about 300,000

Polish soldiers in Soviet prisoner-of-war camps. Among them were many outstanding officers. The Bolsheviks have tried several times to form purely Polish regiments. At present General Sikorski saw no reason why Poland should not assist Russia in the event of the outbreak of war against Germany, after an adequate change in their relations. General Sikorski added that a principle was adopted at the last meeting of the Council of Ministers, according to which the first and main enemy of Poland was Germany, and that, should full Polish sovereignty be recognized within her pre-war frontiers, co-operation between Poland and the Soviet Union would be possible. As long, however, as Russia did not change her basic attitude to Poland and the Poles, so long we also would not change our line of policy, which is the policy of war against Russia, imposed on us by the latter.

Sir Stafford stated that Polish assistance would be priceless, and asked the General, in the event of his return to Russia, to draw up a list of the best Polish officers, as well as prominent and reliable civilians on whom the Polish action might be based in the event of a change of the political conditions in Russia. He would like to have a dozen names (even more, if possible) with a description of these people. He was also of the opinion that, in such an event, General Sikorski should designate at once his man of trust and, if any need arose, also an unofficial representative of the Polish Government who in due time would become the official Polish Envoy in Moscow.

General Sikorski accepted this proposal favourably.

The conversation which ensued dealt with the problem of assistance to the Poles in Russia. The British Ambassador stated that he was unable to do anything for the Poles, and that the Bolsheviks had not only refused all conversations with British representatives on that matter, but had also seen to it that any interventions of that kind should have very unpleasant consequences for the Poles concerned, who became a target for Russian persecution. He quoted the case of six Poles, holders of British passports, former officials of the British Legation in Tallin, who had their domicile in the territory occupied by Germany. In spite of that and in spite of having obtained (illegally, by the way) Soviet exit visas, they were arrested by the GPU at the airport a few moments before taking off.

In these circumstances British assistance can be given only in an unofficial and confidential way, and has to be limited, in principle, to granting visas to British territories.

General Sikorski asked whether it would not be advisable to have a representative of Poland at the British Embassy in Moscow, who, on the one hand, could help in the question of evacuation, and on the other hand, would be a general observer on behalf of Poland.

'Unfortunately,' answered Cripps, 'it is too late for this today. First of all, we would not have received a Russian entrance permit, and even if it had been possible to obtain it, this man would be closely watched and spied upon to such an extent that he would be unable to do anything.'

At this opportunity Sir Stafford told General Sikorski that the evacuation of 800 Czechs was already completed. It had been carried out in great secrecy by a Czech representative, whose name was unknown even to the British Embassy. Sir Stafford suggested that his services should now be used by the Poles.

General Sikorski then recalled the problem of the evacuation of Poles from the Wilno area.

Ambassador Cripps answered that all that the British could do was to grant visas and journey allowances.

General Sikorski offered Sir Stafford adequate sums to be put at his disposal but the Ambassador refused, saying that the British had instructions from the Foreign Office prescribing the use of the Embassy funds for covering all expenses.

Sir Stafford asked that the Polish Government should designate a man of trust who might give relevant information about the Poles applying for visas. Considering the lack of any documents, the possibility exists that some spies might apply for visas, pretending they were Poles.

General Sikorski promised to deal with this matter.

Moreover, the British Ambassador asked that all applications addressed to the British Embassy in Moscow should pass through the Foreign Office for checking, and not be sent, as happens now, directly by various Polish diplomatic posts. Sir Stafford had already raised that matter with the Polish Envoy in Stockholm.

General Sikorski agreed in principle to this demand, with a reservation relating to the Polish Embassy in Tokio, which should be exempted from this rule, and have the right to draw attention to the necessity of granting visas to Poles who have escaped from Siberia, etc.

At the end of the conversation Sir Stafford expressed a wish to maintain the closest contact with General Sikorski, and promised to inform him in time before his return to Russia. He also asked for the memorandum relating to the Russo-German war which General Sikorski had submitted to Prime Minister Churchill.

No. 86

Broadcast by General Sikorski to the Polish Nation on: 'Poland and the German-Soviet war'

London, June 23, 1941   GSHI, PRM, 63
                                                    Official transl. from Polish

What we have been anticipating has occurred. Though sooner than we had expected. The Nazi-Bolshevik combination which was at the source of the terrible disaster that brought about the fate of Poland has been shattered. Since dawn of June 22 the former accomplices are at strife.

Such a sequel is very favourable to Poland. It changes and reverses the former situation. Behold Germany, the foremost foe of the Polish Nation, has torn asunder an alliance which has so long been the source of our greatest misfortunes. By striking at Russia they are undertaking at great risk a task of which the issue is uncertain and to say the least weakening in its accomplishment. The Polish-Russian question which might have shadowed the outlook of many a friend of ours in the West and effected noxious frictions and clashes, I believe may disappear from international politics.

Ever since the Treaty of Brest-Litovsk of 1918 Russia has been continually collaborating with Germany against Poland while that country did not yield to repeated German offers during a period of 10 years proposing a common crusade against Bolshevik Russia. It was not until today that the policy started in Rapallo on April 16th 1922 is falling with clatter to ruins. The Ribbentrop–Molotov Treaty of August 23rd 1939 in which the Soviet Union in concert with the Germans asserted that Poland ceased for ever to exist was its crown point and its consequence. The Soviet Republic aided Hitler in matters concerning military, political and economic domains as well as propaganda. These doings have led to slavery in conquered countries and complete destruction of their culture and their economies.

At this moment we are entitled to assume that in these circumstances Russia will cancel the Pact of 1939. That should logically bring us back to the position governed by the Treaty concluded in Riga on March 18th 1921 between Russia and Poland recognized on March 15th 1923 by the Conference of Ambassadors and on April the 5th by the United States of North America. This Treaty was considered to be founded upon a sound and reciprocal agreement. The political and moral significance of such an act would be tremendous.

Will it not be but natural, even on the part of Soviet Russia, to return to the traditions of September 1918 when the Supreme Soviet Council solemnly declared null all previous dictates concerning the partitions of Poland rather than actively to partake in Her fourth partition?

For the love of their country, their freedom and honour, thousands of Polish men and women, including 300,000 war prisoners, are still suffering in Russian prisons. Should it not be deemed right and honest to restore these people to their liberty?

We also have been taken by surprise with regard to Adolf Hitler's fresh attack against his ally. Not so much by its murderous form against which the Soviets are now crying protest for that is customary to their nature, as by their military character which testifies to a far greater weakness of the German Reich, than we so far suspected.

This attempt to destroy the military power of the Soviet Union in order to avoid a threat to the rear of the German Armies when they assault the British Isles can only mean that the Germans fear that military power. An attempt to provoke internal subversions in Russia points towards apprehension of a revolution at home and indicates a wish to quell the conjectured foreign centre of revolt before it ripens inside the 3rd Reich. The quest at all cost for the raw materials of Russia proves the need of such materials.

In our normal and placid reckonings we were expecting the Germans to terminate the Battle of the Mediterranean upon which they had set out with so great an outlay of resources and men among whom was the flower of German youth. The price they paid for Crete was enormous. It caused no enthusiasm and depression among the German nation. We consequently awaited further development of this onslaught both in the Middle-East and on Gibraltar, much less an interruption of these operations in order to fling the bulk of their forces upon Russia. After that we awaited renewed attempts at invasion of Britain which according to the latest promises of Hitler is to end the war this year. However, in accordance with the drugged Goering's estimation of the situation came the offensive against Russia which is meant to strike the imagination of the German people, raise and strengthen the dented prestige of Hitler's Satraps.

The power of the Luftwaffe is often overestimated in the West. By turning against as strong an adversary as Russia, he exposes his rear and imperils his own country against heavy bombing which has already been undertaken with so great intensity by the Allied Air Force. Overcome by madness and the lust of conquest incomparable with those of Napoleon, he does not consider the losses of the German nation which is to serve as dungheap to his greatness. He offers time for his adversaries to prepare for the ultimate contest. That time will be taken advantage in full and with purpose.

We are not surprised by the guile and cynicism which Hitler once more exposed before the whole world. For Hitler has ever applied to international relations principles and formulas which change likea chameleon's hide, according to the Germanic requirements of the moment.

Since, however, the bloody German Satrap is on this occasion dressing in the luminous attire of a redeemer of the old continent from Bolshevism I therefore declare:

The man who introduced the absolute enslaving of the individual into the 3rd Reich by subordinating him to the interests of the party; he who employs the Gestapo, whose domination is stamped with sadism and atrocity; he who ruthlessly defies God and religion and brings up youth in the spirit of pagan materialism; he who by the most bloody methods imposes, enchains whole nations into slavery; he who destroys completely freedom of thought, of word and of conscience; he who considers that the German race is the only one fit to lord the whole world and would have all humanity locked in a totalitarian prison—that man has not the slightest moral authority to reach for the part of redeemer of a world founded upon Christian culture and civilization.

I esteem that the memory of the ruthless strife carried on against the Church of Rome and for its complete destruction in the 3rd Reich and the attack on Poland will soften down the attitude of the Vatican which Hitler would falsely lure by dreams of progress of the Catholic Church in the East, which that devil incarnate would pretend to encourage. The German propaganda preposterous in its falsehood and insolence is again trying to deceive us. But after two years of brutal war, imposed upon us by Hitler, no one will be deceived.

When in the summer of 1939 Hitler crossed out his anti-Soviet programme and together with Stalin signed a pact of non-aggression it was in conformance with his utilitarian and cynical equity. When at present he is giving the lie to his own propaganda of two past years, which praised and glorified his collaboration with Stalin—he stands before us at the height of his imposture and trumpery, while preaching his Germanic truth.

The victory of Germany over France in 1940 failed to bring the expected termination of the war. The attempted invasion of the British Isles, undertaken nine months ago, also failed completely. Hence, on account of the impossibility to attain a rapid ending of the war with Great Britain, the Germans proceed to change the policy they followed up till now with regard to Russia. They try to subdue that State and make it a passive instrument in the further stages of the struggle against the Democracies. They hope to realize their military aims by crushing and destroying the military power of Russia, by seizing their raw materials, so strongly coveted by Germany— and at the same time making most profit out of propaganda by fighting Communism.

They dream, moreover, of uniting under their leadership the Eastern European States, down from Rumania up to northern Finland including the Ukraine and the Caucasian peoples.

Without committing myself to military prophecies or going to an estimate of these plans I am of opinion that Russia—that enormous and ill-organized country—happens to be a region whence the occupants will draw no immediate gains. These will demand time and great effort and still more German energy. Russia will for long absorb German forces, even in case of military success which may not be so auspicious, as at first it may have seemed to Hitler's advisers. His armies are undergoing further dispersion to an extent which is becoming dangerous even to such a power. These armies may be wanting in the trial contest with Great Britain which according to Hitler's haughty calculations will take place only a few weeks hence. The German tendencies towards Russia are unmistakenly imperialistic. The nations freed by the Germans would become their slaves. The final aim of Hitler is to continue his march against democracy, against Great Britain and the U.S.A. After this war the world will either be totally Nazi or completely free. There can be no other outcome. No one can any longer be misled by the meaning of Hitler's promises and pledges. Agreements signed with Hitler have no longer even the significance of a 'scrap of paper'. To us the Germans will remain the eternal and the irreconcilable foe, with whom there can be neither pacts nor covenants. The Germans must be overthrown, they must be disabled and destroyed in order to provide a place for Poland among the family of free nations.

Countrymen, I am speaking to you on the first anniversary of the tragic fall of France and close to the date when I had that noteworthy conversation with the British Prime Minister Winston Churchill. That conference was to result in the fact that today 'Fighting Poland' is starting by the side of Great Britain over here and in Africa. From that time onward we are most effectively working together both in the military and political spheres in the soundest spirit of friendship and loyalty. During this period the name of the Polish soldier has spread throughout the world the fame of our magnificent air force and our gallant navy. They have gloriously fulfilled their soldier's duty. The first Polish armoured division has been formed in our Army Corps in Scotland—to avenge—when the time has come—the injuries afflicted upon our nation at a moment when it lacked armaments which could equal those of the enemy. The Carpathian Brigade is standing by ready to fight on the African Sector.

We have achieved considerable results. My visit to Canada and the United States of North America was particularly successful. Among the consequences of this visit President Roosevelt has three days ago signed a bill placing Poland on the official list of nations actively engaged in war and possessing the right to a share in the 'Lend and Lease Bill'. The political importance of this decision is vast. For it lays weighty stress upon the fact that Poland, despite the bloody ruffians of Hitler, lives on and fights for her freedom, independence and justice.

No. 87

Declaration made by Mr. Eden in the House of Commons repeating the British pledge relating to the restoration of freedom to Poland

London, June 24, 1941 H.C.Deb., 372/975

The Secretary of State for Foreign Affairs [Mr. Eden]: [. . .]. There is one reference I would ask the House to let me make. At a time like this our thoughts go out with heartfelt sympathy to our Polish Ally. Once again, their soil is a battlefield. Once again their people suffer for no fault of their own. The Polish people have had a hard history. By their courage in a time of unparalleled ordeal, they have earned and they will redeem their freedom. That remains our pledge. [. . .].

No. 88

Letter from General Sikorski to General Macfarlane on conditions of military collaboration between Poland and Russia and on the protection and relief of Polish citizens in the USSR

London, June 24, 1941 GSHI, A.XII. 1/57

I greatly regret that I was unable to meet you before your departure to Moscow. I had hoped to have the opportunity to acquaint you with the situation of the Polish soldiers in Russia, and of my plans and intentions with regard to them in connection with the present state of affairs in Russia.

I must, therefore, confine myself to sending you some material connected with this matter and an instruction for one of the Polish Generals, who is at present a war-prisoner in Russia.

I have had the occasion to discuss the question in detail with His Majesty's Ambassador Sir Stafford Cripps who will be able to give you all required information.

[. . .]. 3. Conditions of military collaboration with Russia.

Collaboration with Russia only possible on condition that Russia:

1. fully recognizes rights founded on the treaty of Riga and repudiates Russo-German treaty of 23rd August 1939,
2. releases all Polish citizens and soldiers from prisons or internment.

The forming of Polish units in Russia depends upon:
— full attribution of sovereignty to those units,
— their employment solely dependable upon the decision of the Polish Government in London.

4. Character and task of military representative of the Polish C.-in-C.
   a. formation of Polish units in Russia in the region East of the line drawn between Astrakhan and Arkhangel,
   b. the care and protection of all Polish citizens in Russia,
   c. conclusion of agreements with Russian Government connected with the improvement of conditions of the Polish citizens in Russia,
   d. liaison military representatives of Allies in Russia,
   e. supplying information to Polish C.-in-C.
5. Liaison.
   a. organization of branch of Polish 2nd Bureau in Russia,
   b. supplying local information,
   c. special code communication with London, either directly or through British means,
   d. Lt.-Colonel Szymański, former Polish Military Attaché in Berlin, to be local D.M.I.

No. 89

Letter from General Sikorski to Mr. Eden on resumption of Polish-Soviet relations with an enclosed suggestion for H.M. Government's declaration

London, July 4, 1941   GSHI, PRM, 39–a

During our last conversation of July 1st we discussed the possibility of a statement on your part regarding Polish-Russian relations. Accordingly I am now enclosing a suggestion for your proposed declaration.

I am not unaware of certain difficulties which you have to consider in this matter. I feel confident, however, that such a declaration on the part of His Majesty's Government would not only be deeply appreciated by the Poles, but would also meet with general approval on the part of all our Allies.

Enclosure

The German attack on Russia has again brought up the question of Eastern Poland. Russia occupied Eastern Poland in accordance with her agreement of August 23rd with Germany and the agreement concerning the German-Russian frontier of 28th September 1939. Neither this nor subsequent Russian annexation of territories of the North and the South of Poland were recognized by H.M. Government nor by any other Government with the exception of Germany and Italy. In attacking Russia, Germany has ipso facto broken the terms of her agreements with Russia.

In view of these new circumstances the Polish Prime Minister, appreciating the importance of a settlement between the two countries attacked in turn by Germany, put out his hand to Russia in a speech of the 23rd June 1941. He proposed a normalization of Polish relations with Russia on condition that the two countries should return to the terms of conventions which bound them before September 1939 and assured to them twenty years of peaceful neighbourship. General Sikorski has also demanded the release by Russia of Polish war prisoners and of the many hundreds of thousands of Polish citizens deported to Eastern Russia.

In his broadcast speech of July 2nd M. Stalin stressed with great vigour the necessity to help all the peoples of Europe who suffer under the yoke of Germany.

Surely Poland is among those nations who suffer most from this oppression.

H.M. Government take this opportunity to emphasize that it is in the interest of war against Germany to reach a settlement between their Polish Ally and Russia who is at present stubbornly defending her own territory.

No. 90

Record of a conversation between General Sikorski and Mr. Eden on re-establishment of Polish-Soviet relations

London, July 4, 1941   GSHI, PRM, 39–b
                                                           Transl. from Polish

Polish Protocol

At Mr. Eden's request General Sikorski arrived at the Foreign Office at 6.15 p.m.

Mr. Eden informed General Sikorski that during the afternoon he had a conversation with Ambassador Maisky who had officially communicated to him the readiness of the Soviet Government to enter into talks on Polish-Soviet problems. Mr. Eden added that Ambassador Maisky was at General Sikorski's disposal.

At the conclusion of his talk with Ambassador Maisky Mr. Eden had made the enclosed note which he read out to General Sikorski. After acquainting himself with its translation General Sikorski said that in the Soviet declaration he sees a clear tendency to revive panslavism, though of a 'red' variety this time. Poland will not be a party to any such proposals which are both unrealistic and harmful. 'Today', added General Sikorski, 'I talked with the Yugoslav Prime Minister and Foreign Minister and with them I discussed the possibilities of creating federal blocs of countries in Central Europe which would provide mutual support for each other. One of such blocs would have Poland as its core and the other would be a Balkan bloc. Blocs of this kind would constitute a serious barrier to German or

Russian imperialism. Whereas a panslav bloc would be but a shield or an extension of Russia.'

General Sikorski's attitude met with Mr. Eden's full understanding. He then called the Permanent Under-Secretary at the Foreign Office, Sir Alexander Cadogan, to whom he repeated General Sikorski's words, adding that he would not make use of them at present in his talks with the Russians, keeping them for later as a very important argument.

Next General Sikorski said that one could not place Polish problems at the same plane with those of Czechoslovakia and Yugoslavia. The figures given by Ambassador Maisky concerning Polish nationals are false and tendentious. According to the calculations of the Moscow *Pravda* there are about 190,000 soldiers in concentration camps, including over 10,000 officers, besides many thousand Poles of military age deported into the depths of Russia. On the other hand in his recent conversation with General Sikorski Ambassador Cripps had said that the Czechs had got all their citizens fit for military service out of Russia, this was mainly about 800 airmen. At present there were no Czechs in the Soviet Union, nor were there any Yugoslavs, according to the Yugoslav Prime Minister. The time of National Committees of the Great War (1914–1918) belongs to the past. Such a proposal would only serve to disclose hidden Soviet designs. Today there exists a lawful Polish Government with which the Soviet Government can talk. It is up to the Polish Government to choose its method of action.

In spite of this General Sikorski does agree in principle to enter into talks with the Soviet Government, with the reservation that he must lay his decision before the Cabinet beforehand. In order to facilitate these talks he considers the following to be fundamental:

1. The Soviet Union acknowledges as null the German-Soviet agreements of August and September 1939.

2. The Soviet Government restores automatically the Polish Embassy in Moscow, recognizing the representative appointed by the Government who might set up citizens' committees, subordinated to the Polish Government, in order to take care of Polish nationals in the Soviet Union.

3. Prisoners of war, political prisoners and deportees into Russia will be freed. From military persons and from persons to be drafted a sovereign Polish army may be created to fight the Germans. This army would come under the Polish C.-in-C. in London.

Mr. Eden accepted the entire statement of the Polish Prime Minister which he is going to communicate immediately to the Soviet Government. Mr. Eden accepted as wholly correct General Sikorski's appraisal of the situation and is of the opinion that the attitude of Russia, which on one hand approaches the Polish Government and on the other proposes the setting up of a Polish National Committee, is 'not correct'. He congratulated General Sikorski on the first success achieved in this supremely difficult question.

To the Polish Prime Minister's question whether there was any news from Ambassador Cripps Mr. Eden read out a despatch from the latter which he had received during the day. Ambassador Cripps reported that he had been summoned by Molotov who had informed him of the instructions issued to Maisky. Ambassador Cripps answered that in his opinion General Sikorski, to whom he had talked immediately before his departure from London and of whose intention he is aware, would adopt a positive attitude to this development. He pointed out that he gave his own private opinion without taking any responsibility for it. The formulation of an answer to these proposals depends on the Polish Prime Minister. He demanded of Molotov immediate release of those in prisons and the conveyance to Moscow of 6 persons from the list handed him by General Sikorski. They are envisaged as representatives of the Polish Government until the nomination of a Polish Representative.

English Protocol

The Soviet Ambassador asked to see me this afternoon when he said that he had brought me a message from his Government. The Soviet Government had been considering their relations with Poland, Czechoslovakia and Yugoslavia. They had taken the decision to give facilities to all three States to form National Committees in the USSR. These Committees would have facilities to form national military forces, Polish, Czechoslovak and Yugoslav. The Soviet Government undertook to supply arms and equipment to these forces. It followed as a result of this that all Polish prisoners of war in Russian hands would be handed over to the Polish National Committee. Their number was not as large as General Sikorski had told me; he understood that there were only 20,000. These forces would fight with the Russian armies against the German aggressor.

With regard to Poland, Soviet policy was to favour the establishment of an independent national Polish State. The boundaries of this State would correspond with ethnographical Poland. From this it might follow that certain districts and towns occupied by Russia in 1939 might be returned to Poland. The form of internal government to be set up in Poland was, in the view of the Soviet Government, entirely a matter for the Poles themselves. If General Sikorski and his Government found these statements of policy acceptable, the Soviet Government were prepared to make a treaty with him to form a common front against German aggression.

The Soviet Government were likewise in favour of the restoration of the independence of Czechoslovakia and Yugoslavia. The internal régime of these states also in their judgment was a matter for the peoples themselves.

I asked the Ambassador whether his Government proposed to make public this important declaration, for clearly it would have considerable effect both on the nationals of the States concerned and also on American opinion. The Ambassador said that he had no information yet as to his Government's intentions in respect of publication but that he supposed that this was contemplated since the decision to recognize National Committees had already been taken.

(Signed) Anthony Eden

No. 91

Record of a conversation between General Sikorski and Ambassador Maisky on the conditions of resumption of Polish-Soviet relations[1]

London, July 5, 1941   GSHI, PRM, 41/4

General Sikorski said that a necessary condition of collaboration between Poland and Russia was a return to normal relations. The Polish people had accepted war with Germany in 1939 on the then existing basis of the Polish State. He was therefore unable now to discuss frontier changes. He must therefore ask that the Soviet Government should explicitly revert to the situation as covered by the Treaty of Riga. This would follow automatically from a Soviet denunciation of the two treaties signed with Germany in August and September, 1939.[2]

Normal relations between the two Governments must be restored and the Polish Government would expect to appoint an Ambassador in Moscow. When these relations had been established, it would be possible to deal with the fate of Polish refugees and prisoners, as well as deportees into Central Asia and elsewhere, in the Soviet Union. General Sikorski drew special attention to the importance which this had for the Soviet Government in that a number of refugees were employed in Soviet industry and if normal relations were re-established and proper conditions provided for Poles in the Soviet Union, all these men would work loyally against Germany and there would be no question of sabotage.

Monsieur Maisky inquired what exactly General Sikorski had in mind in regard to Polish prisoners of war in the Soviet Union.

General Sikorski replied that these men, who according to official Soviet statistics, published recently, number 191,000 men and some 9,000 officers, the majority of whom are in military concentration camps east of the river Volga, should be formed into an independent, sovereign Polish Army in the Soviet Union. If the Soviet Government did not desire the presence of such an army, it might perhaps be possible to transport it elsewhere to continue the fight against Germany.

Monsieur Maisky suggested that this Polish Army would be under the orders of the Soviet General Staff.

General Sikorski replied that that would be so from the point of view of operations, but organically it would be autonomous like the Polish Forces in the United Kingdom. This Monsieur Maisky accepted.

Monsieur Maisky then referred to the attitude of the Soviet Government on the question of an independent Poland. He did not think that it would be profitable at this time to discuss this matter at great length or in detail.

To this General Sikorski replied that he could not accept any departure from the status which existed prior to August 1939. He would not eventually be able to return to his country having agreed to a diminished Poland. Moreover, were he to recognize even implicitly a surrender of Poland to the USSR, it would make it difficult, if not impossible, to create enthusiasm

[1] See Note No. 91.   [2] See doc. Nos. 31, 52.

117

among the Polish soldiers, who are at present in Soviet gaols, concentration camps or deported under distressing conditions. Monsieur Zaleski, the Polish Foreign Minister, remarked that the Germans who are now trying to form in Warsaw a puppet Government are promising the Poles a most considerable extension of their Eastern Boundaries.

Monsieur Maisky said that his Government favoured the formation of an independent national Polish State, and they agreed further that the régime to be established was the exclusive concern of the Poles, but they could not explicitly recognize the frontiers of 1939. Perhaps, however, it would not be necessary to say that now, and the question might be left open.

General Sikorski explained that prior to the present war there were practically no Soviet nationals in the territories occupied by the Soviet Armies in September 1939, moreover as the USSR is not a national State, but a composition of numerous nations ruled by Moscow, she has no grounds to impose strictly ethnographical frontiers on Poland. General Sikorski said that he could agree that this question need not be discussed in detail at present. He could not, however, agree that the Soviet Government should declare that the frontiers of 1939 would *not* be restored.

Monsieur Maisky thereupon inquired whether General Sikorski would be content to leave the frontier question alone and discuss practical arrangements for collaboration against Germany.

General Sikorski said that he would be quite content if the Soviet Government would denounce the two treaties with Germany of August and September, 1939. That would lead to a return to normal relations and the Polish Government will establish their Ambassador in Moscow. For this post he would appoint Professor Bartel if he was evacuated from Lwów. Further, all prisoners should be released. Then Poland would be ready to form an Army on Soviet soil to fight by the side of the Soviet against Germany.

General Sikorski explained that by prisoners he referred to all Poles taken from Poland and kept under restraint in the Soviet Union, including these imprisoned for political reasons.

Some discussion ensued on this point; Monsieur Maisky indicated that this was a complicated question, but undertook to submit it to his Government.

He then summed up what he understood to be the Polish position, namely—

1) Provided the Soviet Government denounce the two treaties with Germany of August and September, 1939, the discussion of frontiers is not material.

2) Return to normal relations between the two Governments and the appointment of a Polish Ambassador in Moscow.

3) Poland would then be prepared to collaborate in the common fight against Germany.

4) A special Polish Army would be formed as a unit on Soviet territory or to be transported elsewhere if that were desired. The exact status of the Polish Army would be assimilated to that of the Polish Forces in the United Kingdom.

5) Polish military and political prisoners to be liberated.

Monsieur Maisky asked whether the Polish Government would agree to the proposal of the Soviet Government for the signature of a treaty and General Sikorski replied that if the above conditions were accepted, he was quite agreeable and he added that there would be a number of matters already mentioned, such as the status of the Polish Forces and the release of prisoners, which could no doubt be incorporated in the treaty.

(Intld.) A.[lexander] C.[adogan]

No. 92

Note from Minister Zaleski to Mr. Eden on the basis for an understanding between Poland and the USSR[1]

London, July 7, 1941   GSHI, A.11. 49/Sow./6

Vu la conversation qui a eu lieu samedi le 5 juillet 1941 entre le Général W. Sikorski, Président du Conseil des Ministres Polonais et M. A. Zaleski, Ministre des Affaires Étrangères, d'une part, et M. Maisky, Ambassadeur de l'URSS d'autre part, en présence de Sir Alexander Cadogan, Principal Sous-Secrétaire d'État aux Affaires Étrangères du Gouvernement de Sa Majesté Britannique, le Gouvernement Polonais tient à souligner ce qui suit:

L'agression par le Reich Allemand de la Pologne en date du 1 septembre 1939 avait été immédiatement précédée par la conclusion d'un accord germano-soviétique en date du 23 août 1939 lequel contenait apparemment des clauses dirigées contre l'existence de l'Etat Polonais.

L'invasion du territoire polonais par les troupes soviétiques en date du 17 septembre 1939 a été suivie par la conclusion du traité germano-soviétique en date du 28 septembre 1939.[2] Cet accord partageait le territoire de l'État Polonais entre le Reich et l'URSS et proclamait la suppression de cet État. Il a été suivi, à son tour, d'une série d'autres actes internationaux conclus entre le Reich et l'URSS ou entre chacune de ces Puissances et des États tiers, affectant tous, l'indépendance et l'intégrité de la Pologne.

Le Gouvernement Polonais a toujours considéré ces accords et actes comme nuls et non-avenus, et il tient à rappeler qu'il a élevé à leur occasion, à des dates diverses, des protestations solennelles. Ces protestations ont été portées à la connaissance des Gouvernements des Puissances alliées et neutres.

Le Gouvernement de la République a également le devoir de souligner qu'en éxécution de ces actes illégaux le Gouvernement de l'URSS a non seulement accompli depuis cette agression, d'innombrables attentats à la souveraineté de l'État et à la propriété publique en Pologne, mais qu'il a en outre crû devoir prendre des mesures affectant gravement les libertés individuelles et la propriété privée de larges masses de ressortissants polonais.

Le Gouvernement Polonais n'entend pas énumérer ici les protestations dont il s'agit, et il se borne à souligner le contenu de la Note en date du 3 mai 1941, qui a été adressée par le Ministre des Affaires Étrangères de Pologne

[1] This note was handed by Minister Zaleski to Ambassador Biddle on July 9, 1941, and by Ambassador Ciechanowski to President Roosevelt on July 25, 1941.
[2] See doc. No. 52.

à LL. EE. les Ministres des Affaires Étrangères des Puissances alliées et neutres, au sujet de l'occupation allemande et soviétique de la Pologne au cours de 1939 et 1940.

Mais, désirant faciliter la tâche des pays alliés qui, contrairement à la Pologne n'ont pas eu à subir d'agression de la part de l'URSS, le Gouvernement Polonais veut faire son possible afin de leur éviter toutes complications dans leurs relations avec l'URSS.

A cette occasion, il y a lieu de rappeler le point de vue formulé dans la lettre du 27 novembre 1939 que le Ministre des Affaires Étrangères de Pologne adressait à S.E. Lord Halifax à la suite de conversations qui venaient d'avoir lieu entre eux, à Londres:

'. . . We had agreed in London that it was premature to take up any definite attitude towards Soviet Russia with regard to their action in Poland and in the Baltic States. We further agreed that, at this stage of the war, it was essential to concentrate all our united forces against Germany, to single out Germany as Enemy No. 1, fully responsible for the aggressive war forced upon the three Allies, for bringing Soviet Russia into action and for all the far-reaching consequences, the moral, material and territorial damages resulting from the war and from the joint action of Germany and Soviet Russia.'

Etant donné que l'Allemagne a dernièrement imposé la guerre à l'URSS et qu'en conséquence celle-ci s'est trouvée contre son gré parmi les nations qui luttent pour la liberté, le Gouvernement Polonais tient à déclarer que non seulement il est décidé à continuer cette politique vis-à-vis de l'URSS mais qu'il serait enclin à voir ses relations avec l'URSS redevenir normales, à conditions toutefois que celle-ci:

1 / s'engage à renoncer intégralement aux traités germano-soviétique du 23 août[3] et du 28 septembre 1939[4] ainsi qu'à tous les accords et actes consécutifs ayant trait à la Pologne. Il sera implicitement entendu que tous les traités et arrangements qui liaient l'URSS à la Pologne avant l'agression allemande seront rétablis.

D'autre part, il sera entendu que les biens enlevés par les autorités de l'URSS en Pologne seront restitués en nature et que les dommages résultant pour la Pologne et ses ressortissants de l'inéxécution des dits traités et arrangements trouveront leur pleine réparation; et enfin que les relations diplomatiques entre la Pologne et l'URSS seront par la suite rétablies.

2 / s'engage à libérer immédiatement:

a / les personnes qui, étant ressortissants polonais au 16 septembre 1939 sont détenues par les autorités soviétiques pour des raisons politiques, b / les ressortissants polonais qui ont été conscrits dans l'armée soviétique, c / les prisonniers de guerre polonais internés dans divers camps à l'intérieur du territoire de l'URSS, d / les ressortissants polonais (hommes, femmes et enfants) qui ont été déportés en masse des diverses régions occupées de la Pologne en URSS, de même qu'à consentir à ce qu'une assistance puisse leur être accordée.

[3] See doc. No. 52.　　　　　　　　　　[4] See doc. No. 31.

Sur ce point (2), il serait indispensable qu'une organisation de secours qui collaborerait officieusement avec les autorités polonaises, puisse être autorisée dès à présent à fonctionner sur le territoire de l'URSS ayant pour tâche de porter secours aux prisoniers de guerre, aux détenus politiques et aux déportés civils en attendant que leur évacuation de l'URSS devienne réalisable.

Le Gouvernement Polonais est en droit de croire qu'il est dans l'intérêt moral et politique de l'URSS de renouer ses relations avec la Pologne dans les conditions définies ci-dessus et ajoute qu'il n'est guère probable que l'URSS veuille continuer à se prévaloir de traités qu'elle avait conclu avec son propre agresseur et relatifs à un territoire que l'URSS ne semble même plus occuper de fait.

Si l'URSS adoptait une telle attitude, elle renforcerait sans aucun doute sa position morale vis-à-vis des democraties qui combattent dans cette guerre et—ce qui n'est pas moins important—vis-à-vis des populations de l'Europe orientale lesquelles y verraient la volonté réelle de l'URSS d'abandonner des méthodes politiques semblables à celles qui ont inspiré et inspirent les agressions allemandes.

Le Gouvernement Polonais désire, afin d'éviter tout malentendu, souligner dès à présent qu'en posant ainsi le problème, il n'entend renoncer, de quelque manière que ce soit, aux droits indiscutables de la Pologne en ce qui regarde ses territoires d'avant le 1 septembre 1939.

Si ce Gouvernement n'a pas d'objection à ce que l'URSS s'abstienne de faire en ce moment une déclaration officielle et précise en ce qui concerne le retour au Traité de Riga de 1921, son attitude est dictée par les considérations suivantes:

(1) Le Gouvernement Polonais désirerait faciliter en ce moment la tâche à ceux de ses Alliés qui entendent maintenir de bonnes relations directes avec l'URSS.

(2) il entend éviter de créer l'impression qu'il existe entre les États qui sont en guerre avec l'Allemagne des difficultés insurmontables.

(3) Le Gouvernement Polonais a lieu de croire qu'en ce qui concerne le Traité de Riga de 1921[5] le Gouvernement de l'URSS peut avoir en vue certaines clauses de ce Traité qui, sans avoir trait aux frontières elles-mêmes et revêtant un caractère technique et transitoire, auraient perdu aujourd'hui, au sens des intérêts de l'URSS, leur actualité et pourraient, en conséquence, être modifiées.

(4) Il se rend compte du fait qu'il est très peu probable que les armées de l'URSS puissent réoccuper elles-mêmes des territoires quelconques appartenant à la Pologne et venant d'être l'objet de l'invasion allemande.

(5) Le Gouvernement Polonais sait, hélas de sa propre expérience, que les obligations stipulées par le Gouvernement de l'URSS ne sont considérées valables par ce dernier que pour autant que ce Gouvernement ne possède ni l'interêt ni la force pour les transgresser.

Le Gouvernement Polonais est obligé de confirmer—ainsi qu'il avait été

[5] See doc. No. 3.

déclaré du côté polonais dans la conversation susmentionnée du 5 Juillet 1941 —qu'il n'est pas seulement incompétent pour renoncer de son propre gré à une partie quelconque du territoire de la Pologne, mais qu'il se garderait, en outre, de vouloir donner l'impression qu'il serait enclin à transiger sur les droits de la République à son intégrité territoriale.

En effet, il y a lieu d'insister qu'une telle attitude:

(1) préparerait en quelque sorte la voie au Reich Allemand que, selon les informations reçues par le Gouvernement Polonais, s'efforcerait déjà à ménager à son profit l'opinion publique polonaise par des soi-disant concessions accordées à l'État. Or il ne faut pas perdre de vue que l'Allemagne serait en raison de son avance militaire non seulement à même de faire de telles promesses mais encore d'y faire face le cas échéant.

(2) Si de tels sacrifices territoriaux au profit de la Russie Soviétique étaient demandés à la Pologne, cela mettrait sans aucun doute en danger la foi des pays de l'Europe Centrale et balkaniques dans le degré de sincérité avec laquelle les Alliés luttent pour la cause de la justice et le respect des traités.

(3) Le Gouvernement Polonais, en luttant aux côtés des Alliés et s'efforçant d'augmenter considérablement les forces militaires polonaises par la création d'une puissante armée formée de volontaires recrutés en Amérique et de prisonniers de guerre actuellement internés en URSS ne saurait en aucune mesure s'attendre a ce que ces forces veuillent participer un jour à la reconquête des territoires polonais des mains des Allemands pour qu'une partie de ces territoires soit ensuite rétrocédée a la Russie.

Le Gouvernement Polonais se voit obligé de souligner que si les soldats polonais devaient, ne fut - ce que pour un instant avoir la suspicion que telles seraient les intentions cachées des Alliés, ce Gouvernement ne serait pas en mesure de leur réclamer le sacrifice du sang qu'ils versent déja journellement pour la résurrection de la Patrie et pour la cause commune des Alliés.

Aussi le Gouvernement Polonais doit souligner que tout en désirant collaborer efficacement avec l'URSS dans la lutte commune contre le Reich Allemand, il interprétera dans le présent comme dans l'avenir les relations entre la Pologne et l'URSS dans le sens des considérations ci-dessus.

No. 93

Memorandum handed by Minister Zaleski to Mr. Eden concerning Polish territories and the Baltic States annexed by the USSR between 1939 and 1940[1]

London, July 8, 1941   GSHI, A.11. 49/Sow./6

It may be expected that within a short time the German armies will expel Soviet authorities from all those territories which in 1939–1940 were militarily occupied and subsequently annexed by the Soviet Government, in agreement with Germany, but against the will of the population. It may also be assumed that Germany will proceed to establish in some at any rate of these territories pseudo-autonomous states, dependent on Berlin, and that she will

[1] See Note No. 93.

re-incorporate into Finland and Rumania the provinces taken from them by Russia.

Whatever the outcome of the German-Soviet war such a development demands particularly skilful and prudent handling by the British and other Allied Governments. Any errors committed at this stage of the situation may adversely affect the course of the war, and in particular may prejudice plans for a better settlement of Europe after the war.

Poland is directly interested in this question: a large part of the relevant provinces belong to the national territory of Poland and the remaining ones to the neighbouring or friendly states of Rumania, Lithuania, Latvia, Estonia and Finland and it will be incumbent upon the Polish Government to pay the greatest attention to a due development of relations with these states after the war.

Considerations to be taken into account on this subject are of both a general and a special character.

General considerations

It is an incontestable fact that Germany has neither legal nor moral right to decide upon the fate of the territories annexed by Russia in 1939–1940. Such a thesis requires no substantiation though the need for its official confirmation may one day arise.

On the other hand neither can the USSR claim any moral or legal right to these territories.

Diplomatic and military activities on the part of the USSR against her Western neighbours took place in 1939–1940 as a result of her previous understanding with Germany as to the partition of Eastern Europe. The purpose of the German Government in bringing about this understanding was a temporary satisfaction of Soviet imperialism before and during the campaigns against Poland and France. The Soviet Government willingly took advantage of this opportunity to gain a strategic starting-point for a revolutionary offensive against Germany in the final stage of the war. Other motives put forward by Russia were either of a secondary nature or were intended to deceive public opinion of the world and of Russia herself. The only European state who recognized the legality of the Soviet annexation was Italy and the German satellites Slovakia and Hungary. Even the Japanese Government has maintained great reserve in this respect. Thus from the standpoint of international law the annexation of the aforesaid provinces by Russia is not only baseless but at the moment when the Soviet troops withdraw from these provinces it becomes pure fiction.

All these territories were incorporated into the Soviet Union by force. Every kind of election and plebiscite as well as other expressions of the will of the people which took place in these territories under terror of the Red Army and the GPU were nothing but a fraud on such a colossal scale as to transcend every Soviet tradition. There is not the slightest doubt that only a negligible proportion of the population reacted favourably to a Soviet occupation. As a result of deportations of the population to Eastern Russia and Central Asia and other outrages of the Soviet police, of a gradual lowering of the standard of life to a general Soviet level and the removal to Russia of stocks of foodstuffs and other goods, of the development of a compulsory collectivization of agriculture and a russification of national institutions and, finally, of widespread reprisals against local Communists, the number of Soviet partisans gradually decreased almost to zero with the duration of the occupation. The same reactions took place in all Soviet-occupied territories from Finnish Karelia to Bessarabia. Numerous revolts of the local populations against Soviet authorities during the whole period of their occupation, and especially since the German attack, are the best proof of such an attitude.

It is fortunate that the British Government have resisted Soviet suggestions for a recognition of the annexations made by Russia since September 1939, for the British Government have thus retained complete liberty of action with regard to these territories and can act in complete harmony with the United States. It is of paramount importance that this liberty of action be maintained throughout the course of the war in spite of the German attack on Russia.

Since the aforesaid territories have now been lost by Russia, it is of the greatest consequence to the future organization of Europe that all steps be counteracted which the German Government, at present occupying the whole of Eastern Europe, takes to mislead the local populations into believing that Britain is opposed to a restoration of national liberties to the nations situated between Germany and Russia. It must be borne in mind that since 1917, and in particular since 1939, hatred and fear of the Soviet, due to both national and social motives, have been steadily growing in all these countries. It is certain that a weakening and even a downfall of the Soviet régime would be received with a feeling of deep relief by all the direct and indirect neighbours of Russia, from Sweden and Hungary to Turkey and Iran. News arriving from these countries since June 22nd corroborates this statement. The present state of military collaboration between the Allies and America on the one hand and Soviet Russia on the other should not divert the Allies' attention from the actual situation in Eastern Europe.

The British Government is looked upon by many peoples as the champion of national freedom. It seems essential that Germany should not be permitted to deprive Britain of this formidable moral asset in respect of the peoples of Central and Eastern Europe. Whatever might have been their local political differences, there has always been a kind of mutual understanding and solidarity between the Central and Eastern European nations. Such feeling is the natural outcome of their deeply rooted fear and distrust of both Germany and Russia. Therefore, should the British Government deviate from their general political principles in the desire to please the Soviet Government, which in a few months' time may no longer exist, such an attitude would be resented by the whole of Eastern and Central Europe. On the other hand, if the British Government adhere to their present attitude, and even make it more general and emphatic, Germany would find it increasingly difficult if not impossible to exploit her theory that Britain is guided only by selfish interests.

Special considerations

a/ Eastern Poland

This question has been the subject of a special Note of the Polish Government, dated July 7th, 1941.[2]

Nevertheless it seems relevant to indicate certain complications which may render the situation of the Poles in Poland difficult. It is not excluded that owing to the attitude of the population the German Government, feeling that they will not be able to master the whole of Poland by police measures only, will make certain proposals to the strongly anti-Russian elements among the Poles. There are indications that the Nazis are considering this possibility. Their proposals will undoubtedly tend to put before the Poles the following alternatives: a/ either the Poles at the price of renouncing some territories in Western Poland will be compensated in the East at the expense of Russia; b/ or the Poles will persist in their intransigent attitude, and then the so-called litigious areas of Eastern and even Central Poland will be surrendered by Germany to the Ukrainians, White Russians and Lithuanians whose Governments will be created and controlled by Germany. The second alternative would result in further extermination of the Polish element in these provinces. It should be noted that the German interpretation of 'litigious areas' is most extensive and that in addition to the whole of the Soviet-occupied territory (Wilno, Lwów, etc.), it includes areas with an insignificant proportion of non-Poles, which were occupied by Germany after the treaty of the partition of Poland of September 28th, 1939[3] (the territories of Chełm and of the Central Carpathians).

b/ Baltic States

The establishment of the three Baltic States, which in a national sense are almost homogeneous, was not so much due to the Allies of the last war as to their own efforts and to some extent to the consequences of the Polish-Soviet war of 1919–1920. Their establishment via facti and in accordance with the will of their peoples after an unsuccessful attempt to impose Soviet rule on them was recognized in the first place by the Soviet Government and later by all other countries. The gradual occupation of these countries by the Soviets in 1940 and their subsequent annexation took place against the will of the population who were desirous of remaining neutral in the present war.

As said at the beginning of this Memorandum, neither Germany nor Russia has any right to decide the fate of these countries. Having withdrawn her minorities from the Baltic States Germany has no longer any real interest there. Russia's interest to use the ports of Latvia and Estonia in addition to her own Baltic ports, may be satisfied by voluntary agreements with these countries without any military occupation, and still more without forcefully

[2] See doc. No. 92.　　　　[3] See doc. No. 52.

imposing on them a social system which they abhor. In Lithuania, which has no ports, Russian interests are non-existing.

Although at present it may seem unsuitable politically it should be realized that the alleged Lithuanian and Latvian Governments of these countries are better qualified to represent their countries than groups of Russian Communists imported from Moscow. One may surmise that in the very near future many, if not all, national and social institutions abolished by Soviet rule will be restored in the three Baltic States. Simultaneously Germany will exploit the populations, which will be more burdensome to them since they have already been subjected to thorough plunder by the Soviets. It may be expected that after a short period of relief, German occupation will become hated by the people and result in anti-German activities which, however, will not be pro-Soviet.

This new situation would give rise to two alternatives. Either it may not be taken advantage of by the Allies, a struggle would then ensue between three elements: pro-German opportunists, Communists and those elements striving for a restoration of their national states. Such chaotic conditions might serve Germany as well as a Communist revolution. Or again, it will come to the knowledge of the Baltic peoples that the Allies recognize the right of every nation to form an independent state resulting in each nation fighting for its own freedom and interests. In such circumstances the discontent of the peoples under German rule may become of real value to the interests of the Allies, as was the case in Norway, Holland, Poland, etc., and consequently be instrumental in bringing about a German defeat.

The alleged members of the Baltic Government (Skírpa, General Rastikis, General Berzins) believe in collaboration with Nazi Germany. It would be an exaggeration to call them Quislings, however. They collaborate with Germany *faute de mieux* as their countries are situated outside the sphere of concrete Allied assistance. Their political existence would automatically come to an end with Germany's defeat and then, if moral help and recognition by the Allies could be accorded them, the democratic elements professing the same principles as Western Europe would come to power in their place.

It would be impossible to accept even tacitly the establishment of the Baltic Governments under German control. At the same time in spite of a negative attitude towards such Governments an opportunity might arise for a public confirmation by the Allies of the principle recognized by them that *every nation* has a right to an independent existence. This principle would implicitly apply to the Baltic countries as such and would mean their right to an existence independent from *both* Germany and Russia within the framework of a new organization of Europe as planned after the defeat of Germany. In this way the Allied Governments would be able to reckon on the active sympathy of six million people and their collaboration in overthrowing the might of Germany.

The incidence that a couple of million people of Baltic extraction are domiciled in America is not unimportant. It is not immaterial whether these people are pro-German or pro-Allied. There, affirmation of the right of all nations to political independence could lead to a movement of free Baltic peoples which in turn might be extended to military activity.

As regards Lithuania, it is possible that the Polish territory of Wilno will be incorporated by Hitler into Lithuania. The Polish Government would doubtless be ready to enter into negotiations with Lithuania, after the war or even during its final stage, with a view to dispelling the political asperity of Polish-Lithuanian disagreements within the framework of the regional organization of this part of Europe. They could not, however, ignore a new attempt to seek discord between Poland and Lithuania by a temporary annexation by German-controlled Lithuania of one of the most homogeneously Polish provinces. This attitude is a direct consequence of the thesis of the integral restoration of Polish national territory which has been put forward by the Note of July 7th, 1941.[4]

c/ Bessarabia and Bukovina

This problem is to a great extent parallel to that of the Baltic States and, moreover, presents certain analogies with the question of Eastern Poland. No State has ever questioned Rumania's right to Bukovina and her title to Bessarabia has been recognized by every State except the USSR. Both these provinces are inhabited by a substantial Rumanian majority. The Soviet Government deemed it necessary to create in 1925 an autonomous Moldavian Soviet Republic along the Rumanian frontier on the left bank of the river Dniester on Ukrainian territory which included only 30% of Rumanians. This was done in order to create a focus of attraction for Bessarabian Rumanians on the other side of the river. Yet in 1940 the Soviet incorporated Bessarabia and Bukovina directly into the Soviet Ukraine without giving them even a semblance of autonomy. These facts, of which allied opinion is to a great extent ignorant, are a proof that in Moscow justice for conquered nations is as empty a phrase as it is for Hitler, and that tactical tricks practised by the Communist do not differ from those practised by Nazi Germany.

Can one be surprised that this conduct on the part of Russia was a great shock to the national feelings of Rumania and that lack of any kind of condemnation of these Soviet annexations on the part of the Allies, at a moment when neutral Rumania was governed by a pro-Allied group of statesmen, facilitated the subjugation of Rumania by Germany?

At present Germany, who herself probably suggested the occupation of Bessarabia to Soviet Russia, poses as the defender of Rumanian rights and interests and urges the return of both provinces. Thus Rumania has become a victim of a particularly perfidious and ruthless game between Germany and Russia.

To the Allies it is not a matter of indifference whether Rumania has to be considered as definitely gone over to the cause of the Axis, or whether there is still a possibility of gaining her collaboration with future Europe. Whatever errors and crimes were committed in 1940 by various Rumanian

[4] See doc. No. 92.

political groups, whatever responsibility lies with the Rumanians, the only way to gain their public opinion in favour of the Allied cause is by a confirmation of the fact that the treaty between Rumania and the Allies of the last war concerning the Eastern frontier of Rumania has not been wiped out by the present-day Allies. As in the case of the Baltic States it would then be possible to turn to the advantage of the Allies the bitterness of the Rumanian population in face of German occupation and their natural sense of affinity with Western Europe which cannot possibly have been extinguished.

No. 94

Record of a conversation between General Sikorski and Minister Zaleski and Ambassador Maisky, held in the presence of Mr. Eden, concerning the resumption of Polish-Soviet relations[1]

London, July 11, 1941 GSHI, PRM, 41/4

M. Maisky: The general position of the Soviet Government as regards the Polish State was that they maintained the point of view previously expressed in favour of the independence of the Polish State within the limits of Polish nationality. This was the Soviet Government's general point of view. They were prepared to accept the Polish suggestion to put aside for the present the question of the frontiers of Poland.

The Soviet Government were prepared also to make a declaration to the effect that the Soviet-German treaties of 1939 regarding Poland are to be considered as non-existent.

As regards the question of the formation of a Polish National Committee, the Soviet Government were animated in making this suggestion by their desire to meet Polish national aspirations, but if the Polish Government finds the creation of such a committee undesirable the Soviet Government does not insist on it.

The Soviet Government were prepared to resume diplomatic relations with the Polish Government and to receive a Polish representative in Moscow.

The Soviet Government favour the creation of an independent Polish army on Soviet soil under commanders appointed by the Polish Government in agreement with the Soviet Government. This army, being part of the forces fighting against Germany, is to be under the general direction of the Soviet High Command.

As regards the Polish prisoners of war, of whom the Polish Government claimed that there were 180,000, 10,000 being officers, the Soviet Government stated that there were only 20,000. The remainder were released as the Soviet Government had not considered it possible to keep these as prisoners of war, and were now dispersed throughout Russia.

This was the message which he had been instructed by his Government to convey to the Polish Government.

General Sikorski: Reserving the final answer of the Polish Government, he would at once observe that, if the Soviet Government renounced the

[1] See Note No. 94.

treaties of 1939 with Germany, this meant, in his view, the return to the legal situation which existed before those treaties were concluded. He had received the approval of Poles in Poland and the United States for this point of view and could not abandon it without losing that approval.

He would not for a moment say that, at the peace conference, Soviet Russia would not be at liberty to put forward all sorts of pretensions, and the Polish Government might also put some forward. But the Polish Government could not recognize the Soviet Government's point of view about the limitation of the Polish State to its ethnographical frontiers.

Secretary of State: There was no question of that.

General Sikorski: According to M. Maisky's declaration, the Polish Government should agree that the future Poland was to be an ethnographical one.

M. Maisky: No; the Soviet Government did not insist that the Polish Government accept their point of view.

General Sikorski: It was necessary to underline certain consequences of the Soviet point of view. For example, what would happen if the Polish and Soviet armies marched victoriously into Polish territory? Who would govern this territory, Poles or Russians? He would be satisfied if M. Maisky said that Poles would govern it.

M. Maisky suggested that at the moment this question was perhaps a little academic.

General Sikorski repeated that he could not accept the Soviet Government's point of view and wanted to make the Polish point of view clear to the Ambassador.

M. Maisky repeated that he only wished to state his Government's point of view about the future limits of the Polish State and did not ask the Polish Government to agree.

General Sikorski: The Polish Government could not accept a declaration regarding the future Poland such as M. Maisky proposed.

M. Maisky: The Soviet Government did not ask for this; they merely stated their point of view.

General Sikorski: If the Polish Government accepted, they would lose the support of Poles abroad. He could not discuss this question. It was not possible that the Soviet Government should make a unilateral declaration on this matter. Any declaration should be bilateral and agreed by both parties. He had understood M. Stalin to say that Russia had occupied Polish territory by arrangement with Germany in order to gain time. If this were so, it was only natural that M. Stalin should now declare that he had only taken that territory temporarily.

M. Maisky: The General has not quoted M. Stalin correctly. The latter had said that his non-aggression pact with Germany was concluded with the object of allowing time for preparation. He did not say anything about territorial arrangements.

General Sikorski: If the Soviet Government denounced their pact with Germany, they should renounce all territorial gains they had got from it.

M. Maisky: The important thing seemed to be to reach an agreement now. If they dwelt on general political matters and questions regarding frontiers, they would not get this agreement now. His statement of the Soviet Government's point of view did not mean that this point of view was to be embodied in a document to be agreed here and now by the Polish Government. The Soviet Government were ready to leave discussion and agreement on this point for the present.

General Sikorski: Some declaration would be necessary and he would make proposals in a few days.

M. Maisky: It was important to state as soon as possible—

[i] That the Treaties of 1939 were dead;

[ii] That diplomatic relations should be restored;

[iii] That the Polish army should be recreated; and

[iv] That both Governments agreed to fight against Germany.

General Sikorski: Two important points would then be lacking:—

[i] The question of Polish political prisoners in Russia. He did not believe the German assertion that all these had been murdered. There must be some still to be released, all of whom were Polish citizens.

[ii] The Soviet Government should restore Government and private property which they had taken from occupied Polish territory.

Secretary of State: Could not these points be raised when diplomatic relations had been restored?

General Sikorski: What were the Ambassador's views on future procedure? Was he authorized to sign an agreement, e.g. a military agreement?

M. Maisky: He was not authorized to sign at the moment, but he would seek authorization if they could agree on something.

Secretary of State: It was important from the point of view of world opinion, particularly in the United States, to conclude a Polish-Soviet Agreement soon. Nothing else could have such a good effect. Should he draft something on the basis of the four points put forward by M. Maisky while the latter sought authority from his Government to sign?

General Sikorski: It was necessary to underline the importance of two points:—[i] The question of the Polish frontier and [ii] that of the prisoners, both prisoners of war and political prisoners.

M. Maisky: The suggestion for the conclusion of an agreement on the basis of the four points he had put forward was his own suggestion, and his Government would have to consider an agreement in that form, though they were agreed on the essence.

Secretary of State: To sum up: it was important to try and get an early agreement. M. Maisky had made a personal suggestion of an agreement on the four points. The Secretary of State would try to put them on paper for both Governments to consider. The question of the frontiers was, in his opinion, not one which really remained outstanding, since, if the four-point agreement was concluded, the Polish point of view was legally safeguarded.

General Sikorski: It was important to be clear that the Polish Government

130

held by the 1939 frontier, and felt that the Poles should take over the administration if the Germans were driven back west of that frontier.

Secretary of State: This question could be discussed later: if the 1939 treaties fell to the ground the legal position was clear. The question of political prisoners, however, remained, and M. Maisky should try and help to meet the Poles in this problem, e.g., by arranging for its discussion when diplomatic relations were restored.

General Sikorski: If the Polish and Soviet Governments reached agreement on the lines proposed, the Polish Government could not understand how the question of the political prisoners could not be automatically settled.

M. Maisky: The exact views of the Soviet Government on this point were not known, but they might feel difficulty in settling this question by a comprehensive promise to release all prisoners. Perhaps something could be done by a private understanding, negotiated by the Polish Ambassador in Moscow.

General Sikorski: The Polish Government could not understand the difficulty of settling this point. They would agree not to publish any agreement about political prisoners, but the Soviet Government ought to be able to appreciate the good impression which the release of those prisoners would make.

M. Maisky: The question was a little more complicated than the General thought. For example, suppose that after Russia occupied Polish territory some Pole had committed a political crime for which he had been sentenced. This would not be a question of military operations. The problem was one that might be considered, but was not so simple as that of prisoners of war.

General Sikorski: This question showed how difficult the frontier question would be. If the Soviet Government did not regard these people as Soviet citizens, their status was regulated by the Hague Conventions. They could only be regarded as having committed political crimes because they remained Polish citizens. It was impossible for the Polish Government to admit the right of the Soviet Government to judge and condemn Polish citizens.

Secretary of State: The General was now asking the Soviet Government to recognize the 1939 frontier as regards the past as well as the present, and to admit that their actions since 1939 in these former Polish territories had been illegal.

General Sikorski: The Polish Government could not agree to reach an agreement with the Soviet Government at the price of selling the Polish political prisoners.

Secretary of State: The Soviet Government would not want to keep these prisoners for ever. What the Polish Government wanted is that they should be freed in the near future. The Soviet Government ought to be able to give a private assurance to this effect.

M. Maisky: The figures which the Polish Government had mentioned were, he thought, exaggerated.

General Sikorski: The principle of the release of political prisoners should be recognized by the Soviet Government. It was a sacrifice for Poland to ignore the Russian aggression of 1939.

M. Maisky: It was not the time to argue about this. Arguments could be used to condemn Polish aggression in the past as well as Soviet aggression. He did not wish to dwell upon the past, but to concentrate on the present and future. An agreement between the Soviet and Polish Governments was important from the point of view of public opinion, and something effective should be made public soon. It was therefore desirable to concentrate on the four points and to make other independent arrangements about the political prisoners, and he was prepared to raise with his Government the possibility of a parallel private agreement on this point.

It was agreed by the Polish representatives and the Soviet Ambassador to proceed on these lines. The aim would be to conclude, first a political agreement, the draft of which, based on M. Maisky's four points, would be communicated by the Secretary of State to the Polish Government and the Soviet Ambassador; and, later, a military agreement. In the meanwhile M. Maisky would sound his Government about the proposed four-point agreement and would seek their views about the private agreement regarding the political prisoners.

A further meeting would be held when M. Maisky had received a reply from Moscow.

No. 95

Proposed political agreement between Poland and the USSR sent by Mr. Eden to Minister Zaleski (points of the Soviet proposal forwarded to the Polish Government after amendment by the Foreign Office)

London, July 11, 1941   GSHI, PRM, 41/1

The four heads of agreement proposed by M. Maisky are:

1. The Soviet Government are prepared to make a declaration to the effect that the Soviet-German Treaties of 1939 about Poland are regarded as non-existent.

2. The Soviet Government are prepared to resume diplomatic relations with the Polish Government and to receive a Polish representative in Moscow.

3. The Soviet Government favour the creation of an autonomous Polish Army on Soviet Soil under a commander appointed by the Polish Government in agreement with the Soviet Government. This Army, being part of the forces fighting against Germany, is to be under the general direction of the Soviet High Command.

4. The two Governments to agree to fight together against Hitler Germany.

No. 96

Draft of the proposed agreement between Poland and the USSR sent by Minister Zaleski to Mr. Eden, in reply to the Soviet proposal of July 11, 1941[1]

London, July 12, 1941   GSHI, PRM, 41/1

In conformity with our understanding of yesterday I am sending you our

[1] See Note No. 96.

suggestions as to the texts which ought to figure under M. Maisky's heads of agreement forwarded to me by Mr. O. Harvey on July 11th.

Projet de déclaration polono-soviétique

Le Gouvernement Polonais et le Gouvernement de l'URSS déclarent ce qui suit:

1 / Le Gouvernement de l'URSS considère comme nuls et non-avenus les traités conclus avec l'Allemagne en date du 23 août 1939 et du 28 septembre 1939, ainsi que tous ses autres accords ou actes de législation interne consécutifs à ces dates et qui demeurent relatifs à la Pologne, et renonce aux bénéfices qu'ils ont pu ou auraient pu assuré à l'URSS.

Les deux Gouvernements reconnaissent le rétablissement des relations contractuelles entre leurs pays sur la base de la dernière déclaration commune polono-soviétique, faite à Moscou, en date du 26 novembre 1938.

2 / Le Gouvernement Polonais et le Gouvernement de l'URSS sont d'accord pour rétablir immédiatement, conformément aux arrangements d'avant 1939, des représentations diplomatiques respectives. Le Gouvernement Polonais aura le droit d'organiser, sur le territoire de l'URSS, un service consulaire pour satisfaire les besoins de ses ressortissants.

3 / Afin d'intensifier la lutte contre l'agresseur commun—le Reich Allemand—le Gouvernement Polonais est d'accord avec le Gouvernement de l'URSS d'organiser sur le territoire soviétique une armée polonaise dont le statut sera celui de l'armée d'un État souverain et ami.

Le Gouvernement de l'URSS s'engage à éviter toute immixtion dans l'organisation intérieure, politique ou militaire, de cette armée, qui sera composée de ressortissants polonais, enrôlés comme volontaire ou à titre de service militaire obligatoire, conformément à la législation polonaise en vigueur. Cette armée sera soumise à l'autorité suprême du Gouvernement et du Haut Commandement Polonais qui sera en droit de l'utiliser contre l'Allemagne—soit sur le front soviétique soit sur un autre théâtre d'opérations.

Un arrangement spécial militaire, conclu entre les deux Gouvernements à la date de ce jour, réglera le statut, l'organisation et le fonctionnement de cette armée.

4 / Le Gouvernement de l'URSS s'engage à libérer immédiatement et à considerer désormais comme des ressortissants d'un État ami, toutes les personnes qui, demeurant ressortissants polonais à la date du 16 septembre 1939, résident actuellement sur le territoire de l'URSS, c'est-à-dire:

a) sont détenues par les autorités soviétiques, comme prisonniers politiques,

b) ont été enrôlées dans l'armée soviétiques comme volontaires ou comme conscrits militaires,

c) sont internées dans des camps de concentration comme prisonniers de guerre,

d) ont été déportées en masse à l'intérieur du territoire de l'URSS.

Le Gouvernement de l'URSS s'engage à rendre aux personnes mentionnées ci-dessus la liberté de circulation, y compris le droit de quitter le territoire soviétique, de leur assurer l'assistance des autorités soviétiques et de leur garantir désormais le traitement le plus bienveillant.

En outre, le Gouvernement de l'URSS reconnaîtra aux personnes ci-dessus mentionnées le droit de bénéficier de la protection diplomatique et consulaire qui sera assurée par les représentations polonaises fonctionnant sur le territoire de l'URSS. Il admettra sur le territoire soviétique des organisations de secours polonaises ou autres qui, d'accord avec le Gouvernement Polonais, seraient chargées d'assister les personnes ci-dessus mentionnées. Il leur accordera à cet effet toutes les facilités indispensables.

Projet de protocole secret Polono-Soviétique

Les deux Gouvernements, considérant comme nuls et non-avenus tous les actes internationaux qui sont intervenus ou qui pourraient intervenir à la suite de diverses agressions allemandes, à commencer par celle du 1 septembre 1939 contre la Pologne, affirment leur ferme volonté de respecter à l'avenir leurs indépendances politiques et intégrités territoriales respectives.

No. 97

Draft agreement between Poland and the USSR proposed by Poland

London, July 13, 1941   GSHI, PRM, 41/1

1/ The Soviet Government will issue a statement denouncing their treaties concluded with Germany and relating to Poland and declaring the restoration of Polish-Russian relations to the status previous to September 1939.

The Polish Government reserves the right to claim reparations at the appropriate time for all damages caused by the USSR on the territory of the Polish State after the entry of the Soviet Armies on September 17th 1939.

2/ The Polish Republic and the USSR will take up normal relations and restore their respective diplomatic representatives immediately following the signature of this agreement.

All Polish citizens who are within the boundaries of the Soviet Union will be returned their freedom. The Polish Government will organize their protection with the assistance of the Soviet Government, and, if necessary, through the intercession of the Red Cross.

3/ An independent Polish Army under Polish Supreme Command will be organized upon USSR territory. During the common struggle within the frontiers of the Soviet Union, it will be operationally subordinated to the Soviet High Command, on the same basis as the arrangement with regard to the Polish Fighting Forces in Great Britain. The organization of this army will be settled in detail by a separate agreement.

If, for any reason whatsoever, the organization of Polish Fighting Forces on USSR territory proved to be impossible, the Soviet Government will encourage and facilitate the evacuation to Great Britain of all Polish citizens fit for military service.

4/ The two Governments mutually undertake to prosecute in common the war against [Hitlerite] Germany.

No. 98

British amendments to the proposed political agreement between Poland and the USSR sent by Mr. Eden to Minister Zaleski[1]

London, July 15, 1941   GSHI, PRM, 41/1

The Government of the USSR and the Government of the Polish Republic have concluded the present Agreement and declare as follows:

Article 1: The Government of the USSR recognizes that the treaties concluded with Germany on August 23rd, 1939, and September 28th, 1939, respectively, are no longer in force, and that the relations between the USSR and Poland in consequence revert to the basis existing before those dates. The Polish Government declares that Poland is not bound by any treaty, agreement or declaration with a third Power directed against the Soviet Union.

Article 2: The two contracting Governments will immediately re-establish diplomatic relations and exchange Ambassadors.

Article 3: The two contracting Governments mutually undertake to render each other assistance and support of all kinds in the war against Hitlerite Germany.

Article 4: An independent Polish army under a Polish Commander-in-Chief will be organized upon USSR territory. So long as this army is employed on the territory of the USSR it will operate under the direction of the High Military Command of the USSR. The organization of this Polish Army will be settled in detail by a separate agreement.

The present Agreement comes into force immediately on signature and is not subject to ratification.

The present Agreement is drawn up in two copies, each of them in the Russian and Polish languages. Both texts have equal force.

Draft Protocol I (for publication)

The two contracting Governments accept the principle that, subject to military considerations in particular cases, Polish citizens who are at present in detention in the territory of the USSR shall be set at liberty.

The application of this principle in respect of such persons, including the arrangements for their protection, shall be settled by discussion between the two contracting Governments, which shall take place through the diplomatic channel as soon as diplomatic relations have been re-established.

[1] See Note No. 98.

The present protocol comes into force simultaneously with the Agreement of today's date.

Draft Protocol II (*not for publication*)

Any claims relating to public or private Polish property in the possession of the USSR are reserved for subsequent discussions between the two contracting Governments.

The present Protocol comes into force simultaneously with the Agreement of today's date.

No. 99

Draft of the proposed agreement between Poland and the USSR (the second Soviet proposal)

London, July 17, 1941   GSHI, PRM, 41/1

Taking into account that the Soviet Government recognizes the Treaties concerning Poland which were concluded between the USSR and Germany in 1939 as invalid, and that the Polish Government declares that Poland is not bound by any Treaty, Agreement or Declaration with a Third Power directed against the Soviet Union, the Government of the USSR and the Government of the Polish Republic have concluded the present Agreement and declare as follows:

1 / The diplomatic relations between the Government of the USSR and the Government of the Polish Republic to be immediately restored and the exchange of Ambassadors effected.

2 / The two Governments mutually undertake to render each other assistance and support of all kinds in the present war against Hitlerite Germany.

3 / The Government of the USSR declares its agreement with the formation on the territory of the USSR, of a Polish Army, its Commander to be appointed by the Government of the Polish Republic in agreement with the Soviet Government. The Polish Army on the territory of the USSR will operate under the direction of the High Military Command of the USSR.

The present Agreement comes into force immediately after its signature and is not subject to ratification.

The present Agreement is drawn upon in two copies, each of them in the Russian and Polish languages. Both texts have equal force.

No. 100

Letter from General Sikorski to Mr. Eden with Polish amendments to the second Soviet proposal of July 17, 1941[1]

London, July 17, 1941   GSHI, PRM, 41/3

According to our promise I am sending you the draft of the agreement presented today by M. Maisky with my observations.

[1] See Note No. 100.

I revert to the original idea of an agreement consisting of four principal points and I suppress the introduction. I have added a sentence to paragraph I, in order to make it absolutely clear that we are returning to the status quo before the war. Therefore also I have consequently suppressed the first paragraph of the Protocol.

I hope to have your full support for this change, so much the more as at present there is not a scrap of Polish territory in Soviet hands.

I cannot accept the necessity to obtain the Soviet agreement to the nomination of a Commander of the Polish Fighting Forces to be formed in the USSR, because it would infringe the sovereignty of the Polish Army. I suggest instead that at a later date a special convention be drawn between the Polish and the Soviet Governments to deal with all military details.

I have also eliminated the word 'reciprocal' in the paragraph concerning the claims inasmuch as there is no question of any damage having been done by the Poles to Russian property, whereas we have sustained tremendous losses in Russian occupied Poland.

Finally, the most important question of the Poles detained on Soviet territory, a question which impresses so heavily the imagination of the masses, must not be settled by a unilateral Soviet Declaration. I therefore consider it necessary to include it as a paragraph in the Protocol.

By confining myself to those minimal changes of the draft submitted by M. Maisky, I wish to help as much as I can to arrive at a rapid conclusion of our agreement with the Soviets, trusting that at the same time a Protocol will be signed by H.M. Government guaranteeing once more the integrity of the Polish territory, as proposed today by M. Zaleski.

Draft Agreement

The Government of the USSR and the Government of the Polish Republic have concluded the present Agreement and declare as follows:

1/ The Soviet Government recognizes the Treaties concerning Poland which were concluded between the USSR and Germany in 1939 as invalid, and recognizes the legal status of the frontiers between the USSR and the Polish Republic as it had existed in July 1939. The Polish Government declares that Poland is not bound by any Treaty Agreement or Declaration with a Third Power directed against the Soviet Union.

2/ The diplomatic relations between the Government of the USSR and the Government of the Polish Republic to be immediately restored and the exchange of Ambassadors effected.

3/ The two Governments mutually undertake to render each other assistance and support of all kinds in the present war against Hitlerite Germany.

4/ The Government of the USSR declares its agreement with the formation on the territory of the USSR of a Polish Army, its Commander to be appointed by the Government of the Polish Republic. The Polish Army on the territory of the USSR will operate under the direction of the High Military Command of the USSR. A special Agreement will settle the details of the organization and utilization of this Army.

The present Agreement comes into force immediately after its signature and is not subject to ratification.

The present Agreement is drawn up in two copies, each of them in the Russian and Polish languages. Both texts have equal force.

Draft Protocol

1 / All practical questions concerning the release of the Polish subjects who are now detained on the territory of the USSR will be considered in a positive spirit after the restoration of diplomatic relations between the USSR and Poland.

2 / The various claims of a public, as well as of a private, nature will be considered in the subsequent negotiations between the two Governments.

No. 101

Suggested draft of a British note to Poland guaranteeing Polish frontiers submitted by Minister Zaleski to Mr. Eden

London, July 17, 1941   GSHI, A.11. 49/Sow./1

Le Gouvernement Britannique, ayant reconnu les frontières occidentales de la Pologne par le Traité de Versailles et les actes y consécutifs, et les frontières orientales par la décision de la Conférence des Ambassadeurs en date du 23 mars 1923,

considérant comme inexistant tous les faits accomplis ou qui seraient accomplis au détriment de la Pologne à la suite de l'agression allemande du 1-er septembre 1939, et

prenant formellement acte des protestations du Gouvernement Polonais contre ces faits accomplis en date du 30 septembre 1939,[1] 21 octobre 1939,[2] 27 octobre 1939,[3] 25 juillet 1940,[4] 16 octobre 1940, a l'honneur d'informer le Gouvernement Polonais qu'il considère comme nuls et non-avenus tous les accords et actes internationaux intervenus ou qui interviendraient à la faveur de l'agression allemande contre la Pologne et préjudiciables aux droits polonais tels qu'ils ont existé au 31 août 1939.

Le Gouvernement Britannique supporte et continuera de supporter le Gouvernement Polonais en tant que seul représentant légitime de toutes les provinces qui composaient l'État Polonais avant l'agression allemande.

[1] See doc. No. 57.   [2] See doc. No. 64.   [3] See doc. No. 65.   [4] See doc. No. 77.

No. 102

Draft of a note sent by Mr. Eden to Minister Zaleski, stating the resolve of the British Government not to recognize territorial changes during the war

London, July 18, 1941   GSHI, A.11. 49/Sow./1

On the occasion of the signature of the Polish-Soviet Agreement of today's date, I desire to take the opportunity of informing you that, in conformity with the provisions of the Anglo-Polish Agreement of August 25th, 1939,[1] His Majesty's Government in the United Kingdom have entered into no undertakings towards the USSR which affect the relations between that country and Poland. I also desire to assure you that, as has been publicly stated by the Prime Minister, His Majesty's Government do not propose to recognize any territorial changes which take place during the war unless they take place with the free consent and good will of the parties concerned.

[1] See appendix No. 5.

No. 103

Letter from General Sikorski to Minister Zaleski asking him to induce the United States Government to issue a declaration on the integrity of Polish frontiers, in connection with the Polish-Soviet Agreement[1]

London, July 19, 1941   GSHI, A.11. 49/Sow./1
                                                                                 Transl. from Polish

I ask you to take the appropriate steps to the effect of inducing the United States Government to issue a declaration similar to that made by the British Government on the occasion of the signature of the Polish-Soviet Agreement. The American declaration may refer to the recognition of our frontiers in 1923.

At the same time, I ask you to inform the Czechoslovak Government of the impending signature as soon as the date of it has been definitely fixed.

[1] See Note No. 103.

No. 104

Polish amendments to the British suggestion of July 18, 1941 with personal letter from General Sikorski to Mr. Eden[1]

London, July 21, 1941   GSHI, PRM, 41/3

At this moment ended the meeting of my Cabinet and I have the greatest pleasure in informing you that after a very long and most difficult discussion my policy concerning the Treaty with the Soviet obtained full support. All the Polish Ministers unanimously accepted the draft of the Treaty provided that today's corrections be approved by the USSR Government. However, further changes would not be acceptable to us.

Enclosed I am returning to you the draft of your note with a small change: the insertion of one phrase as underlined and the omission of the final words. I hope that you will see your way in meeting our wishes which would give a great moral satisfaction to the Polish public opinion.

Our answer will follow more or less the lines of the note I have shown you this morning.

If the USSR Government agrees to the present draft of the Treaty I think

[1] See Note No. 104.

that, as you suggested the signing of it by M. Zaleski and M. Maisky may take place in the Foreign Office and, if possible, in the presence of the Prime Minister, you and myself.

I realize all the tremendous troubles you had in all those negotiations and I thank you from the bottom of my heart for your subtle help and your kind and loyal assistance.

Enclosure

On the occasion of the signature of the Polish-Soviet Agreement of today's date, which Agreement re-establishes relations between Poland and the USSR as they existed before July 1939, I desire to take the opportunity of informing you, that, in conformity with the provisions of the Anglo-Polish Agreement of August 25th 1939, His Majesty's Government in the United Kingdom have entered into no undertakings towards the USSR which affect the relations between that country and Poland. I also desire to assure you that His Majesty's Government do not propose to recognize any territorial changes which took place during the war.

No. 105

Draft of the agreement between Poland and the USSR as submitted to Moscow by Ambassador Maisky[1]

London, July 21, 1941   GSHI, PRM, 41/1

The Government of the Polish Republic and the Government of the USSR have concluded the present agreement and declare as follows:

1 / The Government of the USSR recognizes the treaties concerning territorial changes in Poland which were concluded by the USSR since July 1939 as invalid. The Government of the Polish Republic declares that Poland is not bound by any treaty, agreement or declaration with a third Power directed against the Soviet Union.

2 / Diplomatic relations between the Government of the Polish Republic and the Government of the USSR are to be immediately restored and the exchange of Ambassadors effected.

3 / The two Governments mutually undertake to render each other assistance and support of all kinds in the present war against Hitlerite Germany.

4 / The Government of the USSR declares its agreement with the formation on the territory of the USSR of a Polish Army, its Commander to be appointed by the Government of the Polish Republic. The Polish army on the territory of the USSR will operate under the direction of the High Military Command of the USSR. A special agreement will settle the details of the command, organization and utilization of this army.

The present agreement comes into force immediately after its signature and is not subject to ratification.

The present Agreement is drawn up in two copies, each of them in the Polish and Russian languages. Both texts have equal force.

[1] See Note No. 105.

140

Protocol

1/ All practical questions concerning the release of the Polish citizens who are now detained on the territory of the USSR will be considered and settled in a positive spirit after the restoration of diplomatic relations between Poland and the USSR.

2/ The present Protocol comes into force simultaneously with the Agreement of the . . . July, 1941.

Secret Protocol

1/ The various claims of a public, as well as of a private nature will be considered in the subsequent negotiations between the two Governments.

2/ The present Protocol comes into force simultaneously with the agreement of the . . . July, 1941.

No. 106

Polish-Soviet agreement annulling the Soviet-German treaties of 1939 relating to Poland, restoring mutual diplomatic relations, undertaking mutual aid and support in the present war and formation of a Polish Army on the territory of the USSR. Additional Protocol on an amnesty to be granted to all Polish citizens on the territory of the USSR deprived of their freedom[1]

London, July 30, 1941   GSHI, A.11. 49/Sow./1

The Government of the Republic of Poland and the Government of the Union of Soviet Socialist Republics have concluded the present Agreement and decided as follows:

1. The Government of the Union of Soviet Socialist Republics recognizes that the Soviet-German treaties of 1939 relative to territorial changes in Poland have lost their validity. The Government of the Republic of Poland declares that Poland is not bound by any Agreement with any third State directed against the USSR.

2. Diplomatic relations will be restored between the two Governments upon the signature of this Agreement and an exchange of ambassadors will follow immediately.

3. The two Governments mutually undertake to render one another aid and support of all kinds in the present war against Hitlerite Germany.

4. The Government of the Union of Soviet Socialist Republics expresses its consent to the formation on the territory of the Union of Soviet Socialist Republics of a Polish Army under a commander appointed by the Government of the Republic of Poland, in agreement with the Government of the Union of Soviet Socialist Republics. The Polish Army on the territory of the Union of Soviet Socialist Republics will be subordinated in operational matters to the Supreme Command of the USSR on which there will be a representative of the Polish Army. All details as to command, organization and employment of this force will be settled in a subsequent Agreement.

5. This Agreement will come into force immediately upon its signature

[1] See Note No. 106.

and without ratification. The present Agreement is drawn up in two copies, each of them in the Russian and Polish languages. Both texts have equal force.

Secret Protocol

1. Various claims both of public and private nature will be dealt with in the course of further negotiations between the two governments.

2. This protocol enters into force simultaneously with the Agreement of 30th July 1941.

Protocol

1. As soon as diplomatic relations are re-established the Government of the Union of Soviet Socialist Republics will grant amnesty to all Polish citizens who are at present deprived of their freedom on the territory of the USSR either as prisoners of war or on other adequate grounds.

2. The present Protocol comes into force simultaneously with the Agreement of July 30, 1941.

Władysław Sikorski   I. Maisky

No. 107

Note issued by the Foreign Office in London on non-recognition of any territorial changes in Poland since August, 1939

London, July 30, 1941   GSHI, PRM, 41/3

1. An agreement between the Republic of Poland and the Soviet Union was signed in the Secretary of State's room at the Foreign Office on July 30. General Sikorski, Polish Prime Minister, signed for Poland; M. Maisky, Soviet Ambassador, signed for the Soviet Union. Mr. Churchill and Mr. Eden were present.

2. The agreement is being published.

3. After the signature of the agreement, Mr. Eden handed to General Sikorski an official Note in the following terms:

'On the occasion of the signature of the Polish-Soviet Agreement of today, I desire to take this opportunity of informing you that in conformity with the provision of the agreement of mutual assistance between the United Kingdom and Poland of the 25th of August 1939, His Majesty's Government in the United Kingdom have entered into no undertakings towards the Union of Socialist Soviet Republics which affect the relations between that country and Poland. I also desire to assure you that His Majesty's Government do not recognize any territorial changes which have been effected in Poland since August 1939.'

General Sikorski handed to Mr. Eden the following reply:

'The Polish Government take note of your letter dated July 30 and desire to express sincere satisfaction at the statement that His Majesty's Government in the United Kingdom do not recognize any territorial changes which have been effected in Poland since August 1939. This corresponds with the view of the Polish Government which, as they have previously informed His Majesty's Government, have never recognized any territorial changes effected in Poland since the outbreak of the war.'

No. 108

Statement made in the House of Commons by Mr. Eden concerning the Polish-Soviet Agreement

London, July 30, 1941   H.C.Deb., 373/1502–1504

The Secretary of State for Foreign Affairs [Mr. Eden]: [. . .]. I am very glad to be able to inform the House that an Agreement between the Soviet Union and Poland was signed at the Foreign Office this afternoon. Under that Agreement the Soviet Government recognize that the Soviet-German Treaties of 1939 as to the territorial changes in Poland have lost their validity, while the Polish Government declare that Poland is not bound by any agreement with a third party directed against the Soviet Union. Diplomatic relations will be restored at once and Ambassadors exchanged. The two Governments agree to render each other support of all kinds in the war against Hitlerite Germany. The Soviet Government agree to the formation of a Polish Army on Soviet territory. This Polish Army will be subordinated, in an operational sense, to the supreme command of the Soviet Union. Attached to the Agreement is a Protocol by which the Soviet Government grant an amnesty to all Polish citizens now detained on Soviet territory, either as prisoners of war or on other grounds, as from the resumption of diplomatic relations. Here, perhaps, I may say that arrangements for immediate resumption are being made. [. . .].

I want to say a word in connection with the Note which I handed to General Sikorski. It is stated in paragraph I of the Soviet-Polish Agreement that the Soviet Government recognize the Soviet-German Treaties of 1939 concerning territorial changes in Poland, as having lost their validity. The attitude of His Majesty's Government in these matters was stated in general terms by my right hon. Friend the Prime Minister in the House of Commons on September 5, 1940, when he said that His Majesty's Government did not propose to recognize any territorial changes which took place during the war, unless they took place with the free consent and good will of the parties concerned. This holds good with the territorial changes which have been effected in Poland since August, 1939, and I informed the Polish Government accordingly in my official Note. [. . .]

Mr. Noel-Baker [Lab.]: May I respectfully congratulate the Foreign Secretary on the personal service he has rendered in helping to negotiate this very notable Agreement? Does he think it appropriate and desirable to express to the Governments of our two Allies the appreciation of the Members of this House of the statesmanship and generosity they have both shown?

Captain McEwen [Cons.]: Am I right in assuming that as a result of this Agreement, no guarantee of frontiers in Eastern Europe will be undertaken by His Majesty's Government?

Mr. Eden: Yes Sir. The exchange of Notes which I have just read to the House does not involve any guarantee of frontiers by His Majesty's Government. [. . .]

Mr. Mander [Lab.]: On the question of the guarantee of frontiers, surely the existing guarantees to Poland hold good?

Mr. Eden: There is, as I have said, no guarantee of frontiers.

No. 109

Broadcast by General Sikorski to Poland, in connection with the Polish-Soviet Agreement[1]

London, July 31, 1941   GSHI, A.XII. 30/18. 6

[. . .]. Now that this act [September 28th, 1939][2] has been wiped out, we stand on the threshold of a new era in Polish-Russian relations.

The present agreement only provisionally regulates disputes which have mutually divided us for centuries. But it does not permit even of the suggestion that the 1939 frontiers of the Polish State could ever be in question. It does not allow of any idea that Poland has resigned anything. It restores normal conditions between the two States and recognizes equal reciprocity of assistance. It permits us to form Polish military units from the Polish prisoners of war who hitherto have been languishing in Russia, and yearning for the fight for Poland; it accepts a representative of the Polish Commander in Chief in Russian supreme command, thus giving us the possibility of influencing the course of operations on a world scale. It restores to freedom all Polish citizens in restraint for any pretext on Russian territory, and allows our representative in Moscow to come to the aid of the hundreds of thousands of exiles now suffering throughout the enormous expanses of Russia. In this regard we count on the effective aid of American Polonia. We shall occupy ourselves with the question of restoration of the material damage caused by the war when conditions permit of this.

There is no analogy whatever between the present day and the 1914 war. Today a mortal struggle is being waged for the existence not merely of the Polish State, but of the nation itself. Hitler is consequentially carrying out 'Mein Kampf'. And in 'Mein Kampf' there is a plan for driving the Poles into Siberia. In the event of the defeat and partitioning of Russia, this plan will be carried out. For that matter Herr Greiser foretold as much a week or two ago, when he threatened that 'the Poles will disappear as a nation'.

And so, when the fire of war, continually fed by the sincerest and noblest of Polish blood, is continuing in our country, when Germany in her march eastward is mercilessly trampling down the neighbouring peoples, the Polish Government stands together with Russia, increasing the union of forces against Germany, in the struggle against the plague of invasions and conquests.

Germany always has been, is today, and will be the irreconcilable enemy of Poland. And so more than once in history we have been confronted with

[1] See Note No. 109.   [2] See doc. No. 52.

144

the question: with Germany or with Russia? In 1925 I, as Minister for War, and my co-workers of that time, made our choice. Namely, we decided when working out a plan of defence, that we would seek a relaxation of tension in the East, and concentrate all our efforts on the West. We foresaw that a German aggression would be unavoidable sooner or later. This was after Hindenburg had been elected Reich President, which confirmed us in the conviction that Poland and the whole world was threatened with the unquestionable vengeance of Germany for Versailles. I am sorry that the Government which came later rejected this system of defence, which, as present events testify, was the sole sound one for Poland. But I simultaneously must state that at the crucial moment that Government also, in accordance with the opinion of the country, rejected the secret temptations of the Germans, who wanted to bring Poland into a crusade against Soviet Russia jointly with the Reich. The Nation will reject all idea of any kind of co-operation with Germany. But, led by an infallible instinct, it realizes that in its geographical situation it needs an understanding with one of its great neighbours, in order to resist the other effectively. [. . .].

No. 110

Decree by the Presidium of the Supreme Council of the USSR granting amnesty to Polish citizens deprived of their freedom on the territory of the USSR

Moscow, August 12, 1941   GSHI, A.11. 49/Sow./3
                                            Transl. from Russian: Pol.-Sov.R., No. 33

An amnesty is granted to all Polish citizens on Soviet territory at present deprived of their freedom as prisoners of war or on other adequate grounds.

Chairman of the Presidium of the Supreme
Council of the USSR.
M. Kalinin.
Secretary of the Presidium of the Supreme
Council of the USSR.
A. Gorkin.

No. 111

Extracts from a conversation between Chargé d'Affaires Retinger and Deputy Commissar Vyshinsky on the fulfilment of the Polish-Soviet Agreement of July 30, 1941

Moscow, August 14, 1941   GSHI, PRM, 41/4
                                            Transl. from Polish

In reply to Dr. Retinger's statement Deputy Commissar Vyshinsky emphasized the importance the Soviet Government attached to the Treaty of 30th July. They consider it to be an epoch-making event of historical importance. He affirmed that his Government would endeavour not only to carry on the common war against Hitlerite Germany, but also to establish long-term co-operation between the two sister nations. The Soviet Union was not a monolithic nationalist State, on the contrary, the country was composed of many nations. Therefore, co-operation with the Polish nation could be secured and developed. All nationalities of the Union approved of it. [. . .]. Deputy Commissar Vyshinsky said that, although the Soviet Government were awaiting the arrival of the Polish Ambassador, for the present they noted with satisfaction Dr. Retinger's declaration that the Polish Government was anxious to establish close Polish-Soviet collaboration and that all Poles, whichever province they inhabited, shared that desire. The Soviet Government would support on a large scale all welfare action undertaken by the Polish authorities for the Polish population, and their good will had already been manifested by:

1 / The proclaiming of an amnesty for all Poles living on Soviet territory, in accordance with the stipulations of the Treaty.

2 / The promulgation by the Supreme Council of the USSR of a series of measures and decisions, among others, those with a view to facilitate the organization of the Polish Armed Forces. In connection with the opening of that new era in Polish-Soviet relations, a number of new problems were arising and they should be settled in close co-operation and understanding between the Polish Embassy and the Soviet authorities. In the near future it would be necessary to a/ register the Polish population in the USSR; b/ classify that population and select the group fit for military duties; c/ operate Medical Boards, which the Polish Military Authorities should establish forthwith with the participation of a Soviet representative on them.

Dr. Retinger made a statement to the effect that the Polish Government wished all people unfit for military service to take part in the war effort and, according to their qualifications, work in the war industry. To that Deputy Commissar Vyshinsky replied that the Central Government Organs had already issued instructions to local authorities [Ispolnitelnye Komitety] to ensure employment and accommodation for Poles freed by the amnesty, in particular for women and children. The Soviet authorities were anxious that the thousands of Poles residing in the USSR should work and live in adequate conditions and feel at home in the Union; that those fit to fight should fight and those who wished to work should work. Novikov, the Head of the IV Department of the Narkomindel, was the man to whom the Soviet Government entrusted all those matters relating to Poles in USSR. He should be contacted for settlement of various individual problems.

To Dr. Retinger's request that apart from the capital problems, i.e. army and welfare for Poles, certain secondary, but equally important, questions should also be settled, e.g. the starting of a Polish newspaper and of Polish broadcasts, if possible by allotting one of the broadcasting stations to the exclusive use of Poles, Commissar Vyshinsky replied that, although he could not discuss details, he was certain that the Soviet Government would take a positive view of these problems. They approved of every aspect of collaboration, on the largest scale and in all fields: in the common struggle against Hitler's Germany all kinds of weapons should be used, including propaganda.

No. 112

Polish-Soviet Military Agreement[1]

Moscow, August 14, 1941
GSHI, A.XII. 22/30.1
Transl. from Polish: Pol.-Sov.R., No. 42

1. The military agreement derives naturally from the political agreement of July 30, 1941.

2. A Polish army will be organized in the shortest possible time on the territory of the USSR, wherefore:

   a) it will form part of the armed forces of the sovereign Republic of Poland,

   b) the soldiers of this army will take the oath of allegiance to the Republic of Poland,

   c) it will be destined with the Armed Forces of the USSR and other Allied States for the common fight against Germany,

   d) after the end of the war, it will return to Poland,

   e) during the entire period of common operations, it will be subordinated operationally to the High Command of the USSR. In respect of organization and personnel it will remain under the authority of the Commander-in-Chief of the Polish Armed Forces, who will co-ordinate the orders and regulations concerning organization and personnel with the High Command of the USSR through the Commander of the Polish Army on the territory of the USSR.

3. The Commander of the Polish Army on the territory of the USSR will be appointed by the Commander-in-Chief of the Polish Armed Forces; the candidate for this appointment to be approved by the Government of the USSR.

4. The Polish Army on the territory of the USSR will consist of units of land forces only. Their strength and number will depend on manpower, equipment and supplies available.

5. Conscripts and volunteers, having previously served in the Polish Air Force and Navy, will be sent to Great Britain to complement the establishments of the respective Polish services already existing there.

6. The formation of Polish units will be carried out in localities indicated by the High Command of the USSR. Officers and other ranks will be called from among Polish citizens on the territory of the USSR by conscription and voluntary enlistment. Draft boards will be established with the participation of USSR authorities in localities indicated by them.

7. Polish units will be moved to the front only after they are fully ready for action. In principle they will operate in groups not smaller than divisions and will be used in accordance with the operational plans of the High Command of the USSR.

8. All soldiers of the Polish Army on the territory of the USSR will be subject to Polish military laws and decrees.

Polish military courts will be established in the units for dealing with

[1] See Note No. 112.

military offences and crimes against the establishment, the safety, the routine or the discipline of the Polish Army.

For crimes against the State, soldiers of the Polish Army on the territory of the USSR will be answerable to the military courts of the USSR.

9. The organization and war equipment of the Polish units will as far as possible correspond to the standards established for the Polish Army in Great Britain.

The colours and insignia of the various services and military ranks will correspond exactly to those established for the Polish Army in Great Britain.

10. The pay, rations, maintenance and other material problems will be in accordance with regulations of the USSR.

11. The sick and wounded soldiers of the Polish Army will receive treatment in hospitals and sanatoria on an equal basis with the soldiers of the USSR and be entitled to pensions and allowances.

12. Armament, equipment, uniforms, motor transport, etc. will be provided as far as possible by

a) the Government of the USSR from their own resources,

b) the Polish Government from supplies granted on the basis of the Lend-Lease Act (an Act to promote the defence of the United States, approved March 11, 1941).

In this case, the Government of the USSR will extend all possible transportation facilities.

13. Expenditures connected with the organization, equipment and maintenance of the Polish Army on the territory of the USSR will be met from credits provided by the Government of the USSR, to be refunded by the Polish Government after the end of the war.

This problem will be dealt with in a separate financial agreement.

14. Liaison will be established by

1) a Polish Military Mission attached to the High Command of the USSR,

2) a Soviet Military Mission attached to the Polish High Command in London.

Liaison officers attached to other commands will be appointed by mutual agreement.

15. All matters and details not covered by this agreement will be settled directly between the High Command of the Polish Army on the territory of the USSR and the corresponding authorities of the USSR.

16. This agreement is made in two copies, in the Polish and Russian languages, both texts are equally valid.

Plenipotentiary of the Polish High Command.	Plenipotentiary of the High Command of the USSR.
Szyszko-Bohusz, Brigadier-General.	A. Vassilevsky, Major-General.

No. 113

Protocol No. 1 of the Polish-Soviet military conference

Moscow, August 16, 1941   GSHI, A.XII. 30/18.4

Transl. from Russian

Present:

On behalf of the Command of the Red Army: Maj.-Gen. of Armoured Forces—Panfilov, Colonel—Yevstigneyev.

On behalf of the Polish Command: Lieut.-Gen.—Anders, Maj.-Gen.—Szyszko-Bohusz.

After greeting each other Gen. Panfilov and Gen. Anders considered practical problems.

Gen. Panfilov proposed that the following questions be discussed:

1. Principles of forming the army,
2. What is to be formed and its size,
3. Armament, equipment, provisions, finances, quarters, cultural and educational services and several other questions.

Gen. Anders: Will you please define the total numbers on which we can count in forming the army. Will you also let me have a list of officers and tell me where they are to be found.

Gen. Panfilov: According to our data the effectives of the former Polish Army are concentrated in three principal points:

1) Griazovets Camp in the Vologda region (about 1000 officers);
2) Camps at Suzdal and Yuzhev in the Ivanovo-Vosnesensk region (up to 10,000 persons, other ranks);
3) Starobielsk Camp (up to 10,000 other ranks).

Besides this there is a certain number of Polish citizens in Siberia and in the Urals. Their numbers will be ascertained later.

Gen. Anders: I think that out of this number it will be possible to form two infantry divisions of the light type, about 7 to 8 thousand each, and one Base Camp to make good eventual losses our units would suffer at the front line.

Gen. Panfilov: We think it more appropriate to create at first one division, since however you are thinking of creating two divisions we shall consider the matter and will put it up for decision to the General Staff.

What are your ideas concerning the equipment and the armaments of the army?

Gen. Szyszko-Bohusz: Uniforms and equipment for two divisions are already ordered in Britain and in America and should be supplied soon. We have been already informed about this by Gen. Sikorski. Where arms are concerned we should like to ask for your assistance (rifles, automatic weapons).

Gen. Anders: As regards the call up my personal view is that those should be called up who were mobilized for the Polish Army in 1939. Volunteers should be accepted who did not serve in the army.

Gen. Panfilov: In the camps I have previously mentioned Call Up Commissions should be formed consisting of representatives of the Polish Command, of the Red Army, of the NKVD and of the Medical Corps.

Besides this I should like to know your views on the question of our political objections concerning some officers.

Gen. Anders: I am in complete agreement with this. Should there be people like that amongst them then let us have proofs and we shall remove them ourselves. They will be removed to the Base Camp where a thorough investigation will take place.

Gen. Panfilov: Where Polish citizens who are in [labour] camps are concerned we shall issue instructions to all the Regional Military Commissariats, and we shall jointly consider their applications.

Gen. Anders: I agree.

Gen. Szyszko-Bohusz: We also want your agreement to the creation of a specialized unit for appropriate duties.

Gen. Panfilov: We shall consider this question separately.

Gen. Anders: Can the Poles serving in the Red Army be returned?

Gen. Panfilov: I think this will be possible.

Gen. Anders: Where will be the areas of formation [of the army]?

Gen. Panfilov: Near Orenburg and Saratov. What is your decision concerning financial questions?

Gen. Anders: Just the same as in the Red Army. This goes also for provisioning. I would like to be supplied with establishments of a Red Army division and in order to get acquainted with infantry arms I wish to ask for instructors to be assigned to us.

Gen. Szyszko-Bohusz: Is it possible to receive something on account in order to meet the first expenses?

Gen. Panfilov: We shall provide money and the instructors.

Gen. Anders: I should also like to have your agreement on the question of replacing men in administrative positions with women since we shall need more soldiers at the front line.

Could you also inform me about the effectives of cultural and educational institutions of the Red Army?

Gen. Panfilov: We shall consider the question of women when discussing effectives. Red Army cultural and educational institutions consist of: a club, publication of papers, a cinema, etc.

Gen. Anders: We have one rather delicate question. It is the question of chaplains. We want to have chaplains in our units since for us this is a matter of great importance.

Gen. Panfilov: There will be no objections on our part.

Gen. Anders: I should like to have a list of officers by name very soon, and I should like to have opportunity to see some of them.

I would also like released officers to be directed as soon as possible to the areas where the army is being formed.

Gen. Panfilov: Good. We shall meet again tomorrow and we shall consider the draft of the order for the Call Up Commissions so as to examine it and to sign it jointly. Besides this, you will prepare an order concerning call up which you will sign yourself.

Gen. Anders: Will you please let it be generally known, through the press and the wireless, that I have been nominated Commander of the (Polish) Army and about the formation of the Polish Forces?

Gen. Panfilov: This question will be considered separately.

With this the conversation was concluded.

(signatures) Maj.-Gen. of Armoured Forces—Panfilov, Colonel—Yevstigneyev, Lieut.-Gen.—Anders, Maj.-Gen.—Szyszko-Bohusz.

No. 114

Protocol No. 2 of the Polish-Soviet military conference

Moscow, August 19, 1941   GSHI, A.XII. 30/18.4
                                             Transl. from Russian

Present:

On behalf of the Red Army: Maj.-Gen. of Armoured Forces—Panfilov, Major of State Security—Zhukov.

On behalf of the Polish Command: Maj.-Gen.—Szyszko-Bohusz, Lieut.-Gen.—Anders.

On behalf of the Military Protocol: Colonel Yevstigneyev, Major Kolesov.

After the usual greetings Maj.-Gen. Panfilov acquainted the members of the Commission with the following:

1) The Red Army Command gives its approval to the request of the Polish Army Command for the formation of two divisions of infantry and one reserve regiment in the Soviet Union. The date of readiness for action: 1st October 1941. The divisions are to be formed according to the establishment of a light war-time division of the Red Army. (Ten thousand men each.) Reserve regiment to number 5 thousand.

2) The Red Army Command is assigning the required number of instructors in infantry arms, artillery and other specialists, to the Polish Army in order to acquaint it with the arms from the Red Army earmarked for the Polish Army.

The Commission entrusts to Gen. Anders the task of compiling a numerical list of the specialist instructors for the Polish Army. This list to be ready by the 23rd August 1941.

3) Wishing to placate the Polish Command the Red Army Command accedes to the request of the Polish Command that Poles in units of the Red Army be allowed to volunteer for transfer to the Polish Army. Also, the request of the Polish Command is being granted for an appropriate required number of specialists from the Red Army, necessary for the setting up of cultural and educational institutions (messes, libraries, printing shops, wireless and cinema units) for the newly formed divisions.

4) The Red Army Command assigns the necessary sum in Soviet currency to finance Polish units in the USSR. The commission empowers Gen. Anders to work out, before the 20th August 1941, the necessary requisition for the sum needed.

5) Major of State Security, Comrade Zhukov, hands over to Gen. Anders a list of Polish Army officers, containing 1,658 names.

151

Having heard about the decisions of the Red Army High Command Gen. Anders expresses his thanks for the rapid solution of the most pressing matters and submits the following suggestions:

1. That Polish regulations and instructions, in the possession of the Red Army High Command, be supplied to the Polish Command in an adequate number of copies.

2. That maps of the regions where Polish units in the USSR are being formed be also supplied.

3. That 2 or 3 typewriters with Polish alphabet and the necessary office stationery be also supplied.

The suggestions made by Gen. Anders are accepted by the representatives of the Red Army.

Next, the commission deals with the practical questions connected with the formation of the Polish Army in the Soviet Union.

After long deliberations the commission unanimously reached the following:

1. The Polish Army will be stationed in the following localities:

a. The Polish Army HQ—in Buzuluk
b. One infantry division and the Base Camp—in the camp at Tock
c. One infantry division–in the camp at Tatishchev.

2. The commission unanimously decided that in order to improve the co-ordination of the work of the Polish units with local authorities and with the Command of the Red Army one liaison officer from the Red Army and one liaison officer from the NKVD be assigned to each regiment and division in the process of formation.

3. Not later than by the 22nd or the 23rd August Call Up Commissions are to be set up consisting of representatives of:

a) The Polish Army,
b) the GHQ of the Red Army,
c) Organs of the NKVD,
d) the Medical Directorate of the Red Army.

They are to be sent to the following places:

1) One commission to the Griazovets camp of the NKVD,
2) One commission to the Yuzhev and the Suzdal camps of the NKVD,
3) One commission to the Starobielsk camp of the NKVD.

Membership of the commissions will be decided at the session of the Commission on the 21st August.

4. Gen. Anders is empowered to draft an Instruction for the Call Up Commissions, with the proviso that it will be presented to the Mixed Commission (for the Formation of the Polish Army in the USSR) on the 21st August 1941.

5. The Commission decides that in order to prepare accommodation for the draft units of the Polish formations, not later than by the 25th August 1941, groups of Polish commanders with the appropriate number of officers

and representatives of the Red Army GHQ and of the NKVD, together with work parties, composed of drafted Polish soldiers, will be sent out.

The draft units envisaged for the formation of Polish units will be directed to the regions of formation only when accommodation for them is ready.

6. The Commission recognizes as indispensable that an instruction be issued, through the Red Army, to the Regional Military Commissars telling the latter to make known to Polish citizens within their regions that a Polish Army is being formed and that they have the right to make applications to volunteer for it through the Regional Military Commissariats.

Applications from Polish volunteers received in this way are to be transmitted to the Polish GHQ in Buzuluk for final decision as to their acceptance into ranks of the Polish Army.

7. In connection with the unorganized arrival in Moscow of Polish volunteers the Commission recognizes the need to approach the Military Commander of Moscow for the assignation of some small accommodation to house temporarily detached Polish nationals and to ask that they be directed to the regions of formation as quickly as possible.

With this the sitting was adjourned.

The next sitting of the Commission was convened for the 21st August 1941, at 19.00 hours [. . .].

The original of the protocol was signed by: Major-Gen. of Armoured Forces—Panfilov, Major of State Security—Zhukov, Lieut.-Gen.—Anders, Maj.-Gen.—Szyszko-Bohusz.

No. 115

Note from Chargé d'Affaires Retinger to the People's Commissariat for Foreign Affairs on the application of the Polish-Soviet Agreement of July 30, 1941

Moscow, August 22, 1941 GSHI, PRM, 41/2
Transl. from Polish

I have the honour to submit hereby proposals concerning the temporary decrees made in order to speed up the realization of the decisions of the Additional Protocol to the Agreement between the Polish Government and the Government of the USSR of the 30th July 1941,[1] of article 4 of the same Agreement, as well as of the Decision of the Presidium of the Supreme Soviet of the USSR, of the 12th August 1941,[2] concerning the amnesty to Polish citizens deprived of their liberty on the territory of the Soviet Union.

1. Seeing that because of war conditions the local administrative organs are burdened with several extra duties, which in many cases may hinder the efficient and speedy carrying out of the above-mentioned legal acts, the Embassy of the Polish Republic desires to find, in co-operation with the competent Soviet authorities and in the name of their common interest, such forms of co-operation between administrative organs, the Embassy and the

---

[1] See doc. No. 106. [2] See doc. No. 110.

interested Polish nationals so as not to burden these organs with functions which can be carried out by social agencies.

With this in view I have the honour to ask Your Excellency to cause the issue of a telegraphic directive to local administrative authorities in localities and regions where Polish nationals reside that several (at least three) respectable and trustworthy Polish citizens, living in the given localities, notify the Polish Embassy in Moscow, by telegraph, of their surnames, Christian names, profession, and of the approximate number of their co-citizens. From these names the Embassy will pick, in each locality, or region, one 'homme de confiance' whose duty it will be to approach the Embassy and the local administrative authorities concerning matters affecting Polish nationals to represent with them the interests of the Polish nationals and to provide, as soon as possible, information concerning the numbers, the grouping according to professions, and the most urgent needs of the given Polish community, especially those of women with children, of old people, invalids, etc., and in particular of those who have no adequate means of subsistence.

I have the honour to ask Your Excellency to cause a directive to be issued making the press and the radio publish the above in order to facilitate and to speed up the local registration of Polish citizens after which their individual registration would follow.

2. In accordance with the decisions of the legal enactments mentioned at the outset I have the honour to ask Your Excellency to cause the immediate release from prisons and from places of forced labour of all Polish citizens and their transfer to the temporary assembly stations where they will be sorted out according to sex, age, physical and professional qualifications and whence they will be directed to military camps or to work in industry or on the land. Those unfit to work, especially women with children, juveniles, the old and the invalid, will be directed to localities with the required climatic and health conditions, in principle into the regions where there will be Polish military camps. Soviet authorities will ensure for this category of Polish citizens the appropriate living accommodation, adequate food supplies and their other indispensable needs. Agencies of the Polish Government and Polish Welfare organizations will for their part do what is in their power to come to help Polish citizens who need it, supplying them with clothes, footwear and medicines. The Polish Government, aware of the extent of the war effort of the Soviet Government, has already undertaken steps to secure the supply of a certain quantity of these articles from the United States and from Great Britain but because of transport difficulties they will not, in all probability, be at hand on Soviet territory before eight weeks.

Seeing the very difficult position of Poles being released I have the honour to ask that they be granted a single grant in money to enable them to meet their most urgent needs, as is the case with Polish military persons who are being freed.

3. Concerning persons employed at present in agriculture, in forestry, in industry and in mining and in all sorts of public works in the Soviet Union I have the honour to ask Your Excellency to cause the issuing, as soon as

possible, through the appropriate authorities, of strict directives in order that:

a) Polish citizens, physically unfit for the labour they have been directed to, be transferred to categories of lighter work, more suitable for them, and that persons not fit for work be treated in accordance with the appropriate proposals contained in § 2.

b) Their employment be exclusively in conformity with the norms applying to the local free citizens and that all the regulations concerning protection of labour enjoyed by Soviet citizens be applied in their case.

c) Their food rations be of the highest possible standard.

d) Polish citizens capable of military service be transferred without delay to Polish military camps.

e) Polish citizens, first of all women with children, in cases of well motivated wishes, be allowed to change their place of residence to the locality chosen by them.

4. In order to enable the agencies of the Polish Embassy in Moscow to ascertain the most urgent and the most important problems of the individual Polish communities I have the honour to ask Your Excellency to cause members to be appointed to mixed commissions, each of which would consist of a delegate appointed by the Embassy and of a delegate of the Soviet Government.

These commissions would have to tour at once the regions inhabited by Polish citizens (in particular the Moscow region, Kazakhstan, Novosibirsk and Arkhangelsk regions) and to present to their superiors reports on the condition and the needs of the individual communities, and, in so far as possible, to take part in the sorting out of Polish citizens, as per § 2 and 3. This sorting out should however be started without delay, without waiting for the arrival of the commission.

Because of the need to visit the most important communities before the onset of the autumn season I have the honour to ask Your Excellency to accept the date of 22nd August 1941 as the day of departure of these commissions and to cause the commissions to be assured of air transport. I also have the honour to ask that local authorities be instructed to give the commissions all help required, to inform them efficiently concerning Polish citizens, to provide them with means of local transportation and with accommodation for their work.

I am convinced that in the harmonious relations at present prevailing between the Polish and the Soviet Governments it will be easy to work out the details and to carry out speedily the release of Polish citizens once the general decrees are issued.

Having regard to the fundamental importance of the questions dealt with in the present note I have the honour to ask Your Excellency to enable me to discuss them with you in the nearest future, if possible, on the 25th of this month.

No. 116

Instruction of General Sikorski to Maj.-Gen. Bohusz-Szyszko to amend the tenor of the 2 and 7 paras of the Polish-Soviet Military Agreement of August 14, 1941

London, August 23, 1941   GSHI, A.XII. 22/30.1
                                                          Transl. from Polish

The draft of the Military Agreement presented to me by General Januszajtis differs in many essential points from the draft received by you, General, in London.

These are unacceptable:

1) A paragraph of point 2, imposing on the H.C. the duty of agreeing on all personal issues with the High Command of the USSR—such a ruling was to be accepted only as regards the appointment of the Commander of the Polish Forces on the territory of the USSR.

2) Point 7 does not provide the guarantee that the Polish Forces in the USSR would be used for operational purposes as a whole under Polish Command and the fact that the big units must not be broken up is insufficiently stressed.

[. . .]. Steps must be taken to obtain an additional declaration to this effect under the form of a bilateral protocol including at the same time a statement of the Soviet obligation of assistance to our recruiting boards.

No. 117

Note made by Minister Raczyński from a conversation between General Sikorski and Mr. Churchill on the conditions for creating a Polish Army in the USSR

London, August 23, 1941   GSHI, PRM, 39-b.
                                                          Transl. from Polish

[. . .]. 6) The discussion included Russia and future prospects of the possibility of the support of the Soviet resistance until the winter in order that next spring the USSR might resume her further struggle. [. . .]. With great determination General Sikorski expounded Poland's role in Eastern Europe to Churchill and Winant. He emphasized that it would be a great mistake if the Anglo-Saxon democracies were to underestimate this role, as we should act for them as experts and natural liaison agents in the affairs of Eastern Europe. Unfortunately, at present the opposite holds good. The Great Powers are beginning to act as if they recognized only Russia's role in this part of the world. The General was, and still is, in favour of a sincere understanding with Russia, but on quite different terms. He is for the support of Russia's resolute resistance. He mentioned that since 30th July Russia has been wooing Poland in a quite obvious manner. Ambassador Winant listened very attentively to these statements.

Analysing the present situation Mr. Churchill declared that Stalin's remaining in power was most advantageous for the Allies, to which we agreed. (Mr. Churchill declared that he believed in Soviet, Chinese, etc. 'big masses'). His words betrayed, however, the fear that the Soviet resistance might not last in the long run.

7) In connection with this problem he showed considerable interest in the question of the formation of Polish Forces in Russia. He expressed the hope that our divisions would be organized in places which would enable them to enter into contact with British ones, should any need arise (in the Caucasian area). He asked about their presumable strength but he did not enquire into their fighting value as he was obviously not worried about this point. General Sikorski expounded all the difficulties in organizing a Polish Army in the USSR (the dispersion of soldiers, immense spaces). He asserted that it was also our intention to form the Polish Forces in the proximity of the British ones. He mentioned, however, that the opposite trend existed on the Soviet side. In any case he would give General Anders instructions consistent with Mr. Churchill's point of view. [. . .].

No. 118

Pro-memoria of the People's Commissariat for Foreign Affairs in connection with the Note of Chargé d'Affaires Retinger, dated August 22, 1941

Moscow, August 28, 1941 GSHI, PRM, 41/2
Transl. from Russian

Referring to the Note of the Embassy of the Republic of Poland of the 22nd August[1] the People's Commissariat for Foreign Affairs states that pursuant to the Decree of the Praesidium of the Supreme Soviet of the USSR dated 12th August the following procedure is being applied to Polish citizens whether under arrest or having the status of prisoners of war on the territory of the USSR:

1. The discharge of Polish citizens from prisons has started. They receive railway or waterway tickets to a domicile chosen by them, and also 15 Roubles for every 24 hours as the cost of their maintenance during the journey.

2. All the discharged Polish citizens are given the chance of choosing a domicile wherever they wish, with the exception of some places.

3. All the discharged Polish citizens are given the chance, if they wish so, of remaining in the place in which they have been accommodated so far, and at the same time the Soviet authorities will help them in finding employment.

At the same time it is stated that the Soviet Government do not object to the proposal of the Embassy of the Republic of Poland for it to designate some persons of its trust in the areas inhabited by a considerable number of Polish citizens.

Neither is there any objection to the proposal of the Embassy of the Polish Republic to establish one or more mixed commissions from amongst the representatives of the Soviet authorities and of the Embassy of the PR in order to proceed to a registration of Polish citizens, their resettlement, and finding employment for them.

As regards other questions referred to in the aforesaid Note, they will be dealt with in future.

[1] See doc. No. 115.

No. 119

General Instructions for the Ambassador of the Republic of Poland in the USSR

London, August 28, 1941 GSHI, A.11. 49/Sow./6
Transl. from Polish

Your action in the USSR must be based on our agreement with that country signed on 30th July 1941, by which the state of war between the two countries, started by the Soviet aggression against Poland on 17th September 1939, was brought to an end. The object of our policy towards the USSR must be, in the first instance, to enforce the rights of the Polish Republic to the territories extending to the line laid down by the Treaty of Riga of 1921,[1] and further, to prevent any encroachment on the independence of our policy, in all respects—foreign and domestic affairs, national minorities, economic life—within the territories which the Polish Republic will recover in future. While co-operating with the Government of the Soviet Union you should have those objects in view.

The Embassy should endeavour to rebuild the Polish-Soviet relations which were severed nearly two years ago. This will find its expression in the re-establishment of diplomatic and consular relations. Several important items have not been referred to in the aforesaid agreement, such as the return of the material goods and assets which were taken away from Poland (funds confiscated of State and municipal institutions, banks and private enterprises, also machines, tools, raw material, agricultural implements, livestock, etc.), and cultural assets (libraries, museums, works of art, laboratories. etc.) In spite of the lack of a provision on these matters you should keep these problems in mind.

It is difficult to say now whether this question will become topical during the war or later, after its end, but it is advisable to gather all the relevant data and information now, in order to facilitate to the Polish Government the future enforcement of a claim to these assets, and the request that they be returned to Poland.

After your arrival in the USSR you will have to deal directly with the following issues.

Organization of the Army

As it appears from the report published on 13th September 1940 in the 'Krasnaya Zvezda' (Red Star), the number of Polish servicemen detained in the Soviet prisoner-of-war camps is the following: 10 generals, 52 colonels, 72 lieutenant-colonels, 5,131 regular army officers, 4,096 officers of army reserve, 181,223 other ranks. Similar figures were stated by Premier Molotov in his speech delivered at the Supreme Soviet at the end of October 1939. It is true that Ambassador Maisky declared that there were only 20,000 prisoners-of-war on Soviet territory, but it can be assumed that the actual figure is much higher.

The Embassy has to co-operate with the Polish Military Mission for the

[1] See doc. No. 3.

creation of a Polish Army in the USSR. The Government is aware that the formation of a Polish Army in the USSR will meet with many serious obstacles. It is to be feared that Polish soldiers and officers who have been taken prisoners by Soviet troops and then detained in Soviet camps will not nurture friendly feelings towards their former enemies. These servicemen, after having stayed in camps for such a long time, will, probably, not be in a good physical condition. Physical exhaustion and moral depression, as well as nostalgia, may hamper the formation of a Polish army in the Soviet Union. Jointly with the Military Mission and the Army Command the Embassy is to do everything possible to raise the morale of the former prisoners of war, and to convince them of the necessity of serving their country. You should spare no effort, Mr. Ambassador, to facilitate the hard task of the Military Mission and of the Command of the Polish forces in the East, both in their relations with the Soviet authorities, and with Polish citizens staying in the Soviet Union.

One must keep in mind that the régime of the Soviet Union is based on the Communist doctrine, uniform for all its territories. This doctrine permeates all the cells of Soviet social life. The Soviet army is not only an instrument of State authority, but also of the Communist party. This principle has been ascertained many times in pre-war Soviet Russia, and there is no reason to assume that the present Soviet political leaders have any propensity to forswear it. It is true that, in consideration of Anglo-American public opinion and of the need for assistance from these two countries, the slogans of a world revolution are not being raised for the time being, but any temporary success on the war front could bring about the revival of such slogans, and their triumph over the patriotic slogans launched at present in the Soviet army.

Everything possible must be done to the effect of protecting the Polish troops formed on Soviet territory from the influence of Soviet propaganda, above all by using adequate patriotic propaganda in which all the members of the Embassy should take part.

Should the difficulties arising in connection with the formation of Polish forces in the USSR turn out to be insuperable, an evacuation of our soldiers to Near East countries should be envisaged, where new units of the Polish army could be formed at the side of the British army. A plan for such an evacuation should be prepared beforehand by the Military Mission in agreement with the Embassy, choosing the following routes: the Volga, as far as Astrakhan, from thence to Persia, Syria and Palestine, and also across the Caucasus in the same direction or through Afghanistan to India.

Organization of social assistance to Polish citizens in the USSR

As regards the question of assistance on the part of the Embassy to Polish citizens in the USSR, you must hold the position that such assistance extends to all persons who possessed Polish citizenship on 16th September 1939. Any other interpretation is quite inadmissible for us if only because it would mean the acceptance of a well-known Soviet interpretation of the agreement of

159

30th July 1941. Should you meet, on the Soviet part, with a refusal to carry out our interpretation in practice, in connection with the questions of release, welfare and evacuation, you must not enter into a compromise on this issue until you have received new instructions from the Polish Government. This question may become a fundamental problem in the establishment of good Polish-Soviet relations.

You should try to obtain, in the first instance, the release from prison and camps of all Polish citizens who have been imprisoned or detained on political, social, national and religious grounds, and also request the discharge from the Soviet army and the transfer to new Polish units of all officers and other ranks, who were called up by the Soviet Government in the eastern provinces of Poland after the date of 17th September 1939.

The protection of Polish citizens should be ensured by consular posts. You have to ask for the immediate restoration of the Polish-Soviet Consular Convention of 18th July 1924,[2] which constituted the basis of the functioning of the Polish Republic's consular posts in the Soviet Union. This convention has many important advantages because it guarantees the diplomatic immunity of the members of the consular staff: consuls, vice-consuls and consular attachés.

Considering far-reaching changes due to the war, and also the fact that a great number of deportees were sent to Asiatic Russia, the location of consular posts and their number should depend on these circumstances and, above all, on the number of Polish citizens living in a given area, and the main communication roads along which Polish citizens could be evacuated if need arises. One should have in view two routes: 1) The first, along the Volga river with road-junctions at Kazan and Astrakhan, 2) the second, in the east, along the Trans-Siberian railway with Omsk, Irkutsk and Vladivostok as main points. It would also be desirable to have some supporting bases in the Caucasus, Tiflis and Baku, as well as in Tashkent, whence Polish citizens might be directed to Persia, Afghanistan and India.

The protection of and assistance to Polish citizens should be concentrated in the hands of the head of the consular department of the Embassy. It may be a Consul General, or Head of the Consular Department of the Embassy, with the title of Counsellor to the Embassy, according to Polish consular traditions in the Soviet Union. He should have his office in the same locality in which the Embassy and the central Soviet authorities are residing.

Consulates, or respectively consular agencies, depending on the number of Polish citizens living in the area, should be established as mentioned above; some of them may be wound up after the completion of their task. The officials appointed as Consular agents should have the title of consuls or vice-consuls. The title of consular attaché should be avoided, because in Soviet opinion it is associated with functions of a military nature. The heads of consular posts must be very carefully selected because the conditions of work over there will certainly be very difficult, and greatly differ, as a rule, from

[2] The text of this Convention is not reproduced in this collection; the Convention entered into force on April 2, 1926.

those prevailing in the West. In view of the Soviet attitude that Polish officials in the USSR must not be appointed from among deportees, minor posts should be filled either by officials sent from Great Britain or from the Near East, where a considerable number of former Polish civil servants are staying.

As the action of protection and assistance to the Polish population will be one of the most important branches of the activity of Polish posts in the USSR, and as this work must fit in with the tasks which are within the province of the Ministry of Labour and Social Welfare, a special official will be attached to the Embassy on behalf of the said Ministry, in the capacity of adviser for social and welfare questions. This official's powers are specified in the annexe [not given here]. As far as it is possible the services of Polish refugees should be enlisted for social welfare action by setting up a Central Welfare Committee and local committees. All these institutions, the Central Committee, local committees and the Polish Red Cross, should be entirely under your control, and that of consuls subordinated to you.

Principles and Modes of Welfare Action

As Polish citizens have been deported to the Soviet Union by the order of Soviet authorities, it is these authorities who are responsible for the present position of these people. They must, consequently, provide for the maintenance of those among them who have no adequate means.

Consular offices shall take care that Polish citizens, whatever their national descent or religion may be, should receive the same amount of assistance as Soviet citizens. As the war goes on, it will be impossible to send this population home, and because of that it is imperative to ensure to them the best conditions of life in the Soviet Union. Endeavours should be made to gather Polish citizens in specially selected areas where the climatic conditions are suitable and food supplies are ensured, and which are not far from the evacuation routes. Assistance in evacuation should be given to those citizens whose further stay in the Soviet Union might involve them in some risks, and to those who obtain an assurance of better conditions of life elsewhere.

Social assistance in the USSR, in particular in war-time, will be rather inadequate, and we must reckon with the necessity of providing Polish citizens with financial means, supplies of clothing, and medicines. Supplies of clothing, even second-hand, would be of great help, as clothing in the Soviet Union is extremely expensive and in keen demand. It is therefore a very urgent task that permission be obtained from Soviet authorities for the import, free of custom-duties, of clothing, medicines and food to be distributed among deportees. The Embassy should take appropriate steps for preparing such action.[1]

[1] Subsequent passages of the instruction, omitted here, refer to financial questions, assets of Polish diplomatic and consular posts, the organization of the Embassy and enquiries concerning the fate of some persons missing since September 1939.

General Sikorski's instructions to Lt.-General Anders concerning the political conditions under which the Polish Forces in the USSR should be used

London, September 1, 1941   GSHI, KGA. 7-l
                                               Transl. from Polish

I fully realize that the mission with which I entrusted you involves great responsibility and is of paramount importance for Poland. You will face many times the necessity of taking far-reaching decisions. I should like, therefore, to explain to you some basic ideas, and to supply some supplementary information besides that given to you in letters and dispatches which are rather more of a political nature.

The armed forces, formed on the territory of the USSR, are an integral part of the sovereign army of the Republic of Poland. This is their most important feature which we have to defend, firmly and unrelentingly, even as regards minor issues, and I expect it from you, General.

The German aggression against Russia has started a new phase of the war and has accelerated its progress. Maybe the war will be finished within the next year. But it may last another two years, until such time when the British and American war potential is fully developed. We have continually to reckon with this fact while organizing the Polish armed forces abroad, and consequently also in Russia. We cannot risk their annihilation, although our struggle against the Germans, and lately also against the Italian Fascism, is by no means a token one. The present period is but a period of transition, during which it would be impossible to attain one's final aims. One has to agree to many tactical moves in international politics, but it is not permissible to agree to anything that might harm the Polish cause.

It is in this spirit that I signed the Polish-Russian Agreement after long and laborious negotiations. It is in the same spirit that this agreement will be carried out.

I believe that the USSR Government will understand our position, and will loyally abide by the allied undertakings with the same good faith with which the Government of the Republic of Poland intends to carry them out. So far, the attitude taken by them since the signature of the Agreement of 30th July 1941 lets us hope that it will be so. Nevertheless, I stress most emphatically that Poland upholds now and will uphold in the future the full independence of her political line, and that in no case will she agree to become a tool of the policy of any Power. She desires to preserve her independence in the political field, and to secure the place which is due to her in post-war Europe.

Both in our military and political efforts we side with the camp of great western democracies with which we jointly fight for our common ideals. We wish to co-operate closely and loyally with the USSR, during this war and after it. However, we do not wish to go further than that. Realizing that the New Poland will be basically different from that of yesterday, we shall nevertheless oppose the transplanting of communist ideas on our soil. Neither do we agree to disappear in the Pan-Slav melting-pot.

All my efforts aim at making our position quite clear, and at winning for it recognition and regard. It is for the Ambassador of Poland to the USSR to be the decisive factor in all these matters. He will hand you this letter. Will you please maintain the closest and most friendly relations with him. He is a prominent representative of the Polish Government in Moscow, being, besides, my old personal friend and enjoying my full confidence. I wish and hope that it will be so, and that your personal relations will be the best possible, as this can prove of great value to our cause.

The troops formed and commanded by you must have a high moral sense, and become a valuable and most reliable instrument of the Polish State. They must present a united front and, because of that, keep aloof from politics. I know that you understand this very well, and that under no pretext will you tolerate the instilling of whatever form of politics into the ranks of our Army.

In a dispatch sent to Gen. Szyszko-Bohusz on 23rd August I imparted to him my remarks concerning the Military Agreement, and I showed the way in which small but very characteristic mistakes could be corrected, which could have occurred only through our inadvertence. You will find the relevant indications on these matters in the instruction dealing with military subjects.

I attach the greatest importance to our troops being used for military operations as a whole, obviously under your command. This is indispensable both from the point of view of our prestige, and of operational considerations which do not allow any breaking up of the Polish troops which would lead to sheer waste of their effort. I am absolutely unrelenting on this point since the French campaign, when, owing to jealousy, meanness and envy our divisions were scattered during the training period, and it could not be remedied in June 1940. I think that the Soviet Command will appreciate this principle, and the advantages of its being put into effect. I advise you, however, to be both firm and vigilant in this question of paramount importance for the Polish Army.

I expect from you, General, the same firmness and independence from Soviet military factors in relation to personal and organizational matters. The troops commanded by you depend on the Soviet High Command in what concerns military operations only. Their dependence is explicitly defined in the Military Agreement. In order to emphasize this point and also to help you, I intend to come over there some day and to spend some time among your troops.

I do not overlook the problems of operations and of the use in fighting line of the troops put under your command *after they have attained full combat readiness*. As regards this question, I wish in the first place that the troops may be used in a way enabling them to fulfil single-handed a task which would be important from the point of view of the whole war, and secondly that they may operate as closely as possible with our British Allies. I am writing these words in full agreement with Prime Minister Churchill.

As it appears from General Szyszko-Bohusz's first report, you are completely free to put forward proposals relating to this question. In fact, it was decided in the conversation with Yevstigneyev on 7th August that the Polish Military Mission 'will produce plans concerning the possible course of action to be taken by the Polish military units when they come into action'.

One of the most vital issues for our enemy is to take hold of the oil-fields, and all his operations aim at this. The defence of the oil-fields becomes therefore a very important and self-sufficient task. I consider it to be so important that it deserves to be assigned to our troops in the USSR.

The most appropriate target for the operations of our troops is, in my view, in the direction of the Caucasus and Iran, where, beside operating in a sector of considerable strategic importance, they would have the opportunity of stretching a hand to our British Allies and of fighting side by side with them as well as with the Russian ally.

I ask you therefore to do everything possible to obtain the assignment of the Polish troops in the USSR for this target, so that, in due time, they may be entrusted with a task of their own.

I consider the use of our troops on the Russian western front as undesirable, as they would be diluted there, broken up and playing a secondary role. These harmful consequences would by no means be compensated for by their possibility of reaching Poland at an earlier date.

Will you, please, keep also in mind that our units must be formed in the areas which, 'in all likelihood, are not menaced by evacuation before they attain combat readiness'. I know that you fully realize, my General, the importance of this request.

I am letting you know, moreover, that the British have sent already a full equipment for 50,000 troops, adding to it drill uniforms. The Americans will supply us too. I am so glad that our soldiers will be splendidly uniformed, and that, thanks to British assistance, the Ambassador and you, my General, will be able to secure a strong position in Moscow.

ZWZ, as the home army cadre, is under my direct command. I do not share the view that this organization should be completely inactive during the war. I think that the home country must continue to play an active part in the struggle. Such action must be, however, carried out so as not to expose the organization and home country to enemy reprisals. Enough Polish blood has been shed already, and there is no need to lavish it in order to mark Poland's active part in the camp of the fighting democracies. We must preserve forces as big as possible for the time of the outbreak of an armed rising, and this moment is still far ahead. For this reason I ordered General Rakoń to organize, in close agreement with the Ministry of the Interior, diversions in Germany by Polish workers staying there. He was also ordered to organize diversions in the area adjoining the Polish-Russian frontier. Your assistance in this respect can be extremely valuable. Do organize it under the Ambassador's lead, as he keeps his post in the Cabinet for this purpose. He is very well acquainted with the conditions in which the home country lives and works. I cannot agree, however, to the Soviet Government putting into effect the plans of action which had been prepared before the Agreement with us was signed. It would be contrary to their recognition of the sovereignty of the Polish State, and it would be most dangerous, because it seems they have numerous agents in the ranks of the ZWZ. The latter will be severed from whatever political activity, and this line of policy is binding, in the first place, on Moscow's secret agents. You must constantly keep your eye on this.

On the second anniversary of the outbreak of the war which has so deeply affected you, I send you, my dear General, words of hope for a better future for Poland, together with heartfelt greetings from myself, my wife and daughter.

No. 121

Aide-mémoire of the Foreign Office to the Polish Ministry for Foreign Affairs on the Soviet instigations to sabotage in Poland

London, September 5, 1941   GSHI, A.11. 49/Sow./6

M. Retinger recently received information that the Soviet wireless was about to launch a series of broadcasts urging the Poles to commit all kinds of sabotage. At M. Retinger's request, Sir Stafford Cripps saw M. Vyshinsky on the night of the 29th August, and pointed out to him the need for the most careful co-operation with His Majesty's Government and with the government of any occupied country before any steps were taken to instigate sabotage. M. Vyshinsky accepted the need for this co-operation and said that the steps to which M. Retinger referred had not been planned by the Soviet Government expressly, but were probably the outcome of some departmental plan of the Soviet broadcasting authorities. He promised to go into the matter and see that the broadcasts were carefully prepared so as to avoid the danger to which Sir Stafford Cripps had drawn attention. M. Retinger has asked that this information might be communicated to General Sikorski.

No. 122

Report from Maj.-Gen. Bohusz-Szyszko to General Sikorski on the steps taken in order to obtain a proper interpretation of Articles 2 and 7 of the Polish-Soviet Military Agreement

Moscow, September 11, 1941   GSHI, KGA, 7-b; A.XII. 22/30.10
                                                                   Transl. from Polish

Pursuant to General Sikorski's order of 23rd August 1941 to obtain from Soviet authorities an interpretation of Articles 2 and 7 of the Military Agreement consonant with the basic Polish-Soviet Agreement of 30th July 1941,[1] Maj.-Gen. Bohusz-Szyszko addressed the following letter to the High Command of the Armed Forces of the USSR, at the end of August of the same year:

By order of the President of the Council of Ministers of the Republic of

[1] See doc. No. 106.

165

Poland and C.-in-C. of the Polish Armed Forces General Władysław Sikorski I have the honour to state the following:

1. The Supreme Command of the Polish Armed Forces holds the view that the big Polish military units which are being formed on the territory of the USSR, and which will be sent to the front after having attained full combat readiness, should be grouped into one operational unit, under Polish Command, depending on the Soviet Supreme Command as regards their operational use.

In fact, the use of the joined Polish forces in one operational direction is most essential from moral and propaganda points of view to the Polish Army, Poland and the Allied Powers.

This principle is fully put into effect in Great Britain where the Polish Army Corps holds as its own an operational sector of coastal defence.

2. The Supreme Command of the Polish Armed Forces holds the view that Article 2e of the Military Agreement refers exclusively to those problems and establishments of the Polish Army in the USSR which are connected with the sovereign rights of the USSR, such as transfers of Polish servicemen from other countries to the USSR, or which require co-operation or assistance on the part of the Supreme Command of the Armed Forces of the USSR, as, for instance, pay, supplies, quarters, etc.

It does not extend, on the other hand, as regards the duty of reaching a previous agreement between the Supreme Command of the Polish Forces and the Supreme Command of Soviet Forces, to personal matters which are an integral part of the sovereignty of the Polish State, such as appointing of commanding officers (except the appointment of the Commander of the Polish Armed Forces in the USSR), transfer, distinctions, promotions, etc.

Any other interpretation would not be consonant either with the spirit of the Political Agreement concluded by the two Governments, or with Article 2a of the Military Agreement, signed on 14th August of this year.

In connection with the aforesaid and being fully convinced of good faith and mutual understanding on both sides, as well as in order to avoid any disagreements in the future, the Supreme Command of the Polish Armed Forces proposes to define more accurately the meaning of Articles 2e and 7 by way of a bilateral additional protocol. [. . .].

A verbal reply was given to this request by General Panfilov, the text of which was forwarded by Maj.-Gen. Bohusz-Szyszko to C.-in-C. on 11th Sept. in the following report:

1. On September 10th the Soviet Government officially informed me through the Deputy Chief of Staff, General Panfilov, that they interpreted Article 2, letter 'e', and Article 7 of the Military Agreement in a way agreeing with Polish requests, that is to say that they fully recognize our full independence as regards personal matters and the necessity for using Polish forces as a whole. The Soviet standpoint is confirmed by facts, and in connection with it I do not see any necessity of an additional protocol. This declaration being made verbally I reserved the right to refer to your decision, General.

General Anders holds the view that this declaration is completely sufficient and that further requests are superfluous.

2. The Soviet Government let us know that because of the difficult position as regards supplies they will be unable to keep their promises and can give arms for 1 infantry division only.

3. In relation to the formation of further units I feel there is some hesitation here, due to doubts on the quick arrival of British and American arms.

The same question was also raised by General Wolikowski at the Red Army Headquarters on 19th September. After a week's lapse he received General Panfilov's following declaration, forwarded to General Sikorski on 3rd October:

Re: Verbal statement made by Major-General Panfilov.

This statement runs as follows:

'The High Command of the Red Army, having considered the proposal made by the delegate of the High Command of the Polish Armed Forces Brigadier-General Szyszko-Bohusz regarding the question of defining more accurately the meaning of points 2 and 7 of the bilateral Military Agreement concluded in Moscow on 14.8.1941 between the High Command of the USSR and the Polish High Command, states that there is no reason for re-examining the existing military agreement concluded on 14.8.1941 between the Soviet and Polish High Commands.

'The fears of the Polish High Command that points 2 and 7 might be interpreted in a different way from what was laid down in the aforesaid agreement are groundless, and this has been confirmed if only by the fruitful co-operation between the delegates of the General Staff of the Red Army and the CO of the Polish Army, General Anders, in the question of the formation of the Polish Army on the territory of the USSR.'

No. 123

Two pro-memorias sent by General Sikorski to Mr. Churchill relative to the proposed formation of the Polish Forces in the USSR and a review of the present situation in the USSR[1]

London, September 17, 1941   GSHI, A.XII. 1/56

As you know my greatest concern at the present moment is connected with the formation of a Polish Army and the care of over a million deported Poles in the USSR.

For this reason I am enclosing a note relative to our proposed war-effort in the East and also a short estimate of the present military and economic state of affairs in the USSR.

I will be very grateful to you for giving this vital matter your kind consideration.

Note for the Rt. Hon. Winston S. Churchill, P.C., M.P.,
Prime Minister, relative to the formation of Polish Forces in Russia

Recent reports from Russia lead to a general estimate of our military possibilities on the Eastern Front. There are about 1½ million Poles who have

[1] See Note No. 123.

been deported into Russia. Over 100,000, nearly 60% of whom are trained soldiers, could be called up to the Polish Forces.

Lieut.-General Anders, GO Commanding Polish Forces in Russia, hopes to be able to organize 4 to 6 divisions including special units and services at the disposal of the Army and Army Corps Commands. Unfortunately, the shortage of equipment in Russia does not make it possible to organize immediately a greater number of divisions. The Soviet military authorities have declared their ability to arm one infantry division. This armament, however, will not be complete, particularly in regard to artillery and anti-tank equipment.

The formation of a Polish army in Russia is therefore entirely dependent upon the supply of armament and equipment from Great Britain or the USA.

Two alternatives may be considered with regard to the organization of a Polish army in Russia. This will depend on the available equipment.

Either i/ —one armoured division
          —three infantry divisions (as fully mechanized as possible)
or   ii/ —four infantry divisions
          —two tank brigades co-operating with infantry.

Both alternatives should include: two regiments of heavy artillery (of 3 troops of 3 batteries of 4 guns), two engineer battalions, two signal battalions, two groups of a.a. artillery, two reconnaissance groups, services according to British organization for each division and Army Corps, two mobile hospitals of 600 beds.

Moreover, full kit and personnel equipment will also be required for 50,000 men as well as 5,000 outfits for the women's auxiliary services.

Prevailing conditions in Russia demand the organization of independent supply of provisions. It would be therefore necessary to provide one million iron rations.

The difficulties connected with equipping and supplying of such an army will no doubt be considerable. It is only by overcoming those difficulties, however, that a Polish army can be formed.

It is most important to consider without delay the possibilities of organizing, arming and maintaining the Polish Forces in Russia and to carry out the determined scheme.

I also wish to strengthen the Polish land forces in Britain and Africa by evacuating 8,000 from Russia to Great Britain and 2,000 to complete the Polish Brigade Middle East. All the airmen and seamen will be evacuated to Britain. The first transport of 200 airmen was due to leave Arkhangel on 16th September.

I am convinced that a full support of His Majesty's Government in this direction would greatly facilitate my endeavours.

I am as much concerned with the matter of evacuation to Britain and Africa as with the organization of a Polish Force in Russia. The establishment of our army in Great Britain is not complete and our Brigade in Egypt is already suffering losses and will require complements.

An estimate of the present military and economic situation of the
USSR and a forecast of its development in the immediate future

[. . .]. *Conclusions*

a/ There will be no crisis owing to food shortage, although disorder in
distribution is likely.

b/ There is not yet any danger of oil shortage.

c/ If, as seems probable, the Soviets lose the Donetz and Leningrad
industrial areas and the capacity of the Moscow area is reduced, it is improbable that the Soviet will be able to re-equip their army during the winter
without help from abroad and to resist in the spring of 1942.

No. 124

*Notes on the conversation between General Sikorski and Mr. Harriman on the
supplies of equipment for the Polish Army in the USSR to be demanded from
the Anglo-American Mission at the Moscow conference*[1]

London, September 19, 1941   GSHI, A.11. 49/Sow./4
                                                      Transl. from Polish

Gen. Sikorski greeted Mr. Harriman by wishing him success in his
important mission, and then gave a brief account of the present political and
military situation in Russia. He emphasized the gravity of the military
situation but added that politically the Stalin régime was still strong, which
was to the advantage both of the Polish and the Allied cause. A swing to the
right could bring about a compromise with Germany, and a revolt to the left,
complete anarchy. The Soviet Government was aware that the Polish
element provided support for the existing régime and therefore met every
Polish initiative with confidence: they were anxious to create a Polish Army
as soon as possible,—the G.O.C. of the latter, Gen. Anders, was trusted
implicitly. They insisted that Poles should exert pressure on the Western
Allies to obtain arms and equipment of which they (the Soviets) were short.
At the beginning the Soviet Government promised to arm four divisions,—
now, having lost a great amount of war equipment and many industrial
regions, they have reduced their pledge to one division, and even that was
not supplied up to the agreed standard. Gen. Sikorski showed Mr. Harriman
on a map the location of the Polish Army being organized in Russia (Saratov-
Orenburg), and of their reserve cadres (Novo-Sybirsk). He also explained
his general plan agreed with the British Prime Minister Churchill, the British
General Staff and also with Gen. Wavell. The plan was to move the Polish
Army towards the Caucasus, to create a resistance centre there eventually by
linking up with the British Forces in Persia, to protect the oil fields, and in
the case of a final Russian collapse, to maintain an eastern resistance front and
protect the Middle East. This plan anticipated American assistance and
supplies to be sent by way of the Persian Gulf, Iran and the Caspian Sea.

Gen. Sikorski mentioned that 27,000 volunteers had already reported to
the Polish Army in Russia, and that the creation of an army depended

[1] See Note No. 124.

exclusively on equipment and arms. Great Britain supplied a certain amount of equipment. Gen. Sikorski asked Mr. Harriman, as the Head of the American Mission, to consider his two ardent and insistent wishes:

1/ To take full account of the necessity of supplying arms to the Polish Army in the USSR, and to support that request before his Government.

2/ To support the request for the participation of the Polish Ambassador and Gen. Anders at the Moscow conference whenever Polish problems or interests require it.

Gen. Sikorski added that, right up to the present day, in all his talks in Moscow he had been given to understand that the Soviet authorities would not object to the Polish Ambassador's and Gen. Anders' participation in the conference. As regards the armament for the Polish Army, Gen. Sikorski had been advised in semi-official conversations that the Russians would concede to the Poles priority in obtaining supplies of arms from the West. Gen. Sikorski stressed the importance of the situation, which required a quick decision, and appealed to Mr. Harriman for full support in that matter, and for favourable treatment in Moscow of all the problems of the Polish Ambassador and Gen. Anders. One should consider the circumstances which would arise in the case of Russia's definite defeat, and even of a possible political chaos: in that case the Polish Army might become the leading element, a factor that could dominate the situation and group around them all forces still capable of resistance. Even the Russians took it into account, and that opinion was shared by nearly all the foreign envoys in Moscow, in particular by Ambassador Cripps and Steinhardt; the request of Diplomatic Missions to summon a Polish detachment to Moscow for their protection was a confirmation of the trust in Poles. [. . .].

2. Mr. Harriman stated that he was not entitled to discuss or to promise supplies, he was only a spokesman of the American Government; without the Russians' consent he could not give any definite pledges to the Poles, but he would be glad to confer with the Ambassador and Gen. Anders, and to report all Gen. Sikorski's wishes to the President. He underlined how well disposed President Roosevelt was to the Poles.

[. . .]. Gen. Sikorski in taking leave of Mr. Harriman thanked him for the promised support at the Moscow conference and before the American Government, and he warmly commended to him Ambassador Kot and Gen. Anders with whom Mr. Harriman intended to confer. Gen. Sikorski underlined the importance of the Polish representatives' opinion in Moscow, as they knew the Russian point of view very well.

No. 125

Telegram from General Sikorski to General Ismay concerning the transfer of the Polish Army in the USSR to an area nearer the Caucasus

London, September 26, 1941   GSHI, A.XII. 1/56

Please put the following before General Sir Hastings Ismay:

In view of latest developments on the Eastern front and particularly the rapid German drive in the Southern sector towards the Donetz Basin and the Caucasus the latter has become eminently important to the final issue. The protection of the Caucasian Oil Fields is now vitally urgent. I desire the Polish Divisions to take part in the defence. We are not responsible for delay in their organization or equipment. I do not wish to put forward to the Soviet Government the suggestion of moving the Polish Forces to the Caucasus being most anxious to avoid occasioning any suspicion. I would be most grateful if you will:

1) give your kind assistance in the speeding up of equipment—transport from Arkhangel to the Polish Forces,
2) induce the British representatives to put forward the proposal to move the Polish troops without delay or regard for their stage of organization to the Caucasus and to equip and arm these troops to the extent which will make it possible for them under the prevailing geographical conditions to render vital service both to Soviet Russia and the Allies.

No. 126

Telegram from General Macfarlane to General Sikorski informing of Ambassador Cripps' consent to comply with Polish suggestion of 26 September

Moscow, October 5, 1941   GSHI, A.XII. 1/56

I have discussed your message to General Szyszko-Bohusz with General Ismay and my Ambassador.

1. My Mission will do all it can to help to speed up the transport of equipment from Arkhangel to the Polish forces. I have been pressing the Russian Staff for three weeks to allow me to attach a Liaison Officer to General Anders' Headquarters but have, up to date, failed to obtain their agreement.

2. My Ambassador, General Ismay and I feel that any representation to the Russians regarding the move of the Polish Forces from the Volga area to the Caucasus can only be made by the representatives of the Polish Government in Moscow. We have of course no objection to your representatives stating that in principle we agree that there are arguments in favour of such suggestion.

No. 127

Records of a conversation between Ambassador Kot and Deputy Commissar Vyshinsky relating to the situation of the Polish citizens deported to the USSR, their release from prisons, and the fate of circa 7,500 missing Polish officers. Present also Director Novikov and Secretary of Embassy Arlet, acting as interpreter

Moscow, October 7, 1941[1]   GSHI, A.11. 49/Sow./4
                                                          Transl. from Polish

Ambassador (greeting Mr. Vyshinsky): You will not complain of my being insistent.

[1] The date of this conversation is noted by Prof. Kot as October 6, 1941.

Vyshinsky denies it.

Ambassador: You will not complain of my being insistent because in the course of our last conversation I got your assurance of my receiving some data of great importance for me within five days, and fifteen days have elapsed since then. I understand that both you and the Soviet Government have to deal with many urgent and important matters and I think this is the reason for the delay.

Vyshinsky: In fact, the delay is due to this reason only.

Ambassador: So far as we are concerned we have not been idle, trying on our part to improve the position of the allied Soviet Government in those fields in which we can exercise some influence.

(The Ambassador then shows a telegram of the PAT (Polish Telegraphic Agency) from London relating to Dr. Retinger's interview in The Times and another telegram of the PAT from New York, stating that President Roosevelt at his Press Conference made use of Ciechanowski's letter to Cordell Hull referring to the restoration of religious freedom to the Poles in the USSR. At the same time the Ambassador mentions the protests raised by Roosevelt's declaration in the circles of isolationists and adversaries of a rapprochement with the USSR.) Such are the proofs of our propaganda activity in the spirit of the Polish-Soviet understanding. The war is going on and we try to help our ally as much as we can.

Vyshinsky: This is right in my opinion, the more so as it agrees with the facts.

Ambassador: Unfortunately, it is not so in all fields. So far as religious matters are concerned, it is true that our army has obtained freedom of religious worship, but our civilians are completely deprived of religious care, as there are no churches or priests. The Soviet Constitution guarantees the freedom of religious practices but in fact no religious worship is possible. [...].

Vyshinsky (looking into notes made in his diary under the date of 20th September): The plan of the resettlement of Polish citizens in the German Volga Republic is no longer topical, because on 20th September when it was put forward by you, another plan concerning the resettlement of this territory had already been approved by the Government. I informed the Government of your proposal but I got the reply that other measures had already been taken as regards those territories.

Ambassador: Is there no possibility of putting at least a part of those territories at the disposal of our men? A high NKVD official, who stayed in those parts last month, promised to assign two cantons of the German Volga Republic for the resettlement of the Polish population. (A short discussion ensued on the subject of whether cantons or kolkhozes were meant, some remarks being also made by Director Novikov.)

Vyshinsky: It was quite fortuitous that some Polish citizens had been sent to the German Volga Republic. Before the end of this week, at the latest, a new plan of resettlement of Polish citizens will be approved.

Ambassador: I ask you to discuss this scheme with us before it is finally drafted and submitted to the Government. It would be very difficult to make any changes once it has been approved, and I will be the one made responsible for the way in which this very important matter is solved.

Vyshinsky: The final draft will be submitted to you, and your wishes will be considered as far as possible.

Your inquiries about judges, public prosecutors and former magistrates were forwarded by me to appropriate places, and I expect an answer very soon. The same applies to the statistical data referring to the total number of the Polish population, their place of residence, and respective categories.

The Ambassador asks whether M. Vyshinsky has dealt with any other questions.

Vyshinsky: We have issued orders to interfere with a disorderly mass displacement of the Polish population. Thus, for instance, we stopped the mass movement of the Polish population in Molotov Oblast', of which, by the way, we informed the Embassy. (As a matter of fact, the Embassy did not receive any information on the mass movement of the Polish population in the Molotov Oblast', and Vyshinsky's allegation obviously embarrassed M. Novikov.)

Ambassador: I only hope that it does not mean imposing restrictions on the freedom of movement of Polish citizens for a prolonged period.

Vyshinsky: Certainly not. In the course of this week you will receive not only a scheme for the resettlement of the Polish population but also concrete data relating to the places from which and to which the Poles are moving.

Ambassador: I ask once more for the speeding up of the settlement of these questions.

Vyshinsky: I will work out myself a plan of the welfare organization for Polish citizens, committees, men of trust. I hope this plan will satisfy both sides and will be approved by you. Also the plan of financial settlement is prepared by me in such a manner that it should give concrete results.

Ambassador raises then the question of the slow progress of the release of Polish citizens, and shows telegrams from the World Jewish Congress, enquiring about Professor Schorr and Member of the Diet Sommerstein. A short discussion on the release of our citizens ensues, Vyshinsky and Novikov asserting that many released Polish citizens do not call on the Embassy. The Ambassador replies that Sommerstein, Celewicz and Luckiewicz are in prison at Balashov, and Schorr did not leave the prison of Lubianka until June.

Vyshinsky: I wish you to believe that I take the matter of the release of those men in my hands with pleasure, as I know that there are no obstacles of principle but technical difficulties only. There are, however, some categories of men who must not be released in our common interest. [. . .].

Ambassador: As a matter of fact, I cannot carry out the orders from London and send there many prominent persons needed for completing the National Council, especially those from the Peasant Party. I wish to quote here some figures now. Altogether 9,500 officers were imprisoned in Poland and deported inside the USSR, while there are only 2,000 officers in our army. What happened to 7,500 officers?

173

Vyshinsky and Novikov try to convince the Ambassador that it is quite impossible, are unable, however, to find valid arguments.

Ambassador: We tried to find them everywhere, we thought that they had been delivered to the Germans, we made enquiries in German prisoner-of-war camps, in occupied Poland, everywhere where they might be. I would have understood the missing of some dozens of people, of, let us say, several hundred, but not several thousand.

Vyshinsky and Novikov, very embarrassed, start putting the question themselves: 'What did happen to them?'

Vyshinsky: In the course of our previous conversation I stated that there were 591 Polish doctors; 600 doctors should be the lot. Some may have reported some other profession.

Ambassador: There are only 30 doctors in our army, in fact. Our soldiers' health is rather poor, and there are no doctors to take care of them.

Vyshinsky: I promise to fulfil your request, and to send a greater number of doctors to the army. [. . .].

The conversation lasted from 6.30 p.m. to 7.45 p.m.

No. 128

Letter from General Sikorski to Mr. Churchill on the subject of equipment for the Polish Army in the USSR

London, October 8, 1941   GSHI, PRM, 39-a

I am taking the liberty to write to you on a matter of great urgency as well as of great importance to Poland and, in my opinion, also to the Allied cause in general.

I refer to the Conference recently held in Moscow to discuss the question of supplies of war material to the forces fighting on the Russian front. In view of the formation of considerable Polish fighting units in Russia which are enjoying the statute of Allied forces and are to receive their equipment and arms almost exclusively from Great Britain and the USA, the Conference has acquired a special importance for us. We did not press for a seat at the Conference table as full members, being more interested in the practical than in the formal side of this meeting. In fact, the Polish Government thought themselves justified to expect that the needs and requirements of our armed forces on Soviet territory would be considered apart from those of Russia and thus adequately safeguarded. The friendly assurances which Lord Beaverbrook was kind enough to give me in this respect personally, before his departure for Moscow, confirmed me in this belief. Similar encouragement reached me from the United States where President Roosevelt did not hesitate to extend to Poland the benefits of the Lease and Lend Act. I may perhaps mention confidentially that before the opening of the Conference I was informed of the instructions cabled to Mr. Averell Harriman requesting him to take into special account the requirements of the Polish Army in Russia and to discuss this question directly with the authorized Moscow representatives of the Polish Government.

In view of the above it was with profound regret that I learnt of the decision of the British representative to interpret his instructions as restricting the British contribution in material as destined exclusively for the USSR leaving it to the discretion of the Soviet Government to decide whether they can spare for the use of the Polish Army any of the tanks, armour-piercing and anti-aircraft guns which they receive.

In these circumstances the Conference refrained from making a decision on the question of arms for our troops.

In view of the gravity of the situation which has arisen I am appealing to you to modify the ruling which our British Ally applied in this case. Should it remain unchanged it would place the whole issue at the mercy of the Soviet Government. It would, moreover, seriously jeopardize the adequate armament of the Polish divisions on Soviet territory.

No. 129

Note from Ambassador Kot to Deputy Commissar Vyshinsky concerning the incomplete fulfilment of Soviet obligations towards Polish citizens arising from the Agreement of July 30, 1941

Moscow, October 13, 1941 GSHI, PRM, 41/2
Transl. from Polish: Pol.-Sov.R., No. 34

Referring to the Note of the Chargé d'Affaires *ad interim* of the Republic of Poland addressed to the Commissar for Foreign Affairs, No. 30/41 of August 22, 1941,[1] and the Note Verbale of the Polish Embassy, No. D. 467/41 of September 27, 1941,[2] I have the honour, Mr. Commissar, to inform you of the following:

In both the aforesaid Notes, as in my conversation with you, Mr. Commissar, I emphasized particularly the need for the fulfilment by the Soviet Government of the provisions of the Agreement concluded between the Polish Government and the Soviet Government on July 30, 1941, and of the provisions of the Decree of the Presidium of the Supreme Council of the USSR of August 12, 1941, concerning the release of Polish citizens from prisons, labour camps and localities of compulsory residence at the earliest possible date, at least before the coming winter, during which the departure from many of the camps would be most difficult if not altogether impossible. The question of release was also brought up by the Polish delegation at the two meetings of the Mixed Polish-Soviet Commission, when emphasis was laid on the special urgency of this problem.

During my conversation with you, Mr. Commissar, on September 20, I received your assurance that the Soviet authorities would take care that Polish citizens detained in distant Northern regions, where the climate is unsuitable for Poles, were transported to more suitable districts before the winter season set in. During my conversation on October 7, I quoted figures relating to Polish citizens who were still detained in large numbers in

[1] See doc. No. 115.   [2] Not printed.

camps and mentioned the fact that certain categories among them had been transferred to very remote Northern regions. In spite of repeated Polish requests and the assurances given on behalf of the Soviets, this Embassy has not as yet received the list of localities nor the exact numbers of Polish citizens released.

Contrary to the assurances that except for a small number of individuals suspected, indicted or convicted of espionage on behalf of Germany, whose names and dossiers up to now have not been communicated to the Embassy, all Polish citizens had been set free and that in a small number of cases only was delay caused by purely technical considerations, the Embassy is in possession of information that there are still in a number of prisons and camps thousands of Polish citizens who were not informed of the Agreement concluded on July 30, 1941, or were informed that the provisions of this Agreement and of the Decree of the Presidium of the Supreme Council of the USSR of August 12 did not apply to them.

By way of example, may I state that Polish citizens are still being detained in prison at Saratov, Gorki, Balashov, Tschelabinsk, Kizel and in compulsory labour camps in the Primorski Kray in the North-Eastern extremity of the Yakut district (near the mouth of the Kolyma on the Arctic Ocean), near Aldan, in the region of Tomsk, Karaganda, in the mines of Karabash (Tschelabinsk district), in the Ivgiel camp (Sverdlovsk district), in the Arkhangel district and in the Republic of Komi, along the railway line under construction between Kotlas and Pechora and at other points.

More detailed information concerning the numbers and condition of these Polish citizens is given in the Annexe to the present Note. As will be seen therefrom the local authorities either did not receive detailed orders concerning the treatment of Polish citizens after the conclusion of the Agreement of July 30, or, in some cases, the local authorities were content to deal with the matter in a purely *pro forma* way (the People's Commissariat of Internal Affairs withdrew police supervision of the 2,000 Polish citizens employed in the mines of Karabash-Voloshynowski-Rudnik, but left the persons concerned where they were which actually made their position worse than before), or with a partial execution of the orders issued. It is to be assumed that various considerations have dictated this treatment and in some instances local authorities may have desired to secure for themselves virtually unpaid manpower, whence the tendency to release sometimes elderly, invalid or ailing persons, while the stronger and healthier are retained for compulsory labour.

I have the honour to draw your attention, Mr. Commissar, to another characteristic feature of the conduct of local government authorities towards Polish citizens who are released, or who approach them with the request for employment or for the assignment of a residence. This conduct, without doubt unknown to the central authorities, which should cease in the interests of good relations between the Polish and Soviet Governments, consists in informing those concerned that the blame for their difficult situation rests with the Polish Government and their representatives in the USSR. Naturally Polish nationals are not misled by this, but it arouses unnecessary mistrust among the Polish population.

Information issued abroad by the Polish Government, entirely in line with good Polish-Soviet collaboration, is to the effect that Polish citizens in the Union of Soviet Socialist Republics have been liberated from prisons and camps. I presented to you, on the 7th of this month, copies of communiqués issued by the Polish Telegraphic Agency in London and New York. The Polish Government is of the opinion that such official information should correspond to the real situation of the Polish population in the USSR. In the common interest of both Governments the Polish-Soviet Agreement should be fully carried out so that in foreign countries no elements unfriendly to this collaboration and hostile to the USSR should find in the difficult position of the deported Polish population a theme for their propaganda.

The Polish Government could in no case agree that, as a result of the Agreement of July 30, 1941, the lot of Polish citizens residing in the Union of Soviet Socialist Republics should become worse or that local authorities should carry out its provisions in a manner contrary to the declarations and statements of the representatives of the Soviet Government.

Consequently, in its Note, No. 30/41 of August 22, 1941, the Embassy presented a number of proposals forming a logical whole with a view to the practical solution of the problem of the Polish population in the USSR, in accordance with the interests of this population and of both Governments. The fact that the suggestions contained in point 2 were only carried out in part, and that points 3 and 4 were left completely unfulfilled, means that such Polish citizens as have been released have not been able to improve their living conditions and a large number of them have been forced to wander aimlessly and compelled to camp at railway stations or in the open air in the localities newly chosen for their residence. In view of the approaching winter which in some parts of the Soviet Union has already set in, many of them are threatened with death by starvation. Their position is rendered still worse by the fact that the local authorities not only refuse to carry out the suggestions of the Embassy, but do not even comply with the assurances given by the People's Commissariat for Foreign Affairs contained in the Aide-Mémoire of August 28, 1941, with regard to free railway fares, travelling subsidies, subsistence allowances and, most important of all, employment for the persons released.

I also venture to draw your attention, Mr. Commissar, to the fact that the organization of the Polish Army in the USSR is not progressing in accordance with the letter and the spirit of the Agreement of July 30, 1941, or with the intentions of the two Governments.

The Supreme Command of the Polish armed forces in the USSR has vainly waited four weeks for a decision on the formation of further Polish divisions and the designation of the localities in which this formation is to take place. In consequence, numerous Polish citizens reporting for military service and rallying en masse to the Polish Army stream into the two already overcrowded camps, which lack the necessary number of tents, adequate food supplies and medicines. Thus a situation, harmful alike to the troops and to the common cause, is being created. The local administrative authorities very often do not carry out the instructions issued by the central authorities with regard to questions concerning the Polish Army and create new additional difficulties, as for instance by declining to release from prisons and camps all Polish citizens, military and reservists, and in many instances by detaining the more physically fit elements, which reduces the military value of the units already formed. Moreover, considerable numbers of Polish citizens enrolled in the Red Army and subsequently transferred to the so-called labour battalions, have not up till now been directed to the Polish Army.

Thus the Polish contribution to the common struggle against Germany, contrary to the intentions of the Polish and Soviet Governments and to the unanimous will of the Polish citizens, is being weakened to the detriment of the cause of all the Allies.

In the profound belief that the Soviet Government attaches no less importance than the Polish Government to the development of friendly relations between the two States, I have the honour to request you, Mr. Commissar, to take measures to put into full effect all the proposals contained in the Note of the Embassy of August 22, and in particular the immediate release from prisons, camps and localities of compulsory residence of all Polish citizens, the friendly treatment of those who are unfit for military service and the acceleration of the decision concerning the formation of further large units of the Polish Army, in accordance with the letter and spirit of the Agreement of July 30, 1941.

No. 130

Note on a conversation between Ambassador Kot and Deputy Commissar Vyshinsky on political preliminaries to the visit of General Sikorski to the USSR and on the number of Polish citizens deported and detained in the USSR

Moscow, October 14, 1941
GSHI, A.11. 49/Sow./4
Transl. from Polish

The Ambassador, after a few words of greeting, asked whether Commissar Vyshinsky knew about Gen. Sikorski's proposed visit to Moscow. The Ambassador would like to discuss this visit during the present conversation. Vyshinsky replied that the Ambassador of the USSR in London, Bogomolov, informed the Soviet Government of the intended visit on 11th instant, and on the next day he received the necessary instructions. The Ambassador mentioned that the plan of the visit was conceived in agreement with Mr. Churchill. Vyshinsky confirmed that he was aware of it. The Ambassador stated the following:

I should like to make clear the motives for Gen. Sikorski's journey to the USSR. It is a matter of emphasizing and manifesting to the whole world the readiness of all the Poles for action in the struggle carried on in the East. Gen. Sikorski had intended to come to the USSR at the moment when the Polish Army, now being organized, would have attained a state of full readiness. However, he has advanced the date of his visit deliberately. At a time when the German and isolationist propagandists raise their voice claiming that the allegedly victorious war against the Soviet Union is approaching its end, Gen. Sikorski intends to show to the world that he not only wishes for a Soviet victory, but that he firmly believes in it. It is also necessary to counteract the slogans of Hitlerite propaganda that a war against the Soviet Union is a war for religious freedom, and that it is in the interests of Roman Catholicism. The visit of the head of the Government of a nation widely known as a Roman Catholic one will be in clear contradiction to that propaganda. It will have, apart from its effect in all Roman Catholic countries, a momentous importance for the public opinion in all Slavonic States and the entire Anglo-Saxon world. The press in America and Great Britain will take it up without fail and comment on the fact of the Polish Prime Minister's visit at such a time. From the point of view of Polish problems, Gen. Sikorski's visit is also most important. The Germans begin to approach the Poles and they take steps to win them over, e.g. estates and other property are being restored to Poles who escaped from Soviet occupied territory, or to those who, originating from Eastern Poland, now find themselves in German POW Camps. This action is accompanied by appropriate propaganda. Gen. Sikorski's visit would be a serious blow to German propaganda in Poland, and it would be an appeal to all Poles forcibly mobilized to serve in the German Army, and to the whole Polish nation, to disregard that German move. No one tries to board a sinking ship. I should like to know your opinion of this visit, Mr. Commissar.

M. Vyshinsky (who carefully took note of the Ambassador's declaration, showing some nervousness) replied: The Soviet Government will welcome this visit.

The Ambassador: However, in view of the present state of Polish problems, Gen. Sikorski's visit could not be crowned with complete success. It would be impossible to let him meet on Soviet soil with nothing but complaints from the Polish population. In order to give Gen. Sikorski's visit a reasonable character, the Soviet partner should loyally fulfil his obligations under the Polish-Soviet Treaty. Since an amnesty was proclaimed by the Supreme Soviet of the USSR, two months have elapsed, and a large number of Poles still remain in prisons, labour camps and in places of deportation. We have a number of practical demands, and their speedy fulfilment is of supreme importance to us. Apart from completing the release action, they are concerned with the problem of resettlement, planned in a way that would make it advantageous to Polish citizens; further—with the problem of employment for them, in accordance with their qualifications, and the settlement of the question of welfare and relief action for those Poles who have no means of subsistence.

M. Vyshinsky (in a slightly irritated tone): All the problems now mentioned by you, Mr. Ambassador, are very complex and difficult. It is impossible to settle them in a short time under the present difficult war conditions. [. . .].

The Ambassador: [. . .]. Gen. Anders waited two weeks in Moscow for a decision concerning the formation of further divisions, and he was obliged to leave without obtaining a reply.

M. Vyshinsky: What troops are you talking about, Mr. Ambassador; do you mean the troops which were to be formed in accordance with the Treaty?

The Ambassador: Yes, certainly.

M. Vyshinsky: The Treaty stipulates 2 divisions and one reserve brigade. These have been formed.

The Ambassador: The Treaty knows no such limitations, it stipulates that the number of troops would depend on the manpower available.

M. Vyshinsky: Why are you discussing this with me? Surely I cannot form new divisions. Let the military authorities deal with it.

The Ambassador: Yes, but the military authorities meet with difficulties. That is why I am discussing the matter. If this war is meant to be conducted seriously then all manpower resources should be mobilized.

M. Vyshinsky (irritated, in a rather rude tone): What is the purpose of your saying all this, Mr. Ambassador? You submitted your grievances, we received your Note, and I am dealing with it. Now you are returning to the same subject again. What is the matter?

The Ambassador: Only that all shortcomings and deficiencies in Polish-Soviet relations should be eliminated as soon as possible. Definite orders and instructions should be issued to local authorities, so that by the time of Gen. Sikorski's arrival all these matters in dispute should cease to be a strain on Polish-Soviet relations.

M. Vyshinsky: I cannot guarantee that these questions will be settled before Gen. Sikorski's arrival; the more so, as the problems are so complicated, and war-time conditions make their solution difficult.

The Ambassador: I am fully aware of that but there are certain questions of principle, e.g. the release of prisoners. At the moment of Gen. Sikorski's arrival no Polish citizen should still be in prison.

M. Vyshinsky: As a matter of fact, I wanted to talk about the release. (He takes from Pushkin the statistical report on the release of Poles and dictates):

Among the 387,932 Polish citizens kept in confinement in USSR the following three categories were represented:

I Category: (sentenced or cases being investigated) . . 71,481
II Category: (settled in special settlements, or deported
           to places of compulsory residence) . . 291,137
III Category: (POWs) 25,314

Of all those, 345,511 were released by the 1st October, 1941. Therefore 42,421 persons still remain imprisoned.

The Ambassador (expresses doubts about the accuracy of these data): The one camp at Starobielsk contained more Poles than the total number of POWs given by you, Mr. Commissar.

M. Vyshinsky: Mr. Ambassador, I cannot submit to you but the data in my possession.

The Ambassador: According to Soviet data, among the POWs the officers alone numbered 9,600.

M. Vyshinsky replies. There ensues a long discussion carried out at great speed, partly without interpreting, concerning the accuracy or inaccuracy of the data. The discussion becomes loaded with irritation.

M. Vyshinsky: I frankly admit that we deported certain definite groups: civil servants, officers, police, gendarmes—but not the entire population.

The Ambassador: And the settlers?

M. Vyshinsky: The settlers are included in the same data. (A discussion begins on the term 'deported'. Vyshinsky and Pushkin explain that the figures do not include former Polish citizens who acquired Soviet citizenship on the ground of the Soviet Decree of 1.10.1939. Vyshinsky produces another statistical report, showing the 3 above-mentioned categories with a specification according to Soviet provinces. He states that the Embassy would receive this report on the next day. A discussion on the accuracy of the number of Poles given for various provinces follows.)

M. Vyshinsky (in conclusion explains various individual statistical data): Is the settlement of these matters a condition for Gen. Sikorski's visit, or merely a wish?

The Ambassador: Certainly, a wish only.

M. Vyshinsky: As a representative of the People's Commissariat for Foreign Affairs, and consequently of the Soviet Government, I should be very glad if all these matters could be settled. I am dealing with them personally; but I should like to stress that the Polish-Soviet Treaty was signed by us more from motives of sentiment than of reason (dogovor po tchuvstvu). It is also difficult to say that it has any advantages for us, rather the contrary. We certainly also wish to bring the affairs of the Polish citizens in order and to organize employment for them.

The Ambassador: The whole matter is of considerable sentimental importance for us too. We should like to bring to a happy conclusion all those matters which are still dividing us, so that Gen. Sikorski on his arrival should be free from this burden weighing on our relations. As things stand now he cannot trace a number of his best officers, who are in the USSR, and among them not even his ADC.

M. Vyshinsky: I shall do whatever is possible in our present situation. But perhaps the Mixed Commission should deal with the details.

The Ambassador: The Commission is a useless body and cannot settle anything. On the Soviet side there are no men able to make any decision even in the least important matter.

M. Vyshinsky: In that case, let the Embassy send me in writing all facts on the deficiencies of the local authorities. Let one of the Embassy's six First Secretaries make a list of these matters or even send us the original complaints received by the Embassy.

The Ambassador: We have only three First Secretaries, and one of them is returning to England for reasons of health. We certainly shall convey to you all complaints made by Polish citizens, but I would not like the local authorities to take advantage of it and turn against the complainants.

M. Vyshinsky: We do not even want to know the names of the complainants. We are interested in facts only. And we shall exert pressure on the local authorities. You wrote in your Note that the situation of the released Polish citizens was worse than before. I have obtained a declaration of the NKVD, which we shall also receive in writing, which says that whenever Polish citizens remained on the spot for work, they were employed under the same conditions as free Soviet citizens. Still, as far as written statements are concerned, a Russian poet said: 'gladko pishut na bumagie, no zabyli pro ovragi.' (They write smoothly on paper, but they forgot about the ravines.)

No. 131

Note from General Sikorski to Ambassador Bogomolov urging the release of several thousands of Polish officers who have been found in Soviet military camps

London, October 15, 1941   GSHI, PRM, 41/2

Je vous prie de bien vouloir porter à la connaissance du Gouvernement Soviétique l'assurance, que le Gouvernement Polonais apprécie la bonne volonté demontrée par le Gouvernement Soviétique dans la réalisation de la Convention Polono-Soviétique du 30 Juillet 1941. Cependant certaines difficultés se font jour, qui ne semblent pas être en rapport avec les difficultés provoquées par les opérations militaires. Ainsi la libération immédiate des citoyens polonais, privés de liberté semble nécessaire en vue de l'hiver qui s'approche, ainsi que les moyens de leurs assurer l'existence. Le sort de quelques milliers des officiers polonais, qui ne sont pas rentrés en Pologne et qui n'ont pas été retrouvés dans les camps militaires soviétiques continuent être incertain. Ils sont probablement dispersés dans les régions du nord de l'URSS. Leur présence dans les camps de l'Armée Polonaise est indispensable.

Je vous prie aussi d'attirer l'attention du Gouvernement Soviétique sur la nécessité d'activer l'aide nécessaire pour la formation et l'accroissement de cette Armée.

En même temps j'ai l'honneur de vous communiquer qu'en vue des opérations militaires actuelles, j'ai donné des instructions afin d'intensifier l'action de sabotage et de diversion polonaise en Pologne occupée par les Allemands.

No. 132

Note on a conversation between General Sikorski and Mr. Churchill on the defence of the Caucasus and the suggested transfer of the Polish Army in the USSR to the Caucasus or to the Southern border of the Caspian Sea

London, October 24, 1941   GSHI, PRM, 39–b
                                                              Transl. from Polish

[. . .]. Mr. Churchill informs General Sikorski of the situation in Persia and, in connection with it, of the Soviet requests to Britain. In spite of their difficult position on the main front the Russians continue to maintain an army of occupation in Persia to the strength of five divisions. These troops anger the local population and cause unrest. Those British divisions which could otherwise have been used nearly in full against the enemy now have to fulfil the duties of maintaining order in Persia and defending the population against abuses on the part of the Soviet troops of occupation. Even now, considering the present strength of the British forces there, the railway line linking the Persian Gulf to the Caspian Sea, which is one of the most important means of communication for supplying the Soviet needs by the Allies, is greatly overburdened by supplies for the British forces stationed in Persia. At the same time, the Russians have asked Britain to take over a sector of the Soviet front against the Germans, and to send some (3) divisions of British troops there. Should Britain meet this demand by dispatching some (three?) divisions to the Volga, for instance, the above-mentioned railway line would be overburdened even more. As it is the only available line of communication, its usefulness would be diminished still further in so far as Russia is concerned.

The best solution for England would be the withdrawal of five Soviet divisions from Persia and their transfer to the Caucasus in order to reinforce the defence of that particularly important area for which, as it seems, only five Soviet divisions are available at present. This would have a calming effect in Persia, and would bring some relief to the British forces. Apart from that [it would be advisable] to transfer to the South the greatest possible number of Polish troops who with British aid could be fully equipped and armed during the Winter and ready for action in the Spring. The most appropriate thing from the British point of view would be to transfer these troops to Persia. Should the Russians oppose this move, those troops could, at least, be concentrated on the northern shores of the Caspian Sea, near Astrakhan, to where the British would send the necessary supplies.[1]

Prime Minister Churchill knows that the Russians are opposed both to the first and the second British proposal: they do not wish to leave Persia, even if they should lose Moscow, and although they are facing an immediate threat on the Southern front. On the other hand, they fear the formation of big Polish forces and of their concentration in the South for they might be eventually united with the British forces.

Mr. Churchill proposes to General Sikorski to put in his conversations with Stalin and Molotov a firm request to the effect of transferring the Polish troops to the South, and to offer at that price to intercede with the British Government and support the Soviet request regarding the taking over of a sector of the Soviet front against the Germans by Britain.[2]

The Prime Minister made it quite clear, at the same time, that he could not give any powers to General Sikorski for concrete negotiations on that basis. It would depend on the developments in a constantly changing situation. General Sikorski can, nevertheless, let it be understood that he has good reasons to believe that Great Britain would not decline to compensate the Russians in return for the concessions granted to us by them. Mr. Churchill will take a parallel course of action through British diplomatic channels supporting General Sikorski's moves.[3] The problem is difficult but it is worth the greatest efforts.

Mr. Churchill hopes that the most of Polish forces, three divisions at least, would come within reach of the British strategy.[4] [. . .].

[Personal Notes of Gen. Sikorski:]

[1] Prime Minister Churchill explained that the British would have all the necessary supplies available, but they were still short of rifles.

[2] It appeared from Mr. Churchill's words that he counted besides on support for the British point of view regarding the withdrawal of Soviet divisions from Persia to be used for the defence of the Caucasus.

[3] And, probably, negotiating on the nature, place and extent of the British action 'regarding which'—stated Mr. Churchill—'there exist several alternatives'.

[4] Thinking over Mr. Churchill's line of reasoning, described above, and remembering some significant remarks of his, I am ever more convinced that in spite of the lack of trust and sympathy between the two partners, Great Britain will not be able, under Stalin's pressure, to decline the demand for direct participation of British forces in an action against the Germans on the Russian front. Reckoning with this, Mr. Churchill would like to obtain a countervalue in the form of a Soviet compensation. He was, in fact, quite outspoken in declaring that should the Russians give such a compensation, Great Britain would be ready to increase her contribution.

No. 133

Letter from Mr. Eden to General Sikorski on the British readiness to provide equipment for the Polish Army in the USSR and to suggest her shifting towards Caucasus[1]

London, October 28, 1941   GSHI, A.11. 49/Sow./6

The Prime Minister has passed to me your letter of the 8th October, and has asked me to inform you of the present position as regards the equipment of the Polish Forces in the Union of Soviet Socialist Republics.

On the 13th October I raised this question myself with the Soviet Ambassador. I reminded him of the discussions which had taken place in Moscow during Lord Beaverbrook's visit in the course of which M. Molotov had indicated that while the Soviet Government was not in a position to equip the Polish Forces, they had no objection to our doing so. I therefore informed M. Maisky that we were ready to do our best to provide this equipment, but that it would be easier for us to do so if the Polish troops were placed on the left of the Soviet line, for example in the Caucasus, and thus within easier reach of our communications through Persia. This would have the additional advantage that we should avoid adding to the large flow of supplies via Arkhangel.

[1] See Note No. 133.

I also took this opportunity to draw M. Maisky's attention to the importance of attaching a British liaison officer to General Anders. I said that this would be all the more necessary if we were to undertake the equipment of the Polish Forces, and that we therefore hoped the Soviet Government would see their way to agree.

I have now sent a telegram to Sir Stafford Cripps informing him of my conversation with M. Maisky, and I have asked him to concert with his Polish colleague and with General Macfarlane the best method of securing the agreement of the Soviet Government to the proposals which I made to M. Maisky. I should therefore be grateful if Your Excellency would consider sending to M. Kot any necessary instructions to enable him to concert his action in this matter with Sir Stafford Cripps.

No. 134

Telegram from General Sikorski to Ambassador Kot on the conditions of his intended visit to the USSR, on his plans for shifting the Polish Army from the USSR to Central Asia and for diverting a part of the Polish troops to Great Britain and the Middle East[1]

London, October 28, 1941 GSHI, A.11. 49/Sow./5
Transl. from Polish

On 31st October I shall set off by air for Egypt, and from there—after reviewing the troops—for Russia. My journey, however, depends on the acceptance in principle of the following points by the Soviet Government. I should then discuss their execution with Stalin:

1/ Release from prisons, detention and forced labour camps of all Polish citizens on Soviet territory and the provision of decent living conditions for them;

2/ All soldiers and Polish citizens fit for military service to be used to man the newly forming Polish units;

3/ In view of the inability of the Soviet Government to find equipment and food rations for such numbers, the entire Polish Army would be concentrated, pending their combat readiness, at a point easily accessible for British supplies. In the first line Iran to be considered, alternatively the Caucasus. The British Government undertake, in our and Soviet interests, to arm and feed the Polish Army, demanding in return their move to an area convenient for the transport of supplies.

4/ From the Polish Forces in the USSR 15 to 20 thousand men would be diverted to Egypt and Great Britain.

I am expecting your early reply to London, from where the Foreign Minister, Raczyński, would immediately transmit it to Egypt. Should the reply not be positive, I would end my journey in Egypt in a demonstrative manner, thereby making clear the bad faith of the Soviet Government with regard to the formation of a Polish Army and to the Treaties of 30th July and

[1] See Note No. 134.

14th August. For the sake of our common cause I should, however, prefer to avoid such a demonstration, the more so, as my journey was agreed with all the countries of the democratic camp.

I communicated my demands to Churchill and Eden who, on his part, was to exert pressure on Maisky in the matter of our troops. I instructed our Embassy in Washington to try to obtain an instruction for the American Ambassador in Russia in support of your action.

No. 135

Reply of Ambassador Raczyński to the letter from Mr. Eden regarding the British intervention with the Soviet Government to provide the equipment for the Polish Army in the USSR and to divert a part of the Polish troops to Great Britain and the Middle East

London, October 31, 1941 GSHI, A.11. 49/Sow./6

I am writing to acknowledge receipt of your letter of October 28th, No. c 11419/8090/G, addressed to General Sikorski and to thank you for the information which you were good enough to give him regarding your interventions with the Soviet Government supporting our efforts in the important question of the proper organization, equipment and arming of the Polish army in Russia. Also the attaching of a British liaison officer to General Anders.

Following your suggestion instructions have been sent to Ambassador Kot to concert with Sir Stafford Cripps and with General Macfarlane on further action.

We have received a telegram from our Ambassador in Moscow. It contains information on an improvement in the atmosphere and gives vent to the hope that in connection with General Sikorski's prospected visit it will be possible to obtain from the Soviet Government assurances as to the release of civilian persons still detained and also assurances with regard to the creation of our army.

At the same time Ambassador Kot would be grateful if explicit instructions were given to the British Ambassador in Russia recommending him to assist in the sending of Polish troops to Great Britain and to the Near East. This is necessary as the British competent authorities in Russia appear to have doubts on this matter and are inclined to restrict the dispatch of Polish soldiers to the United Kingdom only to trained air crews.

As you will certainly remember General Sikorski exposed to the British Government the necessity of securing for the Polish Corps now in Scotland and the Polish Brigade in Egypt the urgently needed drafts (about 8,000 and 2,000 respectively). He received from the Prime Minister and from yourself a favourable reply. I am therefore confidently hoping that you will find it possible to give Ambassador Cripps the necessary instructions. It is only after these are received that M. Kot can enter into formal negotiations with the Soviet authorities for the release from Russia of our men.

No. 136

Note from Ambassador Ciechanowski to President Roosevelt concerning the stalemate in the formation of the Polish Army in the USSR and the suggestion of shifting it to Central Asia, with Memorandum[1]

Washington, October 31, 1941   GSHI, PRM, 41/3

Following instructions from Prime Minister General Sikorski, I had the honour to ask that I might be received by you in order personally to submit some details concerning a stalemate which appears to have arisen in connection with the formation of the Polish armed units in Soviet Russia. I have yesterday discussed this matter with Mr. Atherton at the Department of State.

In view of the urgency of the problem which involves the possibility of a speedy organization of Polish Armed Units, likely to attain the figure of about 150,000 eager Polish soldiers, I am taking the liberty of sending you the enclosed memorandum.

General Sikorski informs me that the British Ambassador in Moscow has been instructed by his Government to give full support to the Polish Ambassador's endeavours in this matter.

General Sikorski would be most grateful if you, Mr. President, would grant your invaluable support by influencing the Soviet Government to agree to a favourable solution of this problem so vital to Poland and, in fact, of great importance to the common cause for which we are fighting.

Allow me, Mr. President, to express my thanks for all that you may wish to do in this matter, and please accept the assurances of my highest consideration.

Memorandum

The Polish Ambassador has been instructed by General Sikorski, Prime Minister of Poland, to lay before the President the present situation which has arisen in Russia in connection with the endeavours of the Polish Government to form units of the Polish Army composed of interned Polish military and civilian Poles of military age deported to Russia at the time of the Soviet occupation of Polish territory.

General Sikorski is of the opinion that the common cause requires the utilization of all available man-power, and especially those valuable Polish soldiers at present in Russia, on such fronts where they could most easily be organized and armed, and where there is the greatest need of having considerable armed reserves.

The most recent conversations between the Polish Ambassador to the USSR, Mr. Kot, and the Commissar for Foreign Affairs, Mr. Molotov, cause apprehension to the Polish Government regarding the formation of Polish Armed Forces in Soviet Russia.

These conversations confirm the impression that the Soviet Government tends to limit the Polish Armed Forces to two divisions using the very

[1] See Note No. 136.

numerous remaining former Polish war prisoners and volunteers, for work in factories, mines and agriculture. The reason given is the alleged lack of labour in the USSR.

In the course of the last weeks the transports of former Polish war prisoners in Russia are not being directed to the Polish Training Camps but are being directed via Tashkent to cotton plantations and irrigation and construction works in Uzbekistan, and particularly in the Districts of Nukus and Novourgencz on the Amu Daria river, where the USSR authorities intend to settle 100,000 Poles. It also appears that many Polish prisoners of war have not yet been liberated from prison camps.

Such an attitude on the part of the Soviet Government is not in conformity with the Military Agreement signed with Poland on August 14, 1941.

General Sikorski is of the opinion that this negative attitude of the USSR Government and their claim of not being able to supply equipment and armament for the Polish Armed Forces has been greatly facilitated by the fact that at the Moscow Conference the delegates of Great Britain and the United States, when agreeing to supply heavy armament, tanks and anti-tank guns exclusively to the Soviet Army, did not explicitly designate any of this armament for the Allied Polish Army being formed in Russia.

So far the Soviets have inadequately armed only one Polish Division. The Soviet Government puts forth as an argument lack of material and their inability to arm any further units and even to supply food to the Polish Army.

In view of this situation General Sikorski, Commander-in-Chief of the Polish Army, instructed the Polish Ambassador in the USSR to communicate to Mr. Stalin his intention of coming to Soviet Russia, if the Soviet Government agreed in principle to certain conditions, the application of which could be usefully discussed by the Commander-in-Chief with Mr. Stalin. These conditions are as follows:

The liberation from prisons and camps of forced labour of all Polish citizens at present in the USSR and guaranteeing them human conditions of existence.

All Polish citizens fit for military service to be utilized in Polish camps for the formation of additional Polish armed units by the Polish High Command.

Owing to the inability of supplying equipment and the difficulties connected with the feeding of such a large amount of people by the Soviet Government, this entire Polish Army to be concentrated until ready for action in a locality where it could be easily taken care of by Great Britain. The most convenient locality would be Iran or, as a last resource, the Caucasus could be taken into consideration.

Taking into account Polish and Soviet interests, the British Government expressed their readiness to undertake to equip and feed the Polish Army on condition that it should be located in a place accessible for deliveries of food and material.

About 15,000 to 20,000 Polish soldiers to be evacuated from the USSR to Great Britain and Egypt.

The Polish Government considers that all available man-power, especially qualified soldiers, should be used wherever they are most needed and that the utilization of such valuable trained material on farms and irrigation projects would be unjustified waste, inconsistent with war needs.

Ambassador Biddle has been informed of the above situation and has been supplied with all the data at the disposal of the Polish Government at this time. Apart from that the Polish Prime Minister has informed the Polish Ambassador in Washington that he has discussed these matters with Prime Minister Churchill and Mr. Anthony Eden. Mr. Eden was to try to influence Ambassador Maisky in accordance with the views of the Polish Government on this subject.

Likewise, the British Ambassador in Moscow has been instructed by his Government to obtain the USSR's consent for the evacuation of all Polish military formations to Iran, the British Government declaring that they are ready to undertake the responsibility for their full equipment and armament.

The Polish Ambassador in Washington is instructed by his Government to appeal to the President to lend his valuable support to the endeavours of the Polish Government. Prime Minister General Sikorski believes that, in view of the extensive aid which the United States is at present giving to the USSR, the Soviet Government would undoubtedly give serious consideration to the expression of such support on the part of the President in the matter of the formation of the Polish armed units, in accordance with the fair and legitimate demands of the Polish Government.

No. 137

Note from Ambassador Kot to Commissar Molotov concerning the conditions of the intended journey of General Sikorski to the USSR and his suggestion of previous settlement of Polish requests connected with the execution of the Agreement of July 30, 1941[1]

Kuibyshev, November 1, 1941   GSHI, A.11. 49/Sow./3
                                                 Transl. from Polish

Referring to my conversation with M. A. J. Vyshinsky, Deputy People's Commissar for Foreign Affairs, on 14th October 1941, as well as to my conversation with your Excellency on 22nd October 1941, in the course of which I raised the question of an official visit to the Soviet Union of General Władysław Sikorski, President of the Council of Ministers of the Republic of Poland, I have the honour of informing your Excellency that General Sikorski can leave Egypt for the USSR on about 7th November. . . .

Realizing the importance of his personal meeting with Premier Stalin, your Excellency and the Soviet High Command, for the strengthening of friendly co-operation between the two governments and for the pursuance of the war against the common enemy, General Sikorski desires to hold those conversations in an atmosphere free from a number of essential problems still unresolved or not examined, as their present state would render the

[1] See Note No. 137.

stay of the Polish Premier and C.-in-C. of the Polish Army particularly embarrassing with regard to the Polish population in the USSR, and also to those problems, the satisfactory settlement of which becomes imperative in view of recent developments.

As the purpose and the programme of his journey have been agreed with the British Government, General Sikorski thinks that as long as a propitious atmosphere for conversations does not exist the latter would not produce results corresponding to the interests of both governments and to the common war efforts of the countries struggling against Germany. General Sikorski therefore expects that before fixing the final date of his arrival the Soviet Government will express agreement in principle with the following points which are of primary importance for the Polish Government and people.

1. Speeding up the full execution of the provisions of the Additional Protocol to the Polish-Soviet Agreement of 30th July 1941 and the Decree of the Supreme Soviet of the USSR of 12th August 1941 relating to the amnesty 'for all Polish citizens who are at present deprived of freedom on the territory of the USSR either as prisoners of war or on any other grounds', and ensuring to the Polish citizens who are not enlisted with the Polish Army a suitable employment or means of subsistence.

2. In view of your Excellency's statement in a conversation with myself on 22nd October 1941 about the impossibility of arming and supplying food to such great numbers of men by the Soviet Government, the Polish Army should be concentrated in an area which would enable it to be easily supplied by Great Britain until the troops have attained a condition of combat readiness.

3. In view of the inability of the Soviet Government to find equipment and food rations for such numbers, the entire Polish Army would be concentrated, pending their combat readiness, at a point easily accessible for British supplies.

4. The evacuation of 15,000–20,000 Polish soldiers from the USSR to Great Britain and Egypt.

General Sikorski proposes that the ways in which these requests should be executed, and in particular those under points 2–4, should be settled in his conversations with the Soviet authorities.

Bringing the foregoing matters to your Excellency's notice, by the order of my Government, I take the liberty of expressing my conviction that a satisfactory solution of all these questions and the establishing of a direct contact between Premier General Sikorski and the leading authorities of the Soviet Union, will be not only the turning point in the relations between our States of far-reaching consequences for the future, but will also contribute, in the highest degree, to the strengthening of the common war effort of all the Allies and to their victory over Germany.

Should your Excellency think it proper, I am ready to come to Moscow in order to discuss the matters bearing on General Sikorski's visit to the USSR.

No. 138

Note from Ambassador Cripps on his interview with Deputy Commissar Vyshinsky on the demand of the Polish Government concerning the fulfilment of the Polish-Soviet Agreement of July 30, 1941, with aide-mémoire[1]

Kuibyshev, November 3, 1941   GSHI, A.11. 49/Sow./3

I gave Mr. Vyshinsky an aide-mémoire in the form attached and he told me in reply that he would send it to his Government and endeavour to get me an answer as soon as possible. He added that he had some preliminary observations which he would like to make.

He then stated as follows:

In general principle such questions as were raised were for discussion between the Soviet and Polish Governments. As to the thousands of Polish prisoners remaining in camps, etc.: this statement was without basis as all the prisoners had been released according to the Ukase cited. In the case of persons accused of some crimes, e.g. espionage on behalf of the Germans, the persons implicated were not due for release.

I pointed out that was not so and explained to him exactly how the clause as to the amnesty came to be agreed between myself and M. Stalin and also that there was no exception as to the amnesty as there would have been, had it been intended to exclude any class of Polish citizens.

He agreed that the amnesty was general though the term general was not actually used in the Ukase. But added that there was no contradiction between what he had first said and the view I had expressed of the amnesty. All he suggested was that it was possible that some had not been released who were accused of espionage, he had not said that they had not actually been released. All the persons mentioned in the aide-mémoire had really been released.

There was a difficulty which might account for some individual not being released in regard to the people evacuated from the Ukraine and White Russia, as these had been declared to be Soviet citizens. Also some of the prisoners evacuated from the prisons accused of various crimes had gone in various directions and it might be that the records had got lost or sent to the wrong place. He had no information on the subject and would have to look into it.

It was possible that some were entitled to be released and their cases would have to be looked into.

I asked him what need there was for this as the only thing to be ascertained was whether they were Polish citizens. He replied that the question of their citizenship would have to be enquired into in the first case. On further pressing he said that that was all that would have to be ascertained.

I then said that it was our information that large numbers of Poles remained in camps, etc.; to which he replied that he had no such information, and would I give him the names and the places. I said that I could only repeat to him the list that he had already had from the Polish Ambassador.

[1] See Note No. 138.

He then said that there were only a very small number detained at most, that they had given periodic lists to the Polish Ambassador of the numbers released. It was possible that in the case of those very far away the news of their release had not yet been received.

As to the other question of their feeding they could not give food unless they worked, any more than they would to their own citizens. However everything in the aide-mémoire would be reported to the Government and a reply would be given to the British Government.

He then asked for an explanation of the last paragraph and I told him that as far as I knew General Sikorski wanted these matters settled in principle as he did not want to embark on acrimonious discussions when he came and if they were not so settled he would probably think it wise to delay his visit.

Mr. Vyshinsky thanked me for the explanation and then said that there were no unsettled questions as all due for release had been released and they could obtain work if they liked. He repeated that he was not well up in the matters and would look into them again.

He then returned to the question of feeding and asked me whether it was intended to imply that all who did not work were to be maintained. I replied no, but those that could not work—such as the aged and infirm, invalids, women and children—must be maintained. He then asked why not by the Polish Government. To which I replied because the Soviet Government had removed them from their homes and they were in USSR and not in Poland. Moreover the Polish Government had not got the necessary supplies.

He replied that none got bread free unless they came under some scheme of benefits and that anyway the Poles were being given 15 roubles a day while travelling.

I said that the real question was not who paid for the food, that could be settled hereafter between the two Governments, but it was essential that the people should get the food and not starve. I then cited the case of the 16 people who arrived here dead from the North the other night [of which he] had not before heard and suggested that it must be due to illness. To which I replied that according to my information it was starvation and not illness. I also pointed out that it was said that the Poles were not allowed to get bread at the stations. He said this was not possible as there was no racial distinction in the USSR and if they had money they could buy the bread. He would however check up these things carefully. He agreed that the important thing was for the people to have the bread and the question of who was to pay for it could be regulated after.

I gained the impression that he took the aide-mémoire very seriously and was surprised that he was prepared to go into such a long discussion in an attempt to justify the position of his Government. His preliminary objection to our interfering in the matter was clearly only a formality, and he was most anxious to do what he could to reassure me. I think that he felt that he had failed and for that reason he kept on saying that he was not up in the facts and he would make enquiries, etc.

I am quite sure that he does not think that all the Poles have been released and equally sure that he realizes that his arguments as to spies won't hold water.

On the whole I think that H.M.G.'s intervention may have some effect and I made it quite clear that Sikorski's visit would depend upon the answer that the Soviet Government gave to the Polish questions.

I then asked him about Molotov's return and he said that he would not be back before the holiday when there would be a parade here.

He promised to receive myself and Sir Walter Monckton tomorrow at noon.

Aide Mémoire

His Majesty's Government have been much concerned at information they have recently been receiving from the Polish Government about the difficulties that have arisen over the implementation of the terms of the Agreement of July 30th, 1941, and of the subsequent Military Agreement between the Polish and the Soviet Governments.

The Prime Minister and Mr. Eden have discussed this matter fully with General Sikorski and the Polish Government in London, and they are all in agreement about the desirability of General Sikorski's visiting the USSR.

His Majesty's Government feel some responsibility in the matter owing to the part which they played in assisting the Polish and Soviet Governments to arrive at an agreement in the first instance. In particular, the Soviet Government will recollect that the actual clause about the amnesty for Polish citizens was settled in Moscow between M. Stalin and the British Ambassador.

As a result of conversations which have taken place in London between the British and Polish Governments, and in view of the declaration made by M. Molotov to the Polish Ambassador at Kuibyshev a few days ago to the effect that the Soviet Government were unable to supply the Polish forces with either arms or food in adequate quantities, it has been suggested that it would be best if these forces were to be moved down to the South where they could be equipped by the British authorities and would be more accessible from British sources of supply.

There is a further question, about which His Majesty's Government are much concerned, relating to the amnesty already mentioned above, for which they feel, as already stated, a measure of responsibility. They understand that there are still many thousands of Polish citizens, including many of military age and fit for military service, in prisons, concentration camps and forced labour camps, particularly in the extreme North of the USSR. They do not understand why these persons have not yet been released, as agreed some three months ago and as laid down in the Ukase of the Supreme Council of the USSR of August 8th which was subsequently published.[2] It would seem to them that the immediate release of these Polish citizens is imperative if good relations between the Polish and Soviet Governments

[2] Mistake, should be: Ukase of August 12th.

are to continue. The Soviet Government would no doubt at the same time make whatever arrangements were necessary for these Polish citizens to receive the necessaries of life either by providing them with free work at adequate wages or else by making them the necessary allowances in money or kind.

His Majesty's Government feel impelled to draw the attention of the Soviet Government to the above-mentioned matters since they are most anxious to do all they can to assist in preserving the good relations that exist between the Soviet and Polish Governments.

His Majesty's Government would urge the Soviet Government to give its decision in principle upon the above points at the earliest possible moment, so that it may then be possible for General Sikorski to visit the USSR at an early date.

No. 139

Conversation between Ambassador Kot and Deputy Commissar Vyshinsky on the credits granted by the Soviet Government for the needs of the Polish troops and civilians. Present also M. Pushkin, acting as interpreter, and 1st Secretary of the Polish Embassy W. Arlet

Kuibyshev, November 5, 1941 GSHI, A.11. 49/Sow./4
Transl. from Polish

Vyshinsky: I asked you to call on me, Sir, because I wished to inform you of the recent decision of the Soviet Government on the question of credits for the needs of the Polish Army. Taking as a basis the strength of 30,000 men, pursuant to Art. 13 of the Polish-Soviet Military Agreement, the expenditure on food, maintenance and pay of Polish forces here will be covered from a credit, interest-free, granted to the Polish Government by the Government of the Soviet Union. On 31st December 1941 the total amount of this credit will be 65 million Roubles, divided into the following items:

Maintenance of the troops until 31.10.41 . .	39 Mil. Rb.
Building works for the troops	5 ,, ,,
Maintenance of the troops from 1.11 to 31.12.41 .	17½ ,, ,,
Relief allowances for the civilian population .	3 ,, ,,
Total: about . . .	65 Mil. Rb.

This credit is to be repaid within ten years from the end of the war.

The arrears in officers' and other ranks' pay have probably arisen through the negligence of the Polish and Soviet military authorities. However, in order to pay the arrears as soon as possible, an order will be issued for the sum of 4 million Roubles, to be remitted today into the hands of General Anders.

Ambassador: I am not conversant with the financial problems of the troops. They are within the province of the Military Mission and the High Command of the Polish Armed Forces. In view of that I am unable to express any opinion on the merit of your declaration, Mr. Commissar. General Anders is at present staying at Kuibyshev, and I shall ask him to look into this matter and, on my behalf, I designate M. Strumiłło, Financial Adviser to the Embassy, for the same purpose. What is not quite clear to me is the sum of 3 million as a relief fund for the civilian population. I should be most obliged to you, Mr. Commissar, if you would explain to me for what purpose this sum is earmarked.

Vyshinsky: I know well that these questions interest the army in the first instance, and because of that General Anders will be informed of them by the General Staff. However, I received a special order from Molotov to inform you personally of this decision of the Government, not only because it concerns the army, that is to say, an institution which is particularly near to our hearts, but also because of the sum of 3 million Roubles for the most urgent needs of the civilian population, to be put at your disposal, Mr. Ambassador. It was Molotov also who personally gave the order relating to the payment of arrears to the army and asked me to inform you of it.

Ambassador: The arrears of officers' and other ranks' pay have not arisen through our fault; the indents were submitted in due time to the Quarter-Master General's Department of the Soviet Army, but the reply was that, although there were no objections to the amount requested, a decision of the Supreme Soviet was needed for the payment.

It is the best proof of the high morale of our troops that, although they have not received a farthing for two months, they did not claim the money due to them from the High Command, but continued their training and carried on their military duties. By no means can I agree to the statement that it was our fault.

Vyshinsky: Obviously, our military authorities were guilty. I see that the Narkomindel must look more closely into these matters. I shall take them into my own hands in order to avoid the repetition of such facts in future.

Ambassador: The strength of our army, put at 30,000, also raises some doubts. As far as I remember there are 44,000 soldiers. From what date are your figures taken, Mr. Commissar?

Vyshinsky: This information was received from the General Staff. It corresponds to what has been agreed, namely:

2 infantry divisions @ 11,000 men	22,000
Reserve Centre	5,000
Officer Training Unit	2,000
Staff and services	1,000

Ambassador: As a matter of fact this is not within my province. I shall ask our officers for an explanation. For the time being it is this fund of 3 million Rb. which interests me. Should this sum have any connection with my proposal for a loan, it is clear that I could not accept it. This amount is out of proportion to the actual needs.

Vyshinsky: I told you, Mr. Ambassador, during our last conversation, that as far as this loan is concerned the decision of the Soviet Government was negative, because of, among others, the necessity to abandon the re-settlement plan.

Ambassador: I have just received information from Tashkent that about 300,000 Polish citizens have arrived in Uzbekistan. 100,000 of them are unfit for military service or for work, and they have no means of subsistence whatever. They are invalids, women, elderly people and children. If you compare these two figures, you will see, Mr. Commissar, that the sum of 3 million Rb. will not solve this problem.

Vyshinsky: I have made the position of the Soviet Government on this matter clear. If the Polish Government wishes to help these people, it has to look for other sources, perhaps from some charitable institutions.

Ambassador: I repeat that this sum is no solution at all. Perhaps, being put among military credits, it is destined for the expenses of our soldiers' relatives. Perhaps the Soviet Government could keep this sum, and pay out of it allowances to persons whom it releases from prisons and camps.

Vyshinsky: It is your concern, Mr. Ambassador, how this matter will be settled with your military men. This is all that I wished to tell you today, Mr. Ambassador.

Ambassador: Can you tell me anything about the reply to my Note to Commissar Molotov?

Vyshinsky: I expect the reply tonight, and I shall let you know it immediately.

Ambassador: I shall be most obliged to you.

Vyshinsky: On the same day on which you delivered this Note, I telephoned its text to Moscow, in accordance with your wishes. Yesterday I spoke on the telephone to Molotov who told me he would not delay the reply. The plane from Moscow with our official mail takes off about noon and arrives here before the night, and, unless something unexpected happens causing it to land and spend the night on the way, I expect the answer by tonight or by tomorrow morning at the latest.

Ambassador (taking leave): I shall be at your disposal, Mr. Commissar, when the reply arrives, any time of day or night.

Vyshinsky was much more polite than during the conversation on 2nd October. It seemed that he expected some thanks on the part of the Ambassador for the settlement of the questions raised by him, and he looked disappointed. The Ambassador was reserved and frigidly polite. The conversation lasted half-an-hour.[1]

[1] This document is a copy signed by the First Secretary of the Embassy W. Arlet on 5.11.1941. Prof. Kot in his book *Conversations with the Kremlin* gives different figures so far as the cost of maintenance of the army in particular periods is concerned. However, the total figure is the same.

Telegram from General Panfilov to Lieut.-General Anders announcing the limitation of the Polish Army in the USSR to 30 thousand men

Moscow, November 6, 1941   GSHI, KGA, 7–b
                                                         Transl. from Russian

The High Command of the Armed Forces of the Union has instructed me to let you know that:

1. The total number of the Polish Army on the territory of the USSR for 1941 has been set at 30,000 men, including officers, NCO's and other ranks.

2. On this basis you are empowered to form:

a) two infantry divisions of 11,000 men each . .	22,000
b) one base camp	5,000
c) an officers' school	2,000
d) the army GHQ and ancillary services . . .	1,000
Altogether . . .	30,000

3. Taking the above into account will you please prepare the necessary lists of establishment and let me see them.

These lists must show the amount of pay of officers, NCO's and other ranks.

4. Will you please direct the surplus men in the region of formation to the appropriate localities of residence according to their wishes.

5. In future the issue of food, feedstuffs, equipment and fuel will be carried out in accordance with the numerical state of the Polish Army, not more however than for 30,000 men and the regulation number of horses, motor transport units (according to the agreed establishment and tables).

The food, feeding stuffs, fuel, means of transport, arms and ammunition will be issued against cash, according to the Red Army price list.

6. In future the appropriate rent, as fixed by tariffs, will be collected for the barracks, the accommodation for staffs, the signals facilities, the means of transport and the use of local facilities supplied or put at the disposal of the units commanded by you. It is therefore necessary for the required agreements to be concluded with the supply authorities of the Volga Military Region.

7. The Government of the USSR has placed at the disposal of the Polish Government credits to the amount of 65,000,000 roubles for the needs of the Polish formations in the USSR. Out of this sum you should pay for the food, the feeding stuffs, the fuel, the means of transport, the arms and the ammunition supplied to the Polish units.

The financing of the expenses connected with building construction has been fixed at 5,000,000 roubles. This sum, as well as the 5,000,000 roubles already given you on account, are included in the sum total of credits of 65,000,000 roubles.

In future the organization of Polish units as well as supplying them with food and equipment will be carried out solely through me.

8. Concerning all matters of organization and supply of the units of the Polish Army will you please address yourself to me: The Plenipotentiary of the High Command of the Red Army for the formation of the Polish Army, Moscow, No. 6, Gogolevski Boulevard; or at the same address to the chief of staff for Polish formations, Major W. T. Sosnicki.

No. 141

Note of a conversation between General Sikorski and Mr. Lyttelton on the suggested evacuation of the Polish Army from the USSR

Cairo, November 6, 1941   GSHI, A.11.49/Sow./4
                                                  Transl. from Polish

The conversation centred on the evacuation of the Polish Forces to Persia. Mr. Lyttelton had received an instruction in this matter, from Prime Minister Churchill, signed by the Foreign Secretary, Mr. Eden, which the Polish Chargé d'Affaires had been allowed to read previously. According to the instruction Mr. Lyttelton was to give all his help to the Polish Prime Minister and in fact he did. At the outset he said that he had already studied the problem and had weighed the difficulties. He expected the principal difficulties to lie in communications and organization. Out of the two possible routes only one, through the Caspian Sea, can be reckoned with. The other, more to the East, might prove inadequate.

Mr. Lyttelton pointed out that military matters in connection with Russia come under General Wavell and that he had asked him for an expert to be sent from Basra to Cairo, in order to direct the technical matters.

The Polish Prime Minister, Gen. Sikorski, asked that officers from his staff be allowed to co-operate in drawing up the plans for this operation and that the work be started immediately. Mr. Lyttelton remarked that this co-operation would be very welcome. Gen. Sikorski explained that the morale of the Polish troops in Russia could not be better and that only one per cent could be counted as doubtful owing to Soviet influences.

The Polish Prime Minister made his position regarding the evacuation of the Polish nationals in the Soviet Union quite clear to Mr. Lyttelton and added that he would go to the Soviet Union only if the conditions he had made to Stalin are accepted.

The conversation was of a congenial character and it was obvious that Mr. Lyttelton was striving for a successful solution of the problem.

No. 142

Note from Commissar Molotov to Ambassador Kot concerning the journey of General Sikorski to the USSR[1]

Moscow, November 8, 1941

GSHI, PRM, 41/2
Transl. from Polish

I have the honour of acknowledging receipt of your letter of 1st November by which you informed me that the President of the Council of Ministers of the Republic of Poland, General Sikorski, could leave Egypt for the USSR about 7th November.

I share entirely M. Sikorski's view, stated in your letter, on the great importance of personal contact between the Polish Premier and C.-in-C. of the Polish Army, and J. V. Stalin and the High Command of the Red Army, for the strengthening of friendly relations between the two governments, and also for the pursuance of war against the common enemy.

The question of fixing the final date of M. Sikorski's arrival in the USSR rests entirely with him. The Soviet Government can only state that they are ready to receive M. Sikorski as their guest at any time he might wish. The Soviet Government must state, however, that they do not see any necessity for subordinating the question of fixing the definite date of M. Sikorski's arrival in the USSR to the declaration by the Soviet Government of their agreement in principle to the issues raised under paras. 1–4 of your letter. They consider that these and other issues relating to Polish-Soviet relations are to be examined within the framework of the agreements concluded between the Government of the USSR and Poland. As regards the nature of the issues mentioned in your letter, I feel obliged to state:

1) Pursuant to the Decree of the Praesidium of the Supreme Soviet of the USSR of 13th August, 1941 [this date is given wrongly, it should be 12th August, 1941], on amnesty, all Polish citizens deprived of freedom either as prisoners of war or on any other valid grounds, were released, and specified categories of the persons discharged were given material assistance by the Soviet authorities (free railway and waterway tickets, journey allowances, etc.). The question of providing employment and means of subsistence for those of them who have not been called up by the Polish Army, has been already discussed between us and you, and I can only say that the question should be settled in the same manner as in the case of Soviet citizens, without any special undertaking on the part of the Government of the USSR.

2) The question which Polish citizens should be incorporated into the Polish armed forces rests entirely with the Polish Government within the figures laid down in the Polish-Soviet Agreement [cf. Protocol No. 2 of 19th August, 1941].

3) As regards the designation of localities in which the Polish military units should be stationed, the question is determined by bilateral agreements between Polish and Soviet military authorities, and, if any need should arise of changes, the Soviet Government are ready to take them into consideration.

[1] See Note No. 142.

199

4) There are no obstacles to the evacuation of 15,000–20,000 Polish soldiers from the USSR to Great Britain and Egypt, according to your wishes.

Will you allow me, Sir, to express finally my firm belief that the questions relating to Polish-Soviet relations will always be settled in the spirit of friendly consideration, and the personal meeting of Premier-General Sikorski with the leaders of the Soviet Union will greatly contribute to it.

The question of your coming to Moscow, Mr. Ambassador, I leave entirely with you and, as far as I am concerned, I can assure you that all urgent questions can be discussed by you with my Deputy A. J. Vyshinsky.[2]

[2] Note handed Deputy to Commissar Vyshinsky November 11, 1941.

No. 143

Note from the Polish Embassy in Kuibyshev to the People's Commissariat for Foreign Affairs concerning the conscription by the Red Army of Polish citizens of Ukrainian, White Ruthenian and Jewish origin

Kuibyshev, November 10, 1941 GSHI, A.XII, 22/30.2
Transl. from Polish: Pol.-Sov.R., No. 56

According to information received, the War Commissar for Kazakhstan at Alma-Ata, General Shcherbakov, issued orders that all Polish citizens deported by the Soviet Authorities from occupied Polish territory and possessing documents issued to them by these authorities, endorsed to the effect that they are of Ukrainian, White Ruthenian or Jewish origin, are to be enrolled in the Red Army if they meet the age and fitness requirements.

After an intervention by the interested parties and by a representative of this Embassy, General Shcherbakov declared that he was acting on instructions from the Central Authorities, who are alleged to have directed him to treat as citizens of the USSR all citizens of the Republic of Poland of other than Polish origin possessing Soviet passports. Among others the following Polish citizens, despite protests on their part, were among those conscripted and sent, it would seem, to the Far East: Aleksander Rotstein, Silberspitz and Kotok.

This same discrimination between Polish citizens according to origin or race, devoid of any impartial basis and contrary to the provisions of the Polish-Soviet Agreement of July 30, 1941, is being practised by the military authorities in Alma-Ata, who also explain to the Polish citizens reporting to them to settle various formalities connected with their enlistment in the Polish Army in the Union of Soviet Socialist Republics, that they are acting on instructions from the Central Authorities. Only Polish citizens of Polish origin are given permits to travel to centres where the Polish Army is being organized, while Polish citizens of Ukrainian and Jewish origin are, it seems, categorically refused permits by the aforementioned authorities.

The Polish Embassy has the honour to request the People's Commissariat for Foreign Affairs to cause instructions to be given to the War Commissar in Kazakhstan to apply impartially to all Polish citizens residing in the area under his authority, the principles resulting from the Polish-Soviet Agreement of July 30, 1941, and the Polish-Soviet Military Agreement of August 14, 1941, which guarantee the right to serve in the Polish Army in the USSR to every Polish citizen who is capable of bearing arms.

No. 144

Note on a conversation between Lt.-General Anders, Colonel Yevstigneyev and Colonel Volkovisky on the Soviet restrictions of equipment and food rations to Polish Forces in the USSR

Buzuluk, November 11, 1941　　　　　　　　　　　GSHI, KGA, 7a
　　　　　　　　　　　　　　　　　　　　　　Transl. from Polish

Anders: The number of Polish soldiers in the USSR is very great. Not all of them have been released, there are still thousands of officers in prisons and labour camps in the far North. Those who have been released, as you know, are hurrying to the Buzuluk area. You must remember that I had warned you earlier, at the meetings of the Commission, that this movement would take place spontaneously and gather momentum. When both camps and Buzuluk were filled to capacity the NKVD proposed to direct the constant flow of soldiers to Uzbekistan and some Volga areas. I agreed and sent there as well those men who were not so fit for active service. I have at present 44,000 enlisted soldiers and under no circumstances can I diminish this figure. To send the excess to Tashkent and disperse them to work in various places would completely undermine the morale of the army, and their confidence in me, as their Commander. I cannot agree to it, and should this operation be necessary, I have firmly decided to resign, because in those circumstances I could not assume the responsibility for what might happen.

Volkovisky: It seems to me that the figure of 30,000 as the strength of the Polish Army is provisional. Our present work together should provide the necessary data for moving the proposal for the formation of further units. I think that the present state of things is due to the fact that both sides have committed some mistakes. [. . .]

Anders (interrupting Colonel Volkovisky): I cannot agree with your statement, Colonel. I state very emphatically that there were no mistakes or shortcomings on our part. We put the case clearly and honestly, and if any difficulties or shortcomings arise, it is definitely not our fault.

Volkovisky: In any case, we shall advance the question of further organization of the Polish Army in Moscow.

Anders: Further units must be formed where they will have suitable conditions for accommodation and training. I do not consider the present conditions of the two Polish divisions to be suitable. They have been left in summer camps and have not received the necessary material means for building winter camps, either in due time or in adequate numbers. Moreover, the barracks assigned to them in Belebey were occupied by Red Army units although I had not been advised beforehand of the change of decision. Neither have I received the barracks in Saratov which were promised to me.

Yevstigneyev: What has been done cannot be undone. Still we must see to it that no difficulties arise in future.

Anders: I understand all the difficulties due to the present circumstances, so do my subordinates. I do not exaggerate their importance, but as the C.O. of the Polish Army I cannot agree that my fellow-soldiers should remain another day in prisons and labour camps. Moreover, about 5,000 of my fellow-officers are missing. Neither can I agree to a limit being put to the strength of the Polish Army.

Yevstigneyev: If the figure laid down for 1941 as the strength of the Polish Army was 30,000 it does not mean that there will be no increase in 1942. Personally, I agree with General Anders's statements and I will support the question of the formation of further units.

Anders: To sum up the preceding discussion may I ask you to put the following issues in Moscow quite clearly:

It is necessary— a) to release immediately from prisons and labour camps all our soldiers, and to house them in better conditions;

b) to maintain, in any case, the present strength of 44,000 of the Polish Army until the formation of further units;

c) to release all Polish citizens from the Red Army and Labour Battalions. If I put this issue in third place, it is not because I consider it to be less important but only because these men are at present clothed, have a roof over their heads, and enjoy slightly better conditions of life than the others.

No. 145

Records of the conversation between Ambassador Kot and Deputy Commissar Vyshinsky concerning the detention of Polish officers and Polish civilians contrary to the Polish-Soviet Agreement. Present also Head of the Department of the Narkomindel Novikov and 1st Secretary of the Polish Embassy W. Arlet who made the notes and acted as interpreter

Kuibyshev, November 12, 1941   GSHI, A.11. 49/Sow./4
                                                              Transl. from Polish

Vyshinsky (after having greeted the Ambassador): I apologize for disturbing you again, but I have received some information on the question raised by you in the letter addressed to us on 31st October, 1941. I have here a document consisting of 9 pages and containing a list of places and names, and many detailed data. I ordered the case to be submitted to me immediately, and today I am able to give you some information. For instance: You have stated in your list that in the Altai Land, Topchynsky area, were the following Polish citizens: Witold Górski, Maria Górska and Jadwiga Nagrodzka; they were allegedly refused release. As it appears from the papers in the possession of the NKVD, all these persons had actually been released, and left the place at the beginning of October for an unknown destination. It was said in your letter that a group of Polish citizens remained there. The NKVD organs state that in reality there are no Polish citizens there any more. As you see, it is much easier to make inquiries when exact names are given to us.

Ambassador: Thank you for this information. [. . .].

Vyshinsky: Some time ago you expressed the wish to meet Stalin. I think that you might discuss some matters with him.

Ambassador: I shall consider it an honour. I wish to emphasize, however, that the matter is urgent. I thank you for your proposal but you should keep in mind that General Sikorski will stay in Egypt a short time only. When he finishes his work there he will take off, and it might be too late.

Vyshinsky: I shall ring up Moscow today and discuss the question directly with Stalin. Now, as regards the officers concerning whose release General Sikorski applied to you. Is the Narkomindel in possession of a nominal list? Perhaps M. Arlet can hand the list to M. Novikov?

Ambassador: Two lists of politicians and prominent persons are in the Narkomindel's possession. One was handed personally by me to you, Mr. Commissar, the second was sent to you on my order. So far as officers are concerned, a list was submitted to the NKVD by General Anders, and the list of those who stayed in prisoner-of-war camps at Starobelsk, Kozelsk and Ostashkov and other places is being drawn up at our army head-quarters.

Vyshinsky: I repeat this question, because in my opinion those men have already been released. It remains to find their whereabouts. Should anyone among them be still detained, he will be, of course, released. So far as I am concerned, this problem does not exist at all.

Ambassador: The question is quite simple. The camp authorities at Starobelsk, Kozelsk and Ostashkov possessed exact nominal rolls of Polish militaries detained there. It is sufficient to give an order to release those men according to the said rolls.

Vyshinsky: Certainly, provided they are still there. [. . .].

The conversation lasted 45 minutes. From the very beginning Vyshinsky was all smiles and very courteous, and at the end he was still more cheerful. The Ambassador was rather reserved and uncommunicative at the beginning, but he obviously altered his tone completely in the second part of the conversation.

No. 146

Letter from Lt.-General Anders to the High Command of the Red Army in reply to the Note of the latter of 6th November, 1941, fixing the strength of the Polish Army in the USSR at 30,000 men

Kuibyshev, November 14, 1941

GSHI, PRM, 41/2
Transl. from Polish

Referring to the letter No. 2. of 6th November of this year, signed by the Delegate of the High Command of the Armed Forces of the USSR for the formation of the Polish Army, General-Brigadier Panfilov, I feel it my duty to state the following:

The decision of the High Command of the Armed Forces of the USSR fixing the strength of the Polish Forces on the territory of the USSR at

30,000 men for the year 1941, is not consonant either with the Military Agreement, concluded on 14th August, 1941, or with the tenor of all the subsequent conversations between myself and the representatives of the highest Soviet authorities. As a matter of fact, neither in the Military Agreement, nor in the said conversations, had the strength of the Polish Armed Forces in the USSR been determined, whether for the year 1941, or for any further period.

The decision of the High Command of the Armed Forces of the USSR brought to my notice does not take into consideration any of the requests put forward and justified by me. Not only is this decision quite unexpected to me; it constitutes, moreover, a unilateral settlement by the Soviet High Command of a basic Polish problem which is at the same time an inter-allied one.

As the way in which the matter was settled and brought to my notice leaves me no possibility of taking any further steps relating to the formation of the Polish Armed Forces on the territory of the USSR, and as it undermines at the same time the confidence of the very numerous serviceable Polish citizens who are eager to fight against the Germans, I address myself to the Polish Government through the Ambassador of the Republic of Poland, for the purpose of clearing up this matter with the Soviet Government.

No. 147

Note from Ambassador Bogomolov to General Sikorski in reply to the Polish note of October 15, 1941[1]

London, November 14, 1941   GSHI, PRM, 41/2

En réponse à Votre note du 16 octobre[2] de l'année courante, j'ai l'honneur de la part du Gouvernement Soviétique, de porter à votre connaissance, Monsieur le Président du Conseil des Ministres, que tous les citoyens Polonais, qui, d'après l'ukase du Présidium du Soviet Suprême de l'URSS du 12 août de l'année courante devaient être libérés, sont maintenant libérés et avec cela, les autorités soviétiques ont matériellement aidé aux certaines catégories des libérés et des prisonniers de guerre (voyage gratuit par le chemin de fer et par eau, allocations par jour pour alimentation pendant le voyage, etc.). A tous les citoyens polonais libérés, qui ne sont pas appelés sous les drapeaux à l'armée polonaise, on donne la même possibilité de travailler comme et aux citoyens soviétiques, sans aucuns engagements spéciaux de la part du Gouvernement de l'URSS. Tous les officiers polonais, qui se trouvaient sur le territoire de l'URSS, sont aussi libérés. Les suppositions, exprimées par Monsieur le Président du Conseil des Ministres, que de nombreux officiers polonais sont dispersés dans les régions du nord de l'URSS, sont basées, à ce qu'il parait, sur une information incorrecte. En ce qui concerne votre observation, Monsieur le Président du Conseil des Ministres, au sujet de la nécessité du renforcement de l'aide, de la part du Gouvernement Soviétique,

---

[1] See Note No. 147.   [2] 15 octobre.

dans la formation de l'armée polonaise, ill faut dire, que nous aidons de cette manière infailliblement, conformément à l'Accord militaire entre l'URSS et la Pologne, à quoi la récente décision du Gouvernement Soviétique de donner le crédit au Gouvernement de la République Polonaise pour 65 millions de roubles à l'armée polonaise pour des dépenses jusqu'au 1 janvier de l'année 1942, sert d'example.

Le Gouvernement Soviétique a accueilli avec l'attention spéciale la communication de Monsieur le Président du Conseil des Ministres, concernant l'augmentation, par ses instructions, des actes du sabotage et de l'activité de diversion en Pologne, occupée par les Allemands.

No. 148

Telegram from M. Stalin to Mr. Harriman promising to take Polish wishes into account[1]

Moscow, November 14, 1941   GSHI, A.11. 49/Sow./3

Your telegram of the 12th November received. I have not yet had the possibility to acquaint myself with all the details of the Polish question in the USSR. In the course of two or three days, after studying this question, I will let you know the attitude of the Soviet Government. In any case you should have no doubts that the wishes of the Poles, as well as the interests of the friendly relations between the USSR and Poland will be taken into account by the Soviet Government.

[1] See Note No. 148.

No. 149

Record of a conversation held in the Kremlin between Ambassador Kot and M. Stalin in the presence of Commissar Molotov on the building up of the Polish Army, the fate of the Polish population deported to the USSR and the release of Polish prisoners of war[1]

Moscow, November 14, 1941   GSHI, PRM, 41/4
Transl. from Polish

Kot: It is indeed an honour for me to be introduced to you, Mr. President, whose name is bound with the historic moment of the resumption of mutual relations between Poland and the USSR.

Stalin: I greet you, Mr. Ambassador, with pleasure. We, the men of Soviet Russia, consider that the best relations possible should exist between the Soviet and Polish nations. I hope that, in so far as it depends on our nation, we shall be able to do everything that is necessary in this field. I think we should open a new page in history and base our relations on friendship.

Kot: I have listened to your words, Mr. President, with great pleasure, and, on my part, I can assure you that the leaders of the Polish State and nation are for deep and lasting Polish-Soviet co-operation. In fact, we do not see any reasons for conflicts and no issues which might originate them between us, neighbours as we are.

[1] See Note No. 149.

Stalin: Not only neighbours, but also of the same blood ('iedinokrovni' in Russian).

Kot: In view of the dreadful lesson which Hitler is teaching us and the whole world, we should manifest this consanguinity of ours.

Stalin: You are right.

Kot: Some people assert that there exist some problems which divide us, as for instance the Ukrainian and Lithuanian problems. I think that they can be a factor which might bring us closer together.

Stalin nods assent.

Kot: For the time being, the war continues to absorb all our nation. We wish to contribute everything we possibly can to the camp fighting on our side. Our position is not easy: the Government is abroad, and we have hardly any material means. But in spite of this the Germans have to recognize that the Poles constitute a great force. The Germans know, and fear, that when the decisive moment comes, every Pole under occupation will fulfil his soldierly duty. The Polish nation is already now playing its role in this struggle, thanks to its stubbornness and endurance which make it fight unto the last breath, always loyally on the side of the democratic elements. The Polish nation's love of freedom is certainly well known to you, Mr. President. The Germans could not find a Quisling in Poland, they were unable to set up a puppet government. Moreover, there is one particular feature which is the Polish contribution to the democratic cause. The Poles are the only Catholic nation on the Allied side, that is, the Anglo-Saxon Powers and the Soviet Union. This is a matter of great importance, for Hitler cannot pretend that he is defending religion. The attitude of the Poles prevents the Vatican from siding openly with the Axis Powers. But our most important ambition is to create a Polish Army abroad which will be as large as possible. This war is, in fact, not only yours, it is ours as well. For this reason we ask you for a friendly attitude towards the expansion of our great army. The Poles have proved that they wish and know how to fight against Hitler to their last drop of blood. Our troops are in Egypt, in Palestine, in Great Britain, on the seas and in the air, but the biggest reserve of Polish manpower is in the Soviet Union. This is the great problem that General Sikorski would like to settle with you. General Sikorski is a statesman of great character, a soldier capable of overcoming every obstacle. One of the features of his character is toughness, an unyielding strength of will, which has been proved by the fact that he concluded an agreement with the Soviet Union in spite of existing opposition. He is highly respected by the leaders of the Allied States and there are many indications that together with you, Mr. President, with Churchill and with Roosevelt, he will constitute the group of statesmen who will decide on the future organization of the world.

Stalin: I understand the necessity for the creation of the Polish army. I have met Polish soldiers on many fronts and I appreciate them. That is quite clear. I am ready to give you any assistance. Will you please tell me, Mr. Ambassador, what causes your discontent, as well as that of the Poles in Russia, and what their wishes are. If General Sikorski wishes to come to the

Soviet Union he will be our guest, and I hope that between us we shall be able to reach an agreement.

Kot: Do you wish, Mr. President, to hear our requests and grievances?

Stalin: That is so.

Kot: Our co-operation and our good relations must be based on a favourable atmosphere. The Poles who have suffered so much on account of the Russians since the XVIth century really need such an atmosphere. It is not a question of beliefs only but also of feelings, of warmth. The opinion is widely held by the Russian nation that the Poles are a nation of landlords. This does not correspond to facts. We are a nation of peasants, workers, of wage-earners, a nation deeply and truly democratic. I wish to state that this false opinion is deeply rooted among the minor Soviet officials, and it causes many difficulties to Polish citizens. We should be most grateful to you, Mr. President, if using your authority you would contribute to the alteration of such opinions, which you have already started to do by your gesture towards co-operation with us.

Stalin: In the name of historical truth I must make one thing quite clear. Since the XVIth century not only have the Poles suffered at the hand of the Russians but also vice versa, the Russians at the hand of the Poles, for at that time you have twice occupied Moscow. But let bygones by bygones. I do not doubt that there might be cases of unsuitable behaviour towards the Poles on the part of some authorities. This, however, will be eliminated. I know that the Poles are a nation of peasants and working people. All the conditions favouring the ending of mutual enmity, and our joint struggle against the common enemy Hitlerite Germany exist in fact. As regards the Polish army we contracted an obligation of forming 30,000 troops in 1941, consisting of two infantry divisions, one reserve regiment, an officers' training course and the staff. The first division was to be equipped by the Soviet Union, the second by the Poles. Both divisions, to say vulgarly ('govoria grubo'—in Russian), were to be fed by the Russian people. What the USSR pledged to do, it will do. Is that not so? ('eto pravilno?'—in Russian).

Kot: There is one mistake. The Polish troops ought to be organized in the USSR to the extent allowed by the number of men available. Should we use them in full, we could have an army of 150,000 men, indeed, even greater, but I have taken into account only the men selected from the point of view of physical fitness. We shall try to obtain supplies from abroad.

Stalin: Yes, but there exists a protocol fixing the strength for 1941 at 30,000 men. I do not say that it is our last word, but I stress the existence of this Protocol.

Kot: There are more protocols than one, for instance a protocol drawn up at the first meeting of the Polish-Soviet Military Commission, dated 12th [16th] August as far as I can remember. This protocol states explicitly that the two divisions are but the first stage, consisting of the troops who were to be formed immediately. Even in the following month new protocols were drawn up dealing with further units.

Molotov: But the later protocols have not been either signed or ratified by the Government. Here (holding the protocol in his hand) I have the relevant protocol (fingering a passage of the protocol relating to the date of 1.10.1941).

Kot (pointing to that date): Tell me, please, whether there is any provision here stating that two divisions only should be formed in 1941? All that is said here is that the first two divisions should be ready for action by 1.10.1941. Is that not something quite different? There is no limit to the strength in 1941.

Molotov: Well, you are right. But in any case the later protocols have not been ratified by the Government.

Stalin: The Russians did not violate the protocol. If the Poles are not satisfied, they can propose the conclusion of further agreements. The Russians did not violate their obligations.

Kot: Further units were to consist of three divisions from which, at first, two were to be labour divisions assigned to building works for the army. They were to build winter camps.

Stalin: Yes, but so far you have only two divisions.

Kot: We have two divisions, of which only one is armed, in spite of the assurances that they would both be armed. It was not until September that the Soviet authorities let us know that they were unable to supply arms for the second division.

Stalin: That is true, I remember it.

Kot: I am not a soldier and I do not feel qualified to discuss technical details. Principles, not details, interest me.

Stalin: We, the Russians, are in favour of creating the biggest possible Polish army, ready for war ('voyennosposobnoy'—in Russian). We shall share what we possess and what in our view we are obliged to share, but I must ask the Poles not to forget that the Russians are carrying on a war and that we must arm our reserves, for we have suffered losses. Will you please, Mr. Ambassador, keep in mind that we might be too short of arms and food supplies to supply the front, the reserves and the Polish army as well. We have many millions under arms, and they must be fed. We can arm two Polish divisions; one of them is ready now. I do not object to the formation on Soviet territory of five, six, seven Polish divisions, as many as you have serviceable men for, but, I repeat, we are carrying on a war, we are fighting on a long front, and we may become too short of material to supply this army with arms. The Poles must themselves try to find equipment and arms for these troops. Perhaps the situation will improve after a while, and then it will be a different story ('togda razgovor drugoy'—in Russian).

Kot: I thank you, Mr. President, for this declaration. If I understand you right, we may form as many divisions as we have men for, on condition that we receive the equipment and food from abroad.

Stalin: You have understood my words well.

Kot: It means that all serviceable men will be admitted to the army and there remains only the question of the designation of a place in which these units may be formed. It should be chosen so that the transport of arms and food from abroad will be as easy as possible.

Stalin: I agree in principle. A place will be fixed. But it will not be Uzbekistan, which Polish citizens have been entering illegally.

Kot: Uzbekistan was not our idea, it had been indicated to our military authorities by the Soviet military authorities. I have always been opposed to the helter-skelter movements of the Polish population but despite many requests I could not obtain any satisfactory settlement of this problem. The Soviet authorities themselves directed Poles to Uzbekistan. I have a telegram here to prove it.

Stalin: Where does this telegram come from?

Kot: From Novosibirsk, where local Soviet authorities compelled our people to go south. The people, who were discharged in the North and feared a severe winter, went southwards, and so flooded that area. I consider mass loafing in war-time quite inadmissible, but I was helpless in view of the events.

Stalin: The proper area will be designated tomorrow.

Kot: I reiterate my request that a suitable climate and an area convenient for the transport of supplies from abroad should be chosen.

Stalin: Have you an area in mind for forming troops, or areas for the resettlement of the civilian population? Have they not been designated?

Kot: An excess of recruits for the army arrived in the areas designated for the formation of troops. The Polish military authorities had to direct those people somewhere and they received an indication from the Soviet military authorities to direct the transports to the areas of probable formation of further divisions, to the station Vrevskoye in Uzbekistan, where there existed appropriately large barracks.

Molotov: This place was not given the approval of the authorities, and the sending of men there was unauthorized. The Embassy and its officials sent telegrams to various places inhabited by Poles, instructing them to go to Uzbekistan.

Kot: The Soviet authorities directed those transports to the South. That was the case, for instance, at Farab station. The representatives of the Soviet authorities even sent a telegram to General Szyszko-Bohusz to this effect.

Stalin: I ask you once more, Mr. Ambassador, whether we are considering the question of the areas in which the Polish troops are to be formed or the question of resettlement? Are there one or two problems?

Kot: That is a very difficult question.

Stalin: Which areas shall we designate tomorrow?

Kot: The designation of either is within the province of the Soviet Government. I have already stated our wishes concerning the question of the formation of the army. In so far as the needs of the civilian population are concerned, I ask you to take into account, apart from the importance of the climatic factor, the possibility of finding employment on the spot. There is no need, however, to make a decision tomorrow. I ask you therefore, Mr. President, to postpone this question until General Sikorski's arrival and your conversation with him.

Stalin: I repeat that we would like the Polish army to be as great as possible and well prepared for warfare, but we are carrying on war, and we are not able to maintain more Polish divisions. Perhaps the problem of supplies will improve within three months' time but at present we are organizing a great number of our own divisions. Perhaps it is a matter of two months only.

Kot: Thank you, Mr. President. I shall inform General Sikorski.

Stalin: Are we not allies? Who wants a weak ally? We shall share everything with the Poles in a fraternal manner. We shall do everything possible.

Kot: I perfectly understand all your difficulties. Now, as regards food supplies to the further units of our army, I should like to have your assurance that food will be supplied to them, at least initially.

Stalin: I shall do everything possible.

Kot: The needs of our few divisions stand no comparison with the huge demands of your army.

Stalin: And yet a man who can lift 20 poods (1 pood equivalent to 36,113 lb.) might collapse under the weight of 1 lb. We shall try to do all that is humanly possible, but I cannot make promises which I might not be able to fulfil.

Kot: There is another question of military nature, Mr. President. General Anders, the C.O. of the Polish Armed Forces in the USSR, a valiant and martial general, three times wounded in the September 1939 campaign, received from the Soviet military authorities the order to send 30,000 surplus men away from his camp. He cannot possibly be expected to comply with such an order.

Stalin: Who issued such an order?

Kot (hands over to Molotov the copy of a letter of the Red Army plenipotentiary for dealing with the formation of the Polish Army, dated 8 Nov. 41): Here is a copy of this order.

Molotov hands over the document to Stalin who passes it to a secretary.

Stalin: What is this letter, who signed it?

Interpreter: Panfilov.

Stalin: He has no right to issue such orders (visibly annoyed)—it is therefore not an order.

Kot: I have taken up much of your precious time, Mr. President, but there is still one question I should like to raise. May I speak of it?

Stalin (politely): Please do, Mr. Ambassador.

Kot: You have granted an amnesty to the Polish citizens in the USSR. You made this gesture, and I should be most obliged to you if you would use your influence to effect a full implementation of this order.

Stalin: Are there still any Poles who have not been released?

Kot: Not one officer has returned to us from the camp of Starobielsk which was wound up in the spring of 1940.

Stalin: I shall look into this question ('ia eto razbieru'—in Russian). But things sometimes happen to the released men. What was the name of the officer who commanded in the defence of Lwów? Was it not General Langer, so far as I can remember?

Kot: General Langner, Mr. President.

Stalin: Right, General Langner. We released him as long ago as last year, we brought him to Moscow, we spoke to him, and, meanwhile, he has escaped abroad, probably to Rumania.

Molotov (nods assent).

Stalin: Our amnesty has no exceptions, but there may have been other cases like that of General Langner.

Kot: We have names and lists; for instance, General Stanisław Haller has not been found, and the officers from Starobielsk, Kozielsk and Ostashkov, who were moved in April and May 1940, are missing.

Stalin: We have released all the Poles, even those sent by General Sikorski to blow up bridges and kill Russians, even those men were released. Or rather it was not General Sikorski who sent them, but his Chief of Staff, General Sosnkowski.

Kot: He has already resigned. As regards the men sent here by General Sikorski, you can depend on them totally, they are first-rate men.

Stalin (smiling): I know.

Kot: So I beg you, Mr. President, to issue an order to effect the release of the officers whom we need for the organization of our army. We have official reports stating the dates on which they were moved from the camps.

Stalin: Are there any detailed lists?

Kot: Every name was entered into the lists held by the Russian commanding officers of the camps who used to make a roll-call every day. Moreover, the NKVD interrogated each officer separately. None of the officers who served with the Staff of the army which General Anders commanded in Poland has been returned.

Stalin (who for the last few minutes has been standing and walking by his desk, smoking a cigarette but listening very attentively, rashly approaches the telephone on Molotov's desk and connects himself with the NKVD).

Molotov (stands up and also approaches the telephone): One is not connected like that—(shifts the change-over switch, then sits down again at the conference table).

Stalin (on the telephone): Stalin speaking. Have all the Poles been released from prisons? (A moment of silence, he listens to the telephone)— the Ambassador of Poland is here and he tells me that not all have been released (listens again to the answer, then puts the receiver back)—I, too, should like to put a question to you, Mr. Ambassador. When and where do the Polish troops want to operate against the Germans? Have you any information on this subject? If so, please, tell me.

Kot: I am not a soldier. This is precisely a subject for General Sikorski. I can only say that we Poles do not regard the army simply as a stage-setting. We do not wish to send one or two divisions to the front where they would disappear among the masses of Red Army troops. We would like to have an important army sector assigned to us so that the Poles might make their own impact against Hitler. We would like our army to fight in the East so that our agreement may be sealed by brotherhood in arms.

Stalin: The Czechs formed one battalion and wanted to fight, but I opposed it. I understand your point of view. The Poles should operate as an army corps or an army.

Kot: May I emphasize that as the news of each Polish division formed here reaches Poland, feelings of friendship are fostered, so important for Soviet-Polish rapprochement.

Stalin: Of course, I understand. (Hearing the telephone ring, he gets up and listens, probably to an answer to the question he had put a couple of minutes ago in the matter of the release of Poles. He then replaces the receiver and returns without uttering a word.)

Kot: I wish to thank you, Mr. President, for the further formation of the Polish army and the release of our citizens. These are two great promises. (He gets up to take leave.) Before leaving, I wish to convey my good wishes to you, Sir—may the glory which surrounds you as the defender of Moscow, increase as the war advances with your final victory over Hitler.

Stalin: Thank you, Mr. Ambassador. Can you tell me when General Sikorski's arrival is expected?

Kot: Unfortunately, I have no means of direct communication with Egypt from here. I shall be able to get in touch with him after my return to Kuibyshev. I think it is a question of a few days. I do not wish to take more of your precious time, Mr. President, but I would like to assure you that Poles have a good memory and they will not forget that your name is bound with the agreement with us and with the amnesty.

Stalin: For my part it is essential for me to contribute personally to the restoration of the Polish State, whatever might be its internal constitution.

Kot: I thank you, Mr. President, for this declaration. Would you allow me to note it and to publish it? It would be of enormous importance. Or, perhaps, you would state it publicly.

Stalin: I will do so at the first opportunity.

Kot: I am most grateful to you, Mr. President. Such an announcement would have far-reaching consequences. There is one further question. I know that some time ago you made a decision concerning the appearance of a Polish newspaper. Unfortunately, we have difficulties in this matter.

Stalin (turning partly to Molotov): Is there no Polish newspaper yet?

Kot: Unfortunately not. We have been told that there was no printing-press or, on another occasion, that there were no types.

Stalin (showing obvious discontent): Who said so?

Kot: I prefer not to give the names. But I should be grateful to you if you kindly would give an order on this matter as well.

Stalin: Of course, I will. Do you know Miss Wanda Wasilewska, Mr. Ambassador?

Kot: Of course, she was my pupil. Am I not a university professor by profession?

Stalin: I remember it was exactly a year ago that I spoke to Miss Wanda Wasilewska. I asked her to find some Polish officers who might take in their hands the organization of Polish troops in the USSR. I emphasize that it happened a year ago, that is at a time when the Treaty of Non-Aggression with Germany was still in force. Wasilewska did not find any such officers.

Kot: I thank you, Mr. President, once again for having taken so considerate an attitude towards our needs. May I ask you, Mr. President, for permission to apply to you if, in future, any capital problem should arise?

Stalin: Of course, if you please (he takes leave).

Kot (taking leave of Molotov): Mr. Commissar, I shall have to discuss some further questions with you with which I preferred not to trouble the President; can you receive me to-morrow?

Molotov: If you please (they take leave of each other).

The conversation lasted from 7 p.m. to 9.10 p.m. It was Molotov's interpreter who translated, Ambassador Kot speaking in French, Stalin and Molotov in Russian.

Stalin was very calm and composed all the time. He spoke quietly. Occasionally he showed discontent, for instance when it appeared from Ambassador Kot's words that he had been insufficiently informed by the Soviet authorities. At the beginning of the conversation he was slightly reserved, but with the progress of the conversation he appeared to speak more composedly. During the whole time he addressed the Ambassador in a very courteous manner. He got up twice and walked along the conference table at which the Ambassador was seated. Molotov hardly intervened in the conversation.

No. 150

Pro-memoria on the release of Polish political prisoners and prisoners of war handed by Ambassador Kot to Commissar Molotov

Moscow, November 14, 1941 GSHI, KGA, 7–b
Transl. from Polish

The Agreement of 30th July of this year aims at the establishment of lasting friendly relations between the Republic of Poland and the USSR. The conclusion of this Agreement resulted in uniting both States to the highest degree in their common endeavour to use in full their moral and material means for the struggle against Germany.

Basing their policy on this agreement, the Polish Government were profoundly convinced that all serviceable Polish citizens at present on Russian territory should be conscripted for the Polish Army to fight against Hitler. It is self-evident that those Polish citizens unfit for military service should work to increase Russia's war effort—in conditions, however, not inferior to the conditions of the Soviet citizens, and in a manner corresponding to their professional qualifications, ensuring them a reasonable livelihood.

In the opinion of the Polish Government the fulfilment of these tasks requires:

1. A full execution of the amnesty of Polish citizens through the release of all those who are still detained in prisons or in forced labour camps;

2. The enlistment with the Polish Army of all serviceable Polish citizens.

3. The resettlement, according to a definite plan, of the remaining Polish population, in the areas of suitable climatic conditions, and the provision of work for them corresponding to their individual professional qualifications.

4. The provision of a modest but sufficient livelihood for those Polish citizens who are unfit for work, as for instance children deprived of parents or proper care, women burdened with small children, old people and invalids, out of the funds of the Soviet Union, or alternatively from a loan to be granted to the Polish Government for this purpose.

5. The provision of facilities for the transport and distribution of clothing, medical supplies and food, imported from abroad to assist the Polish citizens, mainly those living in the northern provinces and unfit for work.

6. Permission for the Polish Embassy in the USSR to open an adequate number of welfare-consulary agencies, indispensable, if proper care is to be taken of the Polish citizens. Those agencies would be empowered to supply the Polish citizens with the required identity papers.

The Polish Government is deeply convinced that the drawing of the aforesaid essential conclusions from acts of such exceptional importance as the conclusion of the Agreement of 30th July of this year, and the Decree of the Praesidium of the Supreme Soviet of the USSR of 12th August 1941 on the Amnesty for the Polish Citizens, will closely bind the whole Polish community with the policy for rapprochement and co-operation with the Soviet Union.

No. 151

Record of a conversation held in the Kremlin between Ambassador Kot and Commissar Molotov on the release of Polish citizens still detained in Soviet labour camps and on the Polish relief organization

Moscow, November 15, 1941   GSHI, PRM, 41/4
Transl. from Polish

Kot: I should like, first of all, to make quite clear one question which I did not wish to raise yesterday. Both in a conversation between myself and M. Vyshinsky, and in the conversation between General Anders and some Soviet militaries, we have heard the opinion that in connection with General Sikorski's proposed arrival, some conditions of the nature of an ultimatum were made on the Polish side. This is an obvious misunderstanding which I should like to clear up in the interest of our mutual good relations. I wished simply to settle some questions in which we envisaged certain difficulties before General Sikorski's departure. In the course of yesterday's conversation with President Stalin I preferred not to raise some problems which I would like to put to you today, Mr. Commissar, and it is because of them that I took the liberty of calling on you. Some problems have arisen in the course of the last weeks or even days, like the refusal of a loan, the stopping of the resettlement, interference with the activities of our delegates or even difficulties in obtaining accommodation in Kuibyshev, and all these problems seemed to indicate that General Sikorski's visit was undesirable. As regards military problems, the attempts at limiting the strength of our armed forces to two divisions were also beyond our comprehension, as from the beginning of the conversations between the military delegates no strength limit has ever been mentioned. If such a limit was intended, why then, in the first Protocol, did the Soviet party undertake to issue an announcement, through all voienkomats in the whole territory of the Soviet Union, proclaiming that all the Polish citizens here should report to the Polish Army, and an order be given to release from the Red Army all the Polish citizens who wished to serve with the Polish Army? I would like to show you, Mr. Commissar, some relevant texts, in order to end this misunderstanding.

Molotov: There was in fact some misunderstanding. But to link these misunderstandings and other minor questions, as for instance the question of accommodation in Kuibyshev, with the assumptions that we do not allegedly want General Sikorski's visit, is wrong. If General Sikorski wishes to come to the Soviet Union he will be our guest. As regards the protocols on military problems some of them were approved by the Government, and some not. Nobody intends to end or limit the organization of the Polish Army, but with regard to the further organization no decisions have been taken on account of the difficulties in obtaining supplies. We are unable to approve some proposals made by the Russian Army Command. After yesterday's conversation with Stalin, this problem is to be considered cleared up and exhausted.

Kot: There are four protocols, not one only: that of 16th August 1941 and the subsequent ones. But this problem no longer exists. Yesterday I did not want to give the name of the person who indicated Uzbekistan to us as an area which Poles should enter. Today, however, I wish to give full explanation of this matter. When General Anders proposed the formation of the third and subsequent divisions, he suggested forming them in Uralsk; as regards the fourth and fifth divisions he expressed only the desire that those divisions might be formed also not far from Headquarters. When no decision on Uralsk was coming, and the number of recruits to the army constantly increased, General Fedetov indicated Uzbekistan to General Anders as an area in which our further units might be formed. This was why the military authorities and we ourselves directed Polish citizens to the South. I will produce, Mr. Commissar, the relevant texts, for I found it painful to hear a reproach that the Embassy directed Polish citizens wherever it wished, on its own responsibility, without any agreement with the Soviet authorities. We were authorized to do it.

Molotov: Journeys to the South were not allowed. The fact that the subject had been discussed did not mean that the matter was settled because it was not authorized by the Government. The telegrams sent by the Embassy contained instructions on journeys which were unauthorized by the Soviet authorities.

Kot: As long ago as September, in the conversation with Mr. Vyshinsky, I asked for a plan for the resettlement of the Polish population. Meanwhile life continues as before. Our tragedy consists in the fact that the released men hurried southwards, and all the while we could not obtain any decision on the Soviet part. I argued that such mass wanderings were particularly dangerous in war-time, but as far as we were concerned, we were helpless without the co-operation of the Soviet authorities. Some days ago I produced to Mr. Vyshinsky a list of important issues raised by us in our correspondence with the Narkomindel and which have so far not been settled. I should be grateful to you, Mr. Commissar, if you would ask to see this list and if you would take interest in the way in which these issues have been handled.

Molotov: I am not only ready, but also obliged to help you, Mr. Ambassador. Will you please, however, remember our present situation on the front and all the circumstances connected with it. The resettlement on a big scale of thousands or even millions of people in distress is going on at present. However, let us turn from the past to the future, and I am sure that my Deputy and myself shall do everything in order to settle these problems.

Kot: When I called on you for the first time, Mr. Commissar, you expressed your firm belief that my visit here and co-operation with you would be a success. I answered then that it would be a common success. I remind you of it now deliberately, and I ask you, Mr. Commissar, to help me in achieving this common success. I have a note with me, containing our essential needs and requests. As a matter of fact, this note was ready yesterday, and it refers to some issues a positive decision on which was taken yesterday, by President Stalin (he hands over the note). It refers to questions one and two, that is the release and conscription of all Polish citizens. The question of the resettlement of the Polish population according to plan was within the province of the Mixed Commission, but this commission has simply ceased to exist.

Molotov: What commission?

Kot: A commission composed of the representatives of the People's Commissariat of Foreign Affairs, the People's Commissariat of the Interior, and two representatives of the Embassy. The purpose of this commission was to discuss the wishes of both sides and to find a solution for some urgent matters. I do not remind you of it in order to propose the resumption of the work of this commission, should it have no power for the settlement of important and urgent questions, but as far as we are concerned we put forward a practical proposal in order to prevent any difficulties and confusion.

Molotov: As regards the questions raised under para. 3 they are much more difficult today than was the case a few months ago.

Kot: We had promises referring to public prosecutors, judges and policemen who had been deported to particularly hard areas in the North, but these promises have not been fulfilled.

Molotov: This question is of a practical nature. Many hundreds of thousands, and even millions of men leave the place of their residence, and we require of them to provide for themselves; they have to earn the money to meet their needs. The question will be examined, but the material and transport difficulties are very great indeed.

Kot: I hope, nevertheless, that it will be done. Our men are in a particularly difficult position because, on being released, they own practically nothing.

Molotov: It cannot be helped, people must earn their living. We put aside the sum of 3 million roubles to meet some exceptional cases in our credits for Polish military purposes.

Kot: I cannot accept this sum. A big loan is needed. I reckon upon a generous gesture on your part. The next question is that of a proper use of the professional qualifications of our men, which are being completely wasted. A doctor of medicine or a chemist employed as wood-cutter, or a submarine designer who works as brick-layer, is a sheer waste of the vital forces of our citizens.

Molotov: It will certainly be done, but it can only be done gradually. We, too, cannot help those who move from one place to another in really difficult conditions. In connection with this I wish to refer to a conversation between General Sikorski and our Ambassador Bogomolov to whom General Sikorski said that the leaders of the Soviet Union preferred to employ Polish citizens as forced labourers rather than have them in the ranks of the Polish Army. I was taken aback by General Sikorski's statement because it was quite gratuitous. I had to say that I had never spoken of it with Kot. In fact, I said something different, and that was that the Poles who have not been called up must work wherever they are at the time, and earn their living on the spot.

Kot: There was no question of forced labour. I have simply asked you, Mr. Commissar, what we are to do with the soldiers who report for the army and cannot be admitted because the units are full to capacity. I stated that these men, instead of becoming soldiers, would be obliged to work, while we need soldiers above all. I shall, of course, explain this matter to General Sikorski.

Molotov: The Polish Army is in the process of being organized, but some time must elapse before units are formed. Stalin assured you that two divisions would be armed and maintained, and the men who are to be admitted to further units must work for the time being, or the Polish Government should provide for them, or transport them as Polish citizens to other territories. I should like you to clear the misunderstanding arising from General Sikorski's statement, that the Soviet Government allegedly prefers forced labourers to soldiers.

Kot: Of course, I shall do so, but the problem nevertheless exists for our soldiers that they must work rather than fight.

Molotov: The army will be organized, but only gradually. Therefore, in the meantime, either the Polish Government should assist them, or these people must work as labourers, engineers or employees.

Kot: That is quite clear, but my point of view is that they should become soldiers as soon as possible.

Molotov: I agree.

217

Kot: The Polish Government, for its part, tries to assist its citizens. Some supplies from Great Britain have already arrived at Arkhangelsk, a relief action is being organized in America. We shall receive help from the Red Cross in India. We expect transport facilities from the Soviet authorities for goods of this kind, but it is not right to compare the situation of Soviet citizens compelled to change their place of residence with the situation of the Polish citizens, released from prisons, forced labour camps and places of compulsory residence, who have no financial means and even no clothes. Your citizens have numerous resources. The situation of our citizens requires material help and it accounts for our demand for a loan. It is not the question of assistance to people who are fit to work, but to children, invalids, women with small children. We have to maintain those people, as they are unable to provide for themselves.

Molotov: I shall report the points you have mentioned to the Government.

Kot: On my part I ask you to act as our advocate with the Government. The loan which you will grant to us will yield you a hundred per cent return.

Molotov: I realize that, but will you keep in mind that all our efforts are devoted to the waging of war.

Kot: If I do not establish contacts with Polish citizens living in this country I shall be no better than a laughing-stock. My duty is to enlighten them, to orientate them, to make known the new policy of the Polish Government and its co-operation with the Soviet Union. We must have delegates for this task who will issue passports, carry out welfare work and assist our people. I discussed with the People's Commissariat for Foreign Affairs a plan for the setting up of local committees composed of the representatives of the Polish population concerned. This plan was declined but it was agreed that the Embassy should appoint men of trust and delegates. I received the assurance that local authorities would get instructions to co-operate with them and to facilitate their task. However, many difficulties have arisen in practice. I received a promise that the representatives of the People's Commissariat of the Interior would accompany the circulating delegates. As a matter of fact, where the co-operation of the Soviet authorities is available the results achieved could not be better. The delegates of the Embassy do not intend to do, and they do not do, anything that might be unwelcome to the Soviet authorities. On the contrary, together with them they try to solve difficulties and to put right matters whose settlement is in our common interest. My position cannot be compared with that of other ambassadors who have not such masses of their nationals here. I can refer, for instance, to the case of Mr. Gruja, our delegate in Arkhangel. He cannot establish any contact with the local authorities apart from questions of transport. He is unable to deliver clothing sent from Great Britain to the Polish population in his area although the need for it in the Far North is particularly acute because of the severe winter there.

Molotov: Gruja's example is well chosen indeed. Mr. Gruja came to Arkhangel to take care of transports. Such was the task assigned to him.

Opening a consulate would be unjustified. Did we not accept the principle that consulates are not to be established? It would not be right to agree to the extension of anyone's functions when narrow limits of his powers have been expressly specified.

Kot: The text submitted by me to the People's Commissariat for Foreign Affairs in connection with Gruja's departure left no doubt as to the tasks assigned to him. They were not confined to questions of transport only. Would you please, Mr. Commissar, let me show you this text? From the first I insisted on the definition of the rights and duties of the Delegates which in any case include the gathering of all data and information on the Poles in their area, and supplying them with passports. How can we harmonize the provisions issued by the Soviet Government itself, according to which the Polish population should be provided with passports within a prescribed time, with your declaration on our taking care of the Polish population, if at the same time we are debarred from establishing contact with it? It was the Soviet Government itself who put me in this position. How can we find a solution to this dilemma?

Molotov: As regards the case of Gruja, as far as I know, his attempts at extending the duties assigned to him were not in order. But I shall check this, because what was decided must be carried out. I have to emphasize, however, that there are two different questions here: one is the selection of delegates, and the other—the establishing of consulates, which can be allowed only with the Government's consent. Their functions must be clearly specified, and nothing should be taken for granted.

Kot: Where are the consuls? I will not pursue this question for I am not a professional diplomat, and I am not interested in it. In the present difficult war conditions routine consuls would be unable to fulfil the functions which matter to me. The men must be chosen from among the people on the spot, those directly interested. The only consular function which they will fulfil will be the issuing of passports, and the settlement of this question is in the interest of both governments. I ask you, Mr. Commissar, to look into this matter and to have understanding of the fact that with such functions I can entrust those only in whom I have the fullest confidence.

Molotov: Of course, it is necessary to specify the rights and duties of the delegates and to clear up the whole matter.

Kot: I can issue instructions of co-operation to our citizens only if I maintain contact with them through my emissaries, followers of the same line of policy which I represent, and then enlighten and direct them. In such conditions only I could assume responsibility. I shall submit to the Narkomindel a draft of the definition of the rights and duties of the delegates, we shall discuss it and we shall settle this question as soon as possible in our common interest. May I, at the conclusion of our conversation, present you my congratulations upon everything I have myself seen in Moscow, and which convinces me that you hold a very strong position indeed?

Molotov: I thank you, Mr. Ambassador.

Kot: I should even like to broadcast on the splendid spirit prevailing here, and also on how much the actual situation here differs from the picture spread by the German propaganda.

Molotov: It is true, Mr. Ambassador. The military position of Moscow has improved. We do not want to withhold from either ourselves or others the truth about the gravity of the situation, but I am glad, Mr. Ambassador, to assure you that the position of Moscow is much stronger today than it was exactly one month ago when we were forced to evacuate the embassies. During the last month we have taken serious measures to increase our defences.

Kot: Finally, I wish to assure you, Mr. Commissar, that yesterday I left this room under the spell of the great authority and exceptional charm of President Stalin.

They take leave of each other. (The conversation lasted from 6 p.m. to 7.45 p.m. Molotov's interpreter was translating, the Polish Ambassador spoke in French and M. Molotov in Russian.)

No. 152

Telegram from Minister Raczyński to Ambassador Kot on the decision of General Sikorski to arrive in the USSR at the end of November

London, November 18, 1941   GSHI, A.11. 49/Sow./3
                                      Transl. from Polish

After examining your report on your conversation with Stalin, the Prime Minister asks you to notify the Soviet Government officially of his arrival in the USSR at the end of this month. His departure from Teheran will probably take place on 26th inst. The Prime Minister will be accompanied by: Gen. Klimecki, Dr. Retinger, Lt.-Col. Protasewicz, Lt. Tyszkiewicz and possibly Major Cazalet.

No. 153

Pro-memoria on the release of Polish political prisoners and prisoners of war from the People's Commissariat for Foreign Affairs to Ambassador Kot discussed during a conversation between Ambassador Kot and Deputy Commissar Vyshinsky

Kuibyshev, November 19, 1941   GSHI, A.11. 49/Sow./3
                                      Transl. from Russian

In reply to the Pro-Memoria of the Embassy of the Polish Republic, dated November 14th of this year, handed by M. Kot to V. M. Molotov on November 15th of this year, the People's Commissariat for Foreign Affairs on the order of the Soviet Government has the honour of stating as follows:

1. The amnesty of the Polish citizens has been fully executed. It is self-evident that this amnesty could not apply to persons sentenced for criminal offences or to those former Polish citizens who were Hitlerite agents, Germans, Italians, Rumanians, Hungarians and Finns.

2. The question of the increase of the Polish Army was examined in the conversation between M. Kot and J. V. Stalin on November 14th and the necessary measures have already been taken on this matter.

3. The point of view of the Soviet Government on the question of the removal of the Polish citizens from one area to another was made clear to M. Kot on 2nd November by the Deputy People's Commissar A. J. Vyshinsky. It appears from his statement that any mass movement of Polish citizens is impossible in the present winter conditions, owing to shortage of transport and military needs. It does not debar single Polish citizens from moving to south-eastern areas (namely Southern Kazakstan, Jambul, Semipalatinsk, the Kazak Socialist Soviet Republic). As regards finding employment for Polish citizens corresponding with their qualifications, this problem was dealt with in a personal note of V. M. Molotov of 8th November 1941, and it should be solved, according to the note, in the same way as it is being solved with regard to Soviet citizens, without any special pledges on the part of the Soviet Government, local Soviet authorities having received guiding rules recommending them to help Polish citizens as well as possible under the existing conditions.

4. The proposal of the Embassy relating to ensuring means of existence for those Polish citizens who are unfit for work, either at the expense of the Soviet Government or from the grant of a loan by them to the Polish Government, has been brought to the notice of the Soviet Government and will be examined by them with due attention.

5. The Soviet Government will co-operate in facilitating the transport and distribution in the Soviet Union of the consignments destined for the material and medical assistance of the Polish citizens.

6. In accordance with the system established for the duration of the war the Soviet Government consider it inadvisable to establish Polish consulates or similar institutions on the territory of the USSR. In connection with this point the Soviet Government admit the possibility that the Embassy may delegate temporary agents who will visit certain places in order to issue passports and bring assistance to Polish citizens. The functions and place of residence of those agents will be considered and determined by the People's Commissariat and the Embassy. On the strength of the appointment of these delegates the local Soviet authorities will receive the necessary guidance for co-operating with them.

No. 154

Pro-memoria from Ambassador Kot on the interpretation of the Polish-Soviet Military Agreement and on the subjects of equipment and concentration of the Polish Army with an enclosed letter to Commissar Molotov

Kuibyshev, November 20, 1941 GSHI, KGA, 7–b
Transl. from Polish

Referring to my conversation with President Stalin on 14th November, and with your Excellency on 15th November, in the course of which I undertook to supply the information and legal arguments for the creation of further Polish Divisions in the USSR, as well as the reason for diverting transports of Polish citizens to Uzbekistan, I have the honour to convey to you my 'Notes on the organization and equipment of the Polish Army in the USSR, and on the concentration of Polish citizens in Uzbekistan', with the request to submit it to President Stalin.

I also have the honour to enclose a copy of a Note Verbale of the Polish Embassy to the People's Commissariat for Foreign Affairs, Ref. D/508/41 of October 6th, 1941, concerning the departure for Arkhangel of the 2nd Embassy Secretary, Mr. Józef Gruja, to act there as the Embassy's Delegate in all matters of welfare and transport. The original of that note was handed by me personally to the Deputy Commissar for Foreign Affairs, Mr. A. J. Vyshinsky, on October 6th, 1941. It can be seen from the contents of that note that the accusation of extending Mr. Gruja's powers by the Embassy, without the knowledge of the Soviet authorities, is entirely unfounded and must have arisen through some misunderstanding.

Notes on the organization and equipment of the Polish Army in the USSR and on the concentration of Polish citizens in Uzbekistan.

1/ The Polish-Soviet Military Agreement, signed on 14th August, 1941, stipulated that the numbers of Polish troops to be organized in the USSR would depend on the manpower available and possibilities for equipment (para. 4.) It did not limit by any date or figure the size of the army to be formed.

At a meeting of the Plenipotentiaries of the Red Army Supreme Command with the G.O.C. Polish Army in the USSR and the Chief of the Polish Military Mission, this matter was from the beginning dealt with and discussed on the assumption of the acceptance of that interpretation of the Agreement. There was no difference of opinion in that respect among the members of the Commission.

The above facts are confirmed in the Minutes No. 1 of 16th August, 1941. At that meeting Gen. Anders asked for a full nominal roll of Polish officers, and a complete return of the number of our soldiers residing in the USSR who could be considered available for the organization of the Polish Army. When Gen. Panfilov mentioned the figure of 21,000 men as the point of departure, Gen. Anders estimated that this contingent would form 2 Divisions. Gen. Panfilov then mentioned that the Supreme Command of the Red Army considered it better to begin with the formation of one Polish Division only, and that therefore Gen. Anders' motion of forming two Divisions simultaneously should be submitted to Supreme Headquarters. The figures given by Gen. Panfilov on that occasion represented but a small fraction of our citizens fit for active service, actually residing in the USSR.

At the meeting of the Mixed Commission on 19th August, 1941 (Minutes No. 2), Gen. Panfilov imparted the consent of the Soviet General Staff for the simultaneous formation of 2 Polish infantry Divisions, to be in a state of readiness by 1st October, 1941. These minutes as well as the following ones did not contain any mention that the number of 2 Polish Divisions should be the limit of the strength of the Polish Army in the USSR in 1941—as some Soviet authorities stated at the beginning of November of this year.

The decision of the Red Army Supreme Command to release all Poles, serving in their ranks, for enlistment with the Polish Army (Minutes No. 2, dated 19.8.41) confirms the point of view that the formation of a greater number of Polish Divisions was considered from the very beginning.

Proposals concerning the organization of further Polish Divisions were submitted by Gen. Anders to the Plenipotentiary of the Red Army S.C., Gen. Panfilov, on 12th September, Ref. 100/Org, and on 25th September, 1941 (without reference number). No reply has been received to these proposals.

2/ The question of armament and equipment of Polish Divisions was finally settled at the meeting of the Mixed Commission on August 28th, 1941 (Minutes No. 4). At that meeting Gen. Panfilov informed the G.O.C. Polish Army in the USSR that the Red Army S.C. had decided to supply arms for both Polish Divisions now in process of formation, and demanded the submission of the necessary indents. The indents having been supplied in due time, the Polish units were informed by the Soviet authorities of the dates on which the equipment was due to arrive.

On 10th September, however, the Plenipotentiary of the Red Army S.C. Gen. Panfilov, officially informed the Chief of the Polish Military Mission, Gen. Wolikowski, that in view of the changed situation the Red Army Supreme Command could not fulfil their engagements in respect of the armament of 2 Polish Divisions, and would supply arms for one Division only. Minutes of that conference have still not been supplied by Gen. Panfilov.

In consequence only one Polish Division received arms, and even that not up to scale.

A detailed return of the deficiency in equipment can be presented at any time.

3/ In connection with the question of Polish citizens concentrating in Uzbekistan, it is advised that:

Gen. Anders, G.O.C. Polish Army in the USSR, repeatedly warned the Plenipotentiaries of the Red Army S.C., at the meetings of the Mixed Commission, that the rush of the Polish citizens to join the Polish Army would certainly acquire a spontaneous mass character. With regard to the location of the centres for the formation of troops, Gen. Anders, in his letters of 12th and 25th September, 1941 (copies enclosed), proposed the Ural region for the formation of the 3rd Division, as the area suited best for Polish requirements. At the same time he asked the Soviet authorities to earmark further areas for the formation of the subsequent Polish Divisions. Both these letters remained without a reply.

In the second half of September, Gen. Anders was invited by Gen. Fedotov to the NKVD for a conference concerned with the move of Polish citizens from all directions. Following the instructions of some local authorities and of the Polish Army H.Q., these were streaming towards the already congested areas for the formation of the 1st and 2nd Divisions. Gen. Fedotov, in the presence of Gen. Zhukov, informed Gen. Anders of the plan to direct Polish citizens to Uzbekistan and some Volga regions. Polish rail transports were since then directed to the dispatch areas at the stations Vrievskoye and Farab. That was done in the first instance by the Soviet authorities. They even requested, on several occasions, orders from Gen. Anders to the transport commandants to make them detrain at the above-named stations. According to information in possession of the Embassy, the first telegram of the Polish Military Mission mentioning Vrievskoye as the new destination, was sent from Moscow on 2nd October, 1941. In view of the new situation and on the grounds of information received, that Soviet authorities did not let transports proceed to Buzuluk, Totsk and Tatishchev, the Polish Embassy also answered telegram enquiries from Polish citizens by advising volunteers for the Army to proceed to Farab. This was not however done before 24th October. After a certain time Samarkand was added as a new reporting centre. Maintaining the policy accepted from the beginning, the Embassy continued to warn persons who had at least a minimum means of subsistence not to leave their place of residence.

Under these circumstances, and considering that in most cases transports already on the move were concerned, the Polish Embassy and the H.Q. Polish Army in the USSR cannot be made responsible for the concentration of Polish citizens created in the neighbourhood of Tashkent, Samarkand and Farab, where Polish citizens are now living in the most distressing conditions.[1]

[1] In the archives of the G.O.C. Polish Forces in the USSR (Ref. KGA-7b) a first draft in Russian of the above notes, dated 19th November, is preserved. It differs from the above text considerably in para 3. Enclosures 2, 3, 4 are omitted as being of lesser historical interest.

No. 155

Notes on the conversation between Ambassador Kot and Deputy Commissar Vyshinsky relating to mass removals of Polish citizens from the South to the North, involving great hardship to the people concerned. Present also Director Novikov and First Secretary of the Polish Embassy W. Arlet

Kuibyshev, November 25, 1941   GSHI, A.11. 49/Sow./4
                                                                               Transl. from Polish

Ambassador: When I asked you to receive me today it was because of a very serious and urgent question. I have received from several sources the information that 36,000 Polish citizens are to be transported from Uzbekistan to the Jambul, South-Kazakstan and Semipalatinsk areas, in the period from 25th November to 5th December. I know also that the Soviet authorities in those areas are completely unprepared to receive such a number of people. There are no accommodation, food or catering posts at railway stations over there. Travellers will be provided with bread only for their journey, and no other food will be supplied. The position of those Polish citizens is extremely difficult in all respects. The proportion of small children, women and elderly people among them is very high. They have no suitable clothing because they disposed of it when going southwards. Many are ill. These thousands of Polish citizens came to Uzbekistan in quite a legal way, in circumstances which I have already had the occasion to describe to the Soviet Government. The high proportion of deaths due to starvation and exhaustion shows the results of such transfers of population. During the week between the 7th and 14th November, 70 cases of death have been registered among those travelling to Uzbekistan. What is happening to the Polish citizens is cruel and inhuman, and I cannot understand the purpose of it all.

[. . .]. One does not conduct a war with Hitler in this way. If our people are to perish in this manner it is completely senseless, and I consider that my mission to the USSR serves no purpose. I ask you, Mr. Commissar, to do everything possible to stop this transfer. I feel obliged to raise a protest against this action, because it is an unfriendly act towards myself and the Embassy, towards the Polish Government and the Polish Nation. [. . .].

Vyshinsky: I should like to explain the views of my Government on this question. Speaking about the transfer of the Polish population from Uzbekistan, ordered by the Government, you have to keep in mind the conditions in which the Polish population had moved from the North to the South. This was the cause of all the incidents referred to by you. The wandering of the Polish population southwards was completely planless and disorderly. It is not proper to compare it with the plan for removing 36,500 Polish citizens from Uzbekistan. The former was planless and un-restrained, and as such was instrumental in producing cases of death, reported by you. Should the number of such cases, if there be any, agree with the facts, I can only say that I regret it. I cannot hide, however, that a number of Polish officials gave detailed instructions, sometimes distributed in great numbers: 'Go to Uzbekistan.' It seems (he turns to Novikov) that we raised this question in a conversation with Sokolnicki (Novikov confirms it). The travelling of many thousands of people was bound to cause various tragic incidents. It created many difficult problems in Uzbekistan: the new-comers had no accommodation, work or means of existence. You will certainly remember that we have not contracted any obligation to provide all Polish citizens with jobs, but, in spite of this, our authorities have done and are doing everything possible to provide all fit Poles with a job. The Soviet Government consider that it would be impossible to find enough jobs for such big masses of people in Uzbekistan, and this is why they have issued the order to move them to other areas. The difference between the former movements of the Polish population southwards and the present removal consists in this, that the latter is not nearly so unrestrained and planless as was the former. The Soviet Government provided all the travellers with food for the journey.

[. . .] The aim pursued by the Soviet Government in ordering the transfer cannot in any way encumber our relations with the Polish Government or shake our friendship.

I declare emphatically that such assumptions are very far from the truth. [. . .].

Ambassador: Since September last, that is from the very beginning of my mission, I have insisted on jointly working out a plan for the resettlement of the Polish population. Do you remember?

Vyshinsky: Of course I do.

Ambassador: However, I have received no reply to my requests referring to this matter, although the drawing-up of such a plan would have enabled us to avoid all that happened afterwards.

Vyshinsky: I wished also to propose such a plan, and to settle personally down to this task, but in view of the change of circumstances which you know very well, the Soviet Government was obliged to issue an order to stop all resettlement. It was far from pleasant for me to inform you of this on November 2nd, but I had to do it.

Ambassador: As a matter of fact, two months elapsed between September and the day on which you told me this. The main movement of the population occurred in September and October, and was proceeding in a quite disorderly way.

Vyshinsky: Any resettlement now and in the present circumstances is to be excluded. Speaking to you on November 2nd, I mentioned Semipalatinsk, South Kazakstan and Jambul as the areas suitable for the resettlement of those people who were already on the move, and for those individuals who could afford to pay the costs of the journey. You did not protest against it at that time. [. . .].

Ambassador: Is there any possibility of placing those people in other parts of Kazakstan, in a climate more suitable for them, and of providing them with work corresponding to their qualifications and strength?

Vyshinsky: I shall forward this proposal of yours, Mr. Ambassador, to my Government and, as soon as I get the reply, I shall let you know. In any case I assure you that climatic conditions over there do not differ much. So far as the choice of jobs corresponding to qualifications is concerned it may be that the professions represented by the resettled Polish citizens will be in demand in Kazakstan.

Ambassador: For instance, in the Alma-Ata area the climate is more suitable for our people.

Vyshinsky: I shall inform the Government of your request.

Ambassador: I wish to emphasize that I do not especially care for Uzbekistan. What really matters is to postpone the removal until such time when it can be properly organized. [. . .].

Ambassador: I return once more to this essential question, on account of which I called on you today, Mr. Commissar. It is in our mutual interest that we should either stop the removal of our people from Uzbekistan or limit it. In any case it is imperative to provide those people with clothing, accommodation and work. Should this not be done, there will be a tragedy without remedy. Do you realize what might be the consequences of this in connection with General Sikorski's arrival? [. . .].

Ambassador: Do you know how many Polish citizens are in Uzbekistan, according to Soviet information?

Vyshinsky: Unfortunately, I am not in possession of any information on this matter. [. . .].

The conversation lasted from 9.30 p.m. to 10.50 p.m. After the Ambassador's initial declaration had ended in a protest, Vyshinsky remained very complaisant and courteous. His reply was uttered in a soft voice never used before, and he seemed almost to apologize to the Ambassador. As the conversation proceeded he became obviously nervous but he never lost his self-control, either with regard to the expression of his views or to his manner of speaking.

No. 156

Telegram from M. Stalin to Mr. Harriman on the possibility of settling all fundamental questions relating to the Polish interests in the USSR[1]

Moscow, November 27, 1941   GSHI, A.11, 49/Sow./3

I had recently a conversation with the Polish Ambassador to the USSR Monsieur Kot. I received the impression that the USSR and Poland have all the reasons and possibilities to settle all fundamental questions in which both parties are interested. For your information, I would like to point out that Monsieur Kot did not raise the question, during the conversation, of sending Polish military forces from the USSR to any other country.

[1] See Note No. 156.

No. 157

Note from the People's Commissariat for Foreign Affairs in reply to the note of the Polish Embassy of November 10, 1941, concerning the conscription of Polish citizens of Ukrainian, White-Russian and Jewish origin by the Red Army

Kuibyshev, December 1, 1941   GSHI, A.11. 49/Sow./3
                                                 Transl. from Russian

With reference to the Note of 10th November 1941, No D–740/41 of the Polish Embassy, the People's Commissariat for Foreign Affairs has the honour to communicate the following:

With reference to the fact that citizens of Ukrainian, White-Russian and Jewish nationality, who left the territories of Western Ukraine and Western White-Russia, have been conscripted into the Red Army in the Soviet Republic of Kazakh, the Polish Embassy draws attention to the lack of legal foundation for such action, and is of the opinion that such action is contradictory to the principles laid down in the Soviet-Polish Agreement of the 30th July and Military Agreement of the 14th August 1941.

The People's Commissariat cannot agree to the point of view of the Polish Embassy, there being no foundation, either in the Agreement of the 30th July or in the agreement of the 14th August, for the point of view expressed in the Polish Embassy's Note.

In conformance with the Decree of the Presidium of the Supreme Council of the USSR of the 29th November, 1939, all citizens of the Western districts of the Ukrainian and White-Russian S.S. Republics, which were in the territories of the above-mentioned districts, between the 1–2 November, 1939, in agreement with the Decree re citizenship of the USSR of the 19th August, 1939, acquired Soviet Citizenship. The readiness of the Soviet Government to recognize as Polish citizens, persons of Polish nationality inhabiting the above-mentioned districts till the 1–2 November, 1939, shows the good will and readiness to compromise of the Soviet Government, but can in no case serve as a basis for the analogous recognition as Polish citizens, of persons of other nationalities, in particular, Ukrainian, White-Russian and Jewish; the question of a Polish-Soviet Frontier is not yet settled and is liable to discussion in the future.

As to the reference of the Polish Embassy to the order issued in Alma-Ata by Gen. Shcherbakov, the People's Commissariat for Foreign Affairs possesses information according to which the order on the conscription of the already mentioned citizens into the Red Army was not issued, on the other hand there was a direction concerning their duty to work in the rear areas: a direction which is equally applicable to other citizens of the USSR.

No. 158

Note from the Polish Embassy in the USSR to the People's Commissariat for Foreign Affairs, concerning the non-implementation of the provisions of the Decree of August 12, 1941, on the amnesty of the Polish citizens

Kuibyshev, December 3, 1941 GSHI, A.11. 49/Sow./2
Transl. from Polish

Referring to point 1 of the Aide-mémoire of the People's Commissariat for Foreign Affairs, dated November 19th, 1941, the Embassy of the Republic of Poland has the honour of stating the following:

Acknowledging the declaration of the People's Commissariat for Foreign Affairs on the full application of the measures of amnesty to Polish citizens, the Embassy understands it to mean that the central Soviet authorities have issued appropriate instructions, pursuant to the provisions of the Polish-Soviet Agreement of 30th July, 1941, and of the Decree of the Supreme Soviet of the USSR of 12th August, 1941. However, the Embassy has the honour to draw attention to the circumstance that, contrary to the personal note of the People's Commissar for Foreign Affairs, M. Molotov, of November 8th, 1941, the Aide-mémoire of November 19th, 1941, did not state that the amnesty was extended to all Polish citizens.

In fact a considerable number of Polish citizens are still deprived of freedom, and remain in prisons, forced labour camps or places of compulsory residence.

The Embassy expresses the hope that strong measures will be taken in order to ensure a full and prompt enforcement of the instructions relating to the release of Polish citizens by the executive organs of the State in accordance with the aforesaid legal texts, with the declaration of the Chairman of the Council of People's Commissars of the USSR, J. V. Stalin, made to the Ambassador of the Republic of Poland, Professor Kot, in the conversation of November 14th, 1941, according to which the amnesty granted to Polish citizens was general and unconditional, and with the numerous assurances to this effect on the part of competent Soviet authorities.

As regards the restrictions on the application of the amnesty to some categories of Polish citizens, mentioned in the Aide-mémoire of November 19th, 1941, the Embassy has the honour to state that it cannot agree to their being introduced for the following reasons:

1) The Polish-Soviet Agreement of 30th July, 1941, in its additional Protocol relating to the release of Polish citizens, lays down that: 'as soon as diplomatic relations are re-established, the Government of the Union of Soviet Socialist Republics will grant amnesty to all Polish citizens who are at present deprived of their freedom on the territory of the USSR, either as prisoners of war or on other relevant grounds'. This provision does not mention any restriction of the application of the amnesty in the release of Polish citizens and, furthermore, it prescribes the time within which it should be implemented, this time-limit being overrun by Soviet executive organs on numerous occasions.

2) The Decree of the Supreme Soviet of the USSR of 12th August, 1941, does not mention any restrictions of the amnesty.

3) The Polish Law on citizenship, as well as the whole Polish legislation (like the corresponding Soviet legislation also), makes no restrictive provisions with relation to race or descent; consequently, the fact of possessing Polish citizenship should be the only criterion for applying amnesty provisions to an individual.

4) As regards the nationalities mentioned in the Aide-mémoire of 19th November, 1941, the Embassy does not understand what the People's Commissariat for Foreign Affairs had in mind when referring to Germans, Italians, Rumanians, Hungarians and Finns, as former Polish citizens. Nothing is known to the Embassy about Polish citizens of Italian, Rumanian, Hungarian or Finnish descent on the territory of the USSR, and should such persons be deprived of their freedom on the territory of the USSR and actually possess Polish citizenship, the mere fact of their being Polish citizens should be sufficient ground for extending to them the amnesty measures.

With relation to Polish citizens of German descent, the Embassy has the honour of drawing the attention of the People's Commissariat for Foreign Affairs to the fact that in a great number of cases Polish citizens of German descent who are at present on the territory of the USSR are those who on account of their political beliefs or often anti-Hitlerite activities escaped from the occupied western provinces of Poland to the East and were not claimed back by German authorities. The definite case of such a political figure is a Polish citizen, Jan Kowol, former deputy to the Silesian Diet in Katowice, on behalf of whom the Embassy intervened by Note N.D. 743/41. In these circumstances the Embassy cannot condone the conduct of the Soviet executive organs, for it clashes with the aforesaid legal provisions as regards the general treatment of Polish citizens of German descent. Nothing is known to the Embassy, either, about the deprivation of freedom of all Soviet citizens of German descent (as well as of those of Italian, Rumanian, Hungarian or Finnish descent), and this confirms the fact that the Soviet authorities themselves do not consider all Germans to be protagonists of Hitler and of German imperialism.

5) As regards the category of 'Hitlerite agents', the Embassy takes the view that they not only can but should be deprived of freedom. The Embassy is forced to state, however, that the number of Hitlerite agents among Polish citizens is infinitesimal, while the number of Polish citizens still detained in prisons, as for instance Polish officers who took part in the September 1939 Campaign, can be assessed at many thousands. Moreover, many Poles known for their irreproachable conduct, and even for their active work in the anti-German resistance organizations, have been indicted for espionage on behalf of Germany or other similar offences.

All cases of Polish citizens, suspected of, or indicted for, such offences should consequently be revised and re-considered, and, referring to the conversation between the Deputy People's Commissar for Foreign Affairs M. Vyshinsky, with the Ambassador of the Polish Republic, Professor Kot, on September 20th, 1941, the Embassy has the honour to remind you of the statement according to which the Polish party should be granted the possibility of getting acquainted with the files of such trials, either judicial or administrative, in order to remove any possible disastrous and harmful errors.

6) As regards the category of criminal offenders, the Embassy has the honour of emphasizing that the restriction of amnesty measures relating to them was mentioned for the first time in the aforesaid Aide-mémoire of 19th November, 1941, and as a matter of principle it raises grave doubts because neither the Polish-Soviet Agreement of 30th July, 1941, nor the Decree of the Supreme Soviet of the USSR of 12th August, 1941, make any mention of such restriction. This category probably includes a considerable number of Polish citizens who had nothing to do with criminal offences, and, like the category of 'Hitlerite agents', were put into prisons or forced labour camps for purely political reasons. A typical example of assigning people to this category of offenders is the case of those who were sentenced for illegally crossing the demarcation line between the Soviet and German occupation lines in Poland, or of those who tried to reach Hungary or Rumania in order to enlist with the Polish Army in France, and who were arrested by the Soviet frontier authorities. Here, again, the amnesty measures should be applied in full to that category of people, indicted for criminal offences. A revision appears necessary in those cases, and it may be that among criminal offenders, such as professional criminals whose release is unadvisable for reasons of public safety, there are people who were sentenced on quite different grounds.

At the same time the Embassy has the honour of drawing the attention of the People's Commissariat for Foreign Affairs to the procedure applied at present in the release of Polish citizens which takes place on the strength of a nominal list submitted by the Embassy, as this confirms the fact that the amnesty is not being applied to all Polish citizens by Soviet executive organs. In a number of definite cases the Polish citizens were told that only those would be released who are claimed by name by the Polish authorities. Such an interpretation of the legal provisions relating to the amnesty absolutely contradicts their letter and spirit. The Embassy supplies, as a matter of fact, only a very limited number of names, which is insignificant in comparison with the total number of the Polish citizens who are detained. Submitting a nominal list, the Embassy does not mean to forfeit its claim that the amnesty should be general and does not allow for exceptions.

The Embassy reiterates its request that it should receive a list of Polish citizens who are still detained in prisons and camps, and also of those who have been released, including an indication of the place they went to. The last would present no technical difficulty, while facilitating the task of the Embassy of keeping records, bringing the necessary assistance to the persons concerned, and informing the Polish Government in London as well as the relatives, who for obvious reasons send numerous requests on this matter.

No. 159

Minute of the conversation held in the Kremlin between General Sikorski and M. Stalin on the outstanding problems of Polish-Soviet relations. Present also: Ambassador Kot, Commissar Molotov, Lt.-Gen. Anders

Moscow, December 3, 1941   GSHI, PRM, 41/4
                                      Transl. from Polish: Kersten, No. 17

Gen. S.: I am extremely glad that I can greet one of the real makers of modern history, and congratulate you, Mr. President, on the heroism of the Russian Army in the fight with the Germans. As a soldier I would like to express my admiration for the valiant defence of Moscow led so successfully by you, Mr. President, who himself remains in the capital. Simultaneously I thank you, Mr. President, for the great hospitality which has been extended to me from the very moment I stepped upon Soviet soil.

Stalin: I thank you, Mr. Prime Minister, for what you said and I am very glad to see you in Moscow.

Gen. S.: I will begin by stating that I never have conducted, and never have agreed with the policy directed against Soviet Russia for twenty years. Therefore, I was morally entitled to sign the pact, since it may bring about the final fulfilment of the principles which I have upheld for so long. Furthermore, I have, in this problem so vital for the future, the backing of the Polish nation in our country as well as in all Polish communities, either larger ones like in America where four and a half million Poles live, in Canada and in France where there are six hundred thousand Poles, or in other smaller communities. Those who did not conduct such a policy as mine, I have against me. I would not want that a slow realization of the agreement weaken the policy of approach and of friendly coexistence between our nations. Whether we have really reached a turning point in history depends on a complete and loyal realization of the agreement. This depends on you since your decisions are authoritative in this country. Therefore, it is necessary that our agreement be realized, the chicaneries, annoying our population, disappear. I know perfectly the difficulties in which Russia has found herself. Four-fifths of all the armed forces of the German Reich have been thrown against you. Understanding this I have been the advocate of your cause in London as well as in the United States. A few months ago I already submitted materials proving the necessity of establishing a second front in the West.

Stalin: I thank you, Mr. Prime Minister. It is right and good.

Gen. S.: But this is not an easy task. There exist great difficulties, especially in shipping. The crossing of the English Channel by a large number of armed forces, and the seizure and development of proper positions on the continent, is not a simple task. Operations of this nature have to be prepared very carefully, exactly and concretely; one can't be too insistent on this point, so that another Dakar will not repeat itself.

Molotov: That's right; if such an operation should fail, then morally it would have very negative results.

Gen. S.: I return, however, to our problem. I confirm in your presence, Mr. President, that your declaration about the amnesty is not being fulfilled. Many of our people, a great number of very prominent men, are still kept in labour camps and in prisons.

Stalin [taking notes]: This is impossible, as the amnesty has referred to all and all Poles have been released. [The last words are directed toward Molotov. Molotov nods.]

Gen A. [gives details upon request of Gen. S.]: This is not in accordance with the real facts, since we possess the most concrete data, that from the camps were released firstly, Jews, then Ukrainians, and finally physically weaker Polish labouring groups. Stronger ones were retained, releasing but a small number of them. I have in my armed forces people, who have been released but a few weeks ago from such camps, and they confirm that in individual camps there are still retained in each hundreds and even thousands of our countrymen. Governmental orders are not carried out there, because the commanders of the individual camps, who are responsible for fulfilling the plan of production, do not want to lose their best labouring groups, without which the fulfilment of the plan of production might be at times impossible.

Molotov [smiles and nods his head].

Gen. A.: These people do not understand the real weight of our common problem, and this is extremely detrimental to our common problem.

Stalin: These people should be taken before the courts.

Gen. A.: That's correct.

Gen. S.: It is not up to us to supply the Soviet Government with accurate lists of names of our people; however, complete lists are in the possession of the commanders of the camps. I have with me a list containing the names of approximately 4,000 officers who were deported by force and who presently still remain in the prisons and labour camps. Even this list is not complete, since it contains only names which we were able to take from memory. I ordered that checks be made whether they are in Poland, with whom we have steady contact. It has been proven that not one of them is there, likewise as in our prisoner of war camps in Germany. These people are here. Not one of them has returned.

Stalin: That is impossible, they have escaped.

Gen. A.: Where then could they escape?

Stalin: Well, to Manchuria.

Gen. A.: It is impossible that all could escape, the more impossible considering the fact that since they have been deported from prisoner of war camps to labour camps and prisons, their correspondence with their families has stopped completely. I know perfectly well, being informed by officers who have already returned even from Kolyma, that there is still a large number of officers remaining there, many of them mentioned by name. I know that groups of Poles were already prepared for release and departure, but they were retained at the last moment. I am informed that our people are found even in Novaya Zemlya. The greater number of these officers mentioned in this list, I know personally. Among them are commanders and officers of my staff. These people perish and starve there under the terrible conditions.

Stalin: Surely they have been released, but as yet have not arrived.

Gen. S.: Russia is immense and the difficulties are great. Maybe the local authorities did not carry out the orders. Those who arrive after being released confirm that others who remain there just merely exist and labour. If anyone would succeed to get beyond the boundaries of Russia, he surely would report to me.

Stalin: I want you to know that the Soviet Government has not the slightest reason to retain even one Pole; I released even Sosnkowski's agents who attacked us and murdered our people.

Gen. A.: However, we receive evidence about people, whom we know very well, evidence containing names of prisons and numbers of cells in which they are confined. I know the names of many camps in which an extremely large number of Poles have been retained and must continue to labour.

Molotov: We have retained only those, who, after the war, had committed felony, stimulated diversion, set up radio stations, and the like. You will surely not concern yourself about those.

Amb. K.: Certainly not; however, I have asked many times that lists of these people be given us, because people whom I know as ardent patriots and who are absolutely innocent, are very often charged with this.

Molotov [nods].

Gen. S.: Let's not touch the questions which arose during the war. It would be useful now if you, Mr. President, would make a public statement pertaining to this matter, in order to bring about in Soviet Russia a basic reversal of the situation of the Poles. Certainly they are not tourists here, but people taken by force from their homes. They did not come here by their own will but were deported and have survived tremendous sufferings.

Stalin: The attitude of the population in the Soviet Union toward the Poles is favourable. Only officials can make mistakes.

Gen. A.: It is not only our concern that the officials carry out their orders badly, but it is also our concern that the population should understand that the Poles are gathered in certain places not by their own will. We are particularly interested in good relations with the population.

Gen. S.: In Kuibyshev I saw a transport of our people which impressed me terribly. It is necessary to give them speedy relief. I classify our people into two groups—those who are able to work and they should be given work under best conditions possible.

Stalin: On the same conditions as Soviet citizens.

Gen S.: It does not matter that they be the same, however, simply tolerable ones. The proper use of our people lies in the interest of our joint war efforts. You understand of course, Mr. President, that an expert in building tanks who is now felling trees in a forest, or a distinguished chemist who does physical work on farms, is not properly utilized. The second category of our citizens consists of people unfit for work, old men, women and children, who should all be gathered into places with favourable conditions and climate, so that our Embassy could look after them. From labour camps everyone should be released at once, while those who were deported and who are living in settlements under tolerable conditions may remain there for the time being. An unco-ordinated moving of people back and forth causes only ill feelings, as they find themselves under very severe conditions, and in the result it may come out that I, by making this pact with you, did them only wrong. People even die because of the terrible conditions. These corpses will heavily influence our future relations. These people must be helped instantly, and it is not worth while to bargain over a few million roubles which during the war do not play a part whatsoever. A loan to the Polish Government should be given on a large scale.

It is also necessary that delegates of the Embassy be given permission to enter Polish communities and be granted true and not fictitious right. As for example, our delegate in Arkhangel is not able to give any help to our population, and his work is limited only to the sending out of transports. He cannot even distribute warm clothing to the Polish population. I am also concerned that a mission of the Embassy be set up in Vladivostok. The Polish community in America has collected many things for Poles in Russia, however, they make the shipment dependent upon the condition that it be delivered into Polish hands, to delegates of the Embassy.

Stalin: I agree as to the delegates and also as to Vladivostok.

Molotov: I believe it impossible that your people are still in the camps.

Gen. A.: Nevertheless, I definitely confirm that they are; I repeat that the strongest are retained because they need workers. The retention of our people badly serves our joint cause.

Stalin: This will be settled. Special orders will be given to the authorities, however it should be understood that we are conducting a war.

Gen. S.: And you conduct it well.

Stalin: Oh no, just fairly. Our system of transport was terribly overloaded. We shipped out the wounded, evacuated the population, transferred seventy large factories. We were forced to transfer armed forces back and forth. Your Poles should understand the tremendous difficulties that we had. But it will be better.

Gen. S.: The Polish population should be located in a province with a better climate.

Stalin: We have to think over what regions can be assigned to the Poles. To Fergana and Uzbekistan, we regularly deliver grain, because there we produce cotton and we have even issued special orders prohibiting the raising of grain. From this point of view these territories are not convenient. However, the southern regions of the Semipalatinsk Province would be more adaptable. We can even see how it looks on the map [all rise and approach the map, Stalin points to the map]. Thus, Tashkent, Alma-Ata and the entire southern Kazakhstan.

Amb. K.: The territories around Barnaul and Novosibirsk would be better for those from the Far East.

Stalin: It is cold there but bread is abundant.

Amb. K.: But where can those be sent who are in the Arkhangel Province and in Komi?

Stalin: Also to southern Kazakhstan. [They sit down at the table.]

Gen. S.: Regarding the loan, I think that one hundred million roubles would settle the case for a longer time, if only for the reason that it not cause a bad impression, and so that you would avoid the charge that you make difficulties over such insignificant matters.

Molotov: Of course, we have already given sixty-five million.

Amb. K.: But that was for the armed forces.

Gen. S.: Hitler taught everyone how, without gold and only through labour, great things can be created. Do not follow, Mr. Commissar, the example of the western ministers of treasury who in the beginning bargained for every million.

Stalin [nodding]: Good.

Gen. S.: That is all I wanted to say about the Polish civilian population. Now I must bring up military matters. Should I immediately speak about the whole problem or shall we discuss its elements successively?

Stalin: As you wish, General.

Gen. S.: We Poles do not consider warfare as a symbol but as a true fight.

Stalin [makes a nodding gesture].

Gen. A.: We want to fight for Poland's independence here on the continent.

Gen. S.: In our homeland we have a strong military organization, which I had ordered to remain quiet, because there people are shot for every word. [Stalin nods.] [General Sikorski gives several details pertaining to the methods of fighting of the Polish nation against the Germans.] Our army fights everywhere. In Great Britain we have a corps which needs reinforcements. We possess a navy which performs excellently. We have in action 17 air force units which are equipped with the most modern English planes, and they fight superbly. Twenty per cent of the German Air Force losses in England were caused by Polish pilots.

Stalin: I know that Poles are valiant.

Gen. S.: If they are well led. Thanks to Providence, and thanks to you, Mr. President, we have here with us General Anders, my best soldier, whose eight stars received for wounds prove his valour. You put him into prison because he wanted to join me. This is a loyal leader, not a politician, who will not allow any of his subordinates to conduct any political activity.

Stalin: The best policy is to fight well. [Turning to Anders.] How long did you stay in prison?

Gen. A.: Twenty months.

Stalin: How were you treated?

Gen. A.: In Lwów exceptionally bad, in Moscow slightly better. But you, Mr. President, know yourself what 'better' means in a prison if one is confined for twenty months.

Stalin: Well, such were the conditions.

Gen. S.: I have one brigade in Tobruk which will be transferred to Syria and reorganized into a motorized division with two tank battalions. If the need arises I can transfer it here to the East. We have a few navy vessels. When I had decorated the sailors from one submarine which was stationed in Malta and which had sunk an Italian cruiser and a transport ship, the crew of this submarine became so enthusiastic that after that the submarine entered a Greek port and, even with a damaged periscope, sunk another cruiser and one Greek transport ship. They returned without any losses. The Polish soldier will fight in this manner everywhere, if he is led well. Our homeland is occupied, and we have here the only reserve of our youths. I wish to send to Scotland and Egypt approximately 25,000 as reinforcements. We should form about seven divisions with the rest. This is extremely important for the homeland, which is looking at the Polish army as a symbol of its resistance and independence. We want to fight and that is why our armed forces in Scotland will be used as a vanguard for the establishment of a second front, or will be transferred here to the East. In this case I would personally take the command. The present difficulties of feeding, equipping and training make me anxiously concerned that the formations created under such conditions will be completely useless. Instead of sacrificing health and life for the common cause, people merely exist here or perish in vain. The war will be long. Great Britain and the United States disarmed themselves too much, and their war industry, particularly the American, needs much time to achieve full capacity of production. With time the avalanche of war materials will grow. However, I already have Roosevelt's and Churchill's assurance that they will equip our divisions parallel with yours, without straining the shipment for you, but under the condition that the formation of our armed forces will take place in regions to which supplies can be sent without much trouble. The present state of equipping our divisions is completely inadequate. The divisions under such conditions are incapable of fighting, since they did not receive all of the necessary equipment. General Anders will explain this to you in detail.

Gen. A.: [Explains in detail the state of the equipment received and the entire matter of equipping the Polish armed forces, stressing the insurmountable difficulties, which appear every day.]

Stalin: [Inquires about certain details of artillery equipment.] Russia entered the war with divisions each having 15,000 men, which however in practice proved too large. Therefore, we changed over to a type of light division having a strength of approximately 11,000 men in each.

Gen. S.: The conditions under which the Polish forces are now formed are completely inadequate. The soldiers freeze in summer tents, feel the want of food, and are simply doomed to slow extinction. Therefore, I propose that the entire army and all the people eligible for military service be moved, for instance, to Persia where the climate as well as the promised American and British help would allow these people to recover within a short time and form a strong army which would return here to the front and take over the section assigned to them. This has been settled with Churchill. On my part I am ready to declare that these forces will return to the Russian front, and that they might even be strengthened by several British divisions.

Gen. A.: [Continues to present the situation of the armed forces which are formed at present and confirms that under such conditions of food supplies, housing, sanitation, and of unfavourable climate, the organization of units capable of warfare is completely unfeasible.] This is simply a miserable existence toward which all the efforts of the people are directed, to live and to live very badly! It is, of course, our concern that the Polish army be prepared for war as soon as possible and fight for Poland with our Allies, which under these conditions is absolutely impossible. Therefore, it is essential to transfer the forces into an area with such conditions of climate, food and supply, which would allow the whole problem to be solved. Faced with the difficulties in which Russia finds herself, we must take into consideration the facility of Anglo-American shipping. The most adequate area is Persia. All the soldiers and all men capable of military service should find themselves there. When we take part in fighting, the striking force of our army should not only be a symbol but it should serve towards the aim, the struggle for Poland, for which we are fighting in the entire world.

Gen. S.: I wish the Soviet Government would turn with confidence towards my proposition. I am a person who, when I say yes, then it means yes, when I say no, it means no, and when I say nothing, I either cannot or do not want to tell the truth.

Stalin [expression of excitement and evident displeasure]: I am a person of experience and of age. I know that if you go to Persia you will never return here. I see that England has much to do and needs Polish soldiers.

Gen. S.: We are united with Great Britain by an alliance which she fulfils loyally. We have full sovereignty in Great Britain. I can even bring a corps from Scotland here, and I am sure that no one in England would trouble me about it. Likewise, I can attach the units stationed at Tobruk to our forces here.

Amb. K.: A Pole fights especially well when he is near his fatherland.

Stalin: Iran is not far from here, but the English may force you to fight against the Germans on Turkish territory, and tomorrow Japan may enter the war.

Gen. A.: We want to fight for Poland. We believe that even the strongest air force and navy will not end the war. The battles on the continent will end the war. We all, without exception, love our country and want to enter it first, we want to be ready for fighting as soon as possible, but under the conditions which we now face, it is impossible to prepare ourselves for it.

Gen. S.: England of today and of the past is heaven and earth. The English now have enough armed forces to defend their Isles, therefore, they have no reason not to allow our corps to leave them.

Molotov: [Proposes that General Panfilov be called and gives orders to the secretary who is leaving.]

Gen. A.: [Explains the difficulties of forming forces, the living conditions in Koltubianka, Tatishchev and Tock, and the lack of punctuality in the delivery of food, fodder, equipment, tools, and so on.] This is only a miserable existence and months are wasted. Under such conditions it is impossible to form armed forces.

Stalin [excited]: If the Poles do not want to fight then let them go. We cannot hold back the Poles. If they want to they may go away.

Gen. S.: If we had been allowed to organize ourselves, we would be fighting already. But, so much time was wasted here for which we are not to blame. In the areas where our soldiers are now quartered, we still do not have facilities for their training [an interval of silence]. I, therefore, must ask for another solution.

Stalin: If the Poles do not want to fight here then let them say so, one way or the other. I am sixty-two years old and I know that where an army is formed, there it remains.

Gen. S. [in a sharper tone]: Then please show me another solution, because the proper conditions for organizing of our armed forces are not available here, and I do not want people to perish in vain. I am not presenting an ultimatum, but when there is a severe winter, winds and frost, from which people perish, I cannot look at it and remain silent.

Gen. A.: Where I am the freezing temperatures have already fallen to 33° C. below zero. The people live in simple tents, the majority without heating stoves, which are not supplied to us in a sufficient number. They awaken in the morning with frozen noses and ears. This is not an organization of armed forces but simply sheer existence.

Gen. S.: One cannot throw an untrained soldier against the Germans. One cannot be exposed to disgrace. The Polish Army must be well armed and fight as a body.

Gen. A.: Even so, I have full admiration for our soldiers as they have never complained, in spite of their extreme sufferings during the past two years and in spite of the horrible conditions under which they now live. Only two weeks ago they had received shoes, until then 60% of them were barefoot. They never received their due share of food, and for a long time were not even paid.

Gen. S. [emphatically]: You hurt me, Mr. President, by saying that our soldier does not want to fight.

Stalin: I am rough [Russian 'grubyj'] and I want to know clearly whether you want to fight or not.

Gen. S. [emphatically]: That we want to is proven not by words but by facts.

Gen. A.: That is why we are organizing, in order to fight here and we understand that we will fight on the continent. According to my calculations I can have 150,000 soldiers; this is equivalent to eight divisions. But we do not have quite two divisions, and the formation is limited to that. We do not receive our due share of food and all promises to complete it are not fulfilled.

Stalin [turning to Gen. S.]: As you want, Sir.

Gen. S.: I do not want the matter to be presented in that way. I am still waiting for a new formula and I am ready to accept every just solution.

Stalin [with a shade of irony]: I see that the English are in need of good armed forces.

Gen. S.: This estimate is not exact. In England they value us, but they do not exploit us. I know Churchill very well, and I know that he wants to do all he can to help Russia.

Gen. A.: Sixty per cent of my people are from the reserves, but they must recover from two years of hardship and must be retrained. Volunteers likewise are in very bad shape and must undergo proper training, for which time and proper conditions are necessary.

Stalin [upset]: That means that we are savages, and that we cannot improve anything. It amounts to this, that a Russian can only oppress a Pole, but is unable to do anything good for him. However, we can do without you. We can give back all of them. We will manage ourselves. We will conquer Poland and then we will give her back to you. But what will people say to this? They will ridicule us all over the world that we are not able to achieve anything here.

Gen. S.: I did not receive a reply as to where I am to establish an army so that it could participate in the war but not perish from the horrible climatic conditions. I ask for concrete counterpropositions. I categorically confirm once again that we want to fight for Poland and at your side.

Stalin: When you go to Iran then perhaps you will have to fight in Turkey against the Germans. Tomorrow Japan will enter the war, then against Japan. So as the English will order. Perhaps in Singapore.

Gen. A.: It is on the continent that we want to fight the Germans for Poland. Our people have not seen their country for a long time, and no one loves his country as much as the Poles do. From here it is closest to Poland.

Gen. S.: The patriotism of the Poles does not have to be proven. I confirm that I still have no clear counterproposition.

Stalin: If you insist—one corps, 2 to 3 divisions may leave. However, if you so desire, I shall assign place and means necessary for the forming of seven divisions. I see, however, that the English need Polish soldiers. I, of course, have received Harriman's and Churchill's request to evacuate the Polish Army.

Gen. S.: The English are not so badly off, that the Polish Army formed here should decide their fate. They are slow. However, today they represent a great power. It was I who demanded that Churchill requests the evacuation of our armed forces. I will, however, prove my good will; I am ready to leave the army in Russia, if you assign an adequate region for its concentration and if you assure to it equipment and supplies and proper quarters, and so establish adequate conditions for its training.

Molotov: Panfilov is ready. Gentlemen, do you have any objections against Panfilov entering the room? [All nod, shortly Panfilov, the Deputy Chief of Staff of the Red Army, enters the room.] [A conversation, concerning the conditions for the organization of Polish forces, follows with Stalin, General Anders and General Panfilov; each side brings up various details.]

Gen. A.: I confirm categorically that I do not receive the due share of food nor fodder for horses. The divisions have not received their due rations of food, nor articles of equipment so necessary, like stoves for the tents. Several months have passed since I was promised delivery of tractors, but up to this time they have not arrived. All our requests remain without results, and promises from Soviet military authorities remain unfulfilled. I have typhoid fever in my units, and all my begging for a hospital train has been futile. For several months the soldiers have not received any soap, tools for construction, lumber or nails. The soldiers never receive any vegetables. Many additional food products are never delivered. The means of transportation are absolutely inadequate and in very bad shape. A few weeks ago the food rations were suddenly cut from 44,000 to 30,000. In spite of President Stalin's promise to our Ambassador, that the rations be restored to 44,000, up to now it has not been carried out. On the 1st of December the entire camp in Tock did not receive any food at all. [He enumerates a series of other shortages and lacks of food and supplies.] It does not comply with facts that we did not remind them about it. I myself continuously turned to the Liaison Officer, Colonel Volkovisky, and I myself sent out dispatches and letters. [Panfilov remains silent.] I went after these matters a great deal personally.

Stalin [very sharply to Panfilov]: Who is responsible for this?

Gen. Panf.: Proper instructions were issued, the orders were given by General Khrulov.

Stalin: When did I give the orders for increasing the number of food rations?

Gen. Panf.: Two and a half weeks ago.

Stalin: Why then has the order not been carried out up to now? Shall they eat your directives?

[This entire part of the conversation is conducted in a very harsh tone by Stalin. Panfilov is standing at attention—turning colours.]

Gen. S.: Only the extreme difficulties which we are encountering here, and the bad conditions, have compelled me to present the matter in this way.

Stalin: We can give the Polish Army the same conditions as we give the Red Army.

Gen. S.: Under the conditions existing up to now, not even a corps will be established.

Stalin: I understand that they are bad. Our units are organized under better conditions. I say this sincerely, that if they can give you better conditions in Iran, then as far as we are concerned, we are able to offer only such conditions as we give our Army. Food for our soldiers is better than what the Germans have.

Gen. A.: If they will receive all the food which is due a soldier, then I consider it sufficient, but it should be delivered without those continuous shortages which we encounter. I myself must have the opportunity to manage and establish my own stocks and not live from one day to the next; when a transport does not arrive then people often go hungry.

Gen. S.: I confirm once again our desire for fighting jointly with you against the Germans, our common foe.

Stalin: It seemed to me that the English need your army.

Gen. S.: No, it was I, seeing what difficulties we have to face here, that requested the English and Americans to move our soldiers to better conditions.

Gen. A.: [Gives detailed explanations about the number of Polish soldiers in the area of the southern territories of Russia, enumerating particular localities. A discussion follows about the places where they are being formed. The names of Uzbekistan, Turkistan, and Transcaucasia are mentioned.] I am counting on 150,000 people, that is eight divisions together with the army's maintenance forces. Perhaps there are even more of our people, but among them there is also a great number of Jews who do not want to serve in the army.

Stalin: Jews are poor warriors.

Gen. S.: Many from among the Jews who reported are speculators or those who have been punished for contraband, they never will make good soldiers. Those I don't need in the Polish Army.

Gen. A.: Two hundred Jews deserted from Buzuluk, upon hearing the false report on the bombing of Kuibyshev. More than sixty deserted from the 5th Division a day before the distribution of arms to the soldiers was made public.

Stalin: Yes, Jews are bad warriors.

[A discussion follows among Stalin, Anders and Panfilov concerning armament and its shortages. Verification and calculations are made from lists.]

Gen. S.: When will a new area be assigned to us and when will we learn about the other details pertaining to the organizing of forces?

Stalin: [Deliberates audibly with Panfilov and gives as suggestions names like Uzbekistan, Turkmenistan, and Transcaucasia.]

Gen. S.: After organizing and training, all should be gathered together as one unit, in order to strike as an army, because only such a force will inspire the imagination of the Polish nation.

Stalin: This will require much time.

Gen. A.: No, if everything will be carried out properly then the organization, after the arms are received, will not take much time.

Stalin: [Touches upon the question of the army, without the organization of corps.]

Gen. S.: Maybe this is better. We will agree with this, only the divisions must then be equipped and armed still stronger.

Stalin: The organization without corps is better because the commander of the army delegates all the responsibility to the commanders of the corps, when such exist, and the result is such that no one is responsible for anyone. It would be better that your army have simply seven divisions, as it is in ours.

Gen. S.: I will see to it that equipment comes to you from abroad in a greater volume. With good will this can be done.

Stalin: We will give a part, the English should give the rest. However, the ocean transports do not always arrive on time. They can be late, and this should be kept in mind.

Gen. S.: I must evacuate 25,000 people from here, because I need them for the air force, navy, and panzer units. Besides that we can set up seven divisions. Here, of course, exist our only human reserves. Do you have sufficient airplanes?

Stalin: There is never a sufficient number of airplanes. As to the quantity we are no worse off than the Germans, regarding the quality we are superior. However, in reference to tanks the situation is much worse.

Gen. S.: Libya has destroyed a great part of the German Air Force.

Stalin: For the past 2 months we have not felt the superiority of the German Air Force. They now have very inexperienced pilots, young ones. Their airplanes are relatively slow. And how many airplanes does your air force division have?

Gen. S.: Twenty-seven, eighteen of which are in the first, and nine in the second line.

Stalin: That is equivalent to our air force regiment.

Gen. S.: From England we will be able to send several air force divisions for our army. There the people are anxious for that.

Stalin: [Praises the English airmen who are in Russia.]

Gen. S.: Our airmen have excellent vision and quick orientation.

Stalin: The best and most valiant airmen are Slavs. They act very quickly, because it is a young race which as yet has not been worn out.

Gen. S.: The present war will make the Anglo-Saxons younger. The British are not the French, who really are already finished.

Stalin: I don't agree with this opinion.

Gen. S.: Perhaps the lower class is still good, but the upper class does not represent a greater value [a longer discussion on Pétain, Weygand and others].

Stalin: The Germans are strong, but the Slavs will crush them.

Gen. S.: I now would like to travel in order to inspect the army and visit the centres of the civilian population, and later return once again to Moscow in order to see you again, Mr. President.

Stalin: By all means, I am at your service.

Gen. S.: Tomorrow I shall speak over the radio on behalf of the nations occupied by the Germans. Commissar Vyshinsky was to have sent you the text of my speech.

Stalin: Yes, I read it, it will be good for the broadcast to take place.

Gen. S.: I imagine that it will be useful to the world. The broadcast will be received and transmitted also by the B.B.C. and America.

Stalin: I ordered that here your speech be translated into forty languages.

Gen. S.: I would like you to announce my speech.

I make the suggestion that we sign a joint political declaration. I don't insist upon it of course, but I am leaving its draft with you, Mr. President [hands over a draft of the declaration].

Stalin: Basically I agree. I will read it and tomorrow we will settle it jointly.

Gen. S.: And so, of course, I consider the problem of the armed forces as settled in principle. I will be represented by General Anders in a mixed committee which should be assembled as soon as possible, in order to bring about a final conclusion of these questions. Please appoint your trusted persons for the inspection of the camps.

Stalin: I agree. [He mentions Vyshinsky and Panfilov, asking whether they suit General S.]

Gen. S.: [Replies with approval and bids farewell together with the Ambassador and General A. As they are leaving Stalin asks that General Anders remains.]

[The conversation between Stalin and General Anders lasts for a few minutes. Stalin inquires about his collaboration with Panfilov, to which General Anders stated that this collaboration was proceeding favourably, but that General Panfilov could not accomplish much.]

Gen. A.: Now since you, Mr. President, have promised to do away with the difficulties I believe that the forming of the army will be settled properly.

Stalin: I am very sorry that I did not meet you before.

Gen. A.: It is not my fault that I was not called to you, Mr. President.

Stalin: I will want to meet you from time to time.

Gen. A.: Mr. President, I am always at your disposal to call upon your demand.[1]

[This memo was written under the dictation of General Anders from notes taken by Ambassador Kot.]

Kuibyshev, December 6, 1941.

[1] The conversation lasted for two and a half hours.

No. 160

Note of a conversation between General Sikorski and Stalin during dinner at the Kremlin, Lt.-Gen. Anders taking part

Moscow, December 4, 1941 GSHI, PRM, 41/4
Transl. from Polish

General S.: When yesterday I put forward a proposal for the transfer of the whole Polish Army to Persia, where it would be definitely formed, I did it on the assumption that you did not wish, in fact, a strong Polish army. I now see, I confess, that I made a mistake. I wished to ensure proper conditions for this army to be formed as soon as possible.

Stalin: Because you did not believe in our good faith.

Gen. S.: I also resented your refusal to release from the Red Army and 'labour-battalions' all Polish citizens who had been called up by you on the territories you occupied in 1939.

Stalin: Are we not releasing them now?

Gen. A.: Only now you are beginning to release some people from these battalions, and then only those who are Poles. On the other hand, I was officially told that Byelorussians, Ukrainians and Jews would not be released. Were they not Polish citizens? They have never ceased in fact to be Polish citizens, because your agreements with Germany have been annulled.

Stalin: What do you need Byelorussians, Ukrainians and Jews for? It is Poles you need, they are the best soldiers.

Gen. S.: I do not have individuals in mind, they can be exchanged for the Poles who are Soviet citizens. I am, however, unable to accept, even in principle, any suggestion that the Polish state frontiers could be considered fluid. All Polish citizens within the frontiers of Poland as they existed prior to the war did not cease to be our citizens. One must not create 'faits accomplis' by force. Nobody in the West will agree to it.

Stalin: They took part in the vote and became Soviet citizens.

Gen. A.: They did not do it of their own free will, and, so far as Byelorussians are concerned, they regarded themselves as Poles and were good soldiers in 1939.

Gen. S.: You said yesterday that the world would laugh should the whole Polish Army leave Russia. I have to answer now that the world would have burst with laughter if I accepted a discussion on the 1939 frontiers, and recognition of the facts accomplished by you during the war. We know well, in fact, what all these plebiscites in the Eastern territories were like, the plebiscites which were to settle the question of our eastern frontiers.

Stalin: We shall not quarrel because of frontiers.

Gen. S.: Have you not said yourself that Lwów is a Polish town?

Stalin: Yes, but you will have a dispute about it, not with us but with the Ukrainians.

Gen. A.: Many Ukrainians were and are Germanophils, the present war proves it, and that is why first we, and later on you, had much trouble with them, even with those among them who pretended to be Communists, but who during the retreat of Soviet forces were among the first to shoot at them.

Stalin: Yes, but they were your Ukrainians, not ours. Jointly with you we shall destroy them in future. We shall finish with them once and for all.

Gen. S.: It is not the Ukrainians who matter to me, but the territory in which the Polish element is dominant, and which you have weakened by deporting 2,000,000 Poles into Russia.

Stalin: We should settle our common frontiers between ourselves, and before the Peace Conference, as soon as the Polish Army enters into action. We should stop talking on this subject. Don't worry, we will not harm you.

Gen. S.: The 1939 frontier must not be questioned. You will allow me, Mr. President, to return to this problem.

Stalin: Please, you will be welcome.

The conversation which ensued was held in a friendly spirit. At table Commissar Molotov proposed a toast to General Sikorski.

General Sikorski proposed a toast to the Soviet Army in the person of its Supreme Commander Stalin.

Then Commissar Molotov proposed a toast to Ambassador Kot, and the latter to Commissar Molotov.

Commissar Molotov proposed further toasts to General Anders, General Szyszko-Bohusz, Colonel Okulicki and Captain Klimkowski, as the representative of Polish youth.

All of them answered in turn.

Stalin then delivered a long and important speech, very friendly to Poland. He emphasized that Poland should be big and strong, stronger than ever before. Stalin: . . . 'twice you have conquered Moscow in the past, and the Russians have been several times in Warsaw. We have fought each other continually. It is about time to finish this brawl' (pora konchat' draku mezhdu Polyakami i Russkimi—in Russian).

He spoke about the common effort and struggle against Germany up to the victorious end. He ended by expressing wishes for a common victory over the German aggressor and German savagery which for centuries has been menacing all the Slavs.

After dinner the conversation continued in a very courteous manner. Stalin told some stories from his life (as for instance about an incident at the railway station at Trzebinia, when he spoke in Russian, and about an illegal crossing of the frontier near Bedzin with a Polish guide), and he availed himself of this occasion to make some sarcastic remarks about the Jews.

All the diners were then invited to a cinema which is inside the palace.

During the performance of a film which dealt with war events, Stalin continued a very friendly conversation as between comrades, becoming at times even cordial, with General Sikorski and General Anders. The picture showed the Third Reich's war against Soviet Russia. To Stalin's remark that the picture was made three years ago, that is to say at a time when relations with Germany were apparently most friendly, General Sikorski observed: 'This is not the best horoscope for the declaration which we shall sign presently.'—

'Quite so'—answered Stalin—'but it will be the first time that a declaration has been signed by Stalin and not by Molotov.' 'I thank you,' answered Gen. Sikorski—'and I reckon upon you in future.'

All those present passed to another building to sign the joint declaration.

Stalin ordered the declaration and Sikorski's speech to be translated into 27 languages and to be distributed among Soviet troops, also to be dropped behind the German lines by paratroopers.

'Hitler will be mad with rage and will again bite the carpet out of spite,' observed Molotov. 'You seem to know him intimately,' said General Sikorski.

Taking leave Stalin reminded General Sikorski that he had invited him to come to Moscow for a second time. A visit to a sector of the front in the neighbourhood of Moscow was also announced.

No. 161

Declaration of Friendship and Mutual Assistance signed in Moscow by General Sikorski and M. Stalin[1]

Moscow, December 4, 1941　　　　　　　　GSHI, PRM, 41/1
　　　　　　　　　　　　　　　　　　　Transl. from Polish: Pol.-Sov.R., No. 32

The Government of the Polish Republic and the Government of the Union of Soviet Socialist Republics, animated by the spirit of friendly understanding and fighting collaboration, declare:

1. German Hitlerite imperialism is the worst enemy of mankind—no compromise with it is possible.

Both States together with Great Britain and other Allies, supported by the United States of America, will wage war until complete victory and final destruction of the German invaders.

2. Implementing the Treaty concluded on July 30, 1941,[2] both Governments will render each other during the war full military assistance, and troops of the Republic of Poland located on the territory of the Soviet Union will wage war against the German brigands shoulder to shoulder with Soviet troops.

In peace-time their mutual relations will be based on good neighbourly collaboration, friendship and reciprocal honest fulfilment of the obligations they have taken upon themselves.

3. After a victorious war and the appropriate punishment of the Hitlerite criminals, it will be the aim of the Allied States to ensure a durable and just peace. This can be achieved only through a new organization of international relations on the basis of unification of the democratic countries in a durable alliance. Respect for international law backed by the collective armed force of the Allied States must form the decisive factor in the creation of such an organization. Only under this condition can a Europe destroyed by German

---

[1] See Note No. 161.　　　　　　　　　　[2] See doc. No. 106.

barbarism be restored and a guarantee be created that the disaster caused by the Hitlerites will never be repeated.

For the Government of the	By authority of the
Republic of Poland	Government of the Soviet Union
Sikorski	Stalin

No. 162

Extract from General Sikorski's Broadcast to Polish nation

Moscow, December 4, 1941 GSHI, PRM, 63
Transl. from Polish

I pay homage to the gallant peoples of the Soviet Union, who are defending their own country fearlessly and devotedly against the barbarous German hordes. I express my admiration for the leader of these peoples, Stalin, who plans the defence of Russia. The success with which he is doing this may be seen from the fact that I am speaking from Moscow, which, in Hitler's words, was to be seized by Germany four months ago. I am addressing my country-men, and also, by permission of the Allied Governments, all the peoples who share Poland's fate today.

Mankind is today paying the price for twenty years of illusions, paying in blood and destruction for the material and moral disarmament of so many nations. It is paying for having allowed Germany to rearm on a colossal scale, and to spring a surprise on the democracies by her military might, secretly built up.

The present war is waged not only for disputed territories and the drawing of the frontiers of the countries engaged in it. This appalling conflict is also a world revolution, it is a life and death struggle between democracy and totalitarianism, between two concepts of human life which mutually exclude each other. A new and just world will emerge victoriously from it, a world of free nations, wholeheartedly devoted to freedom, a world built on the unshakeable foundations of true democracy.

Poland was the first country to oppose the military might, unprecedented in history, which in 1939, as the propagandists of the Third Reich today admit, went out to conquer the world. Poland was treacherously attacked, and resisted gallantly, though she lacked modern aircraft and armoured forces. In this way she unmasked Hitler's plans, and gave an example to the nations of Europe of uncompromising struggle. Still, in spite of her fierce resistance, she was defeated. But the Polish nation did not bow to the con-queror, and in spite of unheard-of persecutions, it will never bow. [. . .].

Unfortunately France did not take advantage of the respite afforded to her by the Polish-German war. She did not take advantage of the exhaustion of the Nazi forces in the short but strenuous Polish campaign. But Great Britain, under the inspiring leadership of Mr. Winston Churchill, turned the scales of the war by her indomitable resistance in 1940. As a witness of these events, I can state that the British nation has shown character, courage, and a clear perception of the German menace. At this historic crisis it has shown magnificent moral stamina, and an unusual sense of political and social solidarity.

In future perhaps Germany will succeed in transferring part of her forces from east to west, throwing them against the British Isles. In this case however they will be disappointed, and will suffer defeat on land, at sea and in the air.

Germany owes her initial successes on the eastern front to the element of surprise. She attacked the Soviet Union in the same way in which she attacked other states—treacherously and like a bandit. However Germany was herself surprised by the indomitable fighting spirit of the Soviet Armies, by their tactics and their splendid modern equipment, and by the morale of the peoples of the Soviet Union. The Red Armies have broken the first German onslaught. Their famous Blitzkrieg is already at a standstill. The enormous expanse of Russia, of which the Soviet High Command has cleverly taken advantage, is gradually but continously absorbing the German armed forces. The gallant Soviet soldiers and the Soviet civilian population are inflicting irredeemable casualties on Germany, on a scale so far unknown in the present war. The conquest of vast territories by Germany does not prejudice the final issue, as Germany is not obtaining her strategic aims. Germany is trying to impress upon other people and above all on her own people that the Soviet forces have been destroyed. The course of the war however and events which I myself have witnessed prove this statement to be false.

The authority and prestige of Hitler, so far unconquered on land, is shaken and waning. His hordes will shortly find out for themselves here and in Libya that victory is not their monopoly.

Soviet Russia has, owing to her foresight, a war industry far back in her hinterland, she commands an inexhaustible supply of manpower, and, powerfully backed as she is by Great Britain and the United States, she will quickly replenish her losses and strike increasingly heavy blows at the Nazi war machine. The severe Russian climate is the Red Army's natural ally. It will wear down the German panzer divisions, the state of which is already a source of anxiety to the German High Command. This Command is equally perturbed by the heavy losses in men and material of the Nazi Air Force. It is always a very difficult and lengthy task to make good such losses, and it will be especially so in face of the guerilla warfare, in which the Russians have always been past masters, and which will become still more intensive during the present war.

The consumption of oil is so great in Germany that they had to draw upon their peacetime stocks. Germany will probably make a desperate effort to reach the oil-fields of the Caucasus. However, the lesson which they have just received at Rostov should fill them with some apprehension. [. . .].[1]

During the last two years Hitler has won many battles, devastated many countries, subjugated many nations. He has succeeded in destroying many

[1] Some passages concerning the military and political conditions in the USSR are omitted.

248

towns and burning many villages. He has killed, injured, starved and torn from their homes millions of men. Yet today he is further away from victory than a year ago. He used to promise the German nation that the war would end in 1940 or in 1941 at the latest. In one of his latest speeches he had to use the sibyllic expression 'that this war will end some day'.

Goebbels' propaganda has also lost its offensive drive and its cynical effrontery. The possibility of defeat is discussed in Germany, and the German nation is being made to fear the tragic consequences of defeat. The fear of responsibility for their crimes is intended to stimulate the Germans to further efforts.

A year ago it seemed that Hitler was on the verge of carrying out his much-advertised new order in Europe. Today this New Order of his lies in ruins. The shots recently heard at Nantes, Bordeaux, Prague and Belgrade, the barbarous reprisals in Greece, Norway and Russia, and for more than two years in Poland, show a true picture of the Nazi Order. The mask which covered their perfidy and treachery is off, and the Nazi henchmen are revealed as the champions of bloody tyranny and lawlessness. The policy of so-called collaboration with the Nazi gangsters has brought only humiliation upon all those who trusted the Third Reich, and if they do not awake in time, they will bring their own countries to ruin. Hitler is a devil of destruction, he is unable to build anything positive. Everything he touches is turned to dust, because, in the words of a German poet, this is the 'curse of evil-doing'. There can be neither understanding nor compromise with the Germany of today. [. . .].

There are over 180 million men on the Continent, united in this fashion. This is a powerful army, the more menacing that it holds the front in the rear of the enemy. For the time being this front is silent and underground, but it is no less menacing to the enemy than modern aircraft, armoured divisions and navies. This front is coming into being wherever the jack-boots of the German soldiery have trodden, wherever the blood-thirsty and demoralized Gestapo rules. The conquered nations are waiting impatiently for the day of action and retribution, the hour of which will strike at the moment chosen by us.

We Poles have learnt a lot from this war. United, we fight for a new Poland, whose strength will be based on equality before the law for all her citizens, irrespective of race, rank or religion, on political, social and economic democracy.

When, after victory, we reorganize Europe, we must make an end of petty egoisms, which are the greatest curse of our time. These egoisms have been cleverly exploited by Germany, to set every nation against its neighbours, and to facilitate her conquests in this way.

The new world will be based not on doctrinaire legal formulas but on true international solidarity and on a rational federation of nations.

The war may still last a long time, it will require further efforts on a colossal scale. I know well the material and moral resources of the fighting democracies, backed increasingly by the USA. I therefore believe that we shall win one of the most important victories in the history of the world and that we shall create this time, at the Peace Conference, the lasting foundations for a happy life for the generations to come.

No. 163

Note from the Polish Embassy in the USSR to the People's Commissariat for Foreign Affairs on the subject of Polish citizenship

Kuibyshev, December 9, 1941 GSHI, PRM, 41/2
Transl. from Polish: Pol.-Sov.R., No. 58

The Polish Embassy acknowledges receipt of the Note of the People's Commissariat for Foreign Affairs of December 1, 1941,[1] and has the honour to bring the following to the notice of the People's Commissariat:

1) Polish legislation is founded on the principle of equality before the law of all citizens, regardless of their origin or race. The Polish Embassy is also not aware of any Soviet laws which would introduce or sanction any discrimination or differentiation of this kind.

The Agreement of July 30, 1941,[2] and the Military Agreement of August 14, 1941,[3] do not introduce in any of their provisions relative to Polish citizens (amnesty, military service) the notion of origin or race, and thus they concern all Polish citizens without exception.

In this state of affairs, this Embassy sees no possibility of changing its attitude as expressed in its Note of November 10, 1941,[4] which stated that it was contrary both to the Agreement of July 30, 1941, and the Military Agreement of August 14, 1941, that only Polish citizens of Polish origin should be able to enlist in the Polish Army, while Polish citizens of Ukrainian, White Ruthenian and Jewish origin were enlisted in the Red Army by the War Commissariat in Kazakhstan.

2) The fact of the possession of Polish citizenship by a given person is regulated by Polish law, in particular by the Polish State Citizenship Act of January 20, 1920. For this reason and for the reasons stated above under Paragraph 1, this Embassy has the honour to declare that it finds itself unable to take into cognizance the statement included in the Note of the People's Commissariat for Foreign Affairs of December 1, 1941, to the effect that the Soviet Government is prepared to recognize as Polish citizens only persons of Polish origin from among the persons who found themselves on November 1 and 2, 1939, on the territory of the Republic of Poland temporarily occupied by the military forces of the Soviet Union.

3) The Citizenship of the Union of Soviet Socialist Republics Act of August 19, 1938,[5] cannot be applied to Polish citizens, for its introduction on the territory of the Polish Republic occupied by the Soviet Union from the latter half of September, 1939, until June or July, 1941, would be contrary to the provisions of the IVth Hague Convention of 1907.

4) The Polish Embassy does not connect the matter referred to in Note

[1] See doc. No. 157.   [2] See doc. No. 106.   [3] See doc. No. 112.
[4] See doc. No. 143.   [5] See appendix No. 1.

D. 740/41 of November 10, 1941, with the problem of Polish-Soviet frontiers. The People's Commissariat for Foreign Affairs points out in the Note in question that it does not recognize as Polish citizens persons of Ukrainian, White Ruthenian and Jewish origin who possessed Polish citizenship before November 1–2, 1939, 'because the problem of the frontiers between the USSR and Poland has not been settled, and is subject to settlement in the future'. The Polish Embassy is bound to state that such a thesis is self-contradictory. Maintaining fully the fundamental attitude expressed above in Paragraphs 1–3, this Embassy has the honour to point out that such a view would be tantamount to a unilateral settlement by the Soviet Union at the present time of a problem which, in accordance with this same statement of the People's Commissariat for Foreign Affairs, is subject to settlement in the future.

No. 164

General Sikorski's instruction for Lt.-General Anders on political and military matters[1]

Kuibyshev, December 10, 1941   GSHI, A.XII. 22/30
                                                                                         Transl. from Polish

I. The Polish Army in Russia is an integral part of the Polish Armed Forces, stationed in the Home country, Great Britain, the Middle East, Canada, Switzerland, etc., all of which are, in all respects, subordinated to me as the Commander-in-Chief.

This Army must preserve, in all respects, its distinct national character. This should find its expression in fostering the traditions of the Polish Army and remaining in constant spiritual and ideological union with the Commander-in-Chief and other parts of the Polish Armed Forces.

Special stress must be laid on the close association of the officers with other ranks, and on instilling into the soldiers a feeling of confidence in their superiors.

The special circumstances in which the Polish Army in Russia has to live must neither weaken nor alter these basic features of the Polish Army there. This should guide the Commander of the Army in Russia in his decisions and in the education of the soldier. I attach to this the utmost importance.

II. The nature of your relations with the Ambassador of the Republic of Poland in Russia, as the representative of the Government as a whole, has been defined by previous instructions to you.

I have been able to state that a harmonious co-operation between the Ambassador of the Republic of Poland and yourself has been established. It is all the more indispensable here, as it would be calamitous if anyone were to succeed in bringing about a rift between the particular branches of the Polish State.

You have to inform the Ambassador of any important issue relating to the Army, in order that he may be able to give you full support on behalf of the Government.

[1] See Note No. 164.

III. In organizing the Polish Army in Russia you must base your policy on the following principles:

1. The organization should ensure a continuity of the military effort in Russia; consequently, your aim is not to create the highest possible number of formations, but exactly the number for which you are sure to have sufficient reserves in future. The proportion should be 2 to 1, that is to say for two soldiers in a higher formation or other unit there must be 1 soldier available in a reserve centre.

2. Considering that arms, equipment, and means of transport for the army in Russia, except the 5th Division, will come from Great Britain, the scheme of the organization of divisions and services should be adapted to British establishments, deducting only 1 rifle regiment (brigade) from an infantry division.

Any changes in the organization would only cause confusion in the delivery and distribution of the equipment, and would, therefore, delay the combat readiness of higher formations.

3. I do not say in advance what number of higher formations is to be set up, as this will depend on the available human resources. It seems to me, however, hardly possible to form more than: 4 rifle divisions, 2 armoured support brigades, 2 heavy artillery regiments, 1 engineering regiment, 1 signals regiment @ 2 battalions, 1 anti-aircraft artillery regiment @ 2 batteries, corresponding army services.

The reserve centres of the divisions, grouped eventually in one training division, must be formed simultaneously with the higher formations, that is, from the very beginning.

4. Your greatest difficulties will arise when forming for the future armoured brigades and training army drivers, a great number of which will be required both for higher formations and for army services, to be organized in accordance with British establishments, which are wholly mechanized.

My experience in Great Britain shows that the tank personnel from Poland, where we did not possess a modern, mechanized equipment, has to be trained anew. It is, therefore, imperative, taking into account that we shall attain one day the final stage of organization, to detach the tank and motorized personnel and to start its training as soon as the circumstances allow, for it takes a rather long time.

The Commander of the Army shall investigate the possibility of training the personnel of armoured units in Soviet training centres, assigning some officers for instruction to higher Soviet formations.

IV. Pursuant to the agreement just concluded in Moscow, apart from airmen and seamen 25,000 land troops will be evacuated from Russia. I have appointed Lieutenant-Colonel Tuskiewicz (Staff College) to be officer in charge of the evacuation. He will be directly subordinate to the Commander of the Army.

The Commander of the Army shall assign an adequate number of officers and non-commissioned officers to Lt.-Col. Tuskiewicz in order that he may carry out his task adequately.

Hereunder are the directions for the evacuation:

1. Arkhangel, alternatively Murmansk—Great Britain
2. Ashkhabad—Iran–India, or in case of need, Teheran—Persian Gulf
3. Southern ports of the Caspian Sea—Basra—Persian Gulf

The evacuation should be started as soon as possible. I expect that 2,000 soldiers will be evacuated in December, 1,000 of whom are for the air-force, and that the evacuation will be completed in January and February of 1942.

Among the 25,000 who are to be evacuated there should be 5,000 able men for service in the air-force, apart from those already evacuated and those still remaining in the Russian air-force personnel. There should be no more than 5% of national minorities among the evacuated.

The maximum age of the evacuated must not exceed 36, in equal yearly contingents.

15,000 evacuated men will be assigned by me to Great Britain, as well as all airmen and seamen; 10,000 will go to the Middle East.

There is an evacuation centre in Teheran; the officer in charge is Lieutenant-Colonel (Staff College) Machnowski, subordinate to the Commander of the Polish Armed Forces in the Middle East, and liaison should be established with him.

The closest possible liaison and co-operation should be established with British political and military authorities in the course of the evacuation.

V. The relatives of the troops stationed in Great Britain and in the Middle East should also be evacuated. The Head of the Polish Military Mission should give them all necessary assistance in this respect.

VI. The care of the relatives of Polish soldiers stationed in Russia rests with the Head of the Polish Military Mission who has to submit to me his plan and the conditions of carrying out this care, together with the material needs arising from it.

VII. I approve the formation by the Commander of the Polish Army in Russia of a Women's Auxiliary Service. The women serving with the Army can be used for the following duties: in hospitals as nurses, sisters, for administrative duties, in canteens and reading-rooms, in Headquarters as typists, for draughtsmanship, drivers, army services: seamstresses, laundresses, cooks.

The use of the service of women for any duties below divisional headquarters should be avoided, except for their services in canteens and reading-rooms.

The duties assigned to women at divisional headquarters should be carried out in smaller units by elderly non-commissioned officers or privates, unfit for active military service.

I wish you to note that women serving with the Women's Auxiliary Service should be treated as regular soldiers, and behaviour towards them should be irreproachable in all respects.

It is absolutely inadmissible to treat the WAS on a social footing, and I order the Army Commander to pay special attention to this.

Letter from General Sikorski to Mr. Churchill on the outcome of his journey to the USSR[1]

Teheran, December 17, 1941   GSHI, PRM, 41/3

I feel my visit to Russia resulted in a solution of nearly all the outstanding Polish-Soviet problems and also resulted in some benefit to the Allied cause.

As I wish to convey to you as soon as possible the impressions of my visit to Russia and my interviews with Stalin I am sending you this letter by Mr. Retinger whom I am sending to England ahead of me.

The facts are as follows:

1. Polish Army

If I had insisted on evacuation of the Polish Army as at present formed I am certain I should never have been able to recruit any more Poles—nor should I have obtained any advantages for the Polish civilians now in Russia. Stalin's way of putting it was that 'the world would laugh at him if the Polish Army had to leave Russia'.

It was quite clear to me that Stalin suspected an Anglo-American intrigue at the back of the suggestion. Therefore I immediately and emphatically declared that it was entirely my own scheme based on the reports of General Anders, which proved that under existing conditions our Forces could not possibly be trained in a satisfactory way.

I asked Stalin to state quite definitely what provisions he would make for Polish troops if they remained in Russia. After further conversation I consented to leave them in USSR under the following conditions:

A. That the army would be limited only by the number of Polish citizens available for service. I confidently expect this number to reach 150,000. To those troops will be also added the labour battalions formed previously by the Soviet authorities after the occupations of Eastern Poland.

B. The 25,000 soldiers would be sent to the Middle East or England: this number to be exclusive of the airmen and naval personnel who are being sent to UK.

C. That the Army would be formed in one area and used as one independent operational unit. Up to the present the Russians had wanted to employ the first division, already formed and partially armed, by itself.

Stalin then designated in accordance with my wishes the region between Krasnowodzk-Ashabad-Taskent and Alma Ata, where the climate is mild and the soil fertile, for the Polish Forces. The possibilities of food, clothing and accommodation are better there than elsewhere. This region is on the Persian and Afghanistan frontiers which makes it easier for arms and equipment to be supplied from outside.

D. That the majority of Polish civilians now being moved from place to place would also be sent to the same area. This is for us a very important matter—as at the present moment the conditions under which these people

[1] See Note No. 165.

exist are so bad that anyone used to England could hardly believe life possible under such a state of affairs.

I think it worth remarking that such a Polish Force on Soviet territory may very well play an important role politically and militarily when the war is over, on behalf of Poland and the Allied cause.

In view of the above facts and as it is hoped that the new Polish divisions will be formed very shortly I beg you to consider the problem of their armament and equipment. Full provision for 4 divisions has already been promised by the War Office, I trust additional arms will be made available for 2 or 3 more divisions. I hope that the despatch of these arms may be made simultaneously with the sending of supplies to Russia via Persian Gulf and India. It would be, I consider, most unfortunate if the actual delivery of our arms was in any way mixed up with delivery of arms to Russia. Such a decision would be contrary to our position as a Sovereign Power with an independent Army. It would put me in a false position with Stalin who fully accepted the independent status of Poland—and nothing but misunderstandings would result. I ask you to take personal interest in this matter as it is the most urgent and important question at the present time.

The sending of British divisions to Russia at the present stage of war would —in my opinion—be inadvisable, if for no other reason than the difficulties of transport and feeding. The Poles are, however, more accustomed to hardship and restricted diet. Might not the Polish Fighting Force therefore be regarded as an adequate substitute—especially as by far the largest part of their armaments will have come from Great Britain.

Towards the end of the war I think it will be imperative to have on Russian soil a British and an American division co-operating with the Poles, when the victorious Russian Force will be driving back the Germans into Europe.

My visit to three separate Polish Camps has only endorsed the view I have always had about the magnificent spirit of the Poles. Neither torture nor starvation, gaol or forced labour camps or the assiduous communist propaganda of the Soviet authorities—which continued until my arrival—have had any effect on the minds and spirit of the men. Their only thought is to fight and kill the Germans. There can be no doubt that they constitute the material out of which a first class fighting force can be created which will do honour to Poland and the Allied cause.—I am glad to add that both Stalin and his generals were most appreciative of the qualities of the Polish soldiers. To a man they support my post-war political plan for rapprochement with Great Britain, and of course the United States.

2. The civilian Polish population

In the course of my conversations with Stalin I told him that notwithstanding our agreement and the decree of August 12th there were hundreds of thousands of Poles still detained. I pointed out that various local authorities refused to admit Polish official welfare representatives. Stalin promised to give personal orders about the matter and before I left Russia I heard from

255

all parts of Russia that these orders are being executed as is always the case when Stalin takes a personal hand in any matter.

Furthermore I have every reason to believe that the needs of these people will be met until they join the Polish Army or find suitable jobs.

Our official delegates are now being admitted everywhere.

3. Religious freedom

Full freedom is finally granted for the exercise of religious practice within the Polish Army, for Roman Catholics, Orthodox and the Jews. In my conversation with Vyshinsky he promised me the paragraph 123 of the Russian Constitution granting the religious freedom would not be a dead letter in the future and he himself attended a Catholic service in one of our camps. I am sure that, if not in theory anyway in practice, all the Polish citizens, whatever their creed, will now have freedom in religious worship.

4. International questions

I got the impression that Stalin himself and the Soviet peoples in general are sincere in desiring the Polish-Soviet rapprochement.

The recent joint declaration signed by Stalin and myself[2] declares equality of status as between Poland and the Soviet Union. Apart from condemning Germany—Hitler's Germany—Stalin told me he was strongly in favour of permanently reducing the power of Germany whatever its form of political Government and he added he put no trust even in so-called German communists.

The declaration as well as my broadcast[3] from Moscow, which is really a commentary on it and of which Stalin approved every word, having read it before, binds him more definitely to our and the Allied cause and has considerable significance in that respect as well as in the unification of our efforts.

The Turkish, Swedish and other diplomatic representatives in Russia thanked me for the terms of the declaration particularly where it referred to the independence of foreign states and to 'non-interference' in their internal affairs. This indicates a reasonable assurance that for the time being Stalin has abandoned the idea of universal communism and the international policy of the Comintern.

In my conversation I was of course absolutely sincere and loyal to Great Britain and thereby I hope I may have done something to mitigate Russian suspicion of Great Britain and to have paved the way for Mr. Eden's visit.

I gather you are contemplating the signature of a formal pact between Great Britain, the United States and the Soviet Union. I hope very much that Poland will be included as a signatory and participant in this pact. Of all continental nations and subjected states she is making by far the greatest contribution in the fighting on land, sea and the air. She is also the oldest Ally of Great Britain and now shortly will have an important military force in Soviet Russia.

[2] See doc. No. 161.   [3] See doc. No. 162.

I appeal to you as a true friend of my country to secure a place for Poland in the Supreme War Council which must inevitably soon be formed.

I realize the position in which such a decision may put you as regards the other Allies, however—as I just spoke in Moscow for all of them—I feel a representative of Poland in the War Council could and would represent without bias and loyally the cause of all the suffering nations of Europe.

A delegate from Poland who came to meet me here in Teheran informed me that the Germans are trying to create a nominal Government—based upon the alleged betrayal by Great Britain of her promises given to Poland. The Germans having lost confidence in their crushing victory, do not as yet believe in our complete victory. They still count on a compromise peace and are trying to recover their ground in Poland. I need therefore every argument and assistance to combat this effort.

There are one or two other matters—about which I look forward very much to discuss with you.

I would like you to know how much I value the sympathy and understanding given to me by Sir Stafford Cripps and Gen. Nelson MacFarlane—they have been of greatest help to the Polish soldiers and civilians in these very difficult days.

No. 166

Rules regulating the scope of activities of delegates of the Polish Embassy drawn up in consultation with representatives of the People's Commissariat for Foreign Affairs[1]

Kuibyshev, December 23, 1941

GSHI, A.11. 49/Sow./2
Transl. from Polish: Pol.-Sov.R., No. 70

General Provisions

1. The Delegates of the Embassy of the Republic of Poland in the republics and districts (*oblasts*) where more important concentrations of Polish citizens exist, are the executive representatives of the Embassy authorized to carry out, in close collaboration with the Soviet authorities, such duties towards Polish citizens as arise from the Agreement of July 30, 1941.[2]

2. The functions of Embassy Delegates are temporary. They act as long as concentrations of Poles exist in a given locality, or until they have completed their duty toward Polish citizens, in their capacity as Delegates.

Duties of Embassy Delegates

The duties of Embassy Delegates include the following:

1. To inform the Embassy of the requirements and situation of Polish citizens.

2. To supply Polish citizens with information and guide them according to the spirit of the Polish-Soviet Agreement of July 30, 1941.

3. To register Polish citizens in a given area, to record their movements,

---

[1] See Note No. 166.   [2] See doc. No. 106.

their fitness for military service, for work, and their professional qualifications; to search for missing members of their families and their near relatives.

4. To co-operate with local Soviet authorities in directing Polish citizens to suitable work in accordance with the labour legislation in force in the Union of Soviet Socialist Republics.

5. To exercise due care that Polish citizens unfit for work are assured the minimum means of subsistence, by distributing among them aid in the form of money or in kind, except in cases where the Soviet authorities are obliged to assure them means of livelihood in accordance with existing Soviet legislation.

6. To organize cultural aid for adults and education for youth.

7. To supply Polish citizens with essential documents (passports, certificates, etc.).

8. To receive, dispatch, store and distribute shipments of aid in kind from abroad for the relief of the Polish civilian population.

9. To seek out representatives for regions or localities where Polish citizens are resident. These representatives perform in the districts allotted to them the duties provided under Paragraphs 2, 4, 5, 6 and 7 of the present Regulations, and on instruction of the Delegates the duties provided for in Paragraphs 1, 3 and 8. Candidates for representatives selected by a Delegate are subject to approval by the Embassy. The Delegate exercises direct supervision over the activity of the representatives.

10. In areas where there are no Embassy Delegates, their duties are performed by travelling Embassy Delegates.

Co-operation with Soviet Authorities

1. Embassy Delegates, their deputies and travelling Delegates are appointed by the Polish Ambassador. Their names are immediately notified to the People's Commissariat for Foreign Affairs, which on its part notifies their nomination and the character and scope of their activity to the Soviet authorities of the given Republic or district, instructing them to accord all necessary assistance to the Embassy Delegates.

2. The scope of activity of Embassy Delegates requires their close collaboration with the competent officials of the Soviet authorities in their district, and in particular with the local representatives of the People's Commissariat for Foreign Affairs, *Oblispolkoms, Rayispolkoms,*[3] and the district and regional officials of the People's Commissariat for Internal Affairs. The Embassy Delegates shall acquaint the local Soviet authorities with the situation and requirements of Polish citizens and settle with them all practical questions arising from the situation of the Polish population.

[3] Administrative authorities of provinces and districts.

No. 167

Note from the People's Commissariat for Foreign Affairs to the Polish Embassy in the USSR on the subject of Polish citizenship

Kuibyshev, January 5, 1942　　　　　GSHI, A.11. 49/Sow./3
Transl. from Russian: Pol.-Sov.R., No. 59

In reply to the Note of the Embassy of the Republic of Poland No. 902/41 of December 9, 1941, the People's Commissariat for Foreign Affairs has the honour to communicate the following:

1. After taking note of the considerations set out in the Note of the Embassy of December 9, 1941,[1] on the question of the former Polish citizens forming part of the population of Western Ukraine and Western White Ruthenia— Ukrainians, White Ruthenians and Jews—the People's Commissariat cannot see any reason to change the attitude set forth in its Note of December 1, 1941.[2]

2. The assertion of the Embassy that the law concerning citizenship of the USSR of August 19, 1938,[3] could not be applied to the territories of Western Ukraine and Western White Ruthenia in the period between the middle of September 1939 and the middle of July 1941, as this would be incompatible with the provisions of the IVth Hague Convention of 1907, is incorrect. The provisions of the IVth Hague Convention of 1907, which the Embassy evidently has in view, refer to the régime of occupation on enemy territory, whereas the assertion of 'occupation' in respect to Western Ukraine and Western White Ruthenia is, in this case, devoid of all foundation, alike from the political as from the international point of view, because the entrance of the Soviet forces into Western Ukraine and Western White Ruthenia in the autumn of 1939 was not an occupation but an attachment of the districts mentioned to the Union of Soviet Socialist Republics as the result of the freely expressed will of the population of those districts.

[1] See doc. No. 162.　　　　[2] See doc. No. 157.　　　　[3] See appendix No. 1.

No. 168

Extracts from Commissar Molotov's Note to all the diplomatic missions accredited in Moscow concerning German atrocities against the civilian population of the USSR

Moscow, January 6, 1942　　　　　GSHI, A.11. 49/Sow./3
Soviet Official print

On the instructions of the Government of the USSR I have the honour to bring to your notice the following:

Units of the Red Army, in the course of their continued successful counter-offensive, have liberated a number of towns and rural localities, which temporarily have been in the hands of the German invaders. This liberation has revealed and daily continues to reveal, an unprecedented picture of universal robbery, devastation, abominable violence, outrages and massacres

259

perpetrated by the German Fascist invaders against the peaceful population during their offensive, occupation and retreat.

Abundant documentary material in the possession of the Soviet Government testifies to the fact that the robbing and ruin of the population has been accompanied by widespread bestial outrages and massacres. It has taken place in all districts which have fallen under the heel of the German invaders.

Deliberate Policy of German Government

Irrefutable facts prove that the régime of plunder and bloody terror against the non-combatant population of occupied towns and villages constitutes not merely the excesses of individual German officers and soldiers, but a definite system previously planned and encouraged by the German Government and the German High Command, which deliberately foster the most brutal instincts among soldiers and officers in their army.

Every step of the German Fascist army and its allies on seized Soviet territory of the Ukraine, Moldavia, Byelorussia, Lithuania, Latvia, Estonia, and on the territories of Russian districts and regions brings in its train the destruction of countless material and cultural treasures of our people. The Nazis and their allies rob the peaceful population of property won by its own stubborn labours, and establish a régime of hard labour, starvation and bloody repression before the horrors of which the most terrible crimes that human history ever knew fade into insignificance. [. . .].

During forced labour, they outrageously shoot down people for not fully carrying out the quota of work stipulated. On June 30th the Hitlerite bandits entered the town of Lvov, and the following day they organized a mass slaughter under the slogan: 'Kill off the Jews and Poles.' [. . .].

In the town of Lvov, 32 working women of the Lvov clothing works were raped and then killed by German storm troopers. Drunken German soldiers dragged young women and girls in Lvov to the Kościuszko Park and brutally raped them. [. . .].

According to incomplete data, no less than 6,000 people were shot in Lvov, over 8,000 in Odessa, over 8,500 persons killed or hanged in Kamenetsk Podolsk, 10,500 persons shot by machine-guns in Dniepropetrovsk; over 3,000 local inhabitants were shot in Mariupol, including aged men, women and children, all of whom were robbed and stripped bare before execution. [. . .].

We shall never forgive

The Soviet people will never forgive the atrocities, rape, destruction and mockery which the bestial bands of German invaders have committed and are committing against the peaceful population of our country. They will never forget, nor will they ever forgive, these crimes.

In reporting all these atrocities committed by the German invaders to all Governments with which the USSR has diplomatic agreements, the Soviet Government declares that it lays all the responsibility for these inhuman and rapacious acts committed by the German troops on the criminal Hitlerite Government of Germany.

The Government of the USSR at the same time declares with unshakable confidence that the liberation struggle of the Soviet Union is a struggle for the rights and liberties not only of the peoples of the Soviet Union, but for the rights and liberties of all freedom-loving peoples of the world, and that this war can finish only with the complete destruction of the Hitlerite troops and the complete victory over Hitlerite tyranny.

No. 169

Note from Ambassador Kot to Commissar Molotov on the status of Lwów as a Polish city

Kuibyshev, January 9, 1942 GSHI, A.11. 49/Sow./2
Transl. from Polish: Pol.-Sov.R., No. 81

I have the honour to acknowledge receipt of Your Excellency's Note of January 6, 1942,[1] in which you brought to the notice of all Governments maintaining diplomatic relations with the Soviet Union, the facts concerning the unheard of treatment of the defenceless civilian population by the German Army in the territories temporarily occupied by it as a result of recent war operations.

While fully sharing the Soviet Government's view that responsibility for these inhuman and barbarous actions of the German forces rests with the criminal Hitlerite Government of Germany, I have the honour to remark that this responsibility is also shared to a large extent by the obedient and zealous executors of that Government's will, that is to say German officers, non-commissioned officers and other ranks, and members of the various formations of the German National Socialist Workers' Party who take part in the war operations and in the administration of the occupied territories. I have the honour to recall that in my Note to your Excellency of November 27, 1941,[2] I already pointed out the bestial treatment of the civilian population on the territories of the Republic of Poland by the German Army, and I supplied facts as to pogroms and executions in Lwów, Brześć on Bug, Stanisławów, Komarno and other localities.

At the same time I have the honour to draw Your Excellency's attention to the fact that the inclusion of Lwów among 'other Ukrainian cities' in your Note of January 6, 1942, must be the result of a misunderstanding, for from the historical point of view and from that of international law, and as far as the ethnological constitution of its population is concerned, Lwów was and remains a Polish city.

[1] See doc. Nos. 155 and 168. [2] Not printed.

261

No. 170

Note from the People's Commissariat for Foreign Affairs to the Polish Embassy in the USSR on the release of Polish citizens from prisons and protesting against the word 'occupation' applied to 'Western Ukraine' and 'Western White Ruthenia' [1]

Kuibyshev, January 9, 1942 GSHI, A.11. 49/Sow./3
Transl. from Russian

In reply to the Note No. 926/41 of 3rd December, 1941,[2] the People's Commissariat for Foreign Affairs has the honour to inform the Embassy of the Republic of Poland as follows:

1. The People's Commissariat for Foreign Affairs confirms that its Pro-Memoria of 19th November, 1941,[3] explains precisely the point of view of the Soviet Government on the question of the application of the amnesty to Polish citizens, and that it by no means contradicts the Polish-Soviet Agreement of July 30th, 1941[4] (including the Additional Protocol), and the Decree of the Praesidium of the Supreme Soviet of the USSR. Nor does it contradict the declarations of the Chairman of the Council of the People's Commissars of the USSR, J. V. Stalin, made to the Ambassador of the Republic of Poland, Professor Kot, in the course of the conversation on November 14th, 1941,[5] nor the personal note of the People's Commissar for Foreign Affairs, V. M. Molotov, of 8th November, 1941.[6]

The People's Commissariat considers that it must remind the Embassy that the explanation contained in the aforesaid Pro-Memoria of 19th November of last year, relating to the execution of the amnesty, was given as long ago as August 28th, 1941,[7] in the course of the conversation which took place between A. J. Vyshinsky and M. Retinger on the matter of the application of the Decree of 12th August.[8] This point of view was again reaffirmed in the conversations between A. J. Vyshinsky and M. Kot on October 8th and November 19th, 1941,[9] without any objections on the part of the Embassy.

2. The Pro-Memoria of the People's Commissariat for Foreign Affairs of 19th November stated that it was self-evident that the amnesty could not be extended to Hitlerite agents, and also to persons sentenced for criminal offences.

In objecting to this decision, the Note of the Polish Embassy involves itself in contradictions, for in the same Note of 3rd December there is a statement on the question of Hitlerite agents, who 'not only can, but should be deprived of freedom', and also that criminal offenders must not be released, for reasons of public safety.

The People's Commissariat considers that it must also draw the attention of the Embassy to the fact that it is absolutely inadmissible that, under the conditions of the present war, persons who by their connections or their national feelings might endanger the work of the Soviet Union and of its

[1] See Note No. 170. [2] See doc. No. 158. [3] See doc. No. 153. [4] See doc. No. 106.
[5] See doc. No. 149. [6] See doc. No. 142. [7] Not printed. [8] See doc. No. 110.
[9] See doc. Nos. 127 and 154. The first conversation took place on October 7.

allies, should remain free. The fact that there are no provisions in Soviet legislation imposing restrictions on account of race or nationality, should not be used as a ground for the release of the above-mentioned category of people under present war-time conditions. As regards the case of M. Kowol, quoted as an example, the People's Commissariat replied to the Embassy in Note No. 1 of January 2nd, 1942.

3. The People's Commissariat cannot agree with the statement of the Embassy contained in its Note of December 3rd, 1941, according to which numerous Poles have been sentenced for espionage on behalf of Germany without valid grounds. This statement is absolutely unfounded; the revision of cases of this category does therefore not seem necessary.

4. As regards the remark of the Embassy which stated that, in the course of the execution of the amnesty by local Soviet organs, people detained for political reasons or arrested for illegal crossing of the frontier could also be assigned to the category of criminal offenders, the People's Commissariat states that the possibility of such contingencies is absolutely excluded, because only those people are assigned to the category of criminal offenders and not released, who have been sentenced for criminal offences, like robbery, looting, theft, etc. As regards people sentenced for illegal crossing of the frontier, the amnesty has been applied to them fully, and therefore any revision of the said cases seems unnecessary.

5. The assertion of the Embassy that according to existing practice the release of Polish citizens allegedly takes place only on the strength of nominal lists sent by the Embassy is obviously based on some misunderstanding. The Soviet organs have released Polish citizens irrespective of any lists sent by the Embassy. The Embassy knows well that the lists concerned contain but a few hundred people, while the number of released Polish citizens amounts to hundreds of thousands.

The People's Commissariat knows nothing about cases of Polish citizens being told that their release would take place only on the Embassy's special intervention. Should the People's Commissariat receive, however, information about definite cases of this kind, on the strength of such information proper investigations will be ordered.

6. Relating to the demand of the Embassy that it should receive a list of those Polish citizens who are still detained, the People's Commissariat has the honour to inform the Embassy that such lists will be forwarded as soon as they are sent in by the competent Soviet organs.

7. As there is no reason for returning to the question of the use of the incorrect term 'occupation' applied to the Western Ukraine and Western White Ruthenia, as was done in the Note of the Embassy of 3rd December, the People's Commissariat considers it necessary to state that such assertions are considered offensive to the Union of the Soviet Socialist Republics.

No. 171

Extracts from a report on General Sikorski's journey to the Middle East and Russia, presented by him to the Council of Ministers

London, January 12, 1942 GSHI, PRM-K, 105
Transl. from Polish

[. . .]. The Russo-German war, so much desired by Poland, did not put us in a difficult international position. It is quite obvious that the Great Democracies attached great value to our agreement with Russia. I wish to emphasize, however, in the strongest possible manner that they left the final decision with us, limiting themselves to giving us their full support in our negotiations with Moscow. The Government had to take the decision in their own hands, for the home country was unable to do so. We had to limit ourselves to informing the home country of a new line of policy, which may shape our future for a very long time ahead. But the pace of events was so quick that actual co-operation on the part of our home country in that matter was beyond any possibility. [. . .].

It was quite clear to us that in joining the camp of fighting democracies Russia was bound to review her previous attitude towards Poland. In the past that attitude had found expression in her friendship with a totalitarian Reich and in concurring in the fourth partition of Poland. Thanks to the efforts of our nation and army, Poland became a test-case for the intentions of the Allies, with which Russia had to associate herself. Moreover, Russia was attacked by a common enemy. The whole situation, therefore, underwent a radical change. The fact that by concluding an agreement with us Russia entered upon a course of respect for the sovereign rights of other States and nations is a fact of world-wide importance. It is also important from a purely Polish point of view. [. . .].

We do not know what kind of Poland will emerge from this war. It will depend on the precise balance of forces in the ultimate stage of the war. We hope that it will be to our advantage, and that the Polish State will expand its western frontiers. It is history that pushes us in this direction, providing us with a unique occasion for putting right old wrongs and mistakes and enabling us to reinforce our strategic position in the West, to stem the perennial German drive to the East and to force it back. We shall have to do our utmost in this period in order to lay a firm foundation for a strong Poland, a Poland that will be able to face Germany, by regaining old Slav territories, with wide access to the sea, and secure from the military point of view. Such a Poland, closely allied to Great Britain, should hold a key position in Eastern-Central Europe.

In the East we know only those frontiers within which Poland entered the war, the frontiers established by way of compromise with Russia. It would be a great mistake to allow any official discussion on this subject, and to accept any suggestion that our frontiers are in a state of fluidity. The situation is not yet ripe for any such discussion. Stalin proposed to me a conversation of this nature. He told me of Soviet good will in this direction, and of the assistance which Russia was ready to give us in our disputes with the Ukrainians in the matter of the Polish city of Lwów. He told me of the need to bargain with Russia. He mentioned Poland's mission in the West, and the prospects of her expansion at Germany's cost. I declined these proposals, politely but firmly. Stalin acquiesced, announcing that he would return to the subject at a moment more favourable for us, that is to say, when the Polish Army will begin to fight on the Western front. On the strength of authoritative information I know that the question was not discussed with Mr. Eden during his stay in Moscow. It will, nevertheless, be reopened in a few weeks' time during Molotov's stay in London, and we must be duly prepared for this contingency. Everything possible must be done to win Allied understanding for our rights in the East, and to obtain their full support in accordance with the terms of the Treaty of Alliance. [. . .].

Poland's security is Europe's security. The events of the war which we are now experiencing prove this quite clearly. In order to ensure Poland's safety, we must at the least fight for the frontiers which meet our minimum strategic requirements. Our security must not be thrown into the melting-pot of general security. Let us have no illusions on this point. The frontiers of future States will be of paramount importance for a long time to come. Stalin proposed to me an agreement between Poland and Russia on this issue. Such an agreement should be reached, in his opinion, before the Peace Conference and without any mediation on the part of Great Britain and the United States. I declined this proposal politely, stressing the loyal attitude of our British Ally and emphasizing the value of allied solidarity for all of us, including Russia. This line was maintained during my stay in Russia, and His Majesty's Ambassador and the United States' Chargé d'Affaires in Moscow were duly informed of it. Great Britain and the United States must now maintain this solidarity. In spite of intense German propaganda on that matter, I do not believe that Mr. Eden would sacrifice Poland and recognize Russia's exclusive rôle in Eastern Europe. In any case, it will be up to us to clear up this question and, in connection with it, to take appropriate decisions. [. . .].

Besides the question of frontiers, there may be other sources of conflict with Russia in future. One of them is Russian Pan-Slavism, which we firmly reject. Whether White or Red, it is equally dangerous to both us and the Western Slavs. For this reason we have to warn our refugees and soldiers in Russia against such trends, and in the West try to reach an understanding with Czechoslovakia and Yugoslavia.

I do not doubt that Great Britain, the United States, and our other Allies will understand our position on this question, which is of importance to them too, that they will unite in common cause with us in order to check any Pan-Slav attempts. The Polish-Russian frontier must remain what it has been for centuries, a frontier of Western and Christian civilization.

Another source of conflict with Russia might be the wish to impose a Communist régime on Poland. All attempts of this kind, made in Poland during her occupation, failed. Only part of the Jewish population in our

Eastern provinces joined that movement. But those who were imprisoned in Russia (the common fate of all foreign Communists) after their release—due to our Agreement with Russia—turn back to Poland, whom they slandered but a year ago. [. . .].

One of the most dreaded solutions for us would be a negotiated peace with Germany. For Poland it would be a calamity as great as a lost war. Such a peace could have been concluded only at our cost. Even if we were to recover our devastated provinces, any material and moral indemnification, any firm guarantee for our future, would be out of the question in such an event. Only Germany's total collapse can bring about the desired results. This was the reason for our firm declaration of 4th December, and the fore-shadowing of the severe punishment of all Germans, not only of Hitlerite ones. It should have most favourable repercussions in the West, where not long ago the 'good Germans' had many sympathizers. [. . .].

I wish also to stress that at last our refugees enjoy the freedom of religious worship: the Rev. Prof. Kucharski is in charge of the organization of religious affairs. This freedom is also enjoyed in our Army by all denominations, Catholic, Orthodox and Jewish. Religious worship in the Army has been fully safeguarded. A full religious revival can be observed among our countrymen in Russia. [. . .].

The Polish Army in Russia will be organized without any special limitations. According to estimates which are perhaps too optimistic it will be possible to conscript 150,000 men. This army will be formed in Southern Russia, in the area adjoining Iran and Afghanistan, where Polish refugees are also gathering. [. . .].

25,000 troops and about 1000 to 1500 airmen and sailors will be evacuated from Russia to Great Britain and Egypt. 15,000 troops and all airmen and sailors will be transported to Great Britain, 10,000 to Egypt. The evacuation of these servicemen from Russia will enable us to form a motorized division in the Middle East and to complete the 1st Army Corps in Great Britain. The latter will be reorganized into a motorized and armoured unit. [. . .].

The joint declaration by which Stalin, for the first time, forswore international Communism and recognized the principle of non-interference in the domestic affairs of sovereign States, was warmly welcomed by the representatives of Turkey, Sweden, Greece, Yugoslavia and other States fearing the Red imperialism. Our position in Russia should strengthen the status of Poland as an ally of Western democracies on the European continent. [. . .].

No. 172

Note from the People's Commissariat for Foreign Affairs to the Polish Embassy in the USSR on the status of Lwów, Brześć and Stanisławów and other towns, annexed to the USSR

Kuibyshev, January 17, 1942 GSHI, A.11. 49/Sow./3
Transl. from Russian: Pol.-Sov.R., No. 82

With reference to the Personal Note of Mr. Kot, Ambassador of the

Republic of Poland, of January 9, 1942,[1] the People's Commissar for Foreign Affairs has the honour to present to the Embassy the following declaration on behalf of the Government of the Union of Soviet Socialist Republics:

The People's Commissar deems unjustified the statement by the Embassy in the above-mentioned Note and in certain other documents, in which the towns of Lwów, Brześć, Stanisławów and others on the territories of the Ukrainian SSR and the White Ruthenian SSR belonging to the Union of Soviet Socialist Republics, are referred to as cities which are on the 'territories of the Republic of Poland'.

While finding it impossible to enter into a discussion on the historical and legal bases on which the city of Lwów or any other town on the territories of the Ukrainian SSR and the White Ruthenian SSR belong to the Union of Soviet Socialist Republics, the People's Commissar deems it his duty to inform the Embassy that in future he will not be able to accept for consideration Notes of the Embassy containing declarations of this kind.

[1] See doc. No. 169.

No. 173

Note from the Polish Embassy in the USSR to the People's Commissariat for Foreign Affairs concerning the transfer to the Polish Army of Poles forcibly conscripted by the German Army and at that time being in Soviet captivity

Kuibyshev, January 18, 1942 GSHI, PRM, 72/1
Transl. from Polish: Pol.-Sov.R., No. 51

Referring to its Notes D. 713/41 of November 8, 1941, and D. 48/42 of January 7, 1942, the Polish Embassy has the honour to submit the following for the information of the People's Commissariat for Foreign Affairs:

In the second half of December, 1941, groups of prisoners of war, soldiers of the German Army, passed through Tatishchevo and Saratov; among them were many Polish citizens forcibly conscripted by the German Army. These prisoners on seeing Polish soldiers of the 5th Infantry Division at stations en route asked their countrymen to report their fate to the Polish authorities and to make endeavours to have them set free from prisoner of war camps and enrolled in the Polish Army in formation on the territory of the Union of Soviet Socialist Republics.

Submitting the above for the information of the People's Commissariat for Foreign Affairs, this Embassy has the honour to renew its request that instructions be issued with a view to collecting in a separate centre prisoners of Polish nationality who were forcibly mobilized by the German authorities of occupation, and after particulars as to their identity, etc., have been investigated and their nationality ascertained, make it possible to enlist them in the Polish Army.

Note from the People's Commissariat for Foreign Affairs to the Polish Embassy in Kuibyshev, refusing special treatment for German war prisoners of Polish nationality

Kuibyshev, January 23, 1942   GSHI, A.11. 49/Sow./3

Transl. from Russian: Pol.-Sov.R., No. 52

In reply to the Notes of the Embassy of the Republic of Poland of November 8, 1941, No. 713/41, and January 7, 1942, No. 48/42, and of January 18, 1942—No. 164/42, the People's Commissariat for Foreign Affairs has the honour to communicate the following:

In the Notes mentioned above the Embassy referred to the transfer to the Polish Army in the USSR of Polish citizens, prisoners of war from the German Army, on the assumption that these prisoners surrendered of their own will, supposedly wishing to join the Polish Army in formation on the territory of the USSR.

The People's Commissariat considers itself obliged to declare, that it cannot agree to the Polish Government's proposal and that it sees no grounds for adopting any régime for German prisoners of war of Polish nationality other than the régime established for all German prisoners of war.

Further to the above, the People's Commissariat deems it necessary to inform the Embassy that an overwhelming majority of Poles—soldiers in the German Army—were taken prisoner with arms in their hands, having actively resisted the Soviet forces, and not as a result of voluntary surrender.

No. 175

Note from Ambassador Bogomolov to the Polish Government concerning Minister Raczyński's interview in the 'Sunday Times' of January 11, 1942

London, January 23, 1942   GSHI, PRM, 72/1

L'interview de Monsieur Raczyński, gérant du Ministère des Affaires Etrangères de la Pologne, publiée au 'Sunday Times' du 11 Janvier de l'année courante, contient plusieurs énonciations dont le caractère n'est pas conforme aux intérêts des relations amicales entre l'Union Soviétique et la République de Pologne. Ces énonciations expriment des vues, témoignant la négation du rôle positif de l'URSS dans la solution des problèmes européens, ce que ne corresponde pas à l'ésprit de l'accord entre l'URSS et la Pologne, qui a trouvé son expression dans la déclaration d'amitié et d'assistance mutuelle du Gouvernement de l'URSS et du Gouvernement de la République de Pologne.

En particulier, le Gouvernement Soviétique fait attention à ce que Monsieur Raczyński, ayant parlé de la garantie de l'indépendance de certains états, y compris les États baltiques, et ayant mentionné la situation de ces États en rapport avec la guerre de l'année 1939, a aussi parlé de la défaite ou de la capitulation de ces États, par quoi est dénaturé le cours réel des événements dans la Baltique, qui ont abouti à l'organisation de la République Soviétique Socialiste Lithuanienne, République Soviétique Socialiste Lettone, République Soviétique Socialiste Esthonienne, et à leur entrée volontaire dans l'Union Soviétique.

Parlant, ensuite, de la Confédération future Polono-Tchèque et caractérisant cette confédération comme le centre attractif pour les autres pays, Monsieur Raczyński met la Lithuanie au nombre de ces pays, négligeant ainsi le fait, que la République Soviétique Socialiste Lithuanienne fait partie de l'Union Soviétique.

Le Gouvernement Soviétique juge nécessaire de déclarer a propos de l'interview de Monsieur Raczyński, que plusieurs énonciations dans cette interview ne peuvent que produire l'impression défavorable sur l'opinion publique en l'URSS et ne peuvent pas contribuer au développement des rélations amicales entre l'URSS et la Pologne.

No. 176

Note on a conversation between General Sikorski and Sir Stafford Cripps, relating to the territorial claims put forward by the Soviet Government[1]

London, January 26, 1942
GSHI, PRM, 68
Transl. from Polish

Responding to General Sikorski's request, Sir Stafford Cripps informed him of the state of negotiations between the British and the Soviet Governments concerning the future State boundaries in Europe.

Without concealing his critical opinion of the British Foreign Office, Sir Stafford stated that as long ago as July 1941 he had urged the importance of establishing and putting into practice general principles concerning the frontiers of post-war Europe. At that time Russia was so dependent on Britain's assistance that she would have accepted all proposed conditions. At present, however, in consequence of her military successes, Russia has acquired a much stronger position. In the matter of State frontiers she has established certain principles which she considered as being beyond discussion. In Sir Stafford's opinion the Soviet Government would never alter their point of view in the matter.

The Foreign Minister, Mr. Eden, continued the Ambassador, arrived in Moscow completely unprepared for discussions on principal issues. In consequence no positive agreement could be attained, which again strengthened the position of the Russians. As the military situation became more successful, the Soviet Government became more inflexible.

In European affairs Moscow demanded from Britain the acceptance of these claims: the recognition of the Russian-Finnish frontier of 1940, the incorporation into the Soviet Union of Estonia, Latvia and Lithuania as separate republics; Bessarabia and Northern Bukovina would also become part of the Soviet Union.

[1] See Note No. 176.

By mutual consent Polish-Soviet affairs were excluded from the negotiations and left to be settled between the Polish and Soviet Governments.

General Sikorski stated that the above settlement was not only immoral, but also detrimental to Europe in general, and to Poland in particular. Poland considered Lithuania to be a country within her own sphere of interests. The abandonment of Polish Wilno was out of the question.

Sir Stafford considered that it would be necessary to accept the Soviet terms, as that was the only way of ensuring that Russia would establish the future frontiers of Europe by mutual agreement, that is, by negotiations with Poland.

General Sikorski treated Sir Stafford's point of view with reserve, as he himself could not be certain whether the Soviet Government would keep their engagements. The bitter experience in this respect not only of Poland, but of Great Britain as well, strengthened these doubts. Great Britain would obtain vague promises only in exchange for real and far-reaching concessions. And that would mean a surrender to Stalin.

Sir Stafford Cripps differed, stating that Russia was already becoming aware of the fact that after the war she would find her industry extensively destroyed. For its reconstruction she would need the assistance of the two English-speaking Powers. To General Sikorski's remark that the same consideration could be used now to force Russia to make important concessions, at least in the matter of Lithuania, Sir Stafford replied that Russia excluded whatever negotiations on the subject, and quoted a statement referring to the matter, made by Molotov shortly before the Ambassador's departure from Russia. On the other hand, Sir Stafford personally was convinced that the Soviet Government would keep their promises. Furthermore, it would be better at this stage to have a written statement of the Soviet Government.

General Sikorski considered the importance of Soviet military victories to be overrated. In his opinion, with the spring their successful operations would come to an end, when a German counter-offensive would be launched. Only then would Russia be inclined to make concessions. Therefore, the signing of unfavourable agreements at the moment would be a great error.

The Ambassador expressed an entirely different opinion. He considered that the war could be won by Russia only. And even should a German counter-offensive be crowned with success, it would be of transient importance. In the autumn Russia would regain the lost ground and, according to Sir Stafford, would win the war in 1942, in Berlin. But Russia was defending her own existence above all—and that should not be forgotten.

General Sikorski touched upon the possibility of a joint treatment of Polish problems with the other territorial questions put forward by Russia. He thought it would be essential to do so. Sir Stafford on the contrary considered it neither practical nor possible.

Sir Stafford further informed the General of the temporary deterioration in Anglo-Soviet relations. This was reflected in the fact that he had not been received by Stalin before his departure from Russia.

Sir Stafford's remarks on the future boundaries of Poland were not pessimistic. He stated that Russia was willing to extend Poland's frontiers at the expense of Germany, and above all to annex East Prussia to Poland. Sir Stafford thought that Stalin genuinely believed in the necessity of a strong Poland to serve as a rampart against Germany. But he would like the expansion of Poland to be effected at the expense of Germany only. As far as the Russian-Polish frontier was concerned, Sir Stafford thought that Russia would present rather far-reaching demands. In unofficial Russian circles the 'Curzon Line' had even been mentioned.

'In a word to push Poland from the East to the West,' interrupted General Sikorski at that point, 'but that cannot be done without Polish consent.'

Sir Stafford concluded the conversation, which lasted for about 2½ hours, with cordial and complimentary words about Prof. Kot.

No. 177

Note from Minister Raczyński to Ambassador Bogomolov concerning the failure to set free many thousands of Polish citizens and specifically of Polish officers

London, January 28, 1942   GSHI, A.11. 49/Sow/2

Le Gouvernement Polonais regrette de devoir porter à la connaissance de Votre Excellence que d'après des informations qu'il vient de recevoir la mise en liberté des ressortissants polonais confinés sur le territoire de l'Union des Républiques Socialistes Soviétiques dans des camps de travail et d'autres lieux de détention n'a pas été exécutée d'une façon intégrale. Dans un nombre de cas les autorités locales administratives de l'Union n'appliquent pas, dans toute leur étendue, les dispositions du Decrét soviétique en date du 12 août 1941.

A ce sujet, j'ai l'honneur de mentionner tout particulièrement le fait douloureux que, sur l'ensemble des officiers et soldats enregistrés dans les camps de prisonniers de guerre de Kozielsk, Starobielsk et Ostachkov, n'ont pas été libérés jusqu'à ce jour: 12 généraux, 94 colonels, 263 capitaines et environ 7,800 officiers de rang inférieurs. Il y a lieu de souligner que des recherches effectuées en Pologne et dans le Reich ont permis d'établir avec certitude que les militaires dont il s'agit ne se trouvent actuellement ni en Pologne occupée ni dans des camps de prisonniers de guerre en Allemagne.

D'après des nouvelles fragmentaires qui nous parviennent, une partie des prisonniers se trouverait dans des conditions d'existence très dures dans les îles Francois-Joseph Nouvelle Zemble et sur le territoire de la République de Iakoutsk sur les bords de la rivière Kołyma.

Je tiens à ajouter que la question du sort des ressortissants polonais civils et militaires a été l'objet de plusieures interventions consécutives de l'Ambassade de Pologne à Kuibyshev qui sera en mesure de soumettre sous peu une nouvelle liste nominative de ces personnes au Gouvernement de l'Union. Cette même question a fait, d'autre part, l'objet d'un entretien à Moscou, le 4 décembre 1941 entre M. le Président du Conseil des Ministres Polonais et M. Le Président du Conseil des Commissaires du Peuple. Au cours de cet entretien le Général Sikorski avait été heureux d'obtenir des assurances que les instructions nécessaires seraient données aux autorités soviétiques compétentes et que tous les prisonniers seraient remis en liberté.[1]

En me référant a la lettre et a l'esprit de cet entretien ainsi qu'aux stipulations conclus entre nos deux Gouvernements je ne doute pas que Votre Excellence voudra bien partager ma conviction que l'exécution efficace et rapide, des dispositions du Protocole additionel à l'Accord polono-soviétique signé à Londres, le 30 juillet 1941 au sujet de la libération des ressortissants polonais—emprisonnés ou se trouvant dans des camps de prisonniers, ou camps de travail—est fondée sur des motifs impérieux d'humanité et de justice.[2] Votre Excellence voudra bien sans doute partager également l'opinion du Gouvernement Polonais qu'elle garde une importance essentielle pour le développement favorable de nos relations mutuelles tel que le souhaitent les dirigeants de la politique des deux Pays, unis dans la lutte commune contre l'envahisseur.

En priant Votre Excellence de bien vouloir porter le contenu de cet exposé à la connaissance de Son Gouvernement, je saisis l'occasion de vous transmettre, Monsieur l'Ambassadeur, les assurances de ma très haute considération.

[1] See doc. No. 160.   [2] See doc. No. 106.

No. 178

Letter from General Sikorski to Ambassador Bogomolov stating in connection with Minister Raczyński's interview in the 'Sunday Times' the Polish attitude to the Soviet claims to annexed Polish territories

London, January 30, 1942   GSHI, PRM, 72/1

Me référant à notre entrevue du 23 janvier au cours de laquelle vous avez bien voulu me remettre une notice—au sujet d'un interview du Ministre Raczyński publié dans un journal de Londres—je me permets à mon tour de vous envoyer ci-inclus une déclaration exposant mon point de vue en cette matière en vous priant de bien vouloir la porter à la connaissance de Votre Gouvernement.

Annex.

Comme suite à l'aide-mémoire du Gouvernement de l'Union des Républiques Socialistes Soviétiques, qui m'avait été remis le 23 janvier 1942[1] par Monsieur l'Ambassadeur Bogomolov concernant l'interview accordé au 'Sunday Times' par M. le Ministre E. Raczyński et figurant dans la série des interviews de ce journal avec les membres des Gouvernements alliés, j'ai l'honneur de donner ma réponse dans le même esprit de franchise et de sincérité qui est à la base de ma ligne de conduite politique envers l'Union.

Lorsque j'ai signé les accords du 30 juillet 1941[2] et du 4 décembre 1941,[3] dans lesquels Monsieur le Président Stalin a dans ma conviction pleinement

[1] See doc. No. 175.   [2] See doc. No. 106.   [3] See doc. No. 161.

reconnu la souveraineté et l'égalité de rang de l'État Polonais autant que d'autres états, je ne pouvais pas juger et je ne jugeais pas qu'un rapprochement amical aussi désirable que celui entre la Pologne et l'Union Soviétique dût consister en l'abandon par la Pologne d'une partie de ses territoires occupés par la force des armées soviétiques, en accord avec le Reich Allemand et en la négation de beaucoup de nos droits, à la faveur de résolutions unilatérales prises par le Conseil Suprême de l'URSS. Dans le même ordre d'idées, il ne me semblait guère possible que l'on puisse refuser à un membre du Cabinet Polonais le droit d'exprimer librement sa pensée au sujet de problèmes qui, sinon directement, du moins indirectement—comme dans le cas de la Lithuanie—affectent l'État Polonais. Quant à mon point de vue, il n'a jamais varié; en particulier je l'ai exprimé dans mes discours du 31 juillet 1941[4] (c'est-à-dire au lendemain de la conclusion de l'accord principal) ainsi qu'à Moscou le 4 décembre 1941.[5] En ce qui concerne les frontières de la République, j'ai eu l'occasion de m'entretenir personellement avec Monsieur le Président Stalin et je constate que ce problème était envisagé sous un autre aspect et dans un tout autre esprit.

Quelle est donc cette Pologne pour laquelle les soldats polonais devraient se battre et le peuple polonais verser son sang dans une lutte implacable contre le Troisième Reich si les thèses exposées par le Commissaire du Peuple aux Affaires Etrangères, Monsieur Molotov, dans sa note du 6 janvier 1942, réitérées depuis dans les communiqués soviétiques, devaient devenir des réalités? Depuis mon retour de Russie et la communication qui fut faite par la suite aux Polonais des résultats de ce voyage il y eut un renouveau considérable de l'action subversive en Pologne. Ces 22 cheminots qui tombaient il y a quelques jours à peine le 10 janvier dernier—à Szczakowa—sous les balles de leurs bourreaux nazis avec le cri 'Vive la Pologne' n'auraient certes pas fait le sacrifice de leurs vies pour une Pologne soumise aux influences étrangères ou privée de la plénitude de ses droits souverains, comme elle le serait si des démarches comme celle qui fit Monsieur l'Ambassadeur de l'Union des Républiques Socialistes Soviétiques le 23 janvier 1942 étaient reconnues par le Gouvernement de la République et devenaient de règle dans nos relations mutuelles?

Ainsi qu'il pourrait resulter de l'aide-mémoire qui m'a été remis au nom du Gouvernement de l'Union des Républiques Socialistes Soviétiques, ce Gouvernement semble comprendre d'une façon quelque peu différente de la nôtre les idéals pour lesquels nous luttons et qui trouvent leur expression dans les principes énoncés à ce sujet dans la Charte Atlantique.

C'est en invoquant ces principes et les droits souverains de la Pologne que j'ai l'honneur de déclarer au Gouvernement de l'Union des Républiques Socialistes Soviétiques qu'à l'avis du Gouvernement Polonais, M. le Ministre Raczyński n'a nullement contesté l'utilité d'un rôle positif de l'URSS dans la solution des problèmes européens après cette guerre. Pour ma part, étant convaincu de la nécessité d'instaurer entre le Pologne et l'Union Soviétique une politique d'entente sincère et amicale, je me permets de proposer de

[4] See doc. No. 109.   [5] See doc. No. 162.

suspendre, du moins pour le moment des discussions qui risqueraient d'affaiblir l'énergie indispensable aux Alliés dans leur lutte contre l'ennemi commun.

Je tiens à redire encore, que si je m'exprime avec autant de franchise et de sincérité c'est parce que j'attache à la bonne entente entre la Pologne et l'Union Soviétique la plus haute importance.

No. 179

Notes on a conversation between General Sikorski and Mr. Churchill at Chequers on the problem of Polish-Soviet relations and of Stalin's expansionist aims

London, January 31, 1942

GSHI, PRM, 68
Transl. from Polish

Mr. Churchill asked General Sikorski's opinion on Stalin, whether the General's conversation with him had been satisfactory, whether the problem of Polish frontiers had been discussed, what was the situation on the Eastern front at that time, what was the political situation in Russia and what were the prospects of a German offensive in the spring, and also whether the Germans would be able to hold Smolensk and the Dnieper line. Finally Mr. Churchill asked what would General Sikorski think of his (Churchill's) going to Moscow to see Stalin. This step had been suggested by many British circles.

General Sikorski stated that his conversation with Stalin had been satisfactory. Stalin was a realist with a sympathetic approach to Poland and, unlike Molotov, he was a man with whom it was possible to come to an agreement. Stalin was the omnipotent autocrat of Russia, his decisions were law. However, experience had shown that Stalin's subordinates would create difficulties and obstruct putting into practice matters settled by agreement. These obstructions were considerable. Not long ago the Soviet Government had addressed a note to the Polish Government to which General Sikorski had to reply very categorically, even at the risk of a breach in diplomatic relations.

General Sikorski had sent that note and the Polish reply to Mr. Churchill with a request for support for the Polish point of view. Mr. Churchill promised to acquaint himself with the contents of these notes, and to give his support. Sikorski, describing Stalin, said that he was a man who, having spent a few years in Poland, was convinced that Poland's existence was essential for Russia as a rampart against Germany. He declared to General Sikorski that Poland must arise larger and stronger than before, that East Prussia must belong to Poland, that the Polish Western boundaries must be based on the river Oder. Stalin's tendency to push Poland to the West was obvious. During that official conversation the problem of the Polish Eastern frontiers was not mentioned. During the banquet, however, Stalin broached that subject. General Sikorski declined to discuss it. Stalin also touched upon the Ukrainian problem. He said that the claim for Lwów was not made by him, but by the Ukrainians. The Ukrainians were pro-German, said Stalin, and he proposed to Sikorski that a common action should be undertaken against the Ukrainians. Stalin would like to open the discussion on the Polish-Russian frontier at the time when the Polish Army in USSR was already at the front. General Sikorski warned Mr. Churchill that in consequence of military victories whose importance was but transient, and in view of the world's political situation, Stalin was at the acme of his success and prestige, and would undoubtedly like to take advantage of it. It was clear that he wanted to use the present moment to obtain the consent for annexing the Baltic States, including Lithuania, Bessarabia and Bukovina. He was also dreaming of Bulgaria, the access to the Dardanelles and the Persian Gulf. He would reach out for a free access to the Atlantic through Northern Norway (Narvik). That would be the purpose of a visit of Commissar Molotov to England. General Sikorski warned Mr. Churchill against it and suggested a postponement of Molotov's visit, as the actual time was unsuitable for a discussion. Mr. Churchill's journey to Moscow would be a triumph for Stalin. That idea should be abandoned. Mr. Churchill answered that Molotov's visit was not being considered for the moment, and he made it clear that he did not intend to discuss Stalin's plans of annexation. He added, however, that in the case of victory the demands of Russia aimed at securing the position of Leningrad in the Baltic region and the possession of the Baltic Isles would be justified. It was understandable that Russia would like to protect herself against a possible third German aggression within one century.

General Sikorski was convinced that Stalin, as a staunch Communist and first disciple of Lenin, would tend to introduce communism in Europe from Norway to Greece. Mr. Churchill replied that Great Britain was not afraid of communism. Should Europe accept communism, Great Britain would not oppose it, but she would not permit that any nation be subjected to a communist regime against their will. Mr. Churchill agreed with General Sikorski that Great Britain must support the point of view of the countries threatened by communism from outside.

Reviewing in turn the situation on the Eastern front General Sikorski referred to his appreciation of the situation which he had sent to Mr. Churchill, and to its confirmation which he had found in all the reports coming from occupied Poland, which had also been forwarded to Mr. Churchill. The latter replied that he would study General Sikorski's notes which he had brought along. The General considered that the Germans would at any cost defend Smolensk and the line of the Dnieper which had already been partly fortified.

The internal political situation in Russia was solid. Stalin was more powerful than ever, and should even a German counter-offensive succeed in securing Moscow and Leningrad, Russia would still continue to fight. Speaking of the possibilities of a German offensive in spring, General Sikorski expressed the opinion that the Germans would concentrate their efforts in the South, abandoning the two other principal lines of operations, i.e. Leningrad and Moscow. On that southern sector they would be able to strike much earlier, as spring begins in April on the lower Volga. General Sikorski did not think that Russia would be defeated by Germany, but he foresaw that the counter-offensive, by threatening the Caucasus, might put an end to the present Russian successes. [. . .].

Asked whether he thought that a personal meeting beween Mr. Churchill and Stalin was advisable, General Sikorski replied that he would not consider the present moment as opportune for such a meeting. He added once more that Stalin has reached the peak of his transient successes, and that it would be too great an honour for him to be visited by the British Prime Minister. Mr. Churchill pointed out that he had put the question to hear General Sikorski's reaction, and he believed he would accept the General's opinion. General Sikorski did not conceal, however, that he would view a conference between Stalin and Mr. Churchill with greater confidence, than one between Stalin and Mr. Eden. It did not mean that he had no confidence in Eden personally, but he thought the Foreign Secretary had already gone too far in his talks with Moscow. General Sikorski strongly advised Mr. Churchill against that visit, and Mr. Churchill nodded in approval. [. . .].

Speaking on European problems, Mr. Churchill solemnly assured General Sikorski, also referring to the authority of an agreed opinion between Great Britain and the United States:

/i/ that as long as victory has not been achieved, the problem of the future State boundaries in Europe would be in no way discussed,

/ii/ that the principles of self-determination, proclaimed in the Atlantic Charter, would be the basis of just and peaceful plebiscite voting by which the population of a territory would decide on the incorporation of their land into a given State. However, in territories where the population was so intermixed that it would be impossible to disentangle, a method of resettlement might be adopted.

/iii/ that an exception to the rule would be made with regard to Prussia, in order to make that country harmless in the future. Prussia would be detached from the rest of Germany, and measures would be adopted to break her power. Mr. Churchill did not specify what he understood under the term of Prussia. He included into that denomination the Rhineland, but excluded, on the other hand, Austria, Bavaria, Southern Germany. He did not pronounce himself on Eastern Prussia.

At the end of the conversation Mr. Churchill solemnly reassured General Sikorski, promising that Great Britain and the United States would not allow Poland to be harmed, as they were always mindful of her heroic attitude and the high qualities of the Polish Nation; they would guarantee the restitution of a powerful and independent Polish State and the settlement by agreement with Poland of all the problems concerning her, even indirectly.

No. 180

Telegram from Lt.-General Anders to General Sikorski on the Soviet proposal to send some units of the Polish Army to the front[1]

Buzuluk, February 4, 1942

GSHI, KGA, 9-c
Transl. from Polish

I have to report that, on February 2nd, I had a long conversation with General Zhukov who, in the name of the Soviet Government, raised the following issues:

1) The Soviet Government would like to know when the Polish Army will be ready to fight. I replied that, after the conversations at the Kremlin and the promises to carry out immediately the organization of the Polish Army in the South, I reckoned upon this army achieving its combat readiness not earlier than within 6 months, that is to say on 1st June 1942.

Today, I have to state that the two months which have elapsed since the conversation at the Kremlin have been wasted, and not by the slightest fault of ours. In such circumstances I am unable to state an exact date on which our army would be ready, for this entirely depends on the Soviet authorities, both with regard to the call-up for the army, and the granting of facilities for receiving Anglo-American supplies. Both myself and all my subordinates desire to be ready as quickly as possible, fully realizing the importance of this for Poland.

2) The Soviet Government would consider it proper to send to the front those Polish units which are ready, that is to say the 5th Division which has received its equipment according to Soviet standards. It would be of paramount political and military importance.

I replied categorically that I was opposed to this idea. One division of ours would disappear among the big masses of Soviet divisions and the political and military effect of its action would be nil.

The Polish Army must strike with its full strength, and with a prospect of success. Only then will its action have repercussions in our home country, and the political and military aims pursued by us will be achieved. To throw one single division into battle would undermine the morale of the whole army. Should I receive such an order from the Commander-in-Chief I would be obliged to go with this division to the front, in order that such consequences should be obviated if only partly so, and that my authority in the eyes of my subordinates should not be impaired.

I said at the end that I shall report all this to you, my General, and that I shall let them know the answer.

[1] See Note No. 180.

No. 181

Note from the Polish Embassy in Kuibyshev replying to the Note of the People's Commissariat for Foreign Affairs of January 23, 1942, and demanding the transfer to the Polish Army of German war prisoners of Polish nationality

Kuibyshev, February 6, 1942

GSHI, A.11. 49/Sow./2
Transl. from Polish: Pol.-Sov.R., No. 53

In reply to the Note of the People's Commissariat for Foreign Affairs No. 13 of January 23, 1942,[1] the Polish Embassy has the honour to submit the following:

When it approached the People's Commissariat for Foreign Affairs with the request that Poles be separated from prisoners of war, former soldiers in the German Army, taken prisoner by the Red Army, this Embassy was prompted by the following considerations:

The conscription of Polish citizens by the German Army constitutes a flagrant breach of the fundamental rules of international law, and should be met, in the common interest of all Allied States, not only by condemnation, but also by counter-action both on the part of the Polish Government and on the part of the friendly Government of the USSR. The Germans are endeavouring to mobilize every force to combat the Democracies, and spare no effort to put at the disposal of the German High Command the greatest possible man-power, including even hostile elements. One of the important tasks of both our Governments is to counteract this action.

The Poles, constituting as they do an element decidedly hostile to the Germans, are, as a rule, distributed on conscription by the German Army among different units, in small groups or singly so as to prevent any organized resistance, as for instance mass desertion to the Allied Forces. That the Germans do not trust the Poles conscripted by force is illustrated by the fact that Poles are not admitted to commissioned and non-commissioned rank in the German Army, nor to branches of the service requiring individual action, as for instance tanks, air force, signals, but are given auxiliary duties in supply columns or in infantry units, where an individual soldier surrounded by a mass of Germans would face immediate death at their hands should he lay down his arms.

The Polish Government has, for its part, undertaken appropriate steps on the German-occupied territory of the Republic of Poland to deal with the disastrous results of the conscription of Polish citizens by the German Army, issuing secret instructions to Poles to surrender to the soldiers of the Red Army at the earliest opportunity. The Polish Government intends to extend this action as soon as possible. The principle of deserting from the ranks of the German Army, encouraged on the territory of the Polish Republic, is not fruitless: as best shown by public statements of Soviet authorities. Among others, a report in the *Komsomol Pravda* No. 308 of December 30, 1941, fully

---

[1] See doc. No. 174.

278

supports the attitude adopted in the present Note, and requires no further comment. (A copy of this report is forwarded herewith.)

Besides, last November the Soviet authorities organized a meeting of Slav prisoners of war, former soldiers in the German Army, at which a resolution accepted by all the Slav nations oppressed by Germany was passed. This resolution, signed on behalf of the Poles by Kurt Klauzen, a worker from Bydgoszcz and former soldier of the 106th German Infantry Division, and Ryszard Slibo, from Chorzów, former soldier of the 29th German Infantry Division (*Izvestia*, November 29, 1941)—fully corroborated the correctness of this Embassy's reasoning, submitted to the People's Commissariat in the Notes D. 731/41 of November 8, 1941, D. 48/42 of January 7, 1942, and D. 164/42 of January 18, 1942.[2]

In the opinion of the Embassy, to restrict to propaganda in the Soviet press the results of this action, aimed at encouraging Poles to surrender to the soldiers of the Red Army, is not enough in the present period of friendly collaboration between both States, a collaboration which aims at the fullest mobilization of every force for the fight against the common enemy, and to which expression was given in the Moscow Declaration of December 4, 1941.[3]

At the same time the Polish Embassy has the honour to draw the attention of the People's Commissariat for Foreign Affairs to the undesirable consequences which would ensue should information reach occupied Poland that Poles conscripted by force are treated by the Soviet authorities, on being taken prisoner, in the same manner as German prisoners-of-war. Information of this kind would immediately be utilized by German propaganda not merely to hinder the Polish Government's action with regard to desertion by Polish citizens, but also endanger the principle of Polish-Soviet collaboration on the territory of the Republic of Poland.

This being the state of affairs, this Embassy has the honour to request the People's Commissariat for Foreign Affairs to reconsider its hitherto negative attitude to the transfer of Polish prisoners, former soldiers in the German Army, to the Polish Army in the Union of Soviet Socialist Republics, an attitude expressed in the Note of the People's Commissariat for Foreign Affairs of January 23, 1942.

[2] See doc. No. 173.   [3] See doc. No. 161.

No. 182

General Sikorski's reply to the telegram from Lt.-General Anders stating the conditions under which the Polish Army could be sent to the front

London, February 7, 1942   GSHI, KGA, 9-a
                                              Transl. from Polish

I am taken aback by the suggestion of the Soviet Government, imparted through Zhukov. 1) The date of 1st June of this year, as the date on which the army would achieve its combat readiness, was possible only if the Soviet Government could have supplied the full equipment for all higher formations

279

organized in the USSR. Owing to the waste of time, arising through no fault of ours, the date of combat readiness would have to be fixed in the following way: four months after the date of receiving full equipment for the army. 2) Should the Soviet Government be unable to supply the equipment for the Polish Army in the USSR, it would be impossible for us to state such a date, even approximately, because it would mean our complete dependence on British supplies. The latter cannot arrive immediately, but we insist on them strongly and continually. 3) In no case could I agree to the use of single divisions after they have achieved combat readiness. This reservation was explicitly made in our conversation at the Kremlin. The Polish Army in the USSR can be used as a whole only, under your general operational command; it should consist, at the minimum, of 4 higher formations with their respective services and staffs, on an army scale. Will you please, my General, declare to the Soviet Government on my behalf, that I attach great value to the Polish Army achieving its combat readiness as promptly as possible. However, in no case could I permit troops inadequately armed, organized and trained, to be thrown into battle against such an adversary as Germany. We do not decline to fight. The best proof of this is the underground military action in our home-country, which is gaining strength; but I cannot agree to an utter disregard of such a mighty trump in Allied hands as would be the use of the Army as a whole.

No. 183

A note made for Minister Morawski, Under Secretary of State, by Counsellor Kulski on the subject of opinions expressed by Sir Stafford Cripps (Anglo-Soviet Agreement and Soviet western frontiers) [1]

London, February 10, 1942   GSHI, A.11. 49/Sow./6
Transl. from Polish

From a Person who is usually well informed I have heard the following:

Sir Stafford Cripps in a conversation with the above-mentioned Person expressed the opinion that the British-Soviet agreement would include a recognition of the Soviet frontiers of June 1941, with the reserve that the problem of the Polish-Soviet frontier be left for an ulterior direct understanding between the two Powers concerned. Sir Stafford Cripps admitted that the ultimate fate of the British-Soviet agreement depended on the decision of Washington.

In accordance with information obtained from the same Person, Russia's attitude towards Japan was in no way a counterpart to the British-Soviet agreement. Information, however, has been confirmed that the USSR continued to reinforce their army in the Far East, and that the possibility existed that the re-establishment of diplomatic relations between Australia and the USSR suggested by the High Commissioner to Ambassador Maisky, would be accepted by Moscow.

[1] See Note No. 183.

Although the Foreign Secretary, Mr. Eden, like Sir Stafford Cripps, is in favour of a British-Soviet agreement, the attitude of the Foreign Office is said to be rather reluctant. Sir Alexander Cadogan expressed his dissatisfaction with the Editor of 'The Times' in connection with the recent publication of the well-known article.

The same Person in a conversation with members of the Soviet Embassy in London heard the opinion that Russia supported Polish demands concerning the extension of her frontiers in the West. As an instance, East Prussia was quoted.

There are rumours that before long a Conference of the Danube States would be summoned under Germany's leadership. The purpose of the conference would be the settlement of Danube navigation. The German Government endeavours to obtain Turkey's participation in the conference. It would be worth while to check this item of news through Ankara, as an acceptance of such an invitation by Turkey would be ominous.

No. 184

Note from the People's Commissariat for Foreign Affairs to the Polish Embassy in the USSR, re: organization of Polish Welfare organization

Kuibyshev, February 12, 1942   GSHI, A.11. 49/Sow./3
                                             Transl. from Polish

The People's Commissariat for Foreign Affairs has the honour to acknowledge receipt of the Note of the Polish Embassy, Ref. D.342/42, dated 31st January, 1942.

The People's Commissariat for Foreign Affairs takes note of the statement of the Embassy on the issue of an instruction to their delegates and men of trust to abstain from any unorganized resettlement of Polish citizens, and of the order given by the Polish Military authorities forbidding people due for call-up to the Polish Army to abandon their work until the time when they are duly called, and instructing them that their families should stay where they were.

As to the Embassy's request, presented in the above-mentioned note, concerning the issue of an instruction to the Soviet local authorities to provide for an improvement in the living and working conditions of Polish citizens, it is stated: such an instruction was issued to local authorities at the time of the publication of the Decree of the Praesidium of the Supreme Soviet of the USSR dated 12th August, 1941.[1] That instruction recommended that assistance should be given to Polish citizens in finding work and accommodation for them. Additional instructions to the same effect were issued to local Soviet authorities in January of this year, on receiving from the Embassy the nominal roll of their delegates in various Republics and Provinces. According to that instruction, the Soviet authorities in the respective Republics and Provinces were bound to co-operate with the delegates of the Embassy in

[1] See doc. No. 110.

281

their activities specified in 'The Rules concerning the competence of the delegates of the Polish Embassy', in which the problems referred to by the Embassy had also been mentioned. In addition to the above, on January 29th of this year the Soviet Government issued an instruction for providing special rations and industrial articles to hostels, nurseries and other Polish institutions of similar character, and for supplying with food rations all those Polish citizens unfit for work who could not be put under the care of the above institutions, and also all those Polish citizens working in Soviet enterprises and institutions, as well as their families; and for this to be done on the basis of a ration card system, accepting the basic norms established for analogous categories of Soviet citizens.

The People's Commissariat for Foreign Affairs expects that the Polish Embassy in conformity with the action undertaken by the Soviet Government will endeavour on her part to speed up the intended plans for the improvement of the working conditions of Polish citizens.

No. 185

Report from Maj.-General Wolikowski to Lt.-General Anders on his conversations with General Panfilov dealing with the delay in getting the supplies of arms for the Polish troops, evacuation of a part of them, reduction of contingents and dispatch of a Polish division to the Soviet-German front[1]

Kuibyshev, February 22, 1942   GSHI, KGA, 7-c
                                  Transl. from Polish

Referring to my conversation held in a very friendly spirit with Panfilov on 19th February, 1942, during 3½ hours, I report what follows:

After having read your letter, General, he tried to shift the responsibility for the delay in settling the problems concerning our army onto the Army Staff—the alleged lack of 'indents' which have not been sent either in due time or proper form—inadequate liaison service, etc. I replied stating many instances of our requests remaining unanswered. I availed myself of this opportunity to suggest the transfer of the Mission to Moscow, which would facilitate personal contacts. He agreed in principle, asking for a formal proposal which I submitted at once, and which is to be settled by the Government. I asked also for an officer to be attached from the Army Service Corps to our Headquarters, a request which had been made previously by us. He agreed. An officer of the Army Service Corps in possession of price-lists and formal instructions will be attached to our Army and this, I think, must facilitate the work of the Staff. Then I raised, one by one, all the issues, as ordered by you, General, or respectively known to me from the reports and letters of the Chief of Staff. I shall now deal with each of those issues. [. . .].

2/ Arms for the next (training) division. To my question as to when those arms would be supplied he answered that the arms would be delivered as soon as he received the respective indents, specifying the category and the

[1] See Note No. 185.

place where they should be sent. Such an indent (with a copy for me) is to be established as soon as possible. For the time being I shall insist that the arms, according to the specification established for the fifth division, be put immediately at the disposal of the SAVO[2] being earmarked for our troops. I put this proposal in writing (a copy enclosed herewith) on 21st February.[3] [. . .].

9/ Evacuation. He agrees to the evacuation of 25,000 troops plus 2,000 airmen. He tried to justify himself by saying that he never had any intention to keep them, as it would only increase the number of food-rations, which was obviously not in his interest. Will you, please, give him (enclosing a copy for me) your plan, and state the day on which the evacuation should start. For my part I shall keep an eye on it and forward all the essential technical data which may be transmitted to me by Panfilov. I think that we should establish a list (similar to the form for drivers), forming detachments of 100 to 200 men under command of officers (or non-commissioned officers), each of them being responsible for his detachment.

10/ Conscription and recruitment. To my question as to why conscription is carried out in three republics only he said that a supplementary conscription was ordered in Turkmen and Tadjik republics, and registration all over the territory of the USSR. He is already in possession of the results of the census and will let us know them.

In a few days conscription will be proclaimed everywhere. To my question as to why only the Poles are called up, he answered that the others are 'their citizens'. When I argued saying that it was a strange and unilateral decision to which we would never agree, he answered that it was a political question, and so far as the number of serviceable men is concerned, the number of Poles will be sufficient for the forming of an army according to intentions, and reserves to complete it.

I asked for these statistical data which he had promised to give. My general impression from that conference and from the spirit in which it was held was favourable—one may say that the attitude has changed in our favour.

On his part Panfilov raised three questions: [. . .].

3/ For a long time he tried to convince me of the necessity of dispatching immediately to the front one division, which would constitute a first-rate political asset for them, allowing them to say that the Poles were already fighting.

Judging by the stress he put on this issue, I think that they attach great importance to influencing public opinion in our home-country, and to the impression which would be produced by an action of Poles on the front side by side with them. He used those words at one time.

I replied to him that it would be impossible, that we cannot fight by representation but only as a united force under the command of the commander of our army, and that the repercussions in the home-country are

[2] Srednio Asiatskiy Voyenniy Okrug (Middle Asia Military Command).
[3] Not printed.

great enough owing to the conclusion of the agreement and the fact of the formation of the army. The opinion and the attitude of the home-country is within the province of the C.-in-C. who is the leader of the country. We suffered too much deception owing to the breaking up of our forces in France.

It seems to me that at present, with the approach of Spring and the prospects of ever harder fighting, they will woo us and the home country more and more.

In view of the delay in the arrival of English equipment disclosed in General MacFarlane's statement, and of the combat readiness of our army to be attained next autumn, the pressure on their part for us to send a division to the front will increase, and become ever more difficult to resist. [. . .].

Conversations with General MacFarlane on 19th and 20th February.

In the conversations with me on the questions of evacuation, the General showed much scepticism which, by the way, has been fully warranted so far.

He meets with constant and great difficulties in dealing with every question.

As regards the supplies, he told me that owing to the recent English set-backs, the equipment destined for us was sent elsewhere. One can expect the first consignments at the end of April or in the course of May. So says a telegram from London, dated 6th February.

As regards medical supplies which were already announced, he has no information whether they have reached the Persian Gulf or not.

He stated that 100 lorries, which according to our information were allegedly already in a port of the Persian Gulf, were due in the middle or at the end of March.

No. 186

Note from Ambassador Bogomolov to General Sikorski concerning Minister Raczyński's interview in the 'Sunday Times' of January 11, 1942, and the suggestion of the Polish Government to discontinue further discussion[1]

London, February 28, 1942　　　　　　　　　　　　　　GSHI, PRM, 72/1

Le Gouvernement Soviétique, ayant pris connaissance de l'aide mémoire du Gouvernement Polonais du 30 janvier 1942,[2] constate que le Gouvernement Polonais a estimé possible de prendre l'attitude, laquelle ne diffère pas de l'attitude prise par Monsieur Raczyński dans ses énonciations du 11 janvier de l'année courante. Ces énonciations, dont il s'agit dans l'aide mémoire du Gouvernement Soviétique en date du 22 janvier 1942,[3] ont été déjà caractérisées par le Gouvernement Soviétique comme les énonciations, qui ne correspondent pas aux intérêts des rélations amicales entre l'Union Soviétique et la Pologne.

Le Gouvernement Soviétique, partant des intérêts du développement

[1] See Note No. 186.　　　　　[2] See doc. No. 178.
[3] See doc. No. 175; the date should be January 23, 1942.

efficace de la collaboration entre les deux pays, a jugé comme indésirable la discussion publique des questions, lesquelles les deux Gouvernements ont décidées de laisser temporairement ouvertes. C'est pourquoi, naturellement, le Gouvernement Soviétique n'a pas d'objections contre la suggestion du Gouvernement Polonais de ne pas entrer en discussion pareille, à laquelle les énonciations, analogues aux celles ci-dessus mentionnées, pourrait amener.

Le Gouvernement Soviétique n'estime pas rationnel d'entrer, actuellement, en délibération de plusieurs affirmations incorrectes et des interprétations arbitraires, que l'aide-mémoire de Gouvernement Polonais contient, néanmoins le Gouvernement Soviétique doit souligner la présence à l'Union Soviétique de l'unité complète des vues à l'égard des questions mentionnées, qui, plus tard, doivent être délibérées entre les deux Gouvernements.

No. 187

Note on a conversation between Minister Morawski and Ambassador Bogomolov relating to the post-war organization of the States of Central-Eastern Europe

London, March 2, 1942　　　　　　　　　　GSHI, A.11. 49/Sow./4
　　　　　　　　　　　　　　　　　　　　　Transl. from Polish

[. . .]. Then Bogomolov passed on to the agreement between 8 European States, repeating, perhaps with even more insistence, the arguments used by him in a conversation with me on 10th February. He asked me whether we had taken any new steps in relation to this question, and whether we knew anything about the position taken by Great Britain and the USA on this problem.

I answered that, apart from keeping the F.O. and the American Ambassador well informed on this issue, we had not taken, so far, any special steps, but that we assume from unofficial conversations with the representatives of different States that the idea of establishing permanent co-operation in dealing with Germany meets with increasing sympathy. Neither Great Britain nor the U.S. have, so far, taken any official position on this issue, as we did not insist on it. However, we have no reason to expect any objections from them to the idea of such an arrangement.

Bogomolov replied with some heat, saying that Russia had a loathing for all such pacts which aimed at shaping the future, and in particular for agreements to which she was not a party. 'Have you not the Atlantic Charter, the Declaration signed by 26 United Nations, an agreement concerning the punishment of war-criminals; all these undertakings regard the future although nobody can tell what the future may be. The Soviet leaders consider that, in the present circumstances, it is tanks and not pacts that really matter. In any case, there cannot be and must not be any European arrangement, and especially in Eastern Europe, from which Russia would be excluded. A time will come,' said Bogomolov, 'when the choice will be put before you: Russia or Luxemburg. I know that all of you in Europe are afraid of Bolshevists. However, what would happen should we draw conclusions from Stalin's order, and there are some who interpret it in this way, that we ought to be concerned with our own territories only, and must stop the advance of our army once those territories have been liberated?'

I observed that, personally, I did not see any logical relationship between the idea which we all share, namely that of the necessity for establishing the best possible co-operation between the Allied European States and the Soviet Union, and Russia's demand that those States should not enter into any other commitment without her. It is beyond dispute that those States have, during the war, and will have after it, many aims in common with Russia. It is also obvious that these States are joined by many links, arising from their constitution, their past and the common cultural heritage. Both trends are fully warranted, and there is no discrepancy between them. One must not forget that the idea of the so-called 'New Order' in Europe is a mighty propaganda weapon in Hitler's hands. It is unquestionable that the idea of European unity and organization appeals to many peoples on the European continent, and it may be attractive to American public opinion. It is, therefore, imperative, if only for this reason, to bring about an Allied conception of the future European order. If M. Bogomolov speaks about the possibility of Russia losing all interest in the future outcome of the war, once her territories have been liberated, one is bound to observe that, if this idea is carried out, it might lead to far-reaching developments. I asked him, in this connection, whether he had seen in today's issue of 'France', which he surely reads, a telegram from Stockholm reporting rumours of the impending negotiations between Germany and the USSR on the conclusion of a separate peace-treaty. When Bogomolov denied having read it, and said this news was a piece of German propaganda, I observed that, reading this telegram, my first thought was that it was rather a piece of Soviet propaganda aiming at bringing pressure on the Allies.

No. 188

Report made by Counsellor Weese on the subject of Soviet broadcasts in Polish

London, March 5, 1942 GSHI, MSZ, Coll. 49/Sow. I, No. 66-a
Transl. from Polish

During the last few months Soviet Radio Propaganda broadcast by the Radio Stations: Shevtchenko, Kościuszko, Kuibyshev and others has taken a line far from loyal towards the national and political aspirations of Poland. The Polish-Soviet co-operation in the war was represented so as to obliterate the fact that Poland was a sovereign State having her own territory and separate political aims, and so as to create the impression that her aims were identical with those of other nations which were members of the Soviet Union.

For instance, the Radio Station Kościuszko on 26th January, 1942, issued the following announcement:

'On the 18th inst. a public meeting of representatives of the White-Ruthenian Nation took place in Moscow. All speakers manifested the unbroken will of the White Ruthenian Nation to continue the struggle against Germany and to bring about their reunification with the Soviet Union. In the Ukraine the Germans performed more destruction and cruelties than in White Ruthenia. The Ukrainian Nation fights and makes extreme sacrifices to regain independence and to return to the Soviet Union. We, Poles, can understand their feelings better than anyone, being in the same position as those Nations. The Polish Nation fights as they do, the struggle undertaken in common has a common aim.'

Here the joining of the Soviet Union by Poland is put into the foreground as her final aim. Slightly more refinement is used, on February 28th, by the Kościuszko Station. In presenting the problem they glorify the Red Army and demand the gratitude of the Poles:

We owe our utmost gratitude to the Red Army, and this has been beautifully put into words by Wanda Wasilewska who writes: 'You, Red Soldier, arose to fight the German Army, which had made the whole world tremble. You are carrying freedom to the enslaved nations on your bayonet. Kiev longs for you and so does Białystok and Lwów. You bring destruction to Hitlerism and freedom to the Polish Nation.'

It is difficult not to see the same tendency of reducing the Polish problem to a problem concerning the Soviet Union only, when the Radio Station Kuibyshev announced on February 23rd:

'The victories of the Red Army evoke a vivid response in Polish hearts. After the defeat of 1939 it is the Red Army alone who can bring liberation to Poles. The Red Army is the national army of Poland. Every blow inflicted by the Red Army to Germans lifts the lid of Poland's coffin. The alliance with the Soviet Union opened new perspectives for Poland. Polish people will not wait passively for the Red Army's victory but will take up arms to undermine Germany's might.'

This call to arms addressed to Poles is most frequently repeated in the Polish-language broadcasts from the USSR.

Soviet authorities attach great importance to an immediate mass upheaval against German troops on Polish soil. They endeavour with all available means to push the Poles into organizing them. They do not pay any attention to the interests of Poland regarding the extent of such upheavals nor to the dates when these activities would be opportune. On the contrary, they show impatience and demand that all advice to await a suitable opportunity should be disregarded. The Kościuszko Radio Station broadcast the following appeal on 17th February:

'This is the third year that the Polish Nation has been continuously struggling with the cruel invader. During that period of exertion many Poles have shown incredible heroism and a self-denying spirit of sacrifice for the sake of their beloved country. The deeds of Polish patriots resulted in much damage to the Hitlerites, but all these results are poor in comparison with the might and resources of the enemy. These results are simply nothing when compared with the means at the disposal of Poles dwelling in the very rear of the Germans. Their opportunities are enhanced by the Red Army's

287

victories. These victories bring the battlefield closer to Poland. Therefore the Polish Nation must increase her resistance to the enemy. Polish partisans should operate in thousands, not in small parties. Millions should participate in partisan battles, and the working class should be in the front ranks. Following the example of Poznań, workers from other provinces should take action by organizing strikes and demanding better working conditions. Peasants should support the workers and resist requisitions and drives to build roads and fortifications. When resistance reaches its peak, when hundreds of thousands participate in it, then the occupying forces will lose confidence in their secure position in Poland. That would help the Poles to get in touch with partisans operating on Soviet territory. Hundreds of anti-Hitlerite committees should be organized so that their network covers all the occupied territory. People from all political parties should be admitted to them. Polish brethren! The time has come to start a decisive action against the Hitlerites. The Red Army is approaching and her victories bring nearer the hour of your liberation and the restoration of a Free and Independent Poland.'

The propaganda for establishing anti-German Workers' and Peasants' Committees in Poland has increased and has become gradually more and more pronounced. The Radio Station Kościuszko, discussing the Polish resistance movement, broadcast the following passage on February 27th:

'In towns workers' committees should be organized which would coordinate their activities with the peasants' committees in the country, and would jointly organize resistance against the occupying powers.'

The rôle of such committees during the Russian revolution is all too well known to leave any illusions as to the task which the Soviet Government would like to assign to them in Poland.

The perfidious methods of the Soviet Broadcasting Stations appear in one more instance: they appeal to all Poles, forcibly mobilized to serve in the German Army, to surrender and to join the Polish Army in the USSR to fight against the Germans. At the same time the Soviet Government in a note to the Polish Embassy, dated January 1942,[1] not only refused to permit such POWs to join the Polish Army but stressed that there was no reason for allowing any special treatment to German POWs of Polish nationality.

On February 16th, 1942, Shevtchenko Radio Station made the following remark on the subject:

'News about the organization of a Polish Army in Russia was received with elation. Poles serving in the ranks of the German Army decided to let themselves be captured by the Russians in order to join the Polish Army and so fight for your freedom and ours.'

The Kościuszko Radio Station, on 18th February, 1942, appealing to Poles to perform acts of sabotage, made this broadcast:

'Poles forcibly mobilized to serve in the German Army come over to the Soviet side at the first opportunity. They do it in order to join the Polish Army organized in Russia.'

[1] See doc. No. 174.

On 17th February, 1942, the Shevtchenko Radio Station broadcast an exaggerated statement that Poland received no news from abroad. Such news reaches Poland with great difficulty, and, among other things, Poles know nothing about the Sikorski Government. On the other hand, they are better informed about the situation on the German-Russian front. First news of Stalin's speech of the 7th November, 1941 in commemoration of the October Revolution was received in Poland from leaflets dropped by Soviet airmen.

The political moves towards a Polish-Czech Federation met with unfavourable comments from the Soviet Radio Stations.

Kościuszko Station quotes the negative opinion of a paper issued by the emigré Czecho-Slovak youth movement, concerning a Polish-Czech Federation. They represent the point of view that since Soviet Russia entered the war, a Polish-Czech Federation has lost every significance, as the Soviet Union was not participating in it, and no federation without the Soviet Union could secure the independence of the two countries. The independence and security of Poland and Czechoslovakia could be assured by the Soviet Union only, and 'we share this wise point of view entirely'.

The Kościuszko Radio Station announced on 18th February, 1942:

'On the 15th of February in London a celebration of the 7th anniversary of Czech-Soviet friendship was organized by Czechoslovak Youth and the Foreign Minister Ripka made a speech, saying that nothing would ever alter Czech friendship for the Soviet Union. Czechoslovakia would welcome the steadfast influence of the Soviet Union in Central and Southern Europe. We, Poles, also join in this attitude and we see in the Soviet Union the only possible guarantee of freedom, independence and security.'

No. 189

Letter from General Sikorski to Mr. Eden concerning British-Soviet negotiations, and the main problems of the Allied war policy[1]

London, March 9, 1942   GSHI, PRM, 66

Following our conversation of March 3rd and according to my promise, I would like to bring to your notice some observations on the conduct of the war, particularly in connection with the demands on the part of the Soviet Government which are similar to those that Italy imposed upon the Allies during the last war.

I am examining this problem in the first place from the point of view of the Allies. I am leaving for later the more detailed examination of the relations between Poland and Russia which are becoming confused through the fault of the Soviets and which I desire to render better and to set upon more friendly lines.

The latest events in the Far East are giving occasion in certain circles for excessive pessimism with regard to the situation. This might be detrimental

[1] See Note No. 189.

to the composure of the community, which reacted so magnificently against the direct attacks of the Luftwaffe during the battle of Britain in 1940. Undoubtedly, as a result of errors of many years, the military situation in the Far East is grave. The maritime routes of Great Britain to the Mediterranean, to Russia, America and the Far East, are for the moment imperilled. Almost the whole weight of their defence is borne by the Royal Navy. This, however, is temporary. Public opinion should, therefore, not be permitted to be overcome by inordinate criticism. It remains under the impression of reverses which will turn out to be short-lived, provided the Allies undertake energetic and appropriate counter-measures and awaken to the full advantage the indispensable energy of certain communities.

At the outbreak of the Russo-German war I did not share the general pessimism with regard to the estimation of the power of resistance of Soviet Russia. Today I consider myself, therefore, entitled to state that I do not overrate the significance of the latest Russian successes on the eastern front, where, so far, I have not observed a decisive German defeat. Russia owes her successes in the first place to the severe winter and to the over-confidence with which Hitler and his General Staff judged the Red Army and prepared his forces for the winter campaign. It is perhaps worth while recalling in confidence, that the burning by the secret military organization in Poland of enormous stores of warm clothing assembled from all parts of the Reich during the first days of December 1941 rendered an invaluable service to the Soviet Army. The winter, however, is coming to an end. The German Forces are making preparations for a new offensive. The Soviets should therefore refrain from dictating terms that would necessarily weaken the alliance of Great Britain with the United States at a moment which may prove to be to all of us a turning point. They ought not to disregard the material assistance which is being and should continue to be supplied to them to the utmost extent. This help at the same time provides an honest argument against the political pressure of Russia. Determined military operations aiming at the destruction of Rommel's Army in Libya are also of the utmost importance to Russia. The same applies to the increasing offensive of the RAF which is contributing to victory by the destruction of the principal centres of the enemy's war production and the attacks against the important strategic points. If the establishment of a second front in the West is at present impossible, it is necessary to give direct assistance to the Soviet Army by considerably increasing both naval and air landings on the continent. In connection with the possibility of a second front in Europe, I would like to point out that the fear of a renewal of another 'Dunkirk' is at present unsubstantial. Four-fifths of the German Forces are engaged on the eastern front and the remaining one-fifth has been scattered over vast areas throughout Europe. Moreover, the quality of the German divisions in the West cannot be compared to those of the period of Dunkirk or to the German divisions which will soon be engaged on the eastern front. They are for the most part reserve divisions and consist of conscripts of older age category and incompletely trained.

The development by the Germans of further production facilities also calls for the necessity of rapid action on our part. A single armoured division, employed on the European continent in 1942 at the moment of the fiercest battles on the eastern front, will represent a greater force if compared to the adversary, than five such divisions employed against the Germans in 1943.

We believe that Russia will not lose this war. She may, however, yet lose more than one battle and will be obliged to put herself to a tremendous effort in order to maintain the oilfields of the Caucasus. If the Germans succeed in holding their present line of defence, including the Crimea as a base of operations, they will probably concentrate their main forces in this operational direction and strike towards Rostov. As soon as favourable circumstances prevail, they will also advance on Krasnodarski Kray from Crimea.

We must remember that the Japanese are retaining in permanence in the Far East divisions concentrated against Russia. It is true that the Russo-Japanese relations have lately improved. The Mission of Mr. Sato as Ambassador to Moscow would indicate that the Matsuoka–Stalin Pact of April 13th, 1941, will be maintained. Numerous signs, however, give occasion to doubt the sincerity of this step. They tend to indicate that Japan desires to delude the Soviet Government, in order to surprise the Siberian Red Army, and strike with all the more effect. If, however, Japan, fearing engagement in operations requiring vast land forces, does not actually intend to attack Siberia in the spring, it would mean that she is preparing a campaign in India and, perhaps, an attack on Australia. In that case operations connected with the defence of the Caucasus, the Suez, China and India, or Australia, would constitute a system which is clearly comprehensive to an amateur, and thereby prevent Stalin from complaining against the pretended isolation of Soviet Russia in her struggle with Germany.

The successes of the Japanese, who are operating in vast areas and in dispersed directions, will come to an end when the United States, profiting by the experience of the British Navy, will pass to determined counter-offensive.

The question of a common command of the entire Allied Armed Forces stands foremost among military problems. This matter is of no less importance to Russia. Experience gained during the previous war, when this necessity was not understood until 1917, fully confirms the justice of this principle. It is also underrated by Russia, which is a serious error. The establishment of a supreme command of the Allied Forces would ensure the co-ordination of efforts indispensable towards the attainment of the intended purposes. It would receive the general injunctions from an Inter-Allied War Council, consisting of representatives of nations fighting against the Axis States. It would also be essential that one General-Officer-Commanding the land, naval and air forces would be appointed to every separate operational theatre.

The attainment of numerical and material superiority over the Third Reich is undoubtedly difficult. Owing to the entry into the War of the United States it becomes possible. It could be secured by the quickening of the rate of production, especially in the dock-yards, where the repair and building of new ships is still too slow, and also by intensifying diversion in the occupied countries and bringing about at the right moment the outbreak of insurrections of the subdued nations.

The organization of these risings requires adequate preparations. The conquered nations are in a sense similar to armies finding themselves upon areas forming part of the enemy's bases which, for the moment, are incapable of open action. These nations and in the first place Poland, in spite of brutal extermination, possess considerable numbers of trained soldiers who will play an important part in the successful termination of the war. It would be a cardinal error to disregard or underestimate this factor. Apart from the determination with which their soldiers are fighting, the successes of the Germans and the Japanese should be ascribed to their skilfully organized operations on the rear of their adversaries.

The leaders of the Third Reich are at present feverishly endeavouring to obtain the largest possible contingents from Italy, Hungary, Rumania and Slovakia, for the intended spring offensive. These countries are supporting Germany on the eastern front without much enthusiasm. Let us, therefore, avoid intensifying it through false moves which would immediately be taken advantage of by the adroit German propaganda.

At present, therefore, no decisions should be taken which would weaken the common war effort and fail to ensure the guarantee of security to nations in the future. It is imperative not to yield to the pressure of the Soviet Government, who are taking advantage of circumstances that are favourable to themselves and unfavourable to the Allies, and would like to impose their demands dictated by selfish and erroneously conceived interests.

The recognition by the Allies of these demands which include the incorporation of Lithuania, Estonia, Latvia, Northern Bukovina and Bessarabia, would undermine the foundations for future victory. It would extinguish the faith in our integrity and in the justice of the cause which is being defended with utmost sacrifice on the part of those nations that are inflexibly resisting the Third Reich and her satellites.

The Allies are opposing German aggression under the leadership of Great Britain and the United States. They cannot at the same time recognize the spirit of domination of the Russians which the Poles fearfully apprehend and desire at all costs to avoid.

It would unfavourably influence the attitude of all the neutral countries including Turkey, as well as the Catholics throughout the world. These countries must not be driven to face the choice between the Third Reich and Soviet Russia. At present they are facing only one dilemma: German bondage or freedom.

Would not the recognition of the imperialistic ambitions of Soviet Russia have an evil effect upon the United States and draw away the nations of Latin America? I greatly fear that the efforts of Hitler towards organizing a crusade against bolshevism, which so far proved ineffective, would under such conditions be successful.

Finally, I would like in a few words to draw your attention to the affairs directly connected with my country. The Soviet Government have not succeeded in breaking the spirit of the Poles, either at the time when in co-operation with Germany they occupied by force almost one-half of the territory of Poland, or when they imprisoned and placed in concentration camps one and a half million Polish citizens, many of whom were subjected to the most refined torture. Prime Minister Stalin expressed to me his sincere appreciation of and admiration for the initiative, the endurance and patriotism of the Poles. Is not the present attitude of the Soviet Government with regard to the Polish citizens of foreign descent who have been deported to Russia, dictated by the fact that, after the severe hardship in the prison and concentration camps of Russia, they are in complete unison with the Polish Government concerning the question of the eastern boundaries of the Polish Commonwealth, such as they existed in 1939? The Polish nation, which has exhibited and continues to show such great moral values, has the right to believe in a Poland stronger than the one which opposed the Third Reich. The endless suffering and sacrifice which the Polish people are offering daily on the altar of their country and the common cause, give ground and title of this claim.

I am convinced that the Poland of the future will be determined by the prevailing state and disposition of forces during the final phase of the war. This, however, must not be permitted to be settled today by the arbitrary methods of Bolshevik imperialism.

The Polish–Russian Agreement of July 30th, 1941,[2] as well as the declaration signed by Stalin on December 4th, 1941,[3] would seem to indicate that Stalin had abandoned the idea of a world revolution, that he fully appreciates the solidarity of the Allies and attaches great importance to the moral and material assistance of the Allies. For this reason, I accepted these negotiations and postponed for the time being the question of compensation of the wrongs inflicted on Poland and the Poles between 1939 and 1941.

The Soviet Government are not inspired by their former political realism in their recent proposals, but rather by the revolutionary doctrines of the Comintern, which is reviving under the influence of the Soviet successes during winter months.

It does not lie in my intentions to criticize the Bolshevik régime. If it suits the Russian peoples,—in accordance with the principle of non-intervention in the internal affairs of another state—let them have it. We must, however, insist that the Russian Government recognize the same principle with regard to us. Though conscious of the necessity of far-reaching social reform, we firmly reject the Bolshevik system which does not suit the nations of the West.

Whilst demanding the recognition of the acts which they accomplished by force during the war, the Soviets may insinuate the threat of reaching an agreement with the Third Reich. An indication thereto might be sought in Stalin's order to the troops on February 23rd, 1942. We are fully aware,

[2] See doc. No. 106.   [3] See doc. No. 161.

however, that at present such a step would be impossible. We realize that Hitler's victory would be equivalent to the overthrow of Soviet Russia for whom the solidarity of the Allies is no less important.

The benefits of the pact which Russia desires to conclude would be of doubtful value to herself. On the other hand the prejudice, caused by such an agreement, to Great Britain and her Allies, would be immediate and strengthen Germany and her Associates.

In view of the above, I emphatically protest against the recognition of the territorial claims of the Soviet Government. My point of view is in complete conformity with the policy which Great Britain is conducting since more than two years, expressed in her alliance with Poland concluded on August 25th, 1939,[4] and in your letter of July 30th, 1941,[5] which completes our understanding with Russia and reads: 'I also desire to assure you that His Majesty's Government in the United Kingdom do not recognize any territorial changes which have been effected in Poland since August 1939.'

The present situation requires inspired watch-words as well as action on a large scale. These watch-words must appeal to the imagination of the masses and harden their determination by indicating the necessity of sacrifice and duty. Public opinion in many countries should be guided by this spirit. In order to achieve the purpose, we should assemble all our energy, refraining from dispersing it in diplomatic bargains resulting from imperialistic tendencies. We must not impair the faith of nations in ideals, for which they are fighting. It would be more than political error. It would be a grave military blunder pregnant with incalculable consequences.

These observations may appear unsparing, but they are sincere. I am prompted by the anxiety for our future and our common victory, of which I am no less certain today than I was after the collapse of France, when in all sincerity and trust, I examined the circumstances of the war with your great Leader and Prime Minister, Winston Churchill.

[4] See appendix No. 4.   [5] See doc. No. 107.

No. 190

Telegram from Lt.-General Anders to General Sikorski transmitting the text of Stalin's telegram announcing the reduction of food-rations for the Polish Army in the USSR[1]

Yangi Yul, March 9, 1942   GSHI, KGA, 7-b
                                Transl. from Russian and Polish

C.-in-C. In view of economic difficulties which I had anticipated, and the brunt of which I am bearing now, I applied to Stalin, asking him to enlighten me on this subject. Today, on the ninth of March, I have received the following answer:

'I am in possession of your two telegrams relating to the position of your army with regard to food supplies, and to General Khrulov's dispositions. After having looked into all the information I reached the conclusion that the position of the Red Army with regard to food supplies has become more complicated on account of Japan's aggression against England and the USA. The war in the Far East brought about Japan's refusal to allow transport of grain to the USSR in American ships, and our own tonnage is limited. We expected to receive more than 1 million tons of wheat, and we are receiving less than 100 thousand tons. Because of that the plan of food supplies for the army had to be revised for the benefit of fighting divisions and to the detriment of those which are not engaged in fighting. In spite of that, and not without very great difficulties, I have secured the maintaining of the present ceiling of supplies for the Polish Army in the USSR until March 20th. After that date it will be necessary to reduce the number of food rations for the Polish Army, at least to 30,000. If you think it might be useful you can come to Moscow, and I shall be pleased to hear your views. Yours truly. J. Stalin.'

I informed him immediately that I would fly to Moscow, which was approved and, weather permitting, I shall fly there tomorrow. I consider this question to be very serious and decisive. Whatever may be the outcome, I consider it imperative to store food supplies on the territory of Iran, lest we perish with hunger. In the present position our Army can survive for 5 to 6 weeks, and that only with extreme difficulty. I take into account the necessity of flying directly from Moscow to London. After the conversation with Stalin I shall report immediately on its results through the wireless of the English Military Mission in Moscow.

¹ *This telegram was preceded by a despatch of President Stalin to Lt.-General Anders handed over by Colonel Volkovisky on March 9, 1942, at 7.20 a.m. and answered by Lt.-General Anders at 7.30 a.m. with an announcement of arrival at Moscow as above.*

No. 191

Extract from a conversation between General Sikorski and Mr. Churchill on the Soviet expansionist territorial claims made in the course of British-Soviet negotiations and on the situation of the Polish Army and population in the USSR. Attended by Mr. Eden, Mr. Bevin, Sir Archibald Sinclair, Col. Thompson, Dr. Retinger and Capt. Zamoyski

London, March 11, 1942　　　　　　　　　　　　　GSHI, PRM, 68
　　　　　　　　　　　　　　　　　　　　　　　　　Transl. from Polish

[. . .]. Mr. Churchill then asked whether Gen. Sikorski did not think that the restraint Japan showed in respect of Russia was due to German influence, connected with their attempts at achieving an understanding between the Reich and the Soviet Union. Gen. Sikorski did not think it probable that Germany would seek an understanding with Russia, as it seemed that both sides had burnt their boats. In particular the strongly anti-German feelings of the peoples of the Soviet Union seemed to exclude such a possibility. Obviously, such an understanding was not altogether impossible, but it seemed more than improbable. At present Stalin was making use of his prestige enhanced by military victories, purposely exaggerated, and also of the temporary weakness of the Allies and the setbacks in the Pacific theatre of operations. He did not give proof of the realism which inspired him previously when he came to his first understanding with Great Britain and the Polish Government, nor when, in December 1941, he conversed in the Kremlin with Gen. Sikorski and signed his well-known declaration.[1] His attitude towards Poland had changed and was no longer straightforward. In support of his statement Gen. Sikorski read telegrams received from Russia, amongst them a telegram from Stalin to Gen. Anders,[2] in which Stalin warned Gen. Anders that in view of the difficulty in supplying rations for the fighting forces, and because the promised 1,000,000 tons of wheat from America had failed to arrive, he would be able to send rations for 30,000 Polish troops only, and those on a reduced scale. No rations would be available for the rest of the Polish troops. At the same time Gen. Anders informed Gen. Sikorski that the Polish Army in Russia had food reserves in store for 5 weeks only. For that reason Gen. Sikorski intended to summon Gen. Anders to Great Britain to discuss the situation of the Polish Army in the Soviet Union. Mr. Churchill suggested that the surplus contingent of Polish troops which the Russians were unable to feed should be transferred to Persia where Great Britain would be able to supply rations and armaments. He did not think Gen. Anders would advance the solution of his difficulties by coming to Great Britain. Gen. Sikorski explained that it was done at Stalin's demand. He himself thought that Gen. Anders's presence would be very useful in many ways.

Next Mr. Churchill broached the subject of the military situation on the Eastern front. He asked Gen. Sikorski, as an expert on strategy, when in the latter's opinion a German counter-offensive could be expected, which front-sector would be involved, and what would be the axis of the attack. He also enquired whether a German attack against Turkey was probable. Mr. Churchill thought that Turkey, having 50 divisions and having firmly decided to keep neutral, could avail herself of her favourable defence condition and put up a long resistance.

Even in the case of a Turkish defeat the Germans would come up to attack the main strategic points in Asia Minor with no more than 6 or 8 divisions fit for action.

Gen. Sikorski expected a main German offensive on the Russian front to be launched at the end of May or in June, probably on the Southern sector in the direction of Rostov and the Caucasus. The Germans had concentrated, and were still concentrating enormous forces on the Eastern front. They endeavoured to form new divisions recruited from their allies. They were fully aware of the fact that this decisive war effort may be their last. As regards Turkey, he thought that Germany would make an effort to win Turkey over, to obtain her permission for the passage of German troops with the aim of attacking the Caucasus from the South. He also thought that, should it be proved that the recent bomb attempt on the life of von Papen

[1] See doc. Nos. 159, 160, 161.   [2] See doc. No. 190.

was organized by the Russians, it would certainly produce great distrust of Russia in Turkish public opinion. Gen. Sikorski considered it extremely important to maintain good relations with Turkey, as an infiltration of Germany on the Asia Minor boundary would considerably weaken the defence of the Caucasus, and, on the other hand, the establishment of Germans in Turkey would affect the conduct of the war in the Mediterranean and in Northern Africa.

Gen. Sikorski drew attention to increased German activity in Libya, the Luftwaffe concentration in Sicily and Southern Italy under the command of Gen. Kesselring who also had 2 parachute divisions under his command, and was himself subordinated to Gen. Rommel.

That indicated the probability of a capital German offensive in the Mediterranean, and of an attempt to occupy Malta as a springboard for an attack on Northern Africa and Suez. The offensive would certainly be synchronized with the June operations on the Eastern front. Mr. Eden assured Gen. Sikorski that every effort was being made to maintain the best possible relations with Turkey. They directly depended on the prestige of Great Britain, added Gen. Sikorski, and that would be undermined, should Stalin's conditions be accepted.

Gen. Sikorski expressed his regrets that Sir Stafford Cripps was not participating in the conference, as he could inadvertently exert a detrimental influence by exciting British public opinion in an unwanted direction. Gen. Sikorski availed himself of the presence of Mr. Eden and other members of the British Government to discuss the question of the Soviet claims presented to Great Britain. The Russians aim at concluding at the present stage an agreement which would involve the recognition of Soviet conquests in the West. The General referred to his letter to Mr. Eden, dated 9th March, and he felt that the British Government should be warned of the danger which threatened, should they yield to Soviet pressure, particularly at the present moment, when Russia was taking advantage of her strong position which might prove to be only temporary. Russia's territorial claims could not be justified by any strategic considerations, and were dictated by Russian imperialism. The wish to occupy not only the Baltic States but also Lithuania, Bessarabia and Bukovina clearly showed the imperialist attitude of Soviet Russia (e.g. the annexation of Bukovina would be a stepping-stone to the subjugation of Hungary; Mr. Eden quite agreed with this point of view.) The acknowledging of those far-reaching Russian claims would in the future mean the encirclement of Poland by Russia—in the way she had been encircled by Germany before the war.

As regards the annexation of Latvia and Estonia, Gen. Sikorski did not believe in a Baltic Federation, and therefore Poland was not directly interested, but she would declare herself against that annexation in agreement with the centuries' old tradition of Poland. For Kovno Lithuania, however, he demanded a full and unrestricted independence, notwithstanding any ties that might unite Poland with that country in the future. The Russian-sponsored agreement would mean the elimination of a discussion on Poland's

Eastern frontiers. Thus, in the future Poland would be left to face Russia alone, and it was clear that the latter would demand considerable territorial concessions. Russia might demand a frontier not much different from that established between the Russian and German invasion zones. Gen. Sikorski pointed out that he had signed an agreement with Russia taking on his shoulders the full responsibility for the Nation, whilst the members of his Government were hesitant. When, later on, he discussed and signed the Declaration with Stalin at the Kremlin, he made diligent and most sincere efforts to achieve normal relations and to conclude a lasting agreement with Russia. He had to close his eyes to the monstrously barbarian treatment of the Polish population by the Russians. He was inspired by the conviction that a new era of good neighbourly relations with Russia would begin for the sake of the common cause. The General, however, came to the conclusion that the hostile attitude of the Soviet Government to Poland had not changed at all. Proof of it could be found almost daily in despatches from the Polish Ambassador at Kuibyshev. It was proved by the attitude taken by Soviet authorities towards the Polish population, by the difficulties put in the way of the formation of a Polish Army.—'But still,' intervened Mr. Eden, 'you saved hundreds of thousands of men from death, and you will be able to create a strong army.' 'These Poles'—replied the General—'are now starving and dying of cold, and the organizing of the Army has come to a deadlock.'

The General stated that apart from all that, owing to lack of good will on the Soviet side, such an agreement between Great Britain and Russia could have incalculable consequences on the European continent, in particular in Sweden, Turkey and Poland where the Nation would lose faith in the fairness of the Allies. The Germans would immediately, and perhaps successfully, take advantage of it. They would then have a real foundation for calling a crusade against Russia. Such an agreement could also have a negative effect on the relations between Great Britain and America—whilst in return it would not add a single soldier to the Russian Army.

Gen. Sikorski said to Mr. Churchill that should such an agreement be signed without emendations, and should all the Russian demands, including the annexation of Lithuania, be granted, then the General, who once before had taken the full responsibility for his Nation for a compromise with Russia, could not take it on his conscience this time to accept the far-reaching consequences of such a political step. The General pointed out that he did not intend this statement to sound like a threat, but he felt a warning had to be given at this moment in order to specify mutual responsibilities. Mr. Churchill stressed his great admiration for Poland. He did not share the General's pessimism. He admitted that his own assessment of Russia did not differ much from that given by the General; however, he underlined the reasons which made it necessary to conclude the agreement with Russia. She was the only country that had fought against the Germans with success. She had destroyed millions of German soldiers and at present the aim of the war seemed not so much victory, as the death or survival of our allied nations. Should Russia come to an agreement with the Reich, all would be lost. It must not happen. If Russia was victorious she would decide on her frontiers without consulting Great Britain; should she lose the war, the agreement would lose all its importance. Gen. Sikorski saw another, in his opinion a more probable, alternative, namely the mutual exhaustion of Russia and Germany. Mr. Churchill retorted: 'Then the decisions on peace will be with us, independently of the petty agreements signed today.'

Mr. Eden stressed that the agreement would not settle the Polish frontiers. Gen. Sikorski retorted that the notorious Russian cunning would do the utmost to exclude Great Britain eventually from Polish-Soviet negotiations. Mr. Eden answered: 'We could make a reservation in that respect.' Summing up, Gen. Sikorski said that he could not assume the responsibility for casting the Polish Nation as a prey to the Soviets. He stressed the sufferings and wrongs experienced by Poles in Soviet Russia and the unbelievable brutality and refinement in the tortures inflicted by the Bolsheviks on many Poles. The barbarian methods of the Russians were beyond all belief. There existed a so-called 'Red Book', a report on the conditions existing in the USSR. The book was to be published in America. Gen. Sikorski stopped the publication of that and many other documents referring to Bolshevik cruelty, as he wanted to use every possible means of creating good relations and loyal co-operation with Russia. Both Mr. Churchill and Mr. Eden energetically objected to the publication of such documents. Gen. Sikorski agreed, but said, that if it did not prove possible at least to postpone the dangerous agreement, he would no longer be able to check the propaganda which would expose the real face of the Russians and their brutal imperialism to the world's public opinion. Gen. Sikorski once more warned against hasty decisions in the matter, he expressed his private opinion as to a possible withdrawal by the Russians of their claim concerning Lithuania and even Bukovina, and he drew the attention of the British Government to the grave consequences of a precipitous decision.

Mr. Churchill expressed the hope that during his visit to Washington Gen. Sikorski would discuss the problem with President Roosevelt, and that he would find support for his ideas.

Taking leave of the General, Mr. Churchill warmly wished him a good journey and the best possible success on his important mission, and asked him to convey his warmest greetings to President Roosevelt.

The conference lasted from 13.30 till 15.15. The minutes were kept by Capt. S. Zamoyski. The conversation was held partly in French and partly in Polish, and was translated into English by Dr. Retinger and Capt. Zamoyski.

No. 192

Note from Ambassador Bogomolov to Minister Raczyński in reply to his note of January 28, 1942, concerning the release of Polish citizens and especially of Polish officers

London, March 13, 1942   GSHI, PRM, 72/1

En réponse à votre note du 28 janvier[1] de l'année courante j'ai l'honneur, d'ordre du Gouvernement Soviétique, de porter à votre connaissance ce qui suit:

Le Gouvernement Soviétique ne peut pas être d'accord avec les affirmations que la note du Ministre contient. D'après ces affirmations, la mise en liberté des ressortissants polonais, y compris les officiers et soldats, confinés sur le territoire de l'URSS dans des camps de travail et d'autres lieux de détention, n'aurait pas été exécutée d'une façon intégrale, car, comme on prétend dans cette note, les autorités soviétiques locales n'appliquent pas, dans toute leur étendue les dispositions de l'Ukase du Présidium du Soviet Suprême de l'URSS en date du 12 août 1941,[2] concernant l'amnistie pour les ressortissants polonais.

Dans la réponse, par la note de V. M. Molotov en date du 8 novembre 1941,[3] adressée à M. Kot, et dans l'aide-mémoire du Commissariat du Peuple des Affaires Etrangères en date du 19 novembre,[4] on a déjà annoncé que l'amnistie en faveur des ressortissants polonais avait été strictement exécutée. La vérification correspondente, faite par les organes soviétiques compétents après l'entretien du 4 décembre 1941 entre le Président du Conseil des Ministres de la République Polonaise, Général Sikorski, et le Président du Conseil des Commissaires du Peuple de l'URSS, Y. V. Staline, a complètement confirmé le ci-dessus indiqué et avec cela le Commissaire du Peuple dans l'esprit de la note N.6 du 9 janvier 1942,[5] adressée à l'Ambassade de la République de Pologne, a donné des explications supplémentaires détaillées au sujet de l'exécution de l'amnistie en faveur des ressortissants polonais.

Étant donné que les officiers et les soldats polonais étaient mis en liberté au même titre que les autres ressortissants polonais en vertu de l'Ukase du 12 août 1941, tout ce qui a été dit ci-dessus se rapporte également aux officiers et soldats polonais.

Quant aux déclarations contenues dans la note de Ministre, prétendant qu'il y a jusqu'à présent des officiers polonais qui ne sont pas encore libérés, et que plusieurs de ces officiers se trouvent dans les Îles François-Joseph, Nouvelle-Zemla et sur les bords de la rivière Kolyma, il faut dire que ces déclarations sont sans fondement et se basent évidemment sur l'information incertaine. En tout cas, quand on apprend, qu'il y a quelque part des faits isolés de retard dans la libération des ressortissants polonais, les organes compétents soviétiques prennent immédiatement les mesures nécessaires pour leur libération.

[1] See doc. No. 177.   [2] See doc. No. 110.   [3] See doc. No. 142.
[4] See doc. No. 153.   [5] See doc. No. 170.

Le Gouvernement Soviétique profite de l'occasion pour déclarer qu'il a complètement mis en pratique les mesures concernant la libération des ressortissants polonais, conformément au protocole additionnel à l'Accord Sovieto-Polonais du 30 juillet 1941,[6] et qu'ainsi le Gouvernement Soviétique fait, et à cet égard, tout le nécessaire pour le développement ultérieur favorable des relations soviéto-polonaises.

[6] See doc. No. 106.

No. 193

Record of a conversation between Lt.-General Anders and M. Stalin on the reducing the Polish Army in the USSR to 44,000 and evacuation of the surpluses to Iran

Moscow, March 18, 1942

GSHI, PRM, 72/3
Transl. from Polish: Kersten, No. 20

Punctually at the appointed hour 17.30 the Commander of the Armed Forces in the USSR Divisional General Władysław Anders, accompanied by Staff Colonel Okulicki, were received by President Stalin in the presence of Minister Molotov and a stenographer. Immediately after salutation, President Stalin asked:

'You came to me to find out why the number of rations for the Polish Army had been decreased. I shall answer you with absolute frankness. You see, in October when Harriman and Beaverbrook were here, we made an agreement with America that she will deliver to us monthly 2,200,000 tons of grain. Up to now we should have received from this source 1,000,000 tons of wheat, and to the end of July 1942—1,800,000 tons. Upon that understanding was based the plan of supplying our army with food. The grain should be delivered by American ships, because our own tonnage is limited. How much we received of it—so much as the tears of a cat. I do not blame anybody but till now we have received scarcely 60,000 tons. The Japanese let our ships pass, but they sink American ships, which sail without convoy. They have already sunk four. The war with Japan has shuffled the cards. The American tonnage is not able to deliver us bread. For this reason we were compelled to revise ('pieresmatret') the plan of supplying the army. We were forced to dissolve territorial units stationed behind the army—what you may check at the spot—in order to secure food for the front units, which fight well. We reduced also considerably the cavalry. For these reasons, General Khrulov issued the order that until March 20 you will receive food for the entire force, but after that time only 40,000 rations. I would not like that they say that the Soviet people do not keep promises, but as long as conditions do not change, your army must be limited to three divisions and one reserve regiment.

'Gen. Anders: I understand all this and I came for that reason because I am convinced there must be found a way out of this situation. After the receipt of the telegram from General Khrulov and before I had received your telegram, Mr. President, I did not say anything to anyone. After the receipt of the telegram from you, Mr. President, I informed General Sikorski, from whom I have heard of directing to me 2,000,000 rations, of the contents of the messages. The present size of the army is 75,000 to 78,000 men. I cannot let the rest die from starvation. I see such a solution: Give us food for the entire force up to the time we receive food from England. On this matter I would like to fly to London. General Sikorski agrees to it and wants me to appear there as soon as possible. At present he is flying to Washington and will probably discuss there the matter of supplying our army in the USSR. I would like to do something good for Poland and therefore I search for the best solution. I consider that a scattering of our armed effort is bad and consequently I intend to create a Polish army as strong as possible on the territory of the USSR.

'Stalin: Are the men you are getting in the army good? Are you satisfied with them?

'Gen. Anders: Yes—the average men are quite good so far as morale is concerned; they are physically very exhausted, but they recover very quickly. At present we suffer from an epidemic of typhoid fever. I rely upon getting our men from the construction battalions and from the Russian Army. They are men of young age groups.

'Stalin: Do you know how typhoid fever rages in Poland? We should not have it here. We have enough soap and we should do away with it quickly. How many organized divisions have you?

'Gen. Anders: Six, but not all of them are in full strength, but the others will be ready soon. It is only a question of getting the men, as the command staff is ready.

'Stalin: Is this possible? A pity. In this situation you may have only three divisions—a corps. If you could obtain food supplies from America, then the army may be enlarged.

'Gen. Anders: General Sikorski has just gone by plane to America. I am sure he will do everything possible to secure some assistance.

'Stalin: The transportation of food may be conducted only by England. The Americans send out ships without convoy. The Japanese sink them, but English ships are escorted and all arrive punctually. In this matter I approached Roosevelt, who has not responded to my proposal. If the Englishmen do not deliver food by their own means, the American transportation may be delusive.

'Gen. Anders: The food I have mentioned—2,000,000 rations—promised by General Sikorski will certainly arrive via Iran. I do not know only the exact date. I am sure also that further supplies will arrive.

'Stalin: In this case I shall give you food for 40,000 people.

'Gen. Anders: What about the rest of the people?

'Stalin: Perhaps the rest would go to work on the collective farms.

'Gen. Anders: This is impossible. All Polish citizens able to serve with the army should be with it. They know of the agreement of Mr. President with General Sikorski and of your stipulation. With respect to the morale of the

302

army, it cannot be agreed to. Besides, on the collective farms there is no food and those who are there are also hungry.

'Stalin: Up to now the Polish Army has fed the civilian population from its supplied food. I do not consider it as wrong, and I understand one should help the people.

'Gen. Anders: I admit it was so; the Polish civilian population is in such a condition that we had to help it even at the cost of the military rations. The initiative of doing so came from the soldiers themselves.

'Stalin: It is not allowable to decrease a soldier's ration more as you get physically exhausted men.

'Gen. Anders: I have already prohibited it by order.

'Stalin: I cannot do it otherwise. You will get 44,000 rations. This will be sufficient for three divisions and the reserve regiment. You will have adequate time to organize and train those. We should not press you to go to the front. I understand it will be better for you to go to the front when we come closer to the Polish frontiers. You should have the honour to enter first into Polish lands.

'Gen. Anders: In such a case, if nothing can be changed, the rest should be sent to Iran.

'Stalin: I agree. With us will remain your 44,000 soldiers and the rest will be evacuated. There is no other solution. They will say and say that we have deceived you. I know not you soldiers, but for instance your Kot speaks so of it occasionally and also others say a lot of unfavourable things regarding us. If there were no war with Japan, there would be no need for this discussion. We Soviet people habitually keep our promises.

'Col. Okulicki: Is it possible for you to give us food for the entire force till the time we receive food from the Englishmen. This may not take too long.

'Stalin: Impossible—we do not have food. Front rations cannot be decreased. The Germans have caused hunger in our land. Now we entered into a region which was under occupation for a long time and we cannot absolutely count upon local reserves. Each 1,000 tons of food is of great importance to us and therefore we cannot give you more. My decision is herewith 44,000 rations.

'Gen. Anders: This hurts me much.

'Stalin: It cannot be otherwise. In Byelorussia, where the war is raging at present, the Germans have devoured everything. To the army must be given all. The army which fights cannot go hungry. We cannot give more than 44,000 rations.

'Gen. Anders: How to do it—to send the people for whom there is no food to Iran as quickly as possible? It cannot be done within a few days—they have to be fed of course until they are evacuated.

'Molotov: How many people do you have at present?

'Gen. Anders: According to the last report of March 8—about 66,000; every day arrive 1,000 to 1,500 men, so that today there may be already 80,000 men. This number is increasing steadily and will continue to increase. At the moment the basic problem is the matter of a speedy evacuation to

Iran. A base has to be established in Krasnovodsk; up to now I have not received the required consent; it may be established also in Ashabad.

'Stalin: How much food are the Englishmen able to give you for the evacuees?

'Gen. Anders: At the beginning 27,000 rations for 7 days but the food has to be brought from Pahlevi to Krasnovodsk.

'Stalin (orders to connect him with Gen. Khrulov): Where are your quarters? Is there not malaria?

'Gen. Anders: At present there is the epidemic of typhoid fever. Malaria, dysentery and typhus appear within later periods. Preventive measures are undertaken.

'Stalin: How stands the matter in relation to armament?'

(Gen. Anders hands over a specification to Stalin, who examines it carefully. General Khrulov calls. Stalin asks how many rations does the Polish Army receive. After receiving an answer from Khrulov he returns.)

'Stalin: We extend the time during which we shall issue food for the entire force till the end of March.

'Stalin (takes a seat behind the table): Which division was armed first?

'Gen. Anders: The 5th Infantry Division was armed. Now its armament is scattered among all units for training purposes.'

(Molotov asks General Anders for information how the divisions are numbered.)

'Stalin: We have changed the size of our divisions. We increased them and reinforced their fire power. Instead of 16 guns we give 20 and 12 howitzers. We increased the number of men in companies. The entire force of a division is 12,700 men. Which guns have you received?'

(Col. Okulicki hands over a specification of armament of a 1939 model.)

'Stalin: This armament is very good. Its range is 14 km and it may be used for anti-armour purposes. (He looks at the specification of the armament.) Has the second division got any armament?

'Gen. Anders: No. In spite of several interventions since the visit of General Sikorski and your promises we have not received anything.

'Stalin: It is right, we have made promises to you. Armament for the second division must be given immediately. We produce very much—330,000 carbines monthly and this is not sufficient. (He once again examines the specification of armament.) Is your third division already organized?

'Gen. Anders: Yes; four newly created divisions are almost ready. The organization of the command and staffs is accomplished. These divisions do not have the full strength yet, but they are making up quickly.

'Stalin: Are the divisions numbered?

'Gen. Anders: Yes; from 5 to 10.

'Molotov: How many divisions may be formed out of these 44,000 men?

'Gen. Anders: This I do not know, for it depends upon the strength of a division; if we take into account divisions which you, Mr. President, described, then there would be three divisions and not much will be left for the reserve regiment and additional units out of a division.

'Stalin: It should be sufficient for three divisions and the reserve regiment. Do you have some air force units?

'Gen. Anders: Yes. They are concentrated in one place and have been ready for evacuation since a long time.

'Stalin: Do you want to evacuate them?

'Gen. Anders: According to an agreement with Sikorski, the airmen as well as sailors and 25,000 men should have been evacuated.

'Stalin: Where are the airmen going to?

'Gen. Anders: To England, where they will have good conditions for training.

'Stalin: Are they going to use the southern or northern route?

'Gen. Anders: They will take the southern route through Iran. For a long time they have been ready for evacuation, which in spite of my continued efforts does not move forward.

'Stalin: Do we prevent the evacuation of those airmen to England?

'Gen. Anders: I do not know the reasons why up to now the consent of evacuating them has been withheld, but the matter depends only on your decision. They could be sent away a long time ago.

'Stalin: Why, have you approached Panfilov in this matter?

'Gen. Anders: Yes, many times. I received even a promise, but nothing has been done thus far. Recently my request for establishing a base for them in Krasnovodsk was turned down.

'Stalin: The airmen will be evacuated. Narkomindel has to do it immediately. (Writes in his notebook.)

'Molotov: It will be done.

'Gen. Anders: To settle quickly all formalities, an authorized representative should be appointed here at the spot, because otherwise the matter will again drag along and we shall not reach any result.

'Stalin: Right—such one will be sent. I think General Zhukov may be the best. Where is Zhukov?

'Molotov: He is here in Moscow.

'Stalin: I wonder why he is not in the south.

'Gen. Anders: He was with me all the time and came to Moscow only a few days ago. From the beginning he co-operated with us and will do certainly everything to help us.

'Stalin: Do you have any other needs?

'Gen. Anders: The first and most urgent need is to organize the evacuation, and first of all the base in Krasnovodsk to be able to send away immediately those for whom there are no rations.

'Stalin: All right—this will be done. Anything else?

'Gen. Anders: The second very urgent matter is to direct the drivers and the necessary personnel to receive the motor vehicles and utensils which are there.

'Stalin (makes notes): What else?

'Gen. Anders: The technical conditions of the evacuation shall be arranged with General Zhukov. In connection with the present situation I should go as soon as possible to London and therefore I ask for a plane to Cairo and possibly for an assignment of a representative—maybe someone authorized to make authoritative arrangements.

'Stalin (makes notes): Why do you need there a Russian? In London they will say we have sent with you a guardian from the "Tcheka"; there they will look at this in that way and you may have because of it more unpleasant experience than advantage.

'Gen. Anders: I am not afraid of it. The entire matter of the evacuation, supplies and so forth must be discussed with the English General Staff.

'Stalin (interrupting): This is all right, but in what respect may a Russian help you over there?

'Gen. Anders: Not there, but on my return trip he may render me a great assistance in Teheran, if he has the required authority.

'Stalin (making notes): Yes, the evacuation from Krasnovodsk may not be sufficient and another base may be established in Ashabad, from where the evacuation could be made by land route through Meshed. (Goes to the map, looks for an Atlas and demands some maps.) Our troops may help you in that, for they are familiar with the conditions there. (Quite unexpectedly) I doubt whether the Englishmen will give some armament to you.

'Gen. Anders: They are giving it already.' (Hands over a specification of the first transport of English arms.)

(Stalin takes the specification, studies it and makes some notes.)

'Molotov: It goes through Iran.

'Gen. Anders: Yes, the transport is already on its way and should arrive within a short time. On the territory of Iran there is already for me some sanitary material to set up a hospital. Besides, on the territory of Iran there is a considerable amount of arms of the Iranian Army, which may be easily and quickly shifted to us, if you consent to it.

'Stalin (makes notes): I do not object to it, but there were mostly only carbines and a part of them was already taken by us. (Puts some questions to Molotov.)

'Molotov: Yes—100,000 carbines.

'Gen. Anders: According to my information, there were from 250,000 to 300,000 carbines, furthermore machine guns, guns and anti-aircraft and anti-armour guns. (Takes out a notebook and wants to tell the amount.)

'Stalin: We have not taken all this, and it may be given to you.

'Gen. Anders: All the arms are made for German ammunition. In addition, you have certainly a lot of captured German arms. Our soldiers are very familiar with this armament and therefore it could be used temporarily for training until we receive the English arms.

'Stalin (makes notes): This is quite possible. (A moment of interruption and quite unexpectedly) How many Poles serve as interpreters with the staffs of the Germans?

'Gen. Anders: In each grouping and in each nation there is a certain amount of less valuable men. You too have this kind of people (Stalin assents to) but you cannot draw from this fact any general conclusions. We take care of such people. (Stalin assents to. A map is brought in, Stalin studies it and all others gather around the map.)

'Stalin: Along the Caspian Sea is a route too (indicates on the map) which also may be used.

'Gen. Anders: I have not heard of this route, but know only the route leading through Meshed. (All return to their seats.) In the first days of April as soon as General Sikorski returns, I would like to be in London. The matter is very urgent.

'Stalin: Do you want me to give you a plane to Cairo? (Makes notes.) All right. Is this finally all you wish?

'Gen. Anders: I would like to ask that the Poles who serve with the construction battalions and with the Russian Army be returned to the Polish Army in accordance with your promise, Mr. President.

'Stalin: We may return them, however, you will have to feed them and you do not have the food.

'Gen. Anders: Among them there are excellent young men fit for soldiers. The strongest I shall retain with me and include them in the group of 44,000 men and the rest will be evacuated.

Stalin (makes notes): We shall return them to you.

'Gen. Anders: Apart from those, there are still a lot of our people in prisons and labour camps. Men released recently are steadily returning. We still lack our officers who were taken away from Starobielsk, Kozielsk and Ostashkov. They must still be in your hands. We have collected additional data about them. (He hands over two lists, which were taken by Molotov.) They may have gone astray somewhere. We have traces of their stay on the Kolyma.

'Stalin: I have already given all orders that they should be released. It is said they are even in Francis Joseph land but there is not one of them there. I do not know where they are. Why should I want to detain them? It may be that they are in camps in territories taken over by the Germans and have dispersed there.

'Col. Okulicki: This is impossible—we should know of it.

'Stalin: We have only detained those Poles who acted as spies in the employment of Germany. We have released such men, who afterwards went over to the Germans, as for instance Kozłowski.

'Gen. Anders: Upon Kozłowski has been imposed the death penalty by the Court Martial. I confirmed the sentence and the sentence will certainly be executed, maybe even by our people in the homeland.

'Stalin: Where is Beck?

'Gen. Anders: He is interned in Rumania.

'Stalin: The Germans will, of course, not do him any harm, as he is their friend. And where is Śmigły?

'Gen. Anders: According to information received from the homeland, he is in Warsaw, apparently gravely ill, suffering from angina pectoris.

'Stalin: He is presumably hiding.

'Gen. Anders: Naturally.

307

'Stalin: Certainly Rydz Śmigły proved in 1920 not to be a bad commander. He commanded well in the Ukraine.

'Gen. Anders: Yes, but in this war as Commander in Chief he completely gave up his command after a few days.

'Stalin: The cause of your defeat was the lack of a good intelligence service.

'Gen. Anders: This is not true, we had rather a good intelligence service. The information was very precise, only there was no understanding for utilizing it. I stayed before the outbreak of the war at the frontier of East Prussia and know exactly what was going on the other side opposite me. Likewise I knew exactly about the German concentrations in Slovakia.

'Stalin: Yes, of course, spying in the territory of Germany should not be difficult for you. There you have indeed a lot of Poles.

'Gen. Anders: This is right—I received information from the Mazurs who live in East Prussia.

'Stalin: So the Mazurs are still holding out. That is very good.

'Gen. Anders: Yes, they hold out very well and certainly will hold out to the end. There is still one matter about which I would like to inform you, Mr. President. According to the order received from General Sikorski, namely that the burning of the huge warehouses in Poznań containing warm clothing assembled in the entire German Republic just before the winter, certainly rendered a considerable service to the cause of victory.

'Stalin: Not a bad one.

'Gen. Anders: General Sikorski intended to fly to Washington on March 15; he demands from Churchill and Roosevelt a more serious action on the western front. In his opinion, the organization of one panzer division in 1942 has more importance than the creation of five divisions in 1943. Everything we do proves our friendly attitude towards the USSR.

'Stalin: Hitler is a furious enemy of all the Slav people. He is afraid of the Slavs. (Quite unexpectedly and abstractly) Our airman Lewoniewski, hero of the USSR, a brilliant character, who in spite of persuasions and discouragements attempted to reach his goal. When he lost his life, we sent money to his mother. We wanted to erect a monument on the site of his birthplace.

'Col. Okulicki: His brother, our excellent airman, likewise lost his life.

'Stalin: Yes, I know about that.

'Gen. Anders: Formerly the cavalry was the most important means of defence, in particular our hussars, who today gave the airmen their wings and their armour to their tanks; however, the old cavalry spirit remained. The Slavs are particularly well qualified for flying. Your airmen are indeed famous and our airmen hold first place in England.

'Stalin: Yes, you are correct. The cavalry has a wonderful spirit everywhere. Do you have anything more?

'Col. Okulicki: Not much time remains for completing the evacuation. It is best to make the evacuation from the base of Krasnovodsk, however, the order must be issued immediately, otherwise the evacuation may be postponed and the food supply will be cut off on March 31.

'Stalin: You are right. We must hurry this along. I shall issue proper orders.

'Gen. Anders: If you, Mr. President, authorize General Panfilov to settle the technical problems, I shall discuss them with him and therefore I will not take up your time.

'Stalin: Very well, these matters will be taken care of by Panfilov.

'Gen. Anders: If you, Mr. President, allow, I will summarize our conversation. (Stalin consents.) We, therefore, can reckon that the remainder of the people, for whom there is no allotted food, will be speedily evacuated to Iran.

'Stalin: All right.

'Gen. Anders: In connection with the evacuation and the limiting of the army to 44,000 men, the recruiting will not cease and the Poles from the construction battalions and from the Russian Army will be released and directed to the Polish Army.

'Stalin: All right.

'Gen. Anders: We can depend upon the arms which are in Iran. You do not have any objections to this? May I reveal that to General Sikorski and the Englishmen?

'Stalin: All right; no objections.

'Gen. Anders: In reference to my flight to London, may I count on having a Russian plane to Cairo and back?

'Stalin: Yes; I will see to it that you get the plane, but I shall not send anyone along with you; you have people who do not trust us and they would say that the Tcheka sends along its observer.

'Gen. Anders: I am not responsible for what the foolish people, who are present everywhere, say. Important is only concrete work. I thought that your representative would be of great assistance to me in Teheran.

'Stalin: It is not only the average foolish people who think in that way; recently Grabski, the Chairman of the National Council, wrote a very unpleasant article against us.

'Col. Okulicki: Our dreams for creating here an army as powerful as possible and for the return to the liberated homeland through battle— collapsed today.

'Stalin: Too bad, it cannot be any other way. If it were not for Japan, you could do it. We keep our word to whatever we say. We are not responsible for the change.

'Gen. Anders: We want that our attack be powerful. Only then will it have full effect not only among our soldiers, but particularly in the homeland. Maybe, it will be possible to organize a part of our army in Iran, which later, together with the units that remain in the USSR, would go to the front.

'Stalin (consents): Then you will receive such rations as all our front divisions.

'Gen. Anders: We want to enter first into Polish territory. We know that this is our duty towards our fatherland and that our brothers are waiting there for us impatiently. At the present time, after the decision is made by

309

you, Mr. President, the chief problem is the evacuation, which should begin as quickly as possible.

'Stalin: So it is. I shall order them to check the conditions of railway transportation, sea transportation and army conditions. I shall immediately issue pertinent orders. When are you flying?

'Gen. Anders: Tomorrow it will be impossible as I shall converse with General Panfilov. On the following day I want to leave. This is probably all.'

(He gets up, bids farewell with handshaking; Stalin several times shakes hands with the Commander of the Polish Armed Forces, Molotov bids sincere farewell to all.)

'Stalin: I wish you luck.'

(Stalin responds to a military salutation with a raised hand.)

Termination of the conversation at 19.00 hours.

The tempo of the conversation was lively—the atmosphere friendly.[1]

[1] Recorded by Col. Okulicki.

No. 194

Note on the conversation between General Sikorski and President Roosevelt concerning Soviet territorial claims. Also present: Minister Raczyński and Ambassador Ciechanowski

Washington, March 24, 1942   GSHI, PRM, 71
Transl. from Polish

The problem of Russian territorial claims was approached. Gen. Sikorski stated that he had recently discussed the matter with Mr. Churchill, Mr. Eden and other members of the British War Cabinet. The British Government was unfortunately ready to yield to Soviet pressure and to concede the annexation of the Baltic territories, and also of the Rumanian provinces bordering on Poland. Polish territories were to be excluded from these concessions; that, however, did not alter the fact that their fate would be settled: by their encirclement from the South and from the North, thus making Poland an easy prey for Russia, by leaving the discussion of the Polish-Russian frontier to ulterior negotiations. The Polish Government categorically rejected those demands and objected to such an abandonment of the principles of democracy, proclaimed by the West. The whole country supported him in this matter. As recently as on 20th January all the political parties in Poland had declared their unanimous decision to refuse to yield to German suggestions of a Polish participation in any form in an anti-Russian campaign, in exchange for which the Poles had been offered the re-establishment of normal conditions in Polish territories. It would be difficult to expect an unbroken spirit of resistance to be maintained in the face of monstrous and ever-increasing German reprisals, should public opinion in Poland learn of the concessions intended to be made to Soviet imperialism at the expense of Polish territory. As far as the Baltic countries were concerned, it was against Polish national tradition to deprive any nation of her independence. He was not affected by megalomania, but he must state that Lithuania was very

310

much Poland's concern, and was in the domain of her direct interests. The General finished with a statement that, should those matters of vital interest for Poland become subject to negotiations, the Polish Government would consider it their undeniable right to participate in them. The President replied with emphasis that he shared that point of view, and that the United States Government had decided not to recede from the principle that no territorial questions should be settled before the end of the war. The Soviet Government at present limited their demands to the three Baltic States, Estonia, Latvia and Lithuania, but should that point be conceded to the Russians, then they would certainly put forward analogous claims to other countries' territories, such as Bukovina, Bessarabia, Finland, Northern Norway, etc. etc., and similar claims could also be presented by others. The President was not forgetting the Atlantic Charter which provided for the disarmament of Germany after the war. This done, Germany would no longer be a threat to Russia from the side of the Baltic wall, and Russia's security reasons would no longer be valid.

The President would impart this point of view to Stalin through the Soviet Ambassador, M. Litvinov, explaining that it was 'premature to eat one's pie before it had been baked'. After the war the United States Government would be prepared to discuss Russian demands from the point of view of security; then would be the time for the population of the given countries to express their opinion as regards their future state, but at present these matters could not be settled.

No. 195

Note on the conversation between General Sikorski and the Under-Secretary of State Sumner Welles, concerning Soviet territorial claims. Also present: Minister Raczyński and Ambassador Ciechanowski

Washington, March 25, 1942 GSHI, PRM, 71
Transl. from Polish

The General related his conversations at the Kremlin, and how he personally had avoided a discussion on Russia's territorial claims, which, as Stalin assured him, would have been 'very, very moderate'. Mr. Sumner Welles stated that in the course of discussion there was no difference of principle between the General and the President. He described the démarche made by Maisky in his interview with Mr. Eden, on March 24th. Maisky declared that, as the Soviet Government had never directly approached the United States with their territorial claims, they did not understand the purpose of President Roosevelt's declaration handed over to Ambassador Litvinov to be conveyed to Stalin.[1]

[1] In that statement, made a few days previously to this conversation, President Roosevelt expressed his opinion on the Russian claims which were put forward as being motivated by security reasons. He declared he was willing to discuss the problem of security, but not before the end of the war, and in the light of the then existing situation. (Vide the conversations between President Roosevelt and Count Raczyński on 25.2.42, and Gen. Sikorski on 24.3.42.)

Mr. Sumner Welles wondered what that démarche could mean. Was it just a manifestation of resentment or was it an indication of Stalin's withdrawal in the face of America's objections? Closing that part of the conversation, the Under-Secretary of State declared that he had been instructed by the President to make an official statement defining the attitude of the United States in view of the Soviet pressure; and that was, that as long as the war was in progress, the American Government would not enter into any secret agreements concerning post-war settlements. The American policy was clearly defined in the Atlantic Charter. The settlement of mutual relations between powers, and in particular the question of frontiers between them, must await the end of the war. That decision did not prevent negotiations between individual powers belonging to the United Nations, with a view to defining their claims and points of view.

Washington, 26th March, 1942.

No. 196

Memorandum from the Polish Embassy in London to the
Foreign Office concerning Soviet territorial claims

London, March 27, 1942   GSHI, PRM, 67

In presenting the following observations the Polish Government desire to declare that, ever since the Soviet Union joined the ranks of the Allies, one of the principal aims of Polish foreign policy has been the maintenance and strengthening of the most friendly relations with the Soviet Union. This policy, initiated by the Polish Government in July last, has met with the full appreciation and approval of the Polish people in Poland, who definitely rejected all attempts to involve them in the so-called anti-Bolshevik crusade which is being organized by the Germans on the Continent of Europe.

This policy is not dictated only by the exigencies of the present war arising from the fact that Poland and the Soviet Union are fighting against a common and implacable foe. Loyal collaboration between the two States is, in the opinion of the Polish Government, a guarantee of the future stabilization of the conditions in Europe. This collaboration—if it is to be fruitful—must be based on the genuine respect of each other's independence and on mutual confidence. If this aim is to be realized, territorial solutions in the East which would be likely to sow the seeds of future conflicts between the two States should be avoided.

Good neighbourly relations and friendship between Poland and the Soviet Union are the indispensable conditions of a lasting peace.

II

From the very outset of the war all the Allied and practically all the neutral countries, including the United States of America, gave expression to the opinion that no changes of frontiers whatsoever brought about by violence and aggression can be recognized and that the political status in Europe and in the rest of the world cannot be established before the termination of hostilities. This principle, fully conformant with international law, could only be opposed by States which are themselves committing acts of aggression.

With the lapse of time, while the Continent of Europe was being occupied by Germany and her satellites, Great Britain and the Allied Nations not only maintained this attitude for reasons of morality and international justice, but they have come to the conclusion that the observance of this principle is indispensable for the effective prosecution of the war.

In adopting this attitude the Allies seem to have been guided also by the consideration that it would be impossible to make binding decisions for the future during the fluctuations of war. Moreover, the peoples of the occupied States, though subject today to a reign of terror, are the natural and most valuable partners of the Allies in their struggle for victory. They not only rejected collaboration with Germany but are actively resisting the enemy by organized diversions and preparing for an open revolt against the Germans. The outbreak of this revolt will take place at a suitably selected moment and may become one of the decisive factors in the final outcome of the war. At the same time, the present resistance against the German occupation is immobilizing considerable forces of the enemy and causing him serious difficulties.

Thus, the non-recognition of acts of violence committed by force during the war became a fundamental principle, in the name of which the Democracies are carrying on the struggle. After the collapse of France the British Government embodied this principle as an official doctrine in the Prime Minister's declaration of September 5th, 1940.[1]

A similar principle of the general Allied policy has been clearly formulated in the Atlantic Charter which has been accepted by all the Allies. Meantime, while the war is still being waged, the Soviet Government have put forward the demand that Great Britain should recognize some of the annexations effected in the years 1939–40. Such a recognition would be contrary to both the above-mentioned principles of the Allies' policy as hitherto pursued.

The Polish Government would consider the acceptance of this demand to be detrimental to the general war policy. It would not increase the number of Allied effectives by a single fighting man, nor would it in any way improve the situation of the Allies. On the contrary, it would undermine and diminish confidence in the war policy of the Allies. It would create confusion in public opinion in Europe and beyond. It would dangerously weaken the moral forces of fighting democracy. Compliance with such a demand would be exploited by the enemy not only on the territories of the occupied States but also in neutral countries. This would seem particularly dangerous on the eve of Germany's spring offensive.

At the same time, it is difficult to detect what material advantages in the prosecution of the war against Germany the Soviet Union would obtain from the acceptance of her demands by His Majesty's Government.

[1] See doc. No. 79.

313

The Soviet Union is stubbornly fighting against Germany, for she is fighting in the first place for her own survival. Therefore the rumours spread by Germany, insinuating the possibility of a separate peace with the Soviet Union, are either propaganda or an attempt at blackmail. A comparison of the recent public enunciations of Stalin and Hitler indicates that the war aims formulated in these enunciations are utterly contradictory, and that there is no possibility of a compromise between their respective points of view. It seems that, without exhausting the means still at her disposal, Germany cannot give up the war aims which were publicly formulated at the outset of her campaign against the Soviet Union. It also appears that Germany could make a separate peace with the Soviet Union only in one of the two following circumstances:

1. If her spring offensive were to fail without having achieved its essential strategic objects and

2. if the Soviet Army were defeated, perhaps with the assistance of Japan, whereupon Germany would have achieved her war aims in the East and could simply dictate her conditions. Such considerations, however, are purely speculative at the present juncture.

As far as the Soviet Union is concerned, the war against Germany was imposed upon her and she must carry it on to the end, both in self-defence and in defence of her régime.

III

Independently of the view expressed in Par. II, the Polish Government desire to draw attention to these aspects of the contemplated British-Soviet Agreement, which might infringe upon vital Polish interests. In particular they desire to recall that Point 2b of the Secret Protocol of the Polish-British Agreement of August 25th, 1939,[2] concerning Lithuania amounts to the express recognition by the British Government that the maintenance of the independence of Lithuania is of exactly the same vital interest to the security of Poland as the maintenance of the independence of Belgium and Holland is to the security of Great Britain. The Polish Government have drawn the attention of the British Government to the stipulations of the Protocol in this respect in a Note of December 20th, 1941.

The aforementioned legal text is a consequence of political reality, for an independent Lithuania cannot threaten its neighbours or other States of that region of Europe. On the other hand, the annexation of Lithuania by the Soviet Union would particularly threaten the security of Poland, by prejudicing her position from the North-East and introducing constant friction in her neighbourly relations with the Soviet Union. The latter would not be able to justify on strategic or other grounds, her claims to a country which does not dispose of any harbour worth mentioning on the Baltic and which is inhabited by a predominantly rural population deeply attached to the Catholic Church and to the principle of private ownership.

[2] See appendix No. 4.

314

The Polish Government consider the full sovereignty of Lithuania as a fundamental axiom of their foreign policy and desire to emphasize once more that this axiom does not and cannot unfavourably affect Polish-Soviet relations.

The problem of Lithuania is similar to the question of Bukovina. There is no legal Polish-British act in existence concerning this specific question, because at the time when the alliance between the two countries was being concluded there was no need to deal with it, as Rumania was in possession of a British guarantee [see Pt. 2d of the Secret Protocol] and a defensive alliance between Poland and Rumania was in full force.

The possession of Bukovina has no practical importance for the defence of the Soviet Union. It is a poor province, remote from the sea and from the Danube, connecting Rumania and Poland to whom it assures territorial contiguity. Bukovina was never before in possession of Russia or an object of Russian claims. Soviet claims could only be explained by requirements of an offensive policy in relation to Central Europe and the Balkans.

Furthermore, the acquiescence of the British Government to the passing of Lithuania and Bukovina into Soviet hands would be equivalent to the approval by the British Government of the encirclement of Poland by the Soviet Union from the North-East and South. The strategical position of Poland in the East would then become similar to that existing in 1939 in the West, when after the occupation of Czechoslovakia Germany surrounded Poland from three sides in the same way as would [the Soviet Union] threaten the Polish state in the event of the proposed agreement.

IV

His Majesty's Government are adequately informed that the position of Wilno as a part of the whole principle of integrity of the territories of Poland is fundamental to the Polish state. The Wilno area, inhabited by a Polish population, with a Polish civilization and traditions, became the object of a local dispute which had been exploited by Germany and led to prolonged international discussions.

By Art. III of the Treaty of Riga,[3] concluded in 1921, the Soviet Union undertook to observe a complete désintéressement in the Polish-Lithuanian dispute concerning Wilno. After having been occupied by Soviet troops in September 1939, this area was, until October 10th, 1939, ceded by the Soviet Union to a still independent Lithuania. Seized again in 1940 it was incorporated by force with the Soviet Union as a part of the 'Soviet Republic of Lithuania'. This arbitrary procedure was recognized only by the German Government. The Polish Government protested against it in Notes delivered to the Government of the Allied and neutral States on October 16th, 1939, and in July 1940.[4]

The Polish Government declare that, even an indirect and circumstantial

---

[3] See doc. No. 3.   [4] See doc. No. 63, 77.

questioning of the possession by Poland of the Wilno territory would have to be regarded by them as a manifest infringement of the integrity of the Polish Republic.

The Polish Government consider that discussions regarding matters or problems connected directly or indirectly with vital interests of Poland, in negotiations between the British and the Soviet Governments, would not be consistent with the spirit of the British-Polish alliance.

Even though the question of the Polish-Soviet boundaries were to be excluded from the present British-Soviet discussions, a settlement of their territorial problems in Eastern Europe which would unfavourably prejudice vital Polish interests would not correspond to the spirit of the Alliance. And yet, sustained by this Alliance, Poland did not hesitate, in defence of her integrity, to face this dreadful war and to persevere in the struggle at the cost of ruthless extermination and cruel persecution.

The Polish Government beg to emphasize that the Polish-Soviet frontiers were defined by the Treaty of Riga in 1921. This Treaty was the result of a free decision on the part of both states, which thereby agreed on a compromise between the frontiers of Poland as they existed prior to the Partitions and the Russian frontiers of 1914. In the Polish-Soviet declaration of December 4th, 1941,[5] signed by the Heads of the Polish and Soviet Governments, both parties recognized the necessity of respecting international law, which implies the observance of international treaties. The obligation on the part of Great Britain to respect the integrity of the frontiers of Poland arises from Point 3 of the Secret Protocol to the Polish-British Agreement of August 25th, 1939, as well as from the generally recognized obligations of two allied countries. In his letter to the Polish Prime Minister, dated July 30th, 1941, the British Foreign Secretary stated that His Majesty's Government does not recognize any territorial changes effected in Poland since August 1939.[6] The Polish Government beg to recall that this letter had been the subject of diplomatic negotiations which preceded the signature of the Polish-Soviet Agreement of July 30th, 1941,[7] and thus forms part of this political act, which was achieved with the assistance of the British Government. The political realism by which the Polish side was guided in concluding this agreement brought certain advantages to the general cause of the Allies and particularly to Great Britain.

The Polish Government desire to declare that the surest means of safeguarding the Soviet Union against possible future German aggressions is a strong Poland bound to the Soviet Union by bonds of sincere friendship. The Polish Government are determined to build up such a Poland in complete harmony and friendship with the Soviet Union after victory over Germany has been achieved, when—in their opinion—the question of frontiers would be treated as a whole. That will be the time for the solution

---

[5] See doc. No. 161.   [6] See doc. No. 107.   [7] See doc. No. 106.

of the problem of security which would have to take into account the legitimate and justifiable interests not only of the Soviet Union and Poland but also of other States in Central and Eastern Europe.

No. 197

Minutes made by Counsellor Kulski of his conversation with Mr. Strang concerning British-Soviet political negotiations

London, March 28, 1942   GSHI, A.11. 49/Sow./5
                                            Transl. from Polish

On 27th inst. in the afternoon, that is as soon as the English text of the Memorandum on the British-Soviet negotiations was ready, I called on Mr. Strang and handed him the Memorandum. I wished to hand it directly to Mr. Eden or through Sir Alexander Cadogan, but they were both absent from London on Friday afternoon and on Saturday. Mr. Strang read the Memorandum in my presence and said that he was unable to make any comments before showing it to Mr. Eden. However, all the arguments used in the Memorandum were familiar to him, and he was glad they were couched in the form of an official declaration. I drew Mr. Strang's attention to our wish that the Memorandum should be considered a strictly confidential paper.

Referring to my conversation with Sir Alexander Cadogan I confirmed in my conversation with Mr. Strang that our Prime Minister shared the view of the British Government that any public discussion of the problems connected with the British-Soviet negotiations would be harmful. As a matter of fact, on leaving Great Britain the Prime Minister issued appropriate instructions to this effect. I cannot help observing, however, that discussion on this subject has begun in the British press, namely in The Times, and in the well-known interview granted by Sir Stafford Cripps to the Daily Mail. Once a public discussion has been started in this way, no wonder that it should be continued by the Poles. Moreover, one must not look at the Polish moves only from the point of view of the purposelessness of the discussion at present, as such moves should be considered to be a foretaste of Polish reaction should a British-Soviet Agreement be concluded. It is rather interesting that critical comments of this kind are made by persons who are otherwise deeply convinced of the necessity of fostering good relations between Poland and Russia. Mr. Strang listened to this information with interest, and he did not deny that the discussion had been started by the British side.

As Mr. Strang asked me when approximately we might expect the Prime Minister's return, I availed myself of this opportunity to ask him, once more, to keep me informed of any new facts regarding British-Soviet negotiations, in order that I might advise the Prime Minister in due time.

Letter from Lt.-Colonel Carlisle (War Office) to Maj.-General Klimecki informing him about the first and second stage of the evacuation of Polish forces from the USSR[1]

London, March 30, 1942   GSHI, A.XII. 22/31.3

Lieutenant-Colonel Hulls, our Liaison Officer with the Polish Forces in the USSR, has arrived at Teheran from Krasnovodsk via Pahlevi. He has seen the Soviet authorities who are responsible for arranging the evacuation of the Poles, and informs us that the personnel will arrive in two main echelons.

The first echelon which has already begun to arrive consists of 40,000 men, all of whom should have been landed at Pahlevi by the 6th April. These 40,000 will be moved from Pahlevi according to the arrangements, the general lines of which were communicated to you in my letter of 27th March, 1942.

With the first echelon are 1,500 women and children. They will be taken to Teheran after disinfection, and plans are being made accordingly. The clothes for the women and children will be supplied by the American Red Cross. Plans are being made in conjunction with the Polish Minister for feeding them, and if necessary, the Area Commander will supply the absolute necessities until the arrangements are working.

The second echelon is expected to begin arriving after an interval of some weeks, during which the personnel will be collected from the various labour centres and camps throughout the USSR.

Lieut.-Colonel Hulls, after speaking with the Soviet authorities, expects the second echelon to number 50,000. With the second echelon General Anders hopes to evacuate some 10,000 women and children. This question has, I think, already been raised by the Foreign Office, and is being examined by them. [. . .].

General Anders is expected to arrive in Teheran shortly en route for Cairo, and I should be grateful if you would let me know as soon as you have any information as to the exact date of his departure from Cairo.

The following information has been telegraphed by the British Liaison Officer who, as I informed you in my letter referred to above, had left for Pahlevi where he arrived on the 25th March, 1942, after a journey of ten hours by air.

Major-General Lane saw the Russian Consul, Garrison Commander, and Naval Port authorities on his arrival in Pahlevi, all of whom were helpful. The Persian Governor is also co-operating. [. . .].

Lieutenant-Colonel Ross will be in charge of the British Staff, and also Liaison Officer in Pahlevi, and Brigadier Crampton will be in charge of the evacuation organization at Teheran. [. . .].

I should be very grateful if you would forward to the War Office any information which you may receive from Polish sources on the progress of the evacuation.

[1] See Note No. 198.

No. 199

Telegram from Lt.-General Anders to General Sikorski concerning the evacuation of Polish troops from the USSR

Yanghi-Yul, March 31, 1942   GSHI, A.XII. 30/19.9
                                                Transl. from Polish

General Zhukov in his capacity of plenipotentiary of the Council of People's Commissars let me know, on the USSR Government's order, what follows:

I. The Soviet Government shares the opinion expressed by General Sikorski concerning the establishment of the second front in Europe wherever it can be done, provided that the establishment of such a front would detach at least 40 German divisions from the Eastern front.

It should take place without delay.

II. The Soviet Government, realizing the necessity of evacuation, for economic reasons, of some parts of the Polish Army to Iran, nevertheless considers it necessary that the Polish military effort should not be dispersed but should be carried out in Eastern Europe, as this would enable the Polish Army to be the first to enter the territory of Poland.

In connection with this the USSR Government considers it necessary to form a Polish Army in Iran, where the surplus contingents of conscripts will be sent. In their view these parts of the Army, jointly with the units stationed on Soviet territory, should remain under the command of General Anders.

III. The Soviet Government understands that any partisan moves in the rear, as well as terrorist actions such as the killing of individual Gestapo men or policemen, would only provoke unnecessary losses and reprisals. On the other hand, an operation by resolute men along lines of communication, as, for instance, Warsaw-Baranowicze, would undoubtedly be to the advantage of the common cause.

No. 200

Telegram from General Sikorski to Mr. Churchill on the shifting of the main part of the Polish Forces from the USSR to the Middle East and on the Polish reinforcements to be sent to Great Britain

Washington, April 1, 1942   GSHI, A.XII. 1/57

Thank you for your telegram and your assistance in connection with the evacuation from USSR.

1. Our latest information connected with German intentions regarding Middle East fully confirmed my view of the necessity to form a strong reserve force in the area: Syria, Palestine, Persia. The rapid transfer of a considerable number of fully trained Polish soldiers to that area would be providential.

2. So far 35 thousand soldiers are being evacuated from the USSR. It is difficult to foresee the progress of the further recruitment in Russia and the second echelon of the evacuation. I reckon that another 10–15 thousand may be expected. I fully understand the difficulties of Great Britain connected with the shortage of shipping. Therefore I agree with the policy of transfering

319

the main concentration of the formation of new Polish units (2–3 divisions) to Middle East. This will necessitate the taking of considerable cadres from Great Britain to Middle East. I would like to discuss the details with you personally. I have given necessary instructions to General Klimecki, C.G.S., and will be grateful if preliminary talks were started with the British General Staff.

3. I wish to bring to Great Britain a sufficient number of soldiers from the USSR in order to complete the establishment of the armoured division and the paratroop brigade. I attach great importance to the creation of these units in Great Britain as soon as possible. I am also very anxious to complete the Air Force and the Navy. I would like to fix the minimum required numbers (necessary) with you on my return. They should amount to 17 thousand.

4. I will be very grateful to you for putting pressure on the Soviet Government in order that the recruitment of Polish Forces in the USSR should continue independently of the achievement of the numerical strength of the Army of General Anders as well as of the numbers already evacuated, since complements will be required both for General Anders and in the Middle East. It is possible that General Anders may be needed with his divisions in the Middle East rather than in the USSR.

No. 201

Message from General Sikorski to M. Stalin concerning the evacuation of a part of the Polish Army in the USSR to Iran and the conscription of Polish citizens in the USSR, delivered to Ambassador Bogomolov on April 13, 1942

London, April 9, 1942   GSHI, PRM, 72/1

Le Général Sikorski a été hereux d'apprendre qu'à la suite des conversations tenues en commun à Moscou le Président Stalin ait bien voulu exprimer son consentement définitif à l'évacuation en Proche Orient de soldats polonais en tant que leur nombre dépasse le contingent prévu pour l'armée polonaise en URSS. En éxécution de cette décision 30,000 hommes environ sont arrivés jusqu'à présent en Iran. Ils seront immédiatement encadrés dans les unités polonaises et equipés pour prendre part à la lutte poursuivie par la Pologne contre l'Allemagne ensemble avec l'Union Soviétique et les autres Nations Unies. Le Général Sikorski espère se trouver d'accord avec le Président Stalin pour croire que, vu le développement probable de la situation militaire en Proche Orient et étant donné que ce theatre des operations est intégralement lié au front sur lequel les armées soviétiques livrent d'héroiques combats—il est spécialement indiqué de créer sur ce secteur de fortes unités polonaises.

En outre se pose la question d'un second front en Europe. Le Général Sikorski a fait valoir au Gouvernement Britannique et aussi au Gouvernement Americain son opinion qu'il était indispensable que les Puissances Occidentales entreprennent une action offensive contre l'Allemagne au moment où les forces principales de celle-ci sont engagées sur le front russe. Il a en particulier exposé au Président Roosevelt [la] nécessité de concentrer l'effort principal en premier lieu contre l'Allemagne—point de vue avec lequel le Président s'est trouvé d'accord. Dans des conversations ultérieures avec des personalités officielles americaines le Général Sikorski a repris le même sujet, en insistant sur la nécessité d'accélérer les préparatifs en vue d'une telle opération.

Étant donné que les forces militaires polonaises stationnées en territoire britannique peuvent être appelées a prendre une part active dans une pareille opération, le Général Sikorski attache une grande importance à l'augmentation de leurs effectifs et de leur force de combat.

Il a été hereux de trouver chez le Président Stalin la compréhension de cette nécessité. Il espère de ce fait que malgré les difficultés éprouvées—sera repris et mené à bonne fin le recrutement en URSS des ressortissants polonais appelés au service militaire ainsi que leur évacuation en Proche Orient.

Il espère enfin que le Gouvernement de l'URSS en procédant ainsi et par son respect des droits polonais et son attitude amicale envers les intérêts politiques polonais, facilitera à chaque citoyen polonais valide la participation à la lutte sous l'étandard national en vue d'une victoire commune.

No. 202

Memorandum from Minister Raczyński to Mr. Eden concerning the British-Soviet negotiations on a treaty of alliance[1]

London, April 13, 1942   GSHI, PRM, 67

Referring to the conversation which I had the honour to have with you on April 10th concerning the decision taken by the British Government to enter into negotiations with the Soviet Government on a political agreement dealing with the post-war status of the Continent of Europe—I beg to submit to you the enclosed memorandum expressing the point of view of the Polish Government on the afore-mentioned subject.

Confidential

1. The Polish Government regret that notwithstanding the exchange of views which took place between General Sikorski and Mr. Churchill and also other members of the British Government prior to the General's departure for the United States, and the arguments adduced in the Polish memorandum of March 27th, 1942,[2] the British Government have decided to enter at this early stage into negotiations with the Soviet Government regarding the post-war status of the Continent.

2. The Polish Government consider that pacts and agreements of the nature of the one which is now contemplated by Great Britain and the USSR cannot contribute to the enhancement of the war effort of the United Nations. On the contrary, by desisting from publicly declared principles

---

[1] See Note No. 202.   [2] See doc. No. 196.

of policy they threaten to weaken the determination to fight on, so indispensable in this total war to the forces in the field and also in the countries occupied and oppressed by the enemy.

3. The Polish Government beg to recall once more with the utmost earnestness what they have repeatedly emphasized—and only recently in their memorandum of March 27th—that in addition to her concern for the integrity of the State, Poland has other interests in Eastern Europe which are of fundamental and vital importance to her independent existence. These involve inter alia the future of Bukovina and Lithuania, the latter a country covered by certain stipulations mutually agreed upon between Poland and Great Britain. In the memorandum of March 27th the Polish Government have stated their views on these two questions. They further consider that as these questions are undoubtedly Poland's most immediate concern they cannot be settled without their co-operation and their concurrence.

No. 203

Aide-mémoire from Minister Raczyński to Ambassador Bogomolov concerning Soviet violation of the rights of Polish citizenship and a relief organization for Poles in the USSR

London, April 13, 1942   GSHI, PRM, 72/1

Depuis la visite que le Général W. Sikorski, Premier Ministre de la République de Pologne, avait faite à l'Union des Républiques Socialistes Soviétiques, et depuis la nomination des délégués de l'Ambassade de Pologne qui avaient été institués en vue de l'assistance en faveur des ressortissants polonais, il semblait que la réalisation de l'accord polono-soviétique s'effectuerait sans heurts. En effet, il paraissait que l'accord ne rencontrerait pas d'obstacles susceptibles de ralentir les préparatifs polonais en vue de la lutte commune contre l'Allemagne ou d'empêcher l'amélioration du sort si difficile des ressortissants polonais qui se trouvent sur le territoire de l'Union.

Contrairement à cette attente, les intérêts vitaux de la Pologne en territoire de l'Union des Républiques Socialistes Soviétiques, et plus particulièrement le problème de l'assistance aux ressortissants polonais ainsi que le problème militaire se développent depuis le milieu de mars 1942 d'une façon non satisfaisante.

Bien que les discussions au sujet de la ressortissance n'aient pas abouti à une entente avec le Gouvernement de l'Union, celui-ci oblige les ressortissants polonais à renoncer sur la base de dispositions unilatérales, aux droits et obligations qui découlent de leur caractère de ressortissants polonais, et leur impose des obligations en raison de la nationalité soviétique qu'ils auraient acquise à l'avis des autorités soviétiques.

Il y a lieu de mentionner que les cas de conscription dans l'Armée Rouge de ressortissants polonais de toutes nationalités sont devenues de plus en plus nombreux. Ils se rapportent même à des ressortissants polonais dont la nationalité polonaise est expressément reconnue aux termes de la Note du Commissariat du Peuple des Affaires Etrangères du 1-er décembre 1941.[1]

Malgré les promesses données en ce qui concerne la libération des ressortissants polonais affectés aux bataillons de travail, cette question demeure toujours sans solution.

Il a pu être établi que les autorités administratives enlèvent aux ressortissants polonais les certificats qui leur avaient été octroyés lors de leur libération des camps et des prisons. Le nombre des arrestations, ainsi que des arrêts sévères pour contraventions cependant légères grandit; alors que les représentants des autorités polonaises n'ont pas la possibilité de venir en aide à leurs ressortissants en ce qui regards l'assistance judiciaire.

Dans le domaine de l'assistance sociale, une pression a pu être observée de la part des autorités centrales soviétiques en vue de la limitation des activités des délégués et hommes de confiance de l'Ambassade, bien que leurs compétences aient fait l'objet d'un arrangement préalable avec les autorités de l'Union. En outre, des obstacles se sont faits sentir en ce qui concerne le magasinage et la distribution méthodique des transports venant de l'étranger en vue de cette assistance. Comme exemple l'on peut signaler le cas de la liquidation des dépôts de Novosibirsk, fait—qui a été très durement ressenti dans ce secteur.

Vers la fin du mois de février 1942, l'Ambassade de Pologne a soumis un plan motivé des transferts de personnes, tout en insistant sur les suites véritablement tragiques que comportent les transferts accomplis en absence d'un plan. Ce programme n'a cependant pas été pris en considération; en revanche, tout changement de lieu de domicile a été rendu impossible aux ressortissants polonais dont la situation est quelquefois des plus malheureuses. Ils ont été attachés dans de nombreux cas au lieu de leur dernier séjour par le simple moyen de l'interdiction de la vente à eux de billets ferroviaires. Tous les postes militaires dans les nœuds ferroviaires ont été simultanément supprimés; leur rôle consistait à fournir de la nourriture—acquise par les moyens de l'Ambassade—aux personnes effectuant le voyage.

L'évacuation en Perse d'une partie de la population civile simultanément avec les éléments militaires a été effectuée en fait si brusquement que la sélection des intéressés, par exemple des mères avec leurs enfants, n'a pu être réalisée. Les civils polonais se rendent en grand nombre, de leur propre initiative, à Krasnovodsk avec l'intention de se rendre en Perse, en entraînant ainsi dans le secteur de Krasnovodsk une accumulation humaine privée de toute ressource.

Enfin, il a été établi la tendance de la part des autorités de rendre impossible la continuation de recrutement. C'est ainsi que dans plusieurs 'oblasti' le recrutement de l'Armée Polonaise a été complètement suspendu. Il y a lieu de mentionner en outre que les Commissions de conscription polonaises, instituées en vertu de l'article 6 de l'Arrangement militaire polono-soviétique du 14 août 1941 lequel prévoyait la coopération des autorités

[1] See doc. No. 157.

soviétiques, ont été remplacées entretemps par des organes purement soviétiques, en désaccord avec la stipulation dont il s'agit.[2]

[2] See doc. No. 112.

No. 204

Letter from General Sikorski to Mr. Eden on Soviet territorial claims

London, April 16, 1942   GSHI, PRM, 66

En vous remerciant pour la franchise avec laquelle vous avez bien voulu me fournir hier certains informations sur vos negociations en cours avec l'URSS, je tiens à résumer mon propre point de vue avec la même sincerité. Permettez moi de vous communiquer, en confirmation de l'entretien que nous avons eu tantôt avec vous-même et vos collaborateurs, les considérations que voici:

A aucun moment, que ce soit en URSS même—par la création là-bas d'une armée polonaise—ou ailleurs, je n'ai cessé de fournir des preuves de mon ardent desir de collaborer loyalement avec l'URSS. Je suis toutefois obligé de m'opposer de la façon la plus decidée aux ambitions de la Russie Soviétique qui s'efforce à nouveau de suivre le chemin qu'avait tracé l'impérialisme tsariste et que symbolisait la politique de Pierre le Grand, auquel se refère M. Stalin. C'est à cet impérialisme qui en outre a causé de si grave prejudices à l'Europe et au monde entier que la Pologne devait ses partages. C'est ce même imperialisme qui est au fond des demandes du Gouvernement des Soviets dans les négociations dont il s'agit. L'accord projeté entre le Gouvernement Britannique et l'URSS ne constitue pas hélàs, un acte dirigé contre notre ennemi commun, l'Allemagne, ainsi que cela devrait être le cas en bonne justice, mais plutôt contre les intérêts vitaux de la Pologne, l'alliée de première heure de la Grande Bretagne.

La portée d'une formule generale ayant trait au maintien de nos frontières d'avant le 1-er Septembre 1939, à laquelle vous avez fait allusion, Monsieur le Ministre, ne saurait satisfaire ni nos intérêts, ni vous même, même dans l'hypothèse où M. Stalin entendrait l'accepter.

Je n'ai pas encore connaissance de la teneur de la note que le Gouverne-ment de sa Majesté est en voie de communiquer à notre Ministère des Affaires Étrangères; je demeure néanmoins convaincu que malgré vos observations d'hier, vous serez d'accord avec moi que le point de vue polonais demeure entièrement conforme à l'esprit de l'Accord polono-britannique du 23 Aout 1939.[1]

Je considère l'accord anglo-soviétique projeté, ainsi que je vous l'ai déjà signalé, comme susceptible d'avoir de très graves consequences pour la con-duite ultérieure de la guerre.

S'il est conclu, il équivaudrait en définitive à encercler la Pologne. La propagande ennemie saisirait l'occasion pour l'expliquer à tous les pays interessés que l'URSS a obtenu de la Grande Bretagne une signature

[1] The date of the Treaty should be August 25, 1939.

analogue à celle que le Reich allemand lui avait donné dans l'accord Ribbentrop-Mołotow de 1939. Sacrifier non seulement des intérêts vitaux de la Pologne, mais aussi livrer une partie considerable de l'Europe à la Russie Soviétique dont l'objectif final est de provoquer une révolution mondiale plutôt qu'à mater Allemagne, constitue à mon avis une erreur pouvant engendrer des conséquences incalculables. Tous les pays d'Europe, —allant de Norvège jusqu'au Royaume des Hellènes—défendent un point de vue identique et solidaire, lorsqu'il y va de la sauvegarde de leur indépendence et de leur régime interieur. Et je ne doute pas un instant, que les espoirs placés dans l'URSS pour la voire se substituer en Europe au rôle qui était dévolu naguère à la France, sont des plus illusoires, non seulement pour des raisons d'ordre social, mais aussi géopolitique. Ce rôle devront assumer, à mon avis, les blocs federatifs appelés à tenir en échec l'État allemand, de l'est à l'ouest.

En outre la Fédération future des pays de l'Europe Centrale serait en principe détruite par l'accord. La Russie des Soviets y porterait un coup direct en réclamant pour elle d'une manière aussi artificielle que cynique—la Bukovine, tout comme d'autre part elle réclame la Lithuanie.

L'accord projeté demeure essentiellement contraire aux stipulations que la Pologne a conclu avec l'URSS en 1941. L'accord polono-russe du 30 juillet dernier annulait les conventions passées entre la Russie soviétique et le Reich allemand, au sujet du partage de la Pologne. Il annulait précisément la ligne de démarcation germano-soviétique du 4 octobre 1939, à laquelle l'URSS se refère aujourd'hui comme à sa frontière de 1940 et que le projet d'accord anglo-sovietique confirme.

Il va de soi que la Pologne ne peut prendre aucune part à cette négociation et quelle ne pourra non plus donner son consentement à l'accord lui-même. Mais ainsi que j'ai pu le constater hier avec une douloureuse émotion, ce fait n'est pas susceptible d'exercer une influence sur le cours des négociations, qui se developpent actuellement entre le Gouvernement de sa Majesté et l'URSS.

Il ne m'appartient pas de préjuger de la politique que vont poursuivre à cet égard les États-Unis d'Amérique, bien qu'il est vrai que le Président Roosevelt et son Gouvernement aient entièrement partagé le point de vue et l'attitude de la Pologne à l'endroit des pretentions de l'URSS. Mais je dois exprimer mes craintes fondées sur des observations personelles et des entretiens, que l'accord dont il s'agit risque de renforcer considérablement l'action des isolationistes et de tous les éléments hostiles à la Grande Bretagne et l'URSS, ce qui ne devrait pas rester indifférent à cette dernière Puissance.

Je suis fermement convaincu que l'attitude polonaise, si nettement exprimée au sujet d'un problème si complexe et difficile ne portera aucun ombrage, Mon Cher Ministre, à nos relations personelles, qui sont fondées sur le respect mutuel.

No. 205

Extract from General Sikorski's memorandum to Mr. Churchill on the necessity of forming a second front in Europe and co-ordination of risings in conquered countries with Allied strategy

London, April 13, 1942   GSHI, PRM, 67

I have dwelt on several occasions upon the necessity of establishing a second front against Germany in western Europe.

During my visit to the United States, I was able to ascertain that President Roosevelt, as well as other members of the American administration responsible for the conduct of the war, fully shared my opinion in this respect. I would, therefore, like to revert to this subject and put it before those who are responsible for the general operational leadership in these parts.

I have drawn up a Memorandum relative to this question, which I have the honour to enclose.

Memorandum

There is no doubt that in the nearest future Soviet Russia will have to face a new German offensive. The concentration of the German land forces seems to be drawing to its close. Divisions which had been transferred to western Europe for the winter months of 1941–1942 as well as the newly organized units have either already arrived or are on their way to the eastern front. The Germans will endeavour to crush the Soviet Union by means of operations carried out on a vast scale. It will most probably be their supreme offensive effort, and its result will bear upon the ultimate issue of the world conflict.

The Soviet Government are applying special tactics towards their Allies, whom they maintain in ignorance of their forces and possibilities. It, nevertheless, seems certain that, notwithstanding the great power of resistance of their peoples, the Soviet Government are considering not so much the prospect of a compromise with the Third Reich, as the possibility of a war crisis, if they were left to themselves in complete isolation at the approach of the spring campaign.

Under these circumstances, it would appear correct to anticipate one of the following alternatives with regard to the final issue of the imminent developments on the eastern front:

1. Either Russia will successfully resist the German offensive, and, even in spite of further loss of territory, will occasion the further considerable wastage and exhaustion of the potential of the German armed forces. In this case, no matter how far the Red Armies would be pushed back, the final issue would be evident: Germany would be defeated.

2. Or the German offensive will be sufficiently powerful to threaten the complete destruction of the Soviet Army. In that case, Great Britain with the United States and their co-operating Allies would find themselves in 1943, or perhaps even in the late autumn of 1942, in the face of German forces sufficiently powerful to eliminate any possibility of an allied offensive action on the continent. A similar course of events would completely reverse the

present dislocation of the German armed forces in Europe. The armoured and motorized divisions from the eastern front as well as the major part of the Luftwaffe would take the place of the inferior divisions of the Landsturm, which are at the moment stationed in western Europe, and the second-rate units would be sent to occupy the conquered areas of Russia.

The conclusions are easily drawn and clear.

Should the first alternative arise, it would be necessary to take advantage, even at a great price, of the engagement of the whole German forces on the Russian front and the almost complete exposure in western Europe, in order to obtain a decisive issue by an offensive on the continent and by striking at the heart of Germany.

It would be necessary to commence the immediate realization of the conditions preliminary to this action, which would be started by the attainment of mastery in the air over western Europe and the detailed preparation of a landing.

The second alternative should be avoided at all costs. The defeat of Russia would put in doubt the final issue of the war, or at any rate prolong for many years the armed struggle, which would have to be calculated to exhaust the enemy and leave no possibility to seek an issue by an open battle on the continent. Even in the anticipation of a successful German offensive in the East, the only sure and effective assistance to the Russian effort would be the establishment of a second front. [. . .].

There can be no doubt that independently of the date at which the Allied Forces will be capable of landing on the European continent and regardless of what area is chosen for that purpose, it will be a united and common operation of the land, naval, and air forces.

This operation should be directed by one man in command of the whole armed forces and disposing of one General Staff for the whole of the forces.

Such a Staff should be established without delay, in order to commence the study and preparation of the future, undoubtedly difficult and complex, operations. [. . .].

No. 206

Conversation between General Sikorski and Mr. Harriman in the presence of Dr. Retinger on the attitude of the USA towards Anglo-Soviet negotiations

Washington, April 15, 1942   GSHI, PRM, 71
                                         Transl. from Polish

Harriman began the conversation by saying that he had information from President Roosevelt and from Washington about General Sikorski's visit having been a great success. He knew that the position of the American Government on Russo-British negotiations had been defined, and that they were maintaining a negative attitude towards the impending agreements. The United States adopted a definite position as far as Stalin was concerned, and warned the British Government against nefarious consequences of this agreement. General Sikorski stated that the British Government was carrying out negotiations in secret, and owing to that even the American Government got no full information on that issue. General Sikorski repeated his arguments against the agreement, observing that it was a second Munich only shifted 180 degrees to the left. The signature of this agreement can bring about a split in British public opinion, besides far-reaching consequences which may arise in America and other countries, whether allied or neutral.

Harriman, agreeing with General Sikorski, insisted on his leaving a door open to further negotiations on the part of Poland. He considered that as the American Government were washing their hands of the business, it would be impossible for him to be a go-between, even in a private capacity, in an attempt at a compromise. The Americans were simply 'passing the buck' to the British.

He let General Sikorski understand that Ambassador Winant was among the few Americans who were completely under the spell of Cripps's argument.

The conversation turned then on war strategy, and Harriman asked General Sikorski about his views, and also what he thought of General Marshall; to the last question Gen. Sikorski gave no answer.

Harriman said that two long-range aircraft for flights to Poland would be put at the Poles' disposal within the next weeks. He added that these aircraft had been originally destined for England. The General insisted on getting at least 6 aircraft of this type.

A great part of the conversation was devoted to the question of supplies for Russia. Harriman stated that it was a lie to assert that the Americans delivered only 100,000 tons of grain to Russia instead of the promised 1 million tons; an assertion, by the way, which served—as the General observed—as an argument for Stalin to explain the difficulty in getting food-supplies for Polish divisions over there. Harriman said that the agreement with Russia concerned the delivery of 1 million tons of grain, loco American ports. The transport was to be organized by the Russians, but their shipping arrangements had failed. At present supplies for Russia proceed quite satisfactorily, and Harriman hopes that they will be completed within two months. He complained of the inadequate production of rifles.

No. 207

Telegram from Ambassador Papée to the Ministry for Foreign Affairs on the attitude of the Holy See towards Soviet territorial claims[1]

Vatican City, April 15, 1942 GSHI, A.11. 49/Sow./6
Transl. from Polish

In accordance with the instruction, I informed the Cardinal Secretary of State[2] of our attitude towards Soviet territorial claims. The Cardinal understands our position very well and he sympathizes with us in our action against the annexation of Esthonia, Latvia, Bessarabia, Lithuania and Bukovina by the Soviet Union.

[1] See Note No. 207.
[2] From March 1939 Cardinal Luigi Maglione was Secretary of State.

The Cardinal told me that should the Soviet Union annex Lithuania and Bukovina it would constitute a constant and immediate threat and menace to Poland's safety.

Also my remarks on the undermining of and pernicious influence on neutral countries by the Soviet Union were fully appreciated by the Cardinal.

The Cardinal awaits with great interest information on the results of the voyage of the President of the Council and of yours, Mr. Minister, to the United States.

No. 208

Mr. Eden's reply to the Memorandum from Minister Raczyński of April 13, 1942, concerning the Anglo-Soviet negotiations

London, April 17, 1942   GSHI, PRM, 67

In his note No. 49/Sow./29 of the 27th March, M. Kulski enclosed a strongly confidential memorandum giving the views of the Polish Government on Eastern European problems, with particular reference to the contemplated negotiations for an Anglo-Soviet Treaty.[1] The note which Your Excellency left with me on the 13th April expressly confirmed the contents of this memorandum.[2]

2. These documents have been studied with the greatest care and attention. His Majesty's Government observe that the memorandum gives the reasons for which the Polish Government consider that the negotiations for a political agreement between His Majesty's Government and the Soviet Government at the present juncture are inopportune. The grounds of the Polish Government's criticism are broadly speaking three-fold:

/i/ That the contemplated agreement will be detrimental to the general war policy of the Allies:

/ii/ That it will affect Polish vital interests: and

/iii/ That it will constitute an infringement of the spirit if not of the letter of the Anglo-Polish Agreement of the 25th August, 1939.

3. I wish at the outset to make it clear that the object of the proposed negotiations is not, as stated in your note of the 13th April, the conclusion of a political agreement dealing with the post-war status of the Continent of Europe, but an agreement for Anglo-Soviet collaboration during and after the war, which will take into account on the one hand the desire of the Soviet Government for the security of certain of the Soviet frontiers, and on the other the interests of the United Nations.

4. The first point, namely whether the contemplated agreement is detrimental to the general war policy of the Allies, may well be one on which opinions differ. His Majesty's Government for their part do not share the opinion which the Polish Government have formed. They have naturally taken into full account the interests of all the United Nations in reaching their decision to open negotiations with the Soviet Government, and they would

[1] See doc. No. 196.   [2] See doc. No. 202.

not have embarked on such a course without the firmest conviction of its necessity. Your Excellency will not wish me to enter into an elaborate exposition of the policy of His Majesty's Government, but I can assure you that any agreement which may now be concluded with the Soviet Government will not modify the intention of His Majesty's Government to regard their policy for the post-war settlement in Europe as based upon the principles of the Atlantic Charter, which have already been accepted by the Soviet Government. Secondly, until the war situation is clearer than it is at the present time, His Majesty's Government intend to abide by the principles set out in the Prime Minister's statement of the 5th September, 1940. But His Majesty's Government consider that it is in the general interest of the Allied cause, both for the successful prosecution of the war and also for the elaboration of a satisfactory post-war settlement, that the relationship between the Soviet Union and the Western Powers should be strengthened and placed on a firmer basis of mutual confidence than has existed in the past. This objective cannot be achieved by denying to the Soviet Union a position commensurate with the major part which its victorious armies will inevitably win for it in the period of reconstruction.

5. In the second place, the Polish Government consider that the proposed agreement will affect their vital interests. His Majesty's Government do not presume to assess the vital interests of an ally, but they observe that at the outset of their memorandum of the 27th March, the Polish Government affirm that good neighbourly relations and friendship between Poland and the Soviet Union are the indispensable conditions of a lasting peace. His Majesty's Government welcome this declaration, which applies equally to the relations between the Soviet Union and the United Kingdom. It is the principal object of the negotiations now impending to place Anglo-Soviet relations on a firm basis of confidence, and His Majesty's Government consider that this objective is as much in the interests of Poland as in their own. The policy of His Majesty's Government towards Poland is governed by the Anglo-Polish agreement of the 25th August, 1939. This policy has been confirmed and strengthened by the experiences of the last two and a half years, during which Polish and British forces have fought side by side, on land, on sea, and in the air, and the Polish people have steadfastly refused, in spite of manifold sufferings, to collaborate in any way with the forces of occupation. His Majesty's Government would not therefore be likely to contemplate entering into an agreement with a third party which would injure the interests of so loyal an Ally. The Polish Government will appreciate that any Anglo-Soviet agreement will establish the right of His Majesty's Government to interest themselves generally in the future settlement of Europe, and it could no longer be claimed that any question affecting Polish-Soviet frontiers, for example, is not the concern of His Majesty's Government. In any case His Majesty's Government do not propose to conclude any agreement affecting or compromising the territorial status of the Polish Republic.

6. In this connexion, the Polish memorandum of the 27th March referred to the position of Lithuania and Bukovina in relation to Polish

security. In regard to Lithuania, reference was made in particular to the secret protocol attached to the Anglo-Polish Agreement of the 25th August, 1939, and to the observations contained in Your Excellency's note of the 30th December, 1941. In the latter document Your Excellency quoted Article 2[b] of the Secret Protocol as recognizing implicitly the vital importance of Lithuania to the security of Poland. Your Excellency will, however, recollect that Article 1[a] of the Secret Protocol provided that 'by the expression "European Power" employed in the Agreement is to be understood Germany'. Any implicit recognition by His Majesty's Government of the vital importance of Lithuania to the security of Poland could therefore only apply to the possibility of a threat from Germany, just as the reference in Article 2[b] of the Secret Protocol to the importance of Belgium and the Netherlands to British security could only be held applicable to a case of aggression by Germany. Article 2[b] of the Secret Protocol could therefore only become operative in the event of Poland becoming involved in war with Germany consequent on action by Germany threatening the independence of Lithuania, and it was not in fact suggested that this provision could be invoked by Poland when Lithuania was incorporated into the Soviet Union in 1940.

7. The position is different in regard to Vilna and any other territory within the frontiers of Poland on the 25th August, 1939. The Polish Government have already been assured that His Majesty's Government do not recognize any territorial changes effected in Poland since August, 1939, and it is intended to safeguard this assurance in any agreement which may be concluded with the Soviet Government.

8. As regards Bukovina, the Polish memorandum of the 27th March admits the question of this territory has never been raised in any negotiations between His Majesty's Government and the Polish Government.[3] The memorandum refers however to the British guarantee which Rumania had received at the time of the conclusion of the Anglo-Polish Agreement of the 25th August, 1939. I need not enter into the circumstances in which the Rumanian Government decided to dispense with the guarantee of His Majesty's Government, and eventually to place the full resources of Rumania, including the armed forces of the country, at the disposal of Germany. But His Majesty's Government, who have since declared war on Rumania, cannot regard themselves as in any way bound in regard to future territorial arrangements by an earlier guarantee rejected by the Rumanian Government.

9. His Majesty's Government therefore conclude that their aim in the forthcoming negotiations with the Soviet Government will not conflict in any respect with the obligations which they have assumed to the Republic of Poland. But, as the Polish memorandum suggests, the questions at issue extend beyond the terms of any written document and His Majesty's Government intend to uphold the interests of their Polish Ally, as of their other Allies, to the fullest extent of which they are capable. For this purpose

[3] See doc. No. 196.

they will accept their full share of responsibility for the establishment and maintenance of peace in Europe after the war. But in order to fulfil this task and to prevent the re-emergence of the threat of aggression by German collaboration an agreement with the Soviet Government will be required. It is with the object of placing this collaboration on a firm and enduring footing that His Majesty's Government have undertaken their present negotiations.

No. 209

Note from Minister Raczyński to Mr. Eden concerning Anglo-Soviet negotiations

London, April 21, 1942   GSHI, PRM, 67

I have the honour to acknowledge receipt of your note of the 17th inst., No. C 3438/152/G., in which you were kind enough to inform me of the attitude which His Majesty's Government have taken with regard to the Polish memoranda of March 27th and April 13th concerning the problems of Eastern Europe with particular reference to the contemplated negotiations for an Anglo-Soviet Treaty.

II. The above note deals with the problem from a threefold point of view, dealing with the arguments of the Polish Government to the effect:

1 / that the contemplated agreement will be detrimental to the general war policy of the Allies,

2 / that it will affect vital Polish interests,

3 / that it will constitute an infringement of the spirit if not of the letter of the Anglo-Polish Agreement of August 25th, 1939.

I shall take the liberty to deal with the problem from the same threefold point of view and in reply to state once more briefly the views of the Polish Government with regard to the above points.

III. As far as point 1. is concerned, namely, that the contemplated agreement will be detrimental to the general war policy of the Allies, the Polish Government, in letters from General Sikorski to Mr. Churchill dated March 20th and April 13th, 1942, and in his letters to you of March 8th and April 16th, 1942, and finally in the Memoranda of March 27th and April 13th, 1942, gave expression to their views on the intended settlement, in a bilateral Anglo-Soviet agreement to be concluded in the immediate future in the midst of the war, of a number of territorial questions in Eastern Europe. The Polish Government maintain all their reservations expressed in these documents and based in the first instance on fundamental premises of a moral nature, which are of paramount importance to all the united nations and which were confirmed only recently to representatives of the Polish Government by the responsible leaders of American policy.

The Polish Government do not advance the opinion that the Soviet Union, whose armies have so gallantly opposed the German onslaught in defence of their own territory, should be denied the position of a great power. They consider, however, that the principle of the Atlantic Charter cannot be reconciled with sacrificing weaker nations and states to the interests of a powerful neighbour.

IV. As far as the Polish Government are aware the proposed agreement, though it is being made during a war waged primarily against Germany, does not include any territorial provisions detrimental to the interests of the principal enemy. On the contrary, it may strike German observers as following roughly the line agreed upon in the Molotov-Ribbentrop Agreement of 1939 for the delimitation of the respective spheres of influence of Russia and Germany. It may therefore be said that the projected Anglo-Soviet agreement might, contrary to the spirit of the agreement, become one of the bases on which Germany and Russia may tend to coalesce in future.

The territorial provisions of the projected agreement in no way commit the Soviet Government in relation to Germany, considering that the expansion of Soviet possessions is to be effected not at the expense of Germany but at that of third parties. Being able to prove that in their agreement with Great Britain they have not in any way prejudiced Germany's interests, the Soviet Government would retain a valuable trump card in relation to any, even the present German Government, a fact which would become apparent to all the interested parties as soon as the agreement has become public. Consequently, the agreement should in any case include clauses plainly directed against Germany to which the Soviet Government together with the British Government would contractually subscribe.

V. Point 2. deals with the question of vital Polish interests. The Polish Government, who, on their part consistently aim at the establishment of friendly relations with Soviet Russia, appreciate the reasons which induced Great Britain to seek to consolidate her relations with the Soviet Union by means of a political agreement extending also to the post-war period. Nevertheless the Polish Government fail to perceive any compelling reasons why the agreement should include stipulations, which cannot but weaken the present solidarity existing between the oppressed nations of Europe and the Allies, and which, moreover, directly harm the vital interests of an earlier Ally. The Polish Government have fully explained, in the documents mentioned above and by means of personal conversations, the importance which they attach to the maintenance of the independence of Lithuania and the retention of Bukovina within the area of Central Europe, to which it properly belongs for both historical and geographical reasons. The fulfilment of these two conditions is necessary in order to ensure the independent existence and development of a confederative system in this area, the importance of which for the future of Europe the British Government no doubt recognize.

The Polish Government are grateful to His Majesty's Government for their cordial reference to Poland and her loyalty as an Ally. On their part the Polish Government never had any doubts that the bonds of loyal friendship between Poland and Great Britain, drawn closer on battlefields, will survive all trials and prove their value also in the future settlement of Europe. The Polish Government are glad to receive the friendly assurances of His Majesty's Government in this respect. In their opinion, however, the right of the

United Kingdom to take an active part in this settlement does not require the particular approval on the part of Soviet Russia.

VI. The Polish Government regret that they are unable to agree to the interpretation of the Secret Protocol to the Polish-British Agreement of August 25th, 1939, as set out in paragraph 6. of your note. Article 2, par. 2, of the Agreement covers two distinct conceptions, namely:

1 / A mutual recognition that the independence and neutrality of certain states represents a vital interest for the security of the other party, and 2/a mutual guarantee of armed assistance in the event of aggression by a third European state against the independence and neutrality of these states. The Polish Government agree that by par. 1 of the Secret Protocol the mutual guarantee had become applicable only to Germany. On the other hand the mutual recognition of the vital interests of the other party in the maintenance of the independence of certain states (i.e. Holland, Belgium, and Lithuania) had not been limited in this way, for, on the contrary, par. 1b of the said Secret Protocol clearly states that in the event of an action provided against by Art. 2 of the Agreement and undertaken by other European states than Germany, the two parties are under obligation to consult together on the measures which were to be undertaken in common. It must be concluded therefrom that in the event of a threat to the independence of Lithuania, say, by Soviet Russia, Great Britain is under obligation to Poland to consult with her as to the measures to be undertaken in common. Another conclusion which arises even more clearly is that in such an event, too, Great Britain recognizes that Poland has a vital interest in the maintenance of the independence of Lithuania. The difference in the case of aggression against Lithuania on the part of the Soviet Union consists therein that in such a case Great Britain is under no obligation to give immediate assistance to Poland if the latter would consider it right to take up arms in defence of the independence of Lithuania. Nevertheless, considering that consultation has been provided for in the Secret Protocol for such an emergency, the recognition on the part of Great Britain of the termination by Soviet Russia of the independence of Lithuania, i.e. of a complete cancellation of a vital interest of Poland, could hardly be considered as conformant with the Protocol.

The Polish Government hope that the British Government will recognize the correctness of their interpretation of point 2b of the Secret Protocol in the light of the stipulations of point 1b, to which the British note makes no reference.

The Polish Government take note of the declaration of His Majesty's Government that the state of war between Great Britain and Rumania invalidated the guarantee given to that country by Great Britain. This, however, does not change the fact that the maintenance of the sovereignty of Rumania over Bukovina is of paramount importance to Poland, because in the contrary case the formation of a Central European Confederation with the participation of Hungary and Rumania would become insuperably more difficult.

VII. The Polish Government take note of the renewed confirmation of the guarantee of the British Government that 'in any case His Majesty's Government do not propose to conclude any agreement affecting or compromising the territorial status of the Polish Republic'. In particular the Polish Government note the assurance of His Majesty's Government that the British Government do not recognize any territorial changes effected in Poland since August 1939 and that this assurance refers as much to Wilno as to any other territory, which, on August 25th, 1939, was situated within the frontiers of Poland. As it is His Majesty's Government's intention 'to safeguard this assurance in any agreement which may be concluded with the Soviet Government', the Polish Government confidently expect that His Majesty's Government will be able to carry it out in a way effectively preventing any possibility of misunderstanding on this score.

VIII. The Polish Government are not a participant of the contemplated agreement, they were not informed of the proposal made by the two negotiating parties and they do not know the agreed basis of the understanding. The attitude of the Polish Government regarding the purport of the Agreement, as far as it is known to them, is one of principle. They believe that such an attitude accords with the general interests of the Allies. They are animated by the desire that the moral strength and the fighting spirit of the Allies should not in any way be impaired, especially on the eve of the Spring campaign.

As the agreement is of fundamental importance to Polish interests its conclusion will find the strongest echo among the Polish community in Poland as also among the Poles in foreign countries. Polish opinion will expect an authoritative interpretation of the contents and of the significance of the agreement, and it will not be possible for the Polish Government to refuse to satisfy this expectation of the nation.

No. 210

Reply of Mr. Eden to the letter from General Sikorski of April 16, 1942, on the subject of Anglo-Soviet negotiations

London, April 21, 1942   GSHI, PRM, 66

I wish to thank you for your letter of the 16th April and for the frankness with which you have expressed the views of the Polish Government in regard to the negotiations for a political agreement between His Majesty's Government and the Soviet Government.

You will now have seen my note of the 17th April to Count Raczyński, setting out the attitude of His Majesty's Government. As I suggested in that note, opinions may well differ on the question whether the contemplated agreement is detrimental or not to the general war policy of the Allies. I understand your own point of view and realize the difficulties of the Polish Government and I hope that you will have an equal understanding for our own problems.

The second paragraph on page 4 of your letter suggests that there is a misconception which will, I hope, now have been removed by my note of the

17th April to Count Raczyński. It is of course the case that the Polish-Soviet Agreement of the 30th July last recognized the Soviet-German Treaties of 1939, relating to the territorial changes in Poland, as having lost their validity. There cannot therefore be any question in the contemplated Anglo-Soviet Agreement of confirming the Soviet-German demarcation line of 1940 so far as this resulted from the Soviet-German Agreement of 1939 in regard to Poland. On the contrary, as I stated to Count Raczyński, His Majesty's Government do not propose to conclude any agreement affecting or compromising the territorial status of the Polish Republic, and it is their intention, in any agreement which may be concluded, to safeguard the assurance given to you on the occasion of the Polish-Soviet Agreement last July.

May I in conclusion assure you that His Majesty's Government have given full weight to the arguments you have put forward. I personally have much appreciated the frank and friendly manner in which our conversations have been conducted, and your kind reference to our personal relations which I warmly reciprocate. As you know, it is my intention to keep you informed of the progress of our negotiations with the Soviet Government and I hope that the course of these consultations will help to convince you that we have fully in mind the position of Poland which has made and continues to make so whole-hearted a contribution to the Allied war effort.

No. 211

Record made by Minister Raczyński of a conversation between General Sikorski, Mr. Churchill and Sir Stafford Cripps, held at Chequers in the presence of Mr. Casey,[1] Mr. Duncan Sandys,[2] Minister Raczyński and Dr. Retinger, on the subjects of the Anglo-Soviet Agreement and Soviet Western frontiers

London, April 26, 1942   GSHI, PRM, 68
                                                                          Transl. from Polish

The conversations started at lunch in a wider circle, and were continued in the garden among the group listed above; some of them were held between two persons or more.

Mr. Churchill, passing to the central problem, spoke in a most resolute tone: 'In spite of the opposition in Great Britain on the part of Parliament, the Anglican clergy, not to mention the Catholics, the conservative circles, etc., and in spite of the objections raised by the United States Government, a political treaty with Russia will be concluded. It is not an ideal one. It might cause some deception; nevertheless, this attempt has to be made.' A long, at times highly controversial, discussion followed, which it would be impossible to reproduce in its proper order. The English arguments were: a/ the necessity to create confidence which we failed to win in 1939, before the outbreak of the World War, b/ the present war is the continuation of the preceding world war which Russia had entered with a territory whose return

---

[1] Recently appointed Minister of State (Middle East).
[2] Financial Secretary to the War Office.

336

she is now claiming only partly (that is leaving aside Poland),[3] c/ by granting to Russia the possession of the Baltic and Rumanian territories, Great Britain will win Russia's co-operation in European affairs, and especially the Polish ones, d/ England besides Russia bears the heaviest burden among the Allies, she must adjust her aims to her strength which is limited, she cannot claim the optimum state of things and must be satisfied with what is within her power. There arises, therefore, the necessity of accepting terms which represent the lesser evil—even if this has to be done with a heavy heart. The above-mentioned arguments were developed by Mr. Churchill. Sir Stafford Cripps accentuated them and attempted to supply their motivation. The last argument characterizing the agreement as 'necessary' but, nevertheless, 'evil', was put forward by Mr. Churchill individually. He stated that he had pondered over the negative sides of the agreement and that he deplored them, having, by the way, no deep confidence in Soviet loyalty. He then added that the end of the war was still far away, and that many things might happen meanwhile which, though unforseeable now, could change the course of events. At the same time he raised the following points:

1) During the last war he was alone in helping Sir Edward Grey, and he contributed greatly to the conclusion of the London Treaty, aiming at winning Italy for the Allied camp. That agreement did not enter into force because Italy suffered heavy losses in the war, and had to be saved by England and France. It changed the respective positions of the Allies at that time.

2) The agreement will contain provisions for safeguarding Polish interests, and will ensure Poland, if not complete territorial integrity, in any case her intangibility as a strong and independent State (the Prime Minister Mr. Churchill used the expression 'as a great power, strong and independent', several times.) Sir Stafford Cripps, for his part, emphasized the fact that he considered Poland a most important factor in the stabilization of relations on the European continent.

3) Should Russia, in the course of debates on the Peace Treaty, violate the obligations laid down in the agreement which is now being negotiated, the whole agreement would lose its binding force. Mr. Churchill added that not every treaty which has been signed enters into force. He emphasized, more-over, that he considered the Polish position after the war so important that he would stand at Poland's side with his whole authority, even if it were to bring about his resignation from the post held by him at present.

4) Poland will not be set aside as an ally by Great Britain, she cannot, however, pretend that all her claims should be satisfied or that she should play a role beyond that due to her or above the forces at her disposal. Sir Stafford Cripps supported this argument by saying that there were six claimants to each territory in Europe. 'Why six?'—interrupted General Sikorski—'Usually there are only two, one of them being more often than not German.'

[3] The Soviet claim to Bukovina does not warrant this assertion because Bukovina has never belonged to Russia.

Discussion.

A highly controversial discussion ensued, in the course of which the English partners confirmed that the Russian claims extended to all Baltic States, Bessarabia, and Bukovina, while Cripps stated that the Russians did not wish to go beyond it. In particular those claims did not concern Finland (except for Petsamo 'on account of nickel'), Norway and the Straits. In the heat of the discussion Cripps, who had avoided mentioning the problem of Lithuania, raised doubts as to the justification of Poland's interest in Lithuania. When I interrupted by reminding him of the 400 years of the (Polish-Lithuanian) Union, Cripps retorted that he was speaking about recent years only. I then reminded him of the Agreement of Mutual Assistance (between the United Kingdom and Poland) of August 25th, 1939, in view of which Cripps passed on to arguments based on the mutual balance of forces, which were identical with those put forward by the Foreign Office lawyers.

General Sikorski outlined in strong and grave words the reaction in Europe (from France to Poland). In view of these concessions to Soviet imperialism he mentioned the sacrifice of (our) whole nation, of the army, navy, and air-force, as well as of the people in the home-country. He characterized the difficulties of coexistence with a partner as unreliable as Soviet Russia, whatever the loyalty of the other nation might be. He referred, in particular, to our experience with the Polish Army in Russia, to continuous outbreaks of fresh crises, to which, for our part, we had alluded as little as possible, trying to find satisfactory solutions in the interest of our citizens and of the Polish Army formed in Soviet Russia.

From the point of view of Allied political strategy, the Polish party questioned the purpose of making such costly concessions to Russia, both on moral and political grounds, as it would not add a single soldier to the Allied forces. On the contrary, it would be most harmful to the common war effort. General Sikorski asked point-blank whether Soviet Russia was to repay Great Britain by some reciprocal concessions. Sir Stafford Cripps denied it and declared in particular that the Soviet Government did not raise any claim as regards Persia.

We, the Polish party, pointed out that the territorial concessions made to Soviet Russia would not only fail to safeguard Great Britain against any attempt in the future on the part of Russia to elude the struggle with Germany until the final stage of the war, but they would, on the contrary, strengthen Soviet bargaining power, should a peace by mutual compromise be concluded.

As far as the English side was concerned the whole burden of the discussion was shared by Mr. Churchill and Sir Stafford Cripps, while Mr. Casey and Mr. Sandys listened without intervening. Mr. Churchill seemed to argue without inner conviction, and to state the English arguments with some mental reservations. Several times he confessed that he did not like the whole matter, that it was a violation of the Atlantic Charter, and that he was by no means sure that Soviet loyalty would not eventually fail. On the other hand he stubbornly insisted that England had no choice, that he could not cope with everything nor defend all the rights. Moreover, he returned to the possibility of new circumstances which might change the sense of the agreement at the time of post-war peace arrangements, as it had happened in the past. On taking leave of General Sikorski, Mr. Churchill accompanied him to the hall, and asked him not to judge his attitude towards Poland by the words used by him in the course of the discussion.

Sir Stafford, on the other hand, argued with profound conviction. He repeated the well-known English arguments without showing any scepticism. He emphasized the necessity of avoiding the mistakes committed in 1939, when, in his view, by sacrificing the Baltic States (or as he put it 'Baltic Provinces') it would have been possible to win Stalin as a belligerent on the Allied side. A part of this discussion took place between him and me only. He put forward as an example of Stalin's good faith, the interruption of the campaign against Finland at a time when a complete victory was practically certain. I answered that this example confirmed only the opinion of Stalin's sagacity, as he stopped war against Finland not because he was moderate but out of fear of embroiling himself in a quarrel with England and France, and of facilitating in this way an agreement between 'the Capitalist States against the Soviet Fatherland' which had for a long time, since Lenin, been a source of deep anxiety for Russia. In the course of the general discussion Cripps uttered a vague warning against the action of 'some people close to General Sikorski' directed against the Agreement, an action calculated to infuriate Soviet Russia and to bring about unfortunate consequences for us. In a talk between Cripps and myself the former let me understand that he had in mind an action in the House of Commons circles, aiming at setting the opinion of the House against the Agreement.

In his reply General Sikorski pointed to his constant and consistent attitude towards our Eastern neighbour. While defending essential and basic Polish interests, he showed readiness for friendly and loyal co-operation, above all, in conducting a common struggle against the principal enemy, Germany. He did not engage in an anti-Russian campaign in England nor in America, where he stressed the necessity of far-reaching assistance to the Russian fighting forces. If the American attitude towards Russian claims is negative, it is based on general principles which found their expression in the Atlantic Charter.

Mr. Churchill acknowledged this statement. He expressed the view that he would not consider it inappropriate should Poland make a protest against the provisions of the Anglo-Soviet Agreement and thus safeguard her interests until the moment of the final peace negotiations. General Sikorski reminded Cripps of a conversation with him in the past on the problem of Lithuania. Cripps admitted that if he could freely decide on where Lithuania and Bukovina should belong, he would include both countries in the Central European Federation, adding that he did not favour placing the Lithuanian problem on the agenda of the present Anglo-Soviet negotiations.

In the course of the discussion both Mr. Churchill and Cripps took a favourable attitude towards the plans for a Central European Federation. This led to a discussion on Czech problems.

Mr. Churchill asked whether the frontier problem dividing both countries and 'provoked by the action waged against the Czechs at the period of Munich' had already been settled. He then remarked that Mr. Beneš was 'on very good terms with Russia' and that 'an anti-Russian move on our part might estrange the Czechs'. The Polish party gave an explanation of the problem of Cieszyn (Tesin). As regards the close relations of the Czechs with Russia, we then stated that at the beginning of the Polish-Czech conversations the Czechoslovak Government had declared their 'désinteressement' in the question of Polish-Russian frontiers (we did the same as regards Czech-Hungarian frontiers). It is necessary that the Czechs should avoid repeating the mistake committed 25 years ago and that they should take more account of the neighbour with whom they have a common frontier by Divine Providence than of Russia who impresses them by her size but who has never been, and never will be, their neighbour.

In a talk after lunch General Sikorski reminded Mr. Churchill of a memorandum sent to him not long ago which dealt in part one with the setting up of a common Allied Command, and in part two with a common Staff and a diversionist action in Europe. Mr. Churchill stated that he was interested in part two, but would leave final conclusions with the British General Staff. As regards part one he shielded himself behind the difficulty arising from the participation of 26 States in the United Nations. In his reply General Sikorski underlined the difference between token allies and actual fighting ones.

Mr. Churchill loudly declared his unshakable decision to decline any proposal for a peace by compromise. In the field of strategy Great Britain would limit herself in the current year to air-force action, but on an ever-increasing scale (without any attempt at invasion).

Speaking of India Cripps described the position as improved thanks to his mission. India, he said, would defend herself 'provided there were arms available—even rifles will do for such big masses'.

In a conversation between Mr. Churchill and General Sikorski, the former declared his friendship for Poland several times. Sir Stafford Cripps, too, stated that he reckoned on the maintenance of the closest possible and most sincere personal relations with General Sikorski.

No. 212

Extract from a note of Commissar Molotov to all diplomatic missions in Moscow on the German atrocities in the USSR

Moscow, April 27, 1942   GSHI, A.11. 49/Sow./3

On behalf of the Government of the Union of Soviet Socialist Republics I have the honour to bring the following to your attention:

The Soviet Government is constantly receiving new data and communications testifying that the Hitlerite invaders are carrying on widespread looting and outright extermination of the Soviet population, without hesitating at any crime, at any atrocity or act of violence, throughout the territories which they had temporarily occupied or which they still continue to occupy. The Soviet Government has already made it known that these atrocities are not occasional excesses committed by individual undisciplined military units or by individual German officers and soldiers. At the present time the Soviet Government is in possession of documents recently seized in the headquarters of shattered German units, and these documents prove that the bloody crimes and bestial outrages perpetrated by the German fascist army are committed in accordance with a carefully prepared plan, worked out in every detail by the German Government and in accordance with orders issued by the German High Command. These plans and orders of the German imperialist invaders provide for the wholesale looting of the urban and rural population of our country, for the seizure and exportation to Germany of personal properties belonging to Soviet citizens, as well as properties belonging to the Soviet State; the complete destruction of cities and villages from which the Hitlerites are compelled to retreat under the blows of the armed forces of the Soviet Union; the seizure of lands turned over by the Soviet Government for the perpetual and free use of the collective farms, and the settling upon such seized lands of German 'administrators' and German landlords. They provide for serfdom, slave labour and bondage for our workers and farmers under the domination of the German imperialist invaders; the forcible abduction into Germany for forced labour of several millions of Soviet citizens, from the city and countryside, and their unlawful inclusion in the category of 'prisoners of war'; the liquidation of Russian national culture as well as the national cultures of the peoples of the Soviet Union, with the forcible Germanization of Russians, Ukrainians, Byelorussians, Lithuanians, Latvians, Estonians and other peoples of the USSR; the extermination of the Soviet population, prisoners of war and guerillas through bloody violence, tortures, executions and mass killings of Soviet citizens, regardless of their nationality, social status, sex or age. These are the murderous plans with which the German fascist hordes broke into our country. These predatory Hitlerite plans found their expression in innumerable orders issued by the German military command. The actions of the Red Army, which in fierce battles, step by step, is liberating our cities, villages, districts and regions, have disclosed a truly indescribable picture of how the German fascist army is carrying out the above-mentioned criminal plans of Hitler, Goering and the other rulers who managed to climb to power in present-day Germany, with methodical precision and unheard-of cruelty.

With this note the Soviet Government brings to the attention of all nations new documents and data out of the voluminous material at its disposal, which not only substantiate the planned nature of the atrocities described in the notes of the Government of the USSR of November 25, 1941, and January 6, 1942, but which also prove that the Hitlerite rulers and their accomplices have reached the limit of cruelty and moral degeneration in their criminal and bloody attack upon the liberty, welfare, culture and the very life of the Soviet peoples. [. . .].

[. . .] According to incomplete reports, in three Byelorussian cities alone, the German occupants executed over 28,000 peaceful inhabitants: 6,000 in Vitebsk, 10,000 in Pińsk and over 12,000 in Mińsk. Hundreds of thousands of Ukrainians, Russians, Jews, Moldavians and peaceful citizens of other nationalities perished at the hands of German hangmen in Ukrainian cities. In the city of Kharkov alone, the Hitlerites executed 14,000 persons during the first days of the occupation. [. . .].

The memorandum submitted by the Government of the Polish Republic to the Soviet Ambassador in London, on February 13, 1942, concerning the plight of Soviet prisoners on Polish territory and in a number of occupied Soviet regions, adds innumerable data to our own information of the inhuman treatment given to Soviet prisoners by the German authorities. The Polish memorandum rightly states that 'the treatment of Soviet prisoners probably constitutes the most odious page of German barbarism'. [. . .].

No. 213

Decision of the Polish Government to leave a part of the Polish forces on the territory of the USSR[1]

London, April 30, 1942   GSHI, PRM-K, 105
                                 Transl. from Polish: Pol.-Sov.R., No. 44

The Polish Cabinet expresses its approval of the fact that a number of Polish soldiers have been evacuated from the USSR in accordance with the Agreement of December 1941, and hopes that the Soviet Government will place no difficulties in the way of the further recruiting and evacuation of soldiers and volunteers for the Polish Forces, thus enabling the Polish Army fighting for the common cause of the Allies to increase its strength.

The Polish Cabinet reaffirms that it would be in accordance with Polish interests and with the policy that found expression in the Agreement concluded with the Soviet Government on July 30, 1941, to leave on Soviet territory part of the Polish Armed Forces which would subsequently fight on the Eastern front side by side with the Soviet Army.

[1] See Note No. 213.

No. 214

Aide-mémoire from Minister Raczyński to Ambassador Bogomolov concerning the conscription of Poles in the USSR for the Polish Army

London, May 1, 1942   GSHI, A.11. 49/Sow./2

Au cours des entretiens qui ont eu lieu en décembre dernier entre le Commandant en Chef des Forces Armées Polonaises, le Général Sikorski avec le Président Staline, il a été confirmé la création d'une armée polonaise, qui serait composée de prisonniers de guerre ainsi que de conscrits et volontaires parmi les habitants qui ont été amenés du territoire de la République de Pologne en territoire de l'Union des Républiques Socialistes Soviétiques.

A cet égard, le chiffre de 96,000 avait été fixé avec l'éventualité de l'élever à un plafond plus haut si le réservoir d'hommes s'avérait en fait plus grand.

En même temps il a été établi que tous les marins et aviateurs ainsi que 25,000 militaires de la territoriale seraient évacués en Proche-Orient.

Par la suite, dans une conversation qu'eut lieu entre le Président Staline et le Général Anders le contingent polonais destiné à demeurer sur le territoire de l'URSS avait été fixé, étant données les difficultés d'approvisionnement, au chiffre de 44,000; il fut décidé en outre que tout le surplus ainsi que les recrues et volontaires qui afflueraient, seraient évacués vers le Proche-Orient; la conscription normale devait être continuée.

Comme suite à cet arrangement, environ 30,000 militaires polonais ont déja quitté le territoire de l'Union, à destination de l'Iran. Selon les informations reçues par le Gouvernement polonais depuis le départ de l'URSS du Général Anders, le problème du recrutement polonais s'est en fait heurté, contrairement aux décisions de Moscou, à des difficultés sérieuses qui ont pratiquement empêché sa continuation, et par la suite l'évacuation ultérieure des militaires dont il s'agit.

En revanche, il y a de nombreux cas d'incorporation de ressortissants polonais dans les 'stroi-bataillons' au lieu des centres polonais.

Aux stations-nœuds ferroviaires tous les postes d'approvisionnement et d'enregistrement militaires polonais ont été liquidés par les autorités de l'Union.

Comme suite à l'ordre des autorités de maintenir sur place toutes les personnes, pour des raisons de transport, l'afflux ultérieur vers les centres militaires polonais a été rendu impossible aux conscrits ainsi qu'aux volontaires.

Enfin, dans de nombreux cas, des ressortissants polonais ont été obligés de remettre les certificats qu'ils avaient reçus après leur libération des prisons ou des camps de travail; toutes sortes de difficultés avec les autorités locales en sont la conséquence; ils ne peuvent obtenir du travail et la faim les menace.

Le Gouvernement polonais a l'honneur de souligner qu'à son avis dans la lutte commune de la Pologne et de l'Union des Républiques Socialistes Soviétiques contre le Reich allemand, l'intérêt de deux parties réclame que tous les militaires polonais capables de porter les armes, puissent se trouver dans les rangs polonais là où ils peuvent être équipés et armés sans perte de temps.

Le Gouvernement polonais a l'honneur d'insister sur le caractère urgent de ce problème. En conséquence il prie le Gouvernement de l'Union des Républiques Socialistes Soviétiques de bien vouloir prendre en considération avec bienveillance la situation décrite ci-dessus, en facilitant l'exécution des mesures qui avaient été prévues dans les conversations de Moscou:

a/ en ce qui concerne le complément de recrutement et l'afflux de volontaires, et

b/ en ce qui concerne l'évacuation du surplus de contingent vers le Proche-Orient.

No. 215

General Sikorski's instructions to Lt.-General Anders on the plans for the use of the forces under his command in the general political and military situation

London, May 1, 1942 GSHI, KGA, 7-f
Transl. from Polish

The full understanding of each other's point of view as a prerequisite of mutual confidence is of paramount importance in the relations between a superior and his subordinate. The higher the responsibility of a commander, the more important this factor of mutual comprehension and confidence becomes, and a dry, soldierly order ceases to satisfy. This principle is particularly valid in our present, difficult circumstances.

Since your arrival in London, my General, I have had the opportunity of stating, in the course of a staff conference, that there exist some differences of view on the situation, as well as on the organization and use of the Polish armed forces.

I strongly desire that you should grasp my intentions regarding the Polish armed forces, and because of that I am briefly summing-up my views in writing, to enable you to see my opinions on the general military situation and the plans for the organization, disposition and use of the Polish armed forces, arising from it.

There are three factors on the Allied side which will be decisive for the final outcome of the war. They are:

1. Soviet armed forces.
2. Allied armed forces (in particular those of Great Britain and the United States, and, at their side, a portion of the Polish armed forces).
3. The subjugated countries of Europe.

Ad 1.

Heretofore, in the past stages of the war against the Axis Powers, the biggest role has been, undoubtedly, played by Soviet Russia. In 1941, in spite of enormous losses of men and material, she succeeded in wearing down, to a great extent, the war potential of the Third Reich and, facing $\frac{3}{4}$ of all the German armed forces, in bringing their offensive to a standstill and in imposing on the Germans a winter offensive which was very risky for them. How big were the losses suffered by the Germans is best shown in Hitler's last speech, a speech about which one may say that it is almost defeatist. I was already at that time among the very few who appreciated the possibilities of the Soviet war effort at their true worth. I even stated my opinion in public.

At present Soviet Russia is on the eve of a new German offensive, which may start any moment, although there are many indications that the Germans have different designs. This offensive may take one of the two following courses:

a) Russia will successfully withstand the German onset and, although she may have to surrender considerable portions of her territory, she will stop the German progress eastwards.

It will make no difference wherever this takes place: in the Volga's foreground, on the Volga itself or somewhere further to the east, inside Russia.

Should this occur, jointly with a great weakening of the Russian war potential, that of Germany will also be worn away, perhaps not in a lesser degree than that of Russia. In the event of the battle being on a very big scale it would absorb huge forces, to which strict rules in their husbanding are to be applied.

It would be the last offensive drive on a big scale on the part of Germany, and its collapse would mean a definite Allied victory.

b) Russia is beaten in 1942.

In this case, too, as one can judge from the battle on the Eastern front in 1941, victory would be neither easy nor cheap. German victory in the East could be achieved only at the high cost of an enormous expenditure of German armed forces.

Should this happen, about the end of 1942 or at the beginning of 1943 the centre of gravity of the war would be displaced to the West, and it might happen that the Germans would simultaneously carry out offensive operations in the Middle East.

Such a course of events would mean a long war.

Ad 2.

As you know, General, the armed forces of Great Britain and the United States, owing to the errors committed by the Western democracies within the last twenty years, are not yet quite ready to launch a successful offensive on the European continent. It is, therefore, quite probable that, during the fiercest struggle, Russia may be quite isolated on the land. The contingency is not to be excluded that Germany may be absorbed by the battle in the East to such an extent that the Allied forces in the West, although not fully prepared, may be able to land on the European continent, either to save Russia or to avail themselves of her resolute resistance. President Roosevelt enabled me to foresee such a contingency when he submitted to me his plans of operations which we jointly discussed during my stay in Washington. These plans are fully agreed to by the whole Cabinet and American war leaders. We cannot, therefore, take them lightly.

A successful Allied offensive on the continent would be a finishing stroke for the Reich. In any case, in 1943 the Allied war potential will be so big that such offensive operations on the continent will be within Allied reach.

At the same time I inform you, confidentially, that I obtained an agreement to the assignment of Polish officers, graduated from the Staff College, to a centre where this extremely important matter could be studied.

Ad 3.

The problem of the occupied States in Europe has been heretofore rather underestimated. This factor is, nevertheless, of very great importance, and it may play, in the final stage of the war, a role beyond expectation, provided it is properly used.

Among those States Poland holds the foremost position, and this is well understood by the English and the Americans. Her geographical position, just in the rear of the military operations against Russia, her well built up organization of the Underground Home Army and her will to fight assign to Poland the first place among the subjugated nations.

I inform you, General, that in this field also a definite turn for the better can be noted. We now dispose of means requisite for the home country, the major part of which (so far as this year's budget is concerned) have already reached Poland. A special body will be shortly set up which is to make a serious study of this problem. Other subjugated countries, organized for this purpose for the final stage of the war, will also be represented there but the Polish Government will have a decisive voice in all matters regarding the European continent.

Against this general political and military background I wish now to review my intentions regarding the organization and disposition of the Polish armed forces.

Our war effort, carried on unceasingly and with increasing intensity, has but one aim: Poland, Poland only, a Poland which might be sounder, safer and stronger than the Poland who so resolutely started to fight against the barbarian aggression of our secular enemy. The inheritance left to us after the 1939 campaign, in which we suffered such a shameful defeat, was heavily encumbered. The position regained by us broke down again after France's collapse. Our present position is infinitely better. However, let us not forget at what cost it has been achieved, by Polish blood, suffering and labour.

Which is the shortest way to Poland? From Russia, the Middle East or Great Britain? Nobody can answer this now. However, what matters most is that at least a portion of the Polish armed forces, staying outside Poland, should reinforce the Home Army with modern weapons, in order that the latter may become a centre of order and authority and enable us, in the most efficient way, to take hold of East Prussia, Gdańsk and the German part of Upper Silesia, removing the Germans from those provinces. In this decisive historical moment only accomplished facts will count.

The Polish armed forces must be posted on the existing and future war fronts in such a way that they would be able, in any case, to reach Poland within the shortest possible time. We do not refuse to allow the participation of Polish armed forces in the war. On the contrary. Heretofore, the Polish soldiers have fought on all war fronts. However, I have neither the right nor the intention to risk a concentration of the whole or a major part of the Polish armed forces on one theatre of war, where a possible misfortune could bring about their excessive, if not complete, destruction.

346

Following this line of Policy, I decided to apportion the forces of more or less equal strength between Great Britain, Russia and the Middle East. These decisions have been approved by the Council of Ministers on 30.4.1942.

In Great Britain, where the position is the most favourable from the point of view of military supplies, an armoured-motorized army corps will be gradually built up, consisting of one armoured division and one motorized division, and perhaps, in future, of two armoured divisions and one Parachute Brigade as an advance guard to Poland.

In the Middle East one army corps will be formed consisting of two or three divisions with supporting troops.

In Russia there will be an army corps, or as Stalin calls it, an army, for the time being consisting of three divisions.

The Air Force, apart from army co-operation squadrons, will remain in Great Britain where the conditions for its expansion are the most favourable.

The Navy, and partly also the mercantile marine, will be expanded consistently and according to plan, depending on further arrivals of serviceable men.

We are looking for recruits everywhere. They can be found in Russia, in particular. Whether they will be used most profitably to win the war, waged in common, will depend on the good will of the Soviet Government, whom we have approached by a Note, known to you.

The merging of the Second Army Corps (Middle East) and the Polish Army in Russia under one commander is impracticable in the present circumstances. Apart from the many kilometres of distance separating these two groups, I have to draw your attention, General, to well known difficulties which we constantly meet in Russia in establishing a liaison between them. The union is impossible for this reason also that the Second Army Corps depends from the operational point of view on the British Commander of Middle East Forces, while the Polish troops in Russia, both in the stage of organization and in the event of their being used on the front, depend in the same respect on a Russian commander. A joint command would be, in these circumstances, but a sham.

It may be that in future the union of these two special groups under a joint command will take place, namely in the event of the transfer of the troops from Russia to the Middle East. It seems to me that this would be possible only in the event of the collapse of Russia for an earlier withdrawal of those troops would deprive millions of Poles deported to Russia of their only support.

I have full understanding of the feelings of the soldiers in Russia under your command, General, especially after the last evacuation. I appeal, nevertheless, to their patriotism and to their trained will, which has so well stood the test. They should remain in absolute discipline in a post so important for Poland.

On the other hand, I give you, General, the right to inspect the Second Army Corps on my behalf. I stress by this the union between these groups and, in accordance with Ambassador Kot's proposal, I open to you the possibility of more freedom of movement, and of journeys outside Russia.

I enclose the respective resolutions of the Council of Ministers.[1]

[1] See doc. No. 213.

No. 216

Note from Ambassador Kot to Commissar Molotov on the continuation of the conscription of Poles in the USSR for the Polish Army and evacuation of the surplus quota of the Polish troops to the Middle East

Kuibyshev, May 4, 1942 GSHI, A.11. 49/Sow./2
Official transl. from Polish

Upon instruction of my Government, I have the honour to inform you of the following:

During the conversations which took place in Moscow, in December of last year, between General Sikorski and the President of the Council of People's Commissars of the USSR, Mr. Stalin, it has been decided to increase the Polish Army on the territory of the USSR. This army was being formed from war prisoners, recruits and volunteers—all Polish citizens at the time in the Soviet Union. The number of the army was then established at 96,000, with the provision that in case there would be more men available, this number would be raised. It was also settled that all Polish airmen and sailors, as well as 25,000 soldiers of the land army, would be evacuated to the Near East.

In March of this year, as a result of an instruction restricting the rations for the Polish Army in the USSR, General Anders, the Commander-in-Chief of the Polish Forces in USSR, went to Moscow and was received by President Stalin. During the conversation in the Kremlin, on March 18th, it was decided that, owing to difficulties in supplying food, the number of the Polish Army in USSR would be brought down to 44,000. The surplus of the army, as well as all recruits and volunteers, would be evacuated to the Near East. President Stalin agreed to the continuation of the recruitment of Polish citizens, as well as to the release of those Polish citizens who were incorporated into the Red Army and the so-called 'stroi-bataliony'.[1] They were to be directed to the Polish Army and evacuated with the rest of the recruited surplus.

As a result of this decision around 30,000 Polish soldiers left the USSR for Persia. On the other hand, however, the Polish Government were informed already after the departure of General Anders for London, that the further recruitment into the Polish Army on the territory of the USSR has been practically stopped. In the majority of the districts it has not even been ordered, a fact which completely interrupted the further evacuation to the Near East. At the same time the spontaneous flow of volunteers into the Polish Army was being hampered by administrative measures and on the

[1] Labour-battalions.

348

other hand the number of Polish citizens incorporated into the Red Army and the 'stroi-bataliony',[1] had grown. Besides, Polish military posts in the provinces had to be closed. They had been established—as well as offices of the registration officers—at the time in connection with the recruiting and directing of Polish citizens to the Army and were also centres of sanitation and food distribution on important railway stations.

The Polish Government would like to remind you of the fact that during the December conversations between Prime Minister General Sikorski and President Stalin, as in the March conversation between President Stalin and General Anders, it was stated by both sides that it is in the common interest of the war which Poland and the Soviet Union are waging against Germany, to enable all those fit to serve as Polish soldiers, who are in surplus of the contingent fixed for the Polish Army in the USSR, to join the Polish Forces there, where conditions allow their equipment and armament.

Considering the possibility of military operations, for which this coming year might be decisive, the matter is, in the opinion of the Polish Government, very urgent.

In face of those facts I have been instructed by my Government to ask your Excellency to take most urgent measures in order to bring into effect the decisions taken by the highest authorities of both Governments, that is in the first place the complete recruitment and voluntary enlistment into the Polish Army in USSR, as well as the evacuation to the Near East of the surplus of the agreed contingent resulting from this recruitment and enlistment.

[1] Labour-battalions.

No. 217

Note from Mr. Eden to Minister Raczyński in reply to his note of April 21, 1942, on the subject of Anglo-Soviet negotiations

London, May 6, 1942   GSHI, PRM, 67

I have the honour to acknowledge the receipt of Your Excellency's note of the 21st April, containing further observations from the Polish Government on the contemplated negotiations for an Anglo-Soviet Treaty.

2. The considerations set out in your communication have been noted by His Majesty's Government. As regards the general questions raised, I cannot usefully add anything to the statement of the position of His Majesty's Government contained in my note of the 17th April and in my letter to General Sikorski of the 21st April. I feel it necessary, however, to inform Your Excellency that His Majesty's Government regret that they are unable to agree with the assumption underlying the fourth and fifth sections of your note.

3. In section VI you state that the Polish Government were unable to agree to the interpretation of the Secret Protocol to the Anglo-Polish Agreement of the 25th August, 1939, given in my note of the 17th April. You went on to express the hope that His Majesty's Government would recognize

the correctness of the Polish Government's interpretation of Article 2[b] of the Secret Protocol in the light of the stipulations of Article 1[b], to which no reference had been made in my note of the 17th April.

4. This further explanation of the interpretation placed by the Polish Government upon the Anglo-Polish Agreement and the Secret Protocol suggests however that it does not differ substantially from that of His Majesty's Government. His Majesty's Government have always regarded Articles 2[b] of the Secret Protocol as involving a recognition by them that the independence of Lithuania was of importance to Poland. They take the view, however, that the circumstances which would bring Article 2[2] of the Agreement into operation in consequence of a threat to the independence of Lithuania have not arisen, and that the provision in question would not be applicable if the threat came from the Union of Soviet Socialist Republics. Your note makes it clear that this interpretation is not disputed by the Polish Government.

5. You have, however, referred to the provision for consultation in Article 1[b] of the Secret Protocol. But Article 1[b] in itself could never bring Article 2[2] of the Agreement automatically into operation. The effect of Article 1[b] of the Secret Protocol in relation to any Soviet threat to the independence of Lithuania is that, if Poland became engaged in hostilities with the Soviet Union, or, possibly, if the Polish Government considered that they might become involved in such hostilities, in consequence of a Soviet threat to the independence of Lithuania, they would be entitled to call upon His Majesty's Government for consultation under Article 1[b]. Articles 1 and 2 of the Anglo-Polish Agreement, to which the consultation provided for under Article 1[b] of the Secret Protocol is exclusively restricted, deal entirely with aggression upon one of the contracting parties or action threatening the independence or neutrality of another neutral state resulting in one of the contracting parties becoming engaged in hostilities with the aggressor. If, however, the Polish Government had regarded developments in Lithuania subsequent to the signature of the Anglo-Polish Agreement as justifying a request for consultation under Article 1[b] of the Secret Protocol, His Majesty's Government would have expected such a request to have been put forward at the time of the incorporation of Lithuania into the Soviet Union. No such request was, however, then advanced by the Polish Government, and, since Poland and the Soviet Union are now allies, His Majesty's Government would find difficulty in regarding the provision of Article 1[b] of the Secret Protocol as applicable in existing circumstances. Nevertheless, His Majesty's Government have taken the initiative in informing the Polish Government of their intentions in regard to the contemplated Anglo-Soviet negotiations, and consultation is in fact now taking place between His Majesty's Government and the Polish Government.

6. I trust that the above explanation, coupled with the statements of the attitude of His Majesty's Government set out in earlier correspondence, will convince the Polish Government that, in any negotiations with the Soviet Government, His Majesty's Government intend fully to safeguard the position

of their Polish allies, and do not contemplate any action inconsistent with the provisions of the Anglo-Polish Agreement of 1939 or the Secret Protocol annexed to it.

No. 218

Message from M. Stalin to General Sikorski on the reduction of the strength of the Polish Army in the USSR sent to Minister Raczyński by the Chargé d'Affaires Chichayev

London, May 13, 1942   GSHI, PRM 72/1

Le Président du Conseil des Commissaires du Peuple de l'URSS J. V. Stalin a attentivement pris connaissance du message du Général Sikorski et le remercie pour l'information sur ses entretiens avec le Gouvernement Britannique et avec le Président des États-Unis Monsieur Roosevelt au sujet de la préparation des actions concordées contre l'Allemagne et au sujet de la supposition concernant la participation des forces militaires polonaises à ces actions.

Quant aux suppositions, faites par Général Sikorski, que [le] recrutement en URSS des ressortissants polonais, appelés au service militaire, et leur acheminement seront repris, J. V. Stalin juge nécessaire de rappeler les considérations, exposées par lui au Général Anders le 18 mars 1942, que la fixation définitive des contingents de l'armée polonaise au chiffre de 44,000 était la conséquence des circonstances, dues à la limitation d'approvisionnement des unités militaires, qui ne prennent pas part aux combats.

Vu que jusqu'à présent ces circonstances n'ont pas changé, il n'est pas possible d'apporter des changements quelconques dans les contingents de l'armée polonaise en URSS, fixés au mois de mars de l'année courante.

J. V. Stalin n'a pas de doute à ce que les citoyens polonais, appelés sous leur drapeau national, feront un apport à la lutte commune contre les envahisseurs hitlériens.

No. 219

Note from Commissar Molotov to Ambassador Kot on the discontinuance of the enrolment into the Polish Army in the USSR

Moscow, May 14, 1942   GSHI, A.11. 49/Sow./3
                                                Transl. from Russian

Upon instruction of the Government of the USSR, and in connection with your note of May 4th, referring to measures concerning the Polish Army, on the territory of the USSR, I have the honour to inform you of the following:

During the conversation which took place on March 18th of this year between the President of the Council of People's Commissars of the Soviet Union, J. V. Stalin, and the Commander-in-Chief of the Polish Forces on the territory of the USSR, General Anders, it was decided to reduce the number of the Polish Army to 44,000 men, and to evacuate to Iran contingents of the

Polish Army which would be in surplus of the established number of 44,000 men. This decision, as it is known to the Embassy, was put into effect at the stated time, and thus the evacuation of the Polish military forces from USSR has to be considered as entirely concluded.

As to the proposition of the Embassy to carry on the evacuation of the Polish forces into the Near East and to continue the further recruitment of Polish citizens and the enlistment of volunteers into the Polish Army, I find it necessary to let you know that the realization of this proposition is impossible at the present time for the same reasons for which the numerical strength of the Polish Army in the USSR has been fixed at 44,000 men in March of this year. On the other hand, the reference in your note that apparently the President of the Council of People's Commissars of the USSR, J. V. Stalin, in his conversation with General Anders, confirmed that the recruitment of Polish citizens into military detachments would be continued, and that those Polish citizens who are incorporated into the Red Army and the 'stroi-bataliony'[1] would be directed to the Polish Army and then evacuated to the Near East, is based undoubtedly on a misunderstanding. In reality, J. V. Stalin did not refer to these matters in his conversation with General Anders.

In accordance with the above, the Soviet Government does not see any purpose in undertaking steps which would enable a further recruitment and enlistment of volunteers into the Polish Army on the territory of the USSR for their ultimate departure to the Near East. It also does not see any purpose in renewing the activity of Polish military institutions created in connection with the recruitment into the Polish Army (food stations, sanitary stations, offices of registration officers, and so on).

As to the cases in which Polish citizens have been incorporated into the Red Army and the 'stroi-bataliony'[1] instead of being sent to the Polish Army, a matter which has been referred to in your note, I find it necessary to state that only Soviet citizens are subject to the recruitment into the Red Army and the 'stroi-bataliony'.[1]

[1] Labour-battalions.

No. 220

Note from Minister Raczyński to Ambassador Bogomolov protesting against the activities of Soviet parachutists on the territory of Poland

London, May 16, 1942   GSHI, A.11. 49/Sow./2

D'après les renseignements parvenus récemment au Gouvernement Polonais, des parachutistes soviétiques auraient accompli dernièrement des descentes fréquentes en territoire polonais, notamment dans les districts de Chełm, Zamość, Lublin ainsi que dans les montagnes de Świętokrzysk.

D'après les mêmes renseignements ceux-ci n'ont pu causer comme règle générale que des dommages insignifiants à l'occupant allemand en raison du manque de connaissance de la langue polonaise et du terrain sur lequel il leur échut d'agir. En même temps ils ont exposé la population polonaise à de cruelles répréssailles de la part des autorités militaires allemandes qui ont envoyé dans ces régions des expéditions punitives, tué des habitants et brûlé les villages suspects d'avoir hébergé des parachutistes. Il s'en est suivi une difficulté accrue pour l'organisation polonaise responsable de l'action subversive contre l'ennemi—cette organisation ayant nécessairement vu diminuer l'aide que la population est en état de lui fournir.

C'est donc dans l'intérêt de la cause que nous est commune que j'ai l'honneur de prier Votre Excellence de bien vouloir informer le Gouvernement de l'Union des Républiques Socialistes Soviétiques des faits mentionnés ci-dessus. Votre Excellence voudra sans doute se souvenir de l'entretien du 6 octobre 1941, au cours duquel le Premier Ministre Polonais, le Général Sikorski, a souligné les graves désavantages causés par les descentes en parachute effectuées à l'insu de notre Gouvernement et de nos organisations en territoire polonais occupé par l'ennemi.[1] Il [faut?] ajouter que celles-ci avaient été averties de la décision des autorités militaires de l'URSS d'interdire pour le présent aux parachutistes soviétiques des descentes en Pologne. Ces parachutistes se trouvent de par ce fait sérieusement exposés à l'activité des organizations polonaises qui sont naturellement portées à voir en eux des outils d'une provocation dirigée par des agents allemands.

Il serait superflu d'insister sur l'importance que le Gouvernement Polonais attache à son plan d'activité subversive à l'arrière des armées allemandes.

C'est sous l'empire de cette importante préoccupation que je prie Votre Excellence de porter ce qui précède à la connaissance du Gouvernement de l'Union des Républiques Socialistes Soviétiques.

[1] Not printed.

No. 221

Note from the Polish Embassy in the USSR to the People's Commissariat for Foreign Affairs relating to the Polish citizens still being detained in prisons and forced labour camps

Kuibyshev, May 19, 1942

GSHI, A.11. 49/Sow./2
Transl. from Polish

The Embassy of the Republic of Poland has the honour to inform the People's Commissariat for Foreign Affairs of the following:

The Memorandum enclosed[1] with this Note gives a full account of the position arising from the fact that Polish citizens are still detained in prisons and forced labour camps or forced to stay in banishment, and also from the line of proceeding of the Soviet organs responsible for their release. To some extent, these questions have been already discussed in the Embassy's previous Notes, and in official conversations with representatives of the People's Commissariat for Foreign Affairs.

Stressing the importance of these questions not only for the Polish citizens concerned but also for the Polish Government from the point of view of the

[1] Enclosure to this document, see Note 221.

implementation of the provisions of the Additional Protocol to the Polish-Soviet Agreement of 30th July, 1941, as well as the development of friendly relations between the two States, the Embassy of the Republic of Poland has the honour to ask the People's Commissariat for Foreign Affairs to examine these questions and to take the appropriate favourable measures.

No. 222

Note from Ambassador Kot to Commissar Molotov, in reply to the Soviet Note of 27th April, 1942, and protesting against the inclusion of the Polish town Pińsk in the list of the Soviet towns occupied by German troops

Kuibyshev, May 19, 1942
GSHI, A.11. 49/Sow./2
Transl. from Polish

I have the honour to acknowledge receipt of Your Excellency's Note of 27th April, 1942, describing the action of the German army of occupation aiming at the utter spoliation and destruction of the territories of the Soviet Union which they have temporarily occupied, the spreading of terror among their inhabitants by unprecedented cruelty and exploitation, and the removal of all monuments of native culture and art, the products of centuries of patient and persevering labour. I can find no appropriate terms to express the feelings of revulsion and horror in condemnation of these crimes, which are similar to those committed by the German army of occupation and the administration in the territories of the Republic of Poland, from September 1939 to the present day.

May I express my firm belief that the magnificent attitude of the Soviet people in the Soviet territories temporarily occupied, their stubborn resistance and the struggle carried on against the enemy, will not be vain, and that, thanks to the victories of the Red Army, the sufferings of the people will not last much longer and a better and juster world, based on international law and respect for mutual obligations, will emerge from the present war, waged by the common efforts of the citizens, armed forces and Governments of the Allied countries against German lawlessness, savagery and rule of force in international relations.

As among Soviet towns listed in the aforesaid Note Pińsk was mentioned, I feel obliged to declare, on my part, that the sending of this Note to all States which maintain diplomatic relations with the Soviet Union, as well as its publication in the press, clashes with the point of view expressed in the Aide-Mémoire handed on February 28th, 1942 to the Prime Minister, General Sikorski, by the Soviet Ambassador in London, the relevant passage of which reads as follows: 'In the interest of an effective development of co-operation between the two States, the Soviet Government consider inadvisable a public discussion of the issues which both Governments have decided to leave open for the time being'. It is well known that the Polish Government, maintaining since the beginning of the present war the territorial integrity of the Republic of Poland, consider the town of Pińsk to be

Polish, as it is situated within the frontiers of the Polish State existing before the German aggression of September 1st, 1939.

No. 223

Memorandum from the Polish Ministry for Foreign Affairs to Ambassador Drexel Biddle relating to the Polish problems in the USSR

London, May 29, 1942   GSHI, PRM, 70

1. Polish Forces. In December last Stalin and General Sikorski agreed to the formation of a Polish Army in Russia 96,000 strong. Furthermore 25,000 men were to be sent to Scotland and the Middle East in order to bring the Polish units stationed there to their full strength.

In March last Stalin summoned General Anders and told him that food shortage compelled him to limit the strength of the Polish Forces in Russia to 44,000 and that the remainder were to be evacuated immediately to Persia. Recruiting was to continue. In actual fact 30,000 men were evacuated to Persia but recruiting was stopped.

In April General Sikorski sent a message to Stalin asking him to continue the recruitment and subsequent evacuation of men. A similar request was made by Ambassador Kot. Stalin replied that conditions were unchanged and that he was unable to alter his policy. His message included a hint that should the present Polish Forces be sent to the front-line, he might be willing to recruit more of them but that he felt unable to provide food for troops not actually fighting. He overlooked the fact that Polish soldiers in the camps have not yet been adequately armed and equipped.

On May 14th Molotov replied to Kot confirming Stalin's message and adding that Stalin had made no promise to General Anders to continue recruitment and that the agreed evacuation was considered as altogether completed.

Thus the Polish Forces in Russia have been limited to 44,000 men in military camps and 30,000 evacuated to Persia. This limitation is contrary to the figures agreed upon on several occasions between the Polish and Soviet Governments, as well as to the spirit and the very promises of the agreements binding the two countries. There are in Russia many thousands more able Polish men of military age [at least 60,000] most of whom have had military training and who should obviously be enlisted in the military forces. It is in the common interest of the Allies that they should form part of the military formations in the Middle East and not be dispersed, as they are, throughout the Russian East and in many cases idle and suffering from shortage of food.

The Polish Government's desire is to restart recruitment and, while leaving 44,000 organized forces in Russia, evacuate the remaining men of military age to Persia, where they would join the Polish Army under formation,—unless, in view of a real food shortage in Russia, a solution could be found to supply the newly recruited men in Russia from other countries.

2. Missing Officers. In summer 1940 several thousands of Polish officers

prisoners of war, who were kept in 3 camps in Central Russia [Ostashkov, Starobielsk, Kozelsk], were taken to an unknown destination in the Far North of Russia. Since then they have not been heard of. Their number has been variously described but is usually accepted as 8,300; ⅓ of whom are professional officers and ⅔ reserve officers. The latter are for the most part professional men including about 800 physicians and many University professors and lecturers as well as a number of distinguished specialists. The Polish Military Authorities have lists covering over 4,800 of these officers; these lists have been communicated to Stalin. The Soviet Government have many times been requested to release them. They invariably replied that every available prisoner of war in Russia had already been released. This statement is obviously inaccurate. There are reasons to believe that the officers in question have been deported to Franz-Joseph Islands, North of Spitzbergen, and to North-Eastern Siberia to camps on the River Kolyma, in the North of the Yakut Republic. It is more than probable that most of them have died of hunger, scorbut and cold. If the supposition as to their places of imprisonment is correct there are but two months of summer when for technical reasons they could be brought back to Russia. Or, on the other hand, they could either be brought via the Kolyma River to Alaska or from Franz-Joseph Islands to Iceland. The absence of these officers is the principal reason for the shortage of officers in the Polish Forces in Russia, whither officers from Scotland had to be sent lately. The possible death of these men, most of whom have superior education, would be a severe blow to the Polish national life. Their evacuation during the present summer seems to be the last chance to save those who may still be alive.

3. Polish Children. According to latest dispatches from Russia, the food situation there has lately deteriorated to a very great extent. In the Southern parts of Russia [Central Asia] rations for those who are at work have been limited to 4 oz. of flour daily. Those who do not work receive no rations. Prices on the free market are astronomic and only a small number of privileged people can afford to buy non-rationed food. In consequence many cases of death from starvation are reported and it is likely that their number will increase. The children are the first to succumb. In the Republic of Uzbekistan [Central Asia] between 5 and 14% of Polish children have died of hunger within the last few months.

In these circumstances, if these Polish children in Russia are to be saved from certain death, the evacuation of 50,000 of them, together with several thousands of mothers and guardians [a large proportion of these children are already orphans], is a paramount necessity. The Soviet Government would raise no objection to their evacuation if it were effected in a very discreet manner. They naturally do not want to disclose hunger conditions in Russia. Therefore if these people were evacuated, any information regarding conditions in Russia should be altogether withheld.

Even before receipt of this latest news on hunger conditions in parts of Russia, Ambassador Ciechanowski submitted to Mr. Sumner Welles the desire of the Polish Government to begin a large-scale evacuation of children from Russia. President Roosevelt has very generously taken a personal interest in the matter and instructed the Department of State and the American Red Cross to prepare the evacuation of 10,000 children from Persia to South Africa. Should this evacuation be effected there would be room in Persia for another 10,000 children from Russia. This, however, would mean the salvation of only a small number of the children in question. Truly heroic measures are needed if Polish children, belonging to all classes of society and representing a valuable part of the nation's future, are to be saved.

4. Conclusions. If no political obstacles stand in the way of removing the children in question from Russia to Persia, and thence to other countries in Asia, Africa or even America, the further recruitment and evacuation of soldiers and would-be soldiers, including the aforementioned deported officers, depend on the good will of the Soviet Government. It would appear that all measures available to the Polish Government have already been used with mediocre results [partial evacuation to Persia]. The only hope for a solution to these problems is in the hands of the British and American Governments. The British Government have interested themselves in both these matters, but it is doubtful whether British pressure alone can bring about a positive settlement. It seems, therefore, that the only practical possibility of effecting a change in the policy of the Soviet Government in the above matters would be during the pending conversations in Washington between the United States Administration and the Soviet Foreign Commissar. He will be requesting the assistance of the United States of America in many questions of vital importance for the Soviet Union. While receiving most valuable assistance from the United Nations headed by the United States, it would only be natural that the Soviet Government would feel under an obligation to comply with a request for a change of policy regarding the fate of many thousands of Polish officers and men, whose presence in the Middle East would be a valuable contribution of Poland towards the common cause of the United Nations.

No. 224

Conversation between Ambassador Kot and Deputy Commissar Vyshinsky on the religious organization of the Polish community in the USSR, the evacuation of Polish children from the USSR, and the release of MM. Ehrlich and Alter

Kuibyshev, June 2, 1942   GSHI, A.11. 49/Sow./4
Transl. from Polish

Ambassador: It is more than a month since I had a conversation with you, Mr. Chairman, but today I come to trouble you with many urgent affairs. I may even be unable to exhaust all the topics.

Vyshinsky: Please proceed.

Ambassador: I wish, first of all, to hand you, Mr. Chairman, the photostats of an underground paper 'Rzeczpospolita' (Republic) appearing in Warsaw. An issue of that paper, published as far back as 11th December, 1941, gives not only an exact account of General Sikorski's visit to Moscow, but also the text of the General's broadcast in Moscow, made on 4th December, 1941. As you see, Mr. Chairman, they work very efficiently over there. Will you, please, keep this copy which reflects the reaction of Polish public opinion to this political event?

Vyshinsky (takes the paper and thanks him).

Ambassador: There is another curious reaction to the same event, this time coming from the other, that is, the German, side. I have here the photostat of a paper published by the Germans for Polish officers staying in Prisoner-of-War camps. Will you, please, note the heading of the editorial: 'Sikorski, Anders, Kot and Haller—Kremlin's puppets'?

Vyshinsky: It is very interesting indeed. (He looks at the photos.)

Ambassador: These photostats are far from being perfect because the underground press is sent to London on small films which are developed and printed there. Will you, please, keep this copy too, and show it to President Stalin?

Vyshinsky: Most certainly, I shall send them to Stalin and Molotov. This is very interesting indeed.

Ambassador: I shall not speak to you about a question of great interest to us, that is of conscription and voluntary enlistment for our army, because I am waiting for a report from General Anders who will let me know the results of his conversation with President Stalin.

Vyshinsky: Quite so; as you shall be seeing General Anders very soon, you will have all the necessary information from him.

Ambassador: The third important question is that of organizing religious care for the Polish community in the USSR. This issue has been outstanding for a long time already. I think that the present moment is very propitious for the settlement of the question of providing for the religious needs of Polish citizens here. When I had the occasion to speak to you on this matter in Moscow you asked me to submit a concrete project on this issue. M. Bogomolov told General Sikorski last November that Polish citizens could enjoy full religious freedom. Similar statements and declarations have been made in other places. I keep in mind a conversation between General Sikorski and you, Mr. Chairman, of last December. We try to enlighten international public opinion on religious freedom in the Soviet Union, and I have here a bulletin of the Polish Telegraphic Agency (PAT) with the Rev. Kaczyński's interview with the American press. The Rev. Kaczyński, member of the Polish National Council and a prominent prelate, former head of the Catholic Journalist Agency, in other words, a Catholic Lozovsky, declared in his interview that, while in the German Reich religion is forced to go into hiding, there are all indications that it is coming into the open in the Soviet Union. The Rev. Kaczyński's interview has made a deep impression in the Catholic circles of America (he hands a copy of the PAT bulletin to Vyshinsky). I am not a specialist in these matters, and only now, thanks to Bishop Gawlina's visit to the Soviet Union, have I been able to prepare jointly with him a plan for the settlement of the religious organization of the Polish community here, the outlines of which I wish to hand to you now. This is a strictly minimum programme, and an extremely modest one. (The plan is read out by the interpreter, and Vyshinsky takes note of particular points.) This plan takes into account, in all respects, the Soviet legislation in force, as it aims at setting up a proper organization without causing any difficulties to Soviet authorities. The most difficult problem is, of course, that of the priests. Should we provide for our citizens' religious needs on the same scale as has been the case in pre-war Poland, we would need thousands of priests. We realize that it is impossible to bring here such a number of priests, and we therefore propose 10% of the required number only. Having made a detailed assessment of areas in which the priests should work, we obtained the figure 105. Eleven priests are already working in different places, apart from the military chaplains; they carry out their duties in a private manner. Should the general plan include them, 94 priests would still be needed. I wish to hand you a list of Polish Catholic priests who, so far, have not been released from prisons and labour camps.

Vyshinsky: We have this list already.

Ambassador: This is an amended one. Our previous interventions referred to 57 priests, but, subsequently, we have been informed that some of them are no longer alive. This list is brought up to date. Now, in order to have the required number of priests, we need, as I told you, 94 more priests. If you liberate 50 priests who are still imprisoned, there will be two possible ways of making up the remaining number. I should like to hear your opinion on this point, and, if possible, to obtain the assistance of the Soviet Government. Either you will allow us to use the services of a considerable number of Polish priests who are Soviet citizens, and there must be about a hundred of them over here, or you will agree to the coming of an adequate number of priests from abroad. It is true that out of the priests deported from Poland several were released last autumn and winter, but all of them have been absorbed by the army. According to military regulations a great number of chaplains attached to particular units is needed, and about 20 of them out of the available number have left with the troops evacuated to Persia. I do not raise today the question of Protestant clergymen, because so far we have not come across large groups of Protestants. The question of Jews is not so urgent because, as I understand, there are synagogues in a number of places, but I reserve the right to return to this problem and to submit concrete proposals. I wish also to draw your attention to the fact of a great religious revival among the masses of Poles staying in the Soviet Union. Under the stress of hardship endured in the course of the last years, even those who formerly were indifferent to religion or showed no interest in it are now craving for it and demanding religious care. It is both in the interest of Polish citizens and in that of good Polish-Soviet relations that these questions should be examined and solved on the lines of our plan. If you look at the names of the localities in which we wish to post our priests, contained in our second list handed to you by me today, you will notice that the distances between localities are so great that it would be impossible for one priest to carry out his duties in more than one locality. Summing up, we reduce our demands to a strict minimum.

Vyshinsky: The plan produced by you is not so simple as one might think at first sight. It raises, on the contrary, many very serious objections and difficult points. The Government will, of course, take up a position on it, but I wish to make some points clear at once. In fact, in November 1941, Bogomolov spoke with General Sikorski on these matters, informing him, so far as I can remember, that the conditions and regulations referring to the satisfaction of the religious needs of Soviet citizens, as laid down in the Stalin Constitution, were extended to Polish citizens who are Catholics. What are these rights? The Soviet citizens, and, after Bogomolov's statement, also Polish citizens, can form religious groups and by virtue of agreements with 'gorsoviets' (town soviets) they obtain a place assigned for worship. In the Soviet Union the church is separated from the State which has neither the means nor any reason for supporting any religious group. The Soviet Government cannot assume, therefore, obligations of any kind concerning assistance to the religious life of Polish citizens. I do not prejudice the final answer to this question but I point out the essential difficulties. What can the Government do in a country where the church is separated from the State? Have not our Orthodox citizens their own requests and needs? We do not give them any assistance. Neither do we interfere in their religious problems. Should we settle the question on the lines of the Embassy's plan, we should be obliged to grant special facilities to all the other denominations. You have mentioned Protestants, Mr. Ambassador. Don't we have in the USSR more Protestant Soviet citizens, than Protestant Polish citizens? All denominations would put forward similar demands, Muslims, Armenians, and many others besides. All of them would refer to the special assistance given by the Soviet Government to Polish citizens. All these problems are interdependent, and under no circumstances could I consider them as simple or easy to solve. I thought that the Polish citizens would be able to organize their religious life without any special decision from the Government, which is out of the question, simply by virtue of the Soviet legislation in force and of agreements with 'gorsoviets'. Is there any need to implicate the Government? Why not the Supreme Soviet? What is the need for resolutions? As long as nobody prevents the Poles from enjoying religious freedoms guaranteed by the law, the Governmental Departments have no reason to intervene. What, in general, can the Narkomindel have to do with such matters? One of the points of the plan mentions tax reliefs for Polish citizens of Catholic denomination. It would provoke at once a fully warranted discontent among the other denominations which had not been exempted from the payment of taxes. I shall not conceal from you, Mr. Ambassador, that, contrary to the growth of religious feeling among Polish citizens, just stated by you, the interest in religious matters among our population is dwindling. Nobody wants to study for the priesthood; they prefer to become 'agronomists' and, recently, 'tank-drivers', so much needed by us. You spoke of letting Catholic priests from abroad come here. Having few priests here, the

Orthodox Church would like to let Orthodox priests come to the Soviet Union. We could, for instance, let Orthodox priests, conversant with our language, come from Bulgaria. There are also many Orthodox priests in USA. There is even an Orthodox bishop in New York, a decent, honest patriarch, who allows religious offices to be celebrated for the success of Soviet arms, but this is a matter of no importance to us. As you see, Mr. Ambassador, that would be the second group of difficulties. Now, you have mentioned also Jews, Mr. Ambassador. This I do not understand, as according to our position, which is well known to you, the Jews are Soviet citizens.

Ambassador: I suppose that no Soviet authority would go to the length of asserting that there are no Jews—Polish citizens.

Vyshinsky (ironically): Even if there are, it is not worth while to speak of them. The whole question presented to me by you, Mr. Ambassador, demands review of many other problems. (Smiling) 'One should not be in a hurry with such matters' (in Russian: 'toropitsia ne sleduyet'). We shall give you an answer, of course, in due time.

Ambassador: Our programme is in fact a strict minimum. We do not ask for the establishment of an ecclesiastical hierarchy without which the Catholic Church does not work. What really matters to us, is to ensure religious care for Polish citizens, in accordance with their wishes. We want an assurance that our citizens will have no political troubles on this account, that nobody will persecute them. They are aliens in the Soviet Union, and they do not know what is allowed and what is not. Let them know that they have some definite rights in the religious sphere.

Vyshinsky: Polish citizens can organize their religious life on the same lines as Soviet citizens, in accordance with the legislation in force. Will you please take also into consideration, Mr. Ambassador, that Catholic priests are in a special situation; they have two masters, the State of which they are nationals, and the Holy Father (ironically) to whom they pledge their allegiance.

Ambassador: If there should exist any propensity on the priests' part to carry out a special line of policy, I guarantee that this would not be the case, should they remain under the Embassy's control. As far as the alleged subservience to the Holy Father is concerned, it is, as a matter of fact, not so bad, for the priests keep their attachment to him in their hearts, and it does not prevent them from being politically subservient to their own government.

Vyshinsky: The Soviet Union does not maintain, by the way, relations with the Apostolic See.

Ambassador (jokingly): I do not doubt, nevertheless, that those relations will be eventually established. [. . .].

Ambassador: Here is another important item. Taking into account the shortage of food in the Soviet Union, we should like to proceed to a mass departure of Polish children from here. According to our estimates, there are in the Soviet Union 160,000 children of Polish citizenship. Their departure (the final figure is not yet known, our census not having been

361

completed) would constitute a great relief for yourselves and for us. Do not children belong to a class of population which does not work? Their remaining here, therefore, does not seem pertinent from the economic point of view. We meet, however, with much difficulty in this respect, because the outside world is not very eager to assist us. It would be difficult to place such a quantity of chidren abroad. So far we have obtained permission for the resettlement of 50,000 children only. Many children are dying, the rate of mortality among them is very high, and altogether this is an extremely painful matter for us. The children's departure would relieve us greatly. I understand that there are transport difficulties in war-time but should we use waterways and organize a transport on the Volga it could be done smoothly and promptly. We would provide food for them during the journey, and ask you only for supplies of oatmeal and bread. I should be most obliged if the Soviet Government would agree to give its permission for the departure of those children abroad.

Vyshinsky (speaking very reluctantly): You said, Mr. Ambassador, that there were very many deaths among the children. I feel obliged to state that this is not the case. We received information from the Embassy on high mortality in the Uzbekistan. I ordered the figures to be checked. The answer came without delay. I was able to state that Embassy delegates, and in particular Kazimierczak, the delegate at Samarkand, had misled the Embassy. The data produced by him are based on distorted information. Kazimierczak did not go to the spot at all, and the best thing that can be said about him is that he was led astray. Mortality was limited to single cases, and it is very nearly possible to give the names of those who died. This accounted for the Embassy being panic-stricken, and viewing the position in an overpessimistic way. I think I shall be able to supply the Embassy with an answer within the next days. Kolkhozes are supplying food not only to working people but also to lazy-bones. 50,000 children is quite a fantastic figure, unrealistic. How many children were to go to India? I think 500 (Zorin confirms it). So far they have not been taken away.

Ambassador: Mass mortality among the children is unfortunately a well established fact. I shall take the liberty to submit to you, Mr. Chairman, exact figures relating not to the Far South but to Kuibyshev itself. You will see then how many children died here. You can check it through your officials on the spot.

Vyshinsky: I have never heard of it. There is no such thing as mass mortality. If there are some cases of death, they are quite normal figures, by no means higher than among Soviet citizens.

Ambassador: The Russian climate is not suitable for our citizens. They suffer from very severe winters and excessively hot summers.

Vyshinsky: To carry away 50,000 children is quite a fantastic plan. We are having a war by the way, and quite a hard one too.

Ambassador: May I say that it was not ourselves but the Soviet Government who brought those children over here. Grant us permission to take them away now. [. . .].

362

Vyshinsky (visibly annoyed): You are heaping reproaches on us again. What is the use of ever looking into the past, of reminding the misfortunes of those people, due to the international situation and to various contingencies. [. . .].

Ambassador: I was not prepared for such a reaction to our plan. I was expecting a favourable attitude on your part. Should transport difficulties be so great, we can reckon, it seems, with the assistance of our troops which have recently been supplied with an adequate number of lorries for their needs. It will surely be possible to transport the children by lorries in the South. I ask you, in any case, to submit our plan to the Government which perhaps will take a different view on it as it is in accordance with our and everybody's interests. [. . .].

Ambassador: There is, Mr. Chairman, one more question which has been raised several times by the Embassy. It concerns Ehrlich and Alter, both Polish citizens and Warsaw town-councillors who are kept in prison by you.[1]

Vyshinsky: It is quite impossible for me to discuss this question.

Ambassador: Mr. Chairman, please, do this for me and allow us to take these men away. I shall take full responsibility for their not engaging in anti-Soviet agitation abroad. In asking for this I am prompted by no other reasons than the interest of the war which we wage in common. Nobody will believe that those men were implicated in pro-Nazi activity (he displays leaflets and copies of the correspondence with leading personalities in the United States, emphasizing the protests on the part of the Jewish workers' organizations in the US). Who may need it? Will the common struggle against Germany benefit by it?

Vyshinsky (does not look at the papers): I understand your intentions and feelings, Mr. Ambassador, but I cannot discuss the case of Ehrlich and Alter with you because, as you know, in the view of the Soviet Government those men are Soviet citizens.

Ambassador (jokingly): Do you wish, by any chance, to annex Warsaw after the war? They cannot be your citizens, after all, being Warsaw town councillors, and in your prison already when you proclaimed the annexation of Eastern Poland. [. . .].

The conversation lasted 2 hours and 10 minutes. It was held in a friendly and quiet manner except when the question of the evacuation of children was raised. At that moment Vyshinsky showed excitement and annoyance.

[1] Henryk Ehrlich and Wiktor Alter, prominent Jewish leaders and members of the Executive Committee of the II International, were arrested on 4th December, 1941, on a forged charge of espionage on behalf of Germany, and executed in the course of December. At the time of this conversation they were already dead, but this fact had not been disclosed by the Soviet Government.

Notes made by Dr. Retinger on a conversation between General Sikorski and Mr. Eden in connection with the conclusion of the Anglo-Soviet Treaty. Mr. Strang and Dr. Retinger were also present

London, June 8, 1942 GSHI, PRM, 68
Transl. from Polish

Mr. Eden greeted General Sikorski in a very friendly manner, saying at the beginning of the conversation that during his negotiations with Molotov he had worked as hard for Poland as General Sikorski himself. He let General Sikorski read the text of the Treaty concluded on 26th May, 1942. Mr. Strang then handed the text to Dr. Retinger, so that he might note its most important provisions, asking him at the same time to keep it strictly secret for the time being. Mr. Eden said that the Treaty would be made public by Prime Minister Churchill in the course of the next week. He promised General Sikorski to send him the text of the Treaty officially, three days in advance, so that, in any case, he would receive it before all the other Allied Governments.

General Sikorski congratulated Mr. Eden on the text of the Treaty which in no point harms the rights and interests of the nations on the continent; it should help the Allies in conducting the war and, instead of weakening it, should strengthen their moral position. Then Mr. Eden described his conversations with Molotov who came to London at a British request sent to Moscow after the meeting at Chequers on 26th April between General Sikorski and Prime Minister Churchill. Mr. Eden stated that at the very beginning of the conversations with Molotov he explained to him that he was ready to sign a treaty containing the clauses relating to the Baltic States and to Russia's frontiers in 1940, but he warned Molotov that such clauses would make the worst possible impression on the United States, that an emphatic and public protest would be lodged by the Polish Government, and that it would bring about a weakening, if not the collapse, of the underground resistance of the nations subjugated by Hitler. It would also have, without any doubt, strongly negative consequences in neutral States.

'To sum up,' said Mr. Eden, smiling, 'I repeated all your arguments, General. It is 100% your merit that this treaty has its present shape and not a different one. The United States have also supported your point of view, and therefore 50% of the merit is theirs.'—'And it is 150% your merit, Mr. Secretary, interrupted General Sikorski, that you understood the situation in time and had the courage to take a sharp turn.'—'Yes, but we succeeded because I took your advice. The Poles evidently know the Russians much better than we do. It seems—continued Mr. Eden—as if M. Molotov had received very wide powers (for negotiation) from Stalin' ('or perhaps, interrupted General Sikorski, Stalin feels weaker at present') —'because Molotov, having thought it over for three days, recognized this point of view and withdrew the territorial claims.'

Then Mr. Eden informed General Sikorski of the difficulties that had arisen in the conversations when he wished to introduce into the text a passage explicitly stating the necessity of establishing federal unions in Europe. The Russians opposed it, though they stated that their attitude towards them was not negative.

Replying to General Sikorski's question, Mr. Eden stated on his honour that there were no secret agreements or protocols, and that none would be concluded, as it was contrary to his principles and to his policy, and, moreover, it might have caused great trouble. When Molotov wished—in a question unrelated to territorial issues—to introduce some secret clauses, Mr. Eden reminded him of Lenin's basic arguments of 1918, when in all his declarations concerning international relations, he resolutely fought secret international agreements. Mr. Eden stated that since he became Foreign Secretary he did not conclude any secret agreement, he had only inherited some as for instance the secret protocol with Poland of August 1939. [...].

Mr. Eden further said to General Sikorski that after the signing of the Treaty Molotov spoke to him about the future frontiers of Poland. He repeated Stalin's opinion that after the war Poland should be strong and should receive East Prussia and former Polish territories, lately in German possession, which were indispensable to Poland in the West. At the same time, however, he raised a claim to a rectification of Poland's eastern frontier, mentioning the Curzon Line.

General Sikorski recalled his conversation with Stalin, in the course of which he had refused to discuss the question of the future Polish frontiers during the war. Stalin told him then that he would be satisfied with a 'tiny bit' (tchiut-tchiut in Russian). Now, he is already talking of the Curzon Line. General Sikorski emphasized once more very firmly that, as he was the head of a Government in exile, he was not able to enter a discussion on the question of reductions of Poland's territory and on the flexibility of her frontiers. At this juncture Mr. Eden proposed to General Sikorski a meeting with Molotov before he flew off to Moscow. General Sikorski agreed to it, provided such a meeting would be a meeting of three, that is to say, with Mr. Eden's participation.

Mr. Eden further stated that the signing of the Agreement of 30th July, 1941, by General Sikorski was not only extremely useful to Poland but was a bold, patriotic and wise decision. It was a fundamental act which had a most positive value even as regards the relations of Great Britain with Russia. Mr. Eden added that the present Anglo-Soviet Treaty would not have been concluded but for the existence of the Polish-Soviet Agreement. Instead, the agreement proposed by Russia, and so consistently opposed by General Sikorski, would finally have been signed. Also, the close and friendly military co-operation between the United States and Russia would have been impossible today without the Agreement of 1941. At the same time he emphasized that speaking of the recruitment (for the Polish Army) and the evacuation (of Polish troops from Russia) with Molotov, he had informed M. Molotov, in accordance with the General's letter, of the two naval Polish units lost in battle to the North of Murmansk while on a convoy of military supplies for Russia.

Mr. Eden was well aware of the enormous difficulties which General Sikorski had to overcome in concluding the Polish-Soviet Agreement, and this increased his consideration and respect for the General. He said that the views of those Poles who opposed the agreement were now undergoing a change. Many of them declared they were in favour of it.

No. 226

Note from the People's Commissariat for Foreign Affairs to the Polish Embassy in the USSR stating that the issuing of Polish passports in the USSR will depend on the Soviet permission in each individual case

Moscow, June 9, 1942 GSHI, A.11. 49/Sow./3
Transl. from Russian: Pol.-Sov.R., No. 60

The People's Commissariat for Foreign Affairs taking into consideration that the Polish Embassy and, under the arrangement relating to the scope of action of the Delegates of the Embassy of the Polish Republic, its Delegates in the Republics and Districts of the Union of Soviet Socialist Republics and its representatives are proceeding to issue Polish national passports, has the honour to state that the competent Soviet authorities find it indispensable that, to properly order this matter, the Embassy should present to the People's Commissariat for Foreign Affairs alphabetical lists of Polish citizens to whom it proposes to issue national passports. These lists, made out separately for each district inhabited by Polish citizens, should be presented in four copies with a Russian translation attached to accelerate the procedure. The lists should include all persons above the age of 16. These lists should indicate:

a. Surname, name and father's name;
b. Year and place of birth;
c. Origin;
d. Religion;
e. Present address in full;
f. Citizenship and place of residence until November 1939;
g. If covered by the Amnesty Decree of the Supreme Council of the USSR of August 12, 1941,[1] when and where arrested and sent out, number of jail delivery certificate, when and by what office of the People's Commissariat of the Interior it was issued;
h. If not a permanent inhabitant of Western Ukraine or White Ruthenia, when and how arrived on the territory of the USSR;
i. Whether married or single. If married, place and date of marriage; citizenship of husband and wife since the time of marriage;
j. Present and past citizenship and place of residence of parents.

[1] See doc. No. 110.

These lists may be drawn up in descriptive form or in the form of question-naires.

All objections of competent Soviet authorities to the issue of Polish national passports to these or other persons included in the lists will be notified by the People's Commissariat for Foreign Affairs to the Embassy on the return of these lists.

Persons included in the above-mentioned lists to whom the competent Soviet authorities raise no objection will receive, on presentation of their Polish national passports, permits of residence for foreigners, issued by Militia Headquarters of the respective counties through the Militia Office of their district or town.

The People's Commissariat for Foreign Affairs also has the honour to inform the Embassy that it is indispensable to include in the above-mentioned lists all persons who have already been issued with Polish national passports.

No. 227

Note from Minister Raczyński to Ambassador Bogomolov concerning further enrolment into the Polish Forces in the USSR and the evacuation of surpluses of numerical strength to the Middle East

London, June 10, 1942[1]   GSHI, A.11. 49/Sow./2

J'ai l'honneur d'accuser à Votre Excellence réception du message de Monsieur J. Stalin, Président du Conseil des Commissaires du Peuple de l'Union des Républiques Socialistes Soviétiques, adressé au Général W. Sikorski, Président du Conseil de la République de Pologne, qui me fut transmis le 13 mai 1942[2] par M. Tchitchaiev, Conseilleur d'Ambassade.

En réponse à cette communication j'ai l'honneur de porter à la connais-sance de Votre Excellence que le Général Sikorski, après avoir dûment étudié le contenu de ce message m'a chargé de vous soumettre quelques considérations à ce sujet, en priant Votre Excellence de bien vouloir les faire parvenir à Monsieur le Président du Conseil des Commissaires du Peuple.

Le Gouvernement polonais se rend entièrement compte des difficultés d'approvisionnement existant temporairement en l'Union des Républiques Socialistes Soviétiques et pour cette raison n'a point insisté sur l'augmentation du nombre des rations alimentaires destinées aux armées polonaises en l'Union des Républiques Socialistes Soviétiques.

Le message du Général Sikorski n'avait pas pour but l'augmentation des cadres de l'armée polonaise ni, ce qui s'en suivrait, l'augmentation de l'approvisionnement destiné aux forces armées polonaises se trouvant sur le territoire de l'Union des Républiqes Socialistes Soviétiques.

Le Gouvernement polonais désire pouvoir continuer sur le territoire de l'Union des République Socialistes Soviétiques le recrutement des ressortis-sants polonais capables de porter les armes dans le but d'élargir les cadres de

[1] This Note was drafted on June 5, and later on corrected.   [2] See doc. No. 218.

l'armée polonaise se trouvant en Grande Bretagne et en Proche Orient et donner, par la même, à chaque Polonais apte au service militaire la possibilité de servir activement dans les unités polonaises. Le Gouvernement polonais est prêt à se charger de l'approvisionnement temporaire des troupes en excès du contingent établi de 44,000 hommes, au cours de leur transport à travers le territoire de l'Union des Républiques Socialistes Soviétiques vers les ports méridionaux de la Mer Caspienne, où, le cas échéant, vers Ashabad et Meched. A ces fins une réserve d'un million de rations d'approvisionnement vient d'être déposée à Téhéran et cette réserve pourrait être mise sans délai à la disposition du Général Anders au cas de la reprise de l'évacuation.

Le Gouvernement polonais est décidé d'employer les forces armées polonaises se trouvant en l'Union des Républiques Socialistes Soviétiques, en Proche Orient ou en Grande Bretagne, dans la lutte pour la cause commune contre l'ennemi commun; l'armée polonaise servira par cela même la cause alliée dans son ensemble.

Les pertes subies récemment par les forces armées polonaises sont une preuve éloquente de cette décision du Gouvernement polonais; ces pertes comprennent, entre autres, deux navires de guerre coulés au moment où ils escortaient un transport de matériel de guerre, expédié de Grande Bretagne en l'Union des Républiques Socialistes Soviétiques.[3] Le rôle joué par l'aviation polonaise dans les récentes opérations est illustré par le fait que 101 appareils de bombardement polonais ont pris part dans les derniers raids sur Cologne et la Ruhr.

Il est possible que l'armée polonaise organisée en Proche Orient pourrait —après son équipement et entraînement—être utilisée aussi sur le front de l'Union des Républiques Socialistes Soviétiques, au cas, où la situation militaire l'éxigerait. Certaines unités de cette armée ont déjà pris une part remarquable dans la défence de Tobrouk et dans les combats dans le désert. Le fait que l'armée polonaise n'a pas encore combattu aux cotés de l'Armée Rouge est dû uniquement aux difficultés en matière d'armement éprouvées par l'Union des Républiques Socialistes Soviétiques ainsi qu'aux difficultés ressenties par la Grande Bretagne et les États Unis dans le domaine des transports maritimes.

Si le Gouvernement polonais insiste sur la pleine réalisation des accords conclus par lui avec l'Union des Républiques Socialistes Soviétiques, il le fait donc uniquement dans un intérêt commun bien compris.

Le contingent des armées polonaises en l'Union des Républiques Socialistes Soviétiques fut établi au nombre de 96,000 hommes; en outre 25,000 soldats devaient être évacués en Proche Orient, sans compter 2,000 marins et aviateurs entraînés. Le chiffre total de la force armée, recrutée parmis les ressortissants polonais en l'Union des Républiques Socialistes Soviétiques, devait donc s'élever à 123,000 soldats; en ce moment les contingents prévus pour l'encadrement en l'Union des Républiques Socialistes Soviétiques ne comptent que 44,000 hommes, en dehors des 30,000 déjà évacués. Le Gouvernement polonais est d'avis que pour atteindre le chiffre stipulé de

[3] Trois! depuis quelques jours.

123,000 hommes un complément de 49,000 soldats devrait—après recrutement sur le territoire soviétique, et au cas où ces troupes ne pourraient
entrer dans les cadres de l'armée polonaise en l'Union des Républiques
Socialistes Soviétiques—être évacué en Proche Orient.

En ce référant aux conversations qu'il a eues à Moscou avec Monsieur le
Président du Conseil des Commissaires du Peuple, le Général Sikorski adresse
un appel à Monsieur J. Staline en le priant de vouloir bien rendre possible la
continuation du recrutement des ressortissants polonais en l'Union des
Républiques Socialistes Soviétiques, ainsi que l'évacuation des contingents
dépassant le chiffre de 44,000 soldats, vers l'Iran et la Palestine.

No. 228

*Telegram from General Sikorski to Lt.-General Anders with the instructions
relating to the negotiations with the Soviet Government on the future of the
Polish armed forces in the USSR*[1]

London, June 12, 1942[2]

GSHI, PRM, 73/1
Transl. from Polish

Referring to your telegram No. 701.[3] Your report No. 701 contains some
elements which are extremely dangerous to the whole question. It appears
from it that the position of the Army, which is better than that of the civilian
population, is catastrophic. What conclusions am I to draw from it in relation to the position of hundreds of thousands of civilian refugees? Private
suggestions as to the use of our troops for reinforcement in Syria and Cairo
are absolutely out of touch with reality. I was able to state this beyond doubt
in the course of a long conference with Molotov [. . .]. The Soviet Government
is anxious for our Army to remain in the USSR. Fearing loss of prestige,
they are not willing to agree even to the evacuation of children, but this we
shall probably carry out. It is true that they would like our troops to approach
the front line as soon as possible as it would be evidence of an agreement
between our world and theirs especially in view of the strong position held
by the Polish Government in the West. I raised emphatic reservations
against sending our troops to the front without adequate equipment, and
this met with understanding. Zhukov's requests, put forward allegedly in
the name of the Soviet Government, are made on his purely personal
initiative. He plays a game which, so far, is not quite clear to me, but which
is extremely dangerous for the future of our Army in the USSR. I can
hardly believe that he only wants the departure of the troops to Teheran or
Cairo. I think that his aim is rather the decomposition and the ruin of the
reputation of our army in the USSR, which has not wavered in its resolution
until now in spite of such cruel trials, and today it might collapse. [. . .].

The assertion that the decision to evacuate would enable further recruitment is misleading. Will you, please, my General, be very cautious in

[1] See Note No. 228.
[2] This telegram was despatched on June 11 p.m. and deciphered on June 12 a.m.
[3] Not printed.

your conversations in Moscow. Conferences with Stalin are apparently cordial, but your agreements might be disavowed afterwards, and advantage may be taken to the great detriment of Poland of differences arising between you and the Ambassador. [. . .].

It is the Government only who can defend the interests of Poland and the Army in the USSR, while any transactions through the delegate of the NKVD to the troops formed in the USSR would lead us astray. The question of a further conscription and evacuation is being put forward by me, in my capacity as Head of the Government, in the course of my negotiations with Molotov, and also in my endeavours to win the support of Roosevelt, Churchill and Eden. It is a long and exacting task. I shall inform you of further developments through the Ambassador, because I have declined, for the time being, Molotov's invitation to Moscow. I reckon on your staunch character, power of will and ardent patriotism, and I expect that you will not let the problem of Polish troops in Russia take a bad turn. The Polish Government also expects this from you.

No. 229

Record of the conversation between Ambassador Ciechanowski and Secretary of State Cordell Hull concerning the enrolment of Poles into the Polish Army in the USSR

Washington, June 13, 1942   GSHI, PRM, 71

I—The Polish Ambassador informed the Secretary of State that General Sikorski, Prime Minister of Poland, had made a statement on June 11th, in London, defining the attitude of the Polish Government to the British-Soviet Treaty of Alliance signed in London on the 26th of May, 1942, and published on June 11th, 1942. The most important sentences of this statement are hereto attached.

On behalf of General Sikorski the Polish Ambassador asked the Secretary of State to be kind enough to convey to the President, and to accept for himself and his collaborators at the Department of State General Sikorski's warmest thanks for the invaluable support given to Poland in the course of the discussions leading to the conclusion of this Treaty. The Ambassador assured the Secretary of State that the Polish Government fully realized that American statesmanship and guidance had most effectively contributed to eliminate from its text the territorial clauses liable to endanger the indispensable solidarity of the United Nations.

II—The Polish Ambassador referred to his conversation with the Under-Secretary of State on June 2nd, in the course of which he had the honour to ask for the intervention of the President and the Secretary of State during their conversations with Mr. Molotov concerning the outstanding and difficult problems pending between the Polish Government and the Government of the USSR, in regard to the continuation of recruitment of Polish Nationals in Russia and of their evacuation to Iran, to the liberation of some 8,300 Polish officers who, according to lists in possession of the Polish Government, have not yet been released by the Soviet Government, as well as to the evacuation of 50,000 Polish children at present suffering near famine conditions in the USSR. The Ambassador expressed regret that it had not been possible to raise these problems during the visit of M. Molotov in Washington.

Further recruiting of Polish soldiers in Russia and their speedy evacuation to Iran, where they could be reconditioned, equipped and armed and added to the contingent of some 30,000 Polish military already evacuated from the USSR, is a problem of great importance and urgency not only to Poland, but at this stage of the war it is also of considerable importance to the joint effort of the United Nations. It is certainly of direct importance to Soviet Russia whose Government is so justifiably insistent on the speedy opening up of a second front in order to divert some of the enemy's forces at present concentrating their main effort against Soviet Russia. It would be most regrettable if in this situation the United Nations, including Soviet Russia, were willingly to forego an increase of some 35,000 to 50,000 additional troops composed of keen Polish soldiers, or even unduly to delay their formation into additional units available as a reserve army in the Middle East.

The details of the situation as it now exists in this matter between the Polish and the USSR Government have been explained in the memorandum handed by the Polish Ambassador on June 2nd to the Under-Secretary of State.

In view of the importance of this question, and of the fact that the President has on several previous occasions shown so much kindly understanding of the situation and lent the weight of his valuable and decisive support to the endeavours of the Polish Government,—the Polish Ambassador would be most grateful if the Secretary of State could obtain the President's consent once more to take this matter under consideration and to intervene in Moscow in order to obtain its satisfactory solution in the interests of Poland, of Soviet Russia, and, in fact, of the joint effort of the United Nations.

The Polish Ambassador would also be most grateful if the USSR Government could be made aware that the US Government is interested in the fate of the Polish officers still detained in Russia, probably on the islands of the Arctic Ocean or in the farthest north-eastern region of Siberia. The details of this question are described in the aforementioned memorandum of June 2nd.

The Polish Ambassador expressed the thanks of the Polish Government for the active way in which the question of the evacuation of Polish children from Soviet Russia was being handled on the kind initiative of the President by the Department of State and the American Red Cross, and expressed the hope that its realization could be speedily reached on account of the growing mortality among the Polish children in Russia and its consequent urgency.

Letter from General Sikorski to President Roosevelt asking for his support in the matter of continuation of the recruitment in the USSR and the evacuation of a part of Polish troops from there

London, June 17, 1942   GSHI, PRM, 69

I am writing to express my most cordial thanks for the continuous and fruitful support which you, Mr. President, were kind enough to give to the Polish Government in their defence of Polish interests during the many months of the British-Soviet negotiations. These negotiations finally brought with them the vindication of principles the respect of which is an indispensable condition of a lasting and just peace; ideals for which the Polish nation and its Armed Forces abroad are fighting, and will continue to fight implacably. You, Mr. President, have become the custodian and interpreter of these principles in the sphere of international relations,—in conformity with the age-long traditions of the great North-American democracy of which you are the leader and spokesman.

The political and moral solidarity of the United Nations has been preserved at this crucial moment. German propaganda has been denied an opportunity to exploit for its benefit the agreement of the great democracies with Soviet Russia, while the peoples of the Soviet Union will find a new encouragement in their struggle against the Teutonic invader. I emphasized this view before Mr. Eden and M. Molotov while congratulating them on the favourable results which they were able to achieve. If, however, Soviet Russia is to remain true to the positive political role which it proposes to play, words must be followed by deeds.

Apart from the release of the surviving officers deported to the Northern provinces of Russia, accessible only during the short summer months, the Polish Government, relying on their undoubted rights, are gravely concerned with two main problems. The resumption of recruiting of Polish citizens to the Polish Army, which has been stopped by the Soviet authorities, and their subsequent evacuation,—and secondly the removal of 50,000 children from Russia. The latter have scarcely any chance of surviving the difficult conditions existing in Russia and owing to their poor physical condition are being decimated by disease. They are a priceless treasure vouchsafing the future of the Polish people, which is being ceaselessly exterminated in the homeland. The enclosed photographs show the state of Polish children who arrived in Persia from Russia. These unfortunate children had already spent several months recuperating under the care of the Polish Embassy.

As far as the Polish Army is concerned, the Soviet authorities cannot be said to implement their verbal and written agreements. The Polish Army is not being provided with arms and this fact is being subsequently used as an argument against the Poles. Therefore, it is in the mutual interest of the future relations between Poland and Russia that: 1/ the Polish Army in Russia should be speedily armed and thus enabled to fight against Germany. 2/ The enrolment in the Army should be resumed and at least 49,000 men should be recruited from among the able-bodied Polish citizens covered by the existing but not yet fully executed agreement. One half of this number would reinforce Polish units in the Middle East and in Great Britain. In view of the steady drain on the personnel of the Polish Air Force, the merit of which is generally recognized and of which 101 crews took part in the two recent mass bombing raids on Germany, replacements are indispensable. The same may be said of the Polish Navy, which recently lost three warships and two transports torpedoed by the Germans while in convoys, carrying war supplies to Russia and Libya. The Polish Land Forces which only recently acquitted themselves with credit in Tobruk and the Libyan desert are in a similar position.

If I venture to appeal to you personally, Mr. President, for support in these matters—as I have already appealed to Mr. Churchill—it is because I wish to leave out considerations of prestige voiced by Monsieur Molotov in his conversations with me in London. I believe that should the Soviet Government persevere in their attitude, they could hardly expect to avoid a public discussion on the subject, from which only Germany and her satellites could reap an advantage.

I trust, Mr. President, that you will appreciate the reasons which prompted me to approach you once more with the most earnest appeal for full and strong support by such means and in such ways as you may consider appropriate—to the endeavours of the Polish Government to bring about a resumption of the arbitrarily suspended recruiting and evacuation of the enrolled soldiers and also the removal of 50,000 Polish children from Russia. The very serious food situation in Russia adds urgency to my appeal.

No. 231

Report of Maj.-General Regulski to Maj.-General Klimecki on insistent British demands to proceed to and speed up the further stage of the evacuation of Polish troops from the USSR

London, June 22, 1942   GSHI, A.XII. 22/31.6
                                                              Transl. from Polish

The War Office has inquired of me several times what has happened about the further evacuation of our troops from the USSR to Palestine;[1] it appears, beyond any doubt, from these inquiries that the English are greatly interested in the further stage of this evacuation and that they are anxious for its being speeded up.

Today I was informed by the War Office that the Soviet authorities have requested the English authorities to wind up the evacuation bases at Pahlevi and Kazvin.

These bases, fully manned, wait for the so-called second stage of the evacuation from the USSR.

[1] On June 17 Lt.-Col. Hull sent from Yanghi-Yul a dispatch to the British Military Mission in Moscow on the necessity of interference on the subject of further evacuation of the Polish Army to the Middle East.

The War Office requests that General Anders be ordered to bring appropriate pressure to bear on the speeding up of the further evacuation and asks about the results of his announced negotiations with the Soviet authorities.[2]

[2] After having received this report, on the following day (23rd June) General Sikorski sent a telegram to General Anders, the relevant passage of which runs as follows:

'Today I was informed by the War Office that the Soviet authorities request from the English authorities the liquidation of the evacuation bases at Pahlevi and Kazvin. These bases with full staff and supplies wait for the second stage of the Polish evacuation from the USSR.—As you have promised the War Office to intervene in the question of maintaining those bases and to settle it with the Russians, I order you to report by return of post on the present state of this question.'

No. 232

Extract from a note from the Polish Embassy in the USSR to the People's Commissariat for Foreign Affairs in reply to the Soviet Note of June 9, 1942, on the matter of Polish passports

Kuibyshev, June 24, 1942   GSHI, A.11. 49/Sow./2
                                              Transl. from Polish: Pol.-Sov.R., No. 61

Referring to the Note of the People's Commissariat for Foreign Affairs No. 107 of June 9, 1942,[1] the Polish Embassy, on the instruction of its Government, has the honour to submit the following for the information of the People's Commissariat for Foreign Affairs:

In accordance with the fundamental principles of international law, the Government of the Republic of Poland assert that the matter of Polish citizenship rests with them and they do not consider it possible that, when verifying lists of Polish citizens demanded of the Embassy, the Soviet authorities should decide the citizenship of Polish citizens resident on the territory of the Republic of Poland and who between 1939–1941 found themselves, as is known, not of their free will on the territory of the Soviet Union.

In particular this attitude of the Polish Government is also in accordance with the Agreement concluded on July 30, 1941,[2] between the Government of the Republic of Poland and the Government of the Union of Soviet Socialist Republics. [. . .]. The issue of passports to Polish citizens is carried out by the Polish Embassy and its representatives under existing Polish laws and regulations. According to the Constitution of the Republic of Poland and Polish law, origin, religion, race or place of residence within the frontiers of the Republic of Poland have no influence on the citizenship of a given person.

Taking into consideration that the aforementioned Note of the People's Commissariat for Foreign Affairs is aimed at imposing a procedure in issuing passports, unprecedented in relations between sovereign States, the Government of the Polish Republic see no possibility of discussing the principles of this question on the basis of the suggested procedure.

[1] See doc. No. 126.   [2] See doc. No. 160.

No. 233

Telegram from General Sikorski to Lt.-General Anders and Ambassador Kot containing instructions for the evacuation of Polish troops from the USSR to the Middle East[1]

London, July 2, 1942

GSHI, A.XII. 22/31.6
Transl. from Polish

Under the pressure of the British and American Governments, prompted by the Polish Government, Stalin informed the British Ambassador through Molotov that the Soviet Government agreed to the evacuation of Polish troops from the USSR to the Middle East.

The Polish Government accepted this suggestion and agreed to it in principle, linking up this question with that of a further call-up, the setting up of a reserve centre there and the evacuation of children and civilian population residing in the area in which the troops are quartered.

You have to discuss this and to make the necessary arrangements, fixing the date on which the evacuation will start and carrying it out on the spot. The orders relating to transport and establishment of camps in the Middle East will be issued by the War Office. You have to submit completely to all British instructions on these matters.

I attach great importance to leaving a strong and well organized reserve centre under the command of General Bohusz. It should be able to organize further recruitment and evacuation. You must insist on this very strongly.

[1] See Note No. 233.

No. 234

Aide-Mémoire delivered by the People's Commissariat for Foreign Affairs to the Polish Embassy in the USSR, announcing the closing of the offices of Embassy Delegates at Aldan, Vladivostok and Archangel

Kuibyshev, July 3, 1942

GSHI, A.11. 49/Sow./3
Transl. from Russian

Referring to the proposals recently made by M. Kot and other members of the Embassy on the matter of the activities of the Delegates and men of trust of the Embassy, the People's Commissariat for Foreign Affairs deems it necessary to state the following:

1. In accordance with the opinion expressed by M. Kot that the maintenance of the office of the Embassy Delegate at Aldan is not necessary (because of the small number of Polish citizens in that area), the People's Commissariat considers it necessary to close that office. Neither is there any need for the further activity of the Office of the Embassy Delegate at Vladivostok, as the number of Polish citizens in that area is insignificant (especially after the recent departure of a big group from Magadan, and the interruption of the transport of welfare supplies through the port of Vladivostok because of the war in the Pacific). The People's Commissariat considers also that the maintenance of the office at Archangel serves no purpose,

as its principal task, the settling and providing with jobs of Polish citizens in the areas of Archangel and Vologodsk, is considered to be completed. In connection therewith the competent Soviet authorities have been issued with instructions aiming at the stopping of the activities of the offices at Aldan, Vladivostok and Archangel.

The People's Commissariat cannot agree to the opening of the office of the Embassy Delegate in Bokhara, as it is not necessary in view of the sufficient number of men of trust of the Embassy of the Republic of Poland. As regards the city of Saratov, in view of the small number of Polish citizens there the People's Commissariat does not think it would be necessary to designate a delegate for Saratov, the more so as this post has remained vacant until now. It is also impossible to send a travelling delegate of the Embassy to the areas of Stalingrad and the Caucasus, because of circumstances due to the war.

2. Having examined the proposals of the Embassy relating to the number of permanent officials on the staffs of the offices of Embassy delegates, the People's Commissariat sees no reason for revising its point of view, considering that 5 to 7 permanent officials in each office will be perfectly able to ensure its proper running.

3. The proposals of the Embassy concerning a conditional recognition of the men of trust appointed by the Embassy directly after receipt of the Embassy's notification is unacceptable because such an arrangement might in practice lead to misunderstandings.

No. 235

Record of a conversation between Minister Raczyński and Sir Alexander Cadogan concerning the evacuation of the three Polish divisions left in the USSR and the Memorandum of the Polish Government of July 3, 1942, presented on this occasion to the British Government[1]

London, July 4, 1942   GSHI, A.11. 49/Sow./4
                                          Transl. from Polish: Pol.-Sov.R., No. 47

On July 2, I visited the Foreign Office at the request of Sir Alexander Cadogan, the Permanent Under-Secretary of State, who notified me of the contents of a telegram he had received from Sir Archibald Clark Kerr, British Ambassador in the USSR, who is at present in Moscow. The Ambassador had received from Commissar Molotov a statement of Premier Stalin, in connection with Mr. Churchill's conversation with M. Molotov in London when Mr. Churchill made a suggestion to transfer part of the Polish Forces from Soviet territory to the Middle East. M. Stalin now suggests that three Polish divisions 'well trained, but not yet fully armed' be moved to that region. Sir Alexander Cadogan asked me to notify him as soon as possible of the Polish Government's decision in this matter. He added that the British Government would be satisfied with such a solution and would be

[1] See Note No. 235.

prepared to take immediate steps to receive these Forces and to assure them the necessary equipment.

I promised Sir Alexander a reply in the shortest possible time.

On the evening of July 4, I delivered the enclosed Memorandum to Sir A. Cadogan. The Memorandum defines the conditions which in the opinion of the Polish Government should be fulfilled in the event of the Polish divisions leaving Soviet territory.

Sir Alexander undertook to communicate the contents of the Memorandum to the British Ambassador in Moscow and to instruct him to submit the Polish conditions to the Soviet Government. Sir Alexander added that he was not aware of the reasons for which the Soviet Government had chosen to negotiate with us through the intermediary of the British Government, on grounds which he was in no position to judge. He thought that at the present stage this method should be maintained until the situation cleared in the course of the British Ambassador's introductory negotiations with M. Molotov. In the light of these negotiations we should be able to consider the most suitable steps to be taken next. I agreed to such an attitude.

Memorandum

1. The Polish Government are gratified to be afforded an opportunity to help in the defence of the Near East with the Polish troops from Russia.

2. They are, however, compelled to draw the attention of His Majesty's Government to the duty of the Polish Government to assist their citizens in Soviet Russia. The presence of Polish troops in Russia has up to now enabled the civilian Poles to obtain the necessary means of existence.

3. Therefore the Polish Government feel they are entitled to hope for His Majesty's Government's collaboration in obtaining from the Soviet Government the fulfilment of the following request:

a) After the departure of three Polish divisions from Russia the Polish recruiting centre shall remain in Russia and recruiting of all Polish citizens able to carry arms shall be resumed until such time as the complete mobilization of all available men shall have been effected.

b) Auxiliary military services of women and boy-scouts shall leave Russia together with the aforesaid three divisions as well as the families of the officers and men leaving Russia.

c) The necessary measures shall be undertaken to begin the evacuation from Russia of 50,000 Polish children accompanied by 5,000 mothers or guardians who would be given refuge outside Russia through the collaboration of the British authorities. The Polish Embassy in the Soviet Union, whilst maintaining fully its protection over Poles remaining in the Union on the basis of arrangements now in force, will be given the opportunity to co-operate through its appointed representatives in this evacuation. President Roosevelt has expressed his personal interest in the fate of these children and has pledged the assistance of American authorities in facilitating the withdrawal of a first contingent of 10,000 from Russia in order to save them from starvation.

4. Finally, the Polish Government hope for the collaboration of His Majesty's Government in the further search for the Polish officers missing in Russia. These officers would prove of great service in the formation of Polish divisions after the withdrawal of three divisions. The matter is urgent as it is only in the short summer months that access is possible to the Northern regions to which these officers have presumably been removed.

London, July 3, 1942

No. 236

Note from the People's Commissariat for Foreign Affairs to the Embassy of the Republic of Poland in the USSR, announcing the withdrawal of diplomatic immunity from the Embassy Delegates

Kuibyshev, July 6, 1942   GSHI, A.11. 49/Sow./3
Transl. from Russian

In a number of localities, namely Ashabad, Pavlodar, Petropavlovsk, Samarkand, Chelabinsk and Chimkent, the Polish Embassy has at present entrusted with the duties of Embassy Delegates persons who at the same time occupy various diplomatic posts. In consequence persons who have been appointed secretaries or attachés of the Embassy do not in fact carry out any diplomatic activity, being actually engaged in a work which has nothing to do with their official diplomatic duties; moreover, they retain their diplomatic rights and privileges. This position is absolutely improper.

The People's Commissariat deems it necessary that local Embassy Delegates occupying diplomatic posts be released either from their duties of Embassy Delegates, or from their diplomatic posts, as in future such a cumulation of duties cannot be allowed, and the local Delegates of the Embassy charged at the same time with diplomatic functions will not be treated as persons enjoying diplomatic rights and privileges.

No. 237

Note from the Polish Embassy in the USSR to the People's Commissariat for Foreign Affairs protesting against the infringement of the diplomatic immunity of the Embassy Delegate in Archangel and against the arrest of his staff

Kuibyshev, July 6, 1942   GSHI, A.11. 49/Sow./2
Transl. from Polish: Pol.-Sov.R., No. 71

The Polish Embassy has the honour to call the following to the attention of the People's Commissariat for Foreign Affairs:

After the re-establishment of diplomatic relations between the Polish Government and the Soviet Government as a result of the conclusion of the Agreement of July 30, 1941,[1] the 'Rules governing the scope of activities of Delegates of the Embassy of the Republic of Poland' were established by an exchange of Notes, No. 48 of the People's Commissariat for Foreign Affairs,

[1] See doc. No. 106.

378

of December 23, 1941, and No. D. 1078/41 of the Polish Embassy of December 24, 1941.

On January 23, 1942, during a conversation which aimed at establishing in greater detail the legal status of these Delegates, their privileges and rights, their personal security and the immunity of their archives, correspondence and offices, M. Vyshinsky, Deputy Chairman of the Council of People's Commissars of the USSR, stated to M. Kot, the Polish Ambassador, that when dealing with the problem of Embassy Delegates, the Soviet authorities realized it was indispensable to grant them a special position in relation to the local authorities, who received instructions to treat the Delegates as representatives of a foreign Embassy and as official persons. When asked by the Polish Ambassador whether this statement would be considered a guarantee that the Delegates would enjoy personal immunity, immunity of their archives and official correspondence, freedom to organize their offices and to choose their office staff and the liberty to travel, the Deputy Chairman of the Council of People's Commissars declared that the People's Commissariat for Foreign Affairs had done all in its power to secure these conditions for them, and requested the Ambassador to inform him should any difficulties of a local nature arise, adding that these difficulties would be removed.

On July 2, 1942, at about 4 p.m. M. Józef Gruja, Polish Embassy Delegate in Archangel, 2nd Secretary of the Polish Embassy, was obliged to go on official business to Murmansk, leaving behind as his deputy in Archangel (in agreement with the local authorities) M. Waldemar Kuczyński, one of his officials. A few hours after the Embassy Delegate had left, three officials of the People's Commissariat for Internal Affairs, accompanied by two women employed in the local Intourist Hotel, entered the office of the Archangel Delegate, carried out a thorough search and for several hours questioned the officials present in the Delegate's office. Finally, according to information received by the Embassy, the officials of the People's Commissariat for Internal Affairs took the liberty of removing all the archives and official correspondence of the Embassy Delegate in Archangel, his seal and his money, and after having arrested the officials of the Delegate's office, that is to say, the acting Embassy Delegate, Waldemar Kuczyński, the storekeeper, Anna Witkowska, the assistant storekeeper, Marian Pytlak, and office-worker Zdzisława Wójcik, they drove these persons away to an unknown destination, leaving with M. Kuczyński's wife previously prepared documents concerning the search they had carried out.

In view of the fact,

1. That the action described above was taken by officials of the People's Commissariat for Internal Affairs, a considerable number of hours before this Embassy was informed, on the night of July 3–4, 1942, of the unilateral decision of the Soviet authorities that the maintenance of an Embassy Delegate in Archangel would serve no further purpose because his principal tasks had been carried out—this at a time when even from the Soviet authorities' point of view there existed a Polish Embassy Delegate in Archangel who was acting legally, i.e. in accordance with the Polish-Soviet

agreement, concluded by Notes exchanged on December 23 and 24, 1941, and on January 8 and 9, 1942;

2. That, in connection with the above, the action taken by the officials of the People's Commissariat for Internal Affairs, the entry into the office of the legally officiating Polish Embassy Delegate, the carrying out of a search therein, the violation of the immunity and the carrying away of the archives and official correspondence and a seal and money belonging to the Polish Embassy in the USSR, constitute a flagrant violation of the rights enjoyed by Polish Embassy Delegates and their offices, expressly guaranteed by the Deputy Chairman of the Council of People's Commissars of the USSR;

3. That the Polish citizens acting Delegate M. Kuczyński, in the temporary absence from Archangel of the Embassy Delegate, and the three afore-mentioned officials of the Delegate's office were deprived of their liberty seems all the more unjustified as the Soviet authorities had not only failed to raise any objection or complaint against the activities of the office of the Archangel Delegate, but even expressed, through the medium of M. Novikov in his conversation, on March 9, 1942, with M. Arlet, 1st Secretary of the Embassy, their appreciation of the activities of that office.

The Polish Embassy is obliged:

To regard the action taken by the Soviet authorities in Archangel as altogether inconsistent with the rules and customs accepted in international relations, and as entirely opposed to the principles of friendly collaboration, which found their expression in the Agreement of July 30, 1941,[1] and the Declaration of December 4, 1941;[2]

To protest against this action of the Soviet authorities; and

To ask the People's Commissariat for Foreign Affairs to cause:

1. the immediate release of the officials of the office of the Polish Embassy Delegate in Archangel, that is the Polish citizens: W. Kuczyński, M. Pytlak, A. Witkowska and Z. Wójcik;

2. the immediate restoration to M. J. Gruja, 2nd Secretary of the Polish Embassy, on his return to Archangel, of all the archives and official correspondence of the Polish Embassy Delegate in Archangel and of the seal and money, constituting the property of the Polish Embassy;

3. that investigations be immediately ordered and that the Soviet officials, guilty of taking the action described in this Note, be punished.

[1] See doc. No. 106.　　　　　　[2] See doc. No. 161.

Record of Ambassador Kot's conversation with Deputy Commissar Vyshinsky relating to the difficulties arising in Polish-Soviet relations on the eve of the Ambassador's departure from the USSR.[1] Present also Chargé d'Affaires Sokolnicki, acting as interpreter

Kuibyshev, July 8, 1942   GSHI, A.11. 49/Sow./4
                                             Transl. from Polish

Vyshinsky: The first item I should like to raise, on behalf of the Soviet Government, concerns the evacuation of Polish troops from the USSR. In view of the military position in the Middle East, and in particular in Libya, the Soviet Government informed the British Government that it would not object to the use in the Middle East of the Polish divisions, now stationed in the USSR, for common war aims.

Ambassador: I have been informed of this suggestion by my Government, and by the British Government. The decision in this matter is, of course, outside my province, and depends on direct negotiations between the Polish and British Governments. We have been forming the Polish Army in Russia in order that it should fight against the common enemy on this soil. On the other hand, the circumstances in which the Polish troops in Russia will be evacuated from here are the Embassy's concern.

Vyshinsky: When the Soviet Government agreed to this arrangement, they were aware of acting to the prejudice of their own interests. However, as Polish divisions are to be used elsewhere for a common cause, the Soviet Government did not oppose it.

Ambassador: I wish to observe that these are our best divisions, much better than the troops sent before. We desired to bring about, for the first time in history, comradeship in arms between Poles and Russians, the Polish soldier fighting side by side with the Russian soldier, against the common enemy. However, this is one war, and wherever one fights, it is for the same cause. These three divisions of ours will fight well. They would have been better prepared for immediate military operations, had they received their training equipment in due time, but it is too late now to lament the past.

Vyshinsky: You are quite right. The Soviet Government considered that it was in our common interest—we have to take the requisite measures.

Ambassador: I acknowledge your statement that it is also in Russia's interest that the Polish troops formed in Russia should fight there. I draw your attention to the fact that if Russia had agreed to a further call-up another army could be formed here for operating in the Middle East. There are excellent potential soldiers here, in particular among the peasant population, now scattered from Arkhangel and Vologda, to Krasnoyarsk and Irkutsk, being wasted in wood-cutting and other jobs, and most of them starving.

[1] This conversation was published in full in Prof. Kot's book *Rozmowy z Kremlem* (Conversations with the Kremlin), London, 1959, pp. 281–297. The text is almost identical.

Vyshinsky: This is quite a special problem. Our position was defined in Stalin's reply to General Sikorski's message relating to the question of conscription for the Polish army.

Ambassador: The war may take an unforseeable turn, and it would perhaps be better not to prejudice the future. Later events may impose a revision of this position.

Vyshinsky: The Soviet position has been negative until the present time. The question is within the province of military authorities. So far as I am concerned I cannot go into all these details. It is quite possible that in future the question will be reconsidered, and the position changed. The conscription causes serious political difficulties. Wherever it is carried out, it disturbs the population and puts it in a state of agitation ('volnuyet ludey' in Russian).

Ambassador: I have to emphasize that the call-up for the Polish Army carried out, by the way, by Soviet commissions, has been ordered, so far, in three southern provinces only. Everything went promptly, efficiently and in a quiet way. It was a matter of a few days. [. . .].

Vyshinsky: The third question which I wish to discuss with you today is an interview with President Raczkiewicz, published by the 'Dziennik Polski' (The Polish Daily)—on 30th June, as far as I can remember.[2] There are two sentences in this interview which can be misunderstood:

'The two years' sufferings of Poles in Russia increased their drive towards action, and left no trace of exhaustion or apathy.

'Everywhere I met with one desire only: to revenge the wrongs done to Poland.'

Ambassador: This is obviously due to a printer's slip. President Raczkiewicz is a very tactful person, and he wishes to co-operate with Russia. It is obvious that the second sentence can refer to Germany only.

Vyshinsky: I wish to stress that anything said by me refers to the newspaper and to the juxtaposition of texts, but not to President Raczkiewicz himself.

These were the three items which I wished to discuss with you.

Ambassador: Now it is my turn to raise some matters. The Embassy's First Secretary, M. Maciej Załęski, was arrested at Vladivostok. You were informed of his departure, in the capacity of delegate with the special mission of taking care of the transport of gift parcels sent from the United States, and of assisting the Polish population in those distant areas, such as, for instance, those who stayed at Kolyma. To arrest a diplomat is a violation of one of the basic rules of international law. I do not know the circumstances in which it took place. Apart from that there was certainly violation of the premises and archives. I ask you for an explanation. I do not know the date of the incident. This fact will force us to raise a very strong protest, and to demand the immediate release of M. Załęski.

Vyshinsky: I don't know anything about this arrest, and I shall order the case to be investigated immediately.

[2] The date is exact.

Ambassador: Somebody must have authorized it. It is unbelievable that the NKVD knew nothing about it, and that local authorities acted of themselves.

Vyshinsky: I was absent from Kuibyshev, and I do not know anything about it. If I say that the NKVD was not informed of it, you have no reason, Mr. Ambassador, to disbelieve my words. If he was arrested, it means that there were some good reasons for it.

Ambassador: There can have been no reasons.

Sokolnicki: M. Załęski certainly did not start shooting, when walking along a street. The case is clear. Załęski is a diplomat and it is absolutely forbidden to arrest him.

Ambassador: I ask you for his immediate release.

Vyshinsky: I repeat that I do not know anything about it, and I shall order this case to be investigated.

Sokolnicki: Such an investigation may take a couple of days, whereas the only thing to do is to give on the telephone an order for his release.

Vyshinsky (visibly displeased): I told you that I shall deal with this case. [. . .].

Ambassador: The next question refers to your Note announcing the withdrawal of the diplomatic privileges enjoyed by some of the Embassy Delegates. I regret that such a decision has been taken unilaterally, without consultation with us, and contrary to our previous agreements. I do not intend, however, to contend with it. If even a secretary of the Embassy can be arrested, it convinces me that diplomatic privileges are quite illusory in the USSR. I dismiss, therefore, the need for diplomatic immunity for our diplomats. Because of that, some of them will be recalled by me, and the others will work without diplomatic privileges.

Vyshinsky: It is entirely up to you, Mr. Ambassador, whom you wish to recall, and whom you will maintain in his post without diplomatic status— but I have to ask you not to draw general conclusions from the fact of a diplomat's arrest.

Ambassador: There are two cases, as a matter of fact—is this not enough to justify what I said?

Vyshinsky: The case of Kuczyński and other officials should not be mentioned here. Immunity extends to the person (and premises?), but not to the papers left by a diplomat on the spot.

Ambassador: It is the violation of a principle that matters, and not whether it took place in one or more cases.

Vyshinsky: I contest that the archives of an Embassy Delegate's office are protected by diplomatic immunity. The best proof of our liberal attitude is the case of Rola-Janicki, who was protected by his diplomatic immunity, while working to the detriment of the USSR. We asked only that he should be recalled and leave the USSR.

Ambassador: I see you have more unpleasant things in store for me before I leave the USSR. [. . .].

Ambassador: I ask you, Mr. Commissar, for a frank answer to these

383

questions: What will be the powers of the delegates in future, what may we reckon with, what is to be their personal status, and what guarantees are they to have of the indispensable freedom of action, considering that the existing state of things and the agreement have been violated? How are the people to be despatched, and how are they to communicate with the Embassy? Has this been changed? In what way can a delegate's office contact men of trust in view of so many obstacles?

Vyshinsky: The 'Regulations' defined the rights of the delegates' offices and their functions. There has been no change in this. Should the Embassy wish to propose some amendments to the agreement, we will consider them. I cannot accept the accusation that Soviet authorities violated it. If any misunderstandings have arisen, it was because there were certainly some offences on the part of the arrested men. The delegate's office has no diplomatic immunity.

Ambassador: The agreement was violated by the closing of several offices. Can I, in these circumstances, recall and change delegates, and will their successors be admitted? I asked you, Mr. Commissar, for permission to bring a dozen people here in order that I might ascertain whether they are suitable candidates for the post of delegate or his deputy. So far, only 2 or 3 men have been able to come to Kuibyshev. How can I organize anything in these circumstances? [. . .].

Ambassador (politely and visibly moved): Before my departure I should like to discuss with you, Mr. Commissar, two items which are of enormous importance for the future development of our relations, which should be not only friendly, but cordial. It is the problem of the evacuation of children, a question discussed here several times before. I ask you, Mr. Commissar, to do everything you can in order to induce the Soviet Government to allow the departure from the USSR of the greatest possible number of our children. We have to ensure them elsewhere good living conditions which they have not here. At a time when the Germans are killing our children in masses, every child's life is extremely precious to us. I have in mind all these children, orphan or not, who stay in 'Dietkoms' where they are russified. Can the Soviet Union, which has such a big population, really be bent upon it? I ask you, Mr. Commissar, most cordially, to facilitate the departure of the greatest possible proportion of children from the USSR.

The second question is that of Polish citizens who have not yet been released. There are among them thousands of judges, public prosecutors, policemen and other civil servants; and, which affects me personally most deeply, there is the question of 8,000 officers, none of whom has been released yet. I assume full responsibility for what I am saying. As summer conditions facilitate transport, I ask you to give me an opportunity of contacting them. They are not criminals, those best officers of ours, but prisoners-of-war. It is beyond possibility that such a great number of men should have vanished, and no-one understands it. The fact that they have not been found yet is a thorn in Polish-Soviet relations. I repeat once more, assuming full responsibility for my words, that none of them has been released. I ask you not for an answer, nor for one of those stereotyped phrases used in all the Notes relating to this matter, so sorrowful to us, but for help in finding those men. I address this request to you with very deep feeling, before taking my leave from you, Mr. Commissar, and from the Soviet Government.

Vyshinsky: You know, Mr. Ambassador, that there are many difficulties arising in connection with the evacuation of children, but it is being considered by the Government. I shall not fail to transmit your request. There is no question of russifying the children. This would be contrary to our principles. If we have placed them in 'Dietkoms', it was only in order to save some of them from death.

As regards the detention of Poles in prisons, labour camps, etc., I can assure you, Mr. Ambassador, that I dealt personally with those matters, and I was able to state that they were not there. I see that you are inclined to consider our answers to your enquiries to be purely formal, but I think that this is not the case. They agree with the facts. Apart from a small group of detained pro-Nazi agents there are no other people in detention. There are no officers in the Far North, nor in less distant northern provinces nor anywhere else. Perhaps they are outside the USSR, or, maybe, a number of them have died. Thus, for instance, not long ago the Embassy withdrew its previous request concerning the release of one person because it turned out that this person was found in Poland. All Poles were released, one portion before the outbreak of the war with Germany, another portion after it.

Ambassador: If I spoke of russifying the children I only had in mind quite a natural process, that of the influence of the surroundings. Thus, for instance, not long ago a father who had been compelled to place his child in a 'Dietkom' was unable to speak with him when he came to take him back, because the man was not conversant with the Russian language. He was bitterly disappointed by this.

So far as the officers are concerned, I have to say that the greatest number of enquiries comes from Poland, from the next-of-kin of those men who are very anxious about their fate, because they are not in Poland. Not one of them is there.

Sokolnicki: The case referred to by you, Mr. Chairman, and relating to one person who was found, proves, on the contrary, that we know well what is going on in our country, and should those men be there in great numbers we would have been advised of it.

If our prisoners have been released, I should be obliged to you for giving us the lists of released persons, with the date and place of their release. The Soviet Government used to make such lists several times, and there can be no difficulty in obtaining them.

Vyshinsky: Unfortunately, we have no such lists. [. . .].

Ambassador: I wish at the end of this conversation to say good-bye to you, as I am forced to leave my post for health reasons, namely exhaustion. I came here full of the same good will with which General Sikorski's Government signed the agreement with the USSR. I deeply regret that not everything could be achieved, there having been many small obstacles in the way.

In my view the relations between Poland and the USSR should be regulated by a far-sighted attitude, and not be troubled by pettiness. I have the impression that my mission has contributed to the laying of foundations for such co-operation. The only guarantee of durable friendly relations will depend on Russia's giving to Polish citizens and the Polish State all their due. True friends try to reach a straight understanding. When this happens there will be no warmer friendship than between Poland and the USSR. Hoping for the successful outcome of this war and for great triumphs for your arms, I present my wishes for all success to the Soviet Government, their President Stalin and Commissar Molotov.

I have to express my special thanks to you, Mr. Commissar, for your co-operation with me, and for the understanding shown for Polish affairs. I wish you the successful accomplishment of your tasks, which will have great historical importance.

Vyshinsky: I am awfully sorry that your health has deteriorated, Mr. Ambassador, and I wish you to regain health in order that you may continue your fruitful work for your State. During your stay here in the capacity of Ambassador it was impossible to avoid some difficulties, and not all proceeded smoothly; nevertheless, many positive things have been done. I expect the latter will take more place in your memory than the rest. Our attitude towards Poland, the Polish nation and the Polish State is quite clear. It was defined by comrade Stalin, and to us it is law. Such is also our wish, our views and our aim. I am deeply convinced that Poland will be great and free and independent, as Stalin said. I have reason to believe that our relations will be close and truly friendly, and it is in this sense that we all in the USSR wish to work, and I will also work along this line. I thank you, Mr. Ambassador, for your good wishes, and on my part I express my good wishes for the Polish nation, army and Government for all success in their struggle for the restoration of an independent Polish State, and for the freedom of the Polish nation. Will you please, Sir, accept once more my thanks for your good wishes which I shall immediately transmit to Stalin and Molotov. Please accept also my personal wishes for good health and recovery which would enable you to resume your activity.

The conversation lasted 3 hours and 10 minutes. It could be noted that Vyshinsky tried not to make matters worse. On the whole his behaviour was quiet and courteous.

No. 239

Note from the Polish Embassy in the USSR to the People's Commissariat for Foreign Affairs protesting against the arrest of the secretaries of the Polish Embassy M. Załęski at Vladivostok and M. Gruja at Archangel

Kuibyshev, July 9, 1942　　　　　　　　　　　　　　GSHI, A.11. 49/Sow./2
　　　　　　　　　　　　　　　　　　　　　　　　　Transl. from Polish

The Embassy has the honour of informing the People's Commissariat for Foreign Affairs of the following:

On 8th inst, in the afternoon the Ambassador of the Republic of Poland delivered into the hands of the First Deputy Chairman of the Council of People's Commissars of the USSR and Deputy Commissar for Foreign Affairs, M. A. J. Vyshinsky, a strong protest against the arrest at Vladivostok of the First Secretary of the Polish Embassy, M. Maciej Załęski, and a probable violation of the immunity of his house and archives. Asking for the immediate release of M. Załęski, the Ambassador stated that the arrest of the First Secretary of the Embassy constituted a patent violation of a fundamental principle of international law, namely the right to diplomatic immunity.

The First Deputy Chairman of the Council of People's Commissars, M. A. J. Vyshinsky, stated in his reply that the fact of the arrest of M. Załęski was unknown to him, and that he would deal with the matter.

On the same day, in the evening, the Embassy of the Republic of Poland received information of the arrest of the Second Secretary of the Embassy, M. Józef Gruja; it took place during his official journey, agreed with the People's Commissariat for Foreign Affairs, between Archangel and Murmansk. The Embassy of the Republic of Poland has not been informed by the People's Commissariat for Foreign Affairs of both these facts of arrest, although according to the latest information M. Załęski was arrested on 1st July of this year.

As from the time of the delivery of his declaration by the Ambassador of the Republic of Poland to the First Deputy Chairman of the Council of People's Commissars of the USSR, A. J. Vyshinsky, there elapsed more than 24 hours, and the Embassy has not been informed so far of the release of the arrested persons, the Embassy:

1) reiterates its strong protest against the arrest of the Polish diplomats;

2) requests the immediate release both of the First Secretary of the Embassy, M. Maciej Załęski, and of the Second Secretary, M. Józef Gruja;

3) requests the immediate restitution of all seals, papers, documents and money seized by the Soviet authorities;

4) requests, finally, adequate amends.

No. 240

Note from the People's Commissariat for Foreign Affairs to the Embassy of the Polish Republic in the USSR in the matter of the procedure to be strictly adhered to in issuing Polish passports

Kuibyshev, July 9, 1942

GSHI, A.11. 49/Sow./3
Transl. from Russian

In reply to the Note of the Embassy of the Republic of Poland No. D.2362/42 of 25th June, 1942[1] the People's Commissariat for Foreign Affairs has the honour to point out that in the issuing of Polish national passports it must insist on the application of the procedure of which the Embassy was advised by the Note of the People's Commissariat of 9th June. The attention of the Embassy is drawn to the fact that the issuing of Polish national passports by officials of the Embassy on the territory of the USSR, as well as the issuing of certificates of residence for aliens to the holders of the said passports by the Militia, is allowed only in accordance with this procedure.

[1] The date of this Note should be June 24, 1942; see doc. No. 232.

No. 241

Telegram from Ambassador Kot to the Polish Ministry for Foreign Affairs on the results of the British intervention in Moscow in support of the Polish claims[1]

Kuibyshev, July 9, 1942

GSHI, A.11. 49/Sow./6
Transl. from Polish

On Tuesday night the British Ambassador had a conversation with Vyshinsky. I am under the impression that he strictly adhered to his instructions, ignoring the data supplied to him by me. The position adopted by Vyshinsky was the following:

1. Further recruitment was refused by the Note of 15th May. Vyshinsky will refer the question to the Government, but his personal view was unfavourable.

2. Evacuation of the relatives of troops and of orphan children from the area in which the Polish forces are quartered. It was the only point to which Vyshinsky raised no objection.

3. Evacuation of 50,000 children. His attitude was unfavourable. He tried to argue that it would be impossible to carry out the evacuation in war time. He will refer to the Government.

4. As the requests referring to non-interference on the Soviet part in the welfare action for Polish citizens carried out by the Embassy were put in the Foreign Office instructions inadequately, Kerr dealt with them very vaguely, and Vyshinsky got rid of them by a sweeping declaration that the Soviet Government was not denying the Embassy's rights to carry out this work.

5. The missing 8,000 officers.—Vyshinsky categorically stated that he had

[1] See Note No. 241.

388

already told the Polish authorities several times that all Polish citizens had been released.

I have the impression that in view of the position adopted by Vyshinsky, which in all likelihood will be supported by the Soviet Government, there is no chance of a positive settlement unless the Government impresses upon the Foreign Office the necessity of exercising a strong pressure directly on Maisky.

No. 242

Note from the Embassy of the Republic of Poland in the USSR to the People's Commissariat for Foreign Affairs on the diplomatic status of some of the Embassy's Delegates

Kuibyshev, July 10, 1942   GSHI, A.11. 49/Sow./2
                                           Transl. from Polish

The offices of the delegates of the Embassy of the P.R. existing in a number of places, namely at Askhabad, Pavlodar, Petropavlovsk, Samarkand, Chelabinsk and Chimkent, have been headed so far by persons having diplomatic status and holding the rank of Secretary or—respectively— Attaché of the Embassy. These appointments were agreed with the People's Commissarat for Foreign Affairs in January of this year, and no objection was raised on that occasion on the part of the People's Commissariat for Foreign Affairs against the carrying out by the respective diplomatic officials of the duties of delegates of the Embassy, considering that such duties do not come into collision with diplomatic immunity. In particular, in the conversation on 23rd January of this year with the Ambassador of the P.R., Professor Kot, the Deputy Chairman of the Council of People's Commissars, M. Vyshinsky, stated that the assigning of the duty of a delegate to a diplomatic official did not involve the loss of diplomatic immunity.

In these circumstances, the Embassy of the P.R., contrary to the allegations of the Note of the People's Commissariat for Foreign Affairs No. 128 of 6th July 1942,[1] cannot consider as necessary or pertinent either the withdrawal of diplomatic immunity from the delegates of the Embassy in the above-mentioned localities, or their dismissal from the posts they occupy. Making reservations against such a unilateral solution of a question previously settled by mutual agreement, the Embassy, in view of this situation, nevertheless recalls to Kuibyshev the Attachés of the Embassy Płoski (Petropavlovsk), Lickindorf (Pavlodar), Słowikowski (Chelabinsk), Kościałkowski (Chimkent). The Second Secretary of the Embassy Gruja (Archangel) and the Second Secretary of the Embassy Głogowski (Ashkhabad) are receiving telegraphic orders to remain in their present places of residence until the question of transport offices in those places, through which the welfare supplies, valued at millions of roubles, are sent for the Polish

[1] See doc. No. 236.

population, has been settled by an agreement between the Embassy and the People's Commissariat for Foreign Affairs, as those goods cannot be left without proper care and control. The delegate of the Embassy, M. Heitzman (Samarkand), remains at his post, but as long as he carries out his duties of Embassy delegate he will not use the title of Attaché in dealing with Soviet authorities.

No. 243

Note from the People's Commissariat for Foreign Affairs to the Polish Embassy in the USSR, concerning the status of Embassy Delegates

Kuibyshev, July 10, 1942 GSHI, A.11. 49/Sow./3
Transl. from Russian

In reply to the Note of the Embassy of the Republic of Poland, No. 2795/48 of 6th July 1942,[1] the People's Commissariat has the honour to state that in the light of information received the persons mentioned in the Embassy's Note—Waldemar Kuczyński, Anna Witkowska, Marian Pytlak and Zdzisława Wójcik—were detained in connection with reports on activities hostile to the Soviet Union. This preventive measure undertaken by local authorities in accordance with Articles 143 and 147 of the Code of Civil Procedure of the USSR is understandable in view of war-time conditions and the need to take quick action. Subsequently, the said preventive measures as regards Kuczyński, Witkowska, Pytlak and Wójcik were withdrawn, and all the aforementioned persons were released on the understanding that they must leave the territory of the USSR within the time-limit prescribed by the Soviet authorities.

In connection with the foregoing, the People's Commissariat considers it necessary to declare that the allegations made by the Embassy that the action of the Soviet authorities at Archangel in the said case was contrary to the generally accepted principles of international law, are unfounded. Neither Embassy Delegates nor their deputies and other members of their offices enjoy any diplomatic rights and privileges, as the institution of temporary Embassy Delegates is not customary in diplomatic law, and the valid principles of diplomatic law therefore do not extend to them so far as diplomatic immunity is concerned. This fact is well known to the Embassy, as it appears from several statements of the members of the People's Commissariat, and in particular from a conversation between A. J. Vyshinsky and M. Kot on 23rd January of this year, and a conversation between G. M. Pushkin and M. Arlet on 19th January of this year.

A reference contained in the Embassy's Note of 6th July of this year to an alleged statement by the Deputy Chairman of the Council of the People's Commissars of the USSR on the granting of special rights to Embassy Delegates is absolutely unjustified. As a matter of fact, in a conversation between A. J. Vyshinsky and M. Kot on 22nd January of this year, dealing

[1] See doc. No. 237.

with this question, A. J. Vyshinsky emphasized that the Constitution of the USSR now in force fully ensured the personal rights of all citizens, and the inviolability of their homes and correspondence, which was extended to all aliens living within the territory of the USSR. In view of this there was no need to grant any special guarantees to Embassy Delegates.

In view of the foregoing the People's Commissariat rejects as unfounded the protest lodged by the Embassy in its Note of 6th July of this year.

No. 244

Note of the People's Commissariat for Foreign Affairs to the Embassy of the Republic of Poland, informing of the release of two Embassy Delegates, M. Załęski and M. Gruja

Kuibyshev, July 10, 1942   GSHI, A.11. 49/Sow./3
                                                             Transl. from Russian

In reply to the Note of the Embassy of the Republic of Poland of 9th July 1942, No. 2861/42,[1] the People's Commissariat for Foreign Affairs has the honour of stating that the investigation made by competent Soviet authorities discovered the facts of a hostile activity towards the Soviet Union, carried out by the Embassy Delegate in Archangel, M. Gruja, and by the Embassy Delegate in Vladivostok, M. Załęski, in connection with which M. Gruja and M. Załęski were arrested. It was a preventive measure, taken for the time of the investigation by local organs, prompted by the necessity of taking urgent measures in the war conditions.

It appears now that the local organs did not know that M. Gruja and M. Załęski, being Embassy Delegates, preserved their diplomatic privileges attached to the posts of Secretaries of the Embassy, held by them at the same time. It was out of ignorance of this state of things that the local organs applied the measure of arrest to M. Gruja and M. Załęski, as otherwise it would not have taken place. An order has now been issued to local Soviet organs to release immediately M. Gruja and M. Załęski, and to return to them seals, papers, documents and money.

In view of the foregoing, the People's Commissariat cannot accept the protests raised by the Embassy on 8th July and 9th July of this year and, at the same time, insists on a quick departure of M. Gruja and M. Załęski from the Soviet Union.

[1] See doc. No. 239.

No. 245

Note and Pro-memoria from the People's Commissariat for Foreign Affairs to the Polish Embassy in the USSR relating to the implementation of the Protocol to the Polish-Soviet Agreement of 30th July, 1941 (release of Polish citizens) [1]

Kuibyshev, July 10, 1942
GSHI, A.11. 49/Sow./3
Transl. from Russian

In reply to the Note of the Embassy of the Republic of Poland of 19th May of this year, No. 1545/42 [2], with which a memorandum was enclosed relating to the implementation of the Additional Protocol to the Polish-Soviet Agreement of 1941, the People's Commissariat for Foreign Affairs has the honour to forward to the Embassy a Pro-Memoria dealing with the questions raised in the aforesaid memorandum.

Pro-memoria

The Embassy of the Republic of Poland presented on 19th May, 1942 to the People's Commissariat for Foreign Affairs a memorandum, dealing with the questions connected with the implementation of the Additional Protocol to the Polish-Soviet Agreement of 30th July, 1941. [3]

1. An assertion was made under para. 1 of the said memorandum that the Decree on Amnesty of 12th August, 1941 [4] was issued for form's sake only, and that further steps were required in order to put it into effect. This allegation is completely unwarranted. The Decree of the Praesidium of the Supreme Soviet of 12th August, 1941 was put into effect already in the first days and weeks after its promulgation and the Embassy was duly informed of it by a pro-memoria of the People's Commissariat for Foreign Affairs of 28th August, 1941. [5] It is quite natural that in the war conditions which brought about the disruption of communications with many areas of the USSR the practical measures to be taken in connection with the release of some hundreds of thousands of Polish citizens should have turned out to be very complicated indeed. In spite of that, the release of the greater part of Polish citizens was completed by September, and soon after the remaining Polish citizens were released, apart from a small number of persons who mostly were not qualified for release, for reasons previously communicated to the Embassy.

As regards the reference in the memorandum to the cases, still occurring in November and December, 1941, as well as in January, February and March, 1942, in which some Polish citizens have not yet been released, it should be emphasized that such cases were due to the need for additional checking, and also for the removal, in individual instances, of difficulties in the application of the provisions of the Decree of 12th August, 1941. These difficulties were unavoidable because of the greatness of the task of the implementation of the amnesty pursuant to the Decree of 12th August.

---

[1] See Note No. 245. [2] See doc. No. 221. [3] See doc. No. 106.
[4] See doc. No. 110. [5] See doc. No. 118.

These cases could not be avoided, the more so, as they were connected with the necessity of ascertaining whether there were valid reasons for applying to the individuals concerned the provisions of the aforesaid Decree. The People's Commissariat for Foreign Affairs informed the Embassy of it by its notes and memos, and in particular by its memo of 19th November, 1941,[6] that of 9th January[7] of this year, and in the course of the conferences between Vyshinsky and Kot. One must keep in mind that in connection with the progress at that time of the evacuation of the western provinces of the Ukrainian Socialist Soviet Republic, and the Byelorussian Socialist Soviet Republic it was quite impossible to ascertain quickly enough on what grounds a given citizen had been deprived of freedom, and also to discover his [or her] whereabouts. However, as soon as the required information was obtained, [and not because of the Embassy's intervention, as it is being alleged in the Memorandum] all persons subject to amnesty were released.

[6] See document No. 153.   [7] See document No. 172.

No. 246

Note from Minister Raczyński to Ambassador Bogomolov protesting against the arrest of members and delegates of the Polish Embassy

London, July 11, 1942   GSHI, A.11. 49/Sow./2

En me référant à notre conversation du 10 crt., j'ai l'honneur de porter à votre connaissance, ce qui suit:

Le Gouvernement polonais vient d'être informé que le 2 juillet dernier, pendant l'absence du délégué de l'Ambassade de Pologne, M. Gruja, qui pour des raisons de service a été obligé de se rendre à Mourmansk, des fonctionnaires du Commissariat du Peuple de l'Intérieur ont fait une descente au siège officiel du délégué de l'Ambassade de Pologne a Arkhangelsk. Après avoir perquisitionné les bureaux et emporté tous les documents et le numéraire qu'ils y ont trouvé, les fonctionnaires de la milice ont emmené de force le remplaçant du délégué absent, M. Kuczyński, ainsi que trois fonctionnaires adjoints, Mme Witkowska, et MM. Pytlak et Wójcik. Le lieu de séjour actuel de ces personnes est inconnu. Il y a lieu d'ajouter, que M. Gruja avait notifié d'avance aux autorités locales d'Arkhangelsk son départ, ainsi que le fait qu'il serait remplacé pendant son absence par M. Kuczyński. M. Gruja avait obtenu la reconnaissance par les autorités locales du caractère formel de la situation de M. Kuczyński.

Le lendemain, c'est à dire le 3 juillet,[1] le Commissariat du Peuple des Affaires Etrangères a communiqué par une Note adressée à l'Ambassade de Pologne, sa décision unilatérale de clore les offices des délégués de l'Ambassade de Pologne à Arkhangelsk, à Vladivostok, à Aldan-Yakoutsky, ainsi que celui de Saratov. Dans sa communication, le Commissariat a passé sous silence le fait de la perquisition opérée dans les offices du délégué à Arkhangelsk, ainsi que de l'arrestation du délégué adjoint et de ses collaborateurs. Plusieurs

[1] See doc. No. 234.

393

jours après, l'Ambassade de Pologne à Kuibyshev a appris que M. Gruja, délégué à Arkhangelsk ayant le rang de Secrétaire d'Ambassade et inscrit sur la liste du Corps Diplomatique, a été arrêté dans le train entre Mourmansk et Arkhangelsk. Son lieu de séjour actuel est également inconnu. En même temps la nouvelle est parvenue à l'Ambassade de Pologne, que M. Załęski, Secrétaire de l'Ambassade de Pologne exerçant les fonctions de délégué de l'Ambassade de Pologne a été arrêté par la milice et est détenu en prison. Tout contact entre l'Ambassade et MM Gruja et Załęski est ainsi rompu. Finalement le Commissariat du Peuple des Affaires Etrangères vient d'informer par une Note l'Ambassade de Pologne qu'il cesse de reconnaître dorénavant le caractère diplomatique des délégué locaux de l'Ambassade même en cas où ceux-ci posséderaient ce caractère comme membres de l'Ambassade.

En portant ce qui précède à la connaissance de Votre Excellence, Le Gouvernement polonais se croit obligé d'exprimer l'opinion que la décision unilatérale du Gouvernement soviétique de clore les offices des délégués de l'Ambassade de Pologne, de même que les mesures, prises vis-à-vis des délégués de l'Ambassade de Pologne à Arkhangelsk et Vladivostok et leurs offices, constituent une atteinte aux droits exercés par l'Ambassade de Pologne dans le domaine de l'assistance matérielle aux citoyens polonais en l'Union des Républiques Socialistes Soviétiques, ainsi qu'aux assurances données officiellement à cet égardpar les représentants qualifiés du Gouvernement soviétique.

En effet, le 26 janvier, le Commissaire adjoint du Peuple aux Affaires Etrangères, M. Vychinsky, avait assuré l'Ambassadeur de Pologne que les délégués de l'Ambassade de Pologne en l'Union des Républiques Socialistes Soviétiques seront traités par les autorités soviétiques comme représentants d'une mission diplomatique en l'Union des Républiques Socialistes Soviétiques, c'est-à-dire avec dûs égards et considération. Selon une explication additionelle de M. Vychinsky lui-même, les droits de chaque délégué devaient comprendre l' inviolabilité de sa personne, de ses archives ainsi que de sa résidence. Les assurances de M. Vychinsky ont permis à l'Ambassade de Pologne d'organiser un système d'assitance matérielle aux nombreux citoyens polonais dispersés en l'Union des Républiques Socialistes Soviétiques par l'envoi de différentes marchandises venant du Royaume-Uni et des États-Unis d'Amérique. Dans le cadre de ce système, les délégués de l'Ambassade à Arkhangelsk et à Vladivostok remplissaient un rôle d'une importance toute particulière leurs devoirs consistant à trier les marchandises venues par mer d'après leur destination et à ré-expédier, par voie ferrée, celles parmi ces marchandises qui étaient adressées à l'Ambassade de Pologne à Kuibyshev ou aux autres délégués de l'Ambassade avec siège à l'intérieur de l'Union des Républiques Socialistes Soviétiques. Par ailleurs le délégué de l'Ambassade à Arkhangelsk avait la tâche de distribuer les marchandises en question aux citoyens polonais se trouvant dispersés dans les provinces d'Arkhangelsk et de Vologda, et il demeurait directement responsable de l'assistance qui devait leur être fournie. Ce groupe de citoyens,

15,000 environ, se trouve dans des conditions plus difficiles que les autres groupes de citoyens polonais en l'Union des Républiques Socialistes Soviétiques. Quant au délégué de l'Ambassade à Vladivostok, il remplissait des fonctions similaires d'agent officiel de transmission et de distribution pour les marchandises expédiées des États-Unis à Vladivostok. Ses fonctions locales consistaient à distribuer les secours aux citoyens polonais dispersés dans la province maritime et dans l'extrême orient de l'Union des Républiques Socialistes Soviétiques.

Durant toute la période de l'activité de M. Gruja en sa qualité de délégué de l'Ambassade de Pologne à Arkhangelsk, aucune plainte des autorités locales contre ses activités n'est parvenue à la connaissance de l'Ambassade. Au contraire ces autorités, ainsi que les autorités centrales, ont à plusieurs reprises exprimé leur satisfaction de la façon dont M. Gruja, de même que son personnel, exerçait ses fonctions.

Dans les conditions actuelles, quand par la suite des circonstances militaires l'accès en l'Union des Républiques Socialistes Soviétiques de l'extérieur est réduit à quelques ports, la base de distribution polonaise à Arkhangelsk, sous le régime du délégué de l'Ambassade jouait un rôle de tout premier ordre dans l'organisation de l'assistance matérielle aux citoyens polonais dispersés dans la plus grande partie du Nord et de l'Ouest de l'Union des Républiques Socialistes Soviétiques. C'est par là que sont passés des dizaines de milliers de colis d'un poids total de quelques milliers de tonnes comprenant vivres, médicaments, vêtements et autres articles de première nécessité destinés aux citoyens polonais. Le rythme de ces envois s'accroissait derniérement, bien qu'il ne correspondait pas encore aux réels besoins.

La fermeture de l'office du délégué de Pologne à Arkhangelsk aurait pour conséquence de rendre impossible l'organisation adéquate de la réception et du contrôle des arrivages des marchandises en question, ainsi que de leur distribution à l'intérieur de l'Union des Républiques Socialistes Soviétiques, y compris la distribution directe de l'assistance parmi les 15,000 Polonais de la province Arkhangelsk-Vologda. Si le refus de reconnaître la délégation de l'Ambassade à Archangelsk était maintenue, il en résulterait comme conséquence la désorganisation d'assistance aux citoyens polonais qui vient d'être établie par l'Ambassade de Pologne en l'Union des Républiques Socialistes Soviétiques avec le concours des autorités soviétiques et grâce à l'aide de nombreuses institutions humanitaires britanniques et américaines avec lesquelles l'Ambassade de Pologne maintient un contact continu. Une telle mesure serait inévitablement suivie d'une détérioration de la situation de milliers d'individus et en particulier des enfants. En même temps une grave atteinte serait portée à l'intérêt que les institutions britanniques et américaines témoignent en matière d'assistance aux citoyens polonais en détresse.

Le Gouvernement polonais se refuse à croire que les autorités soviétiques aient pu avoir en vue la cessation de l'assistance aux citoyens polonais en l'Union des Républiques Socialistes Soviétiques qui ont été obligés contre leur gré de quitter leurs foyers en Pologne. Il croit que le Gouvernement soviétique est en plein accord avec le Gouvernement polonais quant à la nécessité et l'urgence qu'il y a de porter secours à ces malheureux. L'organisation de ce secours demande la continuation de l'activité de la délégation de l'Ambassade de Pologne à Arkhangelsk, de même que dans d'autres localités, qui ont été fixées d'avance d'accord entre l'Ambassade et le Commissariat du Peuple des Affaires Etrangères.

J'ai l'honneur de prier Votre Excellence de bien vouloir transmettre au Gouvernement de l'Union des Républiques Socialistes Soviétiques la protestation que le Gouvernement polonais élève contre la fermeture de quatres délégations en question et contre les mesures arbitraires des autorités soviétiques locales quant au délégué adjoint et le personnel de la délégation à Arkhangelsk. En même temps le Gouvernement polonais est en devoir d'élever une protestation énergique contre la violation par le Gouvernement de l'Union des Républiques Socialistes Soviétiques de privilège diplomatique reconnu par ce même Gouvernement, ainsi que contre l'arrestation de deux membres de l'Ambassade dont il fait mention plus haut. Le Gouvernement polonais à l'honneur de demander d'urgence la mise en liberté de toutes les personnes dont il s'agit ainsi que la réstitution des archives et des fonds confisqués à Archangelsk et d'après toute vraisemblance à Vladivostok. Finalement, le Gouvernement polonais prie le Gouvernement soviétique de reconsidérer sa décision concernant la fermeture des délégations et qu'en conséquence il rende possible la ré-ouverture des offices des délégués de l'Ambassade de Pologne à Arkhangelsk, à Vladivostok et à Aldan-Yakoutsky.

No. 247

Aide-mémoire from the Polish Ministry for Foreign Affairs handed to Under-Secretary of State Sumner Welles on the situation of Poles in the USSR

Washington, July 13, 1942   GSHI, PRM, 71

The Ambassador described to the Under-Secretary of State facts relating to the present difficulties in Polish-Soviet relations. He regarded the situation as grave and informed the Under-Secretary that he was instructed to ask that details concerning the recent deterioration of Polish-Soviet relations should be taken under consideration by the Department of State in view of a friendly intervention on the part of the U.S. Government both in Kuibyshev and through Ambassador Litvinov.

The Ambassador described some of the aspects of the present Polish-Soviet relations as follows:

1 / The arbitrary attitude on the part of the Soviet Government of discrimination against Polish deportees who are Jews and the refusal to allow the Polish Embassy in Kuibyshev and its Delegates to remain in contact with, to treat these Jews as Polish citizens, to enlist them in the Polish Army, to evacuate them from Russia, to supply them with articles sent for Polish Relief from the United States for distribution by the Polish Embassy to all Polish citizens.

2/ The recent exchange of messages between General Sikorski and Premier Stalin concerning the continuation of recruitment of Polish military and their evacuation to the Near East together with their families.[1]

3/ The exchange of notes between the Polish Embassy and Mr. Molotov regarding the refusal on the part of the Soviet Government to admit the exclusive right of the Polish Government of determining the Polish citizenship of Poles evacuated from Polish Territory in specific cases, and of direct contact between the Embassy and Polish citizens in matters pertaining to military service and relief.

4/ The recent arrests of members of the staff of the Polish Embassy in Kuibyshev by the Soviet authorities, contrary to definite engagements entered into by that Government in authorizing direct distribution of relief to the Polish citizens in Russia by the said officials of the Polish Embassy, to whom the Soviet Government had granted diplomatic status.

The Polish Government is greatly concerned about the situation which has thus arisen. The exchange of numerous notes concerning these matters and the conversations between the Polish Ambassador in Kuibyshev and the competent Soviet authorities do not appear to have eased the situation. The Polish Government on its part continues to pursue a policy of understanding with Soviet Russia, but this is rendered most difficult on account of the present attitude of the Soviet Government. General Sikorski and Foreign Minister Raczyński have asked the Ambassador to discuss the matter with the Under-Secretary of State and to ask him for the friendly intermediacy of the U.S. Government in obtaining a change of attitude on the part of the Soviet Government.

General Sikorski has replied to the message obtained by him through the British Ambassador from Premier Stalin expressing willingness of the latter to the evacuation to the Near East of three divisions of Polish troops at present ready for action in Russia. While General Sikorski views favourably the evacuation of these troops, especially on account of the urgent demand for a reserve unit in the Near East, he wants to see a contingent of Polish troops fighting alongside of the Soviet armies in Russia. From the message of Premier Stalin it would appear that his suggestion for the evacuation of the said three divisions would be rather in the nature of a liquidation of any further recruitment of Polish troops, than a friendly gesture, which in itself is in the interest of the Soviet Government, of increasing the number of troops active in the Near East.

In view of the present military situation in the Near East in connection with the events in Egypt, it might perhaps be possible for the U.S. Government to express its interest in such an evacuation, and, likewise, to urge upon the Soviet Government that it should allow the Polish Military Command to proceed with the further normal recruitment of Polish soldiers, who are in Russia, in accordance with previous Polish-Soviet agreements.

[1] See doc. No. 201, 218.

The Polish Government is likewise distressed at the unfriendly attitude adopted by the Soviet Government concerning the evacuation of Polish children from Russia. The Polish Government has been informed of the conversations which took place between Ambassador Standley and M. Molotov on this subject in the first days of July and hopes that the U.S. Government will not let the matter rest, as the evacuation of the Polish children has become a matter of the utmost urgency on account of the increasing mortality and the impossibility of adequately looking after them or feeding them inside Russia.

In all these matters the Polish Ambassador encloses more detailed memoranda based on the latest instructions and information received by him from the Polish Government.[2,3]

Memorandum (Enclosure 1)

Reference has been made on previous occasions to some unwarranted accusations emanating from certain Jewish quarters in the USSR and in Palestine regarding the alleged discriminations by the Polish authorities against Polish Jews in Russia in the distribution of relief supplies sent from abroad.

As it has been pointed out on previous occasions these accusations are totally unfounded.

The Polish Embassy in Kuibyshev and the Polish Government in London have evidence given them by various responsible representatives of Polish Jewry to the effect that no such discrimination exists and that all Poles whether Jews or Christians are being treated by the Polish authorities on terms of complete equality.

Two statements testifying that this is a fact can be quoted:

The Polish Embassy in Washington received recently a cable from a member of the Jewish Bund from Kuibyshev in which it is said:

'After due investigation I testify that the distribution of our funds here is highly satisfactory.

The Polish Embassy is doing its utmost to help us in spite of the fact that the Soviet authorities consider us arbitrarily as Soviet citizens.

This Soviet interpretation is causing panic among the Jews. They are not allowed to leave the USSR even if they have Palestine visas because the Soviet authorities refuse to issue exit permits on account that they are regarded as Soviet citizens.'

[2] Enclosure 2 contains a summary of the Note of the People's Commissariat for Foreign Affairs of 9 June, and of the Polish Note of June 24. See doc. No. 226, 232.

[3] Enclosure 4 contains a Memorandum on the further relief for Polish citizens in the USSR.

A Jewish newspaper correspondent S. in Teheran, Iran, made recently the following statement in writing:

'I declare most emphatically that during my stay in Iran I have never noticed any anti-semitism on the part of the Polish civilian authorities in the camp for refugees.

There is no truth in any allegations made to the effect that I have made other statements. I can add that all Polish citizens are receiving equal help and assistance in Iran from Polish authorities.'

Memorandum (Enclosure 3)

In reply to General Sikorski's message regarding Polish military requirements in the USSR, Foreign Commissar Molotov handed the British Ambassador in Moscow the following statement by Mr. Stalin:

Mr. Stalin said in part that he had no objection to the transfer of Polish troops in the USSR to the Near East and suggested that three divisions of these troops be thus transferred.

The Polish Minister for Foreign Affairs thereupon handed the following memorandum to the British Foreign Office in London:

1/ The Polish Government is glad that the Polish Army will be able to help in the defence of the Near East.

2/ The Polish Government is responsible for the care of all Polish citizens in Russia. The presence of Polish troops in Russia is playing an important part in the fulfilment of this obligation.

3/ In this connection the Polish Government will expect the co-operation on the part of the British Government in obtaining from the Soviet Government the fulfilment of the following requests:

    a/ A reserve unit of the Polish Army will be maintained in Russia after the transfer of the three Polish divisions to the Near East; the recruiting will be resumed until the enlistment of all available men is completed.

    b/ Women's auxiliary services, boy scouts, and families of enlisted men must be permitted to leave Russia together with the Army.

    c/ Steps must be taken immediately in co-operation with the Polish Embassy in Russia for the evacuation of 50,000 children with their mothers and (or) women having charge of them.

4/ Furthermore the Polish Government will expect assistance and co-operation of the British Government in its endeavours to locate missing Polish officers who have been deported and who are urgently needed for the setting up of new divisions.

The British Ambassador was instructed by the Foreign Office to hand the reply of the Polish Government to Mr. Molotov's communication.
July 7, 1942.

No. 248

Records of a conversation between General Sikorski and Mr. Eden in the presence of Mr. Strang and Dr. Retinger, on the difficulties arising in Polish-Soviet relations

London, *July 16, 1942*

GSHI, PRM, 68
Transl. from Polish

[. . .]. Mr. Eden also asked Gen. Sikorski about his opinion on recent Soviet propaganda broadcasts relating to military operations. Gen. Sikorski warned him of the aims of this propaganda: questioning the effectiveness of the Allied war effort was a way of finding a scapegoat for Soviet military setbacks in future. The position of the Soviet armies on the front was not so bad as to justify the tone given to the discussion by Soviet propaganda. The way in which they put their request for the second front verged on demagogy, for the creation of such a front depended entirely on the available Allied means. The Soviet High Command had recently spread the news in its three bulletins that three fresh German divisions had arrived on the Eastern front. This amounted to an accusation that the Allies were completely inactive in the West. The Soviet Government warned against overestimating Russian strength and went on to open threats against Great Britain and the USA. Mr. Eden thanked Gen. Sikorski for having drawn his attention to these facts, which were disquieting, and he gave an explanation of the Russo-American communiqué relating to the creation of the second front. He outlined the attitude of the British Government towards this problem and added that the said communiqué was, as a matter of fact, Molotov's only achievement in Washington. Its practical value was, in Mr. Eden's view, rather doubtful. A discussion on this topic ensued, and it was decided that the essential arguments used in its course should remain strictly confidential.

During the discussion on Russia Mr. Eden eventually admitted that Gen. Sikorski was right, for not only loyalty but also a firm determination were needed in all political and diplomatic conversations with Russia. Mr. Eden emphasized that Soviet leaders had no sympathy for Professor Kot. Gen. Sikorski replied that any Polish representative occupying this post and showing Prof. Kot's force of character was bound to meet the same attitude on the part of the Soviets. The Polish Government's confidence in Prof. Kot had only increased. Gen. Sikorski asked Mr. Eden about the British Government's attitude to Polish requests put forward in connection with the evacuation of three Polish divisions to the Middle East. Mr. Eden answered that the British Ambassador had received explicit instructions from his government to give full support to the Polish Government, and to try to approach Stalin on this matter. The Prime Minister, Mr. Churchill, would contact Stalin immediately after this conversation with Gen. Sikorski. A memorandum to be dispatched was delayed in order to include any alterations that might arise from this conversation. Mr. Eden asked General Sikorski which of the four points raised by the Polish Government was considered by them to be the most important. Gen. Sikorski, continuing to support all four points raised by the Polish Government, replied that the questions of the evacuation of children, the re-opening of recruiting centres and a further evacuation of conscripts should be dealt with in the normal way; he agreed with Mr. Eden that the question of the several thousand missing Polish officers was the most difficult one, but stressed that it would be possible to trace them only at this time of the year. The question had been raised by Gen. Sikorski's wife in a letter to Mrs. Roosevelt and, with British support, it would be eventually possible to clear up this case, so deliberately tangled up by the Soviet authorities. It could be done only at this time of the year when communications with the northern provinces of Russia were possible.

The fourth point raised by Poland, namely the release of the arrested members of the Embassy, had already been settled by the Soviet Government. The spiteful attitude displayed by the latter on that occasion showed what value one could attach to Soviet pledges.

Gen. Sikorski observed that in connection with the above mentioned requests he would like to have a conversation with Ambassador Maisky and invite him to luncheon, on Wednesday 22nd. Mr. Eden offered his help and said he would come to the luncheon in order to demonstrate Anglo-Polish solidarity in front of the Russians, provided he had no other engagement on that day. Half-an-hour after lunch, Mr. Eden's secretary informed Gen. Sikorski that Mr. Eden would come to the luncheon accompanied by Mr. Strang.

As regards the evacuation of Polish children from Russia, Mr. Eden declared that the British Government was ready to give all necessary assistance, adding that financial considerations would be disregarded. He pointed out, however, that transport difficulties were very great. The only possibility of solving this question would be to transport the children to food-producing areas instead of leaving them in places which had to be supplied with food. On this matter as well as on the question of refugees the Foreign Office was in close contact with the Polish official in charge of these matters. [. . .].

No. 249

Note from Chargé d'Affaires Sokolnicki to Deputy Commissar Vyshinsky on the Soviet unilateral decision to close the offices and arrest several Polish Embassy Delegates

Kuibyshev, July 19, 1942 GSHI, A.11. 49/Sow./2
Transl. from Polish: Pol.-Sov.R., No. 72

In the course of your conversation with the Polish Ambassador on July 8, 1942, when you discussed with him the latest actions of the Soviet authorities with regard to the network of local offices of Embassy Delegates established in accordance with the corresponding agreements between this Embassy and the People's Commissariat for Foreign Affairs, reference was made to the unilateral decision of the Soviet authorities to close the offices of the Delegates in Aldan-Yakutsky, Vladivostok, Archangel, and Saratov; the arrest of M. M. Załęski, 1st Secretary of Embassy, acting Embassy Delegate in Vladivostok;

the arrest of the entire staff of the office of the Embassy Delegate in Archangel; searches carried out in the offices of the Embassy Delegates in Vladivostok and Archangel; the violation of the immunity of the Embassy's archives in the offices of these Delegates; the seizure by the local authorities of a number of documents, of money and of seals belonging to the Embassy, and the closing and sealing of the Embassy's stores. In the course of this conversation the Polish Ambassador asked a question, which I now again put to you, that is, do the above actions of the Soviet authorities denote a change in the policy of the Soviet Government as initiated on July 30, 1941,[1] in respect of that portion of the Polish population, which as a result of well known events found itself forcibly on the territory of the Soviet Union. It is the opinion of the Ambassador that if this action on the part of the Soviet Authorities was aimed at the destruction of the entire welfare and relief organization for Polish citizens in the USSR, created with such difficulty by this Embassy in agreement with the People's Commissariat, then it would be better to state this clearly instead of creating a fictitious situation in which one cannot be certain of the fate either of people or of institutions.

It was to be inferred from your reply, Mr. Chairman, that the Soviet Government did not propose to change the attitude that it had hitherto adopted towards Polish citizens in the USSR and their relief organization set up by this Embassy, and that general conclusions should not be drawn from specific cases based on misunderstandings of local officials or resulting possibly from criminal actions of individuals.

During the ten days that have passed since the aforementioned conversation took place, this Embassy has been informed of new facts, which seem to signify that the organization of Embassy Delegates on the territory of the USSR is actually being closed down; this is accompanied by the arrest of those members of this Embassy's staff who have been most active in bringing relief to Polish citizens in their districts, the seizure by the local authorities of official archives and documents of this Embassy, the blocking of this Embassy's accounts in branches of the State Bank of the USSR, the closing and sealing by the Soviet authorities of warehouses containing relief goods from the Allied States addressed to the Embassy of the Republic of Poland in the USSR.

Apart from the arrest of M. M. Załęski, 1st Secretary of Embassy; M. Gruja, 2nd Secretary of Embassy and the staff of the Delegate's office in Archangel, already the subject of separate diplomatic correspondence, I am obliged, Mr. Chairman, to bring the following further facts to your notice:

On July 16, 1942, this Embassy received news of a search having been carried out by the local authorities in the office of the Embassy Delegate in Barnaul, the arrest of the Embassy Delegate W. S. Mattoszko and his staff, M. Siedlecki, D. Wajgetner, J. Kowalewski and K. Bartosz, and of the seizure by these same authorities of the archives and seal of the Delegate's office and the closing of the Embassy's current account in the local branch of the State Bank.

[1] See doc. No. 106.

On July 17, 1942, this Embassy received news of a search having been carried out by the local authorities in the office of the Embassy Delegate in Samarkand and the arrest of M. M. Heitzman, Attaché of the Embassy, who enjoys diplomatic immunity, and of the Delegate's staff, K. Kazimierczak, F. Kowol, K. Jaroszewski, and F. Mantel.

On July 18, 1942 this Embassy received news of a search having been carried out by the local authorities in the office of the Embassy Delegate in Kirov, where is located the greatest clearing warehouse on the territory of the USSR for goods arriving from Allied States for the Polish Embassy in the USSR. At the same time M. A. Wisiński, the Embassy Delegate in Kirov whose appointment to this post received the approval of the People's Commissariat for Foreign Affairs on June 26, 1942, was arrested, together with his staff, T. Słucki, F. Dubrawski, S. Fink and Z. Piotrowski.

On July 19, 1942, this Embassy received news that the office of the Embassy Delegate in Petropavlovsk had been *de facto* deprived of its freedom of action, while stores of relief goods sent to the Polish Embassy from Allied States, located at the station of Mamlutka, were closed and sealed by the local authorities.

On the same day, this Embassy received similar information concerning the office of the Embassy Delegate in Siktivkar, where Dr. Winiarczyk, the Embassy Delegate, was arrested.

Further details of the aforementioned steps taken by the Soviet Authorities with regard to the local offices of this Embassy are as yet unknown to me. I do, however, possess information to the effect that telegrams addressed to this Embassy and containing reports on these events, are not delivered to this Embassy and that this Embassy's telegrams to certain of its Delegates and representatives are being intercepted. The dispatches in question included those sent by the Ambassador and intercepted and not delivered to Attachés of Embassy Płoski and Lickindorf and to Secretaries of Embassy Głogowski and Gruja, which contained instructions in accordance with the contents of this Embassy's Note to the People's Commissariat for Foreign Affairs, of July 10, 1942, No. D. 2871/42.[2] This constitutes a new infringement of diplomatic immunity and privileges, established by law and international custom.

Though I intend to return to each of the matters just mentioned on receipt of more concrete and detailed information, I have, perforce, to limit myself at present to protesting against the action of the Soviet authorities in closing down the Embassy's relief organization; and to insist that the Delegates and their staffs who have been arrested, be immediately set free, and that the archives, seals and money belonging to the Embassy be returned.

At the same time I have to state, that as a consequence of instructions issued by the Soviet Authorities during the last three weeks:

1. Four out of the twenty, that is 20%, of the offices of Embassy Delegates established in agreement with the People's Commissariat for Foreign Affairs,

[2] See doc. No. 242.

namely the offices of Embassy Delegates in Vladivostok, Archangel, Aldan Yakutsky and Saratov have been closed down by unilateral order of the Soviet authorities;

2. According to information so far received by this Embassy, five other offices of this Embassy's Delegates, namely those in Barnaul, Samarkand, Kirov, Petropavlovsk and Syktyvkar are *de facto* no longer able to function because the Soviet authorities have arrested most if not all of their staff;

3. In this way the Soviet authorities have actually paralysed the activity of 45% of all the Embassy Delegates, appointed in accordance with a joint agreement between the Embassy and the People's Commissariat for Foreign Affairs, and operating in districts where there are at present more than 170,000 Polish citizens, according to the as yet incomplete registration figures;

4. In view of the fact that the offices of nine Embassy Delegates have been prevented from functioning, the issue of food and clothing to tens of thousands of Polish citizens, some of them in very difficult circumstances, has had to be stopped in the districts served by these Delegates. The same applies to the distribution of financial aid to Polish citizens, unfit for work. Food, clothing, and medical stores, worth millions, and consisting of goods sent to the Polish Embassy in the USSR from Allied States are left entirely unprotected. Further shipments of food, clothing and medical supplies which are on their way to the offices of individual Delegates, will no longer go to persons duly authorized to receive them. Preventive inoculation against typhus will have to be suspended. Homes for orphans and the aged, maintained by individual Delegates, will be left without suitable care;

5. In view of the fact that the relief activities of this Embassy's agencies are being formally or actually rendered impossible, the responsibility for every consequence of this action rests with the Soviet authorities;

6. In view of the effective stopping, closing and sealing by the Soviet authorities of food, clothing and medical stores, collected at great expense and effort by the Polish Government, as well as by the Governments and peoples of the Allied States, destined for Polish citizens in the USSR and delivered to Soviet ports by Polish and Allied sailors, who sacrificed much and risked their lives to accomplish this task,—the responsibility for the destruction and deterioration of these goods which may ensue, must also rest with the Soviet authorities.

No. 250

Aide-mémoire from the Polish Embassy in Kuibyshev to the People's Commissariat for Foreign Affairs protesting against the restrictions imposed on the Delegates' offices in Archangel and Vologda districts

Kuibyshev, July 19, 1942 GSHI, A.11. 49/Sow./2
Transl. from Polish

With reference to the Aide-mémoire of the People's Commissariat for

Foreign Affairs, dated 3rd July, 1942,[1] the Polish Embassy considers it necessary to make the following statement:

1. The scope of action of the Delegates of the Polish Embassy and the plan for the location of their offices throughout the country were established by mutual agreement between the Embassy of the Polish Republic and the People's Commissariat for Foreign Affairs, and were confirmed by an exchange of notes dated 23rd/24th December, 1941, and 8th/9th January, 1942.

This agreement was infringed by the unilateral decision of the People's Commissariat for Foreign Affairs liquidating four out of the twenty established Delegates' Offices, namely those at Archangel, Vladivostok, Aldan-Yakutsk and Saratov. The above mentioned decision was communicated to the Embassy in the Aide-mémoire of July 3rd, 1942, quoted above. The closing down of the Delegates' Offices, however, took place on 29th June, 1942 at Archangel, and on 30th June, 1942 at Vladivostok, i.e. four and three days respectively before the decision was communicated to the Embassy. This fact alone emphasizes the complete disregard for any agreements concluded with the representatives of a foreign Power, and also the wilful character of the measures taken by the Soviet authorities. The People's Commissariat for Foreign Affairs never proposed to the Embassy, either in conversation or in writing, the discussing of a new plan of location for the Delegates' Offices nor the revision of the clauses concerning the competence of the Embassy's Delegates.

It is therefore considered necessary to state that the orders by which the Delegates' Offices at Archangel, Vladivostok, Aldan-Yakutsk and Saratov were liquidated were a unilateral violation of a bilateral agreement still in force, and that consequently these orders could not be considered as compatible with international customs and normal relations between two Powers inspired with the will to co-operate.

2. The Polish Embassy considers it necessary to emphasize that the allegation of the People's Commissariat that the task of resettlement and employment of Polish citizens in the Archangel and Vologda Provinces was completed, is not in accordance with the real state of affairs. This assertion is, moreover, limited to certain tasks only, chosen and considered essential arbitrarily, from among all the duties assigned to the Delegates. According to information in the Embassy's possession these tasks have not been completed, and their settlement is still in progress. The living conditions of the great majority of Poles in the Archangel and Vologda Provinces are among the worst. This, incidentally, has been confirmed by a representative of the People's Commissariat for Foreign Affairs in his conversation with a member of the Embassy, on 11th April, 1942, when discussing the necessity of immediate aid to 800 Polish citizens in the Vologda Province, in the Voshegod, Kharov and Babushkin districts. These people were unemployed and the local authorities could neither find work for them, nor supply them with rations.

[1] See doc. No. 234.

405

The Embassy continually informed the People's Commissariat for Foreign Affairs of the distressing conditions of Polish citizens in the Archangel and Vologda Provinces, as, for instance, in its notes of 31st January, 1942, Ref. D/342/42, and of 23rd February, 1942, Ref. 576/42.[2] These notes pointed out the extreme physical exhaustion of Polish citizens, the impossibility of finding adequate work for them, and, in certain instances, the dismissal of Poles from work, the inadequate supply of rations, etc. These data were supplemented in conversations with members of the People's Commissariat on 17th March, 1942, 11th April, 1942, 17th April, 1942, 21st April, 1942, etc. The Embassy continually received desperate appeals from Poles in the two mentioned provinces for resettlement to more normal living conditions. Unfortunately, all suggestions made by the Embassy with a view to a planned resettlement have not, so far, been considered by the People's Commissariat. Moreover, the most essential duties laid down in the 'Regulations concerning the activities of the Delegates' have never been carried out. For instance, the registration of Polish citizens, which was in full progress in the Archangel and Vologda Provinces, the placing of children and adults, unfit for work, in adequate institutions, the supply of clothes. The Delegate at Archangel received a considerable amount of clothes and footwear and summoned the 'men of trust' to collect these articles for distribution. They arrived at Archangel at the very time when the local authorities were closing down the Delegate's office, and had to depart without any supplies.

The Polish Embassy emphasizes that the maintenance of Delegate's Offices in the above-mentioned territories is absolutely essential. The Embassy, on its part, is ready to open negotiations concerning the location of the Offices in any towns situated on a railway line in the Archangel and Vologda Provinces. Should this proposal be considered unacceptable, the Embassy would suggest the establishment of a travelling Delegate for the two Provinces, in accordance with clause 10, Chapter II of the 'Regulations concerning the activities of Delegates'. Should the Delegates' activities in these two Provinces be still hampered, then the Embassy would renew its proposition of an organized resettlement of Polish citizens, and, above all, of children, from the Archangel and Vologda Provinces to other territories remaining within the boundaries covered by the activities of the Embassy's Delegates.

3. In respect of the personnel of the Delegate's Offices, the Embassy is obliged to point out that M. Vyshinsky, in his conversation with the Polish Ambassador, agreed that this matter should be discussed in detail, and accepted in principle that the number of personnel employed by each Delegate should depend on the number and needs of Polish citizens, the extent of the territory concerned, and the travelling facilities available, etc. Such negotiations have never taken place, and the Embassy considers that the matter should first be the subject of a detailed discussion before it can be finally solved.

4. The Embassy takes note of the People's Commissariat's point of view concerning the appointment of Delegates and 'men of trust', and expects that,

[2] Not printed.

in consequence, the People's Commissariat may find it possible to shorten the time necessary for dealing with the notes from the Embassy. The present routine makes it difficult for Delegates and 'men of trust' to carry out their duties as laid down in the 'Regulations concerning the activities of the Delegates of the Polish Embassy'.[3]

[3] The People's Commissariat for Foreign Affairs announced on July 20 the closing down of the offices of Embassy delegates in Archangel and Vologda.

No. 251

Aide-mémoire handed by Deputy Commissar Vyshinsky to Chargé d'Affaires Sokolnicki on the matter of Embassy Delegates[1]

Kuibyshev, July 20, 1942 GSHI, A.11. 49/Sow./3
Transl. from Russian

It has been established that all the arrested Delegates of the Polish Embassy and their employees, instead of loyally carrying out their duties as laid down in the special 'Regulations', re: the assistance to be given to Polish citizens in close co-operation with the local Soviet authorities, were occupied with anti-Soviet activities and intelligence work. Thus, the institution of special Delegates established with the consent of the Soviet Government to assist the Polish population throughout the country, has not justified itself.

In view of the above-mentioned reasons, the People's Commissariat considers that the further existence of the Delegates' Offices is no longer possible, and, in consequence, has issued relevant instructions to the local Soviet authorities.

[1] See Note No. 251.

No. 252

Note from Chargé d'Affaires Sokolnicki to the Doyen of the Diplomatic Corps Achmed Khan, on the infringement of the diplomatic immunity of members of the Embassy of the Republic of Poland

Kuibyshev, July 22, 1942 GSHI, A.11. 49/Sow./6

J'ai l'honneur de porter à la connaissance de Votre Excellence les faits suivants:

Conformément à un accord spécial conclu avec le Gouvernement Soviétique, l'Ambassade de Pologne en URSS a reçu l'autorisation de créer en province des délégations pour porter l'aide morale, juridique et matérielle aux citoyens polonais qui se sont trouvés en très grand nombre sur le territoire de l'Union Soviétique à la suite des événements de la guerre. Ces délégations ont été gérées par des délégués de l'Ambassade dont 8 étaient choisis parmi les secrétaires et attachés d'Ambassade. Munis des passeports et des visas diplomatiques, ainsi que des 'dip-cartotchki', ils étaient toujours considérés par le Narkomindiel comme membres du corps diplomatique. Ils ne figuraient pas sur la dernière édition de la liste du corps diplomatique car, d'accord avec le NKID, l'Ambassade a réduit le nombre des noms insérés dans la liste à celui des diplomates résidant à Kouibychev pour éviter aux collègues diplomatiques les invitations et échange des cartes de visite inutile.

Vis-à-vis du Narkomindiel ils conservaient toujours la résidence à Kouibychev pendant leur mission temporaire en province et ils rentraient dans le nombre du personnel diplomatique de l'Ambassade.

A la suite des mesures, tout-à-fait inexplicables et contraires au droit des gens, prises par les autorités soviétiques, M. Gruja, II Secrétaire d'Ambassade, et M. Załęski, I. Secrétaire d'Ambassade, ont été arrêté, respectivement à Archangelsk et Vladivostok, le 29 et le 30 juin dernier. Ils ont dû subir un interrogatoire, une révision personnelle avec la réquisition de tous les papiers qu'ils possédaient et ont été soumis au régime stricte de la prison (coupe de cheveux, obligation de nettoyage de la cellule etc.—c'était le cas de M. Gruja; pour les autres—manque d'information).

Après la protestation énergique de l'Ambassade, tous les deux diplomates polonais ont été libérés de la prison avec l'obligation de quitter le pays. M. Gruja se trouve actuellement à Kouibychev, M. Załęski est encore en route, parti de Vladivostok le 16 juillet.

Dans une note du 10 juillet,[1] le Narkomindiel expliquait les arrestations par l'ignorance de la part des autorités locales de la qualité diplomatique de MM. Gruja et Załęski et par les circonstances spéciales de la guerre. Cette ignorance est contredite par les dépositions de M. Gruja qui constate le contraire et qui a eu sur lui sa 'dipcartotchka'. Dans la même note le Narkomindiel accusait les deux diplomates susnommés de l'action hostile envers l'URSS. Le juge d'instruction, cependant, accusait M. Gruja, lors de son interrogatoire, de l'article 58 p. 10 partie 2, pour une action contre-révolutionnaire (propagande ou agitation contre l'URSS), article qui prévoit une peine de mort.

Depuis le 15 juillet les arrestations en masse ont eu lieu parmi les délégués et fonctionnaires des délégations. A l'heure présente on peut considérer comme certain que tous les délégués ainsi que la majeure partie de leurs collaborateurs sont emprisonnés, parmi eux six membres du corps diplomatique: M. Głogowski, II secrétaire d'Ambassade (Ashabad), les attachés d'Ambassade: M. Heitzman (Samarkand), M. Kościałkowski (Czimkent), M. Lickindorf (Pavlodar), M. Płoski (Pietropavlovsk) et M. Słowikowski (rappelé de Tchelabinsk, arrivé à Kouibychev le 16 juillet pour travailler à l'Ambassade ce qui a été annoncé au Narkomindiel le même jour, arrêté le 20 juillet devant la porte de l'Ambassade).

Je n'ai pas manqué de porter immédiatement tous ces faits à la connaisance du Narkomindiel en protestant contre toutes les arrestations et en demandant la libération des détenus. J'ai protesté spécialement contre la violation de l'immunité diplomatique des fonctionnaires d'Ambassade appartenant au corps diplomatique, immunité qui constitue un des principes les plus fondamentaux du droit international.

[1] See doc. No. 244.

J'ai réitéré ces démarches le 20 juillet personnellement auprès de M. Vychynski. Il m'a déclaré que les arrestations ont été faites à cause de l'activité hostile envers l'URSS des fonctionnaires arrêtés et de leur activité d'information. A cause de tout cela les autorités soviétiques ont décidé d'interrompre le fonctionnement des délégations.

J'ai rejeté catégoriquement ces accusations comme étant sans aucun fondement et injustes. J'ai exigé la libération immédiate des arrêtés. Quant aux attachés et secrétaires d'Ambassade, j'ai souligné leur caractère diplomatique. J'ai refuté d'une façon énergique l'assertion de M. Vychynski que les diplomates accusés d'une action hostile au pays ne peuvent jouir de l'immunité diplomatique.

Jusqu'à présent je n'ai reçu du Narkomindiel aucune réponse.

Il faut souligner que la qualité diplomatique des 8 attachés et secrétaires d'Ambassade envoyés temporairement en province n'a jamais été mise en doute par aucun organe soviétique. Cette attitude a été confirmée par la note du Narkomindiel du 6 juillet par laquelle il informait l'Ambassade qu'à l'avenir il ne pourra admettre que les délégués de l'Ambassade puissent en même temps être attachés ou secrétaires d'Ambassade conservant des droits diplomatiques, et que l'Ambassade devrait soit rappeler les diplomates de leur poste, soit annuler leur qualité diplomatique en les laissant à leurs fonctions de délégués.

Les dépêches de rappel envoyées par l'Ambassade aux délégué-diplomates, à la suite de cette note, n'ont pas été remises aux destinataires, ce qui constitue une nouvelle infraction à la liberté de la correspondance diplomatique. Le fait n'aurait peut être aucune influence sur les arrestations des six membres du corps diplomatique, vu le cas de M. Słowikowski, attaché d'Ambassade, qui, rappelé par téléphone et revenu à Kouibychev, a été ici arrêté 4 jours après devant la porte de l'Ambassade.

En informant Votre Excellence, en qualité de Doyen du corps diplomatique en URSS, de tous ces incidents exposés plus haut et qui touchent tout le corps diplomatique, je me permets de La prier de vouloir bien faire les démarches qu'Elle trouvera nécessaires pour faire libérer d'urgence les six membres du corps diplomatique en URSS.[2]

[2] The intervention of Ambassador Achmed Khan played a considerable part in the question of release of the arrested Embassy delegates.

No. 253

Memorandum from Ambassador Ciechanowski to Secretary of State Cordell Hull on the obstacles made by Soviet authorities in the carrying out of the plan for the relief of Polish citizens in the USSR

Washington, July 23, 1942   GSHI, A.11. 49/Sow.6

With reference to the previous memoranda on Polish-Russian relations which the Polish Ambassador personally handed to the Secretary of State on July 13, 1942, additional information has been received from the Polish Government, which the Ambassador submitted in conversation with the Secretary of State on July 23rd, 1942.

According to this information, during the past week two officials of the Polish Embassy in Kuibyshev, M. Gruja and M. Załęski, as well as their collaborators, who had been arrested by the Soviet Authorities, were released by them with the request that they leave the USSR. The Soviet Government gave as reason for this request that these two Polish officials had indulged in activity detrimental to the USSR. Since that time the following delegates of the Polish Embassy for distribution of relief supplies to the Polish population have been arrested: M. Heitzman and his collaborators in Samarkand, M. Mattoszko with practically the entire personnel of his office in Barnaul, M. Wisiński with several collaborators in Kirov, and the Second Secretary of Embassy, M. Głogowski, with part of his personnel in Ashabad.

According to the reports received up to this time, out of a total of twenty offices of such delegates of the Polish Embassy, which had been officially authorized by the USSR authorities to distribute relief among the Polish citizens in the USSR, the following have been closed by the Soviet authorities: the Polish Relief Offices in Archangel, Vladivostok, Aldan, Akmolinsk and Saratov.

The offices at Samarkand, Barnaul, Kirov, Petropavlovsk and Ashabad although not formally closed, are inactive due to the arrest of their personnel. The continued refusal by the Soviet authorities to recognize the personnel appointed by the Polish Embassy to operate the Relief Office in Murmansk and the Polish Relief warehouses in Mamprepk[1] has immobilized all relief activities of both these ports of arrival of Relief supplies.

As a result of this situation about 40% of the Polish civilian population in USSR is deprived of assistance and relief. Consequently there are no proper Polish agencies at the northern ports to take over and handle relief transports arriving there for the Polish population. The warehouses are stocked with valuable goods, without any supervision and will certainly deteriorate and may be stolen. The distribution of clothing, food, medical supplies, vaccines and cash assistance has ceased. Orphanages and invalid asylums are left without care or supervision.

The Polish Chargé d'Affaires, Minister H. Sokolnicki, received the following written declaration of Commissar Vyshinsky on July 20th.[2] [. . .].

The Polish Chargé d'Affaires has rejected the accusations contained in Commissar Vyshinsky's declaration and has requested the immediate release of all the arrested Polish Embassy employees and primarily those with diplomatic status. Although Minister Sokolnicki does not foresee that the USSR authorities will proceed to take legal action against these arrested Polish officials in view of the unfounded accusations made against them, he fears that their detention may be lengthy.

[1] The name of place is distorted. Probably should be Mamlutka, near Petropavlovsk.
[2] See doc. No. 251.

Note from Minister Raczyński to Ambassador Bogomolov protesting against the arrest of the delegates of the Polish Embassy

London, July 24, 1942   GSHI, PRM, 72/1

Le 20 juillet courant Votre Excellence a bien voulu m'apporter la réponse du Gouvernement de l'URSS à la note que je Lui ai adressé le 11 juillet.[1] Vous m'avez communiqué que, d'avis de votre Gouvernement, les gérants et les fonctionnaires des délégations provinciales de l'Ambassade de Pologne en l'URSS se sont rendus coupables d'activités contraires aux intérêts de l'URSS. En même temps vous m'avez communiqué que si les arrestations des délégués possèdant le caractère diplomatique ont pu avoir lieu, cela provenait uniquement du fait que les autorités soviétiques provinciales n'étaient pas entièrement renseignées sur leur statut. Vous m'avez informé que toutes les personnes arrêtées ont été libérées et vous avez demandé qu'elles quittent le territoire soviétique aussitôt que faire se pourra. Vous avez conclu par une affirmation que dans ces conditions vous considérez l'incident comme clos.

2/ Le même jour à Kouibichev le Commissaire Adjoint aux Affaires Etrangères a fait au Chargé d'Affaires de Pologne une déclaration dans laquelle il a affirmé que tous les délégués et leurs fonctionnaires qui venaient d'être arrêtés, au lieu de loyalement remplir leur devoir de porter assistance aux citoyens polonais, poursuivaient des activités hostiles à l'URSS, et s'occupaient en particulier du service de renseignement. Ainsi, selon son avis, l'institution des délégués de l'Ambassade n'avait pas justifié son existence. Jugeant que le maintien de ladite institution n'était plus possible, le Commissariat du Peuple aux Affaires Etrangères avait donné des instructions dans ce sens aux autorités soviétiques locales.

Depuis des informations additionnelles sont parvenues au Gouvernement polonais d'après lesquelles de nouvelles arrestations parmi le personnel des délégations avaient eu lieu, une grande partie des personnes incarcérées n'avait point été mises en liberté, les archives saisis n'avaient point été rendus aux autorités polonaises, et de nouvelles saisies d'archives se seraient produites. En plus, contrairement aux usages universellement reconnus dans les relations internationales et aux assurances que vous avez bien voulu me réitérer, une nouvelle arrestation d'un fonctionnaire polonais jouissant des prérogatives diplomatiques a eu lieu, cette fois à Kouibishev même. En effet le 20 juillet a été arrêté, au seuil de l'Ambassade de Pologne M. Słowikowski, Attaché de cette Ambassade, et notifié comme tel au Commissariat du Peuple pour les Affaires Etrangères.

3/ Les arrestations des délégués et la clôture de leurs bureaux ont porté un coup des plus sévères à l'œuvre de l'assistance polonaise. En effet, les nombreux colis arrivant à Archangelsk, à Mourmansk et à Askhabad ne peuvent pas être réexpédiés à l'intérieur et sont exposés à tous les risques. On m'informe que certaines marchandises, notamment les vivres, se détériorent faute d'arriver à leur destination. Entre temps, les dépôts dans l'intérieur du

[1] See doc. No. 246.

pays se vident et dans de nombreux cas sont déjà vidés, et de ce fait des déportés polonais souffrent de privations supplémentaires et inutiles. On me signale qu'à la date du 18 juillet 40% de l'assistance locale, en chiffres ronds, était déjà arrêté et que des orphelinats, des asiles de vieillards et d'invalides de guerre sont sur le point d'être fermés, faute de ravitaillement. Malgré les immenses efforts de l'Ambassade et des hommes de confiance locaux, la situation de l'organisation polonaise est paralysée et court vers sa fin si des mesures immédiates ne viennent y remédier.

4/ J'ai l'honneur de confirmer par écrit la protestation que je vous ai faite oralement contre les accusations formulées quant aux activités des délégués et de leur personnel et qui équivalent à imputer au mécanisme de secours aux citoyens polonais qu'il était en vérité une organisation dirigée contre l'URSS. Je repousse de la façon la plus catégorique toutes assertions de ce genre, comme portant atteinte à la réputation d'honneur de mon pays et comme incompatibles avec la collaboration qui unit les deux pays dans leur lutte contre l'ennemi commun.

Tous les fonctionnaires polonais en l'URSS, soit arrivés des pays tiers, soit recrutés sur place parmi les déportés, ont de strictes instructions de ne pas se mêler aux affaires de l'URSS et d'éviter toute activité qui porterait le moindre ombrage aux autorités soviétiques. Ces fonctionnaires ne pouvaient non plus ignorer que s'ils déviaient de leur devoir, ils risquaient de compromettre la grande tâche qui leur était confiée. Il est manifeste que les personnes en question ne pouvaient pas se conduire et ne se sont pas conduites d'une façon hostile aux intérêts de l'URSS. Ces accusations sont particulièrement difficiles à admettre quand elles se dirigent contre tout le personnel d'un grand service et en particulier contre des personnes qui, en raison de leurs fonctions diplomatiques, ont été choisies avec un soin tout particulier et jouissent de la pleine confiance du Gouvernement polonais.

5/ Je tiens à souligner qu'à l'avis du Gouvernement polonais il est inadmissible d'interrompre l'assistance aux citoyens polonais en détresse à peine commencée sur une plus ample échelle et au moment, où sa nécessité devient de plus en plus urgente. Les déportés polonais se sont trouvés sur le territoire soviétique contre leur volonté, tandis que leur rôle naturel était de faire face à l'invasion hitlérienne et de grossir les rangs de la résistance à l'ennemi commun, a côté de leurs compatriotes qui participent à cet effort. De plus, comme je l'ai déjà indiqué dans ma Note précédente, le sort de ces malheureuses victimes a vivement ému l'opinion publique aussi bien en Europe qu'en Amérique, qui par l'intermédiaire de ses institutions charitables a pris une part prépondérante dans le financement direct ou indirect de l'assistance aux déportés polonais. L'intérêt commun du Gouvernement soviétique et du Gouvernement polonais éxige qu'il n'y ait pas d'interruption de l'assistance ce qui ne manquerait pas de causer des commentaires adverses dans les milieux intéressés, et que l'organisation de secours puisse reprendre aussi rapidement que possible ses activités normales.

6/ Le Gouvernement polonais qui est resté constamment fidèle aux principes essentiels qui présidaient aux accords polono-soviétiques de l'année dernière,[2] n'a cessé d'y être attaché par des liens fondés sur l'intérêt politique, ainsi que sa conviction loyale. C'est avec un sentiment d'amertume, d'autant plus profond, que le Gouvernement polonais a suivi depuis le début du mois de juillet la marche des mesures prises par les autorités soviétiques dans une question d'un intérêt capital pour la Pologne. Il se refuse de croire que ces mesures répondent à un changement intentionné de la part du Gouvernement soviétique de la politique qui fut à la base de l'Accord du 30 juillet[2] et de la Déclaration du 4 décembre 1941.[3] En même temps il constate que dans les conditions présentes la collaboration nécessaire dans le domaine politique et militaire entre la Pologne et l'URSS ne peut pas être dissociée de la grave question de la situation des citoyens polonais en l'URSS. La protection et l'assistance à ces citoyens constituent un devoir sacré du Gouvernement polonais.

7/ D'ordre de mon Gouvernement je réitère mon énergique protestation contre les arrestations arbitraires des délégués de l'Ambassade et de leur personnel, et tout particulièrement contre la violation répétée et constante du privilege diplomatique des membres de l'Ambassade;

Je constate que ce Gouvernement ne pourrait admettre la compétence de la juridiction soviétique par rapport à l'activité officielle de ses fonctionnaires,

et je me vois obligé d'insister afin que les mesures immédiates soient prises pour la libération de toutes les personnes incarcérées, pour la restitution à l'Ambassade des archives et des fonds des délégations et pour permettre la reprise du fonctionnement de l'organisation de l'assistance polonaise, chargée de porter secours à des nombreuses centaines de milliers des citoyens polonais plongés dans la misère.

[2] See doc. No. 106. [3] See doc. No. 161.

No. 255

Aide-mémoire from Minister Raczyński to Mr. Eden on the difficulties arising in the work of relief for Polish deportees in the USSR[1]

London, July 26, 1942[2] GSHI, A.11. 49/Sow./6

1. The care of the deported Polish citizens in Russia and the help in kind given to them (food, clothing, medicines) was being rendered until July 1942 through the so-called provincial Delegations under the supervision of the Polish Ambassador. The status of the Delegates and their assistants was agreed upon as a result of conversations between the People's Commissariat for Foreign Affairs and the Polish Embassy in Moscow, which were concluded in January 1942.[3] The number of delegates was fixed at twenty, and nineteen offices (all except Saratov) began to function. The offices were in charge of Delegates whom the Soviet Government undertook to treat as representatives

[1] See Note No. 255.
[2] The date of this Aide-mémoire is deduced from other documents.
[3] See doc. No. 166. The date of conversation should be corrected to December 23, 1941.

of the Embassy, assuring their personal immunity as also the immunity of their offices and archives (in a conversation between the Polish Ambassador, Prof. Kot, with the Deputy Commissar for Foreign Affairs, Monsieur Vyshinsky, of January 26th, 1942).[4] In addition the functions of Delegates in the most important centres of welfare and relief were entrusted to political officials of the Embassy included in the lists of the Diplomatic Corps (Archangel, Chimkent, Vladivostok, Samarkand, Ashkhabad). The Delegates functioning in these centres were entitled therefore to enjoy regular diplomatic privileges.

2. As soon as the legal and formal questions were settled and the local offices of the delegations were open, and as soon as the necessary apparatus for the purchase of commodities was organized in Great Britain, Canada, the United States and the Near East, it became possible to begin the work of relief for the deportees. The Polish Government placed considerable funds at the disposal of the relief organization. Moreover, a considerable number of charitable and social organizations and institutions in the United Kingdom, Canada and the United States of America, with the American Red Cross at their head, assisted in the relief activities. The assistance rendered, although inadequate in view of the immensity of the needs, was rapidly growing and the quantities shipped from abroad increased from month to month. During April and May alone, more than 1,500 tons of various commodities were shipped through Archangel. During June the quantity of commodities which were to be shipped through Archangel was larger than that actually shipped during the preceding two months, while still larger quantities were announced to be shipped during July. This relief could have prevented to a certain extent the starvation of and the spread of epidemics among the deportees, especially among children. There exist reliable statistics indicating a very high rate of mortality and it must be borne in mind that owing to the loss of agricultural provinces of Russia resulting from the military operations, the acute shortage of food would become even worse during the period 1942/43, especially in the North of European Russia and in the Central provinces of Asiatic Russia.

3. The principal receiving depôts for all relief shipments were at Archangel, Murmansk and Ashkhabad. The shipments were being checked by the local Delegates, sorted out and forwarded by rail to their various destinations, i.e. to the stores maintained by each Delegation or to Kuibyshev. Certain quantities of commodities were being distributed locally (for instance in the region Archangel-Vologda), as each of the Delegates mentioned above had, in addition to his functions as a shipping agent, the duty to look after the welfare of the Polish population in his own district. The supervision of these transports was all the more indispensable as owing to the acute shortage of all kinds of commodities in Soviet Russia the shipments were being pilfered in spite of the watchfulness of the police.

4. Early in July the Soviet authorities undertook systematic measures of repression towards individual delegates. On July 2nd, while the Delegate in

[4] Not printed. The mentioned conversation took place on January 23, 1942.

Archangel was absent on official duties, the Soviet police arrested the personnel and confiscated the documents and moneys in the offices of the Delegation.[5] The Delegate himself was arrested during his journey. Similar steps were taken with regard to other Delegations; the Delegates and their personnel were arrested while the funds and archives were seized.

5. The position at the present time is as follows:

Of the twenty Delegations it is definitely known that eleven are not functioning at the present time (Archangel, Aldan-Yakutsky, Akmolinsk, Ashkhabad, Barnaul, Kirov, Petropavlovsk, Samarkand, Saratov, Siktivkar, Vladivostok), in which are included the four most important shipping and distributing centres: Archangel, Ashkhabad, Samarkand and Vladivostok. Reports concerning the remaining nine Delegations (Alma-Ata, Chelyabinsk, Chkalov, Chimkent, Jambuł, Krasnoyarsk, Kustanai, Pavlodar, Semipalatinsk) are incomplete owing to the difficulties of internal communications and it is possible that they have been or may be closed down. Of the five diplomatic officials of the Embassy who acted as Delegates two were arrested and released after about a fortnight, while the two others were recently arrested and have not yet been released. At least no information concerning their release has been received. The fifth Delegate has been officially recalled to the Embassy.

6. In this way a state of affairs arose which amounts in fact to the complete paralysing of the relief for the deportees in Russia. The shipments arriving weekly in the ports of Archangel, Murmansk and Vladivostok and the shipments arriving on the Persian-Soviet frontier by the Southern route cannot be forwarded to the interior of Russia owing to the absence of Delegates. Polish stores in these centres include perishable goods and are, moreover, exposed to pilferage. Owing to the closing down of the Delegations in the interior of Russia the distribution of food, clothing, medicines and monetary grants had to be suspended. Preventive vaccination has been interrupted. Orphanages and homes for invalids are without proper supervision. Owing to the interruption of the deliveries of overseas shipments from the ports, the depôts, which are still functioning, will have to be closed down after the exhaustion of the stores. According to the calculations of the Embassy, by July 18th, about 40% of the deportees have been deprived of welfare services. It may be added that apart from the difficulties described above, the local Delegations who are still functioning, are meeting with a systematic refusal of the Soviet authorities to recognize persons selected for the executive personnel of these Delegations.

7. As soon as the arrests and repressions began the Polish Embassy in Kuibyshev and the Polish Ministry for Foreign Affairs repeatedly protested verbally and in writing against the arbitrary measures of the Soviet authorities and demanded the return of the funds and archives and the re-opening of the offices of the Delegations which have been closed down. However, the People's Commissariat for Foreign Affairs in Kuibyshev avoided all discussion on this subject, while the interventions resulted in the release of only a

[5] See doc. Nos. 234, 236, 237, 242, 243 and 245.

few of the arrested persons and the return of a part of the property seized. None of the Delegations, however, has been allowed to re-open its offices.

In his reply to a note of July 11th sent by the Soviet Ambassador accredited to the Polish Government,[6] Ambassador Bogomolov explained on July 20th to the Acting Polish Minister of Foreign Affairs that the Delegates and their personnel were arrested 'owing to their activities harmful to the interests of the Soviets', at a time when the military situation required special caution on the part of the Soviet authorities more particularly in the ports and at other key-points. At the same time Ambassador Bogomolov alleged that the local authorities were not fully informed of the diplomatic standing of those Delegates who enjoyed the diplomatic status. He also stated that all the arrested persons had been released and that they will be obliged to leave Soviet territory as early as possible. While offering this explanation the Ambassador stated that in this way the matter will be closed.

8. In reply the Acting Minister of Foreign Affairs, Count Raczyński, rejected the accusation that reliable Polish officials could have acted in a way damaging Soviet interests, which would be contrary to the definite instructions received by them and which prevented them from any interference in the internal affairs of the USSR.[7] He also stated that he cannot consider the matter as closed, because quite apart from the release of the persons arrested there still remains the practical question of carrying on relief activities directed towards rescuing the deportees from starvation and death. With regard to the desire of the Soviets for the departure from Russia of the Delegates and their personnel, Count Raczyński pointed out that in order to avoid complications detrimental to the rendering of relief it would be desirable if those persons were enabled to depart gradually after the transfer of their duties to their successors. Ambassador Bogomolov stated that this opens a new problem which he will be obliged to submit to his Government.

9. The attitude of the Soviet Ambassador justifies the suspicion that the Soviet Government may altogether refuse to agree to the re-opening of the offices of the Delegations under the direction of other persons to be appointed. Any doubts in this respect or even a delay in the re-opening of the Delegations would naturally lead to the perpetuation of the present state of affairs, i.e. to the cessation of all local relief in the nearest future. In the meantime the relief shipments of a very high value may be wasted. Moreover, in case of an interruption of the overseas supply for the relief of the deportees the charitable institutions, both in Britain and America, may be discouraged in continuing their work the results of which would thus be exposed to great dangers. Last but not least, the health and even the lives of scores of thousands of the deportees would be placed in jeopardy.

10. The accusation that the Delegates and their personnel were engaging in activities hostile to the Soviet Government and even of a 'counter revolutionary character' advanced by the local Soviet authorities must be emphatically rejected. It would be utterly incongruous to assume that any of the

[6] See doc. No. 246. The verbal reply of Bogomolov on July 20 is given in the doc. No. 254.
[7] See doc. No. 254 with Note No. 254.

persons concerned, who had been working with the utmost devotion on behalf of their unfortunate countrymen could expose their and their own fate to the hazards of 'anti-Soviet activities'. However, the raising of this question by the Soviet Government seems to indicate that the repressive measures applied against the Delegates were primarily police measures. The reasons for such a conduct are not clear and could be commented upon only hypothetically.

11. In view of the disaster which threatens or may threaten the large numbers of Polish citizens in Soviet Russia the Polish Government relies on the friendly intervention of the British Government with the Soviet authorities in order to assure that the Polish relief activities should be resumed. The only alternative to the resumption of relief could be the evacuation of the persons concerned, especially children, from Soviet territory. Such an evacuation, however, would have to embrace enormous numbers of people in need of help, thus cancelling all schemes prepared for this purpose up till now.

No. 256

Note from Deputy Commissar Vyshinsky to Chargé d'Affaires Sokolnicki concerning the Offices of the Embassy Delegates

Kuibyshev, July 27, 1942　　　　　　　　　　　GSHI, A.11. 49/Sow./3
　　　　　　　　　　　　　　　　　　　　　　　Transl. from Russian

In reply to your note of 19th July inst.[1] and also to your notes Ref: D.3070/42 of 20th July, D.3095/42 of 21st July, D.3101/42 of 21st July and D.3102/42 of 21st July inst.,[2] I have the honour to inform you of the following:

1. The cessation of further activities of the Embassy's Regional Delegates does not justify the implication that the Soviet Government intends to hamper or to liquidate the welfare work for the Poles in the USSR.

The cessation of the Delegates' activities, as I had the opportunity of informing you in our conversation of 20th July inst., was caused by the findings of the investigating authorities who discovered proof of anti-Soviet activities and intelligence work carried out by the Regional Delegates of the Embassy. The arrangements for continuing the welfare work for Poles in the USSR could be re-considered on receipt of definite suggestions from the Embassy.

2. Referring to the statement in the note of July 19th, that the arrests carried out at Barnaul, Kirov, Petropavlovsk, Samarkand and other places, affected the most active members of the Embassy, employed in the welfare work for Poles, I consider it necessary to stress once more that the arrests of the above-mentioned persons were exclusively caused by their anti-Soviet activities.

3. The information conveyed by you that telegrams sent by the Embassy

---

[1] See doc. No. 249.
[2] The four mentioned notes on individual matters are omitted.

to its Delegates had allegedly been detained has not been confirmed by our investigation, and, therefore, the statement made by the Embassy that such action was proof 'of the violation of privileges and of diplomatic immunity established by international law and usage', is without foundation.

4. Concerning the detention of M. M. Załęski and J. Gruja, the People's Commissariat has already made a statement in their note of 10th July,[3] therefore the matter should be considered closed.

5. The Embassy's Delegates named in the above-mentioned notes of 10th and 21st July: Adam Głogowski, Witold Płoski, Lickindorf, Bohdan Kościałkowski, Słowikowski and also M. Heitzman, whom the Embassy mentioned in the Personal Note of July 19th, were all temporarily detained by the local authorities as a preventive measure in connection with their anti-Soviet activities, as the Embassy was informed on 21st July.

It was brought to the Embassy's knowledge in respect of Adam Głogowski, Witold Płoski, Lickindorf, Bohdan Kościałkowski and Słowikowski, that the order of preventive detention, referred to above, was cancelled on 24th July, and that they were all released on that day.

6. The arrest of Słowikowski and Władysław Zaharjasiewicz was the result of their anti-Soviet and intelligence activities during the period of their employment at the Delegate's Office at Chelabinsk.

7. The protest presented by the Embassy that these arrests were a violation of the diplomatic privileges and rights of these members of the Embassy, established by international law, is entirely unfounded. These rights and privileges vested in the members of the Embassy, temporarily employed on duties of Delegates in the first period of organization, became void on 6th July inst., when the People's Commissariat by their note,[4] Ref. No. 128, informed the Embassy of the discontinuation of this practice, to which the Embassy agreed.

In view of the above, the People's Commissariat cannot accept the Embassy's protest. The question of the release of the remaining Delegates and of their staff, and the restitution of their archives, seals and money, can only be decided on the conclusion of the investigation.

8. Concerning the Embassy's attempt to make the Soviet authorities bear responsibility for the discontinuation of the welfare work for Poles, and also for the consequences of measures taken against the above-mentioned Embassy's Delegates and their staff, the People's Commissariat categorically denies all responsibility, as it must be borne exclusively by those persons who, by their criminal activities, made such measures necessary.

[3] See doc. No. 244.   [4] See doc. No. 236.

Note from Ambassador Bogomolov to Minister Raczyński in reply to the Polish Note of 11th July, 1942, concerning the detention of the Embassy Delegates[1]

London, July 29, 1942

GSHI, A.11. 49/Sow./3
Transl. from Russian

In reply to your Note of 11th July, 1942,[2] handed to me on 13th July, I have the honour, by order of my Government, to inform you of the following points:

Competent Soviet authorities have recently established that Regional Delegates of the Polish Embassy and their staff were indulging in anti-Soviet activities and intelligence work, instead of loyally co-operating with local Soviet authorities in the work of material aid to destitute Polish citizens, as laid down in the 'Regulations concerning the activities of Delegates of the Polish Embassy'. Consequently, all these persons and some of their employees were arrested.

Thus, there is no justification for the further existence of the institution of the Embassy's Delegates, to whose appointment the Soviet Government had agreed, so that they might give material aid to destitute Polish citizens. The Soviet Government, therefore, considered it purposeless to maintain the existence of these Delegates' Offices, and they issued the necessary instructions to their local authorities whilst the People's Commissariat informed the Polish Embassy in Kuibyshev thereof.

In view of these facts the Soviet Government do not consider it possible to re-consider and re-examine the proposals submitted in the Note referring to the resumption of the Delegates' activities throughout the country.

In connection with the protest presented in your Note of 11th July, concerning the arrests of M. Gruja, M. Załęski and a number of other employees of the Embassy's Delegate at Archangel and Vladivostok, I must refer to my explanation given to you on July 20th. It pointed out that analogous protests delivered on 6th and 9th July by the Polish Embassy in the USSR had not been accepted, as they were unfounded. At the same time the Embassy had been informed that M. Gruja and M. Załęski, like the other employees of the Embassy's Delegates at Archangel, had been released, and that their seals, papers, documents and money had been returned to them. It was, however, suggested to them that they should leave the territory of the USSR in view of the compromising evidence held against them.

By order of my Government I must also reject, as entirely unfounded, the protest contained in your Note against the alleged 'infringement by the Soviet Government of diplomatic privileges recognized by themselves'. In fact neither the Regional Delegates of the Embassy, nor their deputies or other staff, enjoyed the rights and privileges of a diplomatic status. The Ministry for Foreign Affairs should be well aware of this fact, and the representatives of the Narkomindel at Kuibyshev stated it repeatedly; in particular

[1] See Note No. 257. [2] See doc. No. 246.

it was pointed out in the conversation between the Deputy People's Commissar for Foreign Affairs A. J. Vyshinsky and Ambassador Kot, on January 23rd. As the institution of temporary Delegates of the Embassy was not a usual diplomatic practice, the binding norms of international law could not provide them with a diplomatic status.

The reference made in the Note to the alleged 'explanations' of A. J. Vyshinsky, 'in the sense that regional Delegates of the Embassy would be regarded as representatives of a diplomatic mission, and that the rights of each Delegate should include his personal immunity and that of his archives and offices', is completely unjustified. In fact, A. J. Vyshinsky, in his conversation with Ambassador Kot on 23rd January, touched upon the problem and explained that the constitution of the USSR fully guaranteed the immunity of persons, dwellings and correspondence of all citizens (as well as of foreigners residing in the USSR,) and therefore there was no need to grant any special guarantees in that respect to the Embassy's Delegates.

Concerning the relief action for Polish citizens, the supposition that the Soviet authorities had the intention of discontinuing that relief work was completely groundless, of which I have the honour to inform you, Mister Minister.

No. 258

Note from the Polish Embassy in the USSR to the People's Commissariat for Foreign Affairs concerning Soviet measures directed against the existence of Polish welfare organizations in the USSR

Kuibyshev, August 13, 1942   GSHI, A.11. 49/Sow./2
                                                Transl. from Polish

Following the conversation of the Chargé d'Affaires a.i., M. Sokolnicki, with Director Novikov, the Polish Embassy has the honour to inform of the following points:

The Embassy has been advised that the Provincial Executive Committee of the Semipalatinsk Province ordered the closing down of the orphanage, established at Semipalatinsk by the Polish Embassy. At the same time the Provincial Executive Committee offered to transfer the orphans, who were Polish citizens, at present living at the Embassy's orphanage, to the local Soviet orphanage. The further issue of food rations to the Embassy's orphanage at Semipalatinsk was refused.

The Provincial Executive Committee of Akmolinsk cancelled the arrangements made for the accommodation of children of Polish nationality, assembled there for further transport to India, and ordered those children to be sent to their previous place of residence. The Akmolinsk Executive Committee also suspended the issue of additional food rations to a children's Home, organized in the Novotcherkassy District by the Polish Embassy.

The Provincial Executive Committee of South Kazakhstan ordered the closing down of a surgery and of a small hospital, organized by the Embassy in the Shauldra District.

The Polish Embassy states that the orders issued by the Provincial Executive Committees of Semipalatinsk, Akmolinsk, South Kazakhstan, liquidating relief institutions for children of Polish nationality as well as medical centres, and also impeding the departure of Polish children to India within the quota agreed with the People's Commissariat for Foreign Affairs, are in contradiction with the point of view expressed by the People's Commissariat for Foreign Affairs, who had given its assurance that the Government of the USSR did not intend to render the relief work for Poles impossible.

All the above quoted orders of the Soviet local authorities, as well as the orders issued by the Executive Committee of the Kustanai Province, of which the People's Commissariat has been informed by the Embassy's Note Ref. D.3411/42, dated 3rd August, 1942,[1] shatter the very foundation of the relief work and of the institutions established for that purpose, though the People's Commissariat agreed to the creating of these institutions, and encouraged the Embassy to organize them.

[1] Not printed.

No. 259

Record of a conversation between Lt.-General Anders and Mr. Churchill in the presence of General Wilson and Colonel Jacob on the general situation on the Russian front and the prospects of evacuation of the Polish Forces to the Middle East

Cairo, August 22, 1942   GSHI, KGA, 7-e

The Prime Minister said that he had studied the documents relating to the organization of the Polish Forces and had remitted them to the CIGS and General Wilson. He understood that General Anders was not authorized to discuss these details.

General Anders agreed that this was so.

The Prime Minister said that on the whole the view of the British authorities coincided with that of General Anders on the general shape that the organization should take, but that it would be best to come to a final agreement in the matter with General Sikorski in London. It was intended to locate the Polish Forces in North Persia where the Tenth Army was being developed as part of the command to which General Wilson had just been appointed.

General Anders said that he thought the chances were in favour of the Germans breaking through the Caucasus, rather than otherwise. The Prime Minister said that he was doubtful on this point. He hoped that the line of mountains and the Volga would both be held until the winter. However, General Anders had personal knowledge in these matters and we were acting on the assumption that he was right.

General Anders said that he would be very glad to fight with his troops as part of General Wilson's Army.

The Prime Minister said that he would personally do his utmost to get the equipment for the Polish Forces as rapidly as possible.

The discussion than turned on the unhappy position of Polish subjects in Russia, on the difficulties of the Polish Embassy vis-à-vis the Soviet Government, and on the question of further recruitment of Poles in Russia. General Anders handed the Prime Minister a note on the latter subject, which the Prime Minister then read.

The Prime Minister said that he was equally anxious to secure as many Poles as possible from Russia to reinforce the Polish Army, and he would consider what action he might take to improve the prospects. He must however be the judge of the moment for making the approach to Stalin. The Russians were now hard pressed and had a natural feeling, that we were somewhat inactive. A more favourable opportunity for taking up this matter with Stalin might soon present itself.

The Prime Minister thought also that it would be well to obtain President Roosevelt's co-operation in this matter, which he wishes to do.

General Anders drew attention to the disappearance of large numbers of his best regular officers who had been imprisoned in Russia. He had been unable to get any news of them whatever. He also emphasized the importance of securing the evacuation of the children who could not be expected to last another winter.

The Prime Minister said that he had given orders that the women and children were to be received from Russia together with the troops. He thought it possible that the Russians were averse to letting the Polish officers go, for fear of the stories that they might spread of the treatment they had received.

General Anders said that he was very satisfied with treatment which the people had received after leaving Russia. He felt it imperative to try to secure the release of the remainder. Stalin's attitude was most illogical. He was refusing further recruiting because the Polish Government had not placed their Army on the Russian Front, whilst at the same time he refused them arms—contrary to his previous agreement—and limited their rations to 26,000, increased to 44,000 on General Anders' personal intervention on March 18th.

There was no justness or honour in Russia, and there was not a single man in that country whose word could be trusted.

The Prime Minister pointed out how dangerous such language would be if it were spoken in public. No good could come of antagonizing the Russians. General Anders said that he fully realized this point and had given strict orders to his people—who fully understood the matter—against saying anything derogatory about the Russians. He had also endeavoured, not entirely without success, to establish good relations with the Russians, particularly during the period prior to their departure.

The Prime Minister said he hoped General Anders would now place himself at General Wilson's disposal so that all necessary arrangements could be made. He felt sure that men in Poland would give a good account of themselves. Their men in the United Kingdom had proved their worth, one of their Fighter Squadrons being admitted to the foremost in Fighter Command.

General Wilson said he understood that General Anders would now be going back to North Persia to supervise the reception of his people, and would then come to Bagdad where he, General Wilson, would be establishing his Headquarters shortly.

The Prime Minister concluded by saying he believes that Poland will emerge from the war a strong and happy country.

No. 260

Lt.-General Anders' memorandum submitted to Mr. Churchill

Cairo, August 22, 1942   GSHI, KGA, 7d

1. On the basis of the Polish-Soviet military agreement (31 July, 1941)[1] and personal promises given by Stalin—all Polish citizens in USSR, released from places of settlement, compulsory labour camps, prisons and the Red Army, were to be directed to the Polish Forces in USSR then being formed.

Up to now the strength of the Polish Army amounts to approximately:

> 33,000 evacuated in March to Palestine,
> 44,000 now in course of evacuation,
> 77,000 approx. total.

During the year after the military agreement was signed the Government of USSR, besides creating many difficulties of a general and individual character to Polish citizens who were seeking their way to the Polish Army, maintained that the Polish Army can but incorporate:

a. citizens of purely Polish blood,
b. Polish citizens who entered the territory under Soviet occupation after 29th November, 1939.[2]

However, even on the lines of the above-mentioned principles—which were never accepted by the Polish authorities—the full possibilities of recruiting have never been exhausted. On the territory of USSR there are still at least 60,000 Poles that should be enlisted into the Polish Army, as they are of purely Polish blood and perfectly fit for military service. The above-mentioned number consists of:

a. those incorporated into the Red Army before 22nd June, 1941,
b. those incorporated into so-called 'Stroj battaliony' i.e. auxiliary labour units. Although a number of such units has been dissolved, the Poles have found themselves still in non-fighting labour units whence they could not escape despite their eagerness to do so,
c. those who from the beginning of their exile are still working in compulsory labour camps and in spite of orders given have not been set free,
d. a great many in prisons and penal servitude—still not released. We have in our Army many men who until April and May, 1942 were still in camps and ignorant of the formation of the Polish Army in USSR.

2. Prisoners of war. There are about 8,300 officers, from former camps in

---

[1] Should be 30 July, 1941.   [2] Probably omitted word 'other' before 'Polish citizens'.

423

Starobielsk and Kozielsk—still in the USSR. Evidence of this number has been strictly and officially compiled. Evidence of their presence in these camps ceased in the spring 1940, when they were deported in small parties to an unknown destination. Not a single man has since been heard of despite promises by the Soviet Government to release the whole number. At present the Soviet Government have withdrawn all promises to search for them, affirming they are not in USSR. We possess however numerous traces of their having been sent to the islands in the Arctic Ocean such as 'Novaja Ziemla' and 'Franz Joseph' and other parts in northern Siberia. We have been denied all opportunity of searching for and rescuing them. These officers represent the best professional elements of the Polish Army.

A similar fate has overtaken the prisoners of war at Ostashkov, where there were over 7,000 men, mostly N.C.O.'s.

Summarizing, it is evident that USSR can and should give at present to the Polish Army in M. E.—at least 60,000 men of purely Polish blood.

No. 261

Note from Minister Raczyński to Ambassador Bogomolov on further enrolment of Polish citizens into the Polish Army

London, August 27, 1942   GSHI, A.11. 49/Sow./2
Transl. from Polish Pol.-Sov.R., No. 48

The Government of the Republic of Poland has been informed by General Anders, Commander-in-Chief of the Polish Armed Forces in the Union of Soviet Socialist Republics, that the authorities of the Union of Soviet Socialist Republics have adopted a negative attitude towards the Polish Government's efforts and endeavours to maintain a reserve depôt on the territory of the Union of Soviet Socialist Republics so as to be able to continue recruiting Polish citizens for the Polish Army.

The authorities of the Union of Soviet Socialist Republics explained their refusal as follows:

'As the Polish Government does not find it possible to use the Polish divisions formed on the territory of the Union of Soviet Socialist Republics on the Soviet-German front, the Government of the Union of Soviet Socialist Republics cannot allow the formation of any Polish units whatsoever nor any recruiting in the Union of Soviet Socialist Republics.'

As regards the adoption by the Government of the Union of Soviet Socialist Republics of such an attitude in a matter as important to the Polish Government as the problem of carrying on recruiting of Polish citizens for the Polish army, I have the honour to inform Your Excellency of the following:

The political Agreement of July 30, 1941,[1] and particularly the Military Agreement of August 14, 1941,[2] provided for the organization of a Polish Army on the territory of the Union of Soviet Socialist Republics, by voluntary

[1] See doc. No. 106.   [2] See doc. No. 112.

enlistment and by normal recruiting. In view of the explicit terms of this Agreement, the Polish Government was entitled to expect that the organization of the army would not meet with any difficulties from the Government of the Union of Soviet Socialist Republics, and that its executive authorities would in the measure of their possibilities extend their help to the Polish Embassy and the Polish Army Command in their efforts to form an Army of Polish citizens capable of bearing arms and willing to fulfill their duty to their country in its Armed Forces. Unfortunately actual events have not justified these hopes of the Polish Government, and the facts given below will show that the authorities of the Union of Soviet Socialist Republics have not lent their support to the development and organization of the Polish Army.

Thus, when in November last, before the recruiting boards were set up, and the strength of the Polish Army already amounted to 46,000 men, the Military Authorities of the Union of Soviet Socialist Republics informed the Polish Command that the strength of the Polish Army could not exceed 30,000 men and that the establishment and rations for the Army had been limited to that number. Although Ambassador Kot immediately intervened with M. Molotov, People's Commissar for Foreign Affairs, this unilateral decision was not changed and as a result the Polish Command was forced to discharge from the ranks of the Army 16,000 soldiers who had enlisted as volunteers. This was the first serious setback that hampered the organization of the Polish Army.

It would have seemed that the problem of the numerical strength of the Polish Army was finally and definitely settled in December of last year during General Sikorski's visit to Moscow.[3] General Sikorski together with Premier Stalin, Chairman of the Council of People's Commissars, established the numerical strength of the Polish Army in the Union of Soviet Socialist Republics at 96,000 men, exclusive of 25,000 men to be evacuated to the Near East to reinforce the Polish units fighting in Libya, and the 2,000 airmen and sailors to be evacuated to Great Britain. Thus the total number of Polish soldiers to be recruited on the territory of the Union of Soviet Socialist Republics was to amount to 123,000.

Hardly had three months elapsed, however, before this decision agreed upon by both parties, underwent an unexpected unilateral change. Thus in March, 1942, the Chairman of the Council of People's Commissars informed General Anders, Commander-in-Chief of the Polish Army in the Union of Soviet Socialist Republics, that the strength of the Polish Army could not exceed 44,000 men and that the surplus over and above that number would be evacuated to the Near East. The decision to reduce the strength of the Polish Army in the Union of Soviet Socialist Republics from 96,000 to 44,000 men was a new obstacle to the organization of the Polish Army.

The Polish Government, thus faced with an accomplished fact, received this decision with genuine regret. The Polish Government had hoped that thanks to the continuation of recruiting for the army, that had been promised to General Anders, a considerable number of soldiers over and above the

[3] See doc. No. 159.

425

established strength of 44,000 would also be evacuated to the Near East to reinforce the Allied armies fighting the enemy. These hopes were openly expressed in General Sikorski's message of April 9, 1942,[4] to the Chairman of the Council of People's Commissars, delivered to Your Excellency on April 13; in my Aide-Mémoire of May 1, 1942,[5] to Your Excellency; in Ambassador Kot's Note of May 4,[6] to the People's Commissar for Foreign Affairs; and in my Note of June 10, 1942,[7] to Your Excellency. I should moreover like to add that in accordance with the Declaration made on December 4, 1941,[8] by General Sikorski and the Chairman of the Council of People's Commissars, which established the bases of co-operation between the Polish Army and the Soviet Army, and in accordance with the frequent public statements made by General Sikorski about the common struggle of the Polish Forces and the Armed Forces of the Union of Soviet Socialist Republics against the German forces, I stated in my Note of June 10, that even those Polish soldiers who had been evacuated from the Union of Soviet Socialist Republics would take part, after they had been adequately equipped and trained and should the necessity arise, in fighting on the territory of the Union of Soviet Socialist Republics, side by side with the soldiers of the Army of the Union of Soviet Socialist Republics.

The answer sent by M. Molotov, People's Commissar for Foreign Affairs, on May 14, 1942,[9] in reply to Ambassador Kot's Note of May 4, surprised and astonished the Polish Government. The reply in question contained a statement that the Chairman of the Council of People's Commissars in his conversation with General Anders never touched upon the problem of continued recruiting for the Polish Army, and further that the recruiting, supply and medical centres of the Polish Army, intended to facilitate the dispatch of volunteers to that Army, must also be closed.

This decision to reduce the strength of the Polish Army, the refusal to allow recruiting and voluntary enlistment, already restricted by the ban on Polish citizens leaving their places of temporary residence and the suspension of railway passes, prove that the Government of the Union of Soviet Socialist Republics did not desire an increase in the strength of the Polish Army on the territory of the Union of Soviet Socialist Republics or in the ranks of the Polish units fighting in the Near East.

The negative attitude of the Soviet Government to the further development of the Polish forces is also proved by the fact that more than 8,000 Polish officers, who in the spring of 1940 were interned in the prisoner of war camps of Ostashkov, Starobielsk and Kozielsk, are still missing despite frequent interventions by the Polish Government, and although incomplete lists of the names of these officers were delivered to the Chairman of the Council of People's Commissars by General Sikorski in December, 1941, and in March, 1942, by General Anders.

Taking into consideration all the aforementioned indisputable facts concerning the organization of the Polish Army on the territory of the Union of

[4] See doc. No. 201. [5] See doc. No. 214. [6] See doc. No. 216.
[7] See doc. No. 227. [8] See doc. No. 161. [9] See doc. No. 219.

Soviet Socialist Republics, I have the honour to inform you, Mr. Ambassador, that the Government of the Republic of Poland considers the allegation that the Polish Army declines to fight shoulder to shoulder with the Army of the Union of Soviet Socialist Republics, as entirely unfounded and inconsistent with the true state of affairs, and that the Government of the Republic of Poland cannot take into cognizance the motives alleged for the refusal to allow further recruiting for the Polish Army.

No. 262

Record of a conversation held in Chequers between General Sikorski and Mr. Churchill on the subject of British support for the Polish claims in Moscow

London, August 30, 1942   GSHI, PRM, 68
                                                            Transl. from Polish

The discussion on Polish-Soviet affairs was initiated by Mr. Churchill at the very beginning of the conversation. Mr. Churchill stated that, at the moment, Great Britain could not demand anything of Russia. First, Great Britain had no military victories to claim, and secondly she could not give Russia any effective assistance, even in the domain of war equipment. 'Being a realist,' said Mr. Churchill, 'I cannot risk a refusal' (je ne peux pas essuyer un refus). However, at the first opportunity, as soon as the situation changes —and Mr. Churchill hoped that in the near future he would be able to offer material aid to the Soviets (he clearly alluded to the possibility of supplying Russia with a large number of operational aircraft), he would exert pressure to make Russia comply with the Polish demands which he considered justified.

Gen. Sikorski reacted very vividly, asking whether at least he could count on British support for American initiative in that respect. Mr. Churchill promised that support unconditionally, stressing that it would be much easier for the Americans than for the British. At that point Mr. Churchill stated emphatically that Great Britain was fully aware of the part played in the war by Poland, of her importance and of his obligations towards her. At the peace conference he would make an all-out effort to obtain the acceptance of all the desiderata, presented by Gen. Sikorski. Here Mr. Churchill drank a toast in honour of Poland.

Mr. Churchill made a short résumé of his conversation with Gen. Anders, whom he esteemed as a good soldier, although he disapproved of his unnecessary criticism of the Russians and of Russia's military operations, and of his pessimism concerning Russia's war potential. He mentioned he thought it incorrect for a general under Gen. Sikorski's command to express such opinions, even in front of Mr. Churchill himself, as that was Gen. Sikorski's exclusive privilege.

Then Mr. Churchill tried to convince Gen. Sikorski that he should go to Moscow to have another talk with Stalin. He was very critical of Maisky and Bogomolov (—and in a private conversation with Sikorski of Molotov as well). He thought Stalin was the only man with whom it was possible to negotiate, and that, by the way, Stalin had many characteristics in common with Gen. Sikorski.

Gen. Sikorski answered that first of all he must go to America.

The British Prime Minister stated that this journey could be very helpful to President Roosevelt in view of his difficulties in connection with the approaching election. So far the campaign had not quite followed his line. Mr. Churchill thought that the postponement of Gen. Sikorski's journey to Moscow would not greatly affect the situation. Here Mr. Churchill sharply criticized the policy of Col. Beck and Gen. Rydz-Śmigły, asking Gen. Sikorski's opinion of these men.

Mr. Churchill was very satisfied with his journey and the effect it had had on the situation at home. 'It would calm', he said, 'the 25 rascals who voted against me' ('les 25 canailles qui ont voté contre moi').

Gen. Sikorski spoke about the Polish National Council.

Mr. Churchill, 'as of old', asked Gen. Sikorski's opinion on the general military situation. He spoke very enthusiastically of Polish air-crews, whose superiority was acknowledged even by British airmen, 'and they are not too bad themselves'.

Gen. Sikorski availed himself of that opportunity to raise the question of a revision of the Polish-British Air Force Agreement. It was indispensable in view of the changed situation, so different from the one before the collapse of France, when the agreement had been stipulated. Mr. Churchill assured Gen. Sikorski that Sir Archibald Sinclair would certainly meet him half-way, as he was a well-known friend and admirer of the Polish Air Force.

Gen. Sikorski also discussed the general aspect of Polish military affairs. It became evident that the information Mr. Churchill had obtained from Gen. Anders concerning Polish plans was not quite correct.

Gen. Sikorski spoke of the problem arising in the Middle East, and, in that connection, he suggested that a senior Polish officer should be appointed to the HQ of the GOC Tenth Army, Gen. Maitland-Wilson. Going on to the affairs of the Polish Army Corps, he suggested the appointment of another senior Polish officer to the HQ of Gen. Brooke.

Mr. Churchill refused this request, stating that he did not want to have a parliament at Headquarters. 'By the way,' he added, 'you know, General, that I entirely accept all your suggestions and advice, and you can always contact me personally; should pressure of work prevent it, then convey your observations in writing to me.'

After a conference, lasting four hours, Mr. Churchill took Gen. Sikorski aside to have a private conversation with him, and once again to summarize the points agreed upon, which were as follows:

1. Support for Polish demands with regard to Russia: in the first stage, by supporting President Roosevelt's initiative, and, should the Military situation improve, and Great Britain give more effective assistance to Russia—by direct British pressure in support of the just Polish demands.

2. Support of Gen. Sikorski's claims at the time of a peace conference,

3. A positive solution of Polish military problems in Scotland and the Middle East,

4. Revision of the Air Force Agreement,

5. General Sikorski's journeys to America and Russia.

No. 263

Note from Minister Raczyński to Ambassador Bogomolov on the closure of the offices of the Polish Embassy Delegates and on a new relief organization

London, September 1, 1942[1]   GSHI, A.11. 49/Sow./2
                                       Official transl. from Polish

Many weeks have passed since the imprisonment of delegates of the Polish Embassy in the Union of Soviet Socialist Republics, the personnel of the delegations and the 'hommes de confiance'. One hundred and thirty Polish citizens, enjoying official status recognized by the authorities of the USSR, who, as I am able to state, in their overwhelming majority carried out with devotion and under difficult conditions their duty of helping and caring for their countrymen, continue to be detained in prison. Repeated interventions of the Polish Government on their behalf, made either through the good offices of Your Excellency or through the Polish Embassy in Kuibyshev, have so far produced no result.

The Polish Government is, naturally, without detailed information concerning the whereabouts and the treatment of the persons imprisoned. Scanty and necessarily casual news which reaches us, however, justifies the fear that their fate is especially hard. At the same time, the welfare machinery to look after Polish citizens in the USSR, which was established with such difficulties, is completely immobilized.

I need not emphasize again, after having done so repeatedly in writing and by word of mouth, that the Polish Government regards the task of looking after the welfare of Polish citizens who found themselves in the territory of the USSR neither of their own free will nor through any fault of theirs, as its fundamental right and duty, which it will not and cannot neglect. Polish citizens, who found themselves in a strange country, in unfamiliar circumstances and environment, torn from their homes and their trades, deprived of all their possessions, have to a higher degree than others become the victims of a situation which is difficult for all, because it was produced by war, and, therefore, they are in greater need of assistance than others. Your Excellency is informed how difficult it was, ever since the conclusion of the Agreement of July 30th, 1941,[2] to find and to agree on the forms of the welfare organization. Here I shall only say that the system finally adopted was the result of prolonged discussions between the Polish Embassy and the authorities of the USSR. The principle of entrusting the responsibility for the whole organization to none other but actually to delegates of the

[1] This note was sent in English translation on September 18 to Mr. Eden, Ambassador Biddle and Ambassador Dormer.   [2] See doc. No. 106.

Embassy with official status and to 'hommes de confiance', was adopted on the initiative of the People's Commissariat for Foreign Affairs after the authorities of the USSR had rejected the proposals for the re-opening of Consulates, for the resumption of the activities of the Polish Red Cross or for the establishment of Social Welfare Committees, whose members were to be elected by the Polish citizens concerned. After toilsome preparations, which dragged on till February/March of this year, the machinery in the field passed the first period of its work in relative peace. It is, however, most significant that as soon as the work developed, when relief for Polish citizens in the form of food supplies, clothing and medicaments began to arrive, the local authorities of the USSR treated the activities of the delegations with suspicion and placed numerous obstacles in the way of the delegates and their collaborators. Moreover, as soon as the stocks arrived and were being more widely distributed, the delegates were arrested, the archives seized and their entire activities liquidated.

I desire to state here with the utmost firmness, and with that frankness which ought to characterize our mutual relations, that the suggestion that the re-creation of the welfare machinery might be separated from the case of the imprisoned delegates, amounts to a complete disregard of realities. Without the release of all the persons arrested and without the restoration of the archives, the re-creation of the machinery for welfare and relief is impossible not only for considerations of principle, but also for purely practical reasons. The deportation and imprisonment of the heads and staffs of the delegations, men enjoying the confidence of Polish citizens, for whose welfare they worked, was bound to produce anxiety and confusion among those citizens. If for no other reason, the very disbelief in the possibility of effective work and the fear of repressions on the part of the Government of the USSR applied on grounds which are incomprehensible to the general public, would make the appointment of new persons competent to carry on social welfare work impossible at a time when their predecessors are suffering the duress of imprisonment for exactly the same work.

I have no desire to criticize in any way or to qualify the administrative institutions and the legal norms in force in the USSR. This is an internal problem of Your Excellency's country, with which no one from outside is entitled to interfere. Your Excellency will agree with me, however, if I say that these institutions and norms differ in many respects from those valid in other European countries, especially in the countries of Central and Western Europe or of America. I am mentioning this only in order to point out that —as it seems—certain functions performed by the delegates in good faith and in full conformity with Western-European conceptions, laws and customs in which they grew up and with which they are familiar, might have conflicted technically with the more rigorous and different regulations in force on the territories of the USSR.

I feel bound, however, to reject categorically the charge of any deliberate action on the part of the delegates detrimental to the USSR. The suggestion that these hundred or so carefully chosen men jointly or severally engaged

430

spontaneously in activities conflicting with the general guiding lines of the Polish Government, is one devoid of all qualities of probability. These general guiding lines imparted to the field personnel by the central Polish authorities through the Polish Embassy were designed solely with a view to directing all the efforts of this personnel towards assuring to the Polish citizens scattered throughout the USSR the utmost assistance and relief. The Polish Government considers this activity to be an integral and essential part of the struggle against the enemy, who is applying biological extermination, as one of the most cruel and at the same time most effective methods of total warfare, against the liberty-loving nations which are opposing him. To this struggle, in which Poland and the Union of Soviet Socialist Republics stand shoulder to shoulder, the Polish Government constantly subordinates all its efforts.

One of the fundamental conditions on which the victory of our common cause depends is the establishment of a relationship of confidence and equitable collaboration between the United Nations. Acting on this principle, the Polish Government endeavoured to give the least publicity to the difficulties which it encountered while carrying out its task of looking after the welfare of Polish citizens in the Union of Soviet Socialist Republics, hoping that, given mutual good will, such difficulties would speedily be overcome. The continuation of the enforced inactivity of the distributing and welfare machinery, however, produced conditions in which—quite apart from the desire of the Polish Government—further discretion is difficult to maintain. The accumulation and partial deterioration of the stocks arriving from America, and the impossibility of distributing them among those for whom they were sent, compel the Polish Government to inform the organizations responsible for their distribution of the state of affairs brought about by the arrest of the delegates.

News concerning the stoppage of the distribution of relief to Polish citizens in the Union of Soviet Socialist Republics has already reached Polish territories occupied by the Germans. It is producing comprehensible anxiety and bitterness, as reflected in the reports which the Polish Government is receiving from its agents, from political organizations and individuals. It would be directly contrary to the intentions of the Polish Government if this anxiety were adversely to influence the fighting spirit of the Polish people in Poland, or if it were to produce an atmosphere, which would make it difficult to consolidate in future the good neighbourly relations between Poland and the Union of Soviet Socialist Republics in the spirit of the declaration signed at the Kremlin on December 4th, 1941,[3] by the Prime Minister of Poland, General Sikorski, and the Chairman of the Council of People's Commissars, Joseph Stalin.

While addressing myself again to Your Excellency to urge the immediate release from prison of the arrested delegates of the Polish Embassy, personnel of the delegations and 'hommes de confiance', and while informing you of my readiness to induce them to depart from Soviet territory immediately

[3] See doc. No. 161.

431

after their release, I am acting not only in conformity with my rights and duties of defending my imprisoned fellow countrymen and collaborators, I am acting not only in the interests of those hundreds of thousands of Poles, who without warning were suddenly deprived of assistance and relief, which under existing conditions of war, is frequently tantamount to protection of their lives. I am acting at the same time on behalf of that higher interest for which Poland and the Union of Soviet Socialist Republics are fighting in the ranks of the United Nations, prompted by what I believe is the common endeavour of our two nations, to lay already now the foundations for the future collaboration of our countries, based on the principles of good neighbourliness.

No. 264

Note from Minister Raczyński to Ambassador Bogomolov concerning air operations over Polish territory

London, September 4, 1942

GSHI, A.11. 49/Sow./2
Transl. from Polish

The Polish Government is in possession of a report from Warsaw on the air bombing of that city by the Soviet air force, on the night of 20th/21st August. The observers of the Polish Government report that bombs were dropped from a considerable altitude which rendered difficult, if not altogether impossible, any precise aiming. In consequence, the residential districts of the city suffered most from that bombing. Amongst the Polish population, about 800 people were killed and about 1,000 injured.

From the description of the second bombardment of Warsaw, carried out by the Soviet air force and related in a Moscow broadcast, on the night of 1st/2nd September, one gathers that, among others, the neighbourhood of the former Polish General Staff Building and the Ministry of War were particularly heavily bombed. The Soviet authorities are presumably aware of the fact that the General Staff Building is situated between the central district of the city, which suffered very much in 1939, and the ghetto created by the Germans. The War Ministry Building was burnt down in 1939. Both these buildings are at a considerable distance from any military objects, and are surrounded by purely residential blocks.

The Soviet Government has certainly been informed that after the siege of Warsaw in 1939 and the destruction of a great number of dwelling houses, and also as a result of the influx of refugees from Western Poland, the density of that city's population, especially in the central area, is nearly twice as great as before the war. In the ghetto district of Warsaw, on the average well over 10 people live in one room. For about fifteen thousand inhabitants in Warsaw there are but 9,000 civilian Germans. According to information received, the plan of establishing a special German residential district has been abandoned, lest it should facilitate its air bombing. The German garrison is quartered in barracks in special town districts.

In these conditions the bombing of the city from a considerable altitude, based on inadequate information on the location of military objectives, transport and industrial centres, etc., would necessarily result in a great number of civilian victims among the Polish and Jewish civilian population, and in consequence it might produce on that population an impression quite opposite to that intended by the Soviet authorities.

The Polish Government fully understands that air bombing of German military objectives must result in material damage and a certain number of casualties amongst the civilian population of Warsaw and other Polish towns. They consider, however, that it is possible, and even imperative, to plan those bombing raids in such a way as to concentrate them on strictly military objectives in the first place.

In view of the aforesaid I would like to return to my original proposal of an understanding between the Polish and Soviet military authorities concerning air operations over Polish territory. Polish military authorities who are in possession of special knowledge of that territory and of the location of military objectives thereon, would be able, by their information, to secure for the Soviet authorities a better effect of air operations against military objects.

I should be grateful to you, Mr. Ambassador, if you would inform the Government of the Union of Soviet Socialist Republics of my proposal, and if you would communicate their reply to me on its arrival.

No. 265

Note from the Polish Embassy in the USSR to the People's Commissariat for Foreign Affairs requesting the release of the arrested Embassy Delegates, representatives and staff

Kuibyshev, September 5, 1942   GSHI, A.11. 49/Sow./2
Transl. from Polish: Pol.-Sov.R., No. 74

With reference to the statement made by M. J. Vyshinsky, Deputy Chairman of the Council of People's Commissars of the USSR, on July 20, 1942, his personal Note of July 20, 1942,[1] Note No. 138 of July 24, 1942,[2] and the Aide-mémoire of the People's Commissariat for Foreign Affairs of July 27, 1942,[3] the Polish Embassy has the honour to communicate the following:

1. This Embassy categorically rejects the allegation contained in the Statement of July 20, 1942, that all the arrested Delegates of the Embassy, and their staffs, instead of loyally carrying out their duties of bringing relief to Polish citizens—were engaged in actions hostile to the Soviet Union and in intelligence work.

It is impossible that all the Delegates without exception, most of the members of their staffs and many of their representatives who were continuously and consistently instructed by the Embassy to co-operate with the Soviet authorities in accordance with the Agreement of July 30, 1941, and the Declaration of December 4, 1941—in the spirit of the common struggle

[1] See doc. No. 251 with note No. 251.
[2] Not printed; it concerns the release of 6 Embassy delegates.   [3] See doc. No. 256.

against Hitlerite Germany, could have at the same time carried on actions hostile to a State allied with the Republic of Poland. Most of these persons, and especially the Delegates, are well known personally to this Embassy and have always shown exceptional ability in social work and devotion to the welfare of the Polish population in the USSR.

The charges brought against those arrested, lacking any semblance of proof, must have been based on some tragic misunderstanding, highly injurious to the persons arrested. Indirectly—in view of the wholesale and simultaneous arrests—it shatters the entire relief organization of the Embassy and in consequence adversely affects, both from the moral and the material point of view, all Polish citizens residing on the territory of the USSR.

This Embassy again asks the People's Commissariat for Foreign Affairs to cause the immediate release of all those arrested, and asserts that their official activities, carried on in conformity with the Rules governing the scope of activity of Embassy Delegates, for instance furnishing this Embassy with information concerning the requirements and condition of Polish citizens, can in no way provide a basis for their being charged with intelligence work in the USSR.

2. This Embassy cannot agree with the statement of the People's Commissariat for Foreign Affairs alleging that up to now the activities of the Delegates have shown their lack of usefulness. The tremendous tasks which the Delegates had to perform were in no way decreased as the same masses of Polish citizens still remain, requiring help and feeling its lack today more than ever. The institution of the Embassy Delegates was created out of practical considerations, and in future the only really practical solution of the problem of relief for Polish citizens in the USSR must be based on some intermediary organization or other to go between the central body—the Embassy—and the field representatives working in Polish centres dispersed throughout the vast territory of the USSR.

3. This Embassy cannot consider as closed the matter of the arrest by the Soviet authorities of Secretaries of Embassy Załęski and Gruja, as well as other Polish diplomats. Avoiding formal discussion as to whether the local authorities were or were not informed of the diplomatic status of these officials who, in point of fact, were well known in the localities where they worked and who possessed diplomatic identification cards issued to them by the People's Commissariat for Foreign Affairs, this Embassy wishes to state that it has not as yet received appropriate satisfaction either for their illegal arrest or for their equally illegal detention in Soviet prisons.

The Embassy wishes also to correct a fundamental inexactitude contained in Paragraph 7 of the Personal Note of July 27, 1942, stating that this Embassy agreed to deprive of their diplomatic rights and privileges, as from July 6, persons with whom Note No. 128 of the People's Commissariat for Foreign Affairs was concerned. To the proposal contained in Note No. 128 of the People's Commissariat for Foreign Affairs 'that Embassy Delegates occupying diplomatic posts, be relieved by the Embassy either of their duties as Embassy Delegates or of their diplomatic posts', this Embassy replied in its

Note No. 8, D-287/42 of July 10, 1942, protesting against a unilateral decision in a matter settled by mutual agreement, and informing the People's Commissariat for Foreign Affairs of its decision to recall from posts as Embassy Delegates persons of diplomatic status, of which decision those concerned were immediately informed by telegraph.

4. The Embassy cannot agree that the return of the official seals, archives and money of the Embassy held illegally by the Soviet authorities, be made conditional on the completion of whatever kind of investigation, and once more requests the People's Commissariat for Foreign Affairs to return them to this Embassy without further delay.

No. 266

Aide-mémoire from the Polish Embassy in the USSR to the People's Commissariat for Foreign Affairs requesting the return of seized records and the release of members of Polish Welfare Missions

Kuibyshev, September 10, 1942 GSHI, A.11. 49/Sow./2
Transl. from Polish

Reference is made to the conversation on 4th August, 1942, between the Assistant People's Commissar for Foreign Affairs, M. Lozowski, and the Chargé d'Affaires, M. Sokolnicki, on the situation arising after the Soviet authorities had liquidated the posts of the Embassy's Delegates and Men of Trust. In that conversation M. Lozowski repeated the assurances, already contained in the Personal Note of the Deputy Chairman of the Council of People's Commissars of USSR, M. Vyshinsky, dated 27th July, 1942,[1] that the Soviet Government intended neither to impede in the least nor, above all, to liquidate the relief work for Poles in the USSR. The problem of organizing this relief work under the new conditions made by the Soviet authorities, was discussed between M. Freyd and M. Zorin on 14th and 18th August.

Following the above-mentioned conversation and considering the experience of the past two months—since the de facto liquidation of the network created by the Delegates, acting in accordance with the principles laid down in 'The regulations concerning the activities of the Embassy's Delegates', of 23rd–24th December, 1941—the Embassy once more wishes to state the following:

The Polish Embassy endeavoured, in spite of the above-mentioned liquidation, to find a practical approach to the problem of relief work for Poles under the changed conditions, because it appreciated the historical importance—not only now, during the war, but in future, after its victorious conclusion—of establishing an era of friendly Soviet-Polish relations, as manifested in the Agreement of 30th July, 1941,[2] and in the Declaration of 4th December, 1941.[3] The Embassy is also aware of how important it is for the Polish Nation, after its many sufferings in this war, to save the hundreds of thousands of Polish citizens who found themselves in very difficult conditions in the USSR.

[1] See doc. No. 255. [2] See doc. No. 106. [3] See doc. No. 161.

In that connection the Embassy met, however, the following difficulties and hindrances:

1 / Under the present system of relief organization, the Embassy remained the general centre of disposition, in agreement with the 'Regulations etc.' The details of the location, composition, situation and needs of the Polish population in various centres were necessarily concentrated in the hands of the Regional Delegates. The apprehension of the Delegates and of the majority of their executive staff, the seizing of their archives and account books, deprived the Embassy of all data indispensable for the planning of relief and the distribution of clothes, food, medical and other supplies from abroad. Without detailed information as to the number of Poles in various centres, their age, sex, profession, state of health and needs, and deprived of all accounts of previous issues of supplies and money subsidies, the Embassy was obliged to carry out its emergency relief work blindly, without any rational and controlled welfare administration. Unable to account for the work already done, without accounts concerning financial aid, without inventories of the supply stores and all the documentation concerning Polish Welfare institutions, which had been created in agreement with the People's Commissariat for Foreign Affairs and other Soviet authorities, the Embassy thinks that it is hardly possible to work out a practical and rational plan for the relief work under the new conditions.

2 / The Embassy endeavoured to obtain the necessary data from their Delegates, and to continue the welfare work in direct contact with them on the largest possible scale. However, the majority of the Delegates, whose names were submitted to the People's Commissariat for Foreign Affairs, have not yet been acknowledged by the People's Commissariat. In consequence, local Soviet authorities, surely acting on general instructions from the central authorities, refuse to co-operate with our men. The excuse given by them is the lack of information as to the consent of central authorities to allow the functioning of the given post of an Embassy's Delegate. In many cases it results in the liquidation not only of the post itself, but also of the existing Polish welfare institutions, such as homes for children, old people or invalids, surgeries, etc.

Moreover, for many weeks the Embassy has had no information about people whom they believed to be continuing their work on the spot and organizing relief and welfare work for Polish citizens, whilst in fact they had been arrested and detained in prison. Under such conditions, without information from Soviet authorities of the arrest of their employees, the Embassy can never be sure which of the Delegates is still working or whose activities have been forcibly brought to an end. This state of affairs, as well as transport, communication and other difficulties resulting from the vastness of the Soviet Union and, finally, the fear of reprisals for any energetic relief move by the Delegates, create a situation in which the relief work for Poles, based exclusively on a network of Delegates, should be considered under present conditions as unpracticable.

As an instance of the conditions under which the Embassy has to work, the following case may be quoted: At the end of last month the Embassy by chance received the information that their Delegates at Bijak, Forgan and Ush-Tobe had been arrested. Only a short time before, large transports of relief goods had been directed to those centres, those very 'men of trust', who by keeping in touch with the Embassy and showing special zeal in their work, had seemed to guarantee the proper distribution of the relief in kind. The arrest by the Soviet authorities of the addressees will certainly create widespread complications, when the transports arrive at those centres. These instances make the Embassy fear similar difficulties in future.

3/ In accordance with information received by the Embassy the Polish population in the USSR welcomed the Polish-Soviet understanding as a guarantee of fruitful co-operation between the two nations. Since the liquidation of the posts of Delegates and their arrest all over the country, and the continuing wave of arrests of 'men of trust' appointed by the Embassy, the Polish population lost their bearings and become an easy prey to fear of the future. In such circumstances the spirit of mutual trust is being destroyed, instead of serving as a genuine and firm foundation for the rapprochement and co-operation of the two neighbouring nations, both now, during this war fought in common, and in future, after its victorious ending.

The Embassy considers that the important task of the care of Polish citizens in USSR undertaken with the co-operation of the two Governments, with the assistance of the Peoples and Governments of other Allied Countries, was largely and tragically impaired as a result of the misunderstandings of the last few months, and that it could be successfully continued only after the creation of conditions allowing for an atmosphere of mutual confidence. Such conditions should allow the Embassy and the Soviet authorities not only to work out a rational plan of further welfare work, but to apply it efficiently.

The Embassy considers that in this matter the following points must be noted:

[1] That all these Embassy employees working in the country who were unjustly arrested should be released, and further arrests of men authorized by the Embassy to carry out welfare work should stop;

[2] That the Soviet authorities should return archives, stamps and money belonging to the Embassy;

[3] That full use should be made of all material aid arriving from abroad;

[4] That appropriate instructions should be issued to the local Soviet authorities advising them to adopt a friendly attitude towards welfare agencies established by the Embassy;

[5] That the principle should be adopted that all misunderstandings and questions in dispute, regarding the welfare work for Polish citizens, should be settled not by a unilateral Soviet action, without informing the Embassy, but by examining the problem in common, in a direct exchange of views and arguments between the People's Commissariat and the Embassy.

However, the Embassy considers that the re-establishment of mutual confidence at all levels of the State administration is the most important condition for an effective welfare action for the Polish population, and therefore it will endeavour to do all in its power to sponsor its return.

No. 267

Note from the People's Commissariat for Foreign Affairs to the Polish Embassy in the USSR on the closing down of the Embassy's Agencies

Kuibyshev, September 16, 1942   GSHI, A.11. 49/Sow./3
                                          Transl. from Russian: Pol.-Sov.R., No. 76

In reply to the Note of the Embassy of the Republic of Poland of September 5, 1942,[1] the People's Commissariat for Foreign Affairs has the honour to communicate the following:

1. The question of the reasons for the arrests of Embassy Delegates and local representatives of the Embassy and the closing of their offices was exhaustively dealt with in the declaration made by M. A. J. Vyshinsky to M. Sokolnicki, Polish Chargé d'Affaires, on July 27,[2] and in a series of subsequent conversations between the representatives of the People's Commissariat and the representatives of the Embassy, and for this reason the People's Commissariat sees no necessity to return to this question. The People's Commissariat for Foreign Affairs can only confirm that, in spite of the repeated declarations of the Embassy concerning the loyalty to the USSR of all its delegates and the alleged lack of grounds for their arrest, the investigation of their actions now in course provides considerable evidence entirely corroborating information in possession of the Soviet authorities, as to their intelligence work hostile to the USSR.

In view of the reasons stated above, the request of the Embassy for the immediate release of the arrested persons cannot be granted, as this question can only be decided after the conclusion of the investigation and will depend upon its results.

2. The question of Embassy delegates in the field, raised in Paragraph 2 of the Note, was fully exhausted in the Personal Note of M. A. J. Vyshinsky to M. Sokolnicki on July 27, 1942,[3] and the People's Commissariat does not see any reason to reconsider its point of view in this matter.

3. The question of the arrest of M. M. Załęski, Gruja and others raised by the Embassy in the first part of Paragraph 3 of its Note, was also exhaustively dealt with in the Notes of the People's Commissariat No. 130 of July 10, 1942,[4] No. 138 of July 24, 1942, and in the Personal Note of M. A. J. Vyshinsky to M. Sokolnicki of July 27, 1942.

As to the question raised in the second part of Paragraph 3 of the above mentioned Note of the Embassy, the People's Commissariat deems it necessary to make clear that in Paragraph 7 of the Note of the People's Commissariat of July 27, the assent of the Embassy was given only to the cessation in future of the state of affairs under which diplomatic collaborators of the

[1] See doc. No. 265.   [2] See doc. No. 256.
[3] Not printed; it concerns the Embassy delegates in Archangel and Vologda.
[4] See doc. No. 244.

Embassy, while discharging the duties of local Embassy Delegates, retained their diplomatic rights and privileges. This viewpoint of the Embassy was confirmed in the Note No. D. 2871/42 of July 10, 1942,[5] concerning Embassy Delegate M. Heitzman in whose case the Embassy consented not to claim diplomatic immunity for him during the period of his activity as Embassy Delegate in Samarkand.

4. To the question raised in Paragraph 4 of the above mentioned Note, the People's Commissariat has already given answer in the Note of July 27, 1942 and for the time being does not see any reason to change its attitude as therein defined.

[5] See doc. No. 242.

No. 268

Reply of Ambassador Bogomolov to Minister Raczyński concerning the bombing of Warsaw

London, October 9, 1942

GSHI, A.11. 49/Sow./3
Transl. from Russian

In reply to your note of 4th September, 1942,[1] I have the honour to inform you of the following:

1/ The Soviet Government cannot accept your allegation concerning the ineffectiveness of the bombing carried out by the Soviet Air Force on military objectives in Warsaw, as according to information, obtained through Soviet military channels, that bombing was entirely successful.

2/ The Soviet Government cannot agree with the statement of the Polish Government that the casualties caused by the Soviet Air Force bombing among the civilian population of Warsaw induced that population to interpret wrongly the aims and objects of these air raids. Such a suggestion is erroneous, as it should be obvious that Soviet bombing of German objectives in Warsaw, and in other towns occupied by the Germans, not only inflicted heavy blows on German war factories, German reserve bases and Army communication lines, but also undermined the prestige of the German Armed Forces and, in the occupied countries, gave the population under German occupation a growing feeling of the approaching defeat of Hitler and the liberation of their native lands from German oppression.

As regards the Polish Government's suggestion about the operations of the Soviet Air Force over Polish territory occupied by the Germans, the Soviet Government will instruct their military authorities to make use of any information submitted by the Polish military authorities with a view to rendering Soviet air bombing of German military objectives in Warsaw even more effective.

[1] See doc. No. 264.

No. 269

Aide-mémoire handed by M. Novikov to Chargé d'Affaires Sokolnicki concerning the investigations in respect of the arrested members of the staff of the Polish Embassy

Kuibyshev, October 16, 1942   GSHI, A.11. 49/Sow./3
                                               Transl. from Russian: Pol.-Sov.R., No. 77

Investigations in respect of the arrested Polish citizens have now been brought to a close.

The cases of 15 persons, namely: F. A. Meller, G. A. Ochnik, G. Malinowski, R. Iliniczowa, J. F. Lubowicki, G. G. Rylko, M. B. Ryczak, M. J. Matuszek, B. B. Kon, S. G. Wachtel, F. J. Mantel, Z. A. Piotrowski, A. A. Juszkiewicz, G. A. Winczewska, and M. W. Nowosad, have been dismissed and orders have been issued to release these persons from detention.

The cases of 16 persons, charged with intelligence work hostile to the USSR, namely: J. J. Mieszkowski, Z. J. Bochniewicz, M. S. Sawicz, W. S. Mattoszko, G. S. Żółtowski, A. P. Saraniecki, Z. M. Kuczyński, M. T. Tworkowski, B. I. Szwajzer, E. G. Stawiński, W. J. Janczuk, W. F. Bugajski, S. A. Winter, F. W. Bednarz, L. M. Artamanowa-Pest and W. W. Zarudny —have been referred to the courts.

In respect to the remaining 78 persons, a decision was reached at a special meeting of the People's Commissariat for Foreign Affairs whereby these persons compromised by actions hostile to the Union of Soviet Socialist Republics are subject to deportation from the USSR.

No. 270

Aide-mémoire from the Polish Ministry for Foreign Affairs sent to the Soviet Embassy to the Polish Government in London concerning the enrolment of German war prisoners of Polish nationality

London, October 22, 1942   GSHI, A.11. 49/Sow./2
                                            Transl. from Polish

At the end of last year the Polish Embassy at Kuibyshev was informed that a great number of Polish citizens, serving in the German Army, had been taken prisoner by the Soviet Army. These Poles had been forcibly mobilized from the Polish territories incorporated into the German Reich, and they were inspired with vivid hatred for the invader. It was their ardent wish to serve with the Polish Army and to fight for the liberation of their native land from the German yoke.

Referring to the above, and anxious to make use of all available forces in the struggle with Germany, the Polish Embassy at Kuibyshev addressed a Note to the People's Commissariat for Foreign Affairs, dated 7th January, 1942.[1] Therein the Embassy requested all Prisoners of War of Polish nationality, forcibly mobilized by the German occupation Forces, to be

[1] Not printed; contents as in doc. No. 173.

assembled at one locality, so that the Embassy may proceed to a recruitment for the Polish Army.

The People's Commissariat for Foreign Affairs in their reply, dated 22nd January, 1942,[2] pointed out that it would not be possible to treat Polish citizens differently from other German Prisoners of War, since they had been taken prisoner when actively resisting the Soviet Army.

The Polish Embassy replied to that Note, on 6th February, 1942,[3] by stressing that Polish citizens found themselves in the German ranks contrary to International Law, and that they continued to be a hostile element within that Army. The Polish Government had already taken action with a view to reducing the ill effects of the mobilization of Polish citizens by Germany: they had issued a secret instruction to Poles to surrender to the Red Army at the first opportunity.

In the meantime public enunciations of Soviet organs confirmed that the appeal propagated on Polish territory for the abandoning of German ranks did not remain without effect. Thus, e.g., the 'Komsomolskaya Pravda' No. 308 of 30th Dec. 1941 published a correspondent's report confirming entirely the point of view of the Polish Embassy at Kuibyshev. Several times Soviet Radio Stations broadcast news on voluntary surrender of Poles. Recently the Soviet Press have reported it, as, amongst others, 'Pravda' on 27th September, 'New Horizons' on 20th September, 1942, etc.

Under these circumstances I would like to come back to the Embassy's Notes of 7th January and 6th February. I wish to emphasize that the Polish Government aims at rallying as many Poles as possible in the common struggle against the German invader, and therefore considers it very important that the Embassy's representatives should be given access to POWs of Polish nationality, that the latter be assembled at one special centre, and that recruiting for the Polish Army among them be rendered possible.

[2] The date should be January 23; see doc. No. 174.   [3] See doc. No. 181.

No. 271

Message from General Sikorski to President Stalin recommending to him the new Polish Ambassador M. T. Romer[1]

London, October 26, 1942   GSHI, PRM, 72/1

Le nouvel Ambassadeur de Pologne est sur le point de remettre ses Lettres de Créance. Je saisis cette occasion, Monsieur le Président, pour recommander à votre bienveillance l'Ambassadeur Romer, qui est un des diplomates polonais les plus expérimentés et qui jouit de la pleine confiance du Gouvernement polonais aussi bien que de mon entière confiance personnelle. Sans aucun doute, il fera tout ce qui sera dans son pouvoir pour assurer l'application, conformément aux instructions qu'il a reçues, d'une politique de confiance mutuelle entre la Pologne et l'Union des Républiques Socialistes

[1] See Note No. 271.

441

Soviétiques, telle qu'elle a été conçue au cours de nos conversations a Moscou en décembre 1941. J'ai le ferme espoir que l'accueil que vous voudrez bien réserver à l'Ambassadeur Romer et ses efforts personnels, contribueront à liquider promptement et entièrement les difficultés qui se sont manifestées au cours des derniers mois dans le domaine de l'organisation du secours pour les citoyens polonais se trouvant sur le territoire de l'Union des Républiques Socialistes Soviétiques et permettront d'intensifier notre collaborations dans la lutte contre l'ennemi commun. Les résultats obtenus dans ces domaines contribueront effectivement, j'en suis sûr, à assurer entre nos deux États une collaboration suivie et harmonieuse dans leur marche vers un avenir meilleur.

No. 272

Aide-mémoire from the Soviet Embassy to the Polish Government in London to Minister Raczyński concerning the closure of offices of Polish Embassy Delegates in the USSR[1]

London, October 28, 1942   GSHI, A.11. 49/Sow./3
                                                                    Transl. from Russian

Recently a number of instances of anti-Soviet intelligence activities have been brought home to a number of Polish citizens, amongst them to some regional Delegates and Men of Trust of the Polish Embassy.

A thorough investigation undertaken in this connection has confirmed the facts, finding that the main role in organizing and operating this criminal scheme by Polish citizens on USSR territory was played by Regional Polish Agents and by a number of members of the Polish Embassy in the USSR.

The investigation against Polish citizens being now completed, the People's Commissariat for Foreign Affairs is able to expound the matter with the required precision, as regards individual groups of Polish citizens as well as the Regional Delegates and official members of the Embassy.

It is known that regional Polish agencies were created with the approval of the Soviet Government in numerous towns of the Soviet Union—amongst others in Archangel, Vladivostok, the Volga towns, and in the Ural, Siberian, Uzbekistan and Kazakhstan provinces. Their purpose was to give material relief to poverty-stricken Polish citizens and also to assist in finding employment for them. It was also within the scope of their duties to assist the Soviet authorities in settling the living conditions of the Polish citizens and inspiring them with the spirit of the Polish-Soviet Treaty of 30th July, 1941,[2] as stipulated in p. 2, of the 'Regulations concerning the activities of the Polish Embassy's Delegates', put into force at the end of December, 1941.

In their effort to give their best assistance to the Polish Government in the task of organizing relief for Polish citizens, the Soviet Government deemed it possible to consent to the establishment of the Embassy's Agencies in 20 localities on Soviet territory, and also to accept the appointment by the Embassy of the so-called 'Men of Trust'. The latter, in principle, performed

---

[1] See Note No. 272.   [2] See doc. No. 106.

the same duties as the Embassy Delegates and were the closest assistants of those, as well as of the Embassy itself, where direct contact with the Polish population was concerned.

Thus, owing to the good will manifested by the Soviet Government in their concern about the needs of the Polish citizens on Soviet territory, a widespread network of Embassy Agencies was created, covering a great part of the Soviet Union. The Soviet authorities bestowed on the Embassy Delegates and its Men of Trust extensive rights for giving material aid to Polish citizens and created appropriate conditions for assisting them in the performance of their duties.

On allowing the establishment of Embassy Delegates, the Soviet Government counted on the loyal performance of their duties by the Polish officials, and also on their loyal co-operation with the local Soviet authorities in the spirit of friendly Polish-Soviet relations.

The Soviet Government did not confine their assistance to issuing administrative measures for assuring for the Polish Delegates full freedom of action amongst the Polish population—the Soviet Government also applied a number of financial and economic measures with a view to increasing and sponsoring the material aid for destitute Polish citizens.

To wit, the Soviet Government granted a loan of 100 million roubles to the Polish Government for relief work amongst Polish citizens. That loan, bearing no interest, was to be repaid in ten years' time, beginning with the sixth year after the end of the war. The Soviet Government also agreed to relieve of customs duties all goods imported from abroad and destined for the indigenous Polish population; they introduced a special reduced railway tariff for those goods; they established special food 'funds', ration-allotments for the various and numerous charitable institutions, invalid- and old people's hostels for Polish citizens, children's homes and nurseries, canteens, etc., organized by the Embassy, and they abolished the duty on passport registration for Polish citizens.

Consequently the Soviet Government took all the necessary measures to satisfy the needs of the Polish population and to secure a widespread and effective activity of Polish institutions serving the material relief work.

The local Soviet authorities fully supported the action of the Polish Delegates and assisted them on a large scale. These authorities, the Executive Committees of the Delegates of Working People's Soviets, bore the main burden and concern for the re-settlement of Polish citizens, for providing them with food-rations, fuel, medical service, employment, etc., which demanded a considerable effort under the particularly difficult war conditions.

In these circumstances Polish Delegates were presented with a great opportunity for effective work in the field of material aid to the destitute Polish citizens. An honest and loyal fulfilment of these obligations with which the Delegates were entrusted by the 'Regulations concerning the activities of the Polish Embassy's Delegates' was all that was required of those Delegates, put in control of the local Polish Agencies. The Soviet authorities

443

were entitled to expect it from them, after having shown so much trust and having created such good conditions for their work.

These expectations, however, have not been justified. In fact, it became evident that Polish local Agencies and a number of their employees and Men of Trust, instead of honestly performing their duties in co-operation with the local Soviet authorities, became engaged in anti-Soviet intelligence work. As the inquest has proved, the Embassy's local Agencies, under cover of their alleged charitable work, in fact organized an action of the intelligence type, grouping about them Polish citizens, systematically occupied with gathering espionage information which was conveyed through them to the agencies.

The findings of the inquest in respect of a number of arrested Polish citizens has established many facts of that kind. It has been proved that the espionage network organized by the Embassy's Delegates paid special attention to the war industries, their capacity and production, and also to the movement of troops and rail and other transport of Red Army units. The employees of the Agencies and some Men of Trust established direct contact with the local population for the purpose of that anti-Soviet intelligence, and once they found themselves on the path of crime, they very often tried to enlist and persuade individual Soviet citizens to become accomplices in their criminal doings.

The inquest has proved that the intelligence espionage action was conducted by the exposed Polish citizens under direct control and by instruction from responsible members of the Embassy. By a special order of the Soviet Government a considerable number of the Embassy's employees, exposed as taking part in the anti-Soviet intelligence scheme, who tried to conceal their criminal 'work' under cover of diplomatic passports, were expelled from the USSR.

Those exposed and expelled from the USSR were: the head of the Polish Military Mission Gen. Wolikowski, who played the most important part in the organization and operation of espionage in the USSR, 1st Secretaries of the Embassy: Arlet and Załęski, who was the Embassy's Delegate at Vladivostok, 2nd Secretaries: Gruja, Delegate for the Archangel Province, and Głogowski; Embassy Attachés: Rola-Janicki, Słowikowski, Płoski, Lickindorf, Kościałkowski, Heitzman and others; most of whom were acting as Embassy Delegates in various territories and provinces.[3]

According to the findings of the inquest, a special activity in anti-Soviet work was shown by the following persons—apart from the above mentioned:

1/ A group of employees of the Agency at Krasnoyarsk Territory: Bochniewicz, Sawicz and others, under the leadership of the former Delegate of the Embassy—Mieszkowski.

2/ A group of employees of the Agency in the Altay Territory—at their head being the former Delegate Mattoszko and Żółtowski.

3/ A group of employees of the Agency of the Semipalatinsk Province: Saraniecki, Kuczyński.

[3] The distorted names were corrected. The names of territories and provinces are given incorrectly in the original.

4/ In the Akmolinski Province: Tworkowski; in the Karaganda Province: Speiser; in the Turkmen Republic: Stawiński; in the Chardjou Province: Janczuk; in the Tashkent Province: Bugajski; in the Fergan Province: Winter; in the Kirgiz Republic: Bednarz; in the Tchkalov Province: Zarudny; and others.

Most of these people, like others against whom legal proceedings have been taken,—admitted their criminal activities and made statements giving detailed information as to the character, the purpose and the methods of their work.

All the sixteen above-mentioned persons have been handed over to the Military Tribunal, indicted of espionage and other hostile activities against the USSR of the most malicious and active kind.

Extending their intelligence action against the USSR, the above-named and other apprehended Polish citizens who, following a Decree of an Extraordinary Session of the People's Commissariat for Home Affairs, are subject to expulsion from the USSR, also indulged in criminal activities of a different character, using other methods. One of the most important features among those was provocation by means of spreading all kinds of slanderous allegations and lies, detrimental to the USSR, with a view to discrediting Soviet authorities and the entire régime. The noisy fascist propaganda among the Polish and also partly among the Soviet citizens, the manifold praising of Hitlerites, the attempt to persuade Polish citizens to go over to the German side, slander and malicious accusations against the Red Army—that was the systematic work done by the Embassy Delegates, their employees and Men of Trust, who have been indicted of the committed crimes. Widespread also was the use by these people of false information depicting the situation of the Polish population in the Soviet Union in the gloomiest colours. A specially popular provocation practice of the indicted employees of the Agencies and Men of Trust was the spreading of false rumours on the alleged high mortality amongst the Polish population.

As an instance of one of the many anti-Soviet activities of the local Polish Delegates, one may quote the mendacious reports of the Agency of the Uzbek Republic.

In these denunciations, the Embassy Representatives for the Uzbek Republic have consciously and falsely reported, e.g., that during the period from 1st February to 20th April, 1942, in the Samarkand District alone, 217 Polish citizens died, and that 70% of these deaths were caused by a state of complete exhaustion. A check on this information, made by the State Control Office of the Uzbek Republic with the participation of Polish representatives (Kazimierczak) has easily proved the complete falsehood of the 'facts' mentioned in these denunciations. The inquest established that during the entire first half of 1942 only 18 Polish citizens died in the Samarkand District, and that there has been not even one case of death from exhaustion, and consequently the denunciations of the Polish Agency in the Uzbek Republic were but a pack of disgusting lies. As the subsequent investigation proved, namely by obtaining a statement from an ex-Man of

445

Trust in the Tashkent Province, Bugajski, these mendacious rumours were spread by him under the instruction from the Embassy Attaché, Powierza.

It should be emphasized that the intelligence and all the other activities, detrimental to the USSR, of the Embassy's local Delegates and of a number of their employees not only remained unchecked by the members of the Polish Embassy, but, as was found during the investigation, in the case of certain Polish citizens these official persons impelled the Embassy representatives to take up that hostile action. That was proved in particular in respect of the 1st Embassy Secretary Arlet, the ex-Attachés Rola-Janicki, Powierza, Gen. Wolikowski, Gruja, Załęski and other Polish citizens, members of the Polish Embassy. What those Embassy Delegates seem to have forgotten was that, whilst spying on the enemy is a necessary and understandable thing, espionage against an ally is neither justified nor can be tolerated.

Having thus infringed the elementary principles and norms of international law, defining the duties and rules of conduct of diplomatic agents in a country offering them hospitality, a number of the Embassy's diplomatic members initiated a criminal action, hostile to the USSR, making use of their diplomatic rights and privileges. Such activities of those persons were displayed in various deeds and acts, by means of which they instigated, organized and controlled the actions of their local agents.

Amongst those absolutely illicit actions which brutally exceeded, as has been mentioned before, the diplomatic duties of an Embassy, was e.g. the organization of an illegal and clandestine messenger service, and the issue of an 'instruction concerning the messengers' mail service'. In that instruction were practical indications for the messengers how to carry out their illegal service, using cypher or code words, etc.

One of such undertakings was also the practice of issuing passports by the representatives of the Polish Embassy, and the promulgation of an 'instruction on the issue of passports', in which, contrary to law, it was proposed that representatives of the Polish Embassy should supply with Polish passports non-Polish citizens, e.g. people possessing Lithuanian, or Soviet-Lithuanian certificates (p. 2, of the 'Regulations'). How unfastidious were some Delegates of the Embassy in the choice of their methods, can be seen from the document—a kind of official instruction, signed by the Attaché Powierza, dated 19th February, 1942, addressed to the Man of Trust for Alma-Ata, Mr. Więcek. In that instruction the following was literally stated: 'In addition to our previous conferences, I impart to you the decision of the Embassy of the Polish Republic concerning your posting: [1]. You are entitled to purchase valuables, proceeding with utmost caution and secrecy.'

It ought to be mentioned that, the moment the People's Commissariat for Foreign Affairs became aware of the facts of hostile anti-Soviet intelligence activities of certain Embassy Delegates, they considered it their duty to forewarn the Embassy, pointing out the serious consequences such activities of Polish official personnel would bring about. This forewarning was made in connection with the discovery of hostile intelligence activities of the 1st Embassy Secretary Arlet, Gen. Wolikowski and Attaché Rola-Janicki.

Disregarding the warning, however, the criminal action of certain members of the Embassy was not discontinued but developed even more widely, and on a larger scale.

It is evident that this state of affairs could not be tolerated, and it was stopped by the Soviet authorities. At the same time was suspended the existence of the posts of Embassy Delegates whose agencies were the source of espionage and anti-Soviet activity.

On 20th July[4] the People's Commissariat for Foreign Affairs informed the Embassy of a number of facts compromising the Agencies and emphasizing that these Agencies were doing intelligence work and acting against the interests of the USSR. In connection with that a number of employees of these agencies were arrested and the institution of Delegates liquidated as not justifying its existence.

All the aforesaid undeniably proves that the Soviet Government and the Soviet local authorities did everything that was possible and necessary to ensure a regular organization and operation of the relief for destitute Polish citizens in the USSR. If, as the Polish Government assures, some difficulties arose in the course of the relief action, then the whole and exclusive responsibility for it remains with the Embassy's Agencies and their personnel, and partly also with the Embassy itself. The Embassy not only failed to ensure a loyal attitude of the Delegates towards their duties, but in the persons of a number of its responsible members impelled these Delegates to enter the path of anti-Soviet criminal activity.

[4] See doc. No. 251.

No. 273

Note from Ambassador Bogomolov to Minister Raczyński denouncing the alleged unwillingness of the Polish Army in the USSR, its Command and the Polish Government to take part in the struggle on the Soviet-German front

London, October 31, 1942 GSHI, PRM, 72/3
Transl. from Russian: Pol.-Sov.R., No. 49

In reply to your Note of August 27, 1942,[1] I have the honour to inform you of the following:

1) As is known, in accordance with the Polish-Soviet Agreement of July 30, 1941,[2] a Military Agreement was signed on August 14, 1941,[3] between the High Command of the USSR and the High Command of the Republic of Poland, with a view to forming on the territories of the USSR a Polish Army for the prosecution of the war against Germany in common with the Soviet armies and those of the other Allied countries.

To carry out this purpose the representatives of the Soviet and Polish High Commands started from the necessity of completing the formation of the Polish Army in the shortest possible time, with a view—as was emphasized on many occasions by the representatives of the Polish High Command,

[1] See doc. No. 261.   [2] See doc. No. 106.   [3] See doc. No. 112.

Generals Anders and Szyszko-Bohusz—to the earliest possible participation of these units in active warfare.

Such a plan for the organization of the Polish Army necessitated the immediate setting up of recruiting boards and that Polish citizens throughout the Soviet Union be at once notified of the formation of a Polish Army, and of the possibility as Polish citizens of joining this Army as volunteers.

As is known, all this was undertaken at the time (the end of August) with the fullest possible co-operation of the Soviet military and local civilian authorities.

Also, at that time an agreement was reached between the Soviet and Polish Commands that the strength of the Polish Army be fixed at 30,000 men (two rifle divisions, one reserve regiment, a military school for officers, the staff and staff offices), and it was decided that the formation of the two rifle divisions and a reserve regiment should be completed by October 1, 1941. This date was decided upon to meet the desire of the Polish Command for the quickest possible organization of a Polish Army. For the same reason, and in accordance with a proposal of the Polish representative (General Anders), it was agreed to send one or the other of these divisions to the Soviet-German front as soon as it was ready.

The Soviet military authorities, acting upon instructions from the Soviet Government, co-operated with the Polish Command in the fullest possible measure to assist it in the most successful solution of all the intricate problems connected with the formation of a Polish Army, namely: food supplies, stocks, billeting of military units, staffs and the various staff institutions, billeting facilities for officers, supplying newly formed units with arms, etc.

As regards the method of providing the Polish forces with supplies, the Soviet Government arranged to ensure that the Polish Army should be included within the Red Army supply system, which greatly facilitated the whole task of forming the Polish units. Thus, food supplies were to be the same as those for the Red Army behind the front, until the advance of the Polish units into the front line. Forage, fuel, grease, training ammunition, were also issued in quantities equal to Red Army standards. To this should be added that the use by the Polish Army of military barracks, staff billets, means of communication, transport, lighting, etc. was paid for according to normal rates fixed for the Red Army.

All these arrangements connected with the formation and maintenance of the Polish Army were financed through a non-interest bearing loan of 65 million roubles made by the Soviet Government to the Polish Government. This loan fully covered all expenses connected with the army until January 1, 1942. In fact the financial credit given by the Soviet Government for the organization of the army exceeded the amount of the non-interest bearing loan, for this loan did not include considerable grants amounting to an additional 15 million roubles made to the officers' corps of the Polish military units in formation.

2) Regardless of the fact that the organization of the Polish divisions was not completed within the period originally fixed, by October 1 of that year,

which indeed could not but create many difficulties and adversely affect the further development of the Polish Army, the Soviet Government expressed itself fully agreeable to the proposal of the Polish Government that the Polish Army be increased to the strength of 96,000 men, including officers, non-commissioned officers and men.[4]

As a result, in December 1941, the Soviet Government gave its consent to this increase and the Polish Army was to be expanded from two divisions to six divisions of 11,000 men each.

Furthermore the Soviet Government consented that the effectives of the schools for officers, the service of supplies, the reserve units and complementary units, and the staffs and personnel of the staff offices, originally fixed at 3,000, be increased to 30,000.

In view of this large increase in the strength of the Polish Army, the Soviet Government also raised the amount of the loan for the maintenance of the Polish Army from 65 million roubles to 300 million roubles, on the same easy terms (non-interest bearing loan, repayment over a period of ten years beginning from the sixth year after the end of the war, etc.).[5]

This increase in the strength of the Polish Army to 96,000, made necessary the establishment of a number of complementary services, both administrative and economic. All these were set up at the time of the transfer of the Polish Army to the Soviet Republics of Uzbek, Kirgiz and Kazakhstan, as desired by the Polish Command.

Climatic conditions were the main reason for this transfer to the Southern regions of the USSR, but it was also connected with the need for more space than was afforded in the central regions for the Polish divisions already organized, and the tens of thousands of Polish citizens to be recruited. This necessarily involved a tremendous amount of work, for camps had to be erected, quarters found for the staffs, locations for the military schools, sanitary institutions and accommodation for the officers, etc.

As may be well understood in these circumstances, the execution of this programme of more than trebling the size of the Polish Army from that contemplated in the original plan (from 30,000 to 96,000) was fraught with many difficulties as regards organization, transport and materials, these difficulties were particularly complicated and increased by the barbarous warfare waged on the Soviet nation by the German occupants. But all these difficulties were overcome and by February-March of 1942, the Polish Army had reached a strength of nearly 70,000 men.

Such an increase in the strength of the Polish Army in a relatively short period, and the increase by more than four and a half times of the expenditure for the maintenance of that army, from 65 million roubles to 300 million roubles, is ample proof of the Soviet Government's interest in the creation of a Polish Army and in assisting the Polish nation to take its honourable place in the war against the Hitlerite brigands.

3) However the further development of the Polish Army met with certain difficulties caused by such unforeseen circumstances as the non-delivery of

[4] See doc. No. 159.   [5] See appendix No. 6.

wheat to the Union of Soviet Socialist Republics from the United States and England as a result of the outbreak of war in the Pacific Ocean.

Since the USSR could not receive supplies of foodstuffs it became necessary to cut down the quantity distributed to the non-fighting divisions of the army, so as to ensure supplies to the fighting forces. As the Polish Commander-in-Chief showed no inclination to direct any of his divisions to the German-Soviet front, and continued to keep the Polish Army well behind the fighting lines, the Soviet Government was compelled to treat these units as a non-fighting force, and accordingly the decision to cut down the rations of non-combatant units was applied to them.[6]

In view of these circumstances the Soviet Government took the following decision as regards the Polish Army: from April 1 of that year the number of rations to be reduced to 44,000 and the Polish Army over and above these 44,000 to be sent to Iran in accordance with the wish of the Polish Government.

This decision was taken by the Soviet Government on March 18. Already at the beginning of April about 30,000 Polish men and officers left the USSR and proceeded immediately, under instructions of the Polish Government to Iran. Some three months after this evacuation of the Polish military units to Iran, the remaining 44,000 men and officers followed in their footsteps, having been sent outside the USSR frontiers by the Polish Government—to Iran, Syria, Palestine and North Africa.

Thus the question of the Polish Army's participation together with the Soviet Armies in the campaign against Hitlerite Germany was removed by the Polish Government from the agenda. The Polish Government came to a negative decision on this problem, despite its previous assurances and despite the solemn declaration it made in this respect on December 4, 1941, that 'the army of the Republic of Poland which is now on the territory of the Soviet Republic will wage war against the German brigands shoulder to shoulder with the Soviet armies'. Such a decision by the Polish Government was however not unexpected. In spite of the repeated assurances of the Polish Commander-in-Chief that he was determined to bring his detachments into action as soon as possible, in actual fact the date of the despatch of these detachments to the front was constantly postponed.

Indeed when the Polish Army was first being organized the date for its readiness for action was fixed, as is well known, for October 1, 1941, and the Polish Command in this connection declared it was considered advisable to send individual divisions to the front as and when their organization was completed and they were ready for action. Though the preparations connected with the different divisions were delayed, even if it were not possible to fulfil this obligation by October 1, it could nevertheless have been done later. However, the obligation has not been fulfilled, and not once has the Polish Command raised the question of sending the organized divisions to the Soviet-German front.

The Soviet Government did not consider it possible to press the Polish

[6] See doc. No. 190.

450

Command in this matter, but nearly five months after the organization of the Polish military divisions had begun, namely in February, 1942, the Soviet Government became concerned as to when the Polish divisions would begin to fight against the Hitlerites. Mention was then made of the 5th Division, which had completed its training. At the same time the Soviet Government emphasized that it was important, both for political and military reasons, that Polish Units which were in readiness should be sent as soon as possible to fight against the Germans. When raising this question the Soviet Government based itself on the clear and explicit provisions of the Soviet-Polish Military Agreement concluded on August 14, 1941, point 7 of which reads as follows:

'Polish units will be moved to the front only after they are fully ready for action. In principle they will operate in groups not smaller than divisions, and will be used in accordance with the operational plans of the High Command of the USSR.'

Regardless of this categorical provision of the Military Agreement, excluding the possibility of any reservation whatsoever or refusal as to the propriety of moving to the front separate units ready to go into action, the Polish Government adopted an entirely different attitude in this matter. In reply to the Soviet Government's question, General Anders informed the Soviet Commander-in-Chief that he considered it inadvisable and purposeless to send single divisions, although the Poles were fighting even in brigades on other fronts.

Incidentally, General Anders gave his promise that the whole Polish Army would be ready to take part in the campaign against the Germans by June 1 of the present year. Neither by June 1 nor at a much later date did the Polish Army, or rather the Polish Command and the Polish Government, show their willingness to fight the Germans on the Soviet-German front. Furthermore the Polish Government even formally declined to move their units to the Soviet-German front on the grounds that 'the employment of single divisions would give no result', that 'the possible readiness for action of one division does not correspond to our expectations' (telegram from General Sikorski of February 7).

4) While refusing to send its army to the Soviet-German front, the Polish Government at the same time obstinately demanded the consent of the Soviet Government to carry out on Soviet territory supplementary recruiting for the Polish Army.

However, as not a single Polish detachment had taken part in active warfare, the Soviet Government was unable to give its consent. J. V. Stalin, Chairman of the Council of People's Commissars of the USSR, in a message addressed to General Sikorski, and V. M. Molotov, People's Commissar for Foreign Affairs, in a Note of May 14, drew the attention of the Polish Government to these circumstances.[7]

Nevertheless the Polish Government repeated its request to carry out

[7] See doc. Nos. 218, 219.

supplementary recruiting for the Polish Army amongst the Polish citizens residing on Soviet territory. In its Note of June 10, however,[8] the Polish Government explicitly stated a projected use of the Polish fighting forces organized in the Soviet Union, that was nothing else but a refusal to use them on the Soviet-German front.

In reply to this statement, transmitted by Mr. Raczyński, Polish Minister for Foreign Affairs, to Mr. Bogomolov, Soviet Ambassador to the Polish Government in London, the Soviet Government informed the Polish Government that in view of the fact that in spite of agreements between the USSR and Poland, the Polish Government did not deem it possible to employ the Polish divisions organized in the USSR on the Soviet-German front, the Soviet Government could not permit the further organization of Polish units in the USSR.

The above facts prove that the Soviet Government used every means to ensure a successful organization and development of the Polish Army on the territory of the Soviet Union, that the Soviet Government made all the necessary arrangements, and supplied all the necessary means and facilities for this purpose.

The agreement of July 30, 1941, and the declaration of December 4, 1941, clearly and explicitly defined the aims of the Soviet Government and the Polish Government, to unite the forces of the Soviet and Polish nations in the common struggle against the Hitlerite brigands and occupants, to create a Polish Army imbued with this high ideal and to give it an opportunity to fight shoulder to shoulder with the Red Army for the independence of their motherland, their homes and their native soil.

The Soviet Government did everything that was necessary for the realization of this aim. The Polish Government took a different path. The Polish Government showed no inclination to send their divisions—neither the first divisions formed, nor those subsequently formed—to the Soviet-German front, they refused to employ the Polish Army on this front against the Germans hand in hand with the Soviet divisions, and thereby declined to fulfil the obligations they had undertaken. Therefore, the Polish Government must assume full responsibility for the breach that has occurred in the continued organization on Soviet territory of their army from among the Polish citizens in the Soviet Union.

[8] See doc. No. 227.

No. 274

Note from the People's Commissariat for Foreign Affairs to the Polish Embassy in the USSR concerning the Welfare Organization for Poles in the USSR

Kuibyshev, November 4, 1942   GSHI, A.11. 49/Sow./3
                                                 Transl. from Russian

In reply to the Notes of the Embassy of the Republic of Poland of

13th August of this year, No. 3514/42[1] and of 6th September of this year, No. 3855/42[2] as well as the Aide-Mémoire of the Embassy of 10th September of this year,[3] the People's Commissariat for Foreign Affairs has the honour to state the following:

1. The examination of the statements put forward in the said Notes and concerning some allegedly illegal measures taken by the Soviet organs in some areas of the Kazakhstan Socialist Soviet Republic, established their being absolutely unfounded. The investigations made in connection with the cases referred to in the Embassy's said Notes proved that the local Polish Delegates took several completely inadmissible actions, to which the Soviet authorities put a stop in due time.

2. In relation to the assertions made in the Embassy's Note of 13th August of this year, the People's Commissariat for Foreign Affairs rejects as senseless the allegations according to which the designs of the Soviet authorities of the areas of Semipalatinsk, Akmolinsk, Southern Kazakhstan and Kustanai were directed against the 'very foundations of the assistance to the Polish authorities and against the welfare organizations', the same remark applies to the allegation which the Embassy considered proper to make in its Aide-Mémoire of 10th September of this year, and which concerns the constant fear of reprisals felt by the 'men of trust' of the Polish Embassy, 'presumably on account of the social activity they develop'.

3. The question of local Polish Delegates raised by the Aide-Mémoire of the Embassy of 10th September of this year should be considered exhausted in view of the decision taken by the Soviet Government in relation to them. The People's Commissariat does not see any reason to re-examine this question at present.

4. In its Aide-Mémoire of 10th September of this year, the Embassy refers to the existence of some difficulties arising in connection with the organization of material assistance to the Polish citizens.

The People's Commissariat considers it necessary to observe that if there are any difficulties in the matter of the welfare organization for Polish citizens, as the Embassy asserts, the responsibility for them rests entirely with the local Polish Delegates, and to some extent also with the Embassy which did not secure the loyal execution by the Delegates of the duties imposed on them.

5. The People's Commissariat is obliged to state that, in spite of its reiterated declarations of readiness to examine the Embassy's concrete proposals relating to the further welfare action for the Polish citizens in the USSR, the Embassy, so far, has not submitted any such proposals. The proposals enumerated by the Embassy under paras. 3, 4, 5 of the final part of the Aide-Mémoire of 10th September of this year, have been fully carried out from the very beginning of the organization of the welfare action for Polish citizens in the USSR, namely: a safe reception of welfare goods and their distribution among Polish citizens in the USSR in need, the providing of the Polish citizens with a service of a network of Polish welfare institutions

[1] See doc. No. 258.   [2] Not printed.   [3] See doc. No. 266.

453

and men of trust, and also a joint examination of differences arising between the men of trust and Soviet representatives. The People's Commissariat sees no necessity for giving any supplementary explanation or taking any new decisions on these matters.

Taking note of the Embassy's declaration that it will do everything possible to restore mutual confidence and loyal co-operation, the People's Commissariat expresses its hope that if the Embassy carries this line of policy into practice, the whole question of assistance to the Polish citizens in the USSR will be worked out without any difficulty.

No. 275

Aide-mémoire from the Soviet Embassy to the Polish Government in London handed to the Polish Ministry for Foreign Affairs dealing with the enrolment into the Polish Army in the Middle East of German prisoners of war of Polish nationality

London, November 6, 1942   GSHI, A.11. 49/Sow./3

En réponse à l'aide-mémoire du Ministère des Affaires Etrangères de la République de Pologne en date du 22 octobre de l'année courante,[1] l'Ambassade de l'Union des Républiques Soviétiques Socialistes auprès du Gouvernement de la République, de Pologne a l'honneur de faire savoir, que le Gouvernement Soviétique ne peut pas consentir à la proposition du Gouvernement Polonais relative à la création d'un régime spécial pour les Polonais—prisonniers de guerre et à leur transfert dans l'Armée polonaise pour des raisons, qui ont été déja expliquées dans la note du Commissariat du Peuple aux Affaires Etrangères No. 13 en date du 23 janvier 1942, remise à l'Ambassade de la République de Pologne à Kouibychev.[2]

[1] See doc. No. 270.   [2] See doc. No. 174.

No. 276

Note from Minister Raczyński to Ambassador Bogomolov on the arrest of Delegates and representatives of the Polish Embassy in the USSR

London, November 17, 1942   GSHI, A.11. 49/Sow./2
                                         Transl. from Polish: Pol.-Sov.R., No. 78

I have already had the honour to inform you in my Notes of July 11,[1] July 24,[2] and September 1, 1942,[3] and in conversations with yourself, that I consider the charges brought against the diplomatic officials of the Embassy of the Republic of Poland in Kuibyshev, its Delegates, representatives and office staffs, to be entirely unfounded. The Memorandum, you delivered to me, Mr. Ambassador, on October 31,[4] repeats these same charges in a form derogatory to the dignity of Polish officials and Polish authorities, to which I am obliged to take categorical exception.

[1] See doc. No. 246.   [2] See doc. No. 254.   [3] See doc. No. 263.
[4] See doc. No. 272. The date of memorandum was October 28.

For my part I desire therefore to further state that, fully maintaining the attitude previously adopted, I most categorically reject the supposition that the distinct instructions of the Polish Government along lines of collaboration with the Union of Soviet Socialist Republics in the struggle against the common enemy, were not carried out by persons who devoted themselves with much sacrifice to the welfare of their fellow citizens dispersed throughout the Union of Soviet Socialist Republics, and many of whom had already had opportunity to give proof of their efficiency and loyalty in carrying out duties entrusted to them in other posts.

After a thorough examination of the matter, for which it is indispensable, as already stated in Ambassador Romer's conversation with Mr. Molotov, People's Commissar for Foreign Affairs, on October 31, 1942, to have all the documents and archives seized from the Embassy Delegates and their representatives by the police authorities of the Union of Soviet Socialist Republics, returned to the Embassy of the Republic of Poland in Kuibyshev, I shall reply to each of the points raised in the Memorandum you delivered to me.

At the same time I should like to express my deep conviction, that an early settlement of this incident would be desirable in the interests of the satisfactory development of mutual relations between Poland and the Union of Soviet Socialist Republics, and should simultaneously include the resumption of relief work for Polish citizens in the Union of Soviet Socialist Republics, and the release of those Delegates and representatives who are still under arrest.

No. 277

General Sikorski's circular letter to the Polish governmental departments relating to the prospects of Polish-Soviet relations

London, November 19, 1942 GSHI, PRM, 73/1
Transl. from Polish

[. . .] in July 1941 I assumed full responsibility for the policy initiated by the agreement with the USSR. The Polish Government continues to follow this line of policy, exclusively dictated by the interests of the Polish State, in spite of all the difficulties raised on the Soviet part. We are doing this being convinced that the Soviet Government will understand this policy one day, and will duly appreciate its importance and value. Our position does not imply that we are ready to make concessions or to condone the aims which may be set either by the Comintern or Russian imperialism. It is quite the opposite.

Offering Soviet Russia a friendly and good neighbourly co-existence as well as genuine co-operation against the Germans, we oppose all the more any plans threatening our independence and our freedom of political decision. We contest and will contest, in the international field, unwarranted opinions that 'Russia invaded our territory in 1939 for the purpose of securing her strategic position'. We contest and will contest any propaganda which tries to make people believe that the 'evacuation' of the Polish population to Russia in 1941 was carried out 'of its own free will', and that thanks to it these elements were 'saved' for Poland. We shall not surrender in front of the repressive measures taken by the Soviet Government against our delegates. We obtained the release of 94 from among those arrested and, refuting the charges of espionage laid against 16 men still remaining in prison, as the expression of the old, hostile trends in Soviet policy, we shall insist on their release and on obtaining full satisfaction. We continue to enquire into the whereabouts of officers, judges, professors, doctors and lawyers, 10,000 of whom are still missing. We start conversations on a complete restoration of the welfare work for our refugees in Russia, and a gradual evacuation of Polish orphan children. We refute all attempts at organizing sabotage and partisan action in the home-country under Communist leadership.

The action against Poland is but a fragment of the action of the Russian Comintern which attempts to embrace all parts of the globe. This fragment is, however, a very important one, because the Polish State bars the way to the progress of Communism towards the West. This mission will be maintained by Poland who, at the same time, offers Soviet Russia her friendship based on the principle of non-interference in her domestic affairs. Neither will Poland forsake another mission, imposed on her by history, and consisting in creative co-operation in organizing federal unions in Central-Eastern Europe, able to offer resistance to German aggression. Today, Soviet Russia opposes this idea but the future will show that this is the only conception able to ensure full economic development to the States of Central-Eastern Europe and security to all States, including Russia herself, in the first instance.

It was not the Polish Government's fault that the Polish Army formed in the USSR had to leave Russia, where, if only owing to war conditions and transport difficulties, it could not attain the indispensable combat readiness. Its transfer to the Middle East should not have any unfavourable bearing on Polish-Russian political relations, neither should it have any influence on the fate of the numerous Poles still remaining in the USSR. It is in their own interest that the Poles retained in Russia should abstain from criticizing Soviet institutions, or in general from doing anything that may attract 'revolutionary vigilance' to them. The Poles over there have but to assist the Russians in fighting enemy sabotage. The Polish Government is well aware of the present difficult position of Poles in Russia, and will do everything possible to help them and alleviate their situation.

The heavy mistakes committed by Soviet Russia, violation of the agreements concluded in 1941 and the resumption of preposterous claims to Wilno and Lwów—will not, nevertheless, drive us into the anti-Soviet camp, which is what the Germans and their allies try to induce us to do. They even begin to talk of the restoration of the Polish State, a Poland bigger than that of 1939. The Poles, who do not give up any of their rights and firmly defend the independence and sovereignty of their country, refute at the same time those preposterous German suggestions, as being a deadly poison for our nation.

Preserving, so far as is possible, full freedom of action in the international field, the Government will continue to follow the Polish line of policy, dictated by the interests of the Polish State only, being convinced that sooner or later Soviet Russia will recognize the advantages arising from the existence of a strong Poland, a Poland keeping an anti-German front-line and playing the rôle which is her due in Central-Eastern Europe, a Poland who at the same time will be eager to maintain friendly relations with Russia. [. . .].

No. 278

Instruction from General Sikorski to Maj.-General Grot-Rowecki concerning Polish-Soviet relations

London, November 28, 1942   GSHI, Coll. 17/2
                                                            Transl. from Polish

[. . .]. The question of the Underground Army's attitude towards the Soviet Union in the ultimate stage of the war, so rightly put by you, my General, is a subject of constant worry to me. You will find it a guiding idea in a memorandum submitted by me to Churchill. Flying off to Washington, at Roosevelt's invitation, I shall put it there as firmly as I did in London, where they finally took the view that the question was not yet ripe for a final discussion. Taking, in principle, a favourable view of my idea of a joint occupation by Anglo-American-Polish troops of the territories occupied at present by Germany, as far as the eastern frontiers of Poland, they postponed any decision on it for the time being. It will also depend on Russia, whose position is constantly strengthening, and on whose assistance Great Britain intends to rely in the second phase of the war, that is in the course of the war against Japan, after Germany's defeat.

The question of the frontiers between Poland and Russia could not be put in a more determined way than by the annulment of the treaties of partition concluded between Germany and Russia. In the course of the last years we have been witnessing events which demonstrated Russia's attitude to the agreements concluded by her. Everything will depend on the actual balance of force at a given moment. I expect that this balance will be favourable for Poland in the ultimate stage of the war. I did not agree to discuss the frontiers of Poland in December, 1941, when Stalin proposed to me a talk on a small frontier rectification and on a closer alliance. Maybe the Polish Government, with British and American support, will eventually induce the Soviet Government to recognize our rights in the East with a simultaneous support for our claims in the West, which include East Prussia, Danzig and such a rectification of our frontiers as may be necessary for the security of our ports on the Baltic; Opole Silesia should return to Poland. I envisage a direct approach to Soviet Russia by us in relation to these questions. I hope to be able to convince Roosevelt of the necessity of keeping a joint and strong line of action with respect to Russia, should the latter try to infringe upon Polish territorial sovereignty. However, I have to reckon also with such developments which might lead to the Red Army entering the frontiers of the

Republic, in pursuit of the enemy. To wage an armed struggle by the Underground Army against Soviet troops entering Poland, would be sheer madness. To keep secret the military organization of whose existence the Soviet Government is well informed, would lead to an open fight of the Soviet troops against the Underground Army, a fight on which Communist propaganda would spread distorted views in the camp of the Allied Nations. In this eventuality I order, therefore, to prepare the Underground Army for coming into the open, and to start its mobilization. Its strength should be as big as possible, and it should emphasize its sovereign status and its positive attitude towards Soviet Russia. I pave the way for such an action of the Army and of the Home country in the international field; for that is where a decision of a political nature will settle our frontiers. It is also imperative that the Home country, and the military organizations in particular, present their totally united front, and that Communist influence does not prevail among them. All the soldiers must be thoroughly enlightened in this sense. It is imperative for the Underground Army to absorb other semi-military organizations, as any sign of disruption would provide an opportunity for the Soviet Union; this would be the greatest calamity, extremely dangerous for Poland. By giving an example of a statesmanlike attitude the Underground Army must become the rallying point for all organizations to whose patriotic feelings it is necessary to appeal. The hour for joint action may strike very soon. We must be prepared for this contingency. I cannot stress strongly enough the great importance of national unity and discipline at such a moment. Traitors, of the kind of Colonel Berling and Wanda Wasilewska, will tread in the steps of Soviet troops entering Poland, and they will do everything possible in order to bring aboutthe disruption of the Polish nation and the undermining of the Polish State.

After my return to London the Government will issue appropriate instructions to its Delegate in the Home country. One of the aims of my journey is to win Roosevelt's support for the contest with anarchy and Communism in Europe by supplying the Continent with huge quantities of food, medicines and clothing. Such assistance will be urgently needed by the Soviet Union as well, and consequently our future rests on strong foundations. [. . .].

No. 279

Note from Minister Raczyński to Chargé d'Affaires Valkov on slanderous broadcasts and requesting the transfer of German war prisoners of Polish nationality to the Polish Army[1]

London, December 15, 1942   GSHI, A.11. 49/Sow./2
                                                Transl.: Pol.-Sov.R., No. 54

Radio stations on the territory of the Union of Soviet Socialist Republics have on several occasions recently broadcast news of the mass participation

[1] See Note No. 279.

of Poles in the German Army, and even of the formation of special Polish units allegedly commanded by Polish officers. This information was given in such a form as to create the impression that there existed voluntary co-operation between the Poles and the German Army against the Red Army.

At the same time the Polish authorities have had the opportunity to ascertain by reports from Poland that many Polish officers and other ranks, residing in territories illegally incorporated in the Reich, have been forcibly conscripted by the German Army and sent to various German fronts. Poles, thus mobilized, have found themselves in Field-Marshal Rommel's army in Libya, and in German units which took part in the fighting at Dieppe. Availing themselves of the first opportunity, these men surrendered to Allied units and are today in the ranks of the Polish Army, preparing to fight against their age-old enemy.

The Government of the Republic of Poland have therefore instructed Ambassador Romer to explain to the Government of the Union of Soviet Socialist Republics the real reasons for the existence of a certain number of Polish soldiers in the German Army. At the same time Ambassador Romer has instructions to submit to the Government of the Union of Soviet Socialist Republics that the aforementioned broadcasts throw a false light upon the part played in the German Army by the forcibly conscripted Poles, whose only desire is to concentrate their efforts against the German oppressor.

Replying to a verbal intervention by Ambassador Romer, the Deputy People's Commissar for Foreign Affairs, Mr. Lozovsky, stated that from investigations carried out among individual prisoners, the authorities of the USSR estimate the number of Polish soldiers at three hundred thousand. The Government of the Union of Soviet Socialist Republics possesses information to the effect that these soldiers are under strong German supervision. Desiring to influence these soldiers by propaganda, the authorities of the Union of Soviet Socialist Republics have distributed to them appeals and proclamations in Polish.

As can be seen from the statement of Mr. Lozovsky, Deputy Commissar for Foreign Affairs, anti-German sentiments prevail among the soldiers referred to, a fact the Polish Government never doubted.

The lowering of Germany's war potential is indisputably an aim common to all the United Nations. Its realization in respect of Polish soldiers conscripted by the German Army against their will and contrary to international law ought in the common interest to belong primarily to the Polish Government. The success of appeals addressed to Polish soldiers in the German Army would beyond all doubt be greater if the Polish Government were in a position to assure them that on surrendering they would be separated and sent to special camps under the care of Polish Authorities and would be able subsequently to transfer to the ranks of the Polish Army.

I am deeply convinced that a considerable number of Poles forcibly conscripted by the German Army and ordered against their will to fight the Allied Armies could already find themselves in the ranks of the Polish Army, thus contributing to strengthen the forces fighting for the common cause.

459

Therefore I should like to express the hope that in view of the increasing importance of this problem, the Government of the Union of Soviet Socialist Republics will take into account the Polish Government's suggestion and reconsider the attitude hitherto adopted towards Poles who are already Soviet prisoners of war, or may be taken as such in the future, and will consider issuing orders to the effect that broadcasts on the territory of the Union of Soviet Socialist Republics should cease to interpret the tragic fate of the victims of this forcible conscription in a way that may prove a source of misapprehension harmful to them.

No. 280

Note from Minister Raczyński to Chargé d'Affaires Valkov refuting the allegations of the Soviet note of October 31, 1942 concerning the Polish Army and its withdrawal from the USSR

London, December 18, 1942   GSHI, A.11. 49/Sow./2
Transl. from Polish: Pol.-Sov.R., No. 50

In respect to the negative attitude adopted by the authorities of the Union of Soviet Socialist Republics with regard to the efforts of General Anders to have one reserve depôt left on the territory of the Union of Soviet Socialist Republics to continue the recruiting of Polish citizens for the Polish Army, I had the honour to represent in my Note of August 27, 1942,[1] addressed to Ambassador Bogomolov, the consistent and sustained efforts of the Polish Government to organize a numerically strong army of Polish citizens, fit for military service and anxious to fulfil their duty to their motherland in the ranks of the armed forces. To recall these continued efforts of the Polish Government I quoted in my Note a series of facts and referred to the abundant correspondence in the matter between the representatives of the Polish Government and the Government of the Union of Soviet Socialist Republics.

I wish to emphasize that in his reply of October 31, 1942,[2] to my Note mentioned above, Ambassador Bogomolov neither questioned nor denied any of the facts quoted by me. On the contrary, Ambassador Bogomolov, referred in his Note to the decision taken on March 18, 1942, to reduce the Polish forces to 44,000 men,[3] a decision which, as I had the honour to remark in my Note of August 27, 1942, was taken unilaterally by the Soviet Government, without any consultation whatsoever with the representatives of the Polish Government, and which was contrary to the bilateral Polish-Soviet understanding of December 3, 1941,[4] on the formation of a Polish Army on the territory of the Union of Soviet Socialist Republics of 96,000 men, apart from the evacuation of 25,000 infantry and 2,000 air and navy personnel. He also emphasized that 'the further development of the Polish Army met with certain difficulties caused by such unforeseen circumstances as the non-delivery of wheat to the Union of Soviet Socialist Republics from the United States and England as a result of the outbreak of war in the Pacific Ocean'.

[1] See doc. No. 261.   [2] See doc. No. 273.
[3] See doc. No. 193.   [4] See doc. No. 159.

So without questioning in any way my statement concerning the negative attitude of the Government of the Union of Soviet Socialist Republics with regard to the numerical development of the Polish Army, moreover, himself emphasizing that the reduction of that Army in March, 1942, was due to the outbreak of war in the Pacific Ocean and not to any fault on the part of the Polish Government, Ambassador Bogomolov arrives at the end of his Note at a conclusion which I completely fail to understand, namely, that it is the Polish Government which should bear the entire responsibility for the discontinuation of the organization of their army from among the Polish citizens living on the territories of the Union of Soviet Socialist Republics.

Before discussing in further detail the various statements made by Ambassador Bogomolov in his Note of October 31, 1942, I wish first of all to observe that a considerable part of this Note is devoted to the enumeration of all measures and facilities granted by the Government of the Union of Soviet Socialist Republics to make possible the creation of a Polish Army. Ambassador Bogomolov includes in this list the setting up of recruiting boards, the notifying of Polish citizens of the organization of a Polish Army, the collaboration of Soviet military authorities with the Polish High Command for the most satisfactory solution of various problems connected with the organization of the Army, viz.: furnishing appropriate premises, barracks, food and other supplies, munitions for training purposes, etc., as well as a non-interest bearing loan originally of 65 million roubles, raised subsequently to 300 million roubles, granted to the Polish Government by the Government of the Union of Soviet Socialist Republics to cover the cost of all the above mentioned services and deliveries in kind.[5] The Polish Government fully appreciated the efforts the Government of the Union of Soviet Socialist Republics made to this end, efforts undoubtedly great and complicated in view of the war waged on the territory of the Union of Soviet Socialist Republics—and this is why they pressed no demands in this respect. If, however, there were serious shortcomings in matters concerning barracks for the army, food supplies, fodder for horses, which led to repeated representations by General Anders and by General Sikorski on December 3, 1941, in his talk with Premier Stalin, Chairman of the Council of People's Commissars, those complaints were not made as a reproach to the authorities of the Union of Soviet Socialist Republics nor to place their efforts in doubt, but to draw their attention to the fact that these shortages and failures to deliver supplies must evidently impair the rapidity with which the Polish Army could be made ready for action.

In his Note of October 31, 1942, Ambassador Bogomolov mentions that in accordance with the understanding between the Soviet and Polish High Commands, the strength of the Polish Army was fixed at 30,000 men and that the formation of two Polish rifle divisions and of one reserve regiment should have been completed by October 1, 1941, and further, that in accordance with the proposal made by General Anders it was agreed to send the divisions as and when formed to the Soviet-German front without delay.[6]

[5] See annex No. 6.   [6] See doc. No. 114.

Ambassador Bogomolov's assertion that the strength of the Polish Army was fixed at 30,000 men is obviously contrary to the Polish-Soviet Military Agreement of August 14, 1941, to which Ambassador Bogomolov frequently refers in his Note. Article 4, of the above mentioned Military Agreement, reads as follows:[7]

'The Polish Army on the territory of the USSR will consist of units of land forces only. Their strength and number will depend on the manpower, equipment and supplies available.'

As results from the above text, the Military Agreement—that is the basic document governing the organization of the Polish armed forces—does not fix any restriction as to the strength, making it dependent solely on the manpower and equipment available. Moreover, at the signature of the Military Agreement, the Polish Government deliberately abstained from putting forward any definite figure as to the strength of the Army, on the assumption that the Polish armed forces fighting against the Germans would include all Polish citizens capable of bearing arms and eager to fulfil on the fields of battle their duty to their motherland. The Polish Government were fully convinced that on the territories of the Union of Soviet Socialist Republics a numerically strong Polish Army could be raised in view of the man-power available there. These hopes of the Polish Government were based on three factors:

1. The number of Polish citizens, prisoners of war according to the figures published in the *Red Star*, the organ of the Red Army, on September 17, 1940 was 181,000 men, including 12 generals, 58 colonels, 72 lieut.-colonels, 5,131 officers of lesser rank and 4,096 reserve officers.
2. In the Army of the Union of Soviet Socialist Republics there were about 100,000 Polish citizens from the classes of 1917, 1918 and 1919, conscripted on Polish territory in the spring months of 1941.
3. Among those deported from Polish territory, there were considerable numbers of men of military age, who could join the Polish Army in formation, as volunteers or regular recruits, according to the provisions of Art. 6 of the Military Agreement of August 14, 1941.

Several months after the conclusion of the Military Agreement, to be exact, on December 3, 1941, a bilateral decision was reached by General Sikorski and Premier Stalin, Chairman of the Council of People's Commissars, with regard to fixing the strength of the Polish Army on the territory of the Union of Soviet Socialist Republics. As I mentioned above and in my Note of August 27, 1942, the Polish armed forces were to consist of 96,000 men, apart from 27,000 men evacuated to the Middle East, or a total of 123,000 men.

As Ambassador Bogomolov in his Note refers to an alleged fixing of the strength of the Polish Army at 30,000 men during General Anders's negotiations with the Soviet High Command, this refers probably to the so-called Protocol No. 2, of August 19, 1941. I desire to recall in this connection the

[7] See doc. No. 112.

explanations communicated by Ambassador Kot to Premier Stalin, Chairman of the Council of People's Commissars, on November 14, 1941, and on November 15, 1941,[8] to M. Molotov, People's Commissar for Foreign Affairs, which were taken into cognizance. Consequently Protocol No. 2 did not contain any limitation of the strength of the Polish Army—as this would have been contrary to Art. 6 of the Military Agreement signed a few days previously—but provided for a gradual formation of the Army by stages, according to the influx of recruits and the supply of technical equipment, which could be delivered to the Polish Army in formation only by the authorities of the Union of Soviet Socialist Republics and without which the formation of any armed force whatever was completely inconceivable. This Protocol, at the wish of the Polish Command—as emphasized by Ambassador Bogomolov in his Note—fixed a short time limit, October 1, 1941, for the organization and military preparedness of two divisions and one reserve regiment. This extraordinarily short period provided for the organization and military training of the Army, on the initiative of the Polish Command, is irrefutable proof of the eager desire of the Polish Army to take part in war operations on the Eastern front at the earliest possible date. It is obvious, however, that the problem of the military training of two divisions and one reserve regiment in a period of six weeks from the date of the signature of the Military Agreement has no connection whatsoever with the totally different problem of the strength of the Polish Army,[9] as a separately organized entity that was to be formed in accordance with the Agreement of July 30, 1941, and of the Military Agreement of August 14, 1941. Therefore I must consider as wholly unjustified the assertion as regards a definite fixing of the strength of the Polish Army at 30,000 men during the negotiations with General Anders. Equally devoid of all foundation is the attempt to represent the understanding of December 3, 1941, which actually for the first time fixed the number of divisions to be formed on the territory of the Union of Soviet Socialist Republics and the number of soldiers to be evacuated, as a concession made to the Polish Government.

In the above-mentioned Note, Ambassador Bogomolov tries to burden the Polish Government with responsibility for the fact that the two divisions mentioned above did not achieve their military preparedness by October 1, 1941, and that these and other divisions were also not ready to fight at a later date, and finally he asserts that the Polish Government deemed it undesirable to send single divisions to the front, and even refused to send their Army to the Soviet-German front.

I wish to draw your attention, M. Chargé d'Affaires, to the fact that the Government of the USSR, at the time of the conclusion of the Military Agreement with the Polish Government were well aware that the Polish Government disposed of considerable man-power out of which many army divisions could be formed, but that on the other hand, they did not possess their own armament or munition factories. Therefore Article 12 of the Polish-Soviet Military Agreement explicitly provided that 'armament, equipment,

<hr />

[8] See doc. Nos. 149 and 151.   [9] See doc. No. 122.

uniforms, motor transport, etc., will be provided as far as possible by (a) the Government of the USSR from their own resources, (b) the Polish Government from supplies granted on the basis of the Lend-Lease Act'.

The first care of the Polish Government when proceeding with the creation of the Polish Army was to take measures to fully provide the troops with the necessary equipment in the shortest possible time. Thanks to the efforts of the Polish Government a few weeks after the conclusion of the Military Agreement shipments of uniforms for the Polish Army were already despatched from Great Britain. General Anders received the first consignment of uniforms and boots from Soviet authorities only on October 23, 1941, and up to that date the soldiers were in rags, and 40% of them went barefoot. During the initial period of the formation of the Army, arms were to be supplied by the Government of the USSR. But it was only on October 22, 1941, that M. Molotov, People's Commissar for Foreign Affairs,[10] notified Ambassador Kot that the Union of Soviet Socialist Republics had some difficulties as regards armaments and asked whether there was any possibility that the Polish Government might obtain armaments from the United States and Great Britain. An identical statement with regard to armament difficulties was made by Ambassador Bogomolov to General Sikorski and myself on October 25, 1941.[11]

If I mention this matter here it is not with the aim of imparting any blame; I merely record facts which show that in spite of the best will on the part of the Polish Government, Polish armed forces could not be adequately armed within the period of time originally fixed and that the Polish Government cannot assume any responsibility on that score.

The Polish Government, informed by the representatives of the Union of Soviet Socialist Republics of the difficulties concerning the arming of the Polish Army, immediately approached the Governments of Great Britain and of the United States with a request for arms and equipment. As you are aware, M. Chargé d'Affaires, the necessity of continuing supplies to the USSR on the one hand, and the imperative need of massing arms and munitions in North Africa on the other, together with complications arising from the great length of the journey were responsible for the fact that the arms could not be delivered at the dates fixed.

As a result it was only possible to arm and equip the 5th Division of the Polish armed forces on the territory of the Union of Soviet Socialist Republics, and even that division very inadequately compared to a Soviet infantry division, so it was in no case ready to fight. The division did not possess any of the eighteen 45 mm. anti-tank guns the establishment called for, it had no 76 mm. anti-aircraft guns (establishment 4), also it did not possess any synchronized anti-aircraft machine guns (establishment 18) nor any 12.7 mm. machine-guns (establishment 9). The 5th Infantry Division had not received any 77 mm. field-guns, although according to the establishment it should have had 18, and finally it was without munition carriers for 77 mm. guns or 104 mm. howitzers. As for the 37 mm. anti-aircraft guns, it had only four

[10] See Note No. 134.   [11] See Note No. 133.

instead of the six called for in the establishment. Finally the 5th Division was also very short of equipment: the division had only 10% of motor-cars, 56% of field kitchens, 80% of two-horse carts, 45% of ambulances, 60% of one-horse carts and 85% of the horses provided for in the establishment. As far as the other divisions were concerned there was actually no question of their being armed, as all they had was only 200 rifles, a number insufficient even for training purposes, so that in order to prevent the soldiers from remaining idle, General Anders was obliged to distribute among them part of the firearms of the 5th Division.

When on March 18, 1942, General Anders informed the Chairman of the Council of People's Commissars of this state of affairs and simultaneously presented him with a list of arms already received and an estimate of additional arms required to complete the needs of the Polish Army, Premier Stalin said: 'You will have enough time to organize and to train your Army. We do not press you to go to the front. I understand that it will be better for you to go to the front when we shall have advanced to the Polish frontiers. You should have the honour to be the first to step on Polish soil.'

The facts quoted by me above prove that if neither the Polish Army as a whole nor any part of it, such as the 5th Division frequently mentioned by Ambassador Bogomolov, took part in the fighting on the Eastern front, it was not because the Government of the USSR deemed it impossible to exert pressure on the Polish Command, but because no part of this Army was either properly trained or adequately armed, consequently, it did not meet the explicit and simple requirements set down in Art. 7 of the Military Agreement, in the following words: 'The Polish units will be moved to the front only after they are fully ready for action.'

In his Note Ambassador Bogomolov also refers to the second part of this Article, which reads: 'In principle they (the Polish units) will operate in groups not smaller than divisions and will be used in accordance with the operational plans of the High Command of the USSR,' and at the same time he expresses the opinion that the sentence quoted above excludes the possibility of any reservation whatever or refusal as to the propriety of moving to the front separate units ready to go into action. Although I have already had the honour of proving that for lack of armaments none of the Polish divisions had reached the stage of full readiness for action, and consequently none was in a position to participate in the fighting, I now take the liberty of drawing your attention, M. Chargé d'Affaires, to the fact that the interpretation of this part of this Article may be twofold, that is to say, that Polish military units not smaller than a division *might* be or *must* be moved to the front. In order to avoid any possible misunderstanding in the matter and to give to this Article a uniform interpretation which would exclude all ambiguity, General Sikorski, on August 23, 1941,[12] instructed General Szyszko-Bohusz to have a further talk with the High Command of the Red Army to explain that the Polish Army on the territory of the Union of Soviet Socialist Republics would operate as a whole under Polish Command and

[12] See doc. No. 116.

that individual Polish divisions would not be sent to the front. Requesting such an interpretation of Article 7, General Sikorski took the stand that not only military considerations but the prestige of Poland demanded that the Polish Army should operate as a whole and have a special sector of the Eastern front entrusted to it under a Polish general. He also took into consideration the propaganda value that the taking over of a particular sector of the front by the Polish Army would have in Poland and in the whole world. The throwing up to the front of one Polish division and the splitting up of the Polish Army into single units would cause not only unfortunate consequences in the organization of the Polish Army, but would also have undesirable effects for the USSR, as far as propaganda was concerned. After carrying out his instructions, General Szyszko-Bohusz informed General Sikorski on September 11, 1941, that he had been officially informed, on September 10, by the Government of the USSR, through the Deputy Chief of Staff, General Panfilov, that the said Government interpreted Article 7 of the Military Agreement in accordance with the suggestion of the Polish Government and recognized entirely the necessity of using the Polish Army at the front as a homogeneous whole. Also in his conversations with the Chairman of the Council of People's Commissars, General Sikorski made explicit reservations against employing individual Polish divisions at the front and against splitting the Polish Army into single units which would be lost in the immense Red Army.[13]

I am obliged to take the most emphatic exception to the assertion of Ambassador Bogomolov that the Polish Government removed from the agenda the question of the participation of the Polish Army in the common fight together with the Soviet forces against the Germans. The Polish Government were and continue to be firmly resolved to respect all Polish-Soviet agreements, the Agreement of July 30, 1941, the Military Agreement of August 14, 1941 and the Polish-Soviet Declaration of December 4, of the same year. Evacuation of a part of the Polish Army, agreed upon in the negotiations between General Sikorski and the Chairman of the Council of People's Commissars, resulted from the necessity of the speediest possible arming of the Polish troops so that they might be thrown into the battle against Germany. An evacuation of part or even the whole of the Polish Army did not exclude a continuation of recruiting of Polish citizens fit for military service as clearly provided for in the Military Agreement and did not depend on the earlier or later participation of the Polish Army in the battles at the front. In accordance with the provisions of the above-mentioned Agreement, recruiting should be continued until the man-power resources of Polish citizens residing in the Union of Soviet Socialist Republics are exhausted. The recruiting was stopped without agreement with the Polish Government, in spite of the fact that being informed of the difficulties in feeding the troops in the rear of the Army, on June 10 of the current year,[14] they made a proposal to the Soviet Government to supply food rations for recruits over and above the figure of 44,000 pending evacuation to the Middle

[13] See doc. No. 159.   [14] See doc. No. 227.

466

East. As you are well aware, M. Chargé d'Affaires, this offer was not accepted by the Government of the USSR and the recruiting of Polish citizens for the Polish Army was stopped.

In the final paragraph of his Note of October 31, Ambassador Bogomolov asserts that in my Note of June 10 of the current year, the Polish Government declared themselves in favour of such a use of the Polish armed forces formed on the territory of the Union of Soviet Socialist Republics that meant nothing else than a refusal to use them on the Soviet-German front. Desirous to demonstrate that the above assertion can be based only on a misunderstanding, I take the liberty of quoting the paragraph of my Note of June 10, referring to the use of the Polish Army on the Eastern front among others. I wrote then: 'The Polish Government are determined to use the Polish Armed Forces now in the USSR, in the Near East or in Great Britain in the struggle for the common cause against the common enemy.' Moreover, I did not preclude in the above mentioned Note the possibility of the return of evacuated units of the Polish Army to the fighting on the Eastern battlefront, as shown by the following sentences: 'It is possible that the Polish Army formed in the Near East may—after it is equipped and trained—also be used on the front of the Union of Soviet Socialist Republics in case the military situation should so require. Certain units of this army have already taken a noteworthy part in the defence of Tobruk and in the fighting in the desert. The fact that the Polish Army has not yet fought side by side with the Red Army is solely due to armament difficulties experienced by the Union of Soviet Socialist Republics as well as to the shipping difficulties that beset Great Britain and the United States.'

As you see, M. Chargé d'Affaires, the excerpts from my Note of June 10, quoted above, are perfectly clear and unequivocal and they contradict Ambassador Bogomolov's assertion concerning the alleged declaration of the Polish Government against the use on the Soviet-German front of Polish armed forces organized on the territory of the Union of Soviet Socialist Republics. All the facts quoted by me above irrefutably testify that the Polish Government, attaching great importance to the possibility of forming a Polish Army on the territory of the Union of Soviet Socialist Republics, fulfilled with complete loyalty all the obligations they assumed, and most zealously spared no efforts to make that Army as strong numerically as possible. The Polish Government also did everything in their power and spared no steps to obtain as soon as possible from the Government of the Union of Soviet Socialist Republics and from the Governments of Great Britain and the United States the necessary arms and equipment for the Polish Army to enable it to take part in the fighting on the Eastern front. It is through no fault of the Polish Government that their efforts in this direction, owing to a whole series of unforeseen circumstances, did not bring the hoped for results within the time foreseen, as a consequence of which the training of the Army and its readiness for action were also delayed. On the other hand, the decision to reduce the strength of the Polish Army and to stop recruiting for that Army was taken by the Government of the USSR alone without any attempt at consultation with the Polish Government in the matter.[15] Consequently, full responsibility for those decisions must be borne solely by the Government of the Union of Soviet Socialist Republics.

Bearing in mind that the interests of the United Nations in the present war against the aggressor States demand that all available man-power be utilized to wage a most successful war against them, and in view of the fact that many thousands of Polish citizens in the Union of Soviet Socialist Republics capable of bearing arms have not yet been recruited for the Polish armed forces, and, moreover, the possibility that when those Polish units already organized enter into action in the near future, casualties and losses must ensue which will necessitate replacements in the fighting ranks,—the Polish Government cannot alter their opinion that the continuation of recruiting for the Polish Army on the territory of the Union of Soviet Socialist Republics, interrupted several months ago, is in the common interest of all Allied Nations.

[15] See doc. Nos. 219 and 238.

No. 281

Note from Chargé d' Affaires Valkov to Minister Raczyński in reply to the Polish note of November 17, 1942 concerning the accusations against Polish Embassy Delegates in the USSR

London, December 18, 1942   GSHI, A.11. 49/Sow./3
                                                Transl. from Russian

Referring to your Note No. 49/Sow/42 of 17th November, 1942[1] I have the honour, on the order of the Soviet Government, to state the following:

1/ The Soviet Government refutes the attempts made in the said Note at questioning the rightfulness and correctness of the charges, stated in the Memorandum of 31st October of this year,[2] on account of espionage and hostile activity towards the Soviet Union of the former Delegates and men of trust of the Polish Embassy in the USSR, indicted for those reasons.

2/ The question of the further fate of the arrested Delegates of the Embassy of the Republic of Poland in the USSR will depend on the findings of the Courts.

3/ So far as documents and archives seized in the course of arrests are concerned, instructions were issued to the respective authorities to return the said documents, with the exception of those which might be required for the impending trials.

4/ As regards the question of the resumption of the welfare action for Polish citizens, it is a question in which the Soviet Government has fully co-operated and continues to co-operate with the Polish Embassy in the USSR; at present this action continues, being based on a wide network of men of trust, and the Embassy's stores in the areas inhabited by Polish citizens.

[1] See doc. No. 276.   [2] See doc. No. 273.

No. 282

Note from Minister Raczyński to Chargé d'Affaires Valkov in reply to the Soviet note of December 18, 1942 and its accusations against Polish Embassy Delegates in the USSR

London, December 23, 1942   GSHI, A.11. 49/Sow./2
Transl. from Polish

Referring to your Note No. 176-b of 18th December, 1942,[1] and in particular to para. 2 of the said Note, announcing the impending trial on the territory of the USSR of the Delegates and men of trust of the Embassy of the Republic of Poland in Kuibyshev, still under arrest, I wish to maintain to the full extent the point of view of the Polish Government laid down in the Notes No. 49/Sow/42 of 11th July, 1942,[2] No. 49/Sow/42 of 24th July, 1942,[3] No. 49/Sow/42 of 1st September 1942,[4] and No. 49/Sow/42 of 17th November, 1942,[5] addressed to Ambassador Bogomolov.

At the same time I wish to emphasize that in their whole welfare action the Polish Government, as well as the Embassy of the Republic of Poland in Kuibyshev and its organs, were prompted exclusively by the desire to take care of the Polish citizens spread all over the territory of the Soviet Union, and to strengthen the bonds of co-operation between the two States, pursuant to the Agreement of 30th July, 1941[6] and the Declaration of 4th December, 1941.[7]

[1] See doc. No. 281.   [2] See doc. No. 246.   [3] See doc. No. 254.
[4] See doc. No. 263.   [5] See doc. No. 276.   [6] See doc. No. 106.
[7] See doc. No. 161.

No. 283

Memorandum of General Sikorski to Under-Secretary of State Sumner Welles on the Polish-Russian frontier

Washington, December 23, 1942   GSHI, Kol. 3/2

1. A lasting peace in Central and Eastern Europe depends on Polish-Russian collaboration, which in turn is subsequent to the settlement of the question of the common boundaries and the loyal observance of treaties binding the two countries.

2. It must be emphasized from the very outset that by the Treaty of Riga in 1921,[1] Poland renounced all claims to about 55% of her former area and has no territorial assertions whatever with regard to the Soviet Union. It should also be borne in mind that the Treaty of Riga resulted from a compromise based on political, economic, and strategic considerations and had never been put in question by either of the contracting Powers until the conclusion of the Ribbentrop-Molotov agreement of 1939.[2]

3. It was not until after the outbreak of the present war and subsequent to the German-Soviet pacts[3] that certain imperialist tendencies of the Soviet foreign policy became evident. Some of them took their origin from the

[1] See doc. No. 3.   [2] See doc. No. 32.   [3] See doc. Nos. 31 and 32.

traditional policy of Russian imperialism, whilst others—which are primarily directed against Poland—are the outcome of the Communist imperialism of the Bolsheviks.

4. The historical claims of the Soviet Government are consistent with the political testament of Peter the Great, in that they incline towards the possession of icefree ports in the Baltic and the command of the Dardanelles. These claims are explained by the Soviet Government, as successor to the Tsarist traditions, under the pretence of strategic and economic necessities. The accomplishment of these designs against the will of the nations concerned is a problem of world politics, and will depend upon the actual disposition of forces between the Great Powers at the time of the termination of the war. The sympathy of the Polish people, who are suffering such extremities on account of their devotion to freedom, are unquestionably on the side of the weaker nations. Poland, however, is not sufficiently powerful to undertake the defence of their interests.

5. The pressure of the Soviet Government in the direction of the eastern borders of Poland and their intentions against Lithuania admit of demands of a more recent period and are dictated by the precepts of Bolshevik Imperialism, for it is evident that the territories seized by Russia in 1939 as a result of the Ribbentrop-Molotov pact,[4] and held for two years on the basis of Russo-German collaboration, have no value to Russia whatever.

6. The northern and central areas are very poor in natural resources. The southern part which contains our only oil-fields is of great importance to Poland, whereas the high cost of production and the comparatively low output [400,000–500,000 tons per annum] would make it insignificant to our neighbour, nor would it bear comparison with his vast capacities or economic facilities of production. In this part of Poland there is also ozocerite, natural gas, potassium chloride, timber and water-power. The industry of these resources forms the basis of a living for many hundred thousands of Polish families inhabiting outside this area.

7. The potential of Poland consists mainly in the large reserves of manpower, whereas the shortage of raw materials does not afford the opportunities for sufficient employment. There is ample scope for the development of economic intercourse between Russia and Poland, provided that political factors do not interfere with the manufacture and exchange of goods. Russia, for instance, imported to the industrial area of Leningrad millions of tons of coal which could be supplied without difficulty by Poland, whereas it was brought from Russian mines across a distance of over 3,000 miles. In exchange, Poland could receive the raw material output of the neighbouring Ukraine and the Caucasus. For the raw iron of Krivy Rog, Poland would be capable of returning manufactured goods satisfying in addition the home market. The industrial development of eastern Poland would be economically justified, besides

[4] See doc. No. 52.

470

being beneficial to the local population, owing to the circumstance that industrial areas are distant from that region on either side of the Polish-Russian border. There are many reasons, besides these, for the anticipation of great results from economic enterprise between Poland and Russia which would be equally advantageous to both countries.

8. The arguments of a strategic nature brought forward by the Soviet Government in justification of their territorial claims with regard to the eastern part of Poland are not convincing. A span of an additional hundred miles could hardly be of significance to a territorial dimension such as Russia, whose width extends over seven thousand miles. The Russian capital is situated one thousand miles from the western borders of the Soviet Empire. A boundary following the so-called Curzon line [along the river Bug] would from the strategic point of view be infinitely more disadvantageous to Russia than the Russo-Polish frontier previous to September 1939.[5] The Bug is a small river that can be waded without difficulty, while the Polesie marshes, even during the present war, have proved to be a natural obstacle of great military significance. They are important to Poland as a defensive barrier, but worthless as a bridge-head for offensive operations.

9. The centuries of political relationship between Poland and Russia, often agitated, have testified to the attainment of valuable results of cultural and economic intercourse, which moreover could be extensively developed in the future. Through the establishment of a larger federated block of nations, Poland would be capable of playing a considerably more active part by the importance of this politically independent organization existing between Germany and Russia and constituting for the latter the most effective barrier of defence against any future German intentions. Moreover such a block could never be a cause of anxiety to Russia, in the sense of a 'cordon sanitaire' as it would be founded on the binding collaboration of all countries bordering on Germany both in the East and in the West, at the time of the German attack.

10. The Polish Prime Minister gave manifest evidence to the importance which he attaches to the problem of Polish-Russian collaboration, when notwithstanding the ordeal suffered by the Polish population during the two years of Russian occupation, following their treacherous aggression of September 17th, 1939,[6] he was the first to extend his hand towards Russia and in July, 1941,[6] to sign an agreement followed by the joint declaration which he later signed with Stalin in Moscow.[7]

11. It is essential that the Polish-Russian frontiers should be firmly established. There must be a dividing line between the Communist conception of the world as represented by the Soviets and the ideals of the Western Democracies based on individual rights. This demarcation should follow the lines established by the Treaty of Riga.

12. The frontiers of the Treaty of Riga are the only ones acceptable to the Polish Nation for the following reasons:[8]

[5] See doc. No. 93.   [6] See doc. No. 106.   [7] See doc. No. 161.   [8] See doc. No. 3.

a/ All historic arguments are in their favour, particularly on the grounds that the whole of the eastern area of Poland including its two principal centres, Wilno and Lwów, was built up and promoted by the effort of Poland alone and owes its culture to Polish civilization. Moreover throughout history Lwów has never belonged to Russia and Wilno was under the domination of that Country only during the period when Poland was partitioned. It would be impossible in any way to take into consideration the so-called plebiscite which was accomplished by the Russians in a unilateral and coercive manner contrary to the will of the great majority of the population.

b/ Both economic and strategic reasons also recommend the maintenance of the frontiers established by the Treaty of Riga.

c/ The inhabitants of those territories also desire to remain within the boundaries of the Polish State. Apart from the inhabitants of Polish nationality, who previous to the war amounted to 70% of the population of Wilno and over 60% in Lwów [whereas there were no Russians in either of these cities] it should be emphasized that the White Ruthenians adhere instinctively to Poland as their Mother Country, a proof of which is available in letters addressed to General Sikorski as Head of the Polish Government, by a number of White Ruthenians who have been deported by the Russians. The Jewish inhabitants of those provinces are equally most eager to return to Poland. This is evident were it not by the great difficulties which the Russians are creating in respect of the admission of Jews to the ranks of the Polish troops raised among the deportees in the Soviet Union. The same sentiment and desire applies to the Polish citizens of Jewish faith in the Middle East, in England or those who have found refuge in the United States.

d/ General Sikorski feels it his duty to declare most emphatically that the whole Polish Nation would repudiate the recognition of any agreement conceding the annexation of those Polish territories to Russia and would in no lesser degree regard as null and void any such commitments on the part of our Ally, than if they had been made by the enemy. Indeed the surrender of any part of Polish territory would provoke a lasting state of tension in that part of Europe and would render impossible any form of collaboration with Russia.

e/ The foremost obligation of the Polish Government is the defence of the integrity of the Republic and consequently the Chief of the Polish Government has not the right whilst on foreign soil, to sign any agreement which might involve a diminution of Polish territory.

13. Nevertheless, in order to give further proof of good will, General Sikorski is prepared to go once more to Moscow and negotiate with Mr. Stalin a pact of friendship with Russia and discuss a number of other matters important to the shaping of future relations between the two Countries.

No. 284

Note from Chargé d'Affaires Valkov to Minister Raczyński containing the refusal of the Government of the USSR to single out German P.O.W.'s of Polish nationality and to transfer them to the Polish Army

London, January 11, 1943   GSHI, A.11. 49/Sow./3
                                              Transl. from Russian: Pol.-Sov.R., No. 55

On behalf of the Government of the USSR I have the honour to remind you that on the question of German prisoners of war of Polish nationality, which is the subject of your Note of December 15, 1942,[1] the People's Commissariat for Foreign Affairs has already had occasion to communicate to you, in the Note of January 23, 1942,[2] that for reasons indicated in this Note it does not find it possible to apply to Poles among German prisoners of war any régime other than that established for all German prisoners of war in general.

The attitude of the Soviet Government, as set forth in the Note of the People's Commissariat for Foreign Affairs of January 23, 1942, was confirmed twice: by the People's Commissariat in Kuibyshev and by the Soviet Embassy in London.

In reply to your Note of December 15, 1942, on the same question I have the honour to inform you that the Soviet Government cannot see any reason to reconsider their decision.

In regard to the Soviet radio broadcasts concerning the creation of Polish units in the German Army under the command of Polish officers, it is necessary to mention that the radio broadcast, the only one of its kind to take place in the course of the last two months, was based on positive facts. In the above broadcast the undeniable fact was recorded of the presence in the German Army of whole groups and units, consisting exclusively of Poles under Polish commanders whose names were given in the broadcast: Maritime Regiment, Colonel Polkowski; Commander of the 4th Company, Colonel Rakowski.

[1] See doc. No. 279.   [2] See doc. No. 174.

No. 285

Note from the People's Commissariat for Foreign Affairs to the Polish Embassy in the USSR claiming as Soviet citizens all persons who on November 1-2, 1939 found themselves on Polish territories occupied by the armed forces of the USSR

Kuibyshev, January 16, 1943   GSHI, A.11. 49/Sow./3
                                              Transl. from Russian: Pol.-Sov.R., No. 62

The People's Commissariat for Foreign Affairs has the honour to inform the Embassy of the Polish Republic of the following:

In connection with the exchange of Notes in the years 1941-1942 between the People's Commissariat for Foreign Affairs and the Embassy, concerning the citizenship of persons who previously lived in the Western districts of the

473

Ukrainian and White Ruthenian Soviet Socialist Republics, the People's Commissariat for Foreign Affairs informed the Embassy on December 1, 1941,[1] that all inhabitants of the above-mentioned districts who found themselves on the territories of these districts at the time of their entry into the Union of Soviet Socialist Republics (November 1–2, 1939), had acquired Soviet citizenship in accordance with the Decree of the Supreme Council of the USSR dated November 29, 1939,[2] and the Citizenship of the USSR Act of August 19, 1938.[3]

In its Note of December 1, 1941, the People's Commissariat for Foreign Affairs informed the Embassy that the Soviet Government were prepared, by way of exception, to regard as Polish citizens persons of Polish origin living in the territories of the above-mentioned districts on November 1–2, 1939. The People's Commissariat for Foreign Affairs is bound to state that despite the good will of the Soviet Government thus manifested, the Polish Government has adopted a negative attitude to the above statement of the Soviet Government and has refused to take the appropriate steps, putting forward demands contrary to the sovereign rights of the Soviet Union in respect to these territories.

In connection with the above, the People's Commissariat for Foreign Affairs, on instructions from the Soviet Government, gives notice that the statement included in the Note of December 1, 1941, regarding the readiness to treat some categories of persons of Polish origin on an exceptional basis must be considered as without validity and that the question of the possible non-application to such persons of the laws governing citizenship of the Union of Soviet Socialist Republics has ceased to exist.

[1] See doc. No. 157.   [2] See doc. No. 71.   [3] See appendix No. 1.

No. 286

Note from Minister Raczyński to Ambassador Bogomolov in reply to the Note of January 16, 1943 on the legal status of Polish citizens in the USSR

London, January 26, 1943   GSHI, A.11. 49/Sow./2

Dans la note de l'Ambassade de Pologne à Kouibychev en date du 9 décembre 1941,[1] le Gouvernement polonais a signifié son refus de prendre acte de la note du Commissariat du Peuple pour les Affaires Etrangères du 1 décembre 1941[2] par laquelle le Gouvernement soviétique se déclarait prêt à exclure, par mesure d'exception et de faveur, certaines catégories de personnes de nationalité polonaise de l'application du décret du Présidium Suprême de l'Union des Républiques Socialistes Soviétiques du 29 novembre 1939[3] ainsi que des lois qui leur confèrent la qualité de ressortissants de l'Union. La note précitée de l'Ambassade de Pologne relevait que l'octroi ou le retrait de la qualité de ressortissants polonais constitue un attribut exclusif et inaliénable de la souveraineté de l'État polonais dont, d'autre part, la législation ne fait pas de destinction de nationalité, de race ni de croyance parmi ses ressortissants.

[1] See doc. No. 163.   [2] See doc. No. 157.   [3] See doc. No. 71.

474

Depuis lors plus d'une année s'est passée au cours de laquelle les catégories mentionnées de Polonais séjournant dans l'Union ont été traitées en conformité avec leur qualité de ressortissants polonais. Toutefois, le Commissariat du Peuple pour les Affaires Etrangères vient d'informer l'Ambassade de Pologne à Kouibychev, par sa Note No. 12 du 16 janvier 1943, que le Gouvernement soviétique croit devoir annuler la déclaration contenue dans la note du 1 décembre 1941 et que, par conséquant la faculté de soustraire à la législation sur la ressortissance de l'Union des dites catégories de personnes de nationalité polonaise est dorénavant supprimée.

Maintenant son point de vue de principe sur le problème de la ressortissance, le Gouvernement polonais constate avec un profond regret que la communication soviétique du 16 janvier 1943[4] est incompatible avec l'esprit de l'Accord polono-soviétique du 30 juillet 1941[5] et de la déclaration commune des deux Gouvernements datée du 4 décembre 1941.[6]

Ces documents sont basés sur la conviction réciproque des deux parties contractantes que le rétablissement entre elles de relations normales et confiantes entraîne, dans l'intérêt de leur collaboration dans la présente lutte contre l'ennemi commun, et dans celui de leur bon voisinage d'après guerre, la négation d'un récent passé qui était contraire à ces arrangements. Aussi ne laissent-ils subsister aucun doute sur l'abolition des accords soviéto-allemands de 1939 et de leurs conséquences politiques et juridiques.

Je rappelle d'autre part, que d'après le point 1. du Protocole Additionnel à l'Accord polono-soviétique du 30 juillet 1941, le Gouvernement soviétique s'était engagé à mettre en liberté tous les ressortissants polonais détenus à quel titre que ce soit sur le territoire de l'Union. A la date du 30 juillet 1941 il n'y avait point sur ce territoire d'autres catégories de ressortissants polonais que celles auxquelles le Gouvernement soviétiques dénie actuellement cette qualité. C'est donc bien à ces mêmes personnes que l'amnistie fut appliquée en leur qualité de ressortissants polonais. Il faut souligner que le point susmentionné, qui avait fait l'objet de laborieuses négociations constitue une des clauses essentielles de l'Accord du 30 juillet 1941.

Le Gouvernement polonais s'est toujours refusé à reconnaître la validité des décisions unilatérales des autorités de l'Union des Républiques Socialistes Soviétiques, survenues à l'époque où il n'y avait point de relations polono-soviétiques et concernant, entre autres, l'imposition de la ressortissance de l'Union aux ressortissants polonais. Il convient d'ajouter, que des décisions de cet ordre sont incompatibles avec le droit international, tel qu'il est défini dans la IV Convention de la Haye de 1907, et avec les stipulations de la Charte Atlantique du 14 août 1941 à laquelle l'Union des Républiques Socialistes Soviétiques a adhéré dans la Déclaration des Nations Unies en date du 1 janvier 1942.[7]

Toujours désireux, en ce qui le concerne, d'entretenir avec l'Union des

[4] See doc. No. 285.　　　[5] See doc. No. 106.　　　[6] See doc. No. 161.

[7] The consequences of Soviet denial of Polish citizenship to nearly all Polish citizens deported to USSR, were examined in many aspects by Polish Ministry for Foreign Affairs during February and March, 1943 (GSHI, PRM, 102/2 and A.11. 49/Sow./6).

Républiques Socialistes Soviétiques les meilleurs rapports basés sur l'observation de tous les traités et arrangements existant entre les deux pays, le Gouvernement polonais se voit obligé d'insister afin que le Gouvernement soviétique réserve à tous les ressortissants polonais qui résident dans l'Union un traitement conforme à l'esprit et à la lettre de l'Accord du 30 juillet 1941 et aux principes d'équité et de liberté sur lesquels repose la collaboration de toutes les puissances unies dans la lutte contre l'ennemi et l'oppresseur commun.

No. 287

Aide-mémoire from Ambassador Raczyński to Ambassador Drexel Biddle on the infringement by the Soviet Government of the rights of Polish citizens in the USSR[1]

London, February 1, 1943   GSHI, A.11. 49/Sow./6

Following up the copies of a Soviet note of January 16th[2] and our answer of January 26th[3] which were handed over to you by Wszelaki, I am taking the liberty to send you enclosed a copy of an Aide-mémoire giving a fuller story of the sabotage by the Soviet Government of one of the essential stipulations of the Polish-Soviet Agreement of July 30th, 1941.[4]

Ambassador Ciechanowski has been instructed to discuss the matter with the State Department, and in his telegram of January 30th he was reporting about a conversation he had with the Department on the subject. It seemed to appear from his telegram that the State Department was not yet then in possession of the Soviet note and of our answer.

I should be extremely grateful to you for letting me know whether these texts have reached the State Department in full through your kind intermediary?

Aide-mémoire

The Polish-Soviet Agreement of July 30th, 1941,[4] which re-established diplomatic relations between Poland and Soviet Russia, included a Protocol, dealing with the position of large numbers of Polish citizens within the Soviet Union.

The first paragraph of the Protocol, which came into force simultaneously with the Agreement, reads as follows:

'As soon as diplomatic relations are re-established, the Government of the USSR shall grant amnesty to all Polish citizens, who at present are deprived of their liberty on the territory of the Soviet Union, either as prisoners of war or on any other adequate grounds.'

---

[1] Identical notes were sent to Mr. Churchill and Mr. Eden on February 5th and a similar memorandum to Under-Secretary Sumner Welles on January 30, 1943. (GSHI, A.11. 49/ Sow./6).

[2] See doc. No. 285.   [3] See doc. No. 286.   [4] See doc. No. 106.

In conformity with this Agreement, the Presidium of the Supreme Council of the USSR issued on August 12th, 1941, a Decree stipulating that:[5]

'Amnesty is being granted to all Polish citizens, who as prisoners of war, or on any other sufficient grounds are at present deprived of their liberty on Soviet territory.'

On the strength of the Decree, many thousands of Polish citizens were released from prisons and labour camps by the Soviet Government and, as stipulated by the Decree, during the first few months of its application no discrimination was made on account of the nationality or religion of the persons concerned. Similar principles were applied in connection with the organization of the Polish Army in the USSR and Polish citizens of various nationalities volunteered to enrol without any restrictions on the part of the Soviet authorities. Already by November 1941, this force rose to 44,000 officers and other ranks and was growing apace.*

2. In November 1941, the Soviet Government unexpectedly changed its attitude towards Polish citizens and proceeded to discriminate between Polish citizens of 'Polish nationality' and Polish citizens of 'other nationalities'. This new attitude was defined in the Note of the People's Foreign Commissariat to the Polish Embassy in Kuibyshev, dated December 1st, 1941,[6] stating that 'in accordance with the Decree of the Presidium of the Supreme Council of the USSR of November 29th, 1939,[7] all inhabitants of the Western districts of the Ukrainian and White-Russian Soviet Republics, who lived in those territories on November 1st/2nd 1939, acquired the citizenship of the USSR in accordance with the Soviet Citizenship Act of August 19th, 1938.[8] The willingness of the Soviet Government to regard as Polish citizens such persons of Polish nationality, who lived on those territories on November 1st/2nd, 1939, testifies to the good will and spirit of compromise of the Soviet Government, but can in no way serve as a basis for the recognition of persons of other nationalities as Polish citizens. . . .'

This Note pretended to restrict the recognition of Polish citizenship only to persons of Polish nationality. The Polish Government have firmly refused to accept this contention. In practice the Soviet authorities insisted on applying their discrimination rigidly in military cases. Polish social welfare on the other hand continued to include a large proportion of Polish citizens of Jewish, Ukrainian and White-Russian nationality.

3. Towards the end of December 1941, the Soviet Government, after prolonged negotiations regarding material help for Polish citizens, agreed to the organization on the territory of the USSR of a network of Polish social welfare centres conducted by about 20 Embassy delegates and over 300 local representatives in the various districts. While this work of relief was fully

---

[5] See doc. No. 110.   [6] See doc. No. 157.   [7] See doc. No. 71.   [8] See appendix No. 1.

* [Remark on the orig. doc.]. By July, 1942, the number increased to 72,000, notwithstanding restrictions introduced by the Soviet authorities with regard to the nationality of those volunteering and, later also of those compulsorily enrolled, whereby Ukrainian, White-Russian and Jewish citizens of the Polish Republic were denied the right to be enrolled into the Polish Army.

under way and when already large quantities of goods were being received from abroad, the Soviet Government ordered in July 1942 the compulsory liquidation of this newly established organization, which had been set up in full agreement with the Soviet authorities. Many persons were arrested, including all the Embassy delegates and over 100 local representatives, as well as numerous employees of the relief officers.

During the ensuing dispute concerning the organization of relief and social welfare for the Poles in Russia, the Soviet Government gave repeated assurances (statements made by Premier Stalin, People's Foreign Commissar Molotov, his assistant M. Vyshinsky and Ambassador Bogomolov) to the representatives of the British, American and Polish Governments, that they have no objections whatever to the continuation of this relief, and only withhold their consent to the re-appointment of the delegates of the Polish Embassy.

4. In order to reach an agreement with the Soviet Government the newly appointed Polish Ambassador, Monsieur Romer, submitted in November and December 1942, plans for a new organization of social welfare. The principles of this new scheme have been accepted by Monsieur Vyshinsky, and the final agreement was to take place after Ambassador Romer's return from London. Quite unexpectedly in the absence of the Ambassador, on January 16th, 1943, in their Note to the Polish Embassy in Kuibyshev, the People's Foreign Commissariat stated that the Soviet Government consider as null and void their declaration made in the Note of December 1st, 1941, exempting persons of Polish nationality from the provisions of the Decree of November 29th, 1939, and of the 'Soviet Citizenship Act' of August 19th, 1938.

Thus, the citizenship of the USSR is enforced without exception on all Polish citizens at present on the territory of the Soviet Union.

5. It is obvious from the above that in the course of the last 18 months the Soviet Government have moved a long way from the principles agreed to in the Polish-Soviet Treaty of July 30th, 1941: On the strength of paragraph 1 of the Protocol to the Polish-Soviet Agreement of July 30th, 1941, all Polish citizens who were at that time on Soviet territory and who were deprived of their liberty were granted amnesty. This implied the recognition by the Soviet Government of their Polish citizenship, as shown clearly by the Decree of the Presidium of the Supreme Council of the USSR of August 12th, 1941, quoted above. In December 1941 the recognition of Polish citizenship was limited exclusively to those of Polish nationality and on January 16th, 1943, an attempt was made to consider even the latter as citizens of the USSR.

Thus, contrary to the letter and the spirit of the Polish-Soviet Agreement of July 30th, 1941, and contrary to the fundamental principles of international law, all Polish citizens are threatened with conscription into the Red Army. At the same time, they are in danger of being deprived of all material help granted to them by the Polish Government, as well as of gifts and assistance so generously offered to them from Great Britain and from the United States of America.

No. 288

Letter from General Sikorski to M. Stalin concerning his forthcoming conversation with Ambassador Romer

London, February 9, 1943   GSHI, PRM, 101/1

Les grandes victoires remportées par l'Armée Rouge sur notre ennemi commun remplissent d'admiration le monde entier. Je tiens, moi aussi, à vous en féliciter sincèrement en votre qualité de Commandant suprême des forces armées soviétiques. Je n'ai jamais douté de leurs succès, car j'en ai toujours reconnu la vraie valeur.

Je regrette que, pour le moment, les forces que je commande ne prennent part à cette lutte que sur des fronts distants, et non pas, à coté des vôtres, sur le front oriental d'Europe. Attendu avec impatience, l'écrasement final de l'Allemagne approche. Il apportera aussi, j'en ai la certitude, l'indépendance de la Pologne. Elle continue en attendant à offrir à l'oppresseur une résist- ance héroïque que n'arrivent pas à fléchir les sollicitations récentes de l'ennemi s'efforçant de gagner la collaboration de la population polonaise par la promesse de renoncer au régime de terreur.

Ainsi, l'issue de la guerre se présente à nous sous aspect rassurant. Cependant, je me vois obligé de vous signaler, en toute sincérité, la pré- occupation croissante qu'inspirent au Gouvernement Polonais et à l'opinion publique de la Pologne les difficultés de plus en plus sérieuses qui se dressent sur la voie de l'entente polono-soviétique inaugurée en 1941 par vous, Monsieur le Président, et par moi-même. Ces difficultés risquent de la compromettre et de mal servir les intérêts de nos deux pays et celui de notre cause commune. Elles ne me semblent ni justifiées ni inévitables, et je persiste à croire qu'examinées de part et d'autre, dans un large esprit de compréhension et de conciliation réciproque, elles peuvent être écartées.

Tel est du moins, le désir du Gouvernement polonais qui reste fermement convaincu de l'utilité de la politique de rapprochement et de collaboration entre la Pologne et l'Union Soviétique, autant en vue de la poursuite de la guerre contre l'Allemagne que des relations futures de bon voisinage entre nos deux pays. Pour être acceptable aux Polonais, pour être durable, pour être jugée conforme aux grands principes qui nous sont communs à tous dans la présente lutte, cette politique ne saurait toutefois, ni en raison du moment, ni à cause de la disproportion des forces en jeu, consister à éliminer les difficultés que se présentent en demandant à la Pologne un abandon quelconque de principe ou des sacrifices unilatéraux. Les épreuves exception- nelles qui mon pays a endurées, et l'attitude qu'il a su leur opposer aux yeux du monde entier, lui valent—je n'en doute pas—une considération spéciale pour ses intérêts et pour ses aspirations au moment où la guerre de libération entre dans une phase décisive.

C'est dans cet esprit que j'ai eu dernièrement l'occasion de procéder à des échanges de vues avec le Président Roosevelt et avec le Gouvernement américain au sujet de la conduite de la guerre et des solutions que pourrait comporter sa conclusion, y compris l'élimination définitive du danger allemand, et la tâche de reconstruction économique de l'Europe de demain. Ces mêmes problèmes font l'objet de consultations du Gouvernement polonais avec le Gouvernement britannique et avec les Gouvernements résidant á Londres des différents pays d'Europe sous l'occupation allemande.

Je n'ai pas manqué de souligner, à plusieurs occasions, que le Gouvernement polonais serait désireux d'étudier, au même titre, les dits problèmes avec le Gouvernement soviétique dans le cadre des relations réciproques créées par l'accord du 30 Juillet 1941[1] et de notre déclaration commune du 4 Décembre 1941.[2]

Si vous partagez mon point de vus à ce propos, je vous serais obligé de bien vouloir consacrer un moment de votre précieux temps, à recevoir l'Ambassadeur Romer qui retourne à son poste après avoir pris contact avec son Gouvernement et avec moi-même, et qui en possession de ma pleine et entière confiance, est chargé par moi de vous exposer les détails de mes récentes négociations et le point de vue du Gouvernement Polonais. Cette entrevue lui donnerait également l'opportunité de vous parler en mon nom, des difficultés polono-soviétiques auxquelles j'ai fais allusion dans cette lettre et qui me semblent mériter notre sérieuse attention.

[1] See doc. No. 106.   [2] See doc. No. 161.

No. 289

Letter from General Sikorski to Mr. Churchill concerning the refusal of the Soviet Government to consider the inhabitants of Polish Eastern territories as Polish citizens and the discontinuation of the relief for the Polish population in the USSR

London, February 9, 1943   GSHI, PRM, 95

On January 16th the Polish Chargé d'Affaires in Kuibyshev received a note from the Soviet Commissariat of Foreign Affairs, in which the Soviet Government declared that henceforth they refuse to recognize as Polish citizens all persons who on November 1st and 2nd, 1939, were domiciled on Polish territories occupied by the Soviet Armies.[1] A translation of this document, together with a copy of the Polish reply of January 26th,[2] refuting Soviet claims and assertions, were communicated without delay by Count Raczyński to Mr. Eden. A few days later Count Raczyński also communicated to the Foreign Secretary reports received from Soviet Russia to the effect that in execution of their threats Soviet authorities actually proceeded to deprive the Poles, whom they themselves have forcibly deported to the USSR, of the protection of the Polish authorities and of the assistance of the Polish Welfare organization. This latter fact, which threatens all Polish citizens on the territories of the Soviet Union with complete extinction, is the immediate cause of my present letter to you.

[1] i.e. at the time of the so-called 'plebiscites', carried out by the Soviet authorities of occupation. See doc. No. 285.
[2] See doc. No. 286.

I need not recall here the principles by which Poland's conduct was guided from the day of the signature of the Treaty of Alliance with Great Britain until today:[3] her straightforward policy and the fidelity of the Polish nation to the common cause. The utterly unyielding attitude adopted uncompromisingly by Poland alone on the Continent of Europe, not only exposed her to all the more cruel oppression at the hands of the enemy, but it failed to protect her from the grievous wrongs suffered at the hands of her Eastern neighbour, who joined the camp of the fighting Democracies nearly two years after the outbreak of the war and even then not on the strength of his own decision but consequent upon the action of Germany.

The Polish Government, acting with the utmost consistency and in close understanding with the British Government, were ready—after the German attack on the Soviets—to forget the wrongs suffered, for the sake of solidarity in the struggle against the common enemy, and ready to continue friendly, neighbourly collaboration after the achievement of victory. This attitude found its expression in the Polish-Soviet Agreement of July 30th, 1941,[4] supplemented by the Declaration made on the same day by the Foreign Secretary Mr. Eden in the House of Commons,[5] stating inter alia, that the British Government '. . . do not recognize any territorial changes which have been effected in Poland since August 1939'.

The Polish Government faithfully abide by the signed undertaking and have on all subsequent occasions declared their readiness to collaborate with Russia not only in matters of direct concern to them but also in general European matters. The Soviet Government, on the other hand, act contrary to the written Agreement in essential and fundamental points. It will suffice to mention the suspension of recruitment for the Polish Army in the Spring, 1942, the formation of which was safeguarded by Article IV of the Polish-Soviet Agreement of July 30th, 1941, and to point out the present attitude of the Soviets with regard to the question of Polish citizenship, which the Government of the USSR attempted at first to restrict or to question and which today they actually deny to all Polish citizens. On this basis the Soviet authorities are proceeding at present with the conscription of Polish citizens for the Red Army and at the same time with the final liquidation of the Polish Welfare organization.

The enclosed Aide-mémoire contains a detailed and up to date account of this matter.[6]

The Soviet actions referred to above are contrary to international law and violate the latter and the spirit of the Polish-Soviet Agreement, concluded with the active participation of our British Ally, and must be regarded as an unfriendly act directed against an Ally fighting in defence of the same cause and of the same proclaimed principles.

Owing to the prohibition of the departures from the USSR of the Polish orphans and members of the families of Polish officers and other ranks, which produced a profound indignation among Polish troops in the Middle East, I

---

[3] See appendix No. 4.
[5] See doc. No. 108.
[4] See doc. No. 106.
[6] Not printed.

have been obliged to issue a secret Order of the day to all units of the Polish armed forces. The difficulties provoked by the Soviets have, in the absence of any reaction on the part of our great Allies, caused profound anxiety and misgivings in Poland.

The Polish Ambassador in Moscow, M. Romer, who came recently to London in order to consult the Polish Government directly, is taking back with him a personal letter from me to M. Stalin, in which I make one more attempt to bring about a friendly turn in our mutual relations.[7]

I am aware of the difficulties in securing a change in Soviet policy in a period of such marked successes of the Red Army. I am equally well aware, however, that in Poland the Germans stint no efforts in order to gain over the Poles against the Soviets.

In order to avert the creation of further accomplished facts by the Soviet Government, I take the liberty, my dear Prime Minister, to request you to cause an immediate intervention on our behalf in Moscow, in defence of the most fundamental rights of allied Poland, in the first place of her right to protect and to succour her own citizens in their dire need.

[7] See doc. No. 288.

No. 290

Note from Ambassador Bogomolov to Minister Raczyński in reply to the Note of January 26, 1943 concerning the legal status of Polish citizens in the USSR

London, February 17, 1943 GSHI, A.11.49/Sow./3
Transl. from Russian: Pol.-Sov.R., No. 64

With reference to your Note of January 26, 1943,[1] I have the honour to inform you that the Soviet Government do not regard it as possible to reconsider the subject of the citizenship of those persons who on November 1-2, 1939, found themselves on the territory of the western districts of the Ukrainian and White Ruthenian Soviet Socialist Republics, since this matter remains wholly within the sovereign rights of the Soviet Union over these territories.

As to your assertion regarding the incompatibility of the Soviet Government's statement of January 16, 1943,[2] with the spirit of the Polish-Soviet Agreement of July 30, 1941,[3] the Declaration of December 4, 1941,[4] the IVth Hague Convention of 1907 and the Atlantic Charter of August 14, 1941, such an assertion is devoid of all foundation. The Soviet Government also emphatically reject the statement of the Polish Government contained in the Note of January 26, about the alleged forcing of Soviet citizenship upon the above-mentioned persons, as entirely unfounded and a distortion of the true state of affairs.

The Soviet Government consider it imperative to recall that citizens of the western districts of the Ukrainian and White Ruthenian Socialist Soviet Republics acquired Soviet citizenship exclusively on the strength of the freely

[1] See doc. No. 286.   [2] See doc. No. 285.
[3] See doc. No. 106.   [4] See doc. No. 161.

482

voiced will of the population which found its expression in the unanimous resolutions adopted by the people's assemblies of the districts in question, and the Decree of the Supreme Council of the Union of Soviet Socialist Republics, issued on November 29, 1939,[5] in accordance with these resolutions.

[5] See doc. No. 71.

No. 291

Excerpts from the minutes of the conversation at the Kremlin between Ambassador Romer and Commissar Molotov on the crisis in Polish-Soviet relations

Moscow, February 20, 1943   GSHI, A.11. 49/Sow./4
                        Transl. from Polish: Pol.-Sov.R., No. 87/1

[. . .]. Romer: We find ourselves at present, Mr. Commissar, in a historical moment as far as Polish-Soviet relations are concerned. The steps we take now will decide the course of those relations for many years to come. Bearing this in mind, I think, we ought to avoid the discussion of such issues as cannot be settled today and which would only strain our relations. On the other hand what we should discuss is the problem of relief for the Poles in the USSR whose fate is causing the Polish Government special concern.

Molotov: The basis of this problem is our Note of January 16,[1] last, in which the Soviet Government declined to recognize as Polish citizens persons who on November 1 and 2, 1939 found themselves in the western districts of the Ukraine and White Ruthenia.

Romer: What are the reasons, Mr. Commissar, for this change in the attitude of the Soviet Government?

Molotov: The reasons are explained in the Note. Our good will did not meet with an appropriate response from the Polish Government. Now we simply confirmed this.

Romer: Truly, Mr. Commissar, I fail to see any motive for this sudden decision which fundamentally changes the problem of relief for the Polish population.

Molotov: Mr. Ambassador, December 1941 went by and so did the whole of 1942 and in spite of this the Polish Government never accepted the proposals put forward by the Soviet Government.

Romer: The January Note came unexpectedly at a time when negotiations concerning relief for the Poles were well advanced and reaching their final stage. I fail to understand what new development occurred to bring about such a decision on the part of the Government of the USSR.

Molotov: This subject has been discussed not only with you, Mr. Ambassador, but also with your predecessor. The problem could not have come as a surprise after our Note of December 1, 1941;[2] on the other hand, however, the attitude of the Polish Government has remained unchanged ever since. This could not continue.

[1] See doc. No. 285.   [2] See doc. No. 157.

483

Romer: This matter is for us of paramount importance. An attempt to deprive us of hundreds of thousands of Poles who are in the USSR not of their own will, and this at a time when the population of Poland is being decimated as a result of the atrocities committed by the German occupants, is for us a most painful blow and cannot but have a serious effect on Polish-Soviet relations.

Molotov: It is not proper, Mr. Ambassador, to connect this problem with that of German persecutions in Poland. The Government of the USSR has waited long enough for a reply to the proposals it advanced, only by way of exception and good will.

Romer: I point out that this matter has never been raised before in the course of my conversations with you and with Commissar Vyshinsky.

Molotov: On the contrary, Mr. Ambassador, during your tenure of office, we have received Notes in which our attitude was not recognized.

Romer: Am I to understand, Mr. Commissar, that the attitude of the Soviet Government to this problem is connected with the future Polish-Soviet frontier, or is it confined to citizenship?

Molotov: Our Note merely concerns our attitude towards citizenship, which in turn is connected with the problem of the frontiers of the Soviet Union.

Romer: I cannot share your attitude with regard to citizenship, Mr. Commissar. The Government of the USSR could not unilaterally force Soviet citizenship upon Polish citizens. In our eyes, and in the eyes of impartial foreign observers, the matter could only have been settled on the basis of an agreement between the two Governments concerned.

Molotov: No foreign observers will be able to change decisions taken by the Supreme Council of the USSR with regard to the incorporation of the territories in question, which took place on the basis of a plebiscite in which the people freely expressed themselves.

Romer: I do not wish to go deeper into the discussion of this problem. But I shall make two remarks. First—what you referred to as a plebiscite took place within the frontiers set up by the Soviet-German treaty, which the Soviet Government later solemnly renounced in the Polish-Soviet Agreement. Second—Soviet legislation governing citizenship is contrary to its territorial principle as it grants Soviet citizenship not according to domicile, but according to where a given person happened to be at a given time. These are merely incidental remarks independent of the fundamental attitude of my Government to this problem as a whole.

Molotov: Our Note refers to the Soviet citizenship of persons who found themselves on the territories in question on November 1 and 2, 1939. Persons who arrived there subsequent to that date are Polish citizens.

Romer: Does it not then seem unnatural, even from the Soviet viewpoint, that persons who have no connection whatever with these territories should be considered Soviet citizens against their own will?

Molotov: I do not agree with your view. In accordance with Soviet legislation, the Soviet Citizenship Act also applies to persons who came to

Western Ukraine and Western White Ruthenia from the Western districts of Poland.

Romer: I want to make it quite clear, Mr. Commissar. Am I, therefore, to understand that the relief work to assist our people in the USSR is to be regarded as at an end?

Molotov: We examined this problem in our Note of January 16, 1943. Exceptions were made in respect of persons whom we recognize as Polish citizens, that is those who arrived in the territories we consider to be Soviet after November 1 and 2, 1939.

Romer: Practically, one would then be able to count the number of Polish citizens in the USSR on one's fingers. Do you realize, Mr. Commissar, what consequences will result from the application of the Note of January 16, 1943, and in what position the Poles in the USSR will find themselves?

Molotov: Their position will not suffer as a result of it, Mr. Ambassador. All that was being done for them before, we shall continue to do as for our own citizens.

Romer: Irrespective of the deep and painful impression which a decision of this kind would make on the Polish Government and on our people in occupied Poland and abroad, representing as it does, in the present extremely hard circumstances, an entirely unjustified attempt to force foreign citizenship upon a considerable part of our nation, and this against their will, sentiments and traditions which are bound up with the struggle for independence and our most sacred ideals, I want again to draw your attention to the impression this will make abroad, and especially in the countries which collaborated with us in bringing relief to several hundred thousand Polish citizens, and who from one day to the next will learn to their surprise that these people have ceased to be Poles and no longer require their assistance.

Molotov: As you are aware, Mr. Ambassador, there have been for many years a considerable number of Poles in the USSR, Soviet citizens and who have never considered themselves treated any worse than Soviet citizens of other origins. There was never any question of restricting their rights, for our Constitution severely punishes all actions contrary to our principle of national equality. But as regards the subject referred to by you, Mr. Ambassador, I wish once more to state that the entire blame rests with the Polish Government. Now, as early as 1941, we made a concession and agreed not to apply our legislation, showing our good will to recognize Poles as Polish citizens. The Polish Government did not appear to be willing to accept our good will, on the contrary it rejected our proposals. We waited a month, two months, a year—and the attitude of the Polish Government remained unchanged, nor has it changed since your arrival, Mr. Ambassador. Thus, the Polish Government bear the entire responsibility for the consequences.

Romer: I must point out, that the Polish Government never rejected the Soviet Government's readiness to recognize Poles in the USSR as Polish citizens, but it could not accept the terms on which this readiness was conditional, and in particular it had to reject the attempt to distinguish between Polish citizens and divide them into categories for discriminatory treatment, that is unknown to Polish law. I must emphasize once again that this is the first time since I am Ambassador in the USSR that this problem has been raised, and I see no reason for the change made by the Note of January 16, 1943 in the previous attitude of the Soviet Government.

Molotov: I have already stated the position of the Soviet Government, Mr. Ambassador. It is clear and irrevocable.

Romer: The problem is so fundamental and its consequences so serious, that I shall have to inform my Government of your declaration, Mr. Commissar, and at the same time refer the matter to renewed consideration by ourselves. For the time I only renew my request that you transmit the letter of Prime Minister General Sikorski to Premier Stalin and beg him to receive me so that I may submit to him the matters I have already referred to and learn his views on the difficulties in Polish-Soviet relations.

Molotov: I shall forward the letter, Mr. Ambassador, and when I find out about your visit to J. V. Stalin, I shall let you know.

No. 292

Declarations of the Polish National Council concerning Polish-Soviet relations

London, February 20, 1943 GSHI, A.5/3
Transl. from Polish

At its meeting of 20th February 1943 the National Council of the Republic of Poland unanimously passed the following resolution:

After having heard the report on the meeting of the Commission of Foreign Affairs on 18th February, 1943, at which a statement was delivered by the Acting Minister for Foreign Affairs, Raczyński, the National Council states what follows:

The National Council, making common cause with the Government, and upholding the view that the difficulties barring the way to a trustful cooperation between the Allied Nations should be removed, declares that the integrity of the Territory of the Republic of Poland within its frontiers of 1st September, 1939, and its sovereignty, are intangible and indivisible. No unilateral and illegal acts on anybody's part, directed against the territory and sovereignty of the Republic of Poland or against the rights of its citizens, both in the home-country and abroad, are able to change this state of things.

No. 293

Memorandum from Minister Raczyński to Mr. Eden concerning the violations of the rights of Polish citizens by the Soviet Government, the relief scheme and the evacuation of the families of Polish soldiers from the USSR

London, February 23, 1943 GSHI, A.11. 49/Sow./6

Count Raczyński informed Mr. Eden that General Sikorski thanked him

---

[1] This Memorandum followed the conversation between Mr. Eden and Minister Raczyński on February 19, 1943.

for the words of warning which he had conveyed through Sir Alexander Cadogan.

General Sikorski was contemplating a journey to the Middle East to visit the Polish troops in that region. This journey may take place in the course of the month of March.

General Sikorski has received from General Anders a telegram which he deems to be entirely satisfactory.

Count Raczyński pointed out that amongst Polish civilians and soldiers in this country as well as in the Near East there existed a state of excitement which was exploited by irresponsible individuals to launch accusations against the Polish Government on account of their allegedly weak and insufficient reactions to Soviet provocations.

Count Raczyński further set out that strong reasons undoubtedly existed for the excitement prevailing amongst the Poles. The Soviet Government have, in the course of recent months which brought such successes to Russian arms, taken an entirely uncompromising and unfriendly attitude with regard to the most essential Polish interests. In doing so they evinced no respect for the stipulations of the Polish-Soviet Agreement of July 30th, 1941.[2] After arresting the Polish officials dealing with relief for Polish citizens in the Soviet Union and 'men of trust' in the different districts, they have since been continually placing numerous difficulties in the way of Polish relief work. They have prevented the departure from Russia of the families of Polish soldiers in the Middle East and of Polish children, notwithstanding certain promises which had been made of a more liberal attitude in this respect. They finally, on January 16th, denied the right of Polish citizenship to practically all the hundreds of thousands of Poles deported to the Soviet Union.[3] Since then the Soviet authorities have drawn practical conclusions from their note proceeding gradually towards the total liquidation of any Polish activity linked with the Polish Embassy in Kuibyshev. The continuous care expended by the Polish Government and by the Embassy to avoid any step which could be construed as a provocation has not unfortunately brought about any improvement in Polish-Soviet relations. It seems likely that the Soviet-Government are themselves welcoming the growing tension, and that the lack of proper reaction on the part of Poland's Western Allies and friends is interpreted as an argument in favour of still more drastic steps. As pointed out above these have now taken the shape of a direct violation of the spirit of the Polish-Soviet Agreement of July 30th, 1941, and of that of the Atlantic Charter.

The Polish Ambassador in Washington, Ciechanowski, has discussed this matter with the State Department and also directly with President Roosevelt. In the course of these conversations he has not only asked for diplomatic support on the part of the State Department and of the American Ambassador in Russia, but he has also discussed the need for a straightforward declaration reiterating the decision of the United States not to recognize any unilateral act accomplished in the course of the present war by any country

[2] See doc. No. 106.   [3] See doc. No. 385.

whatsoever against the rights or territories of another country. Such a declaration which we hope will be issued jointly or at least simultaneously by both the British and the United States governments would powerfully support and complete any Allied diplomatic action in Moscow. In the case of the British Government the issuing of the declaration seems the more justified and indicated that it would but follow the statement made by Mr. Eden in the House of Commons on the day of the signature of the Polish-Soviet Agreement: 'That His Majesty's Government do not recognize any territorial changes which have been effected in Poland since August 1939.' [4] The declaration would, provided that it is sufficiently clear and unequivocal, go a long way towards restoring the legal position violated by the Soviet decisions. It would vindicate the good faith of Poland and of the Polish Government. At the same time it would be designed to save Great Britain and America a great deal of disappointments and difficulties in the future. A clear and firm attitude shown at a moment when the matter still remains in the domain of principle and not of fact, still less of accomplished facts—appears from every point of view as the best and the safest course.

[4] From the note of Mr. Eden to General Sikorski of July 30, 1941. See doc. No. 107.

No. 294

Declaration of the Polish Government concerning Polish-Soviet relations

London, February 25, 1943 GSHI, PRM, 103/1
Transl. from Polish: Pol.-Sov.R., No. 83

The Polish Government, at a meeting in London on February 25, presided over by General Sikorski, discussed Polish-Soviet relations and issued the following declaration:

The Polish Government affirm that neither before the outbreak of this war nor during it has the Polish nation ever agreed to any co-operation with the Germans against the Soviet Union. In her relations with the USSR Poland has not ceased to be ready to co-operate with the Soviet Union in the prosecution of the war and in maintaining friendly, neighbourly relations after the victory.

The Polish Government repudiate most definitely the malicious propaganda which accuses Poland of indirect or direct inimical tendencies towards Soviet Russia. It is absolutely absurd to suspect Poland of intentions to base the eastern boundaries of the Polish Republic on the Dnieper and the Black Sea, or to impute to Poland any tendencies to move her frontier farther to the east.

The Polish Government, representing Poland in the boundaries in which Poland, first among the Allied nations, took up the fight imposed on her, have, from the moment of the conclusion of the Polish-Soviet Treaty of July 30, 1941,[1] maintained the unchangeable attitude that so far as the question of frontiers between Poland and Soviet Russia is concerned, the

[1] See doc. No. 106.

status quo previous to September 1, 1939, is in force; and they consider the undermining of this attitude, which is in conformity with the Atlantic Charter, as detrimental to the unity of the Allied nations.

The Polish Government consider close co-operation and confidence between all the Allies to be an indispensable factor for victory and a permanent peace, and condemn all acts and suggestions tending to wreck or weaken the common front of the United Nations.

No. 295

Minutes of Ambassador Romer's conversation with President Stalin and M. Molotov, at the Kremlin, during the night of February 26–27, 1943, on some capital issues in Polish-Soviet relations producing a state of tension between Poland and USSR

Moscow, February 26–27, 1943 GSHI, A.11. 49/Sow./4
Transl. from Polish

Stalin: After an exchange of greetings he invites M. Romer to take a seat at the conference table.

Romer: I wish to thank you, Mr. President, for receiving me, and I should like, at the same time, to associate myself with the wishes conveyed to you by the Government of the Republic of Poland on the occasion of the 25th anniversary of the creation of the Red Army, and on its great victories over our common enemy.

Stalin: I thank you for your wishes, and as to my receiving you, that is my duty.

Romer: I prefer not to trouble you with an account of General Sikorski's journey to America, as I had an opportunity of speaking about it with M. Molotov. I wish, instead, to submit another very important issue to you.

Stalin: Please do.

Romer: I should like to speak, in the first instance, of the call-up of Poles to the German army. Quite recently, about 250,000 young men from the western provinces of Poland, which the Reich 'annexed', were enlisted with the German forces. In accordance with our instructions those young men try to evade conscription by all possible means, even by escaping abroad. However, this is not quite practicable, because the number of conscripts who have succeeded in evading military service is, in our view, not very big. Heretofore we have had no exact information about their use at the front, apart from that coming from Soviet sources. We know only that they are assigned to mixed Polish-German units, under strict control of Hitlerite cadres. We know also that not a single officer was called up.

Stalin: We do not know anything about the instructions issued by the Polish Government, enjoining the Poles to evade conscription to the German army. As a matter of fact, information of a different kind reached us. A rather big number of Poles was captured with General Paulus' army.

Romer: Are they young?

Stalin: Yes.

489

Romer: What may be their number, approximately?

Stalin: A couple of thousands. At Leningrad also there were many Poles who surrendered to us, but some others fought there extremely gallantly. So far as I know they were not Mazurs [Polish-speaking population of East Prussia].

Romer: Which part of Poland do they come from?

Stalin: There were among them Poles from Poznań, Cracow and other western provinces. According to our information, it seems ('kak budto'—in Russian) that the Polish Government issued instructions to the Poles to enlist with the German army and then surrender. As regards the instruction enjoining the evading by Poles of service with the German army, the question is not quite clear to me. This is the first time that I hear of it.

Romer: I can assure you, Sir, that there are no Poles who would be willing to enlist voluntarily with the German army. We have information about soldiers of the Red army, taken prisoner, from among whom the Germans form units of volunteers to fight against the USSR. In both cases, this is the effect of German propaganda. I lately came across a German newspaper 'Signal' with photos of the units composed of former prisoners of war, of Ukrainian, Russian, Georgian, Azerbeijanian, etc. descent, ready to fight against the Red Army.

Stalin: Azerbeijanians and others deliberately join such units, and then pass over to us. There is a considerable number of Poles serving with German regiments and staffs in the capacity of interpreters.

Romer: Are they not rather Germans conversant with the Polish language?

Stalin: No, they are Poles, but there are also Russians who advisedly serve the Germans and side with them. There are outcasts in every family ('nyet semyi bez uroda'—in Russian).

In relation to the question of Poles passing over to the Red Army—should the mentioned appeal be launched, the Germans would very soon get wind of it, and they would then scatter the Poles among German units. We witnessed similar cases with Slovaks. The Germans have executed whole units of them. Although the volunteers of Danish, Norwegian, Dutch and other nationalities are grouped in separate units, it does not count for much. We know that there are some disciplinary detachments in the German army which are placed just behind the front-line, and which ruthlessly exterminate all those who refuse to fight. It is much easier for Rumanians and Italians to surrender, who, by the way, eventually got a severe beating and lost all the lust for battle, because they step out in close formations, while the Poles are able to cross the front-line but singly or, at the best, in very small groups. It will be very difficult to organize it.

Romer: You have said, nevertheless, Mr. President, that many Poles have been captured. I think that one should take this problem under consideration. I should be obliged to you, Mr. President, for giving me advice.

Stalin: The passing over to us has to be done during the fight, in difficult conditions, because both the Germans and the Russians are shooting. Our forces suffer losses also from Polish hands; the people, about whom we are speaking try, above all, to save their own skins. It is very difficult to cross the front-line. You ask me, Mr. Ambassador, for advice as how to influence the Poles in the ranks of the German army, how to impress them. It is a very difficult problem, because they are scattered among German soldiers and closely watched.

Romer: It would be best to act in the earlier stages through our underground organizations in the home-country, by means of a skilful propaganda before the call-up, pointing out the possibility of joining the Polish Army after they have crossed over to the Soviet side. This would be the most convincing argument. May I ask what happens to the Poles captured by the Red Army, and how they are treated?

Stalin: They have the usual status of prisoners of war. Those who can work are working, and the sick undergo treatment. They are treated as prisoners of war.

Romer: It would be of utmost assistance to me to obtain an assurance that those Poles who are forced to serve with the German army, and who passed over to the Soviet side of their own free will, would be able to reckon on the possibility of fighting against the Germans under their own national colours, the spies and agents-provocateurs being naturally excluded, after a proper investigation, carried out by competent Soviet and Polish bodies.

Stalin (interrupts): Last year, during the offensive against Moscow, no, it was during the winter, a Polish-Lithuanian battalion, a selected one ('otbornyi batalion'—in Russian) appeared on the front. They fought very gallantly, being devoted to the Germans with utmost conviction. They have been exterminated by us to the last man.

Romer: Does the Soviet Government make any distinction between those prisoners who surrendered of their own free will, and those who were captured carrying arms?

Stalin: Of course, a distinction is being made, but it is difficult to establish it as a rule. During the whole of the present war there was one case only in which 2–3 German battalions killed their officers and surrendered. As a rule the Germans surrender only when they are in circumstances beyond their control, and not because they sympathize with the Soviet State ('ot nuzhdy, a nie ot sochustviya sovietskomu gosudarstvu'—in Russian). Such was the case of the Paulus army. So far as advice to Poles is concerned, it is a very difficult question. Every advice is dangerous. I wish to give the following advice to the Polish Government. I would give an order that the call-up to the German army be evaded. Those who are mobilized should therefore escape to the woods, and join the partisans. In this way, the number of the latter will increase, and thus the diversionist action in the home-country will be reinforced. One should oppose German conscription, go to the woods, join the partisans.

Romer: As I have said, in the western provinces of Poland, that is in those parts of the country in which the Germans call up, there are no big woods, and there is no place in which to hide. As the Soviet Government makes distinction between those who surrendered of their own free will, and those who were captured carrying arms, I do not doubt that a distinction will be made between soldiers of German nationality, and those who belong to friendly nations such as Czechs and Poles. Friends should be treated in a different way from enemies, and they should be won over by a promise that after they have crossed over to our side they will regain freedom and will be able, side by side with the Red Army, to fight against the Germans for the common cause, under their own national colours.

Stalin: Your point of view is right, in principle, Mr. Ambassador. Of course we make a distinction between prisoners of different nationalities. However, one must be cautious. We shall try to make an appeal to the Poles through the Command of the Red Army. There is a snag, however, in this case. After such a loud appeal the Germans will watch the Poles more closely.

Romer: This is why I think it would be better to enlighten the Poles while still in their home-country, through our underground organizations, before they have been called-up; this would raise no suspicion on the German side. What is necessary, however, is a previous assurance from the Soviet Government that it would agree to hand over to the Polish Army those who passed over to the Soviet side of their own free will.

Stalin: Do you know, Mr. Ambassador, what happens to the Slovak soldiers? When the Slovaks began to cross over to the Soviet side, the Germans withdrew those units to the rear behind the front-line. Having those units serving in the rear allowed for a corresponding number of Germans to be released and sent to the front. The same occurs with the Bulgarian army, which indirectly helps the Germans. Should we launch an appeal, the Germans will not let the Poles go to the front, and by assigning them to rear formations, they will have more Germans available for the front. The idea is right that the Poles should serve their country once they have crossed over to the Red Army line, but the question must be examined from all points of view. Should the Polish Underground organizations issue such an order, the Germans would react to it by not assigning Poles to front formations. On the other hand, should big numbers of Poles be enlisted with the German army, the whole sabotage action in the home-country would be brought to a standstill, all over the country, both in its wooded and woodless parts. I do not know myself what would be best. It is difficult to give advice. It seems, however, that it would be better, both for themselves and for the Red Army, if the Poles should evade enlistment with the German army, where, whatever may be their chance of passing over to the other side of the front, many of them would perish in the course of military operations. Have we not a war? The Poles are also being killed. It seems to me that this would be better (Molotov assents). One has to choose between the bad and the worse. It is bad if the Poles who hide in partisan units to evade service in the German army should be forced to leave their families to German reprisals, but it would be still worse if they were in the ranks of the German army. It is a very difficult problem.

Romer: I had it in mind to suggest that only those who, in spite of all their

492

endeavours to evade military service, had been enlisted by force, should pass over to the Soviet side.

Stalin (interrupts): Those who could not escape.

Romer: Quite so. As regards your remark, Mr. President, relating to the assigning of Poles to the units serving in the rear of the German army, it would be possible to order them to carry out judicious acts of sabotage, and to contact partisan units.

Stalin: Perhaps this also. It will be right to induce the Poles to harm the Germans by all possible means. However, those who were unable to pass over to the Red Army, as well as those who could not evade the call up, should be issued with the order to join partisan units. Consequently, those who are at the front should be instructed to surrender, and those who are in rear formations should perform acts of sabotage unless they can join partisan units. In any case such an order must start with making the point that the call up to the German army should be evaded by all possible means.

Romer: And so, Mr. President, may I inform my Government of the agreement of the Soviet Government to put at the disposal of the Polish Army those Poles who might pass over to the Soviet side of their own free will?

Stalin (after a moment of reflection): I cannot say it. We had an experience with the Polish Army which turned out very unfavourably. We might be able eventually to form volunteer units which would fight against the Germans within the ranks of the Red Army. After the war we shall hand those units over to Poland.

Molotov (joining in the conversation): Unfortunately, our experience with the Polish Army finished very badly. So it was, Mr. Ambassador.

Stalin (ironically): Should we form another Polish Army, it will hurry to leave for Iran or Iraq.

Romer: You are joking, Mr. President.

Stalin: These are no jokes. The blood of the Soviet soldier is at stake here.

Romer: The Polish units which could be formed now on Soviet territory could remain here and fight side by side with the Red Army against the Germans. This question could be more closely reviewed between military specialists. I do not exclude, by the way, the possibility of the transfer of the Polish Army in the East, or of a portion of it, to the Soviet front. It would depend, of course, on the decision of the Polish Government and the Supreme Polish and Inter-Allied Command. However, all these questions can be considered, in my view, as open, and they can be cordially discussed in the spirit of common interests.

Stalin: Shall we finish now, Mr. Ambassador, or do you wish to raise some other questions?

Romer: I should still like to discuss the problem of Polish-Soviet relations which unfortunately are passing through a crisis, causing anxiety. We have just ended a friendly discussion on a number of important subjects dealing with military collaboration between our countries. But such collaboration can actually bear fruit only as and when accompanied by mutual friendly

493

feeling. First of all in this connection, the fate of Polish citizens in the Soviet Union is of special interest to the Polish Government and public opinion. The Soviet Note of January 16, 1943,[1] introduced new and unexpected elements and implications which have filled us with deep concern and which it is my duty to elucidate in this conversation with you, Mr. President.

Stalin: I am listening, please.

Romer: As a result of the Agreement of July 30, 1941,[2] the amnesty proclaimed by the Soviet Government affected a vast number of Polish citizens, not excluding national minorities, whose Polish citizenship was only called into question on December 1, 1941,[3] in a note of the People's Commissariat for Foreign Affairs. Set free from camps and prisons our citizens began to rally en masse to the Polish Army then in formation. With the assistance of the Governments of the United States and Great Britain, and of a number of social welfare organizations and institutions, the Polish Government organized relief work on a large scale for their families and for those who remained at work in their places of exile. The need for this relief did not in the least imply a desire to assure to the Polish population an existence in any way privileged as compared with their surroundings, nor even an allegation, never put forward by us, that Polish deportees received worse treatment at the hands of the Soviet authorities than the local population. Their position was worse for other reasons. They had been deported at an hour's notice and as a rule with no money, clothing or food, torn away by force from the surroundings in which they had grown up. Frequently they were separated from their families and were taken under most difficult circumstances to distant, foreign countries, often with extremely severe climates differing greatly from that to which they were accustomed. They were settled among an alien people whose language and customs were foreign to them, and where they lacked the adequate living quarters and vegetable gardens at the disposal of the local population. They were made to do work of which they had no previous experience, for instance intellectuals were given heavy manual work which they had never done before. They were also suffering from disease. For these reasons relief in the form of food, clothing and medical supplies was and remains an absolute necessity.

Stalin: Whom do you refer to as the Polish population, Mr. Ambassador? The whole Polish population which found itself in Western Ukraine and Western White Ruthenia?

Romer: According to Polish legislation, I consider as Polish citizens all those persons who possessed Polish citizenship in 1939. There is a difference of opinion between our two Governments on this subject, the more so since, as was made clear by the Soviet Note of January 16, 1943, and its interpretation which I heard from Commissar Molotov several days ago,—the Soviets extended their citizenship to all persons who were in the disputed territories on November 1 and 2, 1939, even if they found themselves there quite temporarily and by accident and had no connection whatever with the place where they were staying.

[1] See doc. No. 285.   [2] See doc. No. 106.   [3] See doc. No. 157.

494

Molotov: That is not exact. There is reference in the Note to the Citizenship Act[4] which differentiates between permanent and temporary residents: the former have become citizens of the Soviet Union by virtue of the law, while the citizenship of the latter is a matter for individual examination.

Romer: The Note of January 16, 1943, states quite explicitly that all persons present in the disputed territories acquired Soviet citizenship.

Stalin: But at the same time there is reference to the Soviet Citizenship Act.

Romer: May I remark that we have received a number of Notes from the People's Commissariat for Foreign Affairs stating that all residents in these districts have become Soviet citizens. The Polish Embassy in Kuibyshev has even received a written warning that intervention on behalf of individual persons will not be considered until evidence is produced showing the whereabouts of such persons on November 1 and 2, 1939.[5]

Stalin: Distinction is made between those who happened to be in those territories and those who lived there permanently.

Molotov: Citizens of a number of States could have been there at the time, as for example Rumanians, Hungarians, Frenchmen and others, but obviously they did not acquire Soviet citizenship on this account. Our Constitution provides distinctly for such eventualities, which, however, have to be examined individually.

Romer: This is an entirely new situation to me. I find this interpretation, which I hear for the first time, extremely interesting. Hitherto, ever since its Note of December 1, 1941, the Soviet Government has adhered consistently to the attitude that especially that category of Polish citizens who found themselves in the territories in question at the time specified acquired Soviet citizenship.

Stalin: Excuse me, Mr. Ambassador, but persons whose presence in these territories was merely transitory did not automatically acquire Soviet citizenship.

Romer: I can quote a whole series of concrete cases of the attitude hitherto held by the Soviet Government. I do not remember them all, but a classical example is that of the two Warsaw city councillors, Alter and Ehrlich, who despite our objections and representations were classified as Soviet citizens.

Molotov: There may have been individual cases.

Romer: What is then the official Soviet interpretation in this matter, Mr. President? All Soviet Notes and statements have indicated hitherto that in practice all Polish citizens in the USSR have lost their citizenship. We cannot agree to that.

Stalin: The Polish Government persists in considering as Polish citizens all Poles now in the USSR. That is wrong. Truly, a number of Soviet offices have overstepped their authority in certain individual cases, but we must put a stop to extremes. I must moreover point out that it also depends on the person concerned what citizenship he wishes to choose. Thus everybody

[4] See appendix No. 1.   [5] See doc. Nos. 57, 58.

must be asked. Take, Mr. Ambassador, the example of Wanda Wasilewska, a Pole from Warsaw who considers herself a Soviet citizen. The people's wishes must be given consideration, one cannot force citizenship upon them. There is in our Note a reference to the Citizenship Act. I must admit that not all Soviet bureaus have always acted along uniform lines and correctly. But not all the Poles who lived and were domiciled in Polish territory will be Polish citizens. That has to be stopped. There are some who are coming over to us. (Suddenly changing the subject of conversation). It seems to me quite strange that several Polish papers in England and the United States, as well as Polish politicians, some of whom still advocate Pilsudski's line of policy, consider that the Germans are the enemy No. 1 and Soviet Russia the enemy No. 2. What do you think of this, Mr. Ambassador? These people write quite openly about their feelings of hatred towards us, while we do not answer back. Such things will not improve our relations.

Romer: Many Poles, Soviet citizens, have lived in the territories of the USSR for many years. We do not claim them, nor have we ever raised this question.

Stalin: I was thinking of Poles domiciled in the western parts of the Ukraine and White Ruthenia.

Romer: I therefore note, Mr. President, that you recognize the will of each person concerned as an important element in determining his or her citizenship. On our part we shall gladly agree to such a criterion for we have no desire to have citizens who do not wish to be Polish citizens. I must, however, emphasize that a large number of practical issues are bound up with the citizenship problem. Of these I will mention the continuation of relief to our people and permission for individuals to go abroad without of course burdening Soviet railways engaged in war transport. I have in mind particularly Polish children and the families still left in the USSR of soldiers serving in the Polish Army in Great Britain and in the Near East, and also families of Polish State officials and welfare workers. The fact that they are separated from their bread-winners can neither be explained nor understood by any one.

I also attach great value to the question of propaganda, raised by you, Mr. President, in the interest of the improvement of mutual relations between our two countries. I have, however, to state that there have been voices in the Soviet press, which is much more official than ours, raising in an unfriendly manner the question of frontiers, in contrast to the previous glossing over of this subject on both sides. It was done not only by the Soviet press. I could refer here to many broadcasts from Soviet radio stations, such as the Kościuszko, the Kuibyshev and others, which took a hostile attitude towards Poland.

Stalin (interrupting): This is quite impossible.

Romer: I have evidence on this point which I can submit to you in writing.

Stalin: Please do this, Mr. Ambassador.

Romer: I will do so, Mr. President.

Stalin: Our radio stations are State institutions, under our control. It is quite impossible that they could have broadcast such things.

Romer: The Polish Government, in its action and propaganda, assigns the first place to the struggle against Germany, which brings us together in a joint front with the Soviet Union. Critical voices against the latter come from the side of our opposition by way of reaction against unfriendly Soviet orders and declarations. The Polish Government is unable to restrain the voice of the opposition press in foreign territory, especially in America which is beyond our control.

Stalin: Does Grabski belong to the opposition? Is the Polish envoy in Canada in the opposition? General Sikorski stood up for a portion of the press which was attacking us. We bear it patiently, but one cannot be always patient. Should we have an envoy acting in this manner we would have dismissed him at once.

Molotov (interrupts): Yes, yes.

Stalin (continues): The only article criticizing the Polish Government and its policy which ever appeared in the Soviet press was that written by Korneychuk. In this article, written with our knowledge, Korneychuk loyally criticized the Polish standpoint.

Romer: Reverting to the subject of citizenship, in view of the practical consequences involved for hundreds of thousands of our people and thus also for Polish-Soviet relations, I must insist that this be settled not unilaterally but by mutual agreement between our two governments. It is unthinkable that a large and valuable portion of our Nation be thus abruptly cut off against its will from the rest.

Stalin: If we consider the Ukrainians and White Ruthenians as nations, we must recognize that a reunion (vossoyedinenie) has taken place between the lands they inhabit and Soviet White Ruthenia and Soviet Ukraine. Surely the Ukrainians are not Poles! Surely the White Ruthenians are not Poles! We have not joined a single Polish province to the Soviet Union. All Polish territories have been occupied by the Germans.

Romer: Since you refer to the plebiscites in our Eastern provinces, Mr. President, I must recall that they were carried out within the boundaries set up by the German-Soviet agreement which was subsequently solemnly repudiated in the Polish-Soviet Agreement of July 30, 1941.

Stalin: It was the German attack on the USSR which rendered the German-Soviet agreement invalid, and especially the non-agression pact.

Romer: At the time the Soviet Union took our territory we were in opposite camps, and we have not recognized any acts of violence committed at our expense. Since July 30, 1941, we are in the same anti-German camp, which entitles us to expect that no changes will be made in the lands that are ours or in our fundamental rights without our agreement. In default of this we must maintain the attitude that the former Polish-Soviet frontiers, established by the Treaty of Riga, remain always in force.

Stalin (reverting to the previous subject): We do not return answer to the attacks of the Polish opposition press. We keep silence.

Romer: We must have a friendly discussion on all subjects of friction between our two Governments, a friction that is of no benefit to either party but only serves Germany. It is in such a spirit that the problems connected with relief for Polish citizens in the USSR and with their departure should be discussed.

Stalin: What problems?

Romer: This is a historical moment which will decide the course of Polish-Soviet relations for many years to come. We must approach the decisions it calls for with mutual and full understanding and good will, excluding for the time being from our discussions such matters as cannot now be decided and which, if raised, merely lead to friction in Polish-Soviet relations and provoke public controversies.

Stalin: The Soviet Government keeps consistently silent on the subject and so should the Polish Government.

Romer: It is easier to remain silent when one is acquiring something than when one is losing it. As a result of the Soviet Note of January 16th, 1943, we are threatened with a loss of several hundred thousands of our citizens who are all the more important to us as we have lost so many at the hands of the Germans. Furthermore we are threatened with the loss on Soviet initiative of the whole eastern part of our territory. No wonder, then, that Polish public opinion is embittered.

Stalin: The territory we have lost is larger than the whole of Poland.

Romer: But the Red Army has already reconquered vast regions and will undoubtedly regain everything. And, moreover, these territories are only a small part of the Soviet Union.

Stalin: Mr. Ambassador, after the Red Army has beaten the Germans on Russian soil it will enter Polish territory and help to chase the Germans out of Poland and then it will immediately return these lands to the Polish Government, and then, Mr. Ambassador, will you say that this will be a unilateral action adversely affecting mutual relations?

Romer: It will not be as bad as that.

Stalin: Mr. Ambassador, we want a strong Poland; we shall give you the whole of German-occupied Poland regardless of the fact that we are being insulted (niesmotria na to tshto nas rugayut). But we can take these insults on our shoulders!

Romer: Thank you, Mr. President, for these words. I shall remember them. And do you agree with me as to the need for coming to a mutual agreement regarding the problem of the citizenship of Poles at present in the USSR and of further relief and assistance for them from our own resources?

Stalin: There will be Poles who wish to acquire Soviet citizenship.

Molotov: We are, of course, referring to citizens other than those from Western Ukrainian or Western White Ruthenian territories. This problem should furthermore be examined for the purpose of determining the citizenship of persons whose presence in those territories was only temporary.

Romer: According to what Mr. President has said, the will of the persons concerned must be given consideration. Since on the strength of an understanding between the two governments it will be made possible for such persons to express their wishes quite freely, I have no doubt that the atmosphere will be easily and smoothly cleared, since all those in whom we are interested will never reconcile themselves to the thought of parting with their Polish citizenship.

Stalin: It must nevertheless be carried out in accordance with our legislation relating to citizenship. The problem of persons serving in the Red Army presents another difficulty. Out of desire to evade further service, they may express their wish to go, say to Australia in the capacity of Polish citizens. Desertion might thus be facilitated. Apart from the will of the persons concerned, other considerations will therefore have to be taken into account. The nationality of such people and their origin will have to be looked into.

Romer: A problem of vital interest to me in this connection is that of our children. There are several tens of thousands in the Soviet Union and they will be of great value to the future of resurrected Poland. From the point of view of bringing to agreement our conflicting views on citizenship, we attach great importance to the fate of the orphans. We should like to make it possible for these orphans to go to other countries where they would find favourable conditions of existence and education and be a minimum financial burden to the Polish Government.

Stalin: In accordance with our legislation this depends on a variety of factors. It is difficult to generalize.

Romer: I think that the problem of citizenship can only be resolved by means of a formal, bilateral agreement.

Stalin: We cannot infringe our laws.

Molotov: Obviously not.

Romer: We have seen that in the past Soviet legislation did not preclude a large measure of elasticity in its application. I think that on such a premise a way would be found to an understanding on the basis of mutual good will.

Stalin: If conversations take place then all these problems will be cleared up.

Romer: Do you see any possibility, Mr. President, of such negotiations being begun?

Stalin: If you, Mr. Ambassador, see such a possibility, I make no objection.

Romer: Well, we shall go into this matter further.

Stalin: Thus according to you we have as subjects for our negotiations, the question of propaganda, the question of citizenship and the problem of frontiers (vopros o granitsach).

Romer: No, I understood differently and emphasized that in order to improve our relations it would be better to avoid discussing frontiers for the time being; on the other hand I suggested that we should begin negotiations on the subject of preventing unfriendly propaganda on both sides, on the problem of citizenship and its practical consequences.

499

Stalin: Very well, Mr. Ambassador.

Molotov: A declaration of the Polish Government was published in London yesterday. Its contents are unfriendly to the Soviet Union.

Stalin: The declaration is more than a newspaper reply. It is in fact an official statement (eto zayavlenye). Where Soviet territory is concerned there is no Soviet Government prepared to waive (otkazalsia by) any provisions of our Constitution. And the adherence of Western Ukraine and Western White Ruthenia to the Soviet Union has been included in the Constitution.

Romer: On the other hand you will not find a single Pole who would deny that Wilno and Lwów are Polish. I myself so declare it in your presence, Mr. President, with the fullest conviction.

Stalin: I understand your viewpoint. We also have ours. We are quits. Perhaps we should act similarly to the Polish Government as regards frontiers and also publish a statement.

Romer (who at the time of the conversation was not conversant with the resolution of the Polish Government of 25th February 1943,[6] reverts to the subject of negotiations): In the interest of our common front in the fight against Germany which occupies first place in your thoughts and in ours, I insist on agreement, by means of Polish-Soviet negotiations, on the standpoint and behaviour of both parties in the difficult sphere of citizenship and the problems arising from it; also for mutual cessation of public statements and propaganda unfriendly to one another. Would you authorize me, Mr. President, to suggest this to my Government?

Stalin: You are right, Mr. Ambassador. I congratulate you on your good idea. The matter must be examined, we must find out whose citizens these people are, each case must be considered.

Romer: May I count on our being enabled to continue our relief work until our negotiations concerning citizenship are concluded?

Stalin: I do not know, Mr. Ambassador, that depends on the People's Commissariat for Foreign Affairs.

Romer: It is a vital problem for us. We could thus avoid in the event of the suspension of our relief work all consequences which might arise in other countries interested in it, such as England and America. It would be much better if we could reach an understanding without intermediaries.

Stalin: You are right. I cannot promise you anything definite in advance, but negotiations can be started.

Romer: Am I to conduct these negotiations in Moscow with Mr. Molotov, the People's Commissar?

Stalin: Yes, do.

Molotov: If it is convenient for you, Mr. Ambassador, I am at your disposal.

Romer: I shall report the above to my Government and ask for instructions, whereupon I shall take the liberty of communicating with Mr. Molotov. In any case, I consider the attitude of the President as an assurance that the

[6] See doc. No. 294.

500

problems under consideration will be examined with good will and I hope that the negotiations will lead to an understanding which will remove all existing difficulties.

No. 296

TASS statement on Polish-Soviet relations in reply to the Declaration of the Polish Government of February 25, 1943[1]

Moscow, March 1, 1943 GSHI, A.11. 49/Sow./3
Transl. from Russian: Pol.-Sov.R., No. 84

The Soviet news agency issued on March 1 the following official Russian statement replying to the Polish declaration:

The declaration of the Polish Government in London[2] bears witness to the fact that the Polish Government refuses to recognize the historic rights of the Ukrainian and Bielo-Russian peoples to be united within the national States.

Continuing to regard as legitimate the aggressive policy of imperialist States, which partitioned among themselves the traditional Ukrainian and Bielo-Russian lands, and disregarding the universally known fact of the reunion of the Ukrainian and Bielo-Russian peoples within their national States which has already taken place, the Polish Government thus comes out as an advocate of a partition of the Ukrainian and Bielo-Russian lands in favour of the policy of plundering the Ukrainian and Bielo-Russian peoples.

The leading Soviet circles are of the opinion that the denial of the right of the Ukrainian and Bielo-Russian peoples of reunion with their blood brethren bears witness to an imperialist tendency, whereas the references of the Polish Government to the Atlantic Charter have no foundation whatever. The Atlantic Charter does not entitle anyone to encroach on the national rights of the Ukrainians and Bielo-Russians, but on the contrary it has its origin in the principle of the recognition of the national rights of peoples, including the Ukrainian and the Bielo-Russian peoples.

Even the well-known British Minister, Lord Curzon, in spite of his inimical attitude to the USSR, realized that Poland cannot put forward a claim to the Ukrainian and Bielo-Russian lands, but the Polish ruling circles still show no understanding in this matter.

The assertion of the Polish ruling circles that Poland until the beginning of this war refused to collaborate in any way with Germany against the Soviet Union does not correspond with reality. The whole world knows of the pro-Fascist policy of rapprochement with Germany of the Polish Government and its Minister Beck, who tried to oppose Poland to the Soviet Union.

If the present war teaches us something it is above all that the Slav peoples must not quarrel among themselves, but must live in friendship in order to rid themselves of the danger of the German yoke. The Polish ruling circles have learned nothing if they put forward claims on the Ukrainian and Bielo-Russian lands, and thereby cultivate enmity between the Polish people and the peoples of the Ukraine and Bielo-Russia. Such a policy of the Polish

[1] See Note No. 296. [2] See doc. No. 294.

501

leading circles weakens, in the first place, Poland herself and breaks the united front of the Slav peoples in their struggle against German invasion.

The declaration of the Polish Government bears witness to the fact that the present Polish ruling circles do not reflect in this matter the genuine opinion of the Polish people, whose interests in the struggle for the liberation of their country and for the restoration of a strong and united Poland are indissolubly linked with the strengthening to the utmost of mutual confidence and friendship with the brotherly peoples of the Ukraine and Bielo-Russia, as well as with the Russian people and the other peoples of the USSR.

No. 297

Communiqué of the Polish Telegraph Agency concerning the Eastern frontiers of Poland with a reply to the Soviet Declaration on Polish-Soviet relations of March 1, 1943

London, March 5, 1943

GSHI, A.11. 49/Sow./5
'Dziennik Polski' No. 814 of 8.5.1943
Transl. from Polish: Pol.-Sov.R., No. 85

The Polish Telegraph Agency has been authorized by the Polish Government to issue the following reply to the Russian statement:[1]

Until the conclusion of agreements between the USSR and the Third Reich concerning the partition of Polish territories, the Treaty of Riga[2] and its frontier clauses, approved in 1923 by the Conference of Ambassadors and by the United States,[3] were never called in question by Russia. The Russo-German agreements were cancelled by the Polish-Soviet agreement of July 30, 1941.[4] The question of any return to the German-Soviet frontier line of that year requires no further comment.

The so-called 'Curzon line' was proposed during hostilities in 1919–1920 solely as an armistice line and not as a frontier.

The polling ordered by the Soviet-occupying authorities in Eastern Poland in 1939 was contrary to international law. It constitutes one of those unilateral acts which are not recognized by the Allied nations. Therefore it cannot form a basis for any legal acts, and cannot, in particular, deprive Polish citizens of their title to Polish citizenship or to relief organized for their benefit by the Polish Government with the aid of the Governments of Great Britain and the United States.

All German proposals previous to 1939, which were aimed at gaining the co-operation of Poland in military action against Russia, were repeatedly rejected, and this led finally to a German attack on Polish territory in September, 1939.

The declaration of the Polish Government of February 25, 1943,[5] unanimously supported by the entire Polish nation, was not intended to produce controversy which would be so harmful at the present moment. It only stated the indisputable Polish rights to these territories, in which the Polish

[1] See doc. No. 296.   [2] See doc. No. 3.   [3] See doc. No. 4.
[4] See doc. No. 106.   [5] See doc. No. 294.

nation will continue to live in harmony with its Ukrainian and White Ruthenian fellow-countrymen in accordance with the principles proclaimed by the Polish Government. The Polish Government, categorically rejecting the absurd insinuations concerning alleged Polish imperialistic claims in the East, has expressed, and continues to express, to the Soviet Government its readiness for an understanding based on friendly mutual relations.

No. 298

Note from Minister Raczyński to Ambassador Bogomolov protesting against the execution of Alter and Ehrlich[1]

London, March 8, 1943 GSHI, A.11. 49/Sow./2
 Transl. from Polish: Pol.-Sov.R., No. 68

Excerpts have been published in the American and British press of a letter from the Ambassador of the Union of Soviet Socialist Republics in Washington addressed to Mr. William Green, President of the American Federation of Labour, containing information on the execution of Wiktor Alter and Henryk Ehrlich, who were sentenced to death by the Soviet authorities on the charge of complicity in subversive action against the Union of the Soviet Socialist Republics, giving assistance to Polish Intelligence and appealing to the Soviet army to cease bloodshed and conclude an immediate peace with Germany.

In connection with the above information the Polish Government refer to Notes regarding Wiktor Alter and Henryk Ehrlich addressed by the Embassy of the Republic of Poland in Kuibyshev to the People's Commissariat for Foreign Affairs, and beg to state as follows:

1. The Councillor of the capital city of Warsaw, Henryk Ehrlich (born in Lublin in 1882), and ex-Councillor and Sheriff of the city of Warsaw, Wiktor Alter (born in Mława, province of Warsaw, in 1890), were released from prison on September 13, 1941, by the competent authorities of the Union of Soviet Socialist Republics in accordance with the provisions of the Polish-Soviet Agreement of July 30, 1941,[2] and a Decree of the Presidium of the Supreme Council of the Union of Soviet Socialist Republics of August 12, 1941,[3] granting amnesty to all Polish citizens domiciled and detained in the territory of the Union of Soviet Socialist Republics. The fact of their release was communicated to the Embassy of the Republic of Poland at Moscow in a Note of the People's Commissariat for Foreign Affairs on September 23, 1941, which clearly proves that MM. Alter and Ehrlich had been recognized by the Soviet authorities as Polish citizens.

2. Henryk Ehrlich and Wiktor Alter were widely known and distinguished leaders of the Jewish Socialist movement in Poland; furthermore M. Ehrlich was a member of the Executive Committee of the Socialist Labour International, and M. Alter a member of the Executive Committee of the International of Trade Unions.

[1] See Note No. 298. [2] See doc. No. 106. [3] See doc. No. 110.

In consideration of his services with the Jewish labour movement in Poland, the Polish Government had intended to appoint M. Ehrlich a member of the National Council, and with this aim in view had taken steps to facilitate his journey from the Union of Soviet Socialist Republics to Great Britain. M. Alter was to be appointed assistant at the Polish Embassy in Kuibyshev in relief work for Polish citizens on the territory of the Union of Soviet Socialist Republics.

The political and social activities of MM. Alter and Ehrlich, for many years well-known throughout Poland and in international labour circles, their patriotism and loyalty as Polish citizens during the German invasion of Poland and also in the light of the desolation caused throughout the Polish nation and the Jewish population by that invasion, are absolute guarantees that they could not even indirectly have been sympathizers with or tools of any action whatsoever in favour of Germany, and even less so in favour of Hitlerism. At the same time the charge that MM. Ehrlich and Alter worked against the Union of the Soviet Socialist Republics at any period whatever in conjunction with the alleged Polish Intelligence must be firmly rejected as being entirely imaginary and contrary to fact.

On the contrary, it was well known to the Government of the Union of Soviet Socialist Republics that during the period between their release from prison and their re-arrest in December 1941, Henryk Ehrlich and Wiktor Alter proceeded, with the knowledge and consent of the Soviet authorities, to organize in Moscow an International Jewish Anti-Fascist Committee, the object of which was to unite all Jewish masses throughout the world in the war effort against Germany and Hitlerism.

On the strength of the above statement, the Polish Government firmly repudiate the motives put forward in the letter of the Ambassador of the Union of Soviet Socialist Republics in Washington to Mr. Green and protest against the execution by shooting of the Polish citizens Henryk Ehrlich and Wiktor Alter.

No. 299

Excerpts from the Minutes of the negotiations at the Kremlin between Ambassador Romer and Commissar Molotov on the crisis in Polish-Soviet relations

Moscow, March 9, 1943   GSHI, A.11. 49/Sow./4
                                          Transl. from Polish: Pol.-Sov.R., No. 87/3

Romer: Before entering upon the actual subject of our conversation today I regret to have to communicate to you a number of events which to my painful surprise have recently occurred in this territory.

The arrests of local representatives of the Embassy continued throughout the whole second half of 1942 and increased in number in January and February last. In these two months twenty-one representatives were arrested whose names, previously, had been regularly made known to the People's

Commissariat for Foreign Affairs, and who, for the most part, had been confirmed in their functions. The Embassy has not, in one single instance, been informed of these arrests, nor of the reasons thereof.

The authorities have begun to carry out the instructions contained in the Note of the People's Commissariat for Foreign Affairs of January 16 last, concerning citizenship.[1] They are forcing Polish citizens to accept Soviet passports. At Kirov, employees at the local Embassy warehouse were summoned to take out Soviet passports. The vast majority of these employees refused to do so and were arrested together with their families. One of our largest warehouses serving a wide expanse of territory in the Union of Soviet Socialist Republics was thus deprived of its staff and immobilized. In this connection it must be noted that the fate of shipments of relief goods sent from abroad for the Polish population and already under way from Archangel has not yet been ascertained.

A similar procedure was applied at Kirov and Kustanay with regard to all Polish citizens living there; the number of those arrested in these circumstances already amounts to about two hundred.

The same principles are applied with regard to families of members of the Polish armed forces now on active service in Great Britain and the Near East. Thus the People's Commissariat for Foreign Affairs refused to allow a group of families of Polish military men to leave the Soviet Union, although before my departure from Kuibyshev, to be precise on December 23, 1942, that is to say before the issue of the Soviet Note of January 16, 1943, I had received the most formal undertakings from Deputy Commissar Vyshinsky on behalf of the Soviet Government that the permission would be granted. I personally attach great importance to this matter, as it gives me the measure of how assurances given to me are carried out.

On the other hand, the Polish citizenship of Mrs. Wolska from Warsaw has been questioned; she is the wife of the Embassy Delegate at Alma-Ata, who was arrested and then expelled from the Soviet Union. The same applies to Mrs. Bardecka and to the Pająk family whose bread-winners have been deported abroad by the Soviet authorities. The Polish citizenship of Mrs. Eleonora Winczewska has been likewise challenged although she is a Polish citizen from Warsaw who in 1939 was living as a refugee in Wilno, that is to say on territory not within the scope of the Soviet Note of January 16, 1943. I must emphasize that Mrs. Winczewska is now living at the Embassy with the full consent of the Soviet authorities and that she, as well as Mrs. Wolska, is under my protection.

Throughout the territories of the USSR, Polish welfare institutions, such as orphanages, homes for invalids, etc., are being sovietized. The home for invalids and the orphanage at Bolshaya Konstantinovka in the Kuibyshev area, organized by the Embassy on the basis of a special agreement with the People's Commissariat for Foreign Affairs, were taken over in the following circumstances. On February 22, 1943, a Commission composed of members of district and regional authorities arrived on the spot and demanded the

[1] See doc. No. 285.

handing over of the administration of the institution. They declared that these proceedings had been agreed to by the Embassy. In other similar cases the authorities declared that the Embassy no longer existed.

Subsequently, the whole personnel and the adult inmates of the institution were summoned to accept Soviet passports. Terrorized and yielding to direct threats twelve old and ailing persons accepted the Soviet passports. All the other adults in the institution numbering about thirty, were ousted from the building. Later a school-mistress arrived. She is, according to information received, of Volga-German origin. Lessons are in Russian only. The children, regardless of nationality, refuse to be taught in Russian and, despite orders and threats, they sing religious hymns and national songs in Polish.

Before I report on these cases to my Government, I should like to ask you, Mr. Commissar, whether you have any knowledge of these facts and whether they have occurred with the knowledge and consent of the Soviet Government?

Molotov: I have not heard anything about the facts you mention, Mr. Ambassador. I will now reply to your statements, dividing my remarks in two parts:

First: I would advise that the Embassy instruct its representatives throughout the country to conform to the Note of January 16, [. . .], it is not excluded that local authorities may have less misunderstandings because if applied the principles laid down in our Note will make it possible to avoid all incidents.

Second: As regards specific cases in which the Note of January 16 was applied, it is not excluded that local authorities may have carried it out wrongly. For instance, inhabitants of Warsaw do not as a matter of law become Soviet citizens. Such cases of a faulty interpretation of the Note may have occurred, but they were quite accidental. If mistakes were made, they will be rectified. I can assure you of this, Mr. Ambassador. On the other hand I must request that the Embassy co-operate with us in this matter.

Romer: I must remark that the Note of January 16 does not say anything about the taking over by Soviet authorities of Embassy institutions, such as orphanages, homes for invalids, and that we were never notified about this. I must further emphasize in this connection that the local authorities are taking over property owned by the Polish State and I don't know on what grounds this is being done. As for the Note of January 16, it refers exclusively to the legal position of persons regarding themselves and also regarded by us as Polish citizens and on whom Soviet citizenship is now being forced.

I must lay special emphasis on the fact that this action is exceptionally painful to me and that it cannot fail likewise to affect the Polish Government and the Polish people. As you, Mr. Commissar, now appeal to us to co-operate in this matter, I must record that the way the Soviet authorities are proceeding excludes such co-operation on our part. [. . .].

Romer: On what legal grounds are orphanages and other Embassy institutions being taken over by the Soviet administration?

506

Molotov: If we establish that Soviet citizens are found there, then these institutions become subject to appropriation by the Soviet authorities. I desire, Mr. Ambassador, to leave no room for misunderstanding in these matters.

Romer: These institutions and everything belonging to them are the property of the Polish State. As far as citizenship is concerned, however, from our point of view, these people are Polish citizens and, in part, would also seem to remain Polish citizens, even from the Soviet viewpoint. The state of affairs thus created is quite inadmissible. [. . .].

Romer: I am forced to inform my Government about these facts. If we are to discuss in a friendly spirit questions relating to citizenship, in accordance with what was agreed on in my conversation with Marshal Stalin, then I must ask you, Mr. Commissar, what interest can the Soviet Government possibly have in arousing Polish public opinion, and also in exciting public opinion abroad where these facts will undoubtedly become known. I have precise information showing that the local authorities deal with these matters drastically. I think the only reasonable solution corresponding to the spirit of my conversation with Marshal Stalin and with you would be the suspension of all steps of this nature by the local Soviet authorities, at least for the period of the negotiations we are to conduct.

Molotov: The local authorities who received instructions on the grounds of the Note of January 16, must put them into operation. For these authorities the question is not controversial at all and it is their duty to carry out their instructions. The way in which this was done may, indeed, have provoked friction. But I must assure you, that it is the intention of the Soviet Government that conditions of life of the Polish population not only shall not suffer any deterioration but on the contrary be improved.

Romer: I must state once again, that the manner in which these instructions are carried out by the local authorities has been extremely ruthless, and they are applied to matters that have not been agreed upon between us, although the authorities concerned referred to an alleged consent of the Embassy. I see no grounds whatever for taking over welfare institutions of the Embassy and Polish State property assigned to them. [. . .]

Romer: How do you contemplate, Mr. Commissar, the problem of further relief aid and of handling shipments from abroad of food, clothing and medical supplies, as well as their distribution through the Embassy at least to those Polish citizens whose citizenship is regarded by both Governments as incontestable?

Molotov: The Embassy may continue to assist these people.

Romer: But if difficulties are already now being made?

Molotov: We shall elucidate this matter in a spirit of collaboration.

Romer: It would be better to settle this matter at once. I am informed that the activities of the Embassy warehouse at Ashabad through which all shipments of relief goods pass on the southern route are paralysed, since our chauffeurs are not allowed to drive from Ashabad to Badjigiran and the Soviet Embassy in Teheran refuses to grant visas valid for several crossings of the frontier to sixteen chauffeurs of Iranian nationality who were also to bring these goods to Ashabad from Iran. Owing to this, our Ashabad warehouse which serves the greater part of the territory of the Soviet Union is virtually immobilized.

Molotov: It seems to me, Mr. Ambassador, that your views as to the complete cessation of relief work in the interests of the Polish population are exaggerated. This work can be continued and in point of fact is functioning in numerous places. I will have the case of Ashabad investigated.

The main object at present is to ensure that the changeover to new forms of organization, as regards relief work in aid of the Polish population, should not lead to a deterioration of the condition of that population. The Soviet Government is also anxious that not only its material conditions should not be depressed but that its cultural requirements should also be safeguarded. The Soviet authorities have already received detailed instructions to this effect. [. . .].

Romer: And what in your view will be the possibilities of distinguishing between the two categories of people, those who for both sides are and remain indisputably Polish citizens, and those whom the Soviet Government now considers Soviet citizens?

Molotov: This problem is purely practical. It will be dealt with within the scope of our legislation.

Romer: I have precise information, Mr. Commissar, that Polish citizens are being arrested for not accepting Soviet passports and I am unable to reconcile this procedure with the stand taken by Marshal Stalin in his conversation with me.

Molotov: You simplify this matter, Mr. Ambassador. The moment is difficult. Truly there is friction. If a Pole resists the orders of Soviet authorities, we shall deal with that as with a hostile action. [. . .].

Romer: In the cases on which we have most detailed reports, the Soviet authorities failed to take into account the will of individuals. Whereas, during my conversation with Marshal Stalin, the latter laid emphasis on the fact that precisely this factor would have to be taken into serious consideration. We, on our part, give due attention to this circumstance, and therefore you, Mr. Commissar, will not, for instance, have to deal with any claim on our part with regard to the citizenship of Wanda Wasilewska, of whose case mention was made.

Molotov: Your reference to Marshal Stalin is incorrect. Comrade Stalin spoke of two factors and you, Mr. Ambassador, mention only one. Stalin said that one must take into consideration: first Soviet legislation; and second, the will of the citizen. As to Wanda Wasilewska, she voluntarily accepted Soviet citizenship although she was born in Warsaw.

Romer: I very well remember the stand taken by Marshal Stalin and I must emphasize that the Soviet authorities only count with the one of the two factors which, according to the Marshal, were to influence the determination of citizenship, namely, Soviet legislation; but they totally ignore the second factor, the will of the person concerned. Therefore, even in the light of Marshal Stalin's explanations, the procedure applied by the authorities is unfair and unjust.

Molotov: We will verify all these facts, and I will inform you of the outcome.

Romer: I must now ask you to give me some explanation regarding citizenship laws in force in the Soviet Union and also to clear up some points which come to my mind in connection with the Note of January 16.

Molotov: I am listening.

Romer: Leaving aside, for the moment, the Polish stand in the matter of citizenship, and we know it is opposed to that of the Soviets, I would like to be informed, as accurately as possible, about Soviet guiding principles, so as to be able to eliminate from our further discussion that special category of persons whose Polish citizenship is not questioned by the Soviet side. I know from Marshal Stalin's declarations and from your own that such a category of persons actually exists according to your views and that it consists of individuals who found themselves fortuitously in the contested territory on November 1 and 2, 1939. A definition of this category of persons, for which I ask, would restrict the field of our controversial discussion.

Molotov: In the Note of January 16, 1943, two laws are mentioned, the Citizenship Law of the USSR of August 19, 1938[2] and the Decree of the Supreme Council on citizenship of November 29, 1939.[3] They govern this matter. I will endeavour to give you in writing, shortly, a legal definition of the category of persons who do not come under these laws. For the moment I can only explain that the persons we regard as Soviet citizens are those who resided at the time we have in mind in the territories of Western Ukraine and Western White Ruthenia which entered the Soviet Union. In so far as the inhabitants of these territories were not citizens of a second or a third state—for such persons may have been there likewise, for instance Japanese, British, Rumanians or other nationals, as I have already mentioned, and insofar as this is not understood to include persons who were there fortuitously and who consequently after all may not have acquired Soviet citizenship— these cases must be cleared up individually—persons belonging to all remaining categories have become Soviet citizens. As regards military families there may be cases, for instance, the wife of a member of the Polish armed forces now in Iran may not wish to join her husband and desire to retain her Soviet citizenship. When such a person acquires Soviet citizenship, the different citizenship of her husband cannot constitute an obstacle. Cases bearing on citizenship must be dealt with individually. True, persons originating from Warsaw, Poznań and other Polish territories are Polish citizens, but, as I say, their cases ought to be treated individually, for these persons may wish to acquire Soviet citizenship and if they acquire can no longer be regarded as Polish citizens.

Romer: May I request you to send me the text of the Decree of the Supreme Council of November 29, 1939?

Molotov: Yes, I will send it to you.

Romer: In the notes of the People's Commissariat for Foreign Affairs of

[2] See appendix No. 1.   [3] See doc. No. 71.

December 1, 1941[4] and January 16, 1943, the terms citizens of the *oblasti* of Western Ukraine and Western White Ruthenia are used, whereas the Law on Citizenship makes use exclusively of the terms: Citizens of the Soviet Union and citizens of the various Republics forming the Union. How then should one understand the term citizen of an *oblast* which is unknown in law?

Molotov: Mr. Ambassador, all Republics are made up of *oblasti*. Thus, for instance, there can be a citizen of the Kiev *oblast* of the USSR.

Romer: The law says nothing about this. I do not think, for instance, that there can be any such thing as a citizen of the Kuibyshev *oblast*.

Molotov: Yes—yes—there can be such a thing as a citizen of the Kuibyshev *oblast*. But in that case he will be a citizen of the RSFSR and so in all Republics.

Romer: In the Soviet law on citizenship mention is made of citizens of the State, and not of a province, therefore, the use of the term: citizen of an *oblast* in both notes of the People's Commissariat for Foreign Affairs is not clear to me, the more so as at the time in question, the territories referred to did not form a part of the Soviet Union. To whom does the term employed in the Notes actually refer?

Molotov: The Soviet citizens of the *oblasti* of Western Ukraine and of Western White Ruthenia and of the Ukrainian Soviet Socialist Republic and of the White Ruthenian Socialist Republic were until November 1, 1939 in various legal positions, for some were only becoming Soviet citizens while others were already citizens.

Romer: Now, what persons were actually implied in the term used in the Notes of the People's Commissariat for Foreign Affairs, which, as we see, causes such a confusion of legal concept.

Molotov: No law can provide for all practical cases. There is no such thing in the world as a perfect law.

Romer: Has one not to do here, simply with Polish citizens, as the inhabitants of those territories at that time must have been considered even by Soviet legislation?

Molotov: You are quite right, we do not deny this. The population there formerly possessed Polish citizenship.

Romer: We can therefore stand on the ground that in the light of Soviet interpretation, we were dealing with Polish territories and Polish citizens.

Molotov: I do not know what inferences you are making in connection with this matter, or what you are aiming at. Not all *oblasti* entered the Soviet Union at the same time. From part of the *oblasti*, the Soviet Union was formed in 1918. Other *oblasti* belonging to this Republic were incorporated in 1939. The Ukrainian Republic was not erected at one stroke, but step by step. We cannot help that.

Romer: To fix the interpretation of these questions is a matter of great practical importance. As has become manifest, it is impossible to decide upon fundamental principles of citizenship, quite independently of territorial questions, and the Note of the People's Commissariat for Foreign Affairs of

[4] See doc. No. 157.

December 1, 1941 is a signal proof of this. It states clearly that the unsolved question of frontiers between Poland and the Union of Soviet Socialist Republics will be settled in the future.

Molotov: What does your question aim at, Mr. Ambassador?

Romer: I merely quote a sentence from the Note of December 1, 1941, to throw light on the problem of citizenship, in the Soviet interpretation.

Molotov: The question of frontiers will certainly be subject to future settlement. We will further discuss this matter. Do you perhaps wish to enter into a conversation on this subject now?

Romer: No, Mr. Commissar, as I already told Marshal Stalin, I do not think that it would serve a good purpose for our two governments at present, in the interest of an improvement of their relations.

Molotov: The territorial boundary of the Soviet Union as confirmed in 1939 by the Supreme Council, is the frontier of the Soviet Union; however we shall not decline to discuss in more concrete terms the subject of frontiers. Rectifications are possible. I mean a few. In the matter of citizenship I will send you an interpretation in writing.

Romer: Thank you. I should prefer, as a means of facilitating our further conversations, if you would send me a draft of this interpretation first, so that we could still discuss it before it is given final form. I should like, in particular, to emphasize that the discussion on citizenship which we have had was only of an informative nature and that it merely aimed to enlighten me as to the standpoint and views of the Soviet Government in this matter, without affecting any change in the fundamental viewpoint of the Polish Government on this subject. I should like it to be well understood, that in asking you these questions, I do not cease to support entirely our different viewpoint in this matter. I shall inform my Government of the regrettable incidents I communicated to you at the beginning of our conversation today and shall also advise them of your assurance that these facts will be investigated without delay and that the result will be made known to me.

Molotov: I shall do so immediately after I receive the explanations.

Romer: Well, it is always better to clean up all matters in an amicable way, to avoid further incidents that can only complicate the situation.

Molotov: I understand.

Romer: Do you wish to inform me of the date of our next interview, Mr. Commissar, or is it more convenient to you for me to suggest it?

Molotov: I am at your service, Mr. Ambassador.

No. 300

Excerpts from the Minutes of the negotiations at the Kremlin between Ambassador Romer and Commissar Molotov on the crisis in Polish-Soviet relations

Moscow, March 18, 1943   GSHI, A.11. 49/Sow./4
                             Transl. from Polish: Pol.-Sov.R., No. 87/4

Romer: In the course of our last conversation, nine days ago you promised to send me an explanation in writing concerning the manner in which Soviet laws on citizenship are to be interpreted, and also on a number of events affecting our interests, which occurred on Soviet territory.

Molotov: I must also ask you a question. Did you receive the Decree of the Supreme Council of the USSR of November 29, 1939?[1] (The Ambassador nods assent.) I shall now answer your question.

During our last conversation I had not at hand the above Decree. On reading it, I saw that the matter of citizenship is quite explicitly dealt with. The text refers to inhabitants of the districts of Western Ukraine and Western White Ruthenia. Within the meaning of this Decree, therefore, any person who was not an inhabitant of these provinces remains a Polish citizen. The Decree deals with this question quite exhaustively and does not require any further elucidation; it says everything there is to say. [. . .].

Romer: To revert to the written interpretation of Soviet legislation on citizenship which you promised to give me during our last conversation, I again emphasize the great importance I attach to receiving it. The Decree actually speaks of inhabitants whereas the Soviet Notes of December 1, 1941,[2] and January 16, 1943,[3] mention persons who found themselves on the contested territories on November 1 and 2, 1939. All this is not clear, and consequently the local authorities interpret their instructions in a divergent and arbitrary fashion.

Molotov: There is no intrinsic difference in the texts, although different expressions are used. We base ourselves on the Decree. I see no need for issuing an interpretation in writing, since obviously the term inhabitant is perfectly understandable. We refer to permanent inhabitants, residing on this territory. What is it, that is not clear in this?

Romer: Your explanation on this point is valuable to me in itself, but the whole matter nevertheless still presents certain doubts. The question is to define the Soviet principle in accordance with which permanent residence is established.

Molotov: There is no one law in the world that could be applied to all cases arising from life. However detailed a law, it will never decide all possible individual cases. If controversial questions arise, we shall be able to discuss them. Personally, I think, that the law is quite clear.

Romer: But the application of the law is relevant, the more so as it exposes our citizens to still greater hardships.

Molotov: Is it necessary to explain what inhabitant means? During our last conversation you did not have the text of the Decree. Do you really require additional explanations, although in the meantime we sent you the text of the Decree?

Romer: I propose, Mr. Commissar, to postpone this discussion until later, so that the concrete cases I intend to present to you may furnish practical illustrations.

Molotov: Willingly I agree, this will be more appropriate.

Romer: The facts I have to bring to your notice are very painful, because

[1] See doc. No. 71.   [2] See doc. No. 157.   [3] See doc. No. 285.

they do not show that the Soviet authorities act in a way consistent with the spirit of friendship that ought to be the rule between our two governments. I shall divide these facts unto the following categories:

First: The forcing of Soviet citizenship about which we already have information, fragmentary but sufficient to draw the conclusion that this is a mass procedure ordered by the central authorities and applied to the entire Polish population in the USSR. This procedure is carried out on lines of moral and physical compulsion that arouse my deepest indignation, as being inadmissible in relations between Allies and in the midst of a hard war against our common enemy. We have proof that Polish citizens, men and women, subjected to this procedure are detained for examination for days on end, that they are even deprived of food and drink to break their resistance. Such arguments are made use of for this purpose, as statements that there is no longer any Polish Embassy in the USSR, or that Poland no longer exists. Those who resist are thrown into prison. Local authorities do not, as a rule investigate the place of origin of a given person, and consequently do not respect the differentiation implied in the interpretation of the Soviet law on citizenship that I received from Marshal Stalin and from you.

Second: The taking over by the Soviet authorities, Mr. Commissar, of the relief institutions of the Polish Embassy, a proceeding likewise carried out on a mass scale. These institutions—they number about 570—were created and operated on the basis of agreements between the People's Commissariat for Foreign Affairs and the Embassy; they were subordinated exclusively to the latter and had at their disposal, in all cases—in larger or smaller measure—Polish State property, equipment, supplies of food, clothing and medicines, school utensils, etc. On grounds unknown to me and in a totally inadmissible manner, the Soviet authorities are taking over these institutions and disposing of them and also of Polish property without the consent of the Embassy, to whom the rightful ownership of and control over these objects belongs. They do not even give any warning of what they intend to do. As regards the taking over the home for invalids and orphanage at Bolshaya Konstantinovka, in the Kuibyshev district, under conditions I described to you during our last interview, the Embassy has received a Note from the People's Commissariat for Foreign Affairs, dated March 10, giving as justification for all this that no Polish citizens were found there. This allegation has no foundation in truth. It was precisely Polish citizens refusing to accept Soviet passports who together with the manager of the establishment were expelled from it. The citizenship of children was obviously decided by higher authorities without any investigation, despite opposition put up by the children themselves. I am therefore compelled to state once again, that methods of actual terrorism were employed by the local authorities, methods wholly incompatible with the spirit of Polish-Soviet friendship and collaboration.

Molotov: Mr. Ambassador, it is very easy to speak about friendly understanding in the matter of incidents that have occurred, but here I do not see anything of this sort on your part. Your reproaches on this subject are unfounded and out of place. I shall not reply to them.

However, as regards Polish State property, I already told you the last time and I repeat once more, that all losses will be made good.

If the Embassy should obstruct our action, the result will be anything but good. I see that you do not want to get reconciled to our standpoint, and the Embassy still continues to follow its old line of procedure. This has nothing to do with assurances of friendship. I must remark that the Embassy's attitude towards these problems is strange, for it does not issue instructions in accordance with our laws. No good can result from this. All this is quite incomprehensible to me.

Romer: Your expostulation, Mr. Commissar, I shall answer later when I substantiate my statement with facts. I will now submit to your consideration a further series of facts, and, in doing so, I would—in connection with point three—emphasize that the Embassy has been exposed of late to various vexations and difficulties. Even I, personally, have trouble when I speak over the telephone with Kuibyshev. Long distance telephone calls of the Embassy are not attended to. An ever increasing number of telegrams from outlying places are not delivered to the Embassy. Callers leaving the Embassy are forced to show their identity papers and are arrested. Worse, cases are known in which such persons have been beaten up in public. If you so desire, I can give further particulars as well as the dates of the incidents. Families of Embassy officials and of employees of institutions under it in outlying districts are forced to accept Soviet passports.

(The Ambassador deals at length with the cases of Mrs. Zagórska, Mrs. Kasińska, Mrs. Maksymowicz, Mrs. Emchowicz, Mrs. Winczewska, Mrs. Wolska and of MM. Kutyba, Cygler and Wójtowicz, and shows that none of the persons involved originated from the contested territories or were resident therein.)

I will now revert to the matter touched on by you, Mr. Commissar, concerning the taking over of relief institutions by the Soviet authorities. I am obliged to emphasize, once more, that the Embassy never agreed thereto and was not even notified by the People's Commissariat for Foreign Affairs in this matter, and that a policy of accomplished fact is being applied. The institutions are closed down before the question of citizenship of the staff and inmates has been established. This is not indicative of any good will on the part of the Soviet Government. I suggest, on my part, that the local authorities discontinue this action at least until our conversations have been brought to a close, as they are intended to bring about a friendly settlement of pending difficulties. At the present juncture it is difficult to arrive at an understanding. Whilst we are discussing questions of principle, things are happening out there in the provinces that are apt to change the whole situation. The Polish Government cannot be indifferent to these happenings.

Molotov: I would like to ask, Mr. Ambassador, at what you are actually aiming? We shall verify the individual facts mentioned by you. (Molotov repeats this twice.) What more can you wish? If you start by not recognizing our laws, then all attempts to achieve an understanding will be futile. From the conversations we have had hitherto I have gained the impression that you continue uninterruptedly to maintain your standpoint of not recognizing the Decree of November 29, 1939.

I will make several remarks:

First: I have the impression that what you actually have in mind is that we should ask each individual inhabitant of Western Ukraine and Western White Ruthenia what citizenship he wishes to retain. Here I must state that there can be no question of any individual citizen, who acquires Soviet citizenship by virtue of the Decree declaring his or her consent. That would be contrary to Soviet legislation.

Second: Within the meaning of the Decree the place of birth of a given citizen is irrelevant; what is relevant, however, is whether that citizen resided in the territory of Western Ukraine and Western White Ruthenia.

Third: I should like to emphasize that if the Embassy hampers our action of issuing passports to Soviet citizens in accordance with our Decree, and if it induces such persons not to accept Soviet passports, then no good will come of it. There will be unnecessary incidents. If, however, the Embassy will cooperate with us in a helpful spirit then we shall be able to investigate individual cases very carefully and rectify any possible mistakes. You certainly do not possess, Mr. Ambassador, general information as to how this whole action is being carried out.

Romer: On the contrary, Mr. Commissar, I have a large number of facts affecting not only Embassy officials. I can for instance mention the case of Mrs. Sigmund, born and domiciled in Warsaw, now residing at Kustanay, a daughter of the well-known writer Adolph Nowaczyński.

Molotov: We will verify these facts.

Romer: Persons who know beyond any doubt that even within the meaning of the Decree they may retain their Polish citizenship and who consequently refuse to accept Soviet passports, are sentenced to imprisonment for this in violation of every principle of law. I can in this respect refer to the cases of three employees of the Embassy's warehouse at Kirov who were sentenced each to two years in prison. What I want is that the local authorities should not consider the question of citizenship from different angles, and that we should draw practical conclusions from the facts, Mr. Commissar.

Molotov: Right!

Romer: I wish to obtain a precise definition of that special category of persons who even from your viewpoint, for all that it does not as we know correspond to our own, remain Polish citizens within the meaning of the Decree.

Molotov: I agree with you, Mr. Ambassador, that persons not falling within the scope of the Decree may be classed separately as Polish citizens. However as Soviet legislation on citizenship is questioned on the Polish side, I must remark that our authorities will execute the legal enactments that are binding upon them. What I am concerned with is that no obstacles, in the nature of a demonstration, be placed in the way of these orders.

Romer: The Embassy never did anything of the sort, but on the contrary always advised Polish citizens to loyally obey orders of the authorities. On the other hand, our citizens must have the possibility of appealing to the superior authorities and also to their Embassy, against decisions which they consider legally unjustified. I may add that, as bearers of Soviet passports thrust upon them by sheer force, they are—under severe penalties—deprived of the possibility of applying to the Polish Embassy and that they would likewise not be in a position to appeal against the unjust decisions of which they may be victims. I am, therefore, first of all anxious to make sure that Soviet authorities do not wrongly interpret the rules set down by the law. Besides, I should like to point out once more, that the local authorities compel the Polish population by various means to accept Soviet passports and that they destroy and deride their national identity papers, which justifies the terms used by me in presenting this matter. I recall that according to the statements of Marshal Stalin, the free will of the persons concerned was also to be an important factor in deciding the question of citizenship. Do you authorize me to assure my Government that in the future, at least pending the termination of our conversations, the method of compulsion in the question of citizenship will be abandoned?

Molotov: I do not agree, Mr. Ambassador, I cannot agree. The authorities are carrying out the Soviet law on citizenship, and they cannot remain passive in the face of resistance. You refer to your conversation with Comrade Stalin and you say, you had the impression that he made the matter of citizenship dependent upon an expression of will. The case of Wanda Wasilewska was mentioned then, and the question was whether she wished to be a Polish or a Soviet citizen. Such individual cases may arise, when Polish citizens not falling within the scope of the Decree are concerned. But it appears, Mr. Ambassador, that you wish that every citizen be asked his opinion.

Romer: I should like to further discuss the category of persons of incontestable citizenship.

Molotov: We will verify these cases.

Romer: The local authorities undoubtedly are acquainted with a series of successive Soviet legal enactments of various dates, the Amnesty Decree, the Note of December 1, 1941, the Note of January 16, 1943. The contents of these documents differ in each case. This leads to a variety of interpretations and is a source of confusion for local authorities, as they do not know how to proceed with regard to Polish citizens, and unnecessary incidents arise. In my view—quite apart from the conflict of principle existing between us—the local authorities ought to receive more precise instructions.

Molotov: If local authorities have applied the law wrongly, Mr. Ambassador, we shall check these facts. But, I should like to remark that the Decree on Citizenship of November 29, 1939, and the Soviet Note of January 16, 1943, constitute the basis of action by our authorities.

Romer: I revert to the discussion we had at the beginning of our conversation today. A more precise definition of the terminology used in Soviet legislation as to who is a resident of the contested territories will contribute to remove friction and difficulties.

Molotov: I do not see any need or necessity to further elaborate such a definition. We shall never reach an ideal formula. Everybody understands what is meant by inhabitant. It is better to deal with these cases individually.

Romer: There can be no question of individual cases since the authorities apply the law to all and compel even persons, incontestably Polish citizens in the meaning of Soviet law itself, to accept Soviet passports.

Molotov: These facts must be verified.

Romer: I am in possession of accurate information. Nine days ago you promised to send me an interpretation in writing. The facts occurring throughout the country are becoming more numerous and causing many unnecessary additional difficulties.

Molotov: There will be no difficulties; the local authorities apply the laws correctly. [. . .].

Romer: I revert now to the matter of Embassy institutions and relief establishments taken over by Soviet authorities. Would you be willing to authorize me to assure the Polish Government that this action will be suspended at least for the duration of the conversations now proceeding between us?

Molotov: The principal consideration by which we are actuated is that the condition of the Polish population should not be impaired. I do not exactly know how far the transfer of these institutions to Soviet administration has been accomplished. But I can state that the entire property of the Embassy and all the possessions of the Polish State will be restored in full or compensation paid.

Romer: In each of these 570 institutions are objects belonging to the Polish State. I make the formal proposal that the action of taking over these establishments be stayed until we reach an agreement.

Molotov: The interests of the Embassy shall be safeguarded in any case.

Romer: But here we deal with the infringement of property rights and management of these Embassy institutions.

Molotov: To avoid misunderstandings, let me quote an example: if butter was taken away, the same quantity of butter will be returned.

Romer: Is the administration of the said institutions being changed?

Molotov: You will understand that at present a large number of persons belonging to the management have turned out to be Soviet citizens.

Romer: It would appear to be fairer, if the questions themselves were first cleared up and deductions reached later, after this has been done. Meantime the institutions should be able to carry on as heretofore. Moreover, there are many children there whose citizenship has not yet even been verified.

Molotov: There are institutions where the employees may have been ill or unable to fulfill their duties, and others which do not function properly. For this reason the Soviet administration was bound to intervene and appoint people who will better fulfil their tasks. The procedure, Mr. Ambassador, is of no importance, what really counts is that the population should not suffer.

517

Romer: Only the Embassy could decide who worked well in its own institutions. I really do not see any valid grounds on which the local authorities can interfere in the matter. And I must further remark that the Embassy issues instructions to these institutions, supplies them with funds and assistance in kind, and that it is not even notified when they pass into other hands. This causes unprecedented and most harmful confusion.

Molotov: The main thing, Mr. Ambassador, is that the material condition of the population should not suffer.

Romer: Have any instructions been given out by the central authorities for these institutions to be taken over? Why were we not notified of this in advance?

Molotov: I repeat once more that the central authorities, acting on the grounds of the decision of the People's Commissars of January 15, 1943, gave categorical orders to the local authorities that the taking over of these institutions by the Soviet Administration must not entail any hardship on the population. But I wish to emphasize that the Embassy will have very little to say in the matter of institutions whose staff and inmates are now for the most part Soviet citizens. The majority of these people acquired Soviet citizenship by virtue of our Note of January 16, 1943. Today is March 18, and the whole matter is now about to be closed.

Romer: How could it happen that the Embassy was not previously notified of this decision nor of the orders issued under it which do not respect Polish State property? Besides, this is wholly contrary to our previous agreements, under which the relief institutions of the Embassy were called into being.

Molotov: The authorities have received instructions to the effect that the situation of the Polish population must not suffer any deterioration.

Romer: It is also our concern, and it was precisely thanks to the work of the Embassy in the field that the Polish population was provided with substantial relief.

Molotov: The Embassy will not lose a farthing.

Romer: That matter, in truth, is secondary. But the violation of principle is inadmissible.

Molotov: Persons who are found to be Soviet citizens must obey the orders of the authorities who are—as a matter of fact—concerned in not allowing the situation of the population to deteriorate. The authorities have been instructed to see to this, irrespective of the sentiments of individual persons.

Romer: I must emphasize once more that the taking over, by an officially recorded act, of relief institutions belonging to the Embassy is illegal and incompatible with their interests, as well as with those of persons benefited by them.

Molotov: What are you aiming at?

Romer: I want the transfer of these establishments to the Soviet Administration to be suspended. I repeat my question whether I may assure my Government that this will be done?

Molotov: I have already told you that the central authorities formally ordered the local authorities to take over these institutions. Apart from this, these institutions have now become Soviet institutions, since the persons serving them are now Soviet citizens. The inviolability of the property of the Polish State will be safeguarded.

Romer: How do you contemplate the question of further relief in kind now due to arrive, bought or ordered abroad by the Polish Government and already shipped with the collaboration of Allied Powers, or donated by friendly Governments and welfare institutions in allied and neutral countries? I am now looking at the practical side of the problem.

Molotov: In principle, I regard all assistance as being desirable if it serves the interests of the Polish population. I am ready to discuss this matter separately.

Romer: Finally, I would like to ask you, Mr. Commissar, to give me an assurance that compulsory methods in the matter of citizenship will not be applied.

Molotov: I regard this demand as unfounded, since our Administration is proceeding in accordance with the instructions.

Romer: Then I have no other choice but to appeal to my Government. And may I count on receiving a written interpretation of the term inhabitant, as contained in the Decree of November 29, 1939?

Molotov: I have already answered this question, Mr. Ambassador.

No. 301

Note from Minister Raczyński to Ambassador Bogomolov containing the protest of the Polish Government against the imposition of Soviet citizenship upon Polish citizens

London, March 29, 1943 GSHI, PRM, 101/1
Transl. from Polish: Pol.-Sov.R., No. 66

It has come to the knowledge of the Polish Government that the Government of the Union of Soviet Socialist Republics, on the strength of the Notes of the People's Commissariat for Foreign Affairs addressed to the Polish Embassy at Kuibyshev on December 1, 1941,[1] and January 16, 1943,[2] and in disregard of the reservations expressed by the Polish Government on each occasion, and invoking the Decree of the Presidium of the Supreme Council of the Union of Soviet Socialist Republics of November 29, 1939,[3] has proceeded to force Soviet citizenship upon Polish citizens who find themselves in considerable numbers and not of their will on the territories of the Union of Soviet Socialist Republics.

In these circumstances the Polish Government deem it necessary to declare once more that in the light of the Polish-Soviet Agreement of July 30, 1941,[4] which is binding on both parties, they consider the principles

[1] See doc. No. 157. [2] See doc. No. 285.
[3] See doc. No. 71. [4] See doc. No. 106.

underlying the attitude of the Government of the Union of Soviet Socialist Republics in this matter as unjustified and unfounded, because:

a) The aforesaid attitude is contrary to Paragraph 1 of the Supplementary Protocol to the above-mentioned Agreement of July 30, 1941, granting amnesty to all Polish citizens within the Union of Soviet Socialist Republics, which bilateral legal instrument cannot be infringed or changed by any unilateral Soviet order.

b) The Decree on citizenship of the Supreme Council of the Union of Soviet Socialist Republics of November 29, 1939, resulting from the Soviet-German treaties of 1939 referring to territorial changes in Poland,[5] and invoking *expressis verbis* one of these treaties, must obviously have lost its validity together with these same treaties from the moment of the German aggression against the Union of Soviet Socialist Republics on June 22, 1941, as recognized by the Government of the Union of Soviet Socialist Republics in Article 1 of the Polish-Soviet Agreement of July 30, 1941.

In view of the fact that regardless of the outcome of the present conversations in Moscow between the two Governments which seek agreement on their attitude in this matter in the spirit of mutual friendliness and collaboration that underlies their present relations, the Government of the Union of Soviet Socialist Republics has not agreed to the suspension, at least during the course of the conversations in progress, of the execution of its orders in respect of Polish citizens in the Union of Soviet Socialist Republics, the Polish Government find themselves regretfully compelled to lodge a determined protest against this and to declare that they cannot recognize this infringement of the sovereign rights of the Polish State; they reserve to themselves the fundamental right to call into question in the future all *de facto* conditions both as regards general matters and those affecting individual citizens, resulting from the aforesaid attitude of the Government of the Union of Soviet Socialist Republics; and the right to claim compensation for any losses sustained by Polish citizens in consequence of this attitude.

[5] See doc. No. 52.

No. 302

Note from Minister Raczyński to Ambassador Bogomolov protesting against taking over by the Soviet authorities of the Polish agencies in the USSR

London, March 30, 1943   GSHI, PRM, 101/1
                               Transl. from Polish: Pol.-Sov.R., No. 80

The Polish Government has received information to the effect that the Government of the Union of Soviet Socialist Republics has proceeded to take over the administration of the relief institutions (orphanages, homes for invalids, etc.) of the Polish Embassy in the Union of Soviet Socialist Republics.

The above-mentioned institutions were set up on the strength of an agreement between the Polish Embassy and the Government of the Union of Soviet Socialist Republics contained in the Note of the People's Commissariat for Foreign Affairs of February 12, 1942.[1] In this Note the Polish Embassy was assured that the aforesaid institutions would receive food allotments (*fondy*) from appropriate Soviet organizations, and was encouraged to set up these institutions on the understanding that from then on the responsibility for the welfare of Polish citizens would rest with the Polish Embassy. In a verbal statement made by a representative of the People's Commissariat for Foreign Affairs to a representative of the Polish Embassy on September 26, 1942, the Government of the Union of Soviet Socialist Republics expressed its consent to the further extension of the network of the Embassy's relief institutions.

In accordance with the above, the Embassy set up on the territory of the Union of Soviet Socialist Republics, at considerable effort and great expense, several hundred relief institutions, and supplied them throughout their existence with substantial quantities of foodstuffs, clothing and medical supplies from abroad, either purchased by the Polish Government, or presented as a gift by Allied Governments and scores of welfare associations in Allied and neutral countries.

To the surprise of the Polish Government the Soviet authorities have recently begun to take over the administration of these institutions and, I state with regret, the Soviet Government did not even deem it necessary to inform the Polish Embassy thereof. In taking over the administration of these relief institutions the local Soviet authorities are at the same time dismissing some of the employees and inmates and are introducing different educational methods for those children remaining there.

The Polish Government also learned with regret that independently of the outcome of the present conversations in Moscow between the two Governments, with a view to reaching an agreement on their attitude in this matter, in the spirit of mutual friendship and collaboration underlying their present relations, the Government of the Union of Soviet Socialist Republics has not agreed to the suspension, at least during the course of the conversations now in progress, of the execution of its orders in respect of Polish citizens in the Union of Soviet Socialist Republics.

In such circumstances, the Polish Government find themselves regretfully compelled to lodge a determined protest against the very fact of removing the relief institutions from the administration of the Polish Embassy, as well as against the procedure adopted by the Soviet authorities in the matter. In the legal and *de facto* status of institutions, functioning on the basis of a bilateral agreement between the two Governments and disposing of property belonging to the Polish State, no changes could be made unless by mutual agreement of the two parties.

At the same time the Polish Government reserve their right to demand from the Government of the Union of Soviet Socialist Republics the restoration of

[1] See doc. No. 184.

all property belonging to the Polish State or to institutions taken over by Soviet authorities in these circumstances, also compensation for all damage and loss already sustained, or which may in future be sustained or brought to light in connection with the taking over of the Embassy's relief institutions.

No. 303

Note from Ambassador Bogomolov to Minister Raczyński in reply to the note of March 8, 1943 protesting against the execution of W. Alter and H. Ehrlich

London, March 31, 1943   GSHI, A.11. 49/Sow./3
                            Transl. from Russian: Pol.-Sov.R., No. 69

In reply to your Note of March 8, 1943,[1] I have the honour to inform you that the Soviet Government reject the entirely unfounded protest of the Polish Government concerning the execution of Ehrlich and Alter, sentenced on account of their activities directed against the USSR at the end of the year 1941, which went so far as to appeal to the Soviet armies to cease this bloodshed and to conclude an immediate peace with Germany; this at the time of the hardest struggle of the Soviet armies against the advancing armies of Hitler.

[1] See doc. No. 298.

No. 304

Note from Ambassador Romer to Commissar Molotov concerning the issuing of Polish passports to persons, whose Polish citizenship is 'unquestionable'

Kuibyshev, March 31, 1943   GSHI, A.11. 49/Sow./2

Au cours des conversations que j'ai eues avec Monsieur le Maréchal Stalin, Président du Conseil des Commissaires du Peuple en date du 26 février 1943,[1] et avec Votre Excellence, les 9 et 18 mars 1943,[2] il est clairement apparu qu'indépendamment du problème contesté entre nos deux Gouvernements, de la ressortissance d'une grande partie de la population polonaise séjournant actuellement dans l'Union Soviétique, les ressortissants polonais qui, en raison des hostilités, se sont accidentellement trouvés dans les provinces polonaises occupées par l'Armée Rouge dans la deuxième quinzaine du mois de septembre 1939, tout en ayant leur résidence d'avant-guerre dans d'autres provinces de la Pologne, continuent être considérés comme ressortissants incontestablement polonais autant par le Gouvernement polonais que par le Gouvernement soviétique.

Dans ces conditions, et en vue de limiter l'objet du litige, l'Ambassade de Pologne se propose de procéder à la délivrance de passeports polonais précisément à cette catégorie des ressortissants polonais incontestés. Etant donné que, jusqu'à présent, les autorités locales soviétiques se refusaient, à défaut d'instructions explicites, à munir les porteurs de passeports polonais de permis de séjour pour étrangers ('vid na jitielstvo dlya inostransta'), j'ai

[1] See doc. No. 295.   [2] See doc. Nos. 299 and 300.

l'honneur de prier Votre Excellence de bien vouloir prendre des mesures afin que les organes compétents de l'administration soviétique soient dûment instruits à ce sujet et autorisés à collaborer avec l'Ambassade de Pologne à l'effet de régulariser le séjour en territoire de l'Union Soviétique de cette catégorie au moins des ressortissants polonais.

Ce problème me semble d'autant plus urgent que, ces derniers temps, les cas deviennent de plus en plus fréquents où les autorités soviétiques locales invitent les ressortissants polonais, qu'elles ont reconnus comme tels, à se procurer à l'Ambassade de Pologne des passeports nationaux et leur imposent à cette fin des délais généralement trop courts et impossibles à observer en raison des distances, des lenteurs de correspondance et des difficultés techniques comme celle p.ex. d'obtenir des photographies.

Me conformant au désir que Votre Excellence a bien voulu m'exprimer au cours de notre conversation du 18 mars, j'ai l'honneur de Lui faire parvenir, ci-joint, un projet de procédure et d'échange d'informations sur l'identité des ressortissants polonais de ladite catégorie, à instituer entre le Commissariat du Peuple aux Affaires Etrangères et l'Ambassade de Pologne.

Je vous serais obligé de bien vouloir me communiquer aussitôt que possible les observations que ce projet vous aura suggérées ou bien de me convoquer à l'effet d'en discuter le contenu.

No. 305

Communiqué issued by Berlin Broadcasting station on the discovery of graves of Polish officers in the Smoleńsk area

Berlin, April 13, 1943, 9.15 p.m.   'Pariser Zeitung', No. 104 of April
                                                        14, 1943.
                                            Transl. from German

It is reported from Smoleńsk that the local population has indicated to the German authorities a place in which the Bolsheviks had perpetrated secretly mass executions and where the GPU had murdered 10,000 Polish officers.[1] The German authorities inspected the place called Kosogory, which is a Soviet summer resting place, situated 12 kilometres west of Smoleńsk, and made the most horrific discovery. A great pit was found, 28 metres long and 16 metres wide, filled with 12 layers of bodies of Polish officers, numbering about 3,000. They were clad in full military uniform, and while many of them had their hands tied, all of them had wounds in the back of their necks caused by pistol shots. The identification of the bodies will not cause great difficulties because of the mummifying property of the soil and because the Bolsheviks had left on the bodies the identity documents of the victims. It has already been ascertained that among the murdered is a General Smorawiński from Lublin. These officers had been previously in Kozielsk near Orel, from whence they had been brought in cattle wagons to

[1] The region of Smoleńsk fell into German hands between 17 and 24 of July 1941. The hill Kosogory forms the northern part of Katyń Wood.

523

Smoleńsk in February and March, 1940, and further on, taken in lorries to Kosogory where all were murdered by the Bolsheviks.

The discovery of and search for further grave pits is taking place. Under layers dug up already, new layers are found. The total figure of the murdered officers is estimated at 10,000 which would more or less correspond to the entire number of Polish officers taken as prisoners of war by the Bolsheviks. Norwegian press correspondents who arrived to inspect the place, and with their own eyes could ascertain the truth, have reported about the crime to the Oslo newspapers.

No. 306

Communiqué issued by the Soviet Information Bureau attacking the German propaganda in connection with the murder of Polish officers in the Smoleńsk area

Moscow, April 15, 1943 GSHI, A.11. 49/Sow./6
'Soviet War News', London, No. 541
of 17 April, 1943

In the past two or three days Goebbels' slanderers have been spreading vile fabrications alleging that Soviet authorities effected a mass shooting of Polish officers in the spring of 1940, in the Smoleńsk area. In launching this monstrous invention the German-Fascist scoundrels do not hesitate at the most unscrupulous and base lies, in their attempt to cover up crimes which, as has now become evident, were perpetrated by themselves.

The German Fascist reports on this subject leave no doubt as to the tragic fate of the former Polish prisoners of war who in 1941 were engaged in construction work in areas west of Smoleńsk and who, along with many Soviet people, residents of the Smoleńsk region, fell into the hands of the German-Fascist hangmen in the summer of 1941, after the withdrawal of the Soviet troops from the Smoleńsk area.

Beyond doubt Goebbels' slanderers are now trying by lies and calumnies to cover up the bloody crimes of the Hitlerite gangsters. In their clumsily concocted fabrication about the numerous graves which the Germans allegedly discovered near Smoleńsk, the Hitlerite liars mention the village of Gnezdovaya. But, like the swindlers they are, they are silent about the fact that it was near the village Gnezdovaya that the archaeological excavations of the historic 'Gnezdovaya burial place' were made.[1]

Pastmasters in such affairs, the Hitlerites stoop to the clumsiest forgeries and misrepresentation of facts in spreading slanderous fabrications about some sort of Soviet atrocities allegedly perpetrated in the spring of 1940, and in this way try to shake off their own responsibility for the brutal crimes they have committed.

These arrant German-Fascist murders, whose hands are stained with the blood of hundreds of thousands of innocent victims, who methodically

[1] The railway station Gniezdovo is twelve kilometres to the west of Smoleńsk, and Katyń Wood is situated four kilometres further in the same direction.

exterminate the populations of countries they have occupied without sparing children, women or old people, who exterminated many hundreds of thousands of Polish citizens in Poland itself, will deceive no one by their base lies and slander.

The Hitlerite murderers will not escape a just and inevitable retribution for their bloody crimes.

No. 307

Communiqué issued by the Polish Minister of National Defence concerning the fate of Polish prisoners of war in the camps of Kozielsk, Starobielsk and Ostashkov and the appeal to the International Red Cross for investigation[1]

London, April 16, 1943   GSHI, PRM, 102/4
                                            Transl. from Polish: Pol.-Sov.R., No. 39

On September 17, 1940, the official organ of the Red Army, the *Red Star*, stated that during the fighting which took place after September 17, 1939, 181,000 Polish prisoners of war were taken by the Soviets. Of this number about 10,000 were officers of the regular army and reserve.[2]

According to information in possession of the Polish Government, three large camps of Polish prisoners of war were set up in the USSR in November 1939:

1) in Kozielsk, east of Smoleńsk,
2) in Starobielsk, near Kharkov, and
3) In Ostashkov, near Kalinin, where police and military police were concentrated.

At the beginning of 1940 the camp authorities informed the prisoners in all three camps, that all camps were about to be broken up, that prisoners of war would be allowed to return to their families and, allegedly for this purpose, lists of places to which individual prisoners wished to go after their release were made.

At that time there were:

1) In Kozielsk, about 5,000 men, including some 4,500 officers.
2) In Starobielsk, about 3,920 men, including 100 civilians; the rest were officers of whom some were medical officers.
3) In Ostashkov, about 6,570 men, including some 380 officers.

On April 5, 1940, the breaking up of these camps was begun and groups of 60 to 300 men were removed from them every few days until the middle of May. From Kozielsk they were sent in the direction of Smoleńsk. About 400 people only were moved from all the three camps in June, 1940 to Griazovetz in the Vologda district.

When after the conclusion of the Polish-Soviet Treaty of July 30, 1941,[3] and the signing of the Military Agreement of August 14, 1941,[4] the Polish Government proceeded to form the Polish Army in the USSR, it was expected

---

[1] See Note No. 307.   [2] See doc. Nos. 177 and 280.
[3] See doc. No. 106.   [4] See doc. No. 112.

that the officers from the above-mentioned camps would form the cadres of senior and junior officers of the army in formation. At the end of August 1941 a group of Polish officers from Griazovetz arrived to join the Polish units in Buzuluk; not one officer, however, among those deported in other directions from Kozielsk, Starobielsk and Ostashkov appeared. In all therefore about 8,000 officers were missing, not counting another 7,000 NCO's, soldiers and civilians, who were in those camps when they were broken up.

Ambassador Kot and General Anders, perturbed by this state of affairs, addressed to the competent Soviet authorities enquiries and representations about the fate of the Polish officers from the above-mentioned camps.

In a conversation with Mr. Vyshinsky, People's Commissar for Foreign Affairs, on October 6, 1941, Ambassador Kot asked what had happened to the missing officers. Mr. Vyshinsky answered, that all prisoners of war had been freed from the camps and therefore they must be at liberty.[5]

In October and November, in his conversations with Premier Stalin, Mr. Molotov and Mr. Vyshinsky, the Ambassador on various occasions returned to the question of the prisoners of war and insisted upon being supplied with lists of them, such lists having been compiled carefully and in detail by the Soviet Government.

During his visit to Moscow, Prime Minister Sikorski in a conversation on December 3, 1941, with Premier Stalin, also intervened for the liberation of all Polish prisoners of war, and not having been supplied by the Soviet authorities with their lists, he handed to Premier Stalin on this occasion an incomplete list of 3,845 Polish officers which their former fellow-prisoners had succeeded in compiling.[6] Premier Stalin assured General Sikorski that the amnesty was of a general and universal character and affected both military and civilians, and that the Soviet Government had freed all Polish officers. On March 18, 1942, General Anders handed Premier Stalin a supplementary list of 800 officers.[7] Nevertheless not one of the officers mentioned in either of those lists has been returned to the Polish Army.

Besides the interventions in Moscow and Kuibyshev, the fate of Polish prisoners of war was the subject of several interviews between Minister Raczyński and Ambassador Bogomolov. On January 28, 1942, Minister Raczyński, in the name of the Polish Government, handed a Note to Soviet Ambassador Bogomolov, drawing his attention once again to the painful fact that many thousand Polish officers had still not been found.[8]

Ambassador Bogomolov informed Minister Raczyński on March 13, 1943, that in accordance with the Decree of the Presidium of the Supreme Council of USSR of August 12, 1941, and in accordance with the statements of the People's Commissariat for Foreign Affairs of November 8 and 19, 1941, the amnesty had been put into full effect, and that it related both to civilians and military.[9]

On May 19, 1942, Ambassador Kot sent the People's Commissariat for

[5] See doc. No. 127. The date should be October 6.
[6] See doc. No. 159. [7] See doc. No. 193. [8] See doc. No. 177.
[9] See doc. Nos. 142 and 154.

Foreign Affairs a Memorandum[10] in which he expressed his regret at the refusal to supply him with a list of prisoners, and his concern as to their fate, emphasizing the high value these officers would have in military operations against Germany.

Neither the Polish Government nor the Polish Embassy in Kuibyshev has ever received an answer as to the whereabouts of the missing officers and other prisoners who had been deported from the three camps mentioned above.

We have become accustomed to the lies of German propaganda and we understand the purpose behind its latest revelations. In view however of abundant and detailed German information concerning the discovery of the bodies of many thousands of Polish officers near Smoleńsk, and the categorical statement that they were murdered by the Soviet authorities in the spring of 1940, the necessity has arisen that the mass graves discovered should be investigated and the facts alleged verified by a competent international body, such as the International Red Cross. The Polish Government has therefore approached this institution with a view to their sending a delegation to the place where the massacre of the Polish prisoners of war is said to have taken place.

[10] See doc. No. 221.

No. 308

Statement of the Polish Government concerning the discovery of the graves of Polish officers near Smoleńsk

London, April 17, 1943   GSHI, PRM, 102/4
                            Transl. from Polish: GSHI, Wyc.11/8

No Pole can help but be deeply shocked by the news, now given the widest publicity by the Germans, of the discovery of the bodies of the Polish officers missing in the USSR in a common grave near Smoleńsk, and of the mass execution of which they were victims.

The Polish Government has instructed their representative in Switzerland to request the International Red Cross in Geneva to send a delegation to investigate the true state of affairs on the spot. It is to be desired that the findings of this protective institution, which is to be entrusted with the task of clarifying the matter and of establishing responsibility, should be issued without delay.

At the same time, however, the Polish Government, on behalf of the Polish nation, denies to the Germans any right to base on a crime they ascribe to others, arguments in their own defence. The profoundly hypocritical indignation of German propaganda will not succeed in concealing from the world the many cruel and reiterated crimes still being perpetrated against the Polish people.

The Polish Government recalls such facts as the removal of Polish officers from prisoner-of-war camps in the Reich and the subsequent shooting of them for political offences alleged to have been committed before the war, mass arrests of reserve officers subsequently deported to concentration camps, to die a slow death,—from Cracow and the neighbouring district alone 6,000 were deported in June, 1942; the compulsory enlistment in the German army of Polish prisoners of war from territories illegally incorporated in the Reich; the forcible conscription of about 200,000 Poles from the same territories, and the execution of the families of those who managed to escape; the massacre of one-and-a-half-million people by executions or in concentration camps; the recent imprisonment of 80,000 people of military age, officers and men, and their torture and murder in the camps of Maydanek and Tremblinka.

It is not to enable the Germans to make impudent claims and pose as the defenders of Christianity and European civilization, that Poland is making immense sacrifices, fighting and enduring suffering. The blood of Polish soldiers and Polish citizens, wherever it is shed, cries for atonement before the conscience of the free peoples of the world. The Polish Government condemn all the crimes committed against Polish citizens and refuse the right to make political capital of such sacrifices, to all who are themselves guilty of such crimes.

No. 309

Note from Minister Raczyński to Ambassador Bogomolov demanding an explanation of the fate of Polish prisoners missing in the USSR

London, April 20, 1943   GSHI, PRM., 101/1
                                            Transl. from Polish: Pol.-Sov.R., No. 41

Foreign telegraph agencies publish a report of the German military authorities concerning the discovery at Kozia Góra near Katyń in the vicinity of Smoleńsk of a mass-grave containing the bodies of the Polish officers allegedly killed in the spring of 1940. During the first few days 155 bodies were identified among which the body of Major-General Mieczysław Smorawiński is supposed to have been found.

This report, although emanating from enemy sources, has produced profound anxiety not only in Polish public opinion but also throughout the world.

In a public statement on April 17, 1943, the Polish Government categorically condemned Germany's attempt to exploit the tragedy of Polish prisoners of war in the USSR for her own political ends. But more than ever the Polish Government unalterably maintains its attitude that the truth about this case so cynically exploited by Hitlerite propaganda must be fully elucidated.

You are no doubt aware, Mr. Ambassador, that after the conclusion of the Polish-Soviet Agreement of July 30, 1941, the Polish Government repeatedly approached the civil and military authorities of the USSR with requests for information concerning the prisoners of war and civilians who were in the camps of Kozielsk (East of Smoleńsk), Starobielsk (near Kharkov) and Ostashkov (near Kalinin).

According to information of the Polish Government there were in all at the beginning of 1940, 15,490 Polish citizens, including 8,700 officers, in the three above-mentioned camps. From April 5, 1940, until the middle of May, 1940, the Soviet authorities proceeded to break up these camps, deporting the inmates in batches every few days. Prisoners of the Kozielsk camp were deported in the direction of Smoleńsk, and from all the three camps only 400 men were transferred in the last batches, first to the Yukhnovski camp (railway station Babynino) and subsequently in June 1940, to Griazovetz in the Vologda district.

When, after the signing of the Polish-Soviet military agreement on August 14, 1943, the Polish Government proceeded with the organization of the Polish Army in the USSR, the camp of Griazovetz, to which in the meantime military and civilian prisoners from other camps had arrived, was also broken up and from the above-mentioned group of 400 prisoners more than 200 officers reported for service in the Polish Army before the end of August, 1941. All the other officers however, who were deported to an unknown destination from the camps of Kozielsk, Starobielsk and Ostashkov, have neither been found nor have they given any sign of life. So it became apparent that more than 8,000 officers were missing who might have supplied the cadres of senior and junior officers of the army in formation and who would have been of inestimable value in the military operations against Germany.

From October 1941, both Ambassador Kot and General Anders, Commander-in-Chief of the Polish Army in the USSR, constantly intervened, both orally and in writing, in the matter of the missing officers. Ambassador Kot discussed this subject with Premier Stalin, with Mr. Molotov, People's Commissar for Foreign Affairs, and with Mr. Vyshinsky, Deputy People's Commissar for Foreign Affairs, demanding a list of the prisoners detained in the three camps mentioned above and an explanation as to their fate. During his visit to Moscow in December, 1941, General Sikorski also intervened in the above matter in a conversation with Mr. Stalin and on that occasion handed him a list containing the names of 3,845 Polish officers. On March 18, 1942, General Anders gave Mr. Stalin, Chairman of the Council of People's Commissars, a list of 800 officers. On January 28, 1942, I had the honour to send you, Mr. Ambassador, a Note in which I emphasized the anxiety of the Polish Government at the failure to find many thousands of Polish officers. Lastly, on May 19, 1942, Ambassador Kot sent the People's Commissariat for Foreign Affairs a Memorandum in which, reverting again to the question of the missing officers, he expressed his regret at the refusal to supply him with the list of prisoners, and his concern as to their fate.[1]

I regret the necessity of calling your attention, Mr. Ambassador, to the fact that the Polish Government in spite of reiterated requests, has never received either a list of the prisoners or definite information as to the whereabouts of the missing officers and of other prisoners deported from the three camps mentioned above. Official, verbal and written statements of the representatives of the USSR have been confined to mere assurances that,

[1] See doc. No. 307.

in accordance with a Decree of the Presidium of the Supreme Council of the USSR, dated August 12, 1941, the amnesty was of a general and universal character as it included both military and civilian prisoners, and that the Government of the USSR had released all the Polish officers from prisoner of war camps.

I should like to emphasize that the Polish Government, as can be seen from their many representations quoted above, entirely independently of recent German revelations, has never regarded the question of the missing officers as closed. If, however, as shown by the communiqué of the Soviet Information Bureau of April 15, 1943, the Government of the USSR would seem to be in possession of more ample information on this matter than was communicated to the representatives of the Polish Government sometime ago, I beg once more to request you, Mr. Ambassador, to communicate to the Polish Government detailed and precise information as to the fate of the prisoners of war and civilians previously detained in the camps of Kozielsk, Starobielsk and Ostashkov.

Public opinion in Poland and throughout the world has rightly been so deeply shocked that only irrefutable facts can outweigh the numerous and detailed German statements concerning the discovery of the bodies of many thousand Polish officers murdered near Smoleńsk in the spring of 1940.

No. 310

Telegram from M. Stalin to Mr. Churchill on the subject of the accusation made by the Polish Government against the USSR on account of the discovery of Polish officers' graves in Katyń

Moscow, April 21, 1943　　　　　　　　　　Cor. Churchill–Stalin. I, No. 150

The behaviour of the Polish Government towards the USSR of late is, in the view of the Soviet Government, completely abnormal and contrary to all the rules and standards governing relations between two allied states.

The anti-Soviet slander campaign launched by the German fascists in connection with the Polish officers whom they themselves murdered in the Smoleńsk area, in German-occupied territory, was immediately seized upon by the Sikorski Government and is being fanned in every way by the Polish official press. Far from countering the infamous fascist slander against the USSR, the Sikorski Government has not found it necessary even to address questions to the Soviet Government or to request information on the matter.

The Hitler authorities, having perpetrated a monstrous crime against the Polish officers, are now staging a farcical investigation, using for the purpose certain pro-fascist Polish elements picked by themselves in occupied Poland, where everything is under Hitler's heel and where no honest Pole can open his mouth.

Both the Sikorski and Hitler Governments have enlisted for the 'investigation' the aid of the International Red Cross, which, under a terror régime of gallows and wholesale extermination of the civil population, is forced to take part in the investigation farce directed by Hitler. It is obvious that this 'investigation', which, moreover, is being carried out behind the Soviet Government's back, cannot enjoy the confidence of anyone with a semblance of honesty.

The fact that the anti-Soviet campaign has been started simultaneously in the German and Polish press and follows identical lines is indubitable evidence of contact and collusion between Hitler—the Allies' enemy—and the Sikorski Government in this hostile campaign.

At a time when the peoples of the Soviet Union are shedding their blood in a grim struggle against Hitler Germany and bending their energies to defeat the common foe of the freedom-loving democratic countries, the Sikorski Government is striking a treacherous blow at the Soviet Union to help Hitler tyranny.

These circumstances compel the Soviet Government to consider that the present Polish Government, having descended to collusion with the Hitler Government, has, in practice, severed its relations of alliance with the USSR and adopted a hostile attitude to the Soviet Union.

For these reasons the Soviet Government has decided to interrupt relations with that Government.

I think it necessary to inform you of the foregoing, and I trust that the British Government will appreciate the motives that necessitated this forced step on the part of the Soviet Government.

No. 311

Communiqué issued by the International Committee of the Red Cross on the conditions of its participation in the identification of the bodies discovered in the Smoleńsk area

Geneva, April 23, 1943   Report of the ICRC, I/428–9

The 'Report of the International Committee of the Red Cross on its activities during the Second World War' quotes the following circumstances that caused the issue of the below Communiqué.

'On April 15, 1943, the ICRC received from the German Red Cross a request to take part in the operations of disinternment; all facilities were offered for the immediate departure of an ICRC delegation. In a second application, the German Red Cross asked the assistance of the Committee in identifying bodies which, they stated, were the bodies of Polish officers reported missing in the USSR and "who were stated to have been murdered by the Bolshevists".

On April 17, the Polish Government in London also asked that representatives of the ICRC "should be allowed to examine on the spot the situation described by the German communiqués".

On account of the publicity this case received throughout the world, the ICRC made known their answer in a press communiqué, on April 23, as follows:[1]

[1] This answer was sent to the Polish Ministry for Foreign Affairs on April 22, 1943.

"The German Red Cross and the Polish Government in London have applied to the ICRC, asking it to participate in the identification of the bodies which have been discovered, according to German reports, in the vicinity of Smoleńsk. The ICRC have replied in both cases that, in principle, it would be ready to lend assistance in appointing neutral experts, on condition that all the parties concerned ask them to do so, in conformity with the memorandum sent by the ICRC on September 12, 1939 to the belligerent States, and in which the Committee established, at the outbreak of war, the principles according to which it could ultimately take part in such investigation." [2]

Shortly after, on May 4, the Polish Government withdrew their application. The German Government never confirmed the requests made by the German Red Cross. As for the Soviet Government, it never sent any request to the Committee on the subject. For these reasons, the conditions laid down by the Committee were not met. The Committee therefore took no part, even indirectly, in the investigation of the case known as the Katyń Forest Affair.'

[2] This memorandum was published in *Revue internationale* Geneva, issue: September 1939, pp. 766–769. Abbreviation: ICRC = International Committee of the Red Cross.

No. 312

Telegram from Mr. Churchill to M. Stalin on the tension in Polish-Soviet relations caused by the discovery of graves in Katyń

London, April 24, 1943   Cor. Churchill–Stalin, I, No. 151

Ambassador Maisky delivered your message to me last night. We shall certainly oppose vigorously any 'investigation' by the International Red Cross or any other body in any territory under German authority. Such investigation would be a fraud, and its conclusions reached by terrorism. Mr. Eden is seeing Sikorski today and will press him as strongly as possible to withdraw all countenance from any investigation under Nazi auspices. Also we should never approve of any parley with the Germans or contact with them of any kind whatever and we shall press this point upon our Polish allies.

2. I shall telegraph to you later how Sikorski reacts to the above points. His position is one of great difficulty. Far from being pro-German or in league with them, he is in danger of being overthrown by the Poles who consider that he has not stood up sufficiently for his people against the Soviets. If he should go we should only get somebody worse. I hope therefore that your decision to 'interrupt' relations is to be read in the sense of a final warning rather than of a break and that it will not be made public at any rate until every other plan has been tried. The public announcement of a break would do the greatest possible harm in the United States, where the Poles are numerous and influential.

3. I had drafted a telegram to you yesterday asking you to consider allowing more Poles and Polish dependents to go into Iran. This would allay the rising discontent of the Polish army formed there and would enable me to influence the Polish Government to act in conformity with our common interests and against the common foe. I have deferred sending this telegram in consequence of yours to me in hopes that the situation may clear.

No. 313

Note from Commissar Molotov to Ambassador Romer concerning the severance of relations between the Soviet Government and the Polish Government

Moscow, April 25, 1943 GSHI, A.11. 49/Sow./3
Transl. from Russian: Pol.-Sov.R., No 88

On behalf of the Government of the Union of Soviet Socialist Republics, I have the honour to notify the Polish Government of the following:

The Soviet Government consider the recent behaviour of the Polish Government with regard to the USSR as entirely abnormal, and violating all regulations and standards of relations between two Allied States. The slanderous campaign hostile to the Soviet Union launched by the German Fascists in connection with the murder of the Polish officers, which they themselves committed in the Smoleńsk area on territory occupied by German troops, was at once taken up by the Polish Government and is being fanned in every way by the Polish official press.

Far from offering a rebuff to the vile Fascist slander of the USSR, the Polish Government did not even find it necessary to address to the Soviet Government any enquiry or request for an explanation on this subject.

Having committed a monstrous crime against the Polish officers, the Hitlerite authorities are now staging a farcical investigation, and for this they have made use of certain Polish pro-Fascist elements whom they themselves selected in occupied Poland where everything is under Hitler's heel, and where no honest Pole can openly have his say.

For the 'investigation', both the Polish Government and the Hitlerite Government invited the International Red Cross, which is compelled, in conditions of a terroristic régime, with its gallows and mass extermination of the peaceful population, to take part in this investigation farce staged by Hitler. Clearly such an 'investigation', conducted behind the back of the Soviet Government, cannot evoke the confidence of people possessing any degree of honesty.

The fact that the hostile campaign against the Soviet Union commenced simultaneously in the German and Polish press, and was conducted along the same lines, leaves no doubt as to the existence of contact and accord in carrying out this hostile campaign between the enemy of the Allies—Hitler— and the Polish Government.

While the peoples of the Soviet Union bleeding profusely in a hard struggle against Hitlerite Germany, are straining every effort for the defeat of the common enemy of the Russian and Polish peoples, and of all freedom-loving democratic countries, the Polish Government, to please Hitler's tyranny, has dealt a treacherous blow to the Soviet Union.

The Soviet Government is aware that this hostile campaign against the Soviet Union is being undertaken by the Polish Government in order to exert pressure upon the Soviet Government by making use of the slanderous Hitlerite fake for the purpose of wresting from it territorial concessions at the expense of the interests of the Soviet Ukraine, Soviet Byelorussia and Soviet Lithuania.

All these circumstances compel the Soviet Government to recognize that the present Government of Poland, having slid on the path of accord with Hitler's Government, has actually discontinued allied relations with the USSR, and has adopted a hostile attitude towards the Soviet Union.

On the strength of the above, the Soviet Government has decided to sever relations with the Polish Government.

No. 314

Telegram from M. Stalin to Mr. Churchill informing him of the severance of the relations between the Soviet Government and the Polish Government

Moscow, April 25, 1943   Cor. Churchill–Stalin, I, No. 152

I have received your message concerning Polish affairs. Thank you for your sympathetic stand on this issue. I must tell you, however, that the matter of interrupting relations with the Polish Government has already been settled and that today V. M. Molotov delivered a Note to the Polish Government. All my colleagues insisted on this because the Polish official press is not only keeping up its hostile campaign but is actually intensifying it day by day. I also had to take cognizance of Soviet public opinion, which is deeply outraged by the ingratitude and treachery of the Polish Government.

As to publishing the Soviet document on interrupting relations with the Polish Government, I fear that it is simply impossible to avoid doing so.

No. 315

Telegram from Mr. Churchill to M. Stalin on the severing of relations between the Soviet Government and the Polish Government

London, April 25, 1943   Cor. Churchill–Stalin, I, No. 153

Mr. Eden saw General Sikorski yesterday evening. Sikorski stated that so far from synchronizing his appeal to the Red Cross with that of the Germans his Government took the initiative without knowing what line the Germans would take. In fact the Germans acted after hearing the Polish broadcast announcement. Sikorski also told Mr. Eden that his Government had simultaneously approached Monsieur Bogomolov on the subject. Sikorski emphasized that previously he had several times raised this question of the missing officers with the Soviet Government and once with you personally. On his instructions the Polish Minister of Information in his broadcasts has reacted strongly against the German propaganda and this has brought an angry German reply. As a result of Mr. Eden's strong representations Sikorski has undertaken not to press the request for the Red Cross investigation and will so inform the Red Cross authorities in Berne. He will also restrain the Polish press from polemics. In this connection I am examining the possibility of silencing those Polish newspapers in this country which attacked the Soviet Government and at the same time attacked Sikorski for trying to work with the Soviet Government.

In view of Sikorski's undertaking I would now urge you to abandon the idea of any interruption of relations.

I have reflected further on this matter and I am more than ever convinced that it can only assist our enemies, if there is a break between the Soviet and Polish Governments. German propaganda has produced this story precisely in order to make a rift in the ranks of the United Nations and to lend some semblance of reality to its new attempts to persuade the world that the interests of Europe and the smaller nations are being defended by Germany against the great extra-European Powers, namely the Union of Soviet Socialist Republics, the United States and the British Empire.

I know General Sikorski well and I am convinced that no contacts or understanding could exist between him or his Government and our common enemy, against whom he has led the Poles in bitter and uncompromising resistance. His appeal to the International Red Cross was clearly a mistake though I am convinced that it was not made in collusion with the Germans.

Now that we have, I hope, cleared up the issue raised in your telegram to me, I want to revert to the proposals contained in my draft telegram to which I referred in my message of April 24th. I shall therefore shortly be sending you this earlier message in its original form. If we two were able to arrange to link the matter of getting these Poles out of the Soviet Union it would be easier for Sikorski to withdraw entirely from the position he has been forced by his public opinion to adopt. I hope that you will help me to achieve this.

No. 316

Note from Ambassador Romer to Commissar Molotov stating the reasons for his refusal to accept the Soviet note of 25 April, 1943, concerning the severance of relations between the Government of the USSR and the Government of Poland

Moscow, April 26, 1943
GSHI, A.11. 49/Sow./2
Transl. from Polish: Pol.-Sov.R., No. 89

You were good enough to receive me today at 0.15 a.m. at your own invitation and for the purpose of reading to me a Note dated April 25, 1943, signed by yourself and addressed to me, notifying me of the decision of the Soviet Government to sever relations with the Polish Government. Upon hearing the text of the Note, I declared that there was nothing I could do but accept with regret the news of this decision of the Soviet Government, which will be held fully and exclusively responsible for this step. At the same time, however, I most emphatically refused to be a party to the motives and conclusions set forth in the Note that was read to me, and which ascribed to the Polish Government in an inadmissible form, conduct and intentions entirely inconsistent with the facts, thus making it impossible for me to accept your Note. I stated, moreover, that contrary to the allegations contained in the Note, the Polish Government had striven for close on two years to obtain from the Soviet Government information concerning the fate of the missing Polish officers, and had as recently as the 20 inst., returned to this matter in a Note to Ambassador Bogomolov.

Since, despite my refusal to accept the Note, I received it later at my hotel in a sealed envelope of the People's Commissariat for Foreign Affairs, I have the honour to return it herewith in conformity with my attitude as set forth above.

No. 317

Telegram from President Roosevelt to M. Stalin expressing the hope that the severance of relations between the USSR and Poland will be only temporary

Washington, April 26, 1943   Cor. Roosevelt–Stalin, II, No. 81

I received your telegram during an inspection trip which I was making in the western part of the United States. I fully understand your problem but at the same time I hope that you can find a way in this present situation to define your action as a suspension of conversations with the Polish Government in exile in London rather than to label it as a complete severance of diplomatic relations between the Soviet Union and Poland.

I cannot believe that Sikorski has in any way whatsoever collaborated with the Hitler gangsters. In my opinion, however, he has erred in taking up this particular question with the International Red Cross. Furthermore, I am inclined to think that Prime Minister Churchill will find a way of prevailing upon the Polish Government in London in the future to act with more common sense.

I would appreciate it if you would let me know if I can help in any way in respect to this question and particularly in connection with looking after any Poles which you may desire to send out of the Union of Soviet Socialist Republics.

Incidentally, I have several million Poles in the United States, a great many of whom are in the Army and Navy. I can assure you that all of them are bitter against the Hitlerites. However, the overall situation would not be helped by the knowledge of a complete diplomatic break between the Soviet and Polish Governments.

No. 318

Statement of the Polish Government concerning the decision of the Soviet Government to sever relations with the Polish Government[1]

London, April 28, 1943

GSHI, PRM, 103/1
Official transl. from Polish

The Polish Government affirm that their policy, aiming at a friendly understanding between Poland and Soviet Russia on the basis of the integrity and full sovereignty of the Polish Republic, was and continues to be fully supported by the Polish Nation.

Conscious of their responsibility towards their own nation and towards the Allies, whose unity and solidarity the Polish Government consider to be the corner-stone of future victory, they were the first to approach the Soviet Government with a proposal for a common understanding, in spite of the many tragic events which had taken place from the moment of the entry of the Soviet Armies on the territory of the Republic, i.e. September 17th, 1939.

Having regulated their relations with Soviet Russia by the agreement of July 30th, 1941, and by the understanding of December 4th, 1941, the Polish Government have scrupulously discharged their obligations.

Acting in close union with their Government, the Polish people, making the extreme sacrifice, fight implacably in Poland and outside the frontiers of their country against the German invaders. No traitor Quisling has sprung from Polish ranks. All collaboration with the Germans has been scorned. In the light of facts known throughout the world the Polish Government and Polish Nation have no need to defend themselves from any suggestion of contact or understanding with Hitler.

In a public statement of April 17th, 1943, the Polish Government categorically denied to Germany the right to abuse the tragedy of Polish Officers for her own perfidious schemes.[2] They unhesitatingly denounce Nazi propaganda designed to create mistrust between Allies. About the same time a note was sent to the Soviet Ambassador accredited to the Polish Government asking once again for information which would help to elucidate the fate of the missing officers.

The Polish Government and people look to the future. They appeal in the name of the solidarity of the United Nations and the elementary humanity for the release from the USSR of the thousands of the families of Polish Armed Forces engaged in the fight or preparing in Great Britain and in the Middle East to take part in their fight—tens of thousands of Polish orphans and children for the education of whom they would take full responsibility and who now, in view of the German mass slaughter, are particularly precious to the Polish people. The Polish Army, in waging the war against Germany, will also require for reinforcement all fighting Polish males who are now on Soviet soil, and the Polish Government appeal for their release. They reserve their right to plead the cause of all these persons to the world. In conclusion,

[1] This statement was transmitted by the BBC on April 28 with the omission of a few sentences.　　　　　　　　　　　　　　　[2] See doc. No. 308.

the Polish Government ask for the continuation of relief welfare for the mass of Polish citizens who will remain in the USSR.

In defending the integrity of the Polish Republic, which accepted the war with the Third Reich, the Polish Government never claimed and do not claim, in accordance with their statement of February 25th, 1943, any Soviet territories.[3]

It is and will be the duty of every Polish Government to defend the rights of Poland and of Polish citizens. The principles for which the United Nations are fighting and also the making of all efforts for strengthening their solidarity in this struggle against the common enemy, remain the unchanging basis of the policy of the Polish Government.

[3] See doc. No. 294.

No. 319

Telegram from M. Stalin to President Roosevelt assuring him that Poles in the USSR would be able to leave the country without any difficulty

Moscow, April 29, 1943   Cor. Roosevelt–Stalin, II, No. 82

I am sorry to say your reply did not reach me until April 27, whereas on April 25 the Soviet Government was compelled to interrupt relations with the Polish Government.

As the Polish Government for nearly two weeks, far from ceasing a campaign hostile to the Soviet Union and beneficial to none but Hitler, intensified it in its press and on the radio, Soviet public opinion was deeply outraged by such conduct, and hence the Soviet Government could no longer defer action.

It may well be that Mr. Sikorski himself has no intention of collaborating with the Hitler gangsters. I should be happy to see this surmise borne out by facts. But my impression is that certain pro-Hitler elements—either inside the Polish Government or in its environment—have induced Mr. Sikorski to follow them, with the result that the Polish Government has come to be, possibly against its own will, a tool in Hitler's hands in the anti-Soviet campaign of which you are aware.

I, too, believe that Prime Minister Churchill will find ways to bring the Polish Government to reason and help it proceed henceforward in a spirit of common sense. I may be wrong, but I believe that one of our duties as Allies is to prevent this or that Ally from taking hostile action against any other Ally to the joy and benefit of the common enemy.

As regards Polish subjects in the USSR and their future, I can assure you that Soviet Government agencies have always treated and will continue to treat them as comrades, as people near and dear to us. It should be obvious that there never has been, nor could have been, any question of their being deported from the USSR. If, however, they themselves wish to leave the USSR, Soviet Government agencies will not hinder them, just as they have never done, and will, in fact, try to help them.

538

No. 320

Telegram from Mr. Churchill to M. Stalin appealing for the resumption of relations between the Government of the USSR and the Government of Poland

London, April 30, 1943   Cor. Churchill–Stalin, I, No. 154

I cannot refrain from expressing my disappointment that you should have felt it necessary to take action in breaking off relations with the Poles without giving me time to inform you of the results of my approach to General Sikorski, about which I had telegraphed to you on April 24th. I had hoped that, in the spirit of our treaty of last year, we should always consult each other about such important matters, more especially as they affect the combined strength of the United Nations.

2. Mr. Eden and I have pointed out to the Polish Government that no resumption of friendly or working relations with the Soviets is possible while they make charges of an insulting character against the Soviet Government and thus seem to countenance the atrocious Nazi propaganda. Still more would it be impossible for any of us to tolerate enquiries by the International Red Cross held under Nazi auspices and dominated by Nazi terrorism. I am glad to tell you that they have accepted our view and that they want to work loyally with you. Their request now is to have dependents of the Polish army in Iran and the fighting Poles in the Soviet Union sent to join the Polish forces already allowed to go to Iran. This is surely a matter which admits of patient discussion. We think the request is reasonable if made in the right way and at the right time and I am pretty sure that the President thinks so too. We hope earnestly that remembering the difficulties in which we have all been plunged by the brutal Nazi aggression, you will consider this matter in a spirit of collaboration.

3. The Cabinet here is determined to have proper discipline in the Polish press in Great Britain. The miserable rags attacking Sikorski can say things which German broadcasts repeat open-mouthed to the world to our joint detriment. This must be stopped and it will be stopped.

4. So far this business has been Goebbels' triumph. He is now busy suggesting that the USSR will set up a Polish Government on Russian soil and deal only with them. We should not, of course, be able to recognize such a Government and would continue our relations with Sikorski who is far the most helpful man you or we are likely to find for the purposes of the common cause. I expect that this will also be the American view.

5. My own feeling is that they have had a shock and that after whatever interval is thought convenient the relationship established on July 30th, 1941, should be restored. No one will hate this more than Hitler and what he hates most is wise for us to do.

6. We owe it to our armies now engaged and presently to be more heavily engaged to maintain good conditions behind the fronts. I and my colleagues look steadily to the ever closer co-operation and understanding of the USSR, the United States and the British Commonwealth and Empire, not only in

the deepening war struggle, but after the war. What other hope can there be than this for the tortured world?

No. 321

Communiqué issued by the Polish Government on the failure of the Polish appeal to the International Red Cross organization in Geneva to investigate the graves in Katyń

London, April 30, 1943　　　　　　　　　　　　　　　　GSHI, Wyc.11/8

In their communiqué issued on April 28th, the Polish Government did not revert to their appeal to the International Red Cross Committee to investigate the graves of Polish officers found near Smoleńsk, the discovery of which was exploited by German propaganda.

In their reply to the Polish Government the International Red Cross Committee explained the difficulties which they found in the way of complying with the Polish request.[1]

In the circumstances the Polish Government regard their appeal as having lapsed.

[1] See doc. No. 311.

APPENDIX No. 1

Citizenship of the Union of Soviet Socialist Republics Act[1]

Moscow, August 19, 1938

GSHI, A.11. 49/Sow./3
Transl. from Russian

Article 1

Pursuant to Article 21 of the Constitution of the Union of Soviet Socialist Republics there is one citizenship of Union for all the citizens of the USSR. Each citizen of a Republic of the Union is a citizen of the USSR.

Article 2

Citizens of the USSR are:

(*a*) all those who until 7th November, 1917 were subjects of the former Russian Empire and have not forfeited Soviet citizenship;

(*b*) those who have acquired Soviet citizenship by means established by law.

Article 3

Aliens, of whatever nationality or race, can acquire the citizenship of the USSR at their own request by a decision of the Praesidium of the Supreme Soviet of the USSR or the Praesidium of the Supreme Soviet of the republic on the territory of which they reside.

Article 4

Release from the citizenship of the USSR is granted by the Praesidium of the Supreme Soviet of the USSR.

Article 5

Contracting marriage by a citizen of the USSR, of either sex, with a person who is not a Soviet citizen does not effect a change of citizenship.

Article 6

In the event of a change of nationality of parents, whereby both become citizens of the USSR or both forfeit citizenship of the USSR, a respective change of the citizenship of children who have not attained the age of 14 is effected. A change of citizenship of children between the ages of 14–18 can take place only with their consent. In other cases the change of citizenship of children below the age of 18 can take place only in the usual way.

---

[1] The organ of the Central Committee of the All Union Communist Party *Pravda* in its issue of August 18, 1938 (No. 227), published a long article by N. A. Bulganin reviewing the Draft Act which was laid before the Second Session of the All Union Soviet of the USSR, and, in its issue of August 20, gave a detailed account of the discussion on the preceding day ending with unanimous approval of the new Act. There appeared also in the same issue a commentary on the approved Act under the title 'The High and Honourable Position of a Citizen of the USSR' (vysokoye i pochetnoye zvaniie grazhdanina SSSR).

Article 7

A person may be deprived of the citizenship of the USSR by virtue of:

(*a*) a judgement of the court in cases specified by law;

(*b*) a special decree, in each particular case, of the Praesidium of the Supreme Soviet of the USSR.

Article 8

Persons residing on the territory of the USSR who, pursuant to this Act, are not citizens of the USSR and are not in possession of evidence establishing their foreign citizenship, are considered stateless.

Moscow, the 19th of August, 1938

> Chairman of the Praesidium of the Supreme Soviet of the USSR
>
> (–) M. Kalinin
>
> Secretary of the Praesidium of the Supreme Soviet of the USSR
>
> (–) A. Gorkin

APPENDIX No. 2

Extracts from the minutes of fourth and fifth meetings of Anglo-Franco-Soviet Military Delegations on the passage of Soviet troops through Polish territory

Moscow, August 14 and 15, 1939   D.Brit.F.P., VII/570–575

The following Heads of Delegations were present: Marshal of the USSR Voroshilov, Kommandarm I. Shaposhnikov, Général d'Armée Doumenc, General Valin, Admiral The Hon. Sir Reginald A. R. Plunkett-Ernle-Erle-Drax, Air Marshal Sir Charles Burnett and Major-General T. G. G. Heywood.

Meeting of August 14, 1939. Marshal Voroshilov was in the chair. [. . .]

21. Marshal Voroshilov opened the meeting. He then stated that, at the last meeting, Général Doumenc had given him a draft of the principles on which the co-operation of the three Powers might be based. It was evident that the principles contained in this draft would be the basis of a military convention if this were reached. The Soviet Mission therefore consider that these principles are very important, and must request more time in which to study the draft.

Admiral Drax and Général Doumenc agreed that the discussion of the draft should be postponed until the Soviet delegation had had the necessary time for consultation. [. . .]

24. Général Doumenc, turning to the eastern front, said that the initial front would be that of the Polish and Roumanian armies, on that front also assistance and additional communications would be required; if circumstances rendered it possible and desirable, there might be an intermediate front, but that is a matter for Marshal Voroshilov to decide. There was also the very important question of sea communications between the two fronts, which, it had been agreed, should be studied later. In addition, there are two points on which co-operation is essential:

/i/ Joint action against the communications of the Fascist Powers.

/ii/ Joint action of the independent fighter and bomber air forces of the three Powers.

It has already been agreed to study these questions in due course.

25. Marshal Voroshilov said that Général Doumenc's exposé was not sufficiently clear. He must ask to be exused for speaking so abruptly, but soldiers could speak their minds to one another. He did not understand what part it was suggested that the Soviet Army should play.

Général Doumenc said that the enemy must never be allowed to break through the Soviet Western Frontier, and he presumed that the Red Army would concentrate on that Frontier.

Marshal Voroshilov stated that his Front was always occupied. The Fascist Powers would never break through whether the Delegations reached agreement or not. [. . .]

28. Marshal Voroshilov said that though the Red Army is well disposed for the defence of its own frontiers, it is not well disposed for offensive operations. He wanted to know how, in the opinion of the British and French General Staffs, the Soviet land forces can act in case of aggression. He would put the following precise questions:—

Do the British and French General Staffs think that the Red Army can move across North Poland, and in particular the Wilno Salient, and across Galicia in order to make contact with the enemy? Will Soviet troops be allowed to cross Roumanian territory?

Admiral Drax said it would be a great help to Poland and Roumania to know that the Red Army was massed behind them, and ready to advance to an agreed line upon which the Germans must be held. Further, in his opinion, as operations developed these two countries would solicit the support of the Soviet Army.

Général Doumenc agreed and stated that the concentration areas of the Red Army as indicated by the Marshal appeared to him to be most suitable for this purpose. The weakest points on the Polish-Roumanian Front would be their flanks and points of junction. [. . .]

31. Marshal Voroshilov said that with Soviet troops operating against East Prussia and in Galicia, and England and France operating in the West, it would be the end of Germany. The question of a passage of Soviet troops through Poland and Roumania was therefore of primary importance to the Allied cause. He noted with interest Admiral Drax's suggestion that Poland and Roumania might be overrun, and if they did not ask for Soviet assistance in time they might become German provinces. He did not disagree with this suggestion, but felt that everyone present should note it. If these countries asked for support too late they would be destroyed, which would be against the interests of the three contracting Powers. Preliminary steps must therefore be taken to obviate this danger. The allies would have to make use of the forces of these States. [. . .]

35. [. . .] on reopening the meeting General Heywood, on behalf of the British and French Delegations, made the following statement to the Soviet Delegation:—

'We have already given our personal opinion quite clearly, and we take note of Marshal Voroshilov's summary of the situation. But it must not be forgotten that Poland and Roumania are sovereign States, and that the authority required by the Soviet Mission must be obtained from these two Governments. This becomes a political question, and we therefore suggest that the Soviet Government should ask the Polish and Roumanian Governments for the answer. This is obviously the most simple and direct procedure. If the Marshal specially wishes it, we are prepared to refer to London and Paris, to ask if our Governments would be ready to ask the Polish and Roumanian Governments the following question:—

If the USSR is our ally, would the Polish and Roumanian Governments respectively be prepared, in the event of aggression by Germany, to permit Soviet troops to enter Polish territory in the Wilno Gap and in Galicia, and also to enter Roumanian territory in order to co-operate in operations against Germany?' [. . .]

36. [. . .] When the meeting reopened, the following statement was read by the stenographer of the Soviet Delegation:—

'The Soviet Military Mission, in answer to the communication of the British and French Delegations, points out:—

/a/ The Soviet Military Mission does not forget that Poland and Roumania are sovereign States. On the contrary, on account of this indisputable fact the Soviet Military Mission asks the British and French Delegations the following question:—

Will the Soviet Military Forces be allowed to pass through Polish territory, that is through the Wilno Gap and Galicia, and through Roumanian territory, in the case of aggression against Britain and France or Poland and Roumania? This question is the more apt in that France has already a treaty with Poland and Britain has guaranteed the integrity of Poland.

/b/ The Soviet Military Mission is in agreement with the British and French Delegations in their opinion that this is a political question.

/c/ As regards the view of the British and French Delegations that the simplest method would be for the Soviet Government to address itself directly to the Governments of Poland and Roumania: since the Soviet Union has no military agreement with Poland or Roumania, and since the danger of aggression in Europe is most likely to affect Poland, Roumania, France and England; to that extent the question of the rights of passage of Soviet Armed Forces across Poland and Roumania, and also the question of the co-operation of the Soviet Armed Forces against aggression over the territory of these countries, should be decided by the Governments of France and Great Britain in consultation with the Polish and Roumanian Governments.' [. . .]

Minutes of Meeting of Anglo-Franco-Soviet Military Delegations held in Moscow on August 15, 1939.

Admiral Drax was in the chair. [. . .]

41. Kommandarm I. Shaposhnikov stated:—

'At the previous meetings we have heard the dispositions of the French Armies in the West. To fulfil the request of the French and British Missions, I will now expound the plan of deployment of the Armed Forces of the USSR on its Western Frontier. Against aggression in Europe, the Red Army will deploy in the European part of its territory and will dispose on the Front: 120 infantry divisions, 16 cavalry divisions, 5,000 heavy guns and howitzers, 9,000–10,000 tanks, from 5,000–5,500 fighter and bomber aircraft (excluding army co-operation aircraft). In these figures the following are not included: garrisons of the fortified areas, air defence troops, coast defence units, depôt troops, line of communication and base area troops.' [. . .]

APPENDIX No. 3

Extracts from notes made by Mr. Roberts on
Anglo-Franco-Soviet Military Conversations between August 19 and 21, 1939

London, August 23, 1939   D.Brit.F.P. VII/559–560

[. . .]. 'Sir H. Kennard saw Colonel Beck after his French colleague [Ambassador Noël] and our Military Attaché [Col. Sword] saw the Polish Chief of Staff on August 19. Both repeated their objections to our proposals[1] and expressed strong suspicion that the Russian objective was to obtain a handle to occupy Polish territory permanently, particularly the White Russian districts in eastern Poland. Colonel Beck's concessions were: *a/* that the Polish attitude might be modified if war actually broke out, and *b/* to refer the matter to the Polish Government. On the evening of August 19 Colonel Beck, after consultation with Marshal Śmigły-Rydz, returned the considered reply of his Government that they could not agree to proposal. It was agreed with Colonel Beck that these exchanges should be regarded as purely unofficial and that the greatest secrecy should be maintained.'
[. . .]

'H.M. Chargé d'Affaires in Paris [Mr. Campbell] saw M. Bonnet on August 19. The latter strongly held the view that we must compel the Poles to agree to accept Russian assistance.[2] M. Bonnet thought it would be an impossible position if

---

[1] The views of Polish official quarters are expressed in other documents of the same collection. So M. Beck 'considered [on August 18] that if Poland agreed to passage of Russian troops across Polish territory this would lead to an immediate declaration of war on the part of Germany.' He said on the same day 'that the mere fact that the Soviets mentioned these two avenues [i.e. Vilna gap and Eastern Galicia] showed that they were not in good faith and that they merely wished to separate Poland from Roumania and from Baltic States'. A day later Polish Minister had a 'feeling that Marshal Voroshilov was attempting today to reach in a peaceful manner what he had attempted to obtain by force of arms in 1920'.

Polish General Staff expressed at this time the opinion that 'should the Soviet troops be confined to a strip of territory in for instance Vilna area they would be presumably required to operate through Lithuanian territory' and 'that the Soviet intention was merely the occupation of Polish territory and that they had no intention of employing Soviet troops in offensive operations'. 'However Polish General Staff were prepared [on August 20] to consider a memorandum regarding military collaboration with the Soviet Union based on staff conversation in Moscow on condition that it should be made clear to the Soviet Government that there was no question of the Polish Government hesitating or reflecting in any way over the main points at issue' (D.Brit.F.P., VII, doc. Nos. 52, 60, 70, 88 and 94).

[2] The French Government was under pressure of Soviet demands in Moscow of August 15 (see Appendix No. 2) and therefore 'urged with every argument at their command that Polish Government should immediately give their consent in whatever form they preferred'. British statesmen made their way by persuading the Poles to give Soviet Forces every facility for rendering Russian collaboration effective on their soil. In consequence the British claimed only a 'Polish tacit consent in principle [confined] even to purely staff discussion of military aspects of passage . . . without necessarily involving Governments of the respective countries', in order to prevent war breaking out and to secure necessary time 'until Polish General Staff had been able to give fuller consideration to strategic factors involved' (i.e. in admission of Soviet troops to the concentration areas in Poland). 'Both West Powers perceived in Polish attitude some apprehension as to possible effect of any understanding with

France and Great Britain had to fight to protect Poland, who had refused such help, and he suggested that we might bring pressure upon M. Beck in connection with the negotiations for our political treaty with Poland which had not yet been finally signed.' [. . .]

'Basing themselves upon Colonel Beck's admission that the position would be different in time of war and his insistence that the démarche should be regarded as non-avenue the French interpreted his attitude as justifying them in returning an affirmative reply to Marshal Voroshilov's enquiry.' [3] [. . .]

Russia on the Ukrainian population [. . .] and [a suspicion] that Russia intended to attack East Prussia through Lithuania which would certainly provoke German attack on Lithuania and might end by a German threat to Polish northern flank.' From these premises the British drew the conclusion the 'no Pole would ever expect to recover any territory occupied by Soviet troops' (D.Brit.F.P., vol. VII, doc. Nos. 27, 38, 70, 87, 90 and enclosure in No. 155).

[3] The interpretation by the French Government of their part as guarantor of Poland is to be seen—according to the words noted by Mr. Strang: 'the solution [was] not to take literally the objections of M. Beck, whose real desire was probably not to know anything at all about the question' and 'to give the Soviet delegation an affirmative answer in principle which might help on the military negotiations'. This attitude agreed with M. Bonnet's 'instruction to sign whatever arrangement might best serve the common interest' and 'to go ahead at liberty with the Russians'—'claiming freedom from any obligations towards Poland' (D.Brit.F.P., vol.VII, Nos.115 and 152).

547

APPENDIX No. 4

Extracts from a conversation between Marshal Voroshilov and Général Doumenc on conditions of a military convention

Moscow, August 22, 1939   D.Brit.F.P. VII/609–11 and 613

[. . .] Marshal Voroshilov: I beg Général Doumenc to show me the document he has received from his Government, and of which I have been informed by letter. I should also like to know if the English Mission has received a reply to the same question.

Général Doumenc: I have no document, but my Government has informed me that the reply to the basic, essential question is in the affirmative. In other words, the Government has empowered me to sign a military convention under which authorization will be given for the passage of Soviet troops at the points specified by you, that is to say, the Corridor of Vilno, and, if the actual circumstances demand it, Galicia and Roumania.

Marshal Voroshilov: Is that the French Government's message?

Général Doumenc: Yes, the French Government has given me these instructions.

Marshal Voroshilov: And the British Government?

Général Doumenc: I do not know if Admiral Drax has received a similar reply from the British Government, but I know that the Admiral is of opinion that the Conference can go on.

Marshal Voroshilov: Then the English Delegation knows of this communication?

Général Doumenc: Yes; I told the Admiral that the French Government's reply had arrived. And I am nearly certain that the same reply will be given by the English Government. But, as I am responsible for the military questions and Admiral Drax more particularly for the naval ones, this reply is sufficient to allow the work of our Conference to proceed.

Marshal Voroshilov: It may be that the English Delegation agrees that Général Doumenc should take charge of the military questions. But it seems to me that the English Mission has, if not a dominant rôle, at least an equal one, in all our conversations. Hence it will clearly be difficult for us to continue the work of the Conference. [. . .]

Général Doumenc: I think that we shall only now need three or four days to sign the Military Convention. The situation is sufficiently clear. The statement made by General Shaposhnikov is an excellent basis on which to build the Convention. For my part I am ready to subscribe to the fundamental proposals made by General Shaposhnikov.

Marshal Voroshilov: Apart from our proposals, there must also be Anglo-French suggestions. We still have to agree on very many practical points.

Général Doumenc: Quite. General Shaposhnikov said that he intended to put a series of questions. I will answer them with pleasure.

Marshal Voroshilov: Please allow us to wait until the situation is clear, that is to say, until we have the British Government's reply and until the position of Poland and Roumania seems clear to us. Then we will meet again. If these things do not happen, then it will be useless for us to meet again, because in such a case no result will be possible. It is essential that the reply should indicate definitely that Poland is being kept informed. It is equally necessary that the British and French Government's reply should be made in accord with the Polish and Roumanian Governments. We do not want Poland to boast that she has refused our aid—which we have no intention of forcing her to accept. [. . .]

Marshal Voroshilov: Our Delegation has already given its reply. Until we receive a clear answer to the questions put, we will not work.

Général Doumenc: Practical questions are not always easily and rapidly disposed of. Practical questions also need to be studied closely, and I propose that we should continue this work. It will be useful to do so before the conclusion of the convention, without, however, binding either of the parties.

Marshal Voroshilov: We cannot lose time over useless work. When complete clarity has been established and all the replies have been received, then we will work. [. . .]

APPENDIX No. 5

Text of the Anglo-Polish Agreement of Mutual Assistance and the Secret Protocol

London, August 25, 1939   H.M.S.O., Cmd 6616, Poland No. 1(1945)

The Polish Government and the Government of the United Kingdom of Great Britain and Northern Ireland:

Desiring to place on a permanent basis the collaboration between their respective countries resulting from the assurances of mutual assistance of a defensive character which they have already exchanged;

Have resolved to conclude an Agreement for that purpose and have appointed as their Plenipotentiaries:

The Polish Government:

    His Excellency Count Edward Raczyński, Ambassador Extraordinary and Plenipotentiary of the Polish Republic in London;

The Government of the United Kingdom of Great Britain and Northern Ireland:

    The Rt. Hon. Viscount Halifax, K.G., G.C.S.I., G.C.I.E., Principal Secretary of State for Foreign Affairs;

Who having exchanged their Full Powers, found in good and due form, have agreed on the following provisions:—

Article 1

Should one of the Contracting Parties become engaged in hostilities with a European Power in consequence of aggression by the latter against that Contracting Party, the other Contracting Party will at once give the Contracting Party engaged in hostilities all the support and assistance in its power.

Article 2

/1/ The provisions of Article 1 will also apply in the event of any action by a European Power which clearly threatened, directly or indirectly, the independence of one of the Contracting Parties, and was of such a nature that the Party in question considered it vital to resist it with its armed forces.

/2/ Should one of the Contracting Parties become engaged in hostilities with a European Power in consequence of action by that Power which threatened the independence or neutrality of another European State in such a way as to constitute a clear menace to the security of that Contracting Party, the provisions of Article 1 will apply, without prejudice, however, to the rights of the other European State concerned.

Article 3

Should a European Power attempt to undermine the independence of one of the Contracting Parties by processes of economic penetration or in any other way, the Contracting Parties will support each other in resistance to such attempts. Should the European Power concerned thereupon embark on hostilities against one of the Contracting Parties, the provisions of Article 1 will apply.

Article 4

The methods of applying the undertakings of mutual assistance provided for by the present Agreement are established between the competent naval, military and air authorities of the Contracting Parties.

Article 5

Without prejudice to the foregoing undertakings of the Contracting Parties to give each other mutual support and assistance immediately on the outbreak of hostilities, they will exchange complete and speedy information concerning any development which might threaten their independence and, in particular, concerning any development which threatened to call the same undertakings into operation.

Article 6

/1/ The Contracting Parties will communicate to each other the terms of any undertakings of assistance against aggression which they have already given or may in future give to other States.

/2/ Should either of the Contracting Parties intend to give such an undertaking after the coming into force of the present Agreement, the other Contracting Party shall, in order to ensure the proper functioning of the Agreement, be informed thereof.

/3/ Any new undertaking which the Contracting Parties may enter into in future shall neither limit their obligations under the present Agreement nor indirectly create new obligations between the Contracting Party not participating in these undertakings and the third State concerned.

Article 7

Should the Contracting Parties be engaged in hostilities in consequence of the application of the present Agreement, they will not conclude an armistice or treaty of peace except by mutual agreement.

Article 8

/1/ The present Agreement shall remain in force for a period of five years.

/2/ Unless denounced six months before the expiry of this period it shall continue in force, each Contracting Party having thereafter the right to denounce it at any time by giving six months' notice to that effect.

/3/ The present Agreement shall come into force on signature.

In faith whereof the above-named Plenipotentiaries have signed the present Agreement and have affixed thereto their seals.

Done in English in duplicate, at London, the 25th August, 1939. A Polish text shall subsequently be agreed upon between the Contracting Parties and both texts will then be authentic.

(L.S.) Edward Raczyński
(L.S.) Halifax

PROTOCOL

The Polish Government and the Government of the United Kingdom of Great Britain and Northern Ireland are agreed upon the following interpretation of the Agreement of Mutual Assistance signed this day as alone authentic and binding.

1 /a/ By the expression 'a European Power' employed in the Agreement is to be understood Germany.

/b/ In the event of action within the meaning of Article 1 or 2 of the Agreement by a European Power other than Germany, the Contracting Parties will consult together on the measures to be taken in common.

2. /a/ The two Governments will from time to time determine by mutual agreement the hypothetical cases of action by Germany coming within the ambit of Article 2 of the Agreement.

/b/ Until such time as the two Governments have agreed to modify the following provisions of this paragraph, they will consider: that the case contemplated by paragraph /1/ of Article 2 of the Agreement is that of the Free City of Danzig; and that the cases contemplated by paragraph /2/ of Article 2 are Belgium, Holland, Lithuania.

/c/ Latvia and Estonia shall be regarded by the two Governments as included in the list of countries contemplated by paragraph /2/ of Article 2 from the moment that an undertaking of mutual assistance between the United Kingdom and a third State covering those two countries enters into force.

/d/ As regards Roumania, the Government of the United Kingdom refers to the guarantee which it has given to that country; and the Polish Government refers to the reciprocal undertakings of the Roumano-Polish alliance which Poland has never regarded as incompatible with her traditional friendship for Hungary.

3. The undertakings mentioned in Article 6 of the Agreement, should they be entered into by one of the Contracting Parties with a third State, would of necessity be so framed that their execution should at no time prejudice either the sovereignty or territorial inviolability of the other Contracting Party.

4. The present protocol constitutes an integral part of the Agreement signed this day, the scope of which it does not exceed.

In faith whereof the undersigned, being duly authorized, have signed the present Protocol.

Done in English in duplicate, at London, the 25th August, 1939. A Polish text will subsequently be agreed upon between the Contracting Parties and both texts will then be authentic.

(signed) Edward Raczyński
(signed) Halifax

Contemporary interpretative note relating to the Secret Protocol to the Anglo-Polish Agreement on Mutual Assistance of August 25th, 1939, made by the Legal Adviser to the Polish Ministry of Foreign Affairs, Dr. W. Kulski

The Secret Protocol gives an authentic interpretation of the Open Agreement, binding either party. Para. 1/a/ specifies that by the expression 'a European Power' employed in the Agreement is to be understood Germany. The Agreement, therefore, applies fully to Germany only; but the Secret Protocol in para. 1/b/ which immediately follows, adds an obligation binding either party in the event of a direct or indirect aggression 'by a European Power other than Germany'. In this event the contracting parties have the obligation to 'consult together' not on the question whether they have to take action in common, but on 'the measures to be taken in common'. The conclusion can be drawn from it that in the event of Russia's direct or indirect aggression against Poland, Great Britain is not bound, as is the case in the event of German aggression, 'to give at once all the support and assistance in her power' (Art. 1 of the Open Agreement), but she is, nevertheless, under obligation to take jointly with Poland such measures as may be determined by way of a joint consultation. The kind and extent of such measures are a matter for consultation, but the basic obligation of action in common stands as it is laid down in para. 1/b/. It means that the attitude consistently adopted by the British Government since October 1939, according to which Great

Britain did not admit any obligation towards Poland, so far as the relations of the latter with Russia were concerned, is not consonant with the text of the Secret Protocol.

Para. 1/b/ extends this obligation (in the event of aggression by a European Power other than Germany) to all hypothetical cases laid down in art. 1 and 2 of the Open Agreement. Among such 'hypothetical cases' are enumerated, in accordance with para 2/b/ of the Secret Protocol, a menace to the Polish interests in the Free City of Danzig, as well as the threat to the independence of Lithuania which is mentioned on the same foot with Belgium and Holland. It means that para. 2/a/ recognizes the existence of special Polish interests not only in the Free City of Danzig but also in Lithuania, on the same foot as the British interests in Belgium and Holland. On the other hand, so far as Latvia and Estonia are concerned, para 2/c/ recognizes Poland's indirect interests in those countries to the same extent as Russia's interests.

Para 2/a/ regarding Rumania refers to the previous obligations of both countries: the guarantee given by the United Kingdom and the Rumano-Polish Treaty of Alliance.

Para. 3 contains a provision forbidding the conclusion by one of the Contracting Parties of an agreement with a third party regarding military assistance, the text of which might prejudice either the sovereignty or the territorial inviolability of the other Contracting Party. That paragraph was introduced because of the Russian request put forward in Moscow, in the course of Anglo-French-Soviet conversations, for the right of passage for the Russian Army and of establishing operational bases in the Wilno area and in Eastern Galicia. Great Britain was, consequently, fully aware of contracting an obligation, should she conclude later an agreement with Russia, binding her to refuse her consent to such requests, infringing upon the sovereignty and territorial inviolability of Poland.

In close connection with it is the Article of the Open Agreement referring to the guarantee of the independence of either party. This guarantee was given on the day of signature, that is on 25th August, 1939, and this date has a double significance: 1) two days before the German-Soviet Treaty had been signed, and Great Britain had to reckon since that date with a possible threat to Poland from two sides: from Germany and Russia. In spite of it Great Britain contracted this obligation of consultation in the event of aggression on the part of Russia, and she bound herself not to agree to an infringement of the sovereignty and territorial inviolability of Poland in future treaties of alliance, 2) Great Britain did guarantee Poland's independence, not in abstracto, as it would be meaningless, but within a definite territory, which was the territory existing at the time of the signature of the Agreement.

Article 7 of the Open Agreement refers also to an explicit obligation of not concluding an armistice or peace treaty, except by consultation. In spite of it Poland was not consulted about the terms of the German surrender.

The Secret Protocol 'constitutes an integral part of the Agreement' (para. 4).

APPENDIX No. 6

Polish-Soviet Agreement on the loan of 100 million Roubles for the financial assistance to the Polish citizens on the territory of the USSR [1]

Kuibyshev, December 31, 1941

GSHI, A.11. 49/Sow/2
Transl. from Polish

The Government of the Republic of Poland, on the one part, and the Government of the Union of the Soviet Socialist Republics, on the other part, conclude this agreement which reads as follows:

Art. 1

The Government of the Union of the Soviet Socialist Republics grants to the Government of the Republic of Poland a loan at the amount of 100 (one hundred) million Roubles for expenditure connected with financial assistance to the Polish citizens on the territory of the USSR.

Art. 2

The repayment of this loan will begin after a period of five years from the termination of the war and will be effected by equal instalments within the following five years.

Art. 3

The amount stated in Art. 1 of this Agreement will be lent to the Government of the Republic of Poland by the Government of the Union of the Soviet Socialist

---

[1] A Soviet loan for the financial assistance to the Polish population in the USSR was, in principle, promised by Stalin to General Sikorski during the visit of the latter to Russia in December, 1941. In the course of a meeting with Deputy Commissar Vyshinsky on December 24, Ambassador Kot raised the question of the implementation of that promise, and was informed by him that a draft agreement had been sent to Moscow for approval. At the following meeting on December 28, Deputy Commissar Vyshinsky handed Ambassador Kot 'plans for a loan for the assistance to the civilian population to the amount of 100 mil. Rb. and for the army to the amount of 300 million'. The Ambassador tried unsuccessfully to obtain more favourable conditions for the repayment of the loan but, on the other hand, he received from the Deputy Commissar 'a statement of Russian readiness to sign the agreement in the course of the current year which would mean that half of the loan could be put into effect during the winter-season (30 million Rb. in January and 10 million both in February and March)'.

This statement was couched in writing in a letter addressed by Deputy Commissar Vyshinsky to Ambassador Kot, in which the order of the payments in single instalments was established. Moreover, the Ambassador received an assurance relating to the 'sale to the Polish population of food and other necessities at official prices'. As far as the question of the loan for the army was concerned, the Ambassador explained that 'in view of its character and the fact that it would be taken on the account of military supplies in kind, he had to consult General Anders before taking any position regarding it', which was bound to delay the signature of the agreement (conversations between Ambassador Kot and Deputy Commissar Vyshinsky on December 24 and 28, GSHI, A.11.49/Sow/4).

Republics by transferring it to a special account to be opened with the State Bank of the USSR bearing the name of the Ambassador Extraordinary and Plenipotentiary of the Republic of Poland.

Art. 4

The Government of the Republic of Poland undertakes to repay the amount of the loan specified in Art. 1 as it may think proper, either in American dollars at the rate of exchange quoted by the State Bank of the USSR on the day preceding the repayment, or in goods, on the conditions to be determined by a special agreement between the parties.

Art. 5

This agreement enters into force on the day of its signature and does not require a ratification.

Made at Kuibyshev, in 2 copies, in Polish and Russian, both texts being authentic.

31 December 1941.

On the strength of Special Powers of the Government of the Republic of Poland	On the strength of Special Powers of the Government of the USSR
(—) St. Kot	(—) A. Vyshinsky

555

APPENDIX No. 7

Polish-Soviet Agreement on the loan of 300 million Roubles for the formation and maintenance of the Polish Army in the USSR [1]

Kuibyshev, January 22, 1942   GSHI, A.11. 49/Sow/2
                                                                Transl. from Polish

The Government of the Republic of Poland on the one part, and the Government of the Union of Soviet Socialist Republics on the other part, conclude the following agreement referring to the question stated hereunder:

Art. 1

The Government of the USSR grants a loan of 300 million Roubles free of interest to the Government of the Republic of Poland, for the expenditure arising from the maintenance of the Polish Army on the territory of the USSR.

Art. 2

The repayment of this loan will start after the lapse of five years from the date of the end of the war, and will be effected by equal instalments within the following five years.

Art. 3

The amount of the loan mentioned under Art. 1 will be transmitted by the Government of the USSR to the Government of the Republic of Poland by turning it to a special account bearing the name of the Commander of the Polish Army in the USSR, to be opened with the State Bank of the USSR.

Art. 4

The Government of the Republic of Poland undertakes to repay the amount of the loan stated under Art 1, as it may think proper: either in American dollars at the rate of exchange quoted by the State Bank of the USSR on the day preceding the repayment or in supplying goods on terms to be specified by a special agreement between the parties.

[1] Unsuccessful attempts were made by Poland to obtain not a definite sum as an immediate loan but current credit whose amount would depend on the actual strength and the material needs of the troops formed in the USSR. A proposal was also made to start the repayment of this credit 10 years after the end of the war. These proposals were rejected by the Soviet Government and this rejection may be connected with the stoppage of some current supplies by Soviet authorities. Thus the Soviet text became the basis of the agreement. The manner in which it was to be put into operation was established by the exchange of letters between the Ambassador and Deputy Commissar Vyshinsky by which the expenditure made theretofore for the needs of Polish troops in the USSR was assessed at Rb. 69 mil. and the number of rations fixed at a maximum of 96 thousand. Standard rates for armament, munitions and clothing of troops, and finally, the way in which the monthly contributions were to be paid were also fixed in the agreement (GSHI, A.11.49/Sow/2-Counter-Propositions of the Polish party with remarks, dated January 15 and the exchange of letters between Ambassador Kot and Deputy Commissar Vyshinsky of January 22, 1942).

Art. 5

The Agreement enters into force on the day of its signature and does not require ratification.

Made at Kuibyshev in two copies, in Polish and Russian, either text being authentic.

On the strength of full powers granted by the Government of the Republic of Poland

(—) St. Kot

On the strength of full powers granted by the Government of the USSR

(—) A. J. Vyshinsky

557

APPENDIX No. 8

Aide-mémoire from the Polish Embassy in Kuibyshev to the People's Commissariat for Foreign Affairs concerning the plight of Polish children in the USSR

Kuibyshev, September 10, 1942　　　　　　　　GSHI, A.11. 49/Sow./2
Transl. from Polish: Pol.-Sov. R., No. 75

The fate of Polish children is a subject of special concern to the Polish Government which is sparing no effort to provide the best possible conditions to enable them to survive the present war. In view of the methods applied by Hitlerite Germany which by mass murder, systematic persecution and de-nationalization is endeavouring to destroy the youth of Poland, every Polish child outside the homeland and especially in Allied and friendly countries is of priceless value to the future of the Polish nation.

One of the ways by which the Polish Government is endeavouring to provide effective relief is the dispatch from abroad of food-stuffs and clothing for Polish children. Last year the extent of such relief in the USSR was quite considerable, but unable as it was to satisfy all needs in the past, it will also not be able to satisfy them in the future.

Conditions for effective relief to Polish children in the USSR were created by the following orders issued by the Soviet authorities in agreement with the Polish Embassy:

1. Granting of special food quotas to Polish citizens, especially to non-working members of families (*izhdiventzy*) which in practice chiefly favoured children;

2. Permission for the Embassy to establish relief institutions in the form of orphanages (*diet-dom*), kindergartens (*diet-sad*), etc.

The order granting food quotas for Polish citizens was only carried out in part and irregularly by the local Soviet authorities. In practice the carrying out of this order varies considerably in different districts and generally the *izhdiventzy* receive no food rations at all, or at the best, in *kolkhoses*, half the bread ration. As the average food ration for a working person amounts to 400 grammes of bread as well as soup, he is in no position to give any of this ration to other members of his family who are not working.

On the whole, while the Embassy Delegates were still functioning, the development of orphanages and kindergartens proceeded satisfactorily. At present, however, the Embassy is continually receiving information that local Soviet authorities are closing the orphanages and kindergartens established with such great difficulty, and even the soup kitchens, especially in the Kazakh SSR. The number of children in relief institutions is constantly decreasing instead of increasing according to needs.

This being the case the Embassy's concern for the fate of Polish children during the approaching winter is easily understood. Parents cannot be expected to be able to feed their children from the modest food rations they receive, and it is doubtful whether it will be possible to set up new relief institutions for children in view of existing conditions.

In order to save Polish children from the consequences of this state of affairs the Embassy deems it necessary—

1. To develop the present system of orphanages and kindergartens in the various

districts and regions, and to extend the system of food quotas to all Polish citizens unfit for work, especially to all children. The Embassy is of opinion that it would be especially desirable to supplement the existing relief institutions for children by setting up in the most suitable places ten or twelve large orphanages, each to accommodate 1500 to 2000 children. The provisioning and administration of such institutions would be considerably easier and more effective. They would remain under the direct control of the Embassy which would supply the staff and provide special food for the children from foreign relief consignments. The local Soviet authorities would provide suitable premises for these institutions and the essential foodstuffs.

2. Since whatever the efforts of the Embassy and the Soviet authorities the proposed measures could not, in existing war conditions, provide for all Polish children requiring assistance, the Embassy renews its suggestion to evacuate a certain number of Polish children from the USSR to those Allied countries which have already declared to the Polish Government their readiness to support these children for the duration of the war. If such evacuation were extended over a long period and consisted of small parties of ten to fifteen children and guardians at a time, it would not require the provision of special transport. The Embassy, on its part, would provide food and medical assistance for the children on their journey.

APPENDIX No. 9

Note from the Polish Embassy in the USSR to the People's Commissariat for Foreign Affairs relating to the evacuation of Polish children from Soviet territory

Kuibyshev, January 23, 1943　　　　　　　　　　　　　　　GSHI. A.11. 49/Sow./2
　　　　　　　　　　　　　　　　　　　　　　　　　　　　Transl. from Polish

The Embassy of the Republic of Poland has the honour to bring the following to the notice of the People's Commissariat for Foreign Affairs.

In the conversation on 5th September, 1942 with the Deputy People's Commissar for Foreign Affairs, M. Lozovsky, the Minister Plenipotentiary Sokolnicki again raised the question of the evacuation of a number of children, Polish citizens, from Soviet territory. In accordance with M. Lozovsky's wishes, M. Sokolnicki sent him an aide-mémoire on 10th September, 1942 containing, among other matters, some proposals relating to the evacuation of a number of Polish children, in small groups and over a rather long period. In reply to the said aide-mémoire, the representative of the People's Commissariat for Foreign Affairs declared on 28th September, 1942 to the representative of the Embassy of the Republic of Poland that the People's Commissariat for Foreign Affairs did not object to the evacuation of a number of orphan children, Polish citizens, and that it was waiting to receive from the Embassy of the Republic of Poland some concrete data, stating the number, place and manner of evacuation of those children.

On the basis of the aforesaid declaration, the Embassy of the Republic of Poland informed the Government of the favourable decision of the USSR Government. In connection with this, the Polish Government approached the British Government who gave its agreement to the reception, within a very short time, of 10,000 Polish children into India and British Africa. The organization of orphanages and transit hostels was started in those countries as well as in Iran, and preparations were made to ensure food supplies and medical care for those children. At the same time, in accordance with the wishes of the People's Commissariat for Foreign Affairs, the Embassy began to work out a plan for the evacuation of some categories of children from different places in the USSR, with the intention of proceeding to the evacuation of about one thousand children every month in the initial stage.

In the conversation on 26th October, 1942 the representative of the Embassy of the Republic of Poland informed the representative of the People's Commissariat for Foreign Affairs that some groups of children were now ready to leave. Having acknowledged this information the representative of the People's Commissariat for Foreign Affairs expressed a wish for the production by the Embassy of a complete plan of evacuation, stating in particular the number of children to be evacuated, the day of their departure and the places from which they would come. At the outcome of the conversation it was explicitly agreed that in view of the difficulties of establishing within a short time a complete and detailed plan, the Embassy would submit the plan of the first stage of evacuation, on the understanding that the following ones would be forwarded to the People's Commissariat as soon as the groups were ready to leave.

In the conversation on 3rd November, 1942 in Moscow the Deputy Chairman of the Council of People's Commissars, M. Molotov, declared to the Ambassador of the Polish Republic, M. Romer, that, without opposing the evacuation in principle, he considered it proper that it should be carried out within a short time.

In the conversation on 12th November, 1942 the Ambassador of the P. R., M. Romer, submitted to the Deputy Chairman of the Council of People's Commissars M. Vyshinsky a definitive plan of the evacuation of 19,000 children, taking into account the possibility of placing 10,000 orphans or semi-orphans in orphanages organized by the Embassy, should the existing welfare institutions be expanded. In view of the aforesaid declaration of the representatives of the People's Commissariat for Foreign Affairs, the reply of the Deputy Chairman of the Council of People's Commissars, given in the course of this conversation, quite unexpectedly reduced the whole problem to the evacuation of 600 children, namely those staying at Ashkhabad or those whose names had been already submitted in the past to the Commissariat for Foreign Affairs. The declaration of the Deputy Chairman of the Council of People's Commissars has radically changed the whole problem of evacuation and frustrated all the preparations of the Government of the Polish Republic, who had good grounds for making them. In these circumstances the Embassy reported the situation to its Government and waits for appropriate instructions.

Without prejudicing the problem as a whole, the representative of the Embassy forwarded on 18th November, 1942 to the People's Commissariat for Foreign Affairs the plan of evacuation of 600 children. In conversations which took place on 27th November, 1942, 4th December, 1942, 21st December, 1942, and 11th January, 1943, the representative of the People's Commissariat for Foreign Affairs was supplied by the representative of the Embassy of the Polish Republic with detailed information on the number of children staying at the time at Ashkhabad and of those who were on the way, as well as information on the groups of children who were to go within the framework of the plan of evacuation of 600 children and the names of persons designated as the guardians of each group of children. In the course of the said conversations the representative of the Embassy asked repeatedly the People's Commissariat for Foreign Affairs to issue orders facilitating the departure from Ashkhabad of the children who had stayed for some time at the Embassy's orphanage and were earmarked for evacuation.

At present, according to the Embassy's information, there are 555 children at the orphanage at Ashkhabad, ready to leave and, moreover, the departure of the following groups of children is being prepared: 40 from Taysset, Irkutsk area, 40 from the Zyrian and Teguldetsk region, Novosibirsk area, 30 from Tomsk, Novosibirsk area, 30 from Semipalatinsk, 40 from Siktivkar, Komi ASSR. At the same time the Embassy states that during the period between 29th September and today, only one group of 61 children has left Ashkhabad.

In view of the fact that detailed plans for the evacuation of the quota of 600 children have been in due time submitted to the People's Commissariat for Foreign Affairs, and that the gathering at the orphanage at Ashkhabad of an excessive number of children is unadvisable for sanitary reasons, the Embassy of the Republic of Poland has the honour to ask the People's Commissariat for Foreign Affairs to issue final orders facilitating the departure abroad of the children, most of whom have stayed several months at Ashkabad, as well as of the above-mentioned five groups of children, whose total number amounts to 594.

NOTES TO DOCUMENTS

No. 1. The above Decree of the Council of People's Commissars was but a step on the way to a new policy, pointed to the West, initiated by Soviet Russia in the autumn of 1918. This new line of policy was based on the guarantee, granted by Germany on 27.8.1918, under the form of an additional protocol to the Treaty of Brest Litovsk, against any further aggression upon the frontiers of Russia, greatly reduced in the South and North. Relying on this pledge and hoping for a prompt collapse of Imperial Germany, Soviet Russia started, in September 1918, preparations for an armed class warfare in Poland, Latvia and Lithuania, on a very big scale, setting up on her territory shadow governments and nuclei of troops, waiting for the end of the German occupation and the rising of new countries. This accounts for the lack of any declaration on the part of Soviet Russia, concerning the independence of Poland, up to that time, except for very general terms of the Decree on the Rights of the Nations of Russia, issued on 15.11.1917. That Decree spoke in a rather ambiguous way about the equality and self-determination of nations 'within the framework of a permanent alliance of the nations of Russia'.

In accordance with this line of policy the subsequent proclamation of the Soviet Government of 13.11.1918, on the annulment of the Treaty of Brest was in fact a reversion to the idea of an alliance of 'working masses' on the ruins of the German and Austro-Hungarian Empires, under the leadership of Soviet Russia; the activity of this new bloc was to be directed 'against the Western bourgeoisie and capitalist pressure' on the recently liberated nations. (Cf. Lionel Kochan, *Russia and the Weimar Republic*, Cambridge, 1954, p. 46; G. Chicherin, *Vneshniya Politika Sovetskoy Rossii za dva goda*, Moscow, 1920, pp. 15–16; J. Mints and H. Gorodetsky, *Dokumenty po istorii grazhdanskoy voyny*, Moscow, 1940, pp. 461–2; *Politika sovetskoy vlasti po natsionalnim voprosam za tri goda*, 1917–1920, Nar. Kom. po Dielam Natsional-nostii, Moscow, 1920, pp. 10–12; T. Komarnicki, *Rebirth of the Polish Republic*, London, 1957, pp. 429 ff.)

No. 2. Similar proposals made in the Note of 22.12.1919, alleged that the obstacles to the conclusion of a peace treaty 'were due to foreign inspirations contrary to the real Polish interests'. The January Note asserted that 'there is no question, territorial, economic or other that might not be settled peacefully . . . in a spirit of good neighbourliness . . .' and as a proof of good intentions expressed Soviet readiness to an armistice line along the actual front line, roughly corresponding to the western ethnographic border of Byelorussia. (Cf. T. Komarnicki, *Rebirth*, pp. 516, 535.) Soviet Notes echoed the resolutions of the VII All Russia Congress of Soviets (18–23.12.1919) censuring the Treaty of Versailles for having imposed heavy burdens and territorial concessions on Central Powers and uttering a warning that 'the Soviet Government will not ask its enemies for peace but it will force them to finish a war, which, so far as Russia is concerned, is a war against the Entente' (Lenin, *Soch.*, XXXI).

As regards the principle of self-determination for such nations as the Ukrainians, Byelorussians and Balts, the plan of the Polish Head of State, Józef Piłsudski, which took a definite shape in the autumn of 1919, consisted in the following: 'The new Poland liberated under his leadership wants freedom and rights not only for herself. She supports and strengthens all movements for independence and all aspirations for autonomous existence of all the nationalities of Russia. . . . Instead of competition between these two Powers [Poland and Russia] for the "borderlands" a new system would have arisen, based on the independence and freedom of these new States' (Sokolnicki, 'Józef Piłsudski a zagadnienie Rosji', *Niepodległość*, vol. II, London, 1950, extract translated by Komarnicki, *Rebirth*, p. 451). This line of policy led to an understanding between Polish and Ukrainian Governments in December 1919, and, eventually to a treaty of political and military alliance, signed on 21–24.4.1920; to co-operation between Poland and Latvia, initiated on 23.10.1919, and sealed by a military convention of 16.1.1920, by which Poland pledged her assistance in the liberation of the occupied parts of Livonia; the guarantee of the intangibility of the demarcation line with Lithuania, given in October and December 1919, was another manifestation of this line of policy.

On 13.3.1920, the Polish Government presented to the Western Powers its proposal according to which 'the fate of the population living to the West of the [old Poland's] frontier of 1772 will be decided in accordance with their wishes'. Explaining this proposal it stated that 'what Poland wished was not annexation of the whole territory included in the old frontiers of the Polish Republic of the XVIII Century, but the disannexation, leaving to the population of this area the opportunity of stating their wishes for the political future'. Meanwhile 'the Bolsheviks asserted that the Ukrainians had already exercised their right to self-determination thanks to the intervention of the Red Army' (Komarnicki, *Rebirth*, pp. 464–5, 533–55, 565–7, 569, 574).

So far as the Soviet attitude towards the principle of self-determination was concerned, it should be noted that the VIII Congress of the Russian Communist Party decided in March 1919 to establish the leadership of 'one and centralised Communist party for the territories of all Soviet republics' which meant that full authority was vested in the designated Russian revolutionaries. Approximately at the same time (10.3.1919) the delegates of town and country proletariate of the Ukraine accepted 'the principles of a constitution for this region proclaiming "the unshakable will of the Ukraine to join the Union of International Soviet Socialist Republics"' (Mikołaj Kowalewski, *Polityka narodowościowa na Ukrainie Sowieckiej*, Warsaw, 1938, pp. 37–42). The same steps were taken by the Soviet Government in relation to Byelorussia (4.2.1919). This line of policy was defined by 'Letter to the workers and peasants of the Ukraine' dated 28.12.1919, in which Lenin asserted: 'If a Ukrainian Communist insists upon the unconditional independence of the Ukraine, he lays himself open to the suspicion that he is supporting this policy not from the standpoint of the temporary interests of the Ukrainian workers and peasants in their struggle against the yoke of capital, but on account of the petty-bourgeois national prejudices of smallholders' (Lenin, *Selected Works*, vol. II, part 2, pp. 310–11).

For all the above stated reasons the interest taken by Poland in the Ukrainian question at the end of 1919 and the beginning of 1920 was instrumental in bringing about the decision of Russian Communists to fight against Poland (A. Yegorov, *Lvov-Varshava*, Moscow, 1929, pp. 10–16; T. Kutrzeba, *Wyprawa kijowska 1920r.*, Warsaw, 1937, pp. 25–7, 39–40, 58–72). In his report made at the opening of the IX Congress of the Russian Communist Party Lenin confessed that 'we received a formal offer of peace from Poland. These gentlemen are in desperate straits, as desperate as those in which their friends the German monarchists are. . . . But the conclusion of peace does not depend on the will of the small states even if they desire it. They are up to their ears in debt to all the countries of the Entente, who are wrangling and competing desperately among themselves. . . . But the measures we take for peace must be accompanied by most intense military preparations, and in no case must our army be disarmed.' In June 1920 Lenin wrote in 'Preliminary draft of theses on the national and colonial questions': 'We need constantly to explain . . . the deception systematically practised by the imperialist powers in creating, under the guise of politically independent states, states which are wholly dependent upon them economically and militarily: under modern international conditions there is no salvation for independent and weak nations but in the union of Soviet republics' (Lenin, *Selected Works*, vol. II, part 2, pp. 326, 328, 469). In October of the same year in his 'Policy of the Soviet Government relating to national problems', Stalin wrote: 'The so-called independence of the so-called independent Georgia, Armenia, Poland, Finland etc. is only an apparent independence covering full dependence of these so-called, let me say, independent States on that of another group of imperialists.' He states that for those States there were only two alternative solutions: 'Either together with Russia—which means the liberation of working masses from imperialist oppression, or together with the Entente—which means an unavoidable imperialist enslavement' (Stalin, *Sbornik Statiei*, Moscow, 1920, p. 93).

No. 3. a/ The fact that the territorial clauses of the Treaty of Riga were settled by way of mutual concessions, was constantly emphasized, in the course of the inter-war period, by Soviet politicians and in Russian official publications. So, for instance, said Adolf Joffe, chairman of the Soviet Delegation to the Peace Conference of Riga, in his closing speech after several months of negotiations: 'I have already experienced the importance for any peace negotiations of the atmosphere in which they are carried on. I should like to emphasize that although international conditions have changed several times during the Polish and Russo-Ukrainian Peace Conference, the atmosphere in Riga was invariably such that it favoured the carrying on of negotiations, and rendered it easier to reach a satisfactory conclusion' (J. Dąbski, *Pokój ryski*, Warsaw, 1931, p. 190).

b/ Still more explicit and going further was the statement made in an article devoted to the Polish-Soviet war of 1918–20, in the Soviet Little Encyclopaedia. The relevant passage in it reads as follows: 'The Treaty of Peace was signed at Riga, in March 1921. The outcome of the war was victorious for the Soviet Republic. The White Poles covered with shame were driven out of the Ukraine, situated to the west of the Dnieper, which they wished to occupy. Poland was forced to accept the peace terms which considerably differed, to our advantage, from those which we had been ready to accept in preliminary negotiations, prior to the offensive of the White Poles' (*Little Soviet Encyclopaedia*, VIII, p. 449, second edition, 1939).

No. 4. The United States Government acceded to this decision by recognizing Poland's sovereignty over her Eastern Provinces on 5.4.1923, and the Polish Government brought it to public notice on 20.4.1923. The decision of the Conference of Ambassadors was a de jure recognition of Poland's frontier with Russia as laid down by the Treaty of Riga and of the line established by the Council of the League of Nations as regards the frontier with Lithuania. The Lithuanian protest against this decision was dismissed by the Council of the League of Nations on 21.4.1923. A group of Ukrainian deputies to the Polish Diet declared at the meeting of the latter on 17.3.1923 that the decision had been made without consulting the Ukrainian people. Let us observe that the decision of 15.3.1923 was made irrespectively of any legal and political conditions; it was only stated in its preamble that ethnographical conditions in the eastern part of Galicia necessitated an autonomous régime. As a matter of fact, the Allied Powers were informed in due time of the promulgation of the Act of 26.9.1922, granting a wider measure of self-government to the voivodeships of Lwów, Tarnopol and Stanisławow. This act only partly put into execution the laws voted in July 1924 (the use of the Ukrainian language in public life and in schools). (Cf. G. P. Pink, 'The Conference of Ambassadors', in *Geneva Studies*, 1942; T. Komarnicki, *Rebirth*, p. 741; A. J. Toynbee, *Survey of International Affairs*, 1920–3, pp. 251–6; *L'Europe Nouvelle*, Paris, 7.4. 1923 (No. 14).)

No. 6. In the course of the negotiations on the Pact of Non-Aggression Poland proposed that a multilateral convention should be concluded, comprising the Baltic States as well as Poland and the USSR, in fact, a regional pact. The Soviet Government, whilst not dismissing the idea of concluding such pacts with the Baltic States, opposed the idea of a regional pact which would be signed jointly by several States. In view of the Soviet opposition the Polish Government abandoned its previous proposal and eventually agreed to the conclusion of separate non-aggression pacts, to be signed within short intervals. It was within this framework that the Soviet Government signed these non-aggression pacts in the following order: with Finland on 21.1.1932, with Latvia on 5.2.1932, with Estonia on 4.5.1932, and with Poland on 25.7.1932. The pact of non-aggression between the USSR and Lithuania was signed on 26.9.1926 (*Poland and the USSR, 1921–41*, Ed. The Polish Research Centre, London, 1941, p. 95).

No. 7. The Convention for the Definition of Aggression was signed simultaneously by eight States. Apart from Poland and the USSR, the following States participated in this convention: Afghanistan, Estonia, Iran, Latvia, Rumania and Turkey (*Poland and the USSR*, p. 101).

No. 9. Beck's visit to Moscow took place in February 1934, three weeks after the signature in Berlin of the Polish-German Declaration of Non-Aggression (26.1.1934). Although the said Declaration expressly stated that all international obligations undertaken by either Government remained in force and were not affected by the Declaration, Beck had the opportunity, in the course of his talks in Moscow, to emphasize that Poland had not undertaken any obligation to co-operate with Germany against the Soviet Union. However, in view of the fact that the Polish-German Declaration was valid for a period of ten years (until January 1944) it was agreed in the Polish-Soviet conversations that the Polish-Soviet Pact of Non-Aggression should be prolonged until 31.1.1945. Thus the date of expiration of the Polish-German Declaration almost coincided with that of the coming to an end of the Polish-Soviet Pact of Non-Aggression.

As Poland and the Baltic States had been negotiating for a Pact of Non-Aggression with the Soviet Union at the same time, Poland requested that the Soviet Union should also prolong its pacts with the Baltic States up to the same date that had been fixed for Poland. The Soviet representative agreed to do so (*Poland and the USSR*, pp. 105–6).

No. 11. On 15.9.1934 a permanent seat in the Council of the League of Nations was offered by the Council to the USSR, and on 18.9.1934 the Assembly of the League of Nations admitted that State to the League of Nations, approving at the same time the preceding resolution of the Council (L.N.M.S., XIV, No. 9, pp. 200–3).

No. 13. Poland's refusal to participate in the proposed Eastern Pact, as well as several declarations made by the Polish Government on its negative attitude as regards any suggestions of joining an 'ideological bloc', pointed to Poland's firm decision to remain aloof from the struggle between Fascism and Communism.

Although the Soviet Union was informed of Poland's opposition to the so-called 'Anti-Comintern Pact', Soviet representatives abroad spread many rumours alleging that Poland intended to join this Pact. In order to stop these rumours, Beck sent on 9.11.1937 a note to all Polish diplomatic posts stating that Poland would not join this pact and that she objected strongly to the formation of 'ideological blocs' between States (*Poland and the USSR*, pp. 109–10).

No. 14. In the late summer of 1938 Polish-Soviet relations were undergoing a period of tension. The violation of Polish frontiers by Soviet planes and a number of frontier-incidents provoked by Soviet frontier guards were assuming disquieting proportions. This state of tension was further increased by a statement which Potemkin made on 23.9.1938 to the Polish Chargé d'Affaires in Moscow after Poland's request to Czechoslovakia to return a part of Tesin Silesia (beyond the Olza river). In his statement Potemkin foreshadowed the possibility of renouncing the Polish-Soviet Pact of Non-Aggression if Poland should take any action against Czechoslovakia.

The fact that the Soviet Union had not been invited to the Munich Conference was very humiliating for her, the more so as she was bound by pacts of mutual assistance (concluded in 1935) with France and Czechoslovakia. The Soviet Government interpreted this isolation as a sign of a political agreement between the Munich powers which might be easily directed against Moscow. Because of these circumstances, as early as October 1938, Soviet policy began its attempts at forming an anti-German front in order to prevent a rapprochement between France and Germany.

Poland did not participate in the Munich Conference and assumed no responsibility for the isolation of the Soviet Union. In fact, Poland made use of the situation and in November 1938 she took the initiative, trying to ease the existing tension. She referred to the agreements in force between the two countries, and in particular, to the Pact of Non-Aggression which, in her view, constituted sufficient basis for the maintenance of mutual peaceful relations. In other words, Poland gave an assurance to the Soviet Union that it had nothing to fear from Poland, and obtained from Russia a confirmation of the pledges relating to the security of Poland's eastern frontier and promises of expanding trade relations. (Cf. J. Growski [Ambassador J. Grzybowski]: 'L'Année brillante de la politique des Soviets et leurs relations avec la Pologne' in the review *La Voix de Varsovie*, Paris, vol. I, No. 2, 15.11.1939, p. 82.)

No. 16. In its editorial of 20.2.1939 *Pravda* called the Soviet-Polish Trade Agreement the first complete commercial treaty between the contracting parties. Many reports from Polish newspapers as well as Soviet statements about the possibility of developing mutual relations between the two countries appeared in subsequent issues of the Soviet organ. It was the belated result of repeated Polish efforts to conclude a Trade Agreement which were hitherto unsuccessful.

No. 18. The Anglo-Polish Agreements of 4–6.4.1939 were followed on 13.4. by a declaration of Daladier who—apart from giving pledges of assistance to Rumania and Greece should they be attacked by a third State—stated that 'France and Poland guaranteed each other immediate and direct aid against any threat direct or indirect, which might aim a blow at their vital interests' (*Documents on International Affairs 1939–1946*, London, 1951; Oxford University Press, I, p. 202).

However, the attitude of the Soviet Union towards this new trend of British policy was becoming ever more critical. According to *Pravda's* editorial of 7.4. (No. 96) the Anglo-Polish Agreement on mutual assistance contained obligations separating those two countries from the rest of Europe. The British Ambassador in Moscow (Sir William Seeds) defined the Kremlin's attitude in his report of 13.4. in the following words: '. . . it does seem to me that as things are now this country [USSR] can properly be tempted to stand aloof and in case of war confine its advertised support of the victim of aggression to the profitable business of selling supplies to the latter'. In the event of Poland's defeat the Ambassador expected also 'an offer by Germany to the Soviet Union of Bessarabia and parts of Poland, not to mention perhaps Estonia and Latvia' (D.Brit.F.P., V, Nos. 52, 170).

No. 19. The occupation of Czechoslovakia by Germany in March 1939 convinced the Soviet Government that the agreement between Germany and the Western Powers was far from firm. In view of the new tension in Europe the Soviet Union was very active in its attempts at extending its influence and reinforcing its position with the neighbouring States, primarily, and with Turkey, Bulgaria, Rumania and Poland secondly. At the end of March 1939 the Soviet Government proposed a unilateral guarantee of their independence to the Baltic States, but this proposal was rejected by them for fear that in the event of their accepting it, the Soviet Union would press for the admittance of Soviet garrisons into their territories. At the end of April the Soviet Government sent Potemkin to Turkey to enquire if Russia could join the political and military agreement between the United Kingdom and Turkey which was at that time under consideration. Ankara promised to start talks with Moscow but only after the conclusion of the treaty of alliance with the U.K.

Potemkin tried then, in a further stage of his journey, to induce Bulgaria to join the Balkan Pact, promising Soviet support to Bulgaria's attempts to recover Southern Dobrudja.

However, on 8.5., Potemkin met with Rumania's express refusal to make any territorial concessions. In the final stage of his diplomatic mission, Potemkin visited Warsaw, but in a conversation with Beck on 10.5. he realized that Poland would oppose any plans according to which Soviet troops could enter the territories of Russia's Western neighbours in the event of a Polish-German war.

A rapprochement between the three Great Powers (France, the U.K. and the USSR) with the aim of checking all future German attempts at territorial expansion was not opposed by Warsaw, on condition that it did not mean that the Western Powers approved the establishing of Russian hegemony in Central Europe. The Polish Government interpreted in this sense the plans for the entry of Soviet troops under the pretext of a silent agreement on the part of the Allies. Such plans would allow Russia to penetrate Central Europe in the name of an anti-German alliance.

In the light of subsequent events, Potemkin's assurances of Russia's 'attitude bienveillante' towards Poland were but a window-dressing for the ambiguous Soviet policy with regard to Germany and the Western Powers. (Cf. Joseph Beck, *Dernier Rapport*, pp. 200–1.)

No. 20. The trade negotiations between the Soviet Union and Germany, which were begun towards the end of 1938, were de facto interrupted in February 1939. On 17.4.1939, Merkalov in a conversation with Weizsäcker, dealing with economic problems, mentioned, for the first time, the necessity of improving political relations between the two countries, adding that Russia was not taking any advantage of the existing tension between Germany and the Western Powers. He said also that ideological differences between States should not affect their mutual relations, citing as an example the correct relations between the Soviet Union and Italy.

A month later, on 17.5., Astakhov in a conversation with Schnurre expressed his great satisfaction at the change of attitude of the German press towards Russia which had taken place since the beginning of May. He emphasized that there were no political differences, as far as foreign policy was concerned, between Russia and Germany, and, consequently, there was no reason for hostility in mutual relations. He referred also, in this connection, to the Treaty of Rapallo.

A few days later, on 20.5., Molotov spoke to the point by declaring that the Soviet Government would be ready to agree to the resumption of trade negotiations should the necessary 'political basis' be created. It was an open offer for a political agreement between the Soviet Union and Germany, put forward by Moscow at the time of Franco-British-Soviet negotiations whose object was to stop further German aggression in Europe. No wonder that it took the Germans by surprise. Schulenburg called it 'suspicious' and thought that its purpose was to exercise pressure on Great Britain. The 'Auswärtiges Amt' ordered him to abstain from any further talks on the matter and to await Soviet initiative. (Cf. D.Germ.F.P., VI, Nos. 215, 406, *442*.)

As a matter of fact the position was more critical than that envisaged by the diplomatic action described above. On 23.5 Hitler took the political decision to strike against Poland, a decision which of course could not be known at that time to the outside world. (Cf. *The Trial of German War Criminals*, I, 165–8 and XXXVII/546–56; D.Germ.F.P., VI, No. 433— a better translation.) The Nuremberg Trial disclosed what had happened on that day at a conference with the commanders of German Armed Forces, in the course of which Hitler emphasized the importance of Poland from the military point of view and outlined his policy towards the Western countries and the Soviet Union as follows:

'The Polish régime will not stand up to Russian pressure. Poland sees danger in a German victory over the West, and will try to deprive us of victory. There is therefore no question of sparing Poland and we are left with the decision: to attack Poland at the first suitable opportunity. [. . .]. A conflict with Poland—beginning with an attack on Poland—will only be successful if the West keeps out of the ring. If that is not possible it is better to fall upon the West and finish off Poland at the same time. Isolating Poland is a matter of skilful politics. [. . .]. Economic relations with Russia are only possible if and when political relations have improved. In press comments a cautious trend is becoming apparent. It is not ruled out that Russia may disinterest herself in the destruction of Poland. If Russia continues to agitate against us, [our] relations with Japan may become closer.'

No. 22. The question whether any Soviet military supplies could be obtained was considered by the Polish authorities in the spring of 1939. The Polish Government had to reckon with the following factors:

—On 28.4. Hitler denounced the Polish-German Non-Aggression Pact (of 24.1.1934) which, as he said, 'the Polish Government have arbitrarily and unilaterally rendered . . . null and void' (D.Germ.F.P., VI, No. 276).

—On 19.5. a Military Convention between France and Poland was eventually signed. Its final stipulations contained a pledge of the extension of French assistance in military supplies for the Polish Army. An additional clause stipulated, however, that 'the convention will enter into force after the signature of the political convention which was being negotiated at the same time' (*Polskie Siły Zbrojne w drugiej wojnie światowej*, Londyn, 1951, Instytut Historyczny im. Gen. Sikorskiego, I/1, p. 94–101 and 'Procès-verbaux des conversations d'État-Majors Franco-Polonaises à Paris', May 1935, reprinted from *Bellona*, London, 1958, No. 2).

—The conversations in Warsaw with the British Military Mission, 23–30.5.1939, made it clear that great difficulties existed in providing the Polish Armed Forces with adequate supplies. It induced the British Government to send later (in July) Ironside to Poland with a mission to explore the measures necessary for meeting the shortage of military equipment in the Polish Armed Forces. (Cf. D.Brit.F.P., V, No. 680, 692, 701, 725 and VI, No. 374; *Polskie Siły Zbrojne*, I/1, pp. 101–5.)

Already in May, in view of the great costs of maintaining the state of alert, the Polish Government applied to Great Britain for a loan in cash (about £60 mil.) but it met with some formal objections. In France as well Polish endeavours to contract a loan in cash have remained unsuccessful for several months. (Cf. D.Brit.F.P., V, 562, 725; VI, 222, 343; *Polskie Siły Zbrojne*, I/1, p. 207.)

No. 24. The assurances given by Sharonov that no German-Soviet trade talks were taking place must be countered with Schnurre's report of 27.7. on his conferences with Astakhov and Babarin. In this memorandum Schnurre took the view that there existed a real possibility of a 'rapprochement' between Germany and the Soviet Union which might be achieved by a resumption of trade relations between the two countries and a revision of their political relations, either within the framework of the Russo-German Treaty of Friendship and Neutrality of 24.4.1926 or within that of a new political agreement. Astakhov shared this view although he expressed some apprehension as to German designs on the Baltic States and Rumania. As far as Poland was concerned he was of the opinion that Gdańsk should return to Germany in one form or another, and that the question of the so-called 'corridor' should be settled in accordance with German wishes. Weizsäcker instructed Schulenburg to approach Molotov with a similar suggestion and also, if the need should arise, to give him an assurance of Germany's respect for the territorial integrity of the Baltic States. (Cf. D.Germ.F.P., vol. VI, Nos. 729 and 736.)

The American views on Soviet foreign policy changed after the departure of the United States Ambassador's in the Soviet Union by Joseph E. Davies in June 1939. The new approach to the situation may be seen from the following extracts of a Memorandum made by Loy W. Henderson on 22.7.1939: '6) The break which took place between Poland and Germany last March, followed by British guarantees to Poland and Rumania, has changed the whole international outlook so far as the Soviet Union is concerned. At present for the first time the Soviet leaders are in no immediate dread of either a German-Polish combination or of a great four-Power European settlement. 7) As a result of this change the Soviet Union has no longer any deep interest in the policy of collective security.

It feels itself relatively safe from a dangerous European attack so long as Poland, supported by Great Britain, is at loggerheads with Germany. It is not anxious to enter into any European arrangement at the present time which may restrict its ability to manœuvre. If it does come to terms with Great Britain, it will do so only on a basis which will give it what amounts to hegemony over Eastern Europe, and which will render impossible for at least many years to come a united Western Europe' (USA, Sov. Union, 774).

No. 25. In the course of a conversation with Molotov on 3.8. Schulenburg stated that 'from the Baltic to the Black Sea, no differences existed between Germany and the Soviet Union' and that the 'Anti-Comintern Pact was not directed against the Soviet Union' (but against the Western democracies as it had been acknowledged by Molotov on 31.5.). Molotov then expressed a desire to conclude an economic agreement and to improve the political relations between the Soviet Union and the Reich. The German representative then expressed Germany's readiness to adopt an attitude towards the Baltic States that 'would safeguard vital Soviet interests in the Baltic Sea'. As regards Poland Germany was ready 'to protect all Soviet interests and to come to an understanding with the Soviet Government on this matter'. However, Schulenburg had the feeling that 'to cause a reversal in the Soviet Government's course will require considerable effort on our [Germany's] part'. (Cf. D.Germ.F.P., VI, No. 766.)

No. 29. The correspondence between the German Foreign Ministry and the People's Commissariat for Foreign Affairs of 14–16.8.1939 enabled the German point of view to be made clear, as is shown by the documents Nos. 26 and 27. Molotov's reply of 17.8 (cf. doc. No. 29) opened up a new prospect for future German-Soviet relations without any reference, however, to a joint settlement of the territorial questions in Europe. Ribbentrop, therefore, insisted in his note of 18.8. on the necessity of reaching a special agreement 'regulating the interests of both parties in the questions of foreign policy of one kind or another; for instance, the settlement of spheres of interest in the Baltic area, the problem of the Baltic States, etc.' Such an agreement was to include a pledge that 'the German Reich and the USSR would in no event resort to war nor to any other use of force', which was ever more imperative in view of events 'which might make the outbreak of an open conflict unavoidable'. Ribbentrop considered, therefore, that his 'visit to Moscow should take place immediately'. In consequence Molotov fixed the date of the German visit for the 26. or 27.8. Hitler's message to Stalin finally led the latter to agree to Ribbentrop's visit to Moscow on the 23.8. for the concluding of the pacts in question. (Cf. D.Germ.F.P., VII, Nos. 113, 125, 142, 149.)

No. 31. After taking the initiative for the conclusion of a political agreement with Germany the Soviet Union tried to keep up the appearances of neutrality in the clash between Germany and the Western Powers. It pretended that its agreement with Germany was simply a trade agreement and an attempt at improving political relations with that country. To the German proposal on 16.8. with reference to Ribbentrop's visit to Moscow, Molotov gave an evasive answer, saying that such a journey should be properly prepared. Urged again on 18.8., Molotov repeated his former argument, adding that the Soviet Government did not welcome the publicity which would be given to such a visit. Eventually, on the following day, because of the German Ambassador's insistence and the information that Germany would like to clarify its relations with the Soviet Union in view of the possibility of a war with Poland, Molotov declared that he agreed to Ribbentrop's coming a week after the publication of the signature of the economic agreement between Russia and Germany, that is, on 26. or 27.8. Thus, the Soviet delaying action lasted three days only and, because of Hitler's letter to Stalin, Ribbentrop came to Moscow on 23.8., that is, on the date chosen by the German Government. (Cf. D.Germ.F.P., VII, Nos. 75, 79, 113, 125, 142, 159.)

No. 41. After 3.9.1939 the Auswärtiges Amt pressed the Russians to speed up the Soviet occupation of Eastern Poland. Molotov tried to explain that the delay was due to the unpreparedness of the Soviet troops for such an operation and he expressed the fear that the Soviet Government might be accused by the Western Powers of an act of aggression. He adhered, nevertheless, to the 'strict execution of the plan adopted' (that is, to the proposed line of demarcation). On 9.9. an agreement was reached as to the date on which the Soviet advance should start. As appears from Schulenburg's report of 10.9, the Soviet Government declared that it intended 'to take occasion of the further advance of the German troops' as this would enable it 'to declare that Poland was falling apart and that it was necessary for the Soviet Union, in consequence, to come to the aid of the Ukrainians and Byelorussians "threatened by Germany". This argument was to make the intervention of the Soviet Union plausible to the masses and at the same time avoid giving the Soviet Union the appearance of being an aggressor.' Between 10. and 13.9. rumours were spread by Soviet authorities about a forthcoming armistice between Poland and Germany 'which would make a new war unnecessary for the Soviet Union'. On 15.9. Ribbentrop informed Molotov that the fall of Warsaw was imminent, and, at the same time, objected to the use of the argument on the part of the Soviet Government, of the German threat to the Ukrainian and Byelorussian population 'as a ground for Soviet action' because 'this would make the two States appear as enemies before the whole world'. Stalin, however, changed the final wording only very slightly, for it ran as follows: 'The Soviet Union considered itself, obligated to intervene to protect its Ukrainian and Byelorussian brothers' and to prevent 'any third powers of might, who could attempt to profit by the chaos which had arisen'. (Cf. D.Germ.F.P., VIII, Nos. 5, 34, 37, 46, 63, 70, 79.)

No. 50. After the German troops had crossed first the river Narew (9/10.9.1939) and a few days later, the Middle Vistula and the San (13/14.9), the leaders of the Soviet Union became anxious lest the Agreement of 23.8. on the delimitation of the Russian and German 'spheres of influence' would be respected. These fears increased still further when between the 14. and 16.9. German troops from both North and South penetrated deeply into the area between the Vistula and the Bug. At the same time the Berlin authorities tried to include into their zone of occupation the Borysław oil centre and the district of Suwałki. On 19/20.9. Ribbentrop eventually abandoned the plan for the seizure of the oil centre as well as the plan for preserving 'a residual Poland'. He obtained, instead, Molotov's assent to the incorporation of the Suwałki district into East Prussia. On the same day of 19.9 the Soviet Government proposed to the German Chancellor a final settlement of the Polish question, receiving a positive answer on 23.9. with the announcement of Ribbentrop's visit to Moscow within a few days' time. In the meantime a Mixed Military Commission at Białystok started to work out a demarcation line between the two zones of occupation. The Soviet Government was represented by Voroshilov and Germany by Köstring. Its work was completed on 22.9. and the findings were published in the communique whose text appeared above. The taking over of the established spheres of influence was to be completed before 4.10. The London *Times* gave the information on the delimitation of the zones of occupation on 23.9. (No. 48.418), adding a note by their special correspondent, entitled 'Germany in the East', which ran as follows: 'For the Western Powers Hitler is the enemy, and to his declaration that "Poland will never arise again in the form laid down by the Versailles Treaty" their only reply is that she will arise in that form, and that to effect it is their pledged duty. So shall Czechoslovakia. As for Hitler's game in White Russia and the Ukraine, they can merely watch it with interest.' (Cf. D.Germ.F.P., VIII, Nos. 70, 78, 90, 94, 103, 109, 114, 115, 122; Weinberg, *Germany*, pp. 55–8.)

No. 52. Before Ribbentrop's visit to Moscow, on 25.9. (cf.: Note to doc. No. 50) Stalin proposed handing over to Germany the whole voivodeship of Lublin and the western part of the voivodeship of Warsaw, in exchange for the surrender of Lithuania to the Soviet

Union. In the name of the Reich Ribbentrop expressed his approval of this transaction, being prompted, according to German sources, by a wish to exploit the fertile land of the Lublin area and—in view of the more distant future—by a wish to keep any initiative in the Polish question in his own hands. Germany retained only a small part of Lithuania, in the neighbourhood of Mariampol, from which frictions later arose between Germany and Russia. It was in these circumstances that the German-Soviet Boundary and Friendship Treaty was signed, on 28.9.1939, a treaty whose purpose was to lay the foundation stone for the exclusive control by the two Powers of the whole of Eastern-Central Europe.

On the day when that treaty was signed, an exchange of letters took place twice between Molotov and Ribbentrop. In the first letter, signed by Molotov, the Soviet Union agreed to a considerable extension of trade relations between the two countries and undertook to supply Germany with raw materials. In the second letter the Soviet Union promised Germany an unrestricted rail transit to and from Rumania along the line Upper Silesia-Lwów-Kołomyja and agreed to increase Soviet oil deliveries.

An attempt to estimate that new agreement from the British point of view can be found in a note of *The Times* of 30.9. which ran as follows:

'The Treaty is not a military alliance automatically involving the Soviet Union in the European war. At the same time, it is difficult to assert that the Soviet Union and Germany are not allies. Russia agrees to support Germany economically and consult with her regarding measures that shall be taken should Great Britain and France now resolve to discontinue the war against Germany. Ribbentrop before leaving [Moscow], indicated that the Soviet Union and Germany had reached an agreement on all Eastern European questions, and would not permit any outside interference.' (Cf. D.Germ.F.P., VIII, Nos. 131, 137, 152, 157–63; Weinberg, *Germany*, pp. 58–9; Rossi, *Deux ans*, pp. 80–1.)

No. 54. On 30.9. an editorial 'Pact of Common Interest' appeared in *The Times*, referring to the Polish frontier with the Soviet Union. 'It is pointed out [in Moscow quarters of diplomatic observers] that Russia has obtained much without entering the war, and can obtain everything she desires without war, should the conflict between the Allies and Germany continue. Moreover, Stalin is withdrawing his forces [according to the Treaty of 28.9.1939] from the purely Polish territory to a roughly ethnographic frontier. This means that only the Ukrainians and White Russians are being taken into the Soviet Union, and it is argued that the Allies, when victorious, would be unlikely to insist on the reincorporation of these peoples in the new Polish State. The Soviet withdrawal could, therefore, be a cautious move by Stalin in order to avoid unnecessary complications.' Similar opinions were expressed in the *Daily Telegraph* of 30.9., and in Churchill's broadcast on 1.10. (Cf. *The Bulletin of International News*, XVI/20.)

No. 63. On 23.10., the Polish Consul-General at Geneva (Kazimierz Trębicki) informed the Secretary-General of the League of Nations that the Polish Government 'having learnt of the Pact of Mutual Assistance between Lithuania and the USSR signed on 10.10.1939, has conveyed to the Lithuanian Government a formal protest against the acceptance by that Government of any territory ceded by the Union of Soviet Socialist Republics and not belonging to the Union'. The diplomatic representatives of the Polish Government had handed to the Governments to which they were accredited a note informing them of this protest. At the request of the Consul-General, the Secretary-General communicated his letter to the States Members of the League on 24.10 (L.N.M.S., XIX, No. 10, October 1939).

No. 65. This protest was communicated by the Secretary-General to the Members of the League of Nations on 28.10. (L.N.M.S., XIX, No. 10, 1939).

571

No. 66. This Declaration was preceded by the ratification of the German-Soviet Pact on the partition of Poland by Hitler on 19,10. and the Presidium of the Supreme Soviet on the following day. In his speech Molotov described the events in the following order: collapse of Poland, occupation of Eastern Poland by Soviet troops, Soviet-German Agreement. This way of presenting the facts was due to his wish to conceal the fact of the previous conclusion of the Soviet-German Treaty which took place on 23.8. and was followed by Secret Protocols signed on 28.9. and 4.10.1939. (Cf. Matuszewski, *G.B.O.*, 18, 35–7; Keesing's, *C.A.*, 1939, p. 3781.)

No. 67. The decision of the Supreme Soviet was based on the alleged 'freely expressed will of the people' of the eastern provinces of Poland on 22.10.1939. It was, however, actually founded on the agreements on the partition of Poland concluded between the German Reich and the USSR in the period from 23.8. to 28.9. and on the occupation after 17.9. by Soviet troops and political agents (numbering about 700,000) of the territories assigned to the Soviet Union. The area occupied by the Soviet troops was of 77,620 sq. miles, with a population in 1939 of 13,199,000, of whom 5,274,000 were Poles, 4,529,000 Ukrainians, 1,945,000 Byelorussians, 1,109,000 Jews, 134,000 Russians, 84,000 Lithuanians and 124,000 people of other nationalities.

As regards the so-called 'election', it must be observed that:

a) The mere fact of putting to vote the question of the sovereignty over an area under military occupation was contrary to International Law, recognized to this limited extent even by the Soviet Union in its treaties and agreements with Poland of 1921, 1929, 1933 and 1934.

b) The election to the National Assemblies of the so-called Western Ukraine and Western Byelorussia was prescribed by the commanders of the troops of occupation in agreement with the organs of the Soviet NKVD.

c) The authorities of occupation imposed the Soviet electoral system which meant that only candidates of one party were admitted. Moreover, the choice of candidates was discussed at public meetings and the voting was indirect, by stages (intermediate electoral bodies).

d) The chairmen of the balloting committees and the leading candidates were mostly Soviet citizens, the majority of them were Russians, and only 110 delegates of Polish nationality were elected out of a total of 921 delegates in Byelorussia and 402 out of the total of 1500 in the Western Ukraine, although the percentage of the Polish population in these territories was respectively 40% and 36·2%.

e) At the beginning of October 1939 the authorities of occupation proceeded to mass arrests of local social and political leaders (about 30,000) and closed all cultural and political associations and editorial boards. In this way the population of those provinces was deprived of all its leaders and debarred from any sources of outside information.

f) The ballot was held on 22.10. under the control of Soviet authorities, with the aid of the police. Secrecy of voting was not observed and all sorts of threats and pressure were exercised on the population which was forced to vote.

g) The results of the ballot were not supervised by an independent body nor by the representatives of the voters, and they were only partly published (it was alleged that official candidates received 90·9% of the votes in the Western Ukraine, and 90·7% in Byelorussia).

h) The National Assemblies of the so-called Western Ukraine and Western Byelorussia were immediately convoked (the respective dates being 26. and 28.10.). They held their meetings for two days under the pressure of Soviet troops and constant outside demonstrations organized by men specially sent for that purpose. They were surprised by an urgent motion proposing incorporation into the USSR which had to be voted openly. A few delegates tried to protest but they were arrested on the spot.

(For the Soviet annexion of Eastern Poland see W. Sukiennicki, *Sprawa aneksji Polski Wschodniej przez Sowiety*, Nov. 1943, GSHI, A.11. 49/Sow./6; *Pravda*, Moscow, of 11,

22 and 25.10.1939; *Czerwony Sztandar*, Lwów, of 5 and 7.10.1939; Special Report No. 1 of the Select Committee on Communist Aggression, Washington, 1954, Government Printing Office.)

No. 72. The stand taken by the British Government towards Soviet Russia was expressed in the speech delivered by Halifax in the House of Lords on 5.12., whose relevant passage ran as follows: 'We have always tried to improve our relations with Russia, but in doing so we had always maintained the position that rights of third parties must remain intact and be unaffected by our negotiations [. . .] I have little doubt that the people of this country would prefer to face difficulties and embarrassment rather than feel that we had to compromise the honour of this country and of the Commonwealth on such issues' (H.L.Deb., v. 115).

This declaration was made after the Soviet aggression against Finland (29.11.) and her appeal to the League of Nations which led to the resolution of the Assembly 'condemning the action of the USSR against Finland' and the expulsion of the USSR from the League ('the USSR has placed itself outside the League of Nations. It follows that the USSR is no longer a Member of the League', L.N.M.S., XIX, Special Supp. to the 1939 December issue).

No. 76. 'A note on a conversation between Zaleski and Lord Halifax on 25.6.1940 (Ch.Pres.P.R.) tells the further story of the said Aide-Mémoire. So far as item 5 of the conversation was concerned, relating to the Prime Minister's Memorandum, Halifax took note of Zaleski's statement, sharing entirely his point of view. He assured him that he was well aware of the fact that the Memorandum aimed at providing some information only and because of that he did not take any steps and did not inform Cripps in Moscow of its contents. He agreed to the complete withdrawal of the Memorandum. In the further course of the conversation it was established that any Polish-Soviet co-operation was not topical.'

No. 78. Towards the end of February 1940 information from various sources began to reach the Polish Government in France on mass-deportations of Polish citizens from the territories occupied by Soviet Russia. This was the first stage of the deportations of the local population, made up of settlers, magistrates, civil servants and police, 120,000 people altogether. The second stage took place in April 1940 and extended to the families of the previously deported, as well as small-holders and farm-hands from the now 'socialized' land estates (irrespective of their national origin), a total of 320,000 people. The third wave of deportations came in June and July 1940, carrying to Russia war refugees from the western provinces of Poland and also the more active elements from among the urban population (a great percentage of which were Jews), altogether 240,000 people. The fourth stage, which was a reaction against the outbreak of the war against Germany, comprised prisoners and detainees from the occupied territory, children from educational establishments and orphanages, railway workers and craftsmen, to the total of 200,000.

Deportations were carried out throughout the whole eastern part of Poland, both of Poles and of national minorities. According to unofficial estimates made by the Polish Embassy in the USSR, among the deportees were 52% Poles, 30% Jews, 18% Ukrainians and Byelorussians. The total number of the deported civilian population was estimated at 880,000 to which have to be added 180,000 prisoners-of-war (there were actually 242,000 at the beginning but a number of these were sent home), 150,000 men conscripted for the Red Army (nearly 3 annual contingents) and 20,000 men enlisted for work in mines. The total figure is therefore 1,230,000 Polish citizens deported, which constitutes 9·3% of the whole population of Eastern Poland, not to mention those inhabitants of Western Poland who took their refuge there. The lowest estimate of the number of deportees was that of 880,000 made in 1944 by the Polish Ministry of Foreign Affairs ('Assessment of the population deported to the USSR', GSHI, B.1703), while all other assessments give much higher figures. For instance, the Intelligence Service of the Home Army in Poland reported that 1,050,000 people were deported, while the statistical data collected by the 2nd Army Corps (published in Polish under the heading *Polska Wschodnia*, 1939–41) by means of a mass enquiry among soldiers, stated the number of deportees as 1,240,000 (together with prisoners-of-war and detainees). The book published by the Polish Ministry of Justice in London, entitled *Stalin and the Poles*, (1949), based on extensive research, states that the number of deportees was 980,000 and that of the arrested persons 250,000. Other categories of displaced persons, such as prisoners, conscripts and mine workers, fluctuate between 394,000 and 430,000. Thus the total number of displaced persons should be a figure between 1,442,000 and 1,660,000. The whole question is discussed by W. Wielhorski in his pamphlet 'Los Polaków w niewoli sowieckiej' (Fate of Poles in Soviet captivity 1939–56), London, 1956. A summary of all these enquiries was given (apart from the aforesaid book *Stalin and the Poles*) in the 'Special Report No. 1 of the Select Committee on Communist Aggression', House of Representatives, 83rd Congress, Second Session, Washington, 1954.

No. 80. From 21.11.1940 the Polish Government was in possession of information from British sources on the readiness of Churchill's Government to give its consent to Soviet proposals for the recognition of the annexation of the Baltic States by approving the existing status quo. This position was supposed not to be in contradiction to Churchill's official declaration of 5.9.1940, on the non-recognition of territorial changes operated during the war. (Cf. Doc. No. 79.) British acquiescence was apparently prompted by the wish 'to check Hitler's diplomatic moves' which became patent at the time of Molotov's visit to Berlin (mid-November). The British assumed that Soviet pressure arose from the wish to free the assets belonging to the Baltic States which remained frozen in English banks and also to obtain possession of a part of the Merchant Navy of those States which was in British service. Halifax's answer which appears in this document did not remove—in Polish views— the danger of creating a precedent of which the Soviet Government would be able to avail itself in the future in relation to its claims of the revision of the Riga Peace Treaty frontier, and also creating a precedent of British readiness to sacrifice it 'should such a sacrifice be necessary for winning the Soviet Union as an ally' (Report of the Polish Embassy in London, Military Attaché, of 15. and 21.11.1940—GSHI, PRM, 20).

No. 83. This protest was raised by the Polish Government on 15.2.1941 on Zaleski's proposal (GSHI, PRM–K, 105). The text which appears in the document was sent to the Foreign Office on 21.2. There is a slight difference between this text and that sent to the U.S. Secretary of State on 19.2. (Cf. USA, Dipl., 1941, I, p. 120.)

No. 85. Sir Stafford Cripps was appointed British Ambassador to the USSR on 6.6.1940. The following year he came to England for consultation with his Government and then returned to his post (Keesing's *C.A.*, 1940, p. 4089, 1941, p. 4633).

No. 91. a) The text quoted above is a note on the conversation of 6.7.1941 'revised with General Sikorski's amendments' in accordance with the exchange of letters between Sikorski and Cadogan on 5–6.7.1941 (GSHI, PRM, 41/4).

b) The question of the future frontiers of Poland was raised in an unofficial conversation after the outbreak of the German-Soviet war. On 27.6. the correspondent of TASS in London, M. Rothstein, told M. Litauer, then Counsellor of the Polish Embassy in London, that 'a democratic Poland which General Sikorski wishes to recreate, and with which the Soviet Union would like to enter into the closest possible relations, must forfeit her former Great Power policy and accept the principle of a national, ethnographic Poland', while

Sikorski (for which he was reproached by Rothstein) began to defend the Treaty of Riga, 'as the basis for the future Polish-Russian frontier' (GSHI, PRM, 41/4).

No. 93. The draft of that memorandum was made on 7.7.1941 but was considerably changed on the following day (GSHI, PRM, 41/3).

On Sikorski's proposal Zaleski told Eden on 8.7. 'that a Polish-Soviet agreement must not be the result of a unilateral declaration of the Soviet Government but should be the consequence of a bilateral agreement and a joint declaration of both the governments concerned'. At the same time he denied the Soviet right to conscript Polish citizens for the Soviet army and emphasized the importance of the fulfilment of the requests raised in the note of 7.7.1941. (Cf. Exchange of letters between Sikorski and Zaleski on 8.7.1941, GSHI A.11.49/Sow/1.)

No. 94. On the morning of 11.7.1941 Eden asked Sikorski and Zaleski to call on him at 3.45 p.m. in order to discuss the bases of the future Polish-Soviet agreement and the question of arranging a meeting with Maisky. When Sikorski and Zaleski called at the Foreign Office at the appointed time, Eden told them that Maisky had already received his Government's answer to the Polish Draft Agreement and was ready to let its contents be made known to them personally. After receiving the requested information about the nature of the proposed conversation Sikorski agreed that Maisky should be called immediately which Eden arranged by telephone. It was in these circumstances that the direct discussion on the Draft Agreement took place (Zaleski's note on the conversation Sikorski-Eden-Maisky on 11.7., GSHI, A.11.49/Sow./1). A record of this conversation was made in English by Mr. Harvey and it is this text that appears in doc. No. 94.

The conversation of 11.7. was reported by Sikorski to the Cabinet at its meeting on the following day. According to this report 'the Polish-Soviet conversation was held in circumstances which were far from favourable for Poland. Public opinion in Britain as well as in America had welcomed with joy the fact that Russia was aligning with Great Britain and the two governments urged a prompt settlement of Polish-Soviet disputes.' The Polish Prime Minister explained further: 'We are on the eve of the conclusion of a British-Soviet military agreement [the agreement was actually signed on that very day and its scope was much wider than originally anticipated], which will greatly strengthen British-Soviet co-operation. Owing to this, pressure on us on the part of our allies for appeasement in Polish-Soviet relations will increase.' On the other hand, Sikorski stated that 'the fact that Poland had never let herself be tempted by suggestions aiming at our participation in an invasion of Russia nor by any "Promethean" combinations for the dismemberment of Russia, was a strong moral argument in our hands'. As regards the conversation itself, Sikorski informed his colleagues that 'he did not leave any room for doubt as to our most firm upholding of the legal position as it existed before September 1939'. Realizing that the Soviet Government feared the formation of a Polish army in Russia he proposed that 'our officers and other ranks should be evacuated from Russia to a territory belonging to the British Empire. However, the realization of such an alternative proposal has so far met insuperable difficulties, although it was studied by the General Staff.' In his further remarks Sikorski revealed that Maisky had let him know that the Soviet Government refused to accept the obligation of the release of political prisoners as well as of a general release of Polish citizens, but at the same time 'expressed Russia's readiness to recognize Polish rights in a number of towns and districts which were under Soviet occupation'. Replying to this statement Sikorski said that he 'decided to reject such a point of view which excluded the release of political prisoners and declared most firmly that the judgment on their political activity was within the sole right of Poland'. At the end of his report the Polish Premier stated that 'the liberation of our refugees and the care of them . . . would be one of the first tasks of our Ambassador in Moscow' (Proceedings of the Council of Ministers, 12.7.1941, GSHI, PRM-K, 104).

575

No. 96. The above initial draft prepared on 11.7. was fuller than the final one, as it contained an attempt to define the principles which inspired the contracting parties concluding the agreement. The articles were arranged in a slightly different manner and there was also a specific pledge of mutual guarantee of territorial integrity and political independence (GSHI, A.11.49/Sow/1).

No. 98. The British amendments were discussed between Sikorski and Eden, in Zaleski's presence, at 10 a.m. on 15.7. To what length the British pressure on Polish representatives went in order to induce them to accept a compromise, appears from the following words spoken by Eden and noted by Zaleski: 'Whether you wish it or not, the treaty must be signed.' The passage of Article I 'the relations between the USSR and Poland in consequence revert to the basis existing before these dates' was according to Zaleski's note proposed and drawn up by Sikorski (who based his remarks on the Polish draft of 13.7.— doc. No. 97) while the initial passage of 'Draft Protocol I': 'The two contracting Governments accept the principle that, subject to military considerations in particular cases, Polish citizens who are at present in detention on the territory of the USSR shall be set at liberty' was drafted by Strang and after some amendments accepted by those present. In the Draft of 13.7. this passage written on the direct instructions of Sikorski ran as follows: 'All Polish citizens who are within the boundaries of the Soviet Union will be returned to their freedom.' Zaleski interpreted the meaning of the whole conversation on 15.7. in the following way: 'It is not the agreement as such that is important for us: we would be ready to sign anything, provided we had an authentic and binding interpretation on the part of England.'

(Cf. Sikorski's letter to Zaleski of 14.7.; a note of Potulicki for Zaleski of 14.7.; a note of Zaleski from the conversation Sikorski-Eden on 15.7. All these documents are in the GSHI, A.11.49/Sow/1.)

No. 100. At midday on 17.7. the Foreign Office received the second Soviet draft through Maisky. Sikorski and Zaleski called on Eden at 4. p.m. and were informed by him of the nature of the Soviet proposals (doc. No. 99). In Zaleski's view 'the whole question of frontiers was relegated to preamble and the question of reverting to normal conditions omitted altogether, while the question of political prisoners was to be settled by an oral declaration by M. Maisky, stating the good will with which it would be treated when the Polish Ambassador would deal with that matter in future. General Sikorski rejected these two amendments on the spot.' The further conversation was devoted to the discussion of the value of the provisions contained in the preamble and Zaleski stressed the point that 'the Poles might be more amenable in the question of negotiations with Russia' should they obtain a British pledge on 'the future order in Europe'. He then produced the relevant text of the proposed British Declaration, using the recent text of the Yugoslav-English Agreement. The meeting was then suspended and all those present left to prepare the amendments. At 7 p.m. Sikorski showed Zaleski the amendments drafted by him together with a covering letter for Eden. All these documents were sent to the Foreign Office late at night. (Cf. notes from the conversations Sikorski-Eden and Sikorski-Zaleski on 17.7.1941, GSHI, A.11.49/Sow/1.)

No. 103. After the outbreak of the Soviet-German war Sikorski's Government placed a high value on obtaining American assistance in the question of the re-establishment of Polish-Soviet relations. With this in view, Ciechanowski had several conversations with Sumner Welles. In the first one (26.6.1941) the representative of the State Department informed him that in the British offer to the Soviet Union the question of assistance to the latter was made dependent on the re-establishment of normal relations between the Soviet Union and Poland. At the same time Sumner Welles declared that the USA would be ready to give assistance to the Soviet Union should the Kremlin ask for it (Report of the Polish Embassy in Washington of 27.6.1941). In the second conversation (7.7.1941) Sumner Welles informed Ciechanowski that the Soviet Government wished only to purchase some military equipment in the US. However, he anticipated some difficulties in bringing about direct Polish-Soviet negotiations in view of Russia's obvious designs to dominate over neighbouring countries. After Ciechanowski's explanation of Poland's aims, Sumner Welles agreed to make public the interest which the US Government was taking in a proper . settlement of the Polish question, both from the legal and the political points of view. At the same time he stressed the great importance for America of the continuation of the Soviet army's resistance, without anticipating, however, the conclusion of a Treaty of Friendship between Moscow and Washington (Report of the Polish Embassy of 9.7.1941). In the third conversation of 12.7., Sumner Welles let Ciechanowski know the point of view of Roosevelt who, two days earlier, in a conversation with Oumansky, drew the latter's attention to the necessity of restoring Polish-Soviet relations to their pre-war condition. Privately, he expressed fear of a dispute which might arise between Poland and the USSR on the question of the revision of their frontiers, especially if such a dispute occurred under outside pressure (Report of the Polish Embassy in Washington of 14.7.1941). The fourth conversation on 22.7. took place at a time when rumours in the press on the difficulties connected with the re-establishment of Polish-Soviet relations, were widely circulating; the State Department was waiting for official news on that matter from London. Sumner Welles spoke about the possibility of evacuating Polish prisoners and technicians from the Soviet Union to Afghanistan and India, and also of organizing relief for Polish refugees on Soviet territory (Report of the Polish Embassy in Washington of 23.7.1941).

It was in these circumstances that Sikorski approached the US Government with a request that the latter should issue a declaration 're-asserting non-recognition of territorial changes (in Poland) brought about by use of force' (doc. No. 103 and Ciechanowski, D.V., 39). Ciechanowski presented this suggestion to the Department of State on 25.7., handing with it a Note (London 7.7., and Washington 24.7., doc. No. 92) which defined Poland's basic position with regard to Soviet Russia. According to Ciechanowski's report 'The State Department took the same view with regard to the re-establishment of Polish-Soviet relations' and 'promised to submit the Note to the President', which was actually done at the beginning of August (cf. telegram of the Polish Embassy in Washington of 27.7. and Cordell Hull's letter of 12.8.1941.—All these documents are in the GSHI, A.11.49/Sow/1, and the whole question with all relevant details is expounded in Langer-Gleason, *U.W.*, pp. 551-7).

No. 104. Polish endeavours on 17.7. to the effect of obtaining a British guarantee for the frontiers of Poland (doc. No. 101) met with F.O.'s refusal on the following day. The British draft declaration of 18.7. (doc. No. 102) induced the Polish Government to present some amendments (doc. No. 104) and also to propose an extension of Soviet obligations in the negotiated agreement (para. 1, doc. No. 99) in the following manner: 'the Soviet Government recognizes the treaties concerning territorial changes in Poland, concluded since 1939, as invalid' (Potulicki's note of 21.7.1941 and the proceedings of the Council of Ministers of the same day).

Maisky immediately received the part of the Polish draft concerning the Agreement with the Soviet Union and after introducing some amendments, transmitted it to his Government in Moscow (doc. No. 105). As far as the British drafts of the Declaration were concerned, the Polish Government envisaged one of two alternative solutions:

a) Should its demands be accepted it intended to issue a declaration defining its position of principle in the following manner:

'The Polish Government has never recognized any territorial changes effected in Poland since the outbreak of the present war, as has been stated in this Government's note dated July 7, 1941, addressed to H.M. Government' (doc. No. 92 and Potulicki's note of 24.7.1941).

b) Should it prove to be impossible to obtain the desired alterations from the British

Government, the Polish Government prepared a declaration whose main point ran as follows:

'The Polish Government [. . .] has the honour to confirm that any territorial changes which have taken place on the territory of the Polish State since the outbreak of the war took place without the free consent and good will of Poland' (Potulicki's note of 21.7.1941).

When Maisky received the information concerning the Polish plan to obtain British pledges, he called on Eden, on 24.7., asking him to introduce the following passage: 'This declaration does not forejudge the position which Great Britain will adopt as regards the future frontiers in Eastern Europe.' Eden told the Polish Government of this fact, adding that probably he would not include the proposed words into his declaration. He preferred to make a statement in the House of Commons at question time, basing it on Churchill's declaration of 5.9.1940 (doc. No. 79 and Zaleski's report of 9.8.1941. All these documents are in the GSHI, A.11.49/Sow/1 and PRM, 41/3).

No. 105. The further course of events is described in 'The Proceedings of the Council of Ministers' of 25.7.1941 (GSHI, PRM–K, 104). At the morning meeting the President of the Council told his colleagues that 'the Soviet Government rejected the amendments, introduced, in agreement with the British Government, into the draft Polish-Soviet Agreement, at the last meeting of the Council on July 22nd [actually 21.7.]. The Soviet Government requests the former wording should be re-introduced as laid down in the first Soviet proposal, with regard to "mutual claims". Very reluctantly and under British pressure only the Soviet Government conceded that the creation of the Polish Army in the USSR should be linked to a special agreement. The Soviet Government insisted on keeping secret the Protocol relating to prisoners and claims. The Soviet Government also accepted reluctantly the passage concerning the annulment of the treaties of the partition of Poland, which will appear as the first article (instead of being put into the preamble), but at the same time it rejected the extension of this clause to all treaties in general, that is, to other treaties than those concluded with Germany. In these circumstances General Sikorski had a long and rather difficult conversation with Mr. Eden who having stated the absolute impossibility of obtaining anything more from the Soviet Government, in spite of all the pressure exercised on it by the British Government, agreed to submit to the British Cabinet a draft note of H.M. Government to the Polish Government to the effect of giving reassurances as regards the integrity of our frontiers, going even further than his proposals at the last meeting of the Council of Ministers on July 22nd [21.7.]. The President of the Council read out this draft note which should constitute a "junctim" with the proposed Polish-Soviet Treaty. The draft states in most emphatic terms the completely negative attitude of Great Britain towards any attempts at imposing on us a revision of our eastern frontiers. At the same time Mr. Eden said, in the most frank and open manner, that, in view of rather warm feelings aroused in British and American public opinion by the unexpectedly stubborn resistance of the Red Army, a refusal to sign the Treaty in its present form would undermine Poland's position in Anglo-Saxon countries. Therefore, fully aware of his responsibility, the President of the Council declares that we have now to take the decision whether to accept the Treaty in its present form or to reject it. There is no hope whatever, either at present or later, of obtaining Soviet consent to a change of the text for better. Neither is there any hope of securing British support on that matter should we reject the draft Treaty, which, by the way, does not differ, from the legal and political points of view, from the text to which the Council of Ministers has agreed. The problem of Wilno is, as a matter of fact, directly connected with the partition of Poland between Russia and Germany, and the annulment of the treaties of partition makes invalid all legal titles based on them. Clearly the fact that the protocol should remain secret and that the Soviet Government has refused to accept the term "settled" instead of "considered" with relation to prisoners, shows Soviet bad faith, placing us in a very awkward tactical position. In consequence thereof we shall be unable to prove to the Polish people that we have secured the possibility of the release of the victims of the Soviet rule of terror. We shall be obliged, of course, to inform our home country of the whole treaty including the protocol. [. . .] There exists beyond any doubt the great danger that, should we reject the present treaty, the Soviet Government might enforce its will by forming a sort of National Committee assuming the character of a government and entrust the latter with the task of creating a Polish army. As the rejection of the treaty will certainly arouse much bitterness among the Poles in Russia who have suffered so much and who were beginning to hope for their liberation and the possibility of doing some useful work for their country, one must reckon that some leaders there may be ready to come to terms with the Soviet Government and take the matter into their own hands.'

'Minister Zaleski sees the main obstacle in the fact that the protocol is to remain secret. He considers, however, the situation to be pretty desperate and making it very difficult for us to withdraw. He fears that our position might be misunderstood in the home country. The insistence on the initial wording of article 1 shows unwillingness to surrender Wilno to us. British reassurances, of course, greatly improve the situation; they cannot, however, satisfy us, because the British do not wish to guarantee the return to 1939 frontiers.' But the Minister considers it possible 'that Britain could use, at least, a formula binding her also for the future—for instance for the duration of the Peace Conference'.

At the evening meeting on the same day 'the Council of Ministers having heard the report of the President of the Council which states that the British Government agreed to the proposed draft of the British Note and to the publication of a communiqué which will disclose the actual tenor of the Protocol without mentioning the Protocol itself, unanimously voted for the signature of the Treaty, which, in view of Minister Zaleski's resignation, should be signed by the President of the Council'.

Finally, at the meeting of the Council of Ministers on 28.7., the President of the Council stated the following facts: 'In order to ease the situation arising from the resignation of three ministers, the President of the Republic proposed that the signature of the Treaty should be postponed. Owing to the fact that a few days ago the negotiations have been moved to Moscow, there exist great possibilities of improving the Treaty, by acceptance and even by extension of some amendments proposed by General Sikorski.'

In proof of this progress the President of the Council asserted that 'it was possible to force the Soviet Government to accept several provisions of the highest importance, first of all the inclusion of the passage referring to the forswearing of the treaties of partition into the text proper of the treaty, as well as of the paragraph emphasizing our sovereign rights over the Polish army in Russia, and of a British Note going far beyond Zaleski's proposals'. 'It has also been agreed in general terms what Mr. Eden should say in the House of Commons in reply to a question there with regard to the consonance of the British Note with the British Constitution. Mr. Eden will quote Churchill's statement of September of last year on the non-recognition of all territorial changes operated by force, without Poland's consent. In this way the sentence which previously appeared in the Note will be transferred to the statement which is not an official document. The disclosure of the secret protocol to the Treaty by way of a British communiqué, should an appropriate formula not be agreed by Moscow, was imposed on the Soviet Government.'

In these circumstances, on 28.7., Sikorski expected that the signature of the Treaty could take place on the following day, provided the President of the Republic granted full powers to this effect.

No. 106. The last attempts of the Polish Government to improve the text of the Polish-Soviet Treaty were summed-up in Sikorski's letter to the President of the Republic, dated 29.7.

'Already on Saturday, July 26, 1941, some vague information was received from Ambassador Cripps according to which there were prospects of a successful outcome of his endeavours. On Sunday 27th, confirmation of this news was received, without any further details. On Monday 28th, Mr. Eden let me know that Ambassador Cripps had received directly from Stalin and Molotov an affirmative reply on the following points:

1. A reference to the territorial changes in Article 1, which will run as follows: "The USSR recognizes that the agreements with Germany of 1939, concerning territorial changes, have become invalid". In the course of negotiations it was made clear that a special reference to the Wilno area was not only superfluous because the question is implied in the annulment of the agreements with Germany but also that there was no point in doing so, because, as Mr. Maisky declared, Russia had not concluded any agreement with Lithuania with reference to the Wilno area.

2. A general clause was inserted relating to the release of Polish detainees, deportees and prisoners-of-war; this clause will appear in the open treaty, which, as we know, is of primary importance, in relation both to Poland and to the outside world.

3. The word "mutual" in the clause relating to public and private claims is to be omitted.

4. As regards Soviet agreement to the appointment of the Commander of the Polish Armed Forces in the USSR, it was stated that it was difficult to dispense with this agreement, because a similar clause, even more far-reaching, was inserted into the treaty concluded between the USSR and Czechoslovakia. The matter has no real significance because of the principle laid down in the treaty, that questions referring to the command, organization and use of our army will be dealt with in a special agreement; the subordination of the Polish Army to the Soviet Supreme Command is reduced to operational matters, which—as a matter of fact—is unavoidable (a similar clause does not appear, by the way, in the Czecho-Slovak-Soviet treaty); moreover, we obtained the concession that a representative of our High Command will be attached to the Soviet Supreme Command, a concession which we did not obtain either in France or in Great Britain' (GSHI, PRM, 60).

The question of securing the U.S. support for the improvement of the text of the Polish-Soviet Treaty continued to absorb the Polish Ministry of Foreign Affairs. On 28.7. Zaleski urged Ciechanowski to induce the State Department to intervene with the British Foreign Office on the matter of the intangibility of Polish frontiers (GSHI, A.11.49/Sow/1, Dispatch of the Ministry of Foreign Affairs No. 281 and 283 of 28. and 29.7.1941).

On 30.7., the State Department was considering the possibility 'of securing for the Polish Government permission [?] to issue a statement that in signing the agreement with Soviet Russia it had not in any way admitted any change in its pre-war territorial boundaries or the existence of any basis for the discussion of such changes' (Langer-Gleason, U.W., p. 556, and a dispatch of the Polish Embassy No. 198 of 30.7.). However, on the following day Sumner Welles stated in reply to Ciechanowski: 'that the American Government did not desire to intrude upon the negotiations and that the British Note to the Polish Government seemed to cover the matter'. In accordance with this statement the Acting Secretary of State said in his statement to the press on 31.7.: 'The United States does not recognize any change in Poland's status as a free, sovereign and independent nation. [. . .] The Russian-Polish Agreement . . . is in line with the United States' policy of non-recognition of territory taken by conquest', (Langer-Gleason, U.W., p. 556 and the dispatch of the Polish Embassy No. 200 of 31.7.). Thus, the U.S. 'Administration was anxious to defer the question of Poland's boundaries till the war was over'.

The signature of the Treaty took place at 4.15 p.m. on 30.7., in the Foreign Secretary's room. No full powers were shown, similarly to proceedings at the signature of the British-Soviet Treaty. The ceremony proceeded in the following manner as described by an official British report: 'It was a simple ceremony and there were both Polish and Russian texts of Agreement. They were signed in turn by M. Maisky and General Sikorski, each signing the text in his own language first. After the signature of the Agreement Mr. Eden and General Sikorski exchanged the Notes, the text of which was given in the preceding column'. (Cf. doc. No. 107.)

The President of the Republic made a reservation on 1.8., according to which such an agreement 'could establish general lines only for the actual conduct of the signatories'. (Exchange of letters between the President of the Republic and Sikorski, dated 31.7. and 1.8.1941, GSHI, PRM, 60.)

The concurrence of views between the Head of State and the Head of the Government was eventually established on 19–20.8.1941, when both parties recognized that 'the Polish-Soviet

Treaty ceased to be a matter of dispute between the President and the Council of Ministers' and that the principles on which co-operation between them was based remained in force. (Cf. the correspondence between Raczkiewicz and Sikorski of 7, 10, 19 and 20.8. and the proceedings of the Council of Ministers of 27.10.1941—all these documents are in GSHI, PRM, 60 and PRM–K, 104.)

A note made by Arlet on his conversation with Cripps on 8.8.1941 throws some light on the origin of some clauses of the Treaty: 'The final text of the Treaty was established by him [Cripps] during a conversation with Stalin. Ambassador Cripps expounded, in particular, on circumstances in which the term "amnesty" was introduced (being, probably, aware of the comments which this term might rouse). He alleged that Stalin was opposed to a general solution of the question of Polish prisoners-of-war, detainees and conscripts, and to the insertion into the Treaty of any terms which might put the USSR into an unfavourable light. Cripps related to have then argued that, should the resumption of Polish-Soviet relations start by negotiations on the release of one or other category of Polish citizens, a difficult situation would be created from the very beginning. Mutual recriminations, arguments on the Polish side about the injustice of the arrests, and, on the Soviet side, about the alleged guilt of the victims of their repressive measures, would inflame discord from the first moment, and this should be avoided if the agreement was to be genuine. "Make a gesture", Cripps is alleged to have said to Stalin. "Show the world that you sincerely desire an agreement." This seemed to be the clinching argument, according to Sir Stafford's statement.

'As regards the question of Polish participation in the Soviet Supreme Command, according to his relation it was discussed in the following manner. Stalin said that he had no idea what a "joint command" meant in practice. Cripps then proposed that a Polish representative should be attached to the Soviet Command and thus the points in dispute were settled' (GSHI, PRM, 41/5).

No. 109. The Polish-Soviet Agreement was widely discussed in the press as well as Sikorski's speech. The first editorial comment appeared in *The Times* (1.8.1941) under the heading 'Peace and Power'; it asserted that 'leadership in Eastern Europe is essential if the disorganization of the past twenty years is to be avoided'; [. . .] 'this leadership can fall only to Germany or Russia. Neither Great Britain nor the United States can exercise, or will aspire to exercise, any predominant rôle in these regions'. This article induced Raczyński to ask the British Government for an explanation. Eden gave him cause for satisfaction by issuing a statement on 19.8., in which the British Government dissociated itself from the opinion expressed in *The Times*, (PRM, 39–b). The problem of the future of the European continent which had arisen in this connection provoked a discussion in the English press. *Time and Tide* (16.8.) expressed reservations on the plans for the surrender of British influence on the European continent: 'The solution recommended by *The Times* oddly resembles the "new order", the difference being that instead of Germany and Italy, the leadership is bestowed on Russia. Before this unexpected proposal we must take fresh stock. We and America shall have the obligation to lead and protect the smaller States in Europe.' Among other English newspapers, the *Manchester Guardian* wrote in a conciliatory mood: 'The question of Poland's eastern frontier [. . .] has been left open. It could never have been decided of itself, for it will be part of a general frontiers settlement in Eastern Europe in which several countries will be concerned. The future eastern frontiers must be made with "the free consent and good will" of both Poland and Russia.' *The Sunday Times* also took the view that the problem which had risen at that time would have to be solved in future, but it outlined the future solution: 'The Anglo-Polish Agreement does not exclude some compromises over the Russo-Polish frontier, if, as highly desirable, she [Poland] receives substantial Baltic enlargement at the expense of Germany' (mentioning: Danzig and all East Prussia).

This discussion took place after the Soviet Government had stated its point of view. The official Soviet organ *Izvestia* published an editorial on 3.8., in which it attacked Polish assertions relating to the return to the pre-war territorial status quo: 'The Soviet Government has recognized that the Soviet-Germany Agreement of 1939 concerning territorial changes in Poland has lost its validity. By this it emphasized that "territorial changes" are not eternal and that frontiers established by such "changes" are not immutable. For instance, we do not consider immutable the Polish-Soviet frontiers established by the Treaty of Riga in 1921, nor do we share the view that "no one dares to presume that the borders of the Polish State of 1939 may be questioned" as expressed by General Sikorski in his speech [of 31.7.1941] . . . The problem of Soviet-Polish frontiers is a matter for the future.'

The Russian emigrés in the West interpreted on the whole the signature of the Agreement as proof of the Polish Government's readiness to make concessions. Typical for these trends of opinion was an article by P. Garvi in *Sozialisticheskii Vestnik*, No. 15, 28.8.1941. He wrote as follows: 'The Soviet Government having conceded to Poland the main point, that is, the annulment of the territorial changes which actually were conquests made jointly with Hitler, did not agree to a reference in the Agreement to the frontiers laid down by the Treaty of Riga, in order to leave the question of their revision open.' It would be possible to come to an agreement after the war 'if Russia and Poland enter the path of a true and far-reaching democracy and if the principle of federation prevails in the reconstruction of Europe'.

The Polish point of view was outlined once more by Stroński in an article entitled 'Polish-Soviet Agreement, Alliance and Recognition of Frontiers' (*Free Europe*, 22.8.) which was a repetition of his broadcast for the BBC on 6.8. According to him 'The essence of the Agreement of July 30 is that the Soviet Union has invalidated the territorial changes in Poland since 1939. Great Britain has declared that she does not recognize the territorial changes effected in Poland since August 1939. The United States has adopted the same attitude [. . .]. We have thus agreements for the recognition of frontiers [with Great Britain] and for mutual help against aggression [with Great Britain and the Soviet Union]. And it is these agreements that constitute a guarantee of our frontiers. No other guarantees exist.'

No. 112. The re-establishment of political relations between Poland and the Soviet Union was initiated by the sending of a Polish Military Mission with Maj.-Gen. Bohusz-Szyszko as its head. Its members left London by air on 2.8.1941. The Mission's principal task was the preparation of a draft military convention in view of the formation of the Polish army in the USSR and the organization of welfare work for released prisoners and deportees. It was understood that the bulk of the Embassy with Kot would follow within 2–3 weeks. The Polish Mission started its work in close touch with Cripps and Macfarlane. Both of them began to press for the prompt arrival of Kot, as in their view the release of prisoners and the gathering of deportees in convenient places would depend on it. As the prompt departure of Kot turned out to be impossible, in order to avoid any semblance of procrastination on the Polish part, on 12.8., Sikorski sent Retinger as chargé d'affaires with the mission to open 'diplomatic channels between Poland and Soviet Russia'. The main effort of the interim Polish diplomatic representation consisted in making administrative arrangements to the effect of the formation of the Polish army and securing consular protection for all deportees. (Cf. Correspondence between Sikorski and Cripps and Macfarlane, dated 2 and 8.8. and 1 and 9.9.1941, GSHI,PRM, 41/3; Reports of Arlet and Retinger, dated 5, 7, 8, 11, 14 and 15.8.1941, GSHI, A.11.49/Sow/2; Zygmunt Bohusz-Szyszko, *Czerwony Sfinks* (Red Sphinx), Rome 1946, pp. 58–61, 93–6, 101–4.)

No. 123. The Memorandum reproduced in this document on the formation of a Polish Army in the USSR was, as a matter of fact, preceded by Sikorski's letter to Churchill, on 11.9.1941. In this letter the Polish Premier was able to provide Churchill with first-hand information:

'General Anders, the G.O. Commanding Polish Forces in Russia, reports that young volunteers are joining the ranks in great numbers. In his opinion, the formation of an army

100,000 strong is merely a matter of procuring equipment and arms. It is significant that in his latest report, General Anders indicates the necessity of supplying mechanized and other armaments from without, whereas three weeks ago he only mentioned clothing equipment. The latter, amounting to 50,000 outfits, has been very promptly and efficiently dispatched by the War Office. It would now be necessary to send another lot for 50,000 men. I have approached the Government of the United States on the subject. I am conscious, however, of their difficulties with regard to supplies and I would like to put this vital matter for your favourable consideration. [. . .] the question of Anglo-American supplies is to the USSR and consequently to the Polish Army in Russia a matter of vital importance. It will no doubt be dealt with at the Moscow Conference. In his last message General Anders reports that no difficulties will be encountered on the part of the Soviet Government with regard to a Polish representative attending the Conference in matters regarding the supply and equipment of the Polish Force in Russia. [. . .].

General Anders has received instructions to gravitate southward with his forces [i.e. to consider the necessity of their shifting southwards]. The first Polish divisions should be formed by the middle of October. The supply and maintenance of the Polish Forces by Great Britain becomes of increasing importance with the prospective southerly move of our troops which moreover it logically demands' (GSHI, PRM, 39-a).

No. 124. The conversation reproduced in this document induced Harriman to seek the State Department's advice on the question of the supplies for Polish forces in Russia. He sent a telegram to the Secretary of State at midnight, of the 20/21.9., in which he wrote: 'would appreciate instructions whether we should attempt to deal with Polish needs direct or should insist that assistance come through the Russians'. Hull's reply (communicated also to Sikorski) ran as follows: 'We feel that it would be preferable to deal with the needs of the Polish forces in Moscow direct with the Poles while you [Harriman] are in the Soviet Union for two reasons: 1) We have already decided that Poland is to receive the benefit of Lend-Lease appropriations. Such a decision has not yet been made with regard to Russia. It would therefore be difficult to furnish through Lend-Lease arms and equipment to the Poles through Russia. 2) It is believed that it would be in conformity with our policy of maintaining as far as possible Polish prestige and influence in Eastern Europe for us to deal direct with the Poles with regard to the supplying of the Polish forces now, as well as in future.' (Cf. Winant's telegram to the Secretary of State of 20.9. and his reply to Biddle of 22.9.1941. USA, Dipl. 1941, I/253–5.)

On the strength thereof on 23.9. the Polish Government sent telegraphic instructions to the Polish Ambassadors in Moscow and Washington, informing them that 'Mr. Harriman asked the President [Roosevelt] not to refuse his assistance emphasizing most strongly our decision to fight against the Germans jointly with Russia and pointing out all the symptoms of a favourable change of the Soviet attitude towards the Church'. In return for undertaking to back Roosevelt's policy (that is, in circulating among American Poles news favourable to the Soviet Union) Sikorski asked that the following Polish requests should be taken into consideration:

'1) that the American Government exercise pressure in Moscow in order to bring about real further progress in the field of freedom of conscience', and 2) that the American Government 'grant an equivalent in prompt and full aid by equipping the Polish army' whose value 'might be most essential and real especially in the Caucasus area'. As both delegates, Beaverbrook and Harriman, declared that they favoured those requests, the Polish Government expected that at the Moscow Conference, they would take a positive stand as regards our requests or at least undertake to support our requests within the prescribed limits. Harriman's report on his journey to the Soviet Union shows to what extent he was interested in the problem of religious freedom. (Cf.: a telegram of the Polish Ministry of Foreign Affairs to Embassies in Moscow and Washington of 23.9.1941. GSHI, A.11.49/Sow/2; Robert E. Sherwood *The White House Papers of Harry L. Hopkins*, London, 1948, I, p. 394.

No. 133. While plans for the transfer of Polish forces from the Volga region to the Caucasus or Central Asia were under discussion, Sikorski had some conversations of an exploratory nature. One of them was with Bogomolov on 25.10.1941, and in the course of it Sikorski uttered the supposition that 'the Soviet Government was unwilling to admit the formation of an army exceeding the strength of two divisions'. Bogomolov denied that his Government had not kept its pledges of the Agreement of 30.7., and took the view that any failure to do so was due to the 'shortage of equipment and arms which the Western Allies should have supplied'. In his further remarks, 'General Sikorski put forward a request for moving Polish army camps southwards, to Persia or Astrakhan, as it would render British assistance in supplies much easier'. The Soviet Ambassador stated that the first direction would be unsuitable because it would obstruct the transport of war material to Russia, as the Persian railways were overstrained (note on a conversation between Sikorski and Bogomolov on 25.10.1941, GSHI, A.11.49/Sow/4a).

Other conversations on that matter were carried out between the Polish Government and the F.O.

On 27.10., Eden informed Sikorski in the course of a conversation that for the last few days 'the Soviet Government had been increasing its pressure in order to bring about a direct participation of British troops in the fight against Germany. In those circumstances and in view of the worsening of the situation on the Russian front, the British Government will probably be forced to engage British forces on that front, without insisting on reciprocal contributions (such as the evacuation of Persia by Soviet troops or the transfer of Polish troops to Persia or near the Persian border).'

On the following day, Eden told Raczyński that 'the Soviet Government stated, through M. Molotov, that the sending of British troops for the defence of the Caucasus would be undesirable. In its view it could not be called a common defence of the Soviet front. The Soviet Government insisted, instead, on the British Army taking over a sector of the front line further north (on the Volga). The British Government considers that request unreasonable, if not unpracticable, on account of difficult communications and supplies. It continues to consider sensible the plan for the withdrawal of five Soviet divisions from Persia to the Caucasus and their joining the Soviet troops posted there, as well as their reinforcement by a few British divisions and a strong British air-force. As a matter of fact, it is unable to accept the Soviet request for engaging 2–3 British divisions on the Volga'. (Cf. notes on the conversations of Sikorski and Raczyński with Eden, 27 and 28.10.1941, GSHI, PRM, 39–b; Churchill, S.W.W. III p. 420. Churchill's telegram to Cripps, 28.10.1941.)

No. 134. On 3.10.1941 Sikorski reviewed the military situation at the Council of Ministers in the following terms: 'For the last few days the Germans have continued to attack the Crimea from land and air. One can say that the Caucasus and its oil-centres are under indirect threat. Only very energetic measures on the part of the British could avert this danger [. . .]. It would be of extreme significance to us if we could secure for General Anders and his troops the defence of the Caucasus' (GSHI, PRM–K, 104). The Polish Premier continued his endeavours to this effect for some weeks, inducing the F.O. to send an instruction to Cripps (22.10.) to intervene with the Soviet Government and request the moving of Polish troops to the southern regions of the Soviet Union (GSHI, A.XII. 22/30 and doc. No. 138). At the same time, on instructions received from the Polish Government, Ciechanowski approached Roosevelt (31.10.) and Kot approached Molotov (1.11.). (Cf. doc. Nos. 136, 137.) In pursuance of the same line of policy—that is, with the aim of raising the Polish military effort to its maximum—Anders submitted to the C-in-C of the Soviet Armed Forces (20.10.), a plan for the expansion of his army, providing for the formation of two new divisions in Uzbekistan, apart from the three already being formed in the Volga area. In view of the shortage of equipment, this plan took into account the possibility of leaving the new units unarmed and using them for work connected with the war effort (GSHI, PRM, 41/2). The Soviet High Command left this proposal unanswered, and even took a step in the opposite direction, by reducing on 27.10. the number of rations for soldiers to 44,000, while Polish civilians had to be satisfied with very meagre assistance. (Report on the state of Army supplies of 1.11.1941, GSHI, A.XII. 22/30.)

The conversation between Kot and Molotov on 22.10. (PRM, 41/4) relevant to those subjects ran as follows:

'Kot: [. . .] We hold enormous potential supplies of serviceable men in Soviet Russia. They must be used properly. We submitted a plan, welcomed by the Soviet General Staff, for the formation of three new divisions [actually, two, and the preparation of one cadre division for full combat readiness]. You realize, Sir, that the war will be long and exhausting. The Poles are very eager to fight and will certainly set their heart on fighting the enemy. I am very anxious now to obtain from the Soviet Government a prompt decision on the choice of the places in which the camps of these three new divisions could be established.' Molotov referred then to the difficulties in obtaining supplies for these new units and put a question: 'What prospects are there that the Polish Government will receive equipment from America and England?' Kot: 'General Sikorski as a military man will be able to give you full information on that matter. It is clear that as regards arms we have no prospects, for the time being, of receiving tanks or armour and anti-armour weapons, but we shall certainly receive all other arms. The most important question, Sir, at this stage with reference to the formation of three new divisions, is the formation of a cadre.' Molotov: then asked again: 'Will they receive food from England or America?' Kot: 'No, Sir, pursuant to our military agreement, food supplies are to be provided by the Soviet authorities.' Molotov: 'The agreement mentions a definite number of divisions, and these have been formed already [cf. doc. Nos. 114, 140, 146, 154, 159]. We have lost the most fertile Ukrainian lands, the Germans are surrounding Moscow and thus the food position is extremely difficult. In this country the Poles must earn their living.' Kot: 'The agreement provided that two divisions and one brigade would be formed but the formation of further units was also taken into consideration. The uniforms for these three divisions will be sent from Britain, and General Sikorski intends to discuss the question of food supplies with the British.' [. . .] Molotov: 'Unfortunately, Sir, in the military field the British are unable to make a landing and thus form a second front which would be a relief to us in our struggle against Germany. As far as we are concerned, we are ourselves obliged to stop forming new units owing to shortage of arms. At the Three Powers' Conference in Moscow [28th Sept.–1st October, attended by Beaverbrook and Harriman] the question of food supplies was raised among other items, and we obtained assurances on the part of the Americans and British on this point. America and Canada must send us flour. As regards the soldiers of whom you propose to form new divisions, I see one solution only in providing them with food, and that is that they should be sent to factories, industrial establishments and the like. Returning to the question of the landing, we must face the fact that the British are unable to effect it, neither can they shift their forces to Soviet territory. This state of affairs does not favour either Soviet interests or those of Great Britain.' Kot: 'I ask you, Sir, not to take any premature decisions in the question of the forming of three new divisions. The Poles are excellent soldiers. The war will be long and hardened soldiers will certainly be much needed.'

The conversation ended with the postponement of a decision on the question of the increase of the strength of the Polish forces. There was, however, very little hope for any change in the unfavourable attitude of Russia. Polish authorities in London were debating at that time the consequences of the Soviet Government's obvious attempts to ignore the Agreement of 30.7. The belief was gaining ground in that quarter that the Soviet Union 'after obtaining a testimony of good conduct from Poland, and being cleared from any blame in dealing with her, did not see any political necessity for further concessions to Poland. We shall not obtain anything through direct contact with Russia, because we cannot repay her for any new services (or even for those promised, but so far unfulfilled) nor can we threaten her. Only England and America who supply her with arms and raw materials can bargain with Russia or ask for services.' These circumstances account for steps taken by the Polish Government with the effect that Cripps and Steinhardt obtained from their Governments binding instructions relating to Polish matters (cf. doc. Nos. 135,

136, 138). In view of Soviet statements on 'the possibility of creating in Russia of only small Polish armed forces', the Polish Ministry of Foreign Affairs drew the conclusion that 'the Soviet Government would prefer rather to agree to a partial evacuation of Polish soldiers from the USSR than to a strong Polish military organization there'. Looking at the military position one could not help observing the fact of the evacuation of Persia by Soviet troops of occupation and a dangerous gap arising therefrom which could not be filled by dispatching British troops in adequate strength. General Wavell also 'could only welcome' a chance of 'getting fresh supplies for his army in Persia—and perhaps in the Caucasus also, in the near future—should Polish troops be shifted there'. (Cf. A political survey of the actual position of the Polish army in Russia, 24.10.1941, GSHI, A.11.49/Sow/5.)

According to Polish opinion, the area of Iran made it possible for the Allied troops there to move along the Caspian Sea and the Black Sea towards Poland. Consequently, it became imperative that a suggestion should be made to the British to shift Anders' troops to Persia; this proposal seemed to be more acceptable to Russia than the Caucasus area which revived bitter memories of Allied intervention in Russia in the years 1918–22. (Remarks on the chances of a partial evacuation of Polish troops from Russia at the end of October 1941, GSHI, A.11.49/Sow/5.) It was in this connection that several times in the course of November 1941 Polish and British specialists examined possible routes of evacuation leading from southern areas of the USSR to Persia. (Cf. doc. Nos. 136, 141.)

Apart from these military plans Sikorski examined ways of ensuring the protection of, and assistance to, Polish deported persons in the USSR. At the beginning it seemed most suitable that a consular convention should be concluded. Two drafts were prepared by the Polish Ministry of Foreign Affairs—one, based on an old Polish-Soviet consular convention of 18.7.1924, the other a legal improvisation which took into account special war conditions. Apart from attempts to find a legal settlement to this question, the Polish Embassy in the USSR tried to bring about a plan for the resettlement and employment of deported persons and to obtain material assistance for them from abroad. However, already at the end of October and the beginning of November, the Soviet Government stated that travels of Polish nationals would not be permitted and the arrival of an American Mission of the Red Cross would be purposeless. At the same time it became clear that it would be impossible, within the framework of Soviet legislation and customs, to secure for Polish exiles the freedom of religious worship similar to that granted to the Polish troops in the USSR. (Cf. doc. Nos. 137, 139 and the Situation of the Polish civilian population in Russia, GSHI, A.11.49/Sow/5.)

No. 136. This personal letter with an enclosed memorandum was handed by Ciechanowski to the State Department on 31.10. The memorandum followed closely the Polish Government's instructions, as it had been the case of the memorandum sent by Raczyński to Eden on 29.10. (GSHI, A.11.49/Sow/6). However, in the letter submitted to the State Department the details concerning the limitation of the strength of Polish forces in Russia and a reference to the British intervention were omitted. In accordance with the request contained in the letter of 31.10., Roosevelt received Ciechanowski on 5.11. (at noon). The conversation dealt with the difficulties connected with the formation of the Polish army in the USSR. Roosevelt, who shared Sikorski's point of view, said that 'to use splendid fighting men as workmen in camps, rather than soldiers, would be contrary to Allied interests; it would be squandering very valuable fighting material'. In order to obviate these difficulties Roosevelt considered that 'it would be advisable and more effective (than a diplomatic intervention) if he [Harriman] addressed a personal telegram to Stalin on this subject'. In his further remarks the President said: 'If for any reason the Russian Government should find it difficult to undertake the feeding and equipment of that Polish army, then the Soviets should do all they can to facilitate the speedy transfer of these Polish troops from Russia to another country, where they would be more accessible to the United States and Britain, who could then ensure their equipment, training, and armament, and put them in the line of battle as soon as possible.' Moreover, the President reviewed the question of assistance to the Polish exiles in Russia, stating that substantial help should come from America (using relief credits voted by Congress). Although anticipating some trouble in granting 'a privileged treatment to one nationality, he took the view that the Polish population should be saved by all possible means'. He charged Sumner Welles with the task to find the ways by which this decision of his could be realized.

On 6.10., the Under-Secretary held a conference with experts in the course of which—as it appears from Ciechanowski's telegram—the following plan of action was adopted: '1) Soviet consent should be obtained for the evacuation of the Polish army to Iran, on account of advantages for Russia who would be thus dispensed from providing food, equipment and armament, and at the same time relieved from the military point of view by a quicker engagement of our troops on the battle front. This point will be settled by Harriman's telegram to Stalin; 2) Supplies, equipment and armament for our army should be prepared for the case of its being shifted to Iran. The strength of these troops was assessed at 150,000 men. Director S[tettinius] and General B[urns] will immediately approach the British Military Mission and Purchasing Commission in order to obtain priority of the Polish Army as regards supplies sent to Iran. General B. has a list of the needs of the Polish army in Russia given by the Premier [Sikorski] to Mr. Harriman and if need arises for the completion of this list he will approach me.' Some members of the Conference expressed doubts whether 'the Soviet Government having already armed two Polish divisions . . . would agree to their going to Iran' but the opinion prevailed that a positive result could be achieved 'by looking at the question broad-mindedly, as at a matter of principle in which general interest is involved and whose positive solution presents some advantage for the Soviets relieving them of the duty of taking charge of the Polish troops in Russia'.

(Cf.: Ciechanowski's report on the conference of 6.11. and his telegram to the M.F.A. London, sent on 6.11. and received 7.11.1941, GSHI, A.11.49/Sow/5.)

No. 137. Sikorski's demands presented on 28.10., postulated under Point 3 'the concentration of the whole Polish army, until it achieved combat readiness, in a place suitable for an easy delivery of English supplies'. He stated expressly that he had in mind 'Iran, in the first place, or eventually the Caucasus area' (doc. No. 134). Kot's Note of 1.11. to the People's Commissariat for Foreign Affairs did not mention, however, any specified country to which that army should be transferred, from which one could assume that movements within the Soviet territory only were envisaged. Neither was this subject raised in the course of the conversation between Kot and Vyshinsky which took place on the occasion of the delivery by Kot of the said Note of 1.11. Kot reported on that conversation in a telegram sent to the M.F.A. on 1.11. (translated by that Office):

'M. Vyshinsky declared: 1/that with the exception of some small groups, the Soviet Government are stopping the transfer of Polish deportees from north to south;

2/that in view of the above the loan requested by the Polish Government is refused;

3/referring to the talks between General Sikorski and Ambassador Bogomolov [25.10.1941], he denied the truth of the information that the Soviet Government were detaining Poles for work, instead of allowing them to join the Polish army.

In reply I [Kot] stated: 1/that the decision to stop the transfer from north to south cannot be used as a pretext to detain Poles who are enlisting in the Army or those who cannot stand the climatic conditions prevailing in the north [. . .].

2/that the Polish Government did not ask for a loan for the purpose of covering the expenses of transfer of the deportees, but for the maintenance of women unfit for work and of children.'

So far as the transfer of Polish units to the south was concerned, Ambassador Kot was under the impression that 'Vyshinsky did not know anything about our [Polish] plans for the expansion of Polish forces, he took the view that it was a new problem and he immediately and strongly stressed the difficulties of the transport of arms and food from abroad'.

The Soviet Government in its Note of 8.11. (doc. No. 142) also considered the possibility of regrouping the Polish Forces inside Soviet territory only, stating that 'the places of stationment of Polish military units depend on a mutual agreement between Polish and

Soviet military authorities and if need for changes arises the Soviet Government is ready to take this under consideration'.

What Kot had actually had in mind appears clearly from his letter to Ciechanowski, in which, enclosing his Note of 1.11., he gave the following interpretation of Point 3 of Sikorski's demands (Kot, *Listy*, pp. 457–459): 'The demand for the transfer of units to the south is a natural consequence of the state of things in the USSR in respect of food, supplies and communications—arising from the war. It was never our aim to evacuate Polish troops from Russia or to form them in areas distant from our home-country, but facts beyond our control came into operation.' Further consequences of Kot's interpretation of Sikorski's intentions are to be seen in the Note to doc. No. 148.

No. 138. The Polish Note of 1.11. was agreed upon with Cripps, who received an instruction from the F.O. to support it with Molotov. However, as regards the request raised in it referring to the evacuation of Polish Forces from the USSR, Sir Stafford decided to intervene only after having received his Government's promise concerning the provision of food for Polish troops abroad. This support was granted on 4.11., when Kot informed the M.F.A. in a telegram: 'Cripps delivered an aide-mémoire supporting our [Polish] requests and firmly unmasking Vyshinsky's tortuous arguments in a long conversation yesterday evening, during which he stressed the importance of General Sikorski's visit' (telegram from Kot to the M.F.A. in London of 1, 2, 3, and 4.10.1941, GSHI, A.11.49/Sow/6). However, until mid-November there appeared instead gradual limitations of the rights of Polish deportees and army by the Soviet Government. (Cf.: doc. Nos. 139, 143, 144, 145, 146.)

No. 142. After receiving the Soviet Note at noon on 11.11., Kot sent the summary of it to the Polish M.F.A. in London by telegram and at the same time sent another summary in English through Macfarlane to the Director of Intelligence in Cairo asking him to hand it to Sikorski. Kot's comments in the latter read:

[. . .] 'Molotov's statement is an endeavour to give the Protocol of 19th August the status of a final agreement, whereas actually it only represented initial technical arrangements between the Russian and Polish Military Authorities. In effect it would practically mean the end of any further recruiting for the Polish Army' (GSHI, A.11.49/Sow/2).

No. 147. Bogomolov handed this Note personally to Raczyński. The latter stated after reading it, that 'it dealt with only one of the points raised in the correspondence between Ambassador Kot and Commissar Molotov. As we [The Polish Government] have incomplete information so far on Molotov's reply to Ambassador Kot's Note, we cannot at the moment take a definite stand'. In conclusion Raczyński assured Bogomolov 'of the wish on the part of Poland to develop co-operation with the Soviet Government' (GSHI, PRM, 41/4).

No. 148. The reasons why the Polish Government asked the State Department for an intervention are stated in the Note of 31.10.1941 (doc. No. 136). In accordance with his promise, on 7.11. Harriman sent, through the U.S. Ambassador, a telegram to Stalin (it was not actually delivered until 14.11.) in which he said: 'The problem of the most efficient method of employing unarmed Polish troops on Russian soil is one that has had deep attention and after consultation with the President and at his suggestion I am telegraphing you direct certain phrases for your consideration [. . .]. The area in which these troops are located borders those vital regions the defence of which is of common interest to all opponents of the Nazi regime. Our suggestion is that these Polish forces, not only with the agreement of but likewise with the assistance of the USSR Government, be assembled and withdrawn to a designated area in Iran. There, with American and British aid, these Polish nationals might be most quickly reconditioned, uniformed and armed to the end that with the greatest possible expedition they become a part of the fighting forces, in the expectation they be returned to the Soviet Russia front [. . .]. An expression of your general views in this regard will be deeply appreciated' (U.S.A., Dipl., 1941, p. 258). Stalin's telegram of 14.11. (doc. No. 148) promised an examination of these proposals, and the way in which they were settled, is described in the subsequent telegram of 27.11. (doc. No. 156).

No. 149. According to Kot (Kot, Rozmowy, p. 127–9), at that moment Stalin whispered as if speaking to himself: 'They say that all of them were released'. Further passages of this conversation ran as follows:

'Stalin: Wasilewska took it upon herself to find Polish officers willing to serve with these units.

Kot: And what has she achieved?

Stalin: There were enough officers willing to serve.

Kot: Why, then, has this army not been formed?

Stalin: There was not one single general ready to take over the command.

Kot: You see, Mr. Chairman, those Polish generals are men of moral standing and of strong character. They refused because they had vowed fidelity to the Polish State and President. And you can take it for granted that now, when the situation has changed and the Polish-Soviet treaty has been signed, Polish generals will not fail to come up to expectation and that, on their Commander-in-Chief, General Sikorski's, order, they will fight side by side with you against Hitler.'

No. 156. A complementary document to this telegram is Harriman's report to Roosevelt and Hull of 29.11. It repeats at the beginning the information contained in Stalin's telegram of 27.11. (doc. No. 156) and continues by analysing the reasons why Kot in his conversation with Stalin on 14.11. (doc. No. 149) failed to raise the question of the withdrawal of Polish Forces from Soviet territory. Harriman said that he approached Raczyński on this subject, who 'advised him that: a) it was either lack of information or inadvertance that led M. Kot to refrain from mentioning the above subject; b) General Sikorski intends to press the subject at his meeting with Stalin; c) the Poles expect to leave, within Russia, the divisions for which the Russians have supplied arms, and they wish to send out for equipping only the unarmed recruits; d) from the discussions between Generals Sikorski and Wavell, it seems clear that India is better than Iran for training and equipping the Polish troops particularly on account of better facilities for the transportation of supplies'.

Harriman 'proposed, subject to the President's and Mr. Hull's approval, to reply to Stalin [. . .] that the suggestion of withdrawing Polish recruits outside Russia is in accordance with the wishes of the Polish Government, as well as of the Government of the United States, and that he is quite sure that the Polish Government has not changed its attitude on this point' (U.S.A. Dipl., 1941, p. 265). The question was eventually discussed between Sikorski and Stalin on 3.12.1941 (doc. No. 159).

No. 161. This declaration was reproduced in full by *Izvestia* and *Pravda* on 5.12.1941. On the following day *Izvestia* commented upon the declaration, emphasizing the importance of the bilateral agreement for the future development of Polish-Soviet relations, which, in its view, was an augury of broader developments in the international field. The English press limited itself to stressing the magnitude of the war effort of the Polish soldiers and civilian population. *The Times* of 9.12. spoke of 'the amazing power of recovery shown by the Polish troops and anticipated 'a very useful contribution to the Soviet war effort by the Polish civilian population'. The *Daily Telegraph* of 9.12. anticipated the formation in the USSR of as many as nine divisions, adding that it would be rather difficult to equip those units. Only the *Manchester Guardian* of 6.12. gave conservative estimates of the Polish potentialities for organizing such an army. On the other hand, the Free French press drew attention to the value of the Polish-Soviet understanding rather from a general point of view. *La France* and *Le Jour* of 6.12. and *La Syrie* saw it as 'laying the foundation stone for a future construction of Central-Eastern Europe' ('les linéaments d'une construction de l'Europe Centrale et Orientale') or, in general, for European stability ('l'équilibre européen').

The results achieved by Sikorski in Moscow were communicated to Polish and British authorities in London, and then passed on to Polish diplomatic posts. On 6.12. Raczyński handed to Eden a personal survey of the situation made by Sikorski. This note emphasized the importance of the agreement from the point of view of international politics: '[. . .] The Polish-Soviet Declaration signed by General Sikorski was largely instrumental in smoothing the conduct of the negotiations and in improving the position of Poland in the USSR. The Declaration was supplemented by the speeches of General Sikorski and Stalin, who emphasized the need for a powerful Polish State. The Declaration, which is based on the principle of parity of the two States, stresses the importance of their collaboration for a durable peace [. . .] General Sikorski concluded by strongly emphasizing that a hundred per cent. Allied solidarity and in particular co-operation and firm support of Poland's interests on the part of Great Britain and the USA were absolutely imperative for the successful achievement of our common aims' (cf.: Sikorski's telegrams to Raczkiewicz, Raczyński and Kukiel of 4.12.; collection of telegrams made by the Polish M.F.A. for Eden of 8.12., GSHI, A.11.49/Sow/5).

The American Embassy in Moscow took great interest in the results of Sikorski's visit from the point of view of the operations in the Middle East and those carried out from the United Kingdom, as appears from the dispatches sent by the Chargé d'Affaires in the Soviet Union to the Secretary of State; the first of these dispatches stated the following: 'I have been informed by members of the British Embassy that the Agreement entered into by Sikorski during his recent visit to Moscow is unsatisfactory to the British Government inasmuch as, if put into operation, it would place too great a burden upon the transport and other services involved in equipping and maintaining the Polish Forces on Soviet territory, while at the same time depriving the British of the use of some fifteen or more thousand of Polish troops in the Near Eastern field. I judge that Sikorski did as he apparently had been requested to do in London, that is to endeavour to obtain Stalin's consent to the transfer of Poles of military age to India and other places in the Near East for equipment and training but that he quickly gave way before Stalin's insistence that the Poles should remain within Soviet jurisdiction.' But the following telegram of 11.12. rectified that information, stating that 'Stalin did agree to the departure from the Soviet Union of 25,000 Polish troops, and he stated that 9,000 of these men will be dispatched to Cairo to reinforce the British troops engaged in the North African campaign and that the remaining 16,000 men will be dispatched to Scotland, where they will join the Polish troops now assembled in the British Isles' (U.S.A., Dipl., 1941, pp. 267–8).

No. 164. This 'Instruction' for the Polish Army in the USSR was followed by orders relating to co-operation in the field of military intelligence and liaison with the home-country, replacing the previous disparate arrangements by uniform rules. The question of linking up Polish Underground activities with the Soviet military operations held the attention of Polish and Soviet authorities after the conclusion of mutual agreements of the summer of 1941. As far back as September, in a conversation with Anders and Retinger, Zhukov drew attention to the need for exchange of information obtained by respective intelligence services and also for an agreement on the co-ordination of sabotage activities on the territory held by the Germans. In the meantime, the Soviet command smuggled many agents and parachutists into Polish territory, who were to penetrate into Underground organizations and carry out the destruction of war industry on a big scale. Moreover,

Polish assistance was requested for Soviet diversions carried out in Poland, Rumania and the Ukraine (Note on a conversation between Anders, Retinger and Zhukov on 4.9.1941–GSHI, KGA, 7; Kot, *Listy*, pp. 82, 88–90, 93–4, 98–9).

Anders gave Sikorski an account of those facts and acquainted him with Soviet intentions in his report of 7.9., but he stressed that he was opposed to the Soviet authorities assuming control in this field as well as to any premature outbreaks in Poland. The C-in-C then, on 12.9.1941, forbade the dispatch of parachutists through Soviet channels. On 9.10. Anders reported that, after a month's co-operation between the two intelligence services, he had ordered the demands for Soviet assistance to be limited to technical help in dispatching military instructors to Poland and in supplying the Underground organizations with money and means of transmission (Report of the Headquarters of the Polish Army in the USSR of 7.9.1941; Anders' letter to Sikorski of 9.10.1941, both documents at GSHI, KGA, 7g; Sikorski's telegram to Anders of 12.9.1941, a wrong date, GSHI, KGA, 9e). In October and November the Polish-Soviet co-operation in the field of intelligence was carried out within the aforesaid limits. On 14.12., during Sikorski's visit to Russia, an agreement was reached between him and Zhukov on this matter. It was decided that the Soviet authorities should stop sabotage work on the territory of Poland and the Poles promised to organize diversions in Byelorussia; a full exchange of military information available in London and Moscow was agreed upon; moreover, the agreement provided for Soviet technical assistance for Polish radio-communication, in exchange for Polish help in smuggling Soviet instructors into the territories adjoining Poland and held by the Germans. However, on 27.12. Zhukov objected to the inclusion in the Proceedings of the conversation, held on 14.12. of the reference to all Polish territories within 1939 borders as the area falling within the province of Polish intelligence services. Immediately, the whole problem of co-operation became questionable and mutual obligations were shelved. Although upholding the line of his instruction of 20.1.1942 Sikorski took care that information of military nature concerning Germany should continue to be transmitted to Moscow through Polish headquarters there, he received no Soviet assistance in return except some technical help in the field of radio-communications. (Summary of the conversation between Sikorski and Zhukov on 14.12.1941; Zhukov's remarks on that summary, 27.12.1941; A telegram from Anders to Sikorski on the amendments to the summary, 12.1.1941; Sikorski's telegram to Anders, 20.1.1942, outlining the principles of co-operation. All these documents are in GSHI, KGA, 7c, b, f, g.)

No. 165. Cf.: Sikorski's telegram to Eden, Teheran, 17.12.1941: 'As appears from an information received by me, the conclusion of a pact between Great Britain, U.S.A. and USSR seems imminent and should it be the case, the Polish Government considers that it would be necessary and important that Poland become the fourth signatory of and party to that pact.'

The reports of the U.S.A. Embassies in Moscow and London, based on British information, give a summary account of Anglo-Soviet negotiations in Moscow (U.S.A., Dipl., 1941, I, pp. 192–205). The aims pursued by Eden in his negotiations with the Soviet representatives appear in the British memorandum which he took to Moscow: 'His Majesty's Government recognize the need in any eventual (territorial) settlement to strengthen the smaller countries of Europe so as to put them both economically and strategically, in a position to resist successfully pressure by Germany. For this purpose they welcome the negotiations between the Czechoslovak and Polish Governments for a confederation. They would hope that this federal system might be extended so as to include other States of Central Europe' (U.S.A., Dipl., 1941, I, p. 203).

The American point of view was expressed in the note of the State Department of 5.12. which stressed that 'in so far as our post-war policies are concerned, it is our belief that these have been delineated in the Atlantic Charter' and 'in order not to jeopardize these aims we shall all share in common looking to an enduring peace, it is evident that no commitments as to individual countries should be entered into at this time'. (Cf.: U.S.A.,

Dipl., 1941, I, pp. 192–195; Churchill S.W.W., III, pp. 469–472; Langer-Gleason, *U.W.*, pp. 824–825.)

In his conversation with Eden, on 18.12., Stalin 'suggested the signature of a secret protocol embodying the joint views of the British Government and the Soviet Government for a settlement of post-war frontiers and outlined in detail his conception of such a settlement for Europe as a whole which was drastic and severe upon Germany. Eden told him that for many reasons it was impossible for him to enter into secret agreement; he was pledged to the United States Government not to do so [. . .] Stalin agreed to this and also to the proposals being communicated to the United States Government' (U.S.A., Dipl., p. 199). On 19.12. Eden told the American Chargé d'Affaires in Moscow that he was afraid that 'Soviet insistence that a commitment be entered into at time recognizing the Soviet frontiers of 1941 may make it impossible for him to reach an understanding with respect to post-war reconstruction'. In this connection he stated that 'the Soviet demands not only embrace the Baltic States and Bessarabia but also seem to imply some expansion to the West, presumably by advancing the Lithuanian borders into East Prussia. It also appears to be desired by the Soviets that in addition to the reestablishment of the Finnish frontier certain additional naval and air bases in Finland must be obtained . . . Eden said, that the Soviet Government would be quite prepared to acquiesce in and support any plans the British Government might have with respect to post-war arrangements such as, for example, the establishment of British bases in Holland or elsewhere on the Atlantic Coast of Europe but that for its part it expects full recognition of its own frontiers and security problems' (U.S.A., Dipl., p. 200).

On 20.12. 'Sir Alexander Cadogan informed me [U.S. Chargé d'Affaires] this evening that it became apparent at the most recent meetings between Eden and Stalin that it would be impossible to reconcile the British and Soviet drafts of the proposed pacts on the joint war effort and post-war problems, in view of the Soviet attitude with respect to the recognition of the 1941 frontiers. It was accordingly agreed that the project to conclude pacts on these two points should be abandoned and that a joint communiqué on the Moscow conversations should be issued instead. This communiqué is to be released on Monday, December 29' (U.S.A., Dipl., p. 204). The communiqué spoke, in fact, only in general terms of a joint struggle against Hitler.

No. 166. One of the main objects, kept in view by the Polish Government in signing the agreement of 30.7.1941 was to ensure the maintenance of relief (clothing, food, medicines) for Polish deportees in the USSR. This work was initiated by the Polish troops as early as September 1941, and was carried out through Polish military centres all over the Soviet territory. It consisted of supplies in kind for the Polish citizens assembling in ever bigger numbers around the areas in which Polish troops were quartered. The building up and the organization of a network of welfare posts became possible only after Sikorski's visit to Moscow, when an agreement was reached (23.12.1941) between Poland and the USSR on the rules defining the powers of the Polish Embassy's local delegates. The welfare network controlled by the Embassy extended to 35 administrative regions (oblasti), in which there were 2,600 Polish settlements.

The regulations defining the powers of the delegates and representatives of the Embassy in relation to the protection and relief work were accepted by the Soviet Government only five months after the signature of the Agreement of 30.7. and the actual organization took shape two months later. This delay was due to the unco-operative attitude of the Soviet Government who rejected several proposals of the Embassy for the opening of Polish consulates or for charging a Committee specially designated for this purpose and composed of members elected by Polish citizens or for the Polish Red Cross taking over that task. In these circumstances, on 19.11.1941 the Embassy submitted a proposal for entrusting Embassy delegates with the care of Polish citizens. The Soviet Government produced a counter-proposal on 3.12. Sikorski's visit eventually rendered possible the settlement of this problem and on 23.12. the regulations concerning the protection of and the care of Polish deportees were approved.

(Cf. Liquidation of the offices of the Delegates of the Polish Embassy in the USSR Official publication (in Polish), Teheran, October 1942; Arlet's report on the liquidation of the offices of Embassy Delegates, 11.8.1942, GSHI, A.11.49/Sow/6; Kot, *Listy*, pp. 28, 87, 95, 104, 106–9, 112–13, 120, 160, 187, 188, 190, 231, 492–3; Kot, *Rozmowy*, pp. 44–5, 47–8, 69–70, 135–7, 140.)

No. 170. The including in a list of Soviet cities of Lwów, Brest and other places situated to the east of the Ribbentrop-Molotov Line as belonging respectively to the Ukrainian and the Byelorussian Soviet Republics, was considered by the Polish Government as contrary to the Atlantic Charter and the Polish-Soviet Agreement of 30.7.1941. The Polish interpretation of the latter was that the disclaiming of territorial conquests and the cancellation of the Russo-German agreements of 1939–40 involved the abandonment of Soviet conquests of the same period, including the annexation of the Eastern Provinces of Poland operated by force and through so-called 'popular consultation' carried out on 22.10.1939. (Cf. notes to documents Nos. 67 and 109 and the memorandum of a conversation between Ciechanowski and Loy Henderson on 29.12.1941–U.S.A., Dipl., 1941, pp. 270–1.)

On the other hand, the Soviet Government, when signing the Atlantic Charter on 24.9.1941, had already stated that 'they subscribed only to the "basic propositions" of the Charter'. D. J. Dallin draws attention to the differences between the Atlantic Charter and the Soviet declaration of 24.9.1941 (*Russia and Post War Europe*, Yale Un. Press, 1943, pp. 136–7): 'Article 1, which states that all contracting "countries seek no aggrandizement, territorial or other", does not and cannot exist in the Soviet program' as 'the Soviet Union . . . is a union of republics which expand gradually through inclusion of new territories.' Article 2 of the Atlantic Charter says: 'They (i.e. signatories) desire no territorial changes that do not accord with the freely expressed wishes of the people concerned.' The Soviet Government subscribes neither to 'the wishes of the majority of the people' nor to the requirement of 'freely expressed will' as this 'presumes a political rivalry of different programs for the support of the people [. . .]. In all cases which have so far occurred in Soviet practice the voters were offered only one program and the voting took place only after military occupation. In general, the Soviet Government is prone to subordinate the territorial to other and, in its opinion, higher aims.'

No. 176. On the same day, 26.1., Raczyński spoke to Eden who stated that 'Soviet pressure on the British Government for the recognition by the latter of Soviet territorial claims to Baltic States, Rumania, Persia, etc.' persisted. 'The British Cabinet has not yet considered this question but it seems that it will be forced to do so very shortly.' In his reply Raczyński observed that 'the Soviet Government seems to try to prejudge the fate of Vilno, considering it as belonging to Lithuania'. In connection with that Raczyński asked the British Government 'not to take any decision without a previous consultation with the Polish Government', in order to maintain a united front in dealings with the Kremlin. He thought it also necessary that 'Great Britain should refuse to enter into any commitments towards the Soviet Union relating to the territorial claims of the latter in Central-Eastern Europe' (a note on the conversation between Raczyński and Eden on 26.1.1942, GSHI, PRM, 68).

No. 180. This telegram, drafted on 4.2., was wired on the following day and decoded on 6.2. On 8.2. Anders wrote a letter to Kot in which, taking his bearings from a conversation with Zhukov, he reviewed the difficulties in the field of material and personnel made by the Soviet authorities in the formation of the Polish Army in Russia (GSHI, KGA, 7g).

No. 183. The opinion expressed by the former Ambassador Cripps was by no means isolated. Some British circles, after Eden's visit to Moscow, intensified their propaganda in favour of granting satisfaction to Soviet claims at the cost of the countries of Central-Eastern Europe. It was *The Times* that took the lead. In its editorial of 12.2.1942 the London paper stated: 'The recent events have shown that the imperative necessities of Russian defence provided a more solid foundation for some past claims than most people in this country were prepared to concede to them at the time' (i.e. in August 1939). On 7.3. *The Times* explained 'that the Soviet intentions nowhere go beyond territories embodied in the Soviet Union, when Hitler marched against it'.

This point of view was contested by *New York Times* whose correspondent, in his article of 14.3., emphasized the reinforcement in Kremlin's pressure in the matter of the recognition by the Western countries of Soviet annexations made in the course of 1939–40 on the territory of the Baltic States and Poland.

The correspondent saw a fresh proof of this attitude in the fact that the Soviet Government decided that the Polish citizens who had stayed on the territories annexed by the Soviet Union in 1939 should be considered Soviet citizens. (Cf. doc. Nos. 157, 170, 172, 175, 178, 181, 186.) Such a capture of living beings clashed, in his opinion, with the results of the conversations between Sikorski and Stalin, which seemed to point to the postponement of the discussion on territorial problems until the end of military operations.

No. 185. Panfilov's consent, given on 19. and 24.2. to Sikorski's requests concerning the evacuation of 27,000 soldiers to the United Kingdom, setting up an evacuation base at Krasnovodsk and the delivery of Soviet arms for a new division, was far from giving immediate results. At the beginning of March further conferences took place between Panfilov, Wolikowski and Macfarlane, in the course of which were discussed the arrangements to be taken for the organization of evacuation in the frontier zone and the delivery of British equipment and arms for the Polish Army in the USSR. So far as the last item was concerned a complication arose in connection with the statement of the British representative from which it appeared that 'the arms which were earmarked for us [Poles] were sent to the Far East and at present the delivery of arms depends on the Inter-Allied Commission in London. They will probably arrive end-April–beginning May, but the instalments will consist of single categories of arms and not of complete arms for the units.' This information gave a shock to Panfilov; he stated however that it would not bring about any change in the delivery of Soviet arms and equipment for the Polish Army. Wolikowski took nevertheless the view, on 10.3., that even if one took into account the great food shortage in the USSR 'the reduction of food rations for Polish troops [to 26,000] was either a pressure aiming at the speeding up of the delivery of arms by England or a kind of political pressure' (Telegrams from the Military Attaché to the Polish Embassy in the USSR to the Chief of the General Staff in London, of 24. and 27.2 and 10. and 12.3. 1942; Report of the Attaché, 25.3. on the conversation with Panfilov and Macfarlane on 4. and 8.3.1942. All these papers are in GSHI, A.XII.22/31.9). The deadlock was eventually overcome during the conversation between Stalin and Anders on 18.3.1942. (Cf. doc. No. 193.)

No. 186. The Soviet point of view on the question of the Polish eastern provinces annexed by the Soviet Union in the course of this war was explained in a conversation which took place on 31.3.1942 between Jankowski and Counsellor Chichayev. 'M. Chichayev in a long statement tried to prove that the Polish-Soviet Agreement had cancelled only the Soviet-German Agreement of September 1939, but had not determined the Polish frontiers in the East. Those frontiers must be determined after the war in the sense of Stalin's declaration. Until then the Soviet Government is bound by the Soviet Constitution only, on the strength of which a part of the Polish territories were incorporated with the USSR. This Constitution can be changed by the Supreme Soviet only, and the signing by the Soviet Government of the Polish-Soviet Agreement could not infringe upon the decisions of the

Supreme Soviet; because of that, so long as the Supreme Soviet has not taken a new decision, all the territories annexed by the USSR are Soviet, beyond any dispute.

Molotov's Note could not omit Lwów, because such a move would place in error and lay astray the public opinion of the USSR, which the Soviet Government did not wish to do.

I wish to add to the foregoing that M. Chichayev referred only to the text of the Constitution and the decision of the Supreme Soviet which is a Soviet organ, without mentioning at all the "plebiscite" as the expression of the will of the local population' (GSHI A.11.49/ Sow/4).

No. 189. Sikorski's letter to Eden of 9.3. was preceded by a conversation between them on 3.3. It appeared from Eden's information that the Soviet representatives in the course of their negotiations with the British had raised the question of the annexation of the Baltic States, Bukovina and Bessarabia only on strategical grounds. The Eastern Provinces of Poland 'were not to be included in the [British-Soviet] Treaty because this was a Polish-Russian question' the settlement of which should be achieved by bilateral negotiations along the lines summed up in Stalin's slogan on 'a strong and powerful Poland', dividing the Soviet Union from Germany. This increase in Poland's position should find its expression above all in the annexation by her of East Prussia. In reply Sikorski once more made a reservation (see note to doc. No. 176) saying that giving a free hand to the Soviet Union in Lithuania would mean the absorption of the Wilno area by Russia, to which no Polish Government will ever agree. In view of the considerable military preponderance of the Soviet Union over the Western countries, Sikorski 'advised Mr. Eden in a most serious way to procrastinate in the negotiations with Russia and not to conclude any treaty with her for the time being'. Eden was aware of the difficulty of reaching a real agreement with the Soviet Union and he rather inclined at that time to an understanding between the three Great Powers, United Kingdom, U.S.A. and the USSR creating 'bonds of a more general and less specified nature'. (GSHI, PRM, 68.)

No. 198. From the beginning of February 1942 the British insistently demanded that the evacuation of part of the Polish troops from the Soviet Union (about 27,000 men pursuant to the agreement of 3.12.1941) be speeded up. These demands were due to the deterioration of the position of British troops in North Africa after Rommel's offensive (24.1.–6.2.), At that time a British-Soviet Commission, without any Polish participation and without any knowledge of the Polish authorities, evolved at Teheran a scheme for the evacuation of part of the Polish troops, who were to be used on the British front. Sikorski protested against such proceedings, and in view of his protest the work of the said commission had to be suspended. (Cf. telegram from the Polish Embassy in Kuibyshev to Sikorski of 9.2. and the reply of the latter of 10.2. in the matter of the British-Soviet conference at Teheran, GSHI, PRM, 73/1.)

Anders' agreement with Stalin of 18.3. (cf. doc. No. 193) speeded up the evacuation to the Middle East of the surplus quota of Polish troops, which had exceeded the strength of 44,000 (the date for their leaving Soviet territory was fixed for 1.4.); it did not, however, change the proportion of the numbers to be sent to the Middle East and to the U.K. (this proportion being 15,000 to 17,000 respectively). However, from 26.3. the War Office tried to reduce the number of troops to be sent to the United Kingdom, because of the shortage of sea transport (without alluding to the position on the front). (Cf. Regulski's Pro-Memorias for the Chief of the General Staff, 19, 24, and 26.3.1942; letter from the War Office to Regulski of 20.3.1942, GSHI, A.XII. 22/31–5.)

The proposal that 10,000 next-of-kin of the soldiers (the initial figure was 15,000)— as agreed upon between Anders and Kerr—should leave Russia with the evacuated troops, was at first opposed by the War Office, which, however, eventually gave its full support to that move. (Cf. Kot's telegrams to Mikołajczyk of 27.3. and to the Deputy President of the Council of Ministers of 30.3.1942, GSHI, A.XII. 22/31.8; letter from the Polish Embassy in London of 31.3.1942, A.XII. 22/31–5.)

During Sikorski's visit to the United States an increase of the prospective participation of Polish troops in the operations in the Middle East was decided upon (doc. No. 200). Sikorski's telegram to Stalin of 9.4. (cf. doc. No. 201) initiated the execution of the whole plan. However, at the beginning of April, the Soviet Government—contrary to its promises of 18.3.—stated that 'further recruitment had to be discontinued in view of the fact that the proposed quota had been reached', and began to direct Polish conscripts to labour battalions (stroy-battalions). The Polish authorities were not advised of that decision, and the liaison officer of the Soviet High Command, Yevstigneyev, referred to it only casually in a conversation with Wolikowski. Wolikowski strongly protested against such a violation of the agreement, pointing to the importance of the defence of the Middle East from the common Allied point of view and also to the plans for the co-ordination of the operations there with those on the Russian southern front. The number of Polish citizens debarred in this way from joining the Polish forces amounted—according to the estimates of the Military Attaché—to 120,000. (Cf. Wolikowski's telegrams to the Chief of General Staff, dated 13 and 15.4.1942, GSHI, A.XII. 22/31.9.)

No. 202. Raczyński had a conversation with Eden when delivering the note on 13.4.1942. Eden stressed that 'during the Moscow visit he resisted the Soviet request for an immediate conclusion of the treaty', but later 'in spite of General Sikorski's arguments, the British Cabinet stated the necessity for negotiations'. Eden 'recognized direct Polish interest in Lithuania' and 'the serious threat to the plans for the federation of the whole area between the Baltic and Adriatic Seas', should Bukovina be annexed by Russia. He hoped to secure Polish interests, for the time being, 'by repeating in the treaty with Russia the declaration of the British Government of 30.7.1941 on non-recognition of the facts accomplished during the war' (cf. doc. No. 107). Raczyński observed that 'since Hitler's speech of March Russia was unable to withdraw from the war with Germany' for some considerable time (GSHI, PRM, 68).

No. 207. O. Halecki's book *Eugenio Pacelli, Pope of Peace*, New York, 1951 defines the attitude of the Holy See towards the two totalitarian beligerents as follows: 'The Pope was most anxious that the Nazis be defeated in the shortest possible time, so that the free forces of the world would retain enough strength to confront the inevitable challenge of Communism.'

The U.S.A. Government's position on that matter was quite different. Two weeks after the outbreak of the Soviet-German war the State Department transmitted the following suggestion to Pope Pius XII and Cardinal Maglione: 'that the Holy See abstain from anything which might be interpreted as favourable to the Axis in the war against Russia'. A personal representative of the President, Myron Taylor, 'was received by Pius XII on September 9 [1941] and delivered a presidential letter dated September 3, which was to bring about the first major differences of opinion between Washington and the Vatican. The letter began by stating the President's belief that a major shift in the Soviet policy towards religion was impending: "Insofar as I am informed—he wrote—the churches in Russia are open. I believe there is a real possibility that Russia may as a result of the present conflict recognize freedom of religion in Russia, although, of course, without recognition of any official intervention on the part of any church in education or political matters within Russia." ' (Cf. note to doc. No. 124.) '[. . .] The Vatican could not take this statement [a distinction between the Nazi and Communist dictatorship in favour of the latter] seriously in the light of the Russian invasion of eastern Poland and Finland, the seizure of Bessarabia and Bukovina, and the ruthless absorption into the Soviet Union of Latvia, Estonia and Lithuania, which had not been recognized by the U.S. State Department [. . .]. Although the Pope knew that Russia and her supporters excused these acts and the following annexations as having been committed before the Atlantic Charter, no guarantees whatsoever could be found that this policy would not be repeated in the event of a total victory over Hitler and his satellites.' For all these reasons Pius XII 'contented himself with reminding Taylor that the Holy See could not feel justified in sharing the President's optimism regarding "the more favourable official Soviet attitude towards religious worship", nor change its views to the extent of relaxing its vigilance against Communist propaganda.' After Italy's declaration of war upon the United States, '[. . .] Mr. Taylor placed before Pius the President's plan for prosecution of the war, which called for the defeat first of the Germans then of the Japanese, and voiced the White House belief that the Russians would never surrender, no matter how hard pressed'. As to America's attitude to Italy 'the White House let it be known that it was even now not too late for the Italians to turn out the leaders who had plunged them into war and secure for themselves a peace' (o.c., pp. 166–70). In the allocution of Christmas Eve, 24.12.1941, Pius XII dealt with the problem of peace in its external aspect, i.e. between the nations. He stressed then inter alia: 'Within the framework of a new order based upon moral principles, there is no room for the violation of the freedom, integrity, and security of other Nations, whatever be their territorial extent or their capacity for defence; [. . .] there is no room for the suppression, be it open or covert, of the cultural and linguistic traditions of national minorities' (Reginald F. Walker, *Pius of Peace*, Dublin, 1945, p. 137).

No. 213. That resolution of the Council of Ministers was connected with the decisions which Sikorski brought to the notice of senior commanders at the meetings with them in London on 23. and 27.4., confirming them later in his instruction regarding the use of Polish Armed Forces, which was sent to Anders on 1.5. (Cf. doc. No. 215.) This political and military plan consisted of 'apportioning the forces in more or less equal strength between Great Britain, Russia and the Middle East'. The reasons for it were stated by the C-in-C in the following terms: 'I have neither the right nor the intention to risk the concentration of the whole or a major part of the Polish Armed Forces on the one theatre of war, where a possible misfortune could bring about their excessive, if not complete destruction.'

This allocation of the armed forces was connected with the anticipated move towards the Middle East of the troops staying in the USSR and the necessity for reducing the sea-transports to the United Kingdom to 8,000 men. We find an explanation of this position in Sikorski's letter to Churchill, dated 24.4.: 'After having given prolonged and deep consideration to the problem of the Middle East and the future of the Polish Forces in all the theatres of war, I have come to the following conclusion. Although it is against the opinion of some of my collaborators, I have decided that in the interests of the Allied cause, seen as a whole, and in those of Poland herself, the main Polish forces, which had been and I hope will continue to be evacuated from Russia, should remain in the Middle East [. . .]. Nevertheless the following reinforcements are urgently needed for the Polish Forces in England: 1,200 men for the Navy, 1,500 men for the Air Force and 5,500 soldiers for the Armoured Division [. . .]. I have taken my decision in this matter and wish to inform you of it at once' (GSHI, A.XII. 1/52).

On 19.5. the Polish Government reiterated its resolution in the following way: 'The decision of the Council of Ministers of April 30th 1942, stating that it agrees with Polish interests and is in conformity with the line of policy as expressed by the Agreement concluded with the Soviet Government on July 30, 1941, if part of the Polish Armed Forces remains on Soviet territory and later takes part side by side with the Soviet Army in the fight against Germany,—is and will remain the basis of the policy of the Government of the Polish Republic regarding the question of the Polish Army in the USSR. The Council of Ministers again expresses its hope that the Soviet Government will put no obstacles to further recruitment of conscripts and volunteers to the Polish Army, in recognition of the sacrifices which have been brought already by the Polish armed forces for the common cause.'

597

Opening the discussion on that resolution at the meeting of the Council of Ministers on 19.5., Sikorski defended its terms in the following way: 'We shall be forced to insist on the fulfilment of the agreement concluded during my visit in Moscow of last year [December 1941]. Since then this agreement has undergone deep changes. In no case could we give up the surplus quota, existing in the outcome of the agreement concluded at the Kremlin. At present this surplus amounts to 49,000 men. According to initial intentions the army in Russia should have been 96,000 men strong and 27,000 were to be evacuated. As there remain in Russia 44,000 men only, 79,000 should be evacuated, pursuant to our agreement. But out of that number, hardly 30,000 have left Russia. The Soviet Government opposes the resumption of recruitment under the pretext of food shortage. This, however, is not sincere, because we wish to evacuate those men from Russia. It is not our fault if our divisions are not yet on the front, as up to now they have not been given arms [. . .]. The Polish Government will also have to take a very firm stand in the matter of the future rôle of the Polish Army in Russia. The trends of opinion favouring the withdrawal of those troops from Russia, although quite understandable, are hindering the action of the Government which aims at the resumption of recruitment. If we state that in principle we wish to maintain in Russia the three divisions stationed there, trying only to obtain adequate supplies for them—on the lines of the resolution of the Council of Ministers of April 30th— we shall probably succeed in breaking the resistance of the Soviet Government.'

Pursuant to this resolution, the Polish Headquarters in Russia and the General Staff in London had to make appropriate arrangements to the effect of relieving the Russian front. (Cf. doc. No. 205.)

No. 221. The enclosed Memorandum to the Note hereinabove consists of 15 typescript pages. It is a very detailed scrutiny of the evidence relating to the shirking of obligations in the matter of the release of all Polish citizens, deprived of freedom either in their capacity of prisoners of war or convicts on account of various political reasons.

The Memorandum recalls that on the strength of the Decree on Amnesty of 12.8.1941, all the detained had to be automatically released, the more so as Stalin in a conversation with the Polish Ambassador on 14.11.1941, stated that the Soviet 'amnesty must admit no exception'. The putting of this measure into full effect was moreover facilitated by the fact that the Soviet authorities were in possession of complete lists of Polish citizens deprived of freedom, whether dead or alive, as it appears from the information given to the Polish Ambassador by Vyshinsky on 2.11.1941.

In spite of these facts only a small portion of Polish citizens was released from prisons and camps, and the central and local Soviet authorities have constantly shirked the obligations contracted in this matter. They did not reply, either, to the enquiries concerning the fate and the place of confinement of individual Polish citizens, mentioned by name. The Memorandum supports this statement by recalling that the names and places of residence of 4,500 Polish citizens, still remaining in prisons, camps and banishment, were submitted in 42 Notes delivered by the Embassy to the Soviet Government between 8.11.1941 and 1.5.42. In reply to these Notes the People's Commissariat for Foreign Affairs mentioned 1,400 names only in its 38 Notes.

The Memorandum tries to put an end to the sabotaging of the Decree on Amnesty by Soviet authorities, and quotes again the names of prominent Polish personalities still un-released, stating at the same time the position held by them previously in Poland, and, in many cases, mentioning also the time of their arrest and their whereabouts in the Soviet Union.

The Memorandum divides the Polish citizens into categories according to their profession, and also gives the names of persons about whom the Embassy possessed quite reliable information, obtained either from their fellow-prisoners or from relatives in Poland.

The following numbers and categories appear in the Memorandum:

1) Scholars, scientists, members of the teaching profession: university professors and lecturers, teachers—altogether 25 persons; journalists—14 persons.

2) Officers imprisoned in 1939 and put into prisoners-of-war camps at Starobielsk, Kozielsk, Ostashkov and others, transferred from them, at intervals, in May–June 1940, to an unknown destination. The total number of prisoners of war was above 15,000 men, of whom 9,000 had stayed at Kozielsk, Starobielsk and Ostashkov. The nominal rolls of these officers were given to Stalin by Sikorski on 3.12.1941, and by Anders on 18.3.1942. They comprised 4,000 names, among them 12 generals, 94 colonels and lieutenant colonels, 263 majors and about 3,500 junior officers.

3) Former senators, deputies to the Diet and prominent representatives of local self-government bodies, total number—36 persons. The People's Commissariat for Foreign Affairs never gave any information on their whereabouts.

4) Judges, public prosecutors, notaries, solicitors and barristers and senior civil servants, total number—84 men.

In order to find out the fate of the above-mentioned persons and, in general, of all Polish citizens still deprived of freedom, the Memorandum requests: 1) the forwarding to the Polish Embassy by Soviet authorities of complete lists of Polish citizens still detained in prisons and forced labour camps, indicating their whereabouts; 2) the issuing by the authorities in charge of prisons and forced labour camps of an order allowing the detained Polish citizens to correspond with the Polish Embassy and its local Delegates.

Lastly, the Memorandum draws attention to ever more frequent allegations in the Notes of the People's Commissariat for Foreign Affairs that the persons whose names appear on the lists presented by the Embassy actually possess Soviet citizenship, without stating on what grounds those persons are considered Soviet citizens by the Soviet authorities (GSHI, A.11.49/Sow/2).

No. 228. A note on the conversation between Sikorski and Molotov on 11.6. is not available. The text of the telegram quoted in this document can be, to some extent, supplemented by the following passages of the Proceedings of the Council of Ministers of 13.6.: 'The President of the Council had a long conversation with Molotov at a lunch given by Maiski, in the course of which he put forward some capital requests. Although the conversation was apparently very friendly, to the great satisfaction of the British guests, any decision was out of the question and the requests had obviously to be transmitted to Stalin. Molotov, who had come here with quite different expectations and who only after three days' lapse (required for getting in touch with Stalin) agreed to the treaty of May 26th, is today visibly satisfied because after his stay in the West he realized that such a treaty was beneficial to Russian interests. As a matter of fact, by that treaty the Soviet soldier has been given a tremendous impulse in his fight against the Third Reich [. . .]. Molotov asserted that many times in Great Britain and the U.S.A. he had stressed the necessity for a strong Poland. He expressed gratitude for the action developed by the President of the Council in America in favour of Russia. On his part, General Sikorski thanked him for his views, at the same time insisting on the necessity for a fair settlement of the points in dispute between Poland and the USSR. The Governments of Great Britain and the U.S.A. will continue to back our requests in Moscow. They concern the resumption of recruitment and the evacuation of conscripts. They refer to the question of missing Polish officers, the number of whom appears however to be smaller than it was initially anticipated. They refer to the evacuation of Polish children to the British Empire. The execution of these requests is rather difficult during the war. The Polish Government has to cope with tremendous tasks and has grave preoccupations. Molotov alleged that there were questions in which prestige was involved. He promised to submit them to Stalin. General Sikorski approached Churchill and Roosevelt on those matters' (GSHI, PRM–K, 105).

Further details on that conversation were given by Sikorski at the XXVIII meeting of the National Council on 15.6.1942: 'In the conversation Molotov did not raise the frontier question at all. He told me that he had heard in America some echoes of my visit, and that they were positive. He told me that he was able to state that I had favoured the establishing of the second front in 1942, and that I had advocated the question of the supplies of war material for the Soviet Union and the speeding up of the deliveries. On the other hand he told me that while in America he had asserted the necessity for the creation of a strong Poland turned against Germany and that he had even used the word "powerful". This time he did not relate it to the revision of frontiers, but Eden let me know that he spoke nevertheless of such a revision in the sense of the Curzon Line, while Mr. Eden, duly informed by me, refused to discuss that matter' (GSHI, A.5/2).

At the aforesaid meeting of 13.6. the Council of Ministers adopted the following motion proposed by Kwapiński, regarding the question of leaving Polish armed forces in Russia and securing for the Government the share of political control of the decisions of military authorities: 'The Ambassador of the Polish Republic in the USSR should communicate General Sikorski's last message to Stalin [cf. doc. Nos. 201 and 218] to all heads of our posts in the USSR in order to enlighten the local Soviet authorities in a discreet way on our position of principle regarding the Polish Army in Russia. It is particularly important to let the Soviet population know that it was not by our fault that the Polish Army in the USSR has not reached the proposed strength of 96,000 and that it was not by our fault that it does not possess the adequate armament which would enable it to take part in the common struggle against the common enemy so much desired by it. As a matter of fact the Polish Government is unanimous in its resolution to keep the Polish Army in Russia and to use it for the fight side by side with the Soviet Army.' In connection with this Kot was to send his representative to the Polish Army Headquarters in the USSR in order 'to exert a proper influence on behalf of the Polish Republic' by expounding the policy of the Soviet Government and the decisions of the Polish authorities (GSHI, PRM–K, 105).

No. 233. This coded telegram was sent on 2.7.1942 at 9 p.m., but decoded at Yanghi Yul on the following day only, after Anders' take off for Kuibyshev. Kot asserts (Kot, *Listy*, p. 50) that he did not become cognizant of the Soviet proposal until 7.7. The summary of the arrangements for evacuation was transmitted by the C.-in-C.'s Headquarters to Zając on 2.7. (GSHI, A.XII, 22/31.6). British-Soviet conversations in the matter of the evacuation of Polish troops were pursued during Molotov's two visits to London, about 24.5. and 10.6.1942. (Cf. notes to doc. No. 228 and 235, as well as Kot, *Listy*, p. 49.)

No. 235. Kot's telegram to Polish M.F.A., sent on 5.7. from Kuibyshev and decoded in London on the following day, throws some light on the steps taken by British authorities in connection with the second evacuation of Polish troops from the Soviet Union to the Middle East (cf. doc. No. 231 and the note):

'Colonel Hulls telegraphed to London requesting the British Government to exert pressure on the Soviet Government in accordance with the Polish interests. Hulls points out that the lack of interest on the part of Great Britain in the violation of Polish-Soviet agreements will have fatal consequences for British interests. So, for instance, in the Middle East —had England supported Polish interests in Russia, a strong Polish Army would have been in existence for a long time and England would not be obliged to take care of the population whose evacuation has now become imperative. Hulls strongly advises that the question be presented in the same way in Washington. Such is beyond question the point of view of English military circles' (GSHI, A.II.49/Sow/6).

Kot's position on the question of evacuation appears from his telegram of 3.7. to the Polish M.F.A. which received it on the following day: 'Basing my opinion on nearly one year's personal experience of Polish-Soviet relations, I consider it absolutely necessary for the political interests of Poland that, before or during their agreement to the evacuation, the Soviet Government should give a formal pledge to us, to Great Britain and to the United States, regarding: 1) Continuation of conscription of Polish citizens for the Polish Army, all over the territory of the USSR;

2) Evacuation of children, next-of-kin of soldiers, and persons prominent and valuable

to us, independently of the departure of troops, and a guarantee of the provision of food and (two illegible words) for the journey;

3) Further financial assistance from the Soviet Government after the present loans have been consumed.

I consider it my duty to draw your attention to the fact that the present evacuation, so far as the Governments of Gt. Britain and of the United States are concerned, is the last trump card held by us against such a disloyal partner as the Soviet Government. Should the troops be evacuated without the fulfilment of the above conditions, more than 500,000 of our population will face destruction, and Poland's political interests in her relations with Russia will be seriously jeopardized. Further details in next telegram through Army wireless' (GSHI, A.11.49/Sow/6).

The whole problem of evacuation was discussed by the Council of Ministers at its meeting of 6.7. 'which took note of the dispatch of the said memorandum' by the Ministry of Foreign Affairs. The question was reported by Raczyński who stated that 'the conditions put by Kot do not differ very much from the conditions put in our memorandum [. . .] they can be forwarded additionally in the course of the expected negotiations' (GSHI, PRM–K, 105).

No. 241. A similar telegram was sent by Kot to the M.F.A. on 7.7.1942. The full text of the Russian reply to the requests put forward in the Memorandum of 4.7. (transmitted to the Soviet Government through the British Government) was wired in Kuibyshev on 9.7. at 1.57 a.m. and decoded in London on the same day at 1 p.m. (Cf. doc. No. 235.) According to the information obtained by the Polish Embassy in London from the Foreign Office on 10.7., Kerr's impressions from his intervention could be summed up as follows: 'He met with a negative reaction from Vyshinsky on two points, namely—further recruitment, on which Vyshinsky took refuge behind the note delivered in May, and enquiries about the [missing] officers. As regards other points he showed some impatience, but he promised an answer, which does not mean that it should be necessarily negative. Following Kot's request Kerr raised the question of the Women's Voluntary Service and the Scouts, assigning these two categories to the military category, contrary to his instructions [. . .]. Ambassador Kerr expressed the view that 'if the conditions put forward by us had been more limited, the reaction would probably have been different' (GSHI, A.11.49/Sow/6).

No. 245. On nine subsequent pages the Pro Memoria questions the truth of the assertions of the Embassy of the Republic of Poland, but at the same time it does not give any concrete answer to the enquiries as to the fate of the persons whose names appear on the list in the memorandum of 19.5.

The Pro Memoria refutes the allegation that a considerable portion of the Polish officers, prisoners of war, has not yet been released, and states that the Embassy's allegation according to which several thousand Polish officers were still detained in spite of the Decree on Amnesty, was completely unfounded.

Replying to the enquiries relating to 159 detained persons from among scholars and professional men, the Pro Memoria supplies information about 48 people only, twelve of whom died, and six of whom did not allegedly possess Polish citizenship, the remaining ones being either released or their whereabouts being unknown.

The Pro Memoria asserts that an overwhelming portion of detained Polish citizens had been released long before any intervention of the Embassy, and in proof of this assertion it states 10 names, drawing from this the conclusion that hundreds of similar cases can be accounted for. Pro Memoria refutes also the assertion that the People's Commissariat for Foreign Affairs had not supplied exact and detailed information in reply to the Embassy's enquiries about several people, and adds that it was extremely difficult to find some of them, as the information supplied by the Embassy was not complete. Lastly, Pro Memoria states that four from among the people about whom the Embassy was enquiring had not been released immediately after the Decree on Amnesty because of their being indicted on charge of espionage for Germany, and further that a dozen people were being prosecuted, while another twelve people escaped from the Soviet Union to Poland or Germany.

No. 251. This Memorandum was delivered during a conversation between Sokolnicki and Vyshinsky in the presence of Counsellor E. Freyd and Novikov, on 20.7. between 10.30 and 11.30 p.m. Vyshinsky read the passage of his note dealing with the question of Delegates' offices. Sokolnicki firmly refuted the 'charge of the Embassy's enemy action towards the Soviet Union'. Vyshinsky limited this charge to those delegates only 'who were doing everything except keep within their province' and gave a warning that 'all those who were imprisoned on suspicion would be kept under remand' and the Polish warehouses would be sealed. Freyd observed that 'for some reasons [the Soviet organs] do not produce any proof of culpability, and we continue to hear some general accusations but nothing about the facts'. Novikov observed that 'we call counter-revolutionary any action directed against the Soviet State'. In their further remarks the Polish diplomats raised the question of the future shape of the organization for the protection of the Polish population in the USSR. Vyshinky stated that 'he did not know anything about the details of the Embassy's welfare scheme', and he added: 'Please, think it over. I think that we can base our dealings on the idea of men of trust.' In any case he rejected the possibility of maintaining the diplomatic rights of the Embassy official sent for carrying out local duties, and also the idea of granting special privileges to the elected representatives of Polish communities. According to him the only proofs to be admitted were 'the reports of Soviet State organs' and he gave an assurance that if 'he had a talk with M. Arlet [the arrested Secretary of the Embassy] the latter would be forced to confess everything'. At the end Sokolnicki produced a protest against the arrest of the II Secretary of the Embassy A. Głogowski and stated that the Soviet press distorted the text of an interview which President Raczkiewicz had granted to a correspondent of the *Gazeta Polska*. He said also that he had just received information of the shelling by Germans near Murmansk (with considerable losses) of the Polish destroyers *Garland* and *Jastrząb* which protected the Allied convoy bringing arms to the USSR. Vyshinsky confirmed the prohibition of publishing any enquiries about the whereabouts of Polish citizens in the USSR in the Embassy's paper *Polska* (A.II.49/Sow/4). On 21.7. Sokolnicki informed the embassies of the United Kingdom and U.S.A. in the USSR of all these events (A.11.49/Sow/6).

No. 253. In a conversation between Ciechanowski and Sumner Welles, on 23.7., the Polish Ambassador 'asked the Secretary of State to take the above-mentioned matter under serious consideration and kindly to intervene in view of clearing up the situation and of lending the valuable support of the U.S. Government to the endeavours of the Polish Government and the Polish Embassy in Russia to obtain the restoration of harmonious co-operation between the Polish and the Soviet Government regarding the continuation of the distribution of relief to Polish citizens by the Polish Embassy in Kuibyshev'. (Cf. Report of Ciechanowski to the Polish Ministry of F.A. of 25.7.1941, GSHI, A.11.49/Sow/6.)

No. 255. On 22.7.1942, after lunch at Savoy's given by Sikorski, the question of the closing of the offices of the Delegates of the Polish Embassy in the USSR was raised. Among the guests were Eden, Maisky, Bogomolov, Biddle, Dormer, Wunsz King and Strang, and among the Poles: Sikorski, Raczyński, Stroński, Strasburger, Kwapiński and Retinger. Raczyński told the story of the arrests of the Delegates of the Polish Embassy in the USSR and the liquidation of local offices on an order of Vyshinsky (doc. No. 251 and the note). He mentioned further the protest lodged by him with Bogomolov on 20.7. against 'imputing to all Polish Delegates and their assistants a line of conduct departing from their duties and instructions' and also against 'an inadmissible disruption of the whole organization entrusted with the reception of gifts sent by charitable institutions of Great Britain, the United States, Canada, etc., as well as goods bought by the Polish Government'. At the end he stated that although the Polish Government has kept silence so far, it would be impossible to hush up those events in the long run. He pointed to the humanitarian aspect of the question, particularly urgent in view of the impending evacuation of Polish troops from the USSR. Bogomolov then observed that the 'question of the evacuation was raised in Soviet-British negotiations and must be dealt with in future within the same framework'. Sikorski disputed such an interpretation of the negotiations on that issue, saying that 'the decision concerning Polish forces rests with the Polish Government and the Polish C.-in-C.'. The conversation then turned to the question of assistance to the Polish population in the USSR. Eden said that 'even if there might be objections regarding some individuals, the maintenance of the whole relief organization is no less necessary'. Biddle supported him. At the end of the meeting Sikorski explained that 'it was not his intention to trouble his guests with unpleasant occurrences' but the circumstances in which the said events took place in the USSR forced him to expound the whole problem in a larger 'family circle' (GSHI, A.11.49/Sow/4).

No, 257, Bogomolov's note made no mention of the Embassy's rights to ensure the protection of the Polish population in the USSR. (Cf. note to doc. No. 251.) The relevant passage of the conversation between Kot and Vyshinsky on 23.1.1942, ran as follows (Kot, Rozmowy, pp. 208–10):

'Vyshinsky: The position is the following: diplomatic officials who so far had this capacity, whose names were communicated to the Narkomindel and who hold diplomatic cards (Dipkartochki) do not forfeit their rights if they are designated by you to the posts of delegates. Such rights will not be granted to new candidates because it would mean the opening of twenty consulates [. . .]. If Pushkin's [Deputy Head of the Central-European Department] words were understood in this way, that diplomatic officials of the Embassy should forfeit their diplomatic rights in case when they are sent by you somewhere to carry out official duties, this declaration was erroneous and went beyond the instruction given to Pushkin [. . .].

Kot: Shall I understand your declaration, Mr. Commissar, as implying a guarantee of the delegates' personal immunity as well as the immunity of archives and correspondence, and the possibility of organizing an office, selecting the staff and enjoying the freedom of travel? [. . .].

Vyshinsky: You can be completely reassured that the Narkomindel will do everything possible to ensure these conditions [. . .]. In the interest of our smooth co-operation I should like to propose that each delegate should receive a written statement certifying his official capacity which might be produced to local authorities. It would be advisable to refer in this document to The Regulations on the Scope of Activity of the Delegates of the Embassy of the Polish Republic' (see doc. No. 166).

A unilateral revision of that agreement took place on 6.7.1942 when the Narkomindel informed the Embassy in Kuibyshev that from now on 'the local delegates of the Embassy charged at the same time with diplomatic functions will not be treated as persons enjoying diplomatic rights and privileges'. The said note did not mention, however, that the position of all other delegates (without diplomatic rights) was also changed.

Accepting Bogomolov's note from his hands on 29.7. Raczyński declared, 'I refute most firmly the charge brought against our delegates and the staff of delegates' offices alleging an enemy action against the Soviet Union [. . .]. I repeat most strongly the request for the release of the arrested men and the return of all papers and seals seized.' He also drew attention to the contradictions in the attitude of Soviet authorities which on the one hand impose the liquidation of delegates' offices, and, on the other, assert that they 'do not oppose the relief action' organized by the Polish Embassy.

Moreover, Raczyński protested 'against a high-handed action organized by Soviet authorities without our knowledge and consent' aimed at provoking an ill-conceived anti-German diversion on Polish territory on the initiative of Soviet parachutists. (Note on the conversation between Raczyński and Bogomolov on 29.7.1942 and telegram of M.F.A. to Polish Embassy in the USSR of 30.7.1942, GSHI, A.11.49/Sow/4.)

No. 271. Romer took over his post of Ambassador to the USSR as quickly as was possible in the circumstances because of the necessity for bringing about a 'détente' in Polish-Soviet relations and submitting to Soviet authorities 'a new scheme of relief work'. On 25.10 the P.M.F.A. sent the text of Romer's credentials by telegram to the Narkomindel and their original text was deposited with the Soviet Embassy in London. The new Ambassador brought with him Sikorski's personal message to Stalin (doc. No. 271) emphasizing the importance of his mission as regards 'the organization of assistance to Polish citizens' and also 'the intensification of the war effort against the common enemy'. Romer presented his credentials to Kalinin at the Kremlin on 31.10. Romer reported that Stalin had referred several times to the unfortunate consequences arising for Poland from the departure of Anders' troops from Russia, as that army had missed the opportunity of 'undergoing a unique training for battle on the front' and had delayed the moment of 'entering the fight for the independence of its own country'. Romer concluded after that visit that 'Soviet agreement to further recruitment seemed to be out of the question in those circumstances, which has been confirmed by Bogomolov's Note of 31.10. (cf. doc. No. 273). The conversations with Molotov took place in Moscow on 30.10. and 3.11. (the latter being much the more important). The conversations embraced the following items:

a/the protection of and assistance to Polish citizens in the USSR. Molotov's point of view appeared clearly from his utterances: 'without being opposed to the action of men of trust, we are obliged to state that the organization of the Embassy's Delegates did not stand the test [. . .] we have to abide in this field by the decision taken at the beginning of the war: no expansion of consular offices. In my [Molotov's] view the problem of the protection of and the assistance to Polish citizens should be solved on the lines of a purely economic organization, such as stores for relief in kind, hostels, etc.' Romer produced the Polish scheme for that matter which foresaw the distribution of goods through 300–400 men of trust whose activities were to be supervised by some controlling offices with Soviet officials attached to them in the capacity of liaison officers. The whole action would be directed by the representatives of the Polish Embassy and of the Narkomindel. Molotov rejected that scheme as too complicated and proposed instead the setting up of 'an economic centre maintaining contact with warehouses, and the latter with the men of trust. The relief work on the spot should rest on: a warehouse man, his assistant and men of trust. We can reach an agreement on such purely economic lines'. In his telegram of 9.11. Romer gave his view on the Soviet position in this matter: 'Having in mind the possible reactions of international public opinion, the Soviet Government cannot wind up our action completely, but it is obvious that it is trying to get rid of special officials ensuring the relief work on the spot, to limit their scope of activity and the possibility of intervention with authorities as well as their connections with the Embassy and other local relief offices.'

b/The question of charges brought against Embassy Delegates on account of alleged espionage seemed to approach its final stage. Romer said that 'it would be most advisable to dispose as quickly and completely as possible with the accusations and sanctions based on misunderstandings which have often arisen from the fact that our citizens were not fully conversant with the legislation and the procedure in individual cases'. To that Molotov replied that 'As things stand now, it would be impossible for us to stop the proceedings. I assure you nevertheless that we do not intend to have a public trial, or, in general, to make too much of it.'

c/When the question of the deportees' nationality was discussed Romer tried to find common ground by emphasizing the human factor. He pointed to frequent cases of separation of members of one family arising from the fact that Polish soldiers who left the Soviet

Union were recognized as Polish citizens, while the same status was denied to their next-of-kin living in parts of the country distant from the places where the Polish troops were then stationed. He added that it was particularly so in the case of Jewish and Ukrainian families. Molotov refuted the accusation of national discrimination and declared that 'we cannot withdraw from nor abandon our position [Soviet], the whole problem being of primary importance for us [. . .] it might be revised in future should we succeed in settling other capital problems between us'. In this way the problem as such seemed to be beyond the framework of the existing Polish-Soviet agreement.

d/So far as the question of the evacuation of Polish children was concerned it seemed likely about the end of October that the Soviet promise of 28.9.1942 to allow a gradual evacuation of a number of orphans and semi-orphans from the Soviet Union to the Middle East would be fulfilled, at least with regard to groups of children who were already prepared for departure (cf. Appendices Nos. 8 and 9). In the conversation of 3.11. Molotov repeated the permission 'for the evacuation of a definite group of orphans', but opposed 'any systematic evacuation', meaning by this a possible limitation of the departures with regard to both number and dates. The establishment of an evacuation scheme was left for further discussions.

Romer's general remarks on his visit in Moscow (telegram of 8.11.1942):

The growing self-confidence of the Russian nation and 'general ill-feeling towards the Allies for lack of co-operation in the war'.

Readiness to 'enforce concessions on the Western Allies' by surprise moves and secret agreements.

The tendency of the Narkomindel to make void the agreement Sikorski–Stalin of December 1941 (cf. Correspondence between the P.M.F.A. and the Embassy in Kuibyshev, 15, 22, 26.10. and 4, 7, 8, 9, 10 and 15.11.1942, A.11.49/Sow/6; Conversation between Romer and Kalinin on 31.10.1942, A.11.49/Sow/4; Conversation between Romer and Molotov on 30.10. and 3.11.1942, A.11.49/Sow/4).

No. 272. This memorandum was handed on 28.10.1942 by Lozovsky to Sokolnicki. The Polish diplomatist succeeded in convincing the Soviet official of the necessity for transmitting on the telephone the tenor of this document to Romer, who had just arrived and was at that moment presenting his credentials in Moscow. After having read the memorandum at home, Sokolnicki reached the conclusion that it was in fact an indictment of the Embassy itself of 'a hostile and espionage action against the Soviet Union', such charges being 'absolutely unfounded' and 'able to bring about a partial revision of the lines on which Ambassador Romer's conversations were to be held'. Consequently on 29.10, after an exchange of sharp arguments with Lozovsky, he returned the memorandum received on the preceding day.

Apart from this incident, Raczyński categorically rejected these charges in a conversation with Bogomolov on 31.10. On the previous day Romer, meeting Molotov, stated that 'all the charges brought against the Embassy should be directed to the Polish Government in London through the appropriate channel, that is, through Ambassador Bogomolov'. The Soviet Commissar replied that 'the memorandum referred to the past and that past, connected with several unpleasant facts, was being liquidated by it'. This was a mutual declaration on the resumption of co-operation (conversations between Sokolnicki and Lozovsky and Novikov on 28 and 29.10.1941, conversation between Raczyński and Bogomolov on 31.10., conversation between Romer and Molotov on 30.10.1941, GSHI, A.11.49/Sow/4, PRM, 72/3).

No. 279. The Soviet propaganda broadcasts as well as the negative attitude of Soviet authorities towards any action of the Polish Government can be explained by the annexionist designs of the leaders of the Soviet Union, as it appears from the conversation between Jankowski and Valkov on 15.12.1942 in London.

'In M. Valkov's view, it appears from a statement published in the *Polish Daily* that Polish claims, both in the East and in the West, go very far indeed. I [Jankowski] replied that Poland did not raise any claims to Russian territory. By signing the Agreement of 30th July 1941, the Soviet Government cancelled the Soviet-German Treaty on the partition of Poland, and it meant the restoration of the pre-war status so far as Poland is concerned, that is of the frontier established by the Treaty of Riga. The Polish claims in the West concern the territories which are inhabited by a great proportion of Polish population, as, for instance, Opole Silesia and East Prussia. The latter has also a great importance for Poland's security, as it was from that territory that Poland was invaded.

M. Valkov contested my arguments in a lengthy talk, saying that the Russo-Polish Agreement did not contain any reference to Poland's eastern frontiers, and that if such a clause had been included, the Soviet Government would not have signed it, for the incorporation of a part of former Polish territory with the Soviet Union was "final". M. Valkov added that Stalin in his conversation with General Sikorski expressed his favourable view on the creation of a "Great Poland", but a Great Poland "could not rise at the expense of Soviet territory".[. . .]

It should be emphasized that the firm position taken by M. Valkov in relation to Poland's eastern frontier coincides with the broadcasts of the Kościuszko Station and other broadcasts in the Polish language, which in the course of recent days were raising the question of the necessity of a "friendly" settlement of the frontier between Poland and the USSR. I refer, in connection with it, to a speech delivered by M. Beneš advocating the settlement of territorial issues between the Allied Nations still in the course of the war. The said Soviet broadcasts advise that Poland should lean on the Soviet Union because of the constant German menace. They state that "Poland's eastern frontiers should be determined in accordance with the will and wishes of the local population" (Kościuszko Radio Station on 9.12.1942) and that "we will settle the question of the eastern frontier in a friendly way with the Soviet Union, who is our natural ally, even if it should be necessary to make some concessions to the White Ruthenian and Ukrainian minority, in accordance with the wishes of those nations" (broadcast of the Kościuszko Radio Station on 14.12.1942). This is something quite new in Soviet broadcasts which have, so far, abstained from raising territorial issues between Poland and the USSR' (GSHI, A.11.49/Sow/4).

No. 296. a) This *Tass* communiqué appeared also in the Bulletin of the Soviet Embassy in Washington on 4.3.1943, with a very unpleasant comment. The State Department, informed of the latter developments by Ciechanowski, assured him that it would stick to 'principles' in its policy towards the Soviet Union but it postponed an intervention to 'a more suitable moment'. On the other hand, the U.S.A. Ambassador in Kuibyshev pleaded for American mediation in the Polish-Soviet dispute (telegrams of the Polish Embassy in Washington to the P.M.F.A., 5.3. and 7.4., GSHI, A.11.49/Sow/6).

The notes on the conversations held in mid-March between Polish representatives and senior officials of the F.O. and the Ministry of Information show a growing concern about Soviet pressure on Eden (cf. Sikorski's letter to Churchill of 10.3.1943, PRM, 95 ; a note on a conversation between Zarański and Lias on 11.3, A.11.49/Sow/6; Raczyński's speech at the meeting of the National Council on 17.3, A.5/3; Sikorski's report to the Council of Ministers on 18 and 22.3., PRM–K, 106; Churchill's broadcast on the BBC of 21.3.; *The Times* and the *Daily Telegraph* of 22.3.; a letter from Cazalet to Strang explaining the political background of the whole problem, dated 19.6.1943, PRM, 68; all these papers are at the GSHI). British representatives advised the Poles to start direct Polish-Soviet conversations before the opening of the Washington Conference and to make concessions, consisting in the surrender of some Polish territories to Russia, transfer of populations in some (in particular south-eastern) districts and federative agreements (with Lithuania). What the British omitted to refer to in the course of those conversations was the existence of a nearly definitive British agreement to the annexation of the Baltic States, Bessarabia and Bukovina by the Soviet Union, and also of the British proposal to the United States

Government (March 1943) that the Soviet claims should be accepted (cf. Churchill, *W.S.S.*, IV, 293, 672 and Sherwood, II, pp. 710–14).

The Times' editorial 'Security in Europe' of 10.3. openly declared that 'if Britain's frontier is on the Rhine', then 'Russia's frontier is on the Oder'. Therefore, 'the lands between Russia's frontiers and those of Germany should be placed in the hands of governments and peoples friendly to Moscow'. After sharp reactions on the part of the Governments of Poland, Holland, Belgium and Norway, Churchill outlined in his broadcast of 21.3.1943, the programme of a united Europe, which should consist of 'confederations of States side by side with the great powers [. . .], without destroying the individual characteristics and traditions of their many ancient and historic races'.

b) Let us see now what was the attitude of the national minorities of Poland towards the problem of the future of the eastern provinces of the Republic.

In the first period of the war (1941–2) the Ukrainians from Poland expected Russia's collapse and the creation of a more or less independent State, under German leadership. The nucleus of such a State should be, in their opinion, the so-called 'Western Ukraine' (see a report on the Soviet attitude to national minorities in Poland, GSHI, PRM, 74/4). They were far, however, from accepting the Russian 'Big Brother' theory of a great Russian nation absorbing their own (see Small-Stocki, *The Nationality Problem of the Soviet Union*, Milwaukee, 1952, p. 458).

The Byelorussians suffered very much in the course of the war. Those among them who were anti-Communist were deported inside Russia where they remained faithful Polish subjects. Those who remained in the country had to put up with the changing occupations of Soviet and German forces.

The Jews' feelings towards the Polish Republic underwent a radical change in the course of the war. The above-said report on the Soviet attitude towards national minorities of Poland observes that 'the Polish-Soviet pact and the recognition of the Polish State by the Soviet Union was warmly welcomed by the Jews . . . they had endured so many humiliations and suffered so many wrongs in Russia that their feelings towards the Soviet Union were those of scorn, contempt and hatred'. In consequence they now became 'the most ardent defendants of the Polish eastern provinces'.

The Polish Government defined its policy towards the Ukrainians and Byelorussians in a communiqué published on 4.3. (doc. No. 297).

c) As regards the allegations contained in the 'Tass Statement' and referring to the policy pursued by Beck, attention should be drawn to documents 6, 7, 8, 9, 10, 11, 12, 13, 14, 15, 18, 19, 22, 24, 36 of this collection as well as to the diplomatic papers published in the 'Polish White Book', Nos. 15, 16, 48, 53.

No. 298. Further details concerning the case of Henryk Ehrlich and Wiktor Alter were provided by Jacob T. Zukerman in the course of 'Hearings before the Select Committee on Communist Aggression' on 23.9.1954 in New York: 'In October 1939 they [H. Ehrlich and W. Alter] were arrested after the partition of Poland in accordance with the Nazi-Soviet Pact. They were arrested by the Soviet Secret Police.' He referred also to the repercussions abroad of their second arrest in December 1941: 'The deceit in this story goes beyond that of the tragic trip to Moscow. The entire American Labour movement was aroused by their disappearance. It was not known at first that they had been arrested. The late President of the American Federation of Labour, William Green, received assurances from the Soviet Ambassador Maxim Litvinov that he would look into the matter [. . .]. On the heels of William Green's request to Litvinov, the late Wendell Willkie, then a roving ambassador for our Government, made a similar appeal to Stalin and received the same assurances.'

Another witness, Henry Edward Schultz, stated in his evidence on 22.9.1954 that out of 600,000 Polish Jews deported in 1939/40 to the Soviet Union 'about 150,000 returned to Poland at the end of the war. The rest—some 450,000—just vanished' ('Seventh Interim Report of Hearings before the Select Committee on Communist Aggression, House of

Representatives, 83rd Congress, Treatment of Jews by the Soviet', Washington, 1954, Govern. Printing Office, pp. 25, 64).

No. 302. In March 1942 the first manifestations appeared of the new Soviet policy towards the relief work, which consisted in imposing restrictions on the activity of Embassy Delegates by depriving them of the right of intervention with local authorities in favour of Polish citizens. Many of the latter still remained in prisons and concentration camps in spite of Soviet pledges contained in the Amnesty Decree of 12.8.1941. Soon after Soviet authorities began to forbid the Ukrainians, Byelorussians and Jews to receive assistance from the offices of Embassy Delegates. Several conversations between the representatives of the Polish Embassy and the People's Commissariat for Foreign Affairs, held in the period March-July 1942, served no purpose. The obstacles, on the part of local and central authorities to the relief work of Embassy Delegates and regional offices, had not been removed. A few months after the beginning of the distribution of relief goods, the relief network consisted of 19 offices with 387 men of trust, among whom were 297 Poles, 82 Jews and 8 Ukrainians or Byelorussians. Apart from financial help and the distribution of clothes, food and medicines, 82 orphanages were founded for 5,364 children, mostly orphans, embracing 7% of the total number of Polish children in Russia and 70% of the total number of orphans. There were also founded: 175 kindergartens, 111 schools and courses, 10 hospitals and convalescent homes, 71 hostels and homes for the disabled, 1 crèche and 1 laboratory, 191 feeding centres, 117 medical posts and first-aid posts and 47 workshops. The total number of institutions—807.

The assistance in kind on the part of the Polish Embassy in the USSR for deportees from August 1941 to the end of April 1943 consisted of: 1) financial relief through the regional network, totalling the sum of Rb. 111,700,493; 2) individual assistance from the Polish Embassy amounting to Rb. 2,243,756; 3) distribution of the relief in kind containing 101,759 parcels of clothes, food and medical supplies. After the liquidation of relief organizations 56,166 parcels were taken over by the Soviet Government; 4) relief in kind supplied by the Polish Government, American Red Cross and Polish Organizations in America contained: 2,200 sacks of wheat flour, 1,800 sacks of beans, 5,000 kilograms of powdered milk, 400 bales of clothes, 100 cases of clothes, 1,500 bales of blankets and a great quantity of medical supplies (cf. Report on the relief accorded to Polish citizens by the Polish Embassy in the USSR, September 1941–April 1943, London, 1943, GSHI, A.11.49/Sow/6).

The actual Soviet assistance to the civilian population in 1942 was limited to a loan of Rb. 100 millions and to providing accommodation.

The Soviet action against the relief organization started on July 2, 1942, when Soviet police entered the premises of the Embassy Delegates in Arkhangel, seized documents and papers, and arrested the Deputy Delegate and three members of the staff. A few days later the Embassy Delegate in Arkhangel was arrested also. The same occurred with the Embassy Delegate in Vladivostok.

In the course of July the Soviet persecutions continued, 118 people being arrested, of whom 9 were holders of diplomatic passports. In view of the Embassy's protests those 9 members of the Embassy staff were released but 109 people remained in prison. Not until the end of October 1942 were 93 people released and 16 still remained in custody.

With the arrests of Delegates, representatives of the Embassy and members of the staff of relief offices the whole welfare action was disrupted. In spite of increasing difficulties the Polish Government thought that the relief work should not be discontinued and it charged the new Ambassador with the task of resuming the negotiations on the reopening of relief offices, even if they should be organized on different lines. The Soviet Government did not decline that proposal in principle, but the whole idea did not materialize. The Soviet Note of 16.1.1943, stating that all persons staying on the territory which had been occupied by Soviet troops became Soviet citizens, as well as the fact that deportees were forced to take Soviet passports, debarred the latter from the possibility of enjoying the assistance from Polish sources. This was the decisive blow to the existence of Polish relief work. In March the Soviet Government, without any previous warning, took under its own administration all welfare offices still in existence, seized all the warehouses with clothes, food and medicines stored in them and discharged the whole staff.

This confiscation of the property belonging to a State with whom the Soviet Government maintained diplomatic relations was aimed at creating such a tension that the Polish Government should be induced to sever the relations with the Soviet Union. (Cf. Liquidation of the offices of the Delegates of the Polish Embassy in the USSR—Teheran, October 1942, GSHI, A.11.49/Sow/6.)

No. 307. The German reports on the discovery of the graves of thousands of slaughtered Polish Officers at Katyń were discussed on 15.4. at 11 a.m. by General Sikorski with members of his Cabinet. It was decided to send a Note to the Soviet Embassy demanding an explanation, to approach the International Red Cross with a request to investigate the matter, and to publish a statement of the case signed by the Minister of National Defence, responsible for questions relating to Prisoners of War. The Ministers of Foreign Affairs and of Information were to co-operate in preparing the text of the communiqué.

The text was approved by the three Ministers at noon on 16.4. and by Sikorski at 12.30 p.m. and issued at night by the PAT (General Kukiel's note).

INDEX

Krestinsky, Nikolai, Deputy People's Commissar, 14, 22–3, 71–2

Kucharski, Kazimierz, Rt. Rev., 266

Kuczyńska, deportee, 379

Kuczyński, Waldemar, Polish Welfare Officer, 379–80, 383, 390, 393

Kuczyński, Z. M., 440, 444

Kukiel, Lt.-General Marian, Polish Minister of National Defence, 525, 590, 609

Kulski, Władysław, Counsellor of Polish Embassy in London, 280, 317, 329, 552

Kutuzov, 87

Kutyba, Józef, Polish Welfare Officer, 514

Kviring, Emmanuel, Soviet politician, 3

Kwapiński, Jan, Polish socialist leader, 600, 602

Lane, Maj.-General, 318

Langner, Maj.-General Władysław Aleksander, 210–11

Latvia, 3, 12, 16, 19, 40, 52, 68–9, 73, 96–7, 123, 125–6, 260, 269, 292, 297, 311, 328, 341, 552–3, 562–6, 596; see also Baltic States

Laval, Pierre, French politician, 27

League of Nations, 3, 9, 12, 22–3, 64, 68, 71, 564–5, 571, 573

Lechowicz, Edward, Polish Delegate in Riga, 3

Lenin, Vladimir Ulyanov, Chairman of the Council of People's Commissars, 1, 2, 100, 275, 339, 365, 562–3

Leśniowska, Zofia, daughter of General Sikorski, 165

Lewoniewski, Józef, Polish airman, 308

Lewoniewski, Soviet airman, 308

Lias, 606

Libya, 242, 248, 290, 297, 373, 381, 425, 459

Lickindorf, Stanisław, Polish Welfare Officer, 389, 403, 408, 418, 444

Litauer, Stefan, Counsellor of the Polish Embassy in London, 574

Litvinov, Maxim Maximovich, People's Commissar for Foreign Affairs, Soviet Ambassador in Washington, 12, 17, 20–1, 23–4, 71, 80–3, 311, 396, 503–4, 607

Lithuania, and Treaty of Riga, 7; and frontier with Poland, 9, 11, 22; and German-Soviet delimitation, 40, 51–3, 61–4; and accord on Wilno, 62–4, 593; and incorporation into USSR, 68–9, 96–7, 100–1, 268, 341; and Poland's interest in her independence, 123, 125–127, 206, 260, 268–70, 272–3, 275, 292,

297–9, 310–11, 314–15, 328–31, 333–5, 470; and British policy, 330–1, 337–40, 349–50; and 491, 534, 546–7, 552–3, 562, 570–2, 580, 592–3, 595–6, 606

Lloyd George, David, M.P., 55, 57

Lozovsky, Solomon Abramovich, Deputy People's Commissar for Foreign Affairs, 358, 435, 459–60, 605

Lubowicki, J. F., Polish Welfare Officer, 440

Luckiewicz, Polish-Ukrainian politican, 173

Łukasiewicz, Juliusz, Polish Ambassador to France, 21

Lwów (Lvov), 45, 50, 55, 118, 125, 210, 236, 287, 456, 472, 564, 593, 595, 599; and Stalin's allusions, 244, 265, 274–5; and German massacres in, 259–60; and Polish objections against its inclusion among Ukrainian cities, 261, 266–7

Łychowski, Head of the Polish Trade Delegation, 24

Lyttelton, Rt. Hon. Oliver, British Minister of State, 198

McEwen, Captain John Helias F., M.P., 143

Macfarlane, General Sir Frank Noel Mason, Head of British Military Commission in Moscow, 112, 171, 185–6, 257, 284, 582, 588, 594

Machnowski, Lt.-Colonel Feliks, 253

Maglione, Luigi, Cardinal, Secretary of State, 328–9, 596

Maisky, Ivan Michaelovich, Soviet Ambassador to Great Britain, and negotiations of a Polish-Soviet Agreement, 114–19, 129–33, 136–7, 140–2; and Soviet suggestions on National Committees in USSR and of an ethnographical Poland, 116–18, 128; and postponement of the question of frontiers, 118; and opposing general release of Polish prisoners, 131; and his four points, 118–19, 130; and signing the Agreement, 142; and 158, 185–6, 189, 280, 311, 389, 401, 427, 532, 575–80, 599, 602

Maksymowicz, Mrs., deportee, 513

Malinowski, G., Polish Welfare Officer, 440

Mander, Geoffrey Le Mesurier, M.P., 144

Mantel, Feliks, Polish Welfare Officer, 403, 440

Marshall, General George Catlett, US Chief of Staff, 328

Matsuda, Michikazu, Japanese diplomat, 11

Matsuoka, Yosuke, Japanese diplomat, 291

Poland (*contd.*)

253, 318, 323, 356-7, 361-3, 375, 377, 397, 399; and freedom of worship, 256, 266, 357-61;

Children, deported to USSR, and care of, 146, 154-5, 192, 214, 218, 420, 599; and their plight, 224-5, 234, 356-7, 414, 422, 558-9; and evacuation of, 318, 356-7, 361-3, 371-3, 375, 384-5, 388, 401, 417, 421-2, 456, 481, 487, 499, 560-1;

Embassy delegates in USSR, 154, 160-1, 218-22, 234, 255-8, 281-2, 322-3, 362; and closing their offices and withdrawal of diplomatic status, 366, 375-376, 378-80, 382-4, 387, 389-91, 393-7, 401-21, 429-40, 442-7, 452-6, 468-9, 477-8, 487, 504-6, 513-18, 520-1, 593, 602, 607, 609; and arrests of delegates and personnel, 378-80, 382-4, 387-8, 391, 393-6, 401-3, 406-18, 429-35, 608; and 78 persons deported from USSR, 440; and accused of anti-Soviet activities, 442-7, 466; and Polish statements of the case, 454-5, 468-9, 487, 504-6, 513-18, 521, 603, 607, 609;

Political prisoners in USSR, 115, 117-22, 130-42; and Soviet reluctance to release all of them, 130-1; and consent to grant amnesty to all, 142, 172, 179-82; and see Amnesty;

Prisoners of war in USSR, 95, 106-7, 109, 112-22, 128, 130-46, 153-5, 157-9, 180-1, 187-8, 190, 204-5, 230, 423-4, 514, 580-1, 599; and conscription of a part to Red Army, 93, 106-7, 133, 150, 178, 215, 223, 227-8, 307, 309; and missing officers (and o.r.) from the camps of Kozielsk, Starobielsk, Ostashkov, 128, 171, 173-4, 181-2, 190-2, 201-4, 211, 230, 271-2, 300, 307, 355-357, 370-2, 378, 384-5, 388, 399, 401, 422-4, 426, 456, 523-40; and German discovery of Katyń graves, 523-4; and Polish statement of the case, 525-7; and 540, 589, 599, 601, 609;

German prisoners of war of Polish nationality in USSR—request for their special treatment and recruitment into Polish Army, 267-8, 278-9, 288, 440-1, 454, 458, 473; and Soviet refusal, 268, 460, 473, 489-93;

Underground Army (Home Army), 164-165, 590-1, 604; and Soviet sabotage

and parachutists in Poland, 164-5, 352-3, 590-1, 604; and her increasing importance, 346; and her prospective coming into the open if Soviet forces entered, 457-8;

Also see: Aggression; Agreements; Amnesty; Territorial changes

Polkowski, German Colonel, 473

Potemkin, Vladimir Petrovich, Deputy People's Commissar, 28, 30, 47, 80, 82-84, 87-9, 565-7

Potocki, Józef, Polish diplomat, 25

Potulicki, Michał, Counsellor of Polish Foreign Ministry, 576-8

Powierza, Andrzej, First Secretary in Polish Embassy in USSR, 446

Pritt, Denis Nowell, M.P., 93

Protasewicz, Lt.-Colonel Michał, 220

Prussia, Kingdom of, and partition of Poland, 1, 100

Pushkin, G. M., 180-1, 194, 390, 603

Pytlak, Marian, Polish Welfare Officer, 379-80, 390, 393

Raczkiewicz, Władysław, President of the Polish Republic, 382, 579-81, 590, 602

Raczyński, Edward, Polish Ambassador in London and Acting Minister for Foreign Affairs, and Anglo-Polish Agreement, 550-2; and protest against the Soviet-German Agreement on partition of Poland, 55; and Lithuania and Baltic States, 268-9, 272-4, 284-5; and missing Polish prisoners of war, 270-1, 300-1; and Soviet territorial claims, 310-17, 321-3, 329, 332-5; and Anglo-Soviet negotiations, 332-5, 349-51, 593, 595; and Polish Army in USSR, 342-3, 351, 367-8, 376-8, 424-7, 440-441, 447-52, 454, 458-68, 473; and infringement of the rights of Polish citizens in USSR, 332-3, 393-7, 399, 411-20, 429-32, 442-7, 454-5, 474-8, 482, 486-8, 519-22; and Soviet parachutists, 352; and air operations over Poland, 432-3, 439; and execution of Alter and Ehrlich, 503-4; and the Katyń mass murder, 528-30, 609; and 17, 25, 41, 156, 185, 220, 336, 581, 584, 586, 588-90, 601-3, 605-606

Rakowski, German Colonel, 473

Rastikis, General, 126

Regulski, Maj.-General Bronisław, Polish Military Attaché in London, 373, 574, 595